Theodore Dwight Bozeman is professor
of religion and history at the University of
Iowa. He is the author of
Age of Science: The Baconian
American Religious Thought.

TO

LIVE

ANCIENT

LIVES

The Primitivist Dimension in Puritanism

THEODORE DWIGHT BOZEMAN

Published for the

Institute of Early American History and Culture

Williamsburg, Virginia, by the

University of North Carolina Press

Chapel Hill & London

The Institute of Early American History and Culture
is sponsored jointly by the
College of William and Mary and the
Colonial Williamsburg Foundation.

Library of Congress Cataloging-in-Publication Data

Bozeman, Theodore Dwight, 1942–
To live ancient lives : the primitivist dimension in Puritanism /
Theodore Dwight Bozeman.
p. cm.
Bibliography: p.
Includes index.
ISBN 0-8078-1785-6
1. Puritans—New England.   2. Primitivism.   3. New England—Church
history.   4. Massachusetts—Church history.   I. Institute of Early
American History and Culture (Williamsburg, Va.)   II. Title.
F7.B75 1988   87-27803
974'.02—dc 19   CIP

Both the initial research and the publication of this work were made possible
in part through grants from the National Endowment for the Humanities, a
federal agency whose mission is to award grants to support education,
scholarship, media programming, libraries, and museums, in order to bring
the results of cultural activities to a broad, general public.

The paper in this book meets the guidelines
for permanence and durability of the
Committee on Production Guidelines for
Book Longevity of the Council on Library Resources.
92 91 90 89 88   5 4 3 2 1

To Helmut, Helga, & Angelika Wagner

ACKNOWLEDGMENTS

In the writing and revision of the present study I have incurred debts innumerable. The staffs of the Main Library at the University of Iowa, of the American Antiquarian Society, the Massachusetts Historical Society, the Boston Public Library, and the Houghton Library at Harvard University were unfailingly efficient and helpful. Conversations along the way with Paul Christianson, Clark Gilpin, John Morgan, and James C. Spalding smoothed the task more than they may know. A complete draft was read and criticized by Paul Christianson, David D. Hall, Stuart Henry, E. Brooks Holifield, Richard T. Hughes, Sydney V. James, and Michael McGiffert. Leonard Sweet reviewed the chapters on eschatology, and Donald Sutherland the section on legal reform. The late Stephen Botein and Philip Morgan, editors at the Institute of Early American History and Culture, contributed much to the tightening-up of the text and to my rethinking of parts of the argument. Gil Kelly, managing editor at the Institute, copy-edited the final manuscript and greatly improved its grammar and style. I thank William M. Fowler, Jr., for permission to use material in Chapter 3 that originally appeared as "The Puritans' 'Errand into the Wilderness' Reconsidered," in *New England Quarterly*, LIX (1986), 232–251. Progress upon the study was speeded by a research fellowship from the National Endowment for the Humanities, a Development Award and two Old Gold grants from the University of Iowa, and grants for typing and copying expenses from the Graduate College of the University of Iowa. John Boyle, Director of the School of Religion at the University of Iowa, arranged departmental grants for various expenses. Mary Lou Doyle typed a complete early draft of the text and notes. At a later stage, Gerald McDermott and Gary Bailey performed many indispensable operations upon the notes and bibliography.

CONTENTS

ABBREVIATIONS

(Full references to individual works in Bibliography)

AM   John Foxe, *The Acts and Monuments of John Foxe*

AP   [John Field and Thomas Wilcox], *An Admonition to the Parliament*

BR   Samuel Danforth, *A Brief Recognition of New-Englands Errand into the Wilderness*

CC   John Eliot, *The Christian Commonwealth . . .*

CG   John Higginson, *The Cause of God and His People in New-England . . .*

CH   *Church History*

EPM   Patrick Collinson, *The Elizabethan Puritan Movement*

LB   William Keeling, ed., *Liturgiae Britannicae . . .*

ER   Samuel Torrey, *An Exhortation unto Reformation . . .*

HCEI   Essex Institute, *Historical Collections*

MCCP   "A Modell of Church and Civill Power . . ."

MHSC   Massachusetts Historical Society, *Collections*

NEHGR   *New England Historical and Genealogical Register*

NEPW   Urian Oakes, *New-England Pleaded With . . .*

NEQ   *New England Quarterly*

NETI   William Stoughton, *New-Englands True Interest . . .*

PCD   *A Platform of Church Discipline Gathered out of the Word of God*

RMB   Nathaniel B. Shurtleff, ed., *Records of the Governor and Company of the Massachusetts Bay in New England*

SE   Eleazar Mather, *A Serious Exhortation to the Present and Succeeding Generation in New England . . .*

UI   Samuel Willard, *Useful Instructions for a Professing People in Times of Great Security and Degeneracy*

WMQ   *William and Mary Quarterly*

WP   Samuel Eliot Morison et al., eds., *The Winthrop Papers*

WT   Horton Davies, *Worship and Theology in England*

WWP   Edward Johnson, *Johnson's Wonder-Working Providence, 1628–1651*

TO

LIVE

ANCIENT

LIVES

INTRODUCTION

As in so many areas of historical scholarship, so in Puritan studies the interpretive venture often has been influenced, and occasionally dominated, by a wish to explain selected features of recent civilization. In Michael Walzer's succinct summary: "Virtually all the modern world has been read into Calvinism. . . . By one or another writer, the faith of the brethren, and especially of the Puritan brethren, has been made the source or cause or first embodiment of the most crucial elements of modernity." And yet, for all the implied reservation in this passage, Walzer devoted the remainder of his *Revolution of the Saints* to a characterization of the Puritan saint as "the first of those self-disciplined agents of social and political reconstruction [and revolution] who have appeared so frequently in modern history."[1]

In so doing, Walzer joined the large company of those who select and stress the modernizing elements—real or alleged—of the Puritan movement: Max Weber, who argued the classic case for "elective affinity" between "Calvinism" (and Puritanism as its most influential type) and early Western capitalism; Robert K. Merton, who described a "point to point correlation" between values of the "Puritan ethic" and the interests of those who promoted the new natural philosophy of the seventeenth century; Christopher Hill, who views Puritanism as the principal supplier of the new ethic of labor discipline needed in an age of nascent capitalism; David Little, for whom the Puritans are protagonists of "a new [voluntarist, functionalist, and semi-egalitarian] order" informed by "a new authority and a new law" that "strain[ed] toward the creation of a new society"; Sacvan Bercovitch, who assigns to the American Puritans a millennial-progressivist outlook neatly meshed with the "process of modernization"; and many others.[2]

1. Michael Walzer, *The Revolution of the Saints: A Study in the Origins of Radical Politics* (New York, 1969), vii, 300.

2. Max Weber, *The Protestant Ethic and the Spirit of Capitalism*, trans. Talcott Parsons (New York, 1958); Robert K. Merton, *Social Theory and Social Structure: Toward the Codification of Theory and Research*, 2d ed. (New York, 1968), 628–660; Christopher Hill, *Society and Puritanism in Pre-Revolutionary*

In this large body of scholarship construing Puritanism as "an agent of modernization, an ideology of the transition period," the saints' contribution to modernity may be described ironically, as in Weber; or, as in Little, they are conceived as cognizant agents of the "new"; or the entire problematic of intentions and consequences may be ignored. But in every case, attention logically turns to those elements that in some sense succeeded in the modern world, however that may be understood.[3] Elements that resist alignment with the future are permitted to recede into the background. One such element is of crucial importance to the present study. Weber's or Hill's protocapitalists, Merton's or Jones's proponents of the new science, Walzer's or Little's agents of change and radically new social and political order, Bercovitch's millennial futurists—these and many similar renderings of the Puritan reality embody a common assumption about orientations within time and history. They point to a general stance within time that deemphasized the past and began to key toward the future. In proportion as the future tense is highlighted, so the alignments with the past, the old, the first, the archetypal that were definitive for traditional European Christianity (Reformed, or Calvinist, Protestantism included) are presumed to have suffered major erosion distinctively within the Puritan context.

A contrary approach appears in the work of those who regard a persisting traditionalism, perhaps modified but not transformed, as a key index of the movement. For students who judge Puritan spokesmen as "thoroughly medieval . . . in their theology," as "looking backward . . . , not ahead" in scientific and economic matters, or as sponsors of an "exaggerated and persistent traditionalism" in their conception of Christian commonwealth, it is the past tense, the insistent look backward, that receives first billing. Much the same may be said of those interpretations that, while drawing attention to inchoately forward-looking themes, find them "wound in among counter-forces that checked and controlled their free play in behalf of . . . ideals more medieval than modern"; for while Puritanism thus envisaged probably did in the long run facilitate movement toward an

---

England, 2d ed. (New York, 1967), 124–218; David Little, *Religion, Order, and Law: A Study in Pre-Revolutionary England* (New York, 1969), 81–166; Sacvan Bercovitch, *The American Jeremiad* (Madison, Wis., 1978), xi–xv, 3–92.

3. Walzer, *Revolution*, 300.

age of reason and commerce, it was no easy or willing midwife.[4] Here the historical connections are drawn oblique; there was no straight line of development to the increasingly *prospective* standards of the succeeding age. So long as the characteristic values of hot-gospeling, "precise" biblicism, and covenanted behavior held sway, men would walk with their gaze fixed firstly upon the past.

This is not to say that concepts of placement and direction within time receive systematic or, most of the time, specific treatment in the scholarship. Perhaps the closest approach is to be found in the flurry of research in Puritan eschatology, for often enough such a focus has issued in portrayal of the drive for further reformation as essentially a procession into the future. Millennialism, in particular, which a number of writers propound as a generic and central feature of Puritan thought, usually is construed as a preoccupation with time forward toward the climax and end of history. Although their influence has been growing rapidly, these are as yet novel inferences, and they are likely in time to provoke a sharp reaction. In any case, that no general agreement in these matters—or, indeed, any extended review of the issues of placement toward past and present—has emerged in nearly a half-century of zealous scholarship presents yet another sign of unclarity about the content of Puritan concerns. On one point, Charles George obviously was right: for the most part the Puritanism abroad in scholarly parlance is a far too protean construct.[5] The consumer of secondary literature in this area must contend with a parade of contradictory and frequently ill-founded usages, and the common complaint on this score has done little to induce a more considered attention to definition. Here, as we begin to examine a historic standpoint in respect to past and present, we will be brought necessarily to consider the formative meaning of the quest for purity that occupied many thousands of English and colonial American Protestants for a century and more. A description of

4. Robert J. Roth, "The Philosophical Background of New England Puritanism," *International Philosophical Quarterly*, X (1970), 577; Darrett B. Rutman, *American Puritanism: Faith and Practice* (Philadelphia, 1970), 71; Leo F. Solt, "Puritanism, Capitalism, Democracy, and the New Science," *American Historical Review*, LXXIII (1967–1968), 28; Bernard Bailyn, in Robert Keayne, *The Apologia of Robert Keayne* . . . , ed. Bailyn (New York, 1965), ix.

5. See C. H. George, "Puritanism as History and Historiography," *Past and Present*, no. 41 (Dec. 1968), 77–104.

their orientation within time must go hand in hand with an attempt more precisely to identify Puritan content.

Expositors of Puritanism as a distinct religious tradition must take into account two ranges of variation. First, there is the internal variation within the movement at any given time, fanning out across a spectrum from minimal to radical dissent. In reference, for example, to the 1570s, it has proven useful to distinguish between a militant Presbyterian wing, demanding root-and-branch ecclesiastical reform, a more moderate party of passive resisters, and a residual group of earlier antivestment crusaders, now reconciled to the basic structure of the church and little further inclined to outspoken opposition. Second, there is the variation through time, the many shifts in program and emphasis from the original antivestiarian position of the 1560s through, say, the great pietist turn of the 1590s to the era of eschatological excitement and revolutionary reform in the mid-seventeenth century. Amid these diversities, may one discover a coherent Puritan pattern within English religion, a pattern notably distinct within the larger and international movement of Reformed Protestantism?[6]

Discouraged by the notorious difficulty of defining Puritanism and by the failure of research to move discernibly closer to agreement on this elementary issue, a number of historians have turned to tout dissensus as the rule. Thus one authority contends: "The word 'puritanism' is analogous to words such as 'socialism' or 'romanticism.' . . . They are impossible to use precisely . . . [so that] to describe someone as a Puritan is not really to tell us very much about his specific views." Another advertises "a welter of uncertainty among Puritans themselves regarding practically every religious, political, literary, and social notion entertained" in early New England. This work addresses only one side of Puritanism, but it finds there little support for such positions, and none whatever for the opinion

6. In a thoughtful discussion of "the problem of definition" in Puritan studies, John Morgan argues that the presence of internal and chronological variation precludes a substantive definition and recommends abandonment of the term "puritanism." His premise, however, that the act of definition necessarily projects a fixed and compact "essence," is arbitrary. The definition I offer below is designed explicitly to encompass variation. John Morgan, *Godly Learning: Puritan Attitudes towards Reason, Learning, and Education, 1560–1640* (Cambridge, 1986), 9–22.

that "there was no theology separating Puritans from Anglicans or binding Puritans to Puritans."[7]

Responding to the vast scholarship in the area, but guided foremost by a decade of reading in sixteenth- and seventeenth-century materials, I have drawn two conclusions. First, beginning in the 1560s there was for a century and more a distinct pattern of principled dissent within English Protestantism. By virtue of its sustained preoccupation with moral and primitive purity, it logically can be called Puritan. Contained for the most part within the Church of England, it yet embodied discontent with one or more major features of the religious establishment. A common strain in Puritan complaint was that the compromises with tradition embodied in the Elizabethan Settlement arrested at a critically immature stage the "work of God begun amongst us in England" in Henrician and Edwardian times. When Protestants were just "beginning to crawl out of [the popish] puddle," the queen and her episcopal commissioners intervened to "sta[y] the reast fro[m] going forwarde with the building they have begonne." This contention brings us to the often-suggested minimal definition of Puritanism as "the Protestant form of dissatisfaction with the required official religion of England," with its many conservative retentions and its relatively lax, church-typical ethos.[8] It points as well to an officially dominant adversary: English Protestants, including at all times the royal "supreme governor" of the church and, from the early 1580s, a decisive majority on the episcopal bench that basically supported the Elizabethan forms and their later refinements.

In the later 1570s and 1580s, a distinguishable Anglican interest

7. H. F. Kearney, "Puritanism and Science: Problems of Definition," in Charles Webster, ed., *The Intellectual Revolution of the Seventeenth Century* (London, 1974), 255; Kenneth Silverman, quoted in Michael McGiffert, "American Puritan Studies in the 1960's," *WMQ*, 3d Ser., XXVII (1970), 40–41; George, "Puritanism," *Past and Present*, no. 41 (Dec. 1968), 101. For the emphasis upon "dissensus" in American studies of the 1960s, see McGiffert, "Puritan Studies," 40–42. The most detailed and ably argued case for heterogeneity has been made by Philip F. Gura, *A Glimpse of Sion's Glory: Puritan Radicalism in New England, 1620–1660* (Middletown, Conn., 1984).

8. Leonard J. Trinterud, ed., *Elizabethan Puritanism* (New York, 1971), 9, 85; [Robert Crowley], *A Brief Discourse against the Outwarde Apparell . . .* (n.p., 1566), sigs. Civ, Aiv.

appears to have emerged. During these years men were coming of age within the church who had not shared the experiences of the Marian exile, who had enjoyed nurture and advancement within the established framework, and who had little or no taste for further reformation. Stung by Puritan criticism, many of their spokesmen would engage in spirited advocacy of the mandated arrangements of worship, discipline, and polity. During the decade before the start of the Great Migration to New England, some of their number would begin, indeed, to press for select modifications of the liturgy and even to propose revisions of Reformed soteriology, but always in a contra-Puritan, catholicizing direction. Out of the continual collision between approving and reproving attitudes to the prescribed religion grew in time clearly differentiated Puritan and Anglican understandings of the church and its mission.[9]

But this account brings us only to a first plateau in definition. It points to a movement of dissent, to its undercurrent of frustration and its adversarial bent, but it does not supply it with a profile. It does not distinguish Puritan from Anglican, Lutheran, or Anabaptist concepts of Protestant life or locate English Puritanism within the international community of Reformed churches and theologies. It fails to supply the criteria by which, say, the Book of Common Prayer

9. In the present study the intended initial meaning of the term *Anglican* is a positive adherence to the spirit and the general terms of the Elizabethan Settlement. I am well aware that this is a loose designation and that advocacy of the official religion never attained a single and clear-cut intellectual pattern during the period covered. Nevertheless, the wish to preserve the Elizabethan arrangements in the face of Puritan assault was a common interest among many leading churchmen. Then, as these men wedged themselves down in the national church, their thought gradually and naturally tended toward congenial stresses, as upon a church-typical understanding of the Christian community, an authoritarian-pyramidal concept of ecclesiastical authority pressed with a tireless urging to obedience and unity, an orientation to formal and relatively elaborate liturgy, a reliance upon the notion of "things indifferent" to legitimate the standing order of worship and polity, and a special regard for the patristic era in church history. All of these themes stand in tension with the positions of Reformed Protestantism on the Continent and in Scotland, although there were points of contact with Zurich. In my opinion, here is sufficient justification for a preliminary and cautious use of the term *Anglican*. The writings of men like Matthew Parker, John Whitgift, John Bridges, and Richard Hooker reveal that a reasonably clear Anglicanism defined in such terms was well in evidence by 1600.

might be judged impure and a truer mode of Protestant worship envisioned.

Hence the second conclusion: that the distinctive concerns of Puritan dissent tended to emerge from three interlinked agendas. In brief form, these may be termed "moralism," "pietism," and biblicist "primitivism." The defining element of the first, spelled out for the most part with typical Reformed accents, was *a stress upon the moral transformation, performance, and purity of individuals and their communities.* In this category a variety of logically connected themes find their natural place: divine will and rule, the biblical presentation of moral and judicial law, covenant, worldly asceticism, church discipline, and work.[10]

Pietism, the second pattern, was not a marked feature of Puritan dissent before the 1590s, but from that decade an elaborate "practice of piety" became a hallmark of the life and teaching of the famed Spiritual Brotherhood of dissenting but generally moderate clergy and, so far as we can judge, of their more committed lay charges. It carried over as well into the separatist cells that from time to time broke away from the official church. Here the defining element was *a preoccupation with the self and its subjective states, particularly with its inner controls.* In this category the cardinal themes, closely interwoven with the moralist motifs listed above and rendering them ever more strenuous, were preparation for conversion; conversion; the great warfare with flesh, world, and devil; the watch upon behavior; a marked degree of religious insecurity coupled to a quest for the assurance of salvation; introspection; a close attention to psychological dynamics that amounted virtually to a Puritan psychoanalysis;

10. Perhaps most diagnostic here is the "covenant" construct which Leonard J. Trinterud, William A. Clebsch, Jerald C. Brauer, and others have joined in identifying as "the essential [theological] genius of Puritanism." Trinterud, "The Origins of Puritanism," *CH*, XX (1951), 55. See also Trinterud, ed., *Puritanism*, 302–312; Clebsch, *England's Earliest Protestants, 1520–1535* (New Haven, Conn., 1964), vii, 9, 316–317; Brauer, "Reflections on the Nature of English Puritanism," *CH*, XXIII (1954), 100.

Recognition of the Puritan insistence upon a moral reformation both personal and civic is also the point at which historians have been most successful in discovering socioeconomic correlations. See, for example, Keith Wrightson and David Levine, *Poverty and Piety in an English Village: Terling, 1525–1700* (New York, 1979); William Hunt, *The Puritan Moment: The Coming of Revolution in an English County* (Cambridge, 1983).

cases of conscience; disciplines of prayer and meditation; spiritual diaries; holy soliloquies; and sabbatarianism.[11]

Although many of the above themes will be familiar, the proposition that they fall into two coherent thematic programs that articulated much of the conscious intent of a distinct Puritanism would require considerable argument. (To provide this, and to comment on the absurdity of deriving English concerns fundamentally from Calvin, will be the task of another book.) The basic ideas presented here in short compass may supply the reader with a sense of the larger definitional boundaries within which the present work has been conceived, for it too is directed, in part, to the problem of definition. But these pages emphasize the third and least familiar component: biblicist primitivism. Primitivism supplies both a conceptual axis along which neglected root meanings of the Puritan enterprise can be expounded and, at the same time, a host of clues germane to sorting out attitudes toward past and future. In several ways it was precisely a prescription for taking bearings within time.

Consider the following words of counsel offered by John Cotton to his congregation at Boston, Lincolnshire, probably during the 1620s. Openly identifying with "the name of *Puritans*," Cotton addressed the principal issue then fueling his dissatisfaction with the established church:

> No new traditions must bee thrust on us, . . . *But that which [we] have had from the beginning.* Doct[rine:] *True Antiquity . . . is that which fetches its originall from the beginning.* . . . True Antiquity is twofold. 1. From the first Institution . . . of a thing, . . . 2. That which fetcheth its beginning from God, though it were of later times, . . . and as hee is the ancient of dayes, so is that good; as Baptisme and the Lord's Supper, though they were not in the World before Christs comming in the flesh, yet being from God, they have true Antiquity, . . . if [a religious form] have no higher rise than the [early] Fathers, it is too young a device, no other writings besides the Scripture can plead true

11. The fullest modern studies of themes of piety are Charles E. Hambrick-Stowe, *The Practice of Piety: Puritan Devotional Disciplines in Seventeenth-Century New England* (Chapel Hill, N.C., 1982); and Charles Lloyd Cohen, *God's Caress: The Psychology of Puritan Religious Experience* (New York, 1986).

Antiquity, . . . Look whatever comes from God . . . is always
new, and never waxeth old, and as it is new, so it is always old,
. . . All errors . . . are aberrations from the first good estate.
. . . [In sum], *live antient lives;* your obedience must be swayed
by an old rule, walk in the old way.[12]

Here is a set of ideas absolutely fundamental to Cotton's outlook,
which itself could be called new if it had not been there all the time.
Most revealing is the familiar and self-evident priority attached by
Cotton to the "old," the "first," the "beginning," the "original," the
"ancient," and "True Antiquity." Also to be noted are the studiedly
invidious contrasts drawn with the "new," the "young," and the
"later" and the hostility focused upon "aberrations from the first."
These were not stray thoughts, nor evidences of idiosyncrasy. They
were characteristic manifestations of a whole facet of Puritan thought
that I shall label "primitivist," or alternatively, "restorationist" or
"restitutionist." At root it was an affirmation of biblical supremacy,
but the typifying element was *a reversion, undercutting both Catholic
and Anglican appeals to a continuity of tradition, to the first, or primitive, order of things narrated in the Protestant Scriptures.*

Primitivism embraced the conviction that the Christian pilgrimage
forth through the age of reformation and toward the eschatological
climax was simultaneously a retrogression. To move forward was
to strive without rest for reconnection with the paradigmatic events
and utterances of ancient and unspoiled times. Examining these ideas
further, one will confront an entire substructure of meanings that
lent distinct flavor and point to Puritan expression in all periods
and on many levels. In most respects it is unfamiliar to students
in the field.[13] Certainly there is no lack of recognition that Puritan
voices habitually appealed to the ancient nation of Israel or to the

12. John Cotton, *A Practical Commentary . . . upon the First Epistle Generall
of John* (London, 1656), 77–79, 189, 232 (I have changed the order of statements,
and the emphasis upon "live antient lives" is mine).

13. The best study touching upon primitivist themes is James C. Spalding,
"Restitution as a Normative Factor for Puritan Dissent," *Journal of the Ameri-
can Academy of Religion*, XLIV (1976), 47–63. See also John Kenneth Reynold
Luoma, "The Primitive Church as a Normative Principle in the Theology of the
Sixteenth Century . . ." (Ph.D. diss., Hartford Seminary Foundation, 1974);
George Yule, "Continental Patterns and the Reformation in England and Scot-
land," *Scottish Journal of Theology*, XXII (1969), 305–323.

primitive Christian churches; but that appeal, that peculiar rallying to an ancient and primitive standard, remains to be pursued as a factor both major and structural to the meaning of this most powerful early movement in Anglo-American Protestantism.

A word about the limits of the study is in order. The present inquiry does not canvass fully the ranges of variation indicated above. The laborer in this area quickly discovers that the historical remains of English dissent through the century or more after the Elizabethan Settlement are unmanageably vast, scarcely to be covered in full in a lifetime of even rapid research. Further, they must be read in counterpoint with expressions of Anglican opinion defending the established church. For these reasons, and to allow the theme to be rendered in reasonably full detail, an intensive case study appears preferable to a general survey.

The first two chapters trace primitivist strands in English Puritan thought through the period of the Great Migration. Following chapters confront in detail the American data, with particular attention to Massachusetts. This approach seeks to avoid the oft-indulged folly of engaging the American ideas without an adequate grasp of their definitive English origins and careers up to the era of migration. It is perfectly true that " 'Puritan,' like other Old World concepts, . . . suffered an Atlantic sea-change" upon removal to the American wilderness; but in the realm of ideas that change was registered most decisively through a shift in restorationist emphasis and is thus a crucial part of the story.[14] With Puritanism thus followed into the American arena after 1630, the continuing saga of dissenters' primitivism in England thereafter may be left to future students of the phenomenon.

14. Basil Hall, "Puritanism: The Problem of Definition," in *Studies in Church History*, II, ed. G. J. Cuming (London, 1965), 294.

ONE

FOUNDATIONS

OF PURITAN

PRIMITIVISM

*I*t is a familiar assumption, regularly advanced, that "the puritans were above all . . . the people of the Book. What united . . . [them] was their belief in the Bible as the sole authority." Thus innumerable writers recognize that the Puritans insisted "on scriptural sanction for everything," that "Holy Scripture was both the practical and the theoretical fountainhead of the [Puritan] movement," that a "notorious Biblicism" was its "simplest identifying feature," that the "nub" of the issue between Puritans and Anglicans was "the authority of scripture," that Massachusetts "was founded . . . upon the eternal laws of the Bible"—and the like.[1]

And yet, despite the fundamental character and the widespread acceptance of such judgments, few studies of Puritanism give more than passing attention to its distinctive significance *within* this context of "the Book."[2] This and the following chapter will argue that

1. G. R. Elton, *England under the Tudors* (London, 1955), 425; Samuel Eliot Morison, *The Intellectual Life of Colonial New England*, 2d ed. (New York, 1956), 8, 29; Sydney E. Ahlstrom, *A Religious History of the American People* (New Haven, Conn., 1972), 92; James Fulton Maclear, " 'The Heart of New England Rent': The Mystical Element in Early Puritan History," *Mississippi Valley Historical Review*, XLII (1955–1956), 623; Perry Miller and Thomas H. Johnson, eds., *The Puritans*, rev. ed., 2 vols. (New York, 1963), I, 41; Perry Miller, *Orthodoxy in Massachusetts, 1630–1650* (Boston, 1959), 222.

2. The notable exceptions are John S. Coolidge, *The Pauline Renaissance in England: Puritanism and the Bible* (Oxford, 1970); and John R. Knott, Jr., *The Sword of the Spirit: Puritan Responses to the Bible* (Chicago, 1980).

Puritan spokesmen joined a fealty to the supreme book to an asser-
tively primitivist orientation; that concepts such as "novelty," "pattern," "addition," "invention," "simplicity," and "imitation" (all absent from the only study of Puritan vocabulary) mark out a major
coherence in English dissenting thought; and that elemental belief
in the power and exemplary authority of an ancient and "first time"
must be viewed as a sharp qualification of the movement's modernizing tendency.[3] There is no disputing that such recourse to the
long-lost undercut traditionalist ideals—or awakened hungers for
religious and social change that may have facilitated transitions to
early modern civilization. Yet the breeding of modern modes was no
part of the conscious intent of religious reformers whose watchword
was "further reformation." Their allegiance remained tied to a firmly
*retro*spective norm, to a drive toward origins that is at least as archaic
an element within Western life as traditionalism itself.

Examined in detail, Puritan conceptions of biblical word and event
and of their continuing role in postbiblical time fall into a harmonious pattern. As we will emphasize often, the crucial premise was
that the first is best; and that premise, with its own long history in
Western thought, leads us to *myth*. Here, this term will be a fundamental tool, assigned specified meanings that answer to aspects of
Puritan perspective. *Myth* will describe a narrative of events that
occurred in an elite, long-ago Great, or Strong, Time in human (and
divine) history, more precisely the age of wonders reported in the
Old and New Testaments. That age was "mythic," sharply divided
from ordinary human days and ways, because it embodied a variety
of singular qualities. In essence, it was the primal (or "primitive" or
"first") time in which Christianity was given and unfolded in fullness
and in this sense is designated the Puritan *primordium*. It was the
normative time to which the men and women of the present must, in
imagination, "return" for saving guidance and empowerment. And
there they would find the crucial bearings for their own continuing
venture through history.[4]

3. Few of the technically crucial terms in Puritan theology are covered in
M. Van Beek, *An Enquiry into Puritan Vocabulary* (Gronigen, 1969).

4. See Appendix 1 for a fuller discussion of the terminology introduced
here and its application to Puritanism. Of course, Reformed-Puritan thinkers
marked differences between the New and Old Testaments, but they resisted the
dichotomous trends in Anabaptist and (if to a lesser degree) Lutheran thought
and developed a relative stress upon biblical unity.

For centuries before the reign of Elizabeth I, an allegiance to Christianity's primitive era (often the emphasis fell largely upon the New Testament) had provided the cornerstone of an impressively complex set of ideas that, collectively, one may call *primitivism*. To describe, illustrate, and ponder Puritan uses of those ideas and their principles of combination is the overall task, but we begin with a brief overview of the entire pattern in its Puritan adaptation.

1. In Puritan perspective, Holy Scripture was the expressive transcript of the events of Christianity's great and formative time. With more comprehensive intent than did magisterial Protestants generally, certainly more so than their Anglican antagonists, Puritans ascribed normative, exalted, mythic status to the biblical era from Creation to Apocalypse. By virtue of such focus, they acknowledged little historical distance between their own and the primal age. In their view of the church's trek beyond apostolic times, all intervening history, save as it might be invoked for occasional polemical purposes, was darkness and loss. It was not the history that produced them. It was eclipsed by the greatness and originative power of biblical times. For those times and events continually hailed in Puritan rhetoric as primitive, first, or original were the ground of the only true history there was. Students in search of the distinctively Puritan phenomenon within English and early American history, therefore, must learn to reckon both with the assumption that "fullness and force are at the beginning" and with its joint application to the ancient and covenanted people of Israel and to "the primitive church in the golden age."[5]
2. Understood in such terms, the scriptural report was far more than a mere chronicle. The events it depicted were not truly remote. They were dramatic, engrossing, and hence contem-

5. Mircea Eliade, *Myth and Reality*, trans. Willard R. Trask (New York, 1963), 51; Thomas Shepard, *The Works of Thomas Shepard*, 3 vols. (Boston, 1853), I, 144. The Puritan "primitive" time possessed much of the prestige attached to the "best age" in Lovejoy and Boas's typology of chronological primitivism and to the time of the beginnings in Mircea Eliade's analysis of "myth." See Appendix 1.

"Magisterial" Protestants, including all but a handful of the figures mentioned in this study, wished to achieve religious reform with the approval and active sponsorship of duly constituted political authorities.

porary.[6] Sacred writ was therefore experienced as a kind of living theater. Since the joined biblical narratives evoked the one and only signifying history of the race, that history in principle must be immediate to the experience of the present age and reader. Making heavy demands upon visual imagination, it invoked characters and events that, in their lively display and existential gravity, might totally absorb the beholder's attention. Accordingly, in the many forms of biblical nurture sponsored by Puritan interests, the first aim was to abolish objective distance between the precise saint of Elizabethan or Stuart times and the world of biblical report; it was to draw the observer within the horizon of action, to promote self-forgetful identification with the presented events.

3. Dramatic identification was much facilitated by the uniquely elevated character of biblical event. Puritans portrayed the scriptural panorama as sacred, as a continual theophany, as a parade of religious heroics suffused with supernatural presence and power. Organic to it were miracles, prophecies, and prodigious, infallible teaching—all narrated with appropriate flair by chosen "clerks" of the Holy Spirit.

4. Associated with sacred event was the quality of "simplicity."[7] Dress, behavior, doctrine, church order, and, above all, the forms of worship of the primitive times embodied the natural simplicity of divine originals. They stood in judgment upon the present, upon the obscuring accretions and complexities of Catholic and Anglican tradition.

5. A cognate quality of the Puritan primordium was "purity." Certainly in one use in Puritan discourse the term pointed to moral achievement, but it as often drew its peculiar force from association with the mythic and first. Frequently with an emphasis upon church polity and forms of worship, advocates of further reformation identified biblical patterns as "pure"; flowing immediately from the divine source, they were as yet

6. This corresponds to Eliade's thesis that in mythic remembrance "the protagonists of the myth are made present, one becomes their contemporary" (*Myth and Reality*, 19).

7. On this point and the next, note the correspondence with Lovejoy and Boas's "cultural primitivism" (see Appendix 1).

untouched by the corrupting human influences that would begin to operate after the close of the apostolic era.

6. In Puritan theology the biblical world was depicted as a display of authoritative archetypes for redemptively significant human activities in the postbiblical era.[8] If in mythic time all experience was universal experience, then mythic acts were universal acts. This did not mean that primordial action in its entirety was to be imitated; only divinely specified, generalizable, and "significant" action was to be designated as mandatory "pattern" or "example." The construction and application of these criteria often proved difficult, and Puritan thinkers— the Presbyterian-Congregational debates of the seventeenth century supply the fullest instance—occasionally disagreed over the right identification of archetypes.

7. Consistently in Puritan expression, the biblical world of saving origins was comprehended as an order of completed perfection. The realm of sacred pattern was closed, all-sufficient, timeless; it was not relative to the times, places, and changes of history. Subject to no alteration, it held full and equal jurisdiction in any present hour.

8. Since, therefore, the truths that Christians must assimilate were complete and immutable, the role of the intellect in religious matters must be restricted to pliant cognition. Insofar as the Puritans' epistemology assumed the enlarging impact of divine "illumination" upon the mind, it was not strictly empiricist; yet the purpose of that illumination was never to encourage "invention" beyond the presentations of sacred writ, but to spur fuller conformation to its objective content.

9. When they stepped back to see it whole, Puritans perceived the historical career of the Christian church as one of progressive decline. Despite its splendid beginnings, the church had fallen prey after apostolic times to ecclesiastical managers and thinkers who forsook the vision of biblical finality. They made free to create and intrude their own forms and teachings, ever more complex and impure as distance from the primi-

8. The mimetic theme in Puritanism is greatly illuminated by Eliade's discussion of the *gesta* of mythic actors and their function as "exemplary model[s] for all significant human activities" (see Appendix 1).

tive source increased, upon those of the great age. Over the centuries the flow of "human inventions" slowly had eclipsed the formative pattern and intent of the Christian dispensation. By the time of the High Middle Ages the church's degeneration into a new "Popish religion, . . . a meere device of mens braines," was complete.[9]

10. Acknowledging important preparation in Waldensian and Wycliffite dissent, Puritan publicists depicted the great Reformation of the sixteenth century as a partially effective countermovement of reform. It marked a line of ascent reversing the decline of centuries but one that also curved back to restore contact with originals and return Christianity to its primitive foundations. In this context, "reformation" (or "restoration" or "restitution"), describing the distinctive task of Protestant Christians until the approaching end of the world, was distinguished by the prefix *re-*, signifying directedness toward the first and best.

11. When, well into the seventeenth century, Puritan thinkers became interested in the millennial idea, they tied it firmly to primitivist priorities. The expected age of fulfillment was understood in several senses as the climax of Protestant restoration, the finally triumphant reversion to primordial conditions.[10]

These eleven propositions summarize much of Puritan thought about the nature and authority of the Protestant Scriptures. Like the Christianized Aristotelian science of nature or the faculty psychology, primitivist doctrine was a part of the intellectual heritage that Puritans matter-of-factly took over. With but a few exceptions, the primacy of first times or the duty of mimesis was discussed only in passing reference. Puritans might disagree with Anglican apologists about the scope of originals or their jurisdiction in particular cases,

9. John Dod, *A Plaine and Familiar Exposition of the Ten Commandements* (London, 1618), 11. Points 9 and 10 connect with Lovejoy and Boas's "Theory of Decline and Future Restoration" (see Appendix 1).

10. It is a primary insight of Eliade that the millennium anticipated in many Christian eschatologies is a recovery of primordial (biblical) conditions. See Robert A. Segal, "Eliade's Theory of Millenarianism," *Religious Studies*, XIV (1978), 159–173.

but they considered their rationale and credit to stand beyond question. Thus while treatises upon vocational calling, preparation for conversion, or special providences were crucial to the movement's propaganda, probably no sermon or text devoted per se to the explication of firstness, of imitation, or of simplicity ever appeared, although a work like William Whately's *Prototypes; or, The Primarie Precedent Presidents out of the Booke of Genesis* (1640) brought the precedential component clearly enough to the fore.

Hence it might escape the student of this literature that it incorporates a version of Christian primitivism unless attention is directed expressly to the relevant and scattered but pervasive passages. But once those evidences are examined and their implication for Puritan studies is grasped, the inquirer may follow from text to text and theme to theme until the schema stands revealed in all its coherence and power. It will also become apparent that, unlike Aristotelian science, Ramist logic, or the traditional classification of mental faculties—those enormously useful but ultimately disposable tools of Puritan theology and homiletics—primitivism was integral in manifold ways to the very meaning of the Puritan vision both within the English church and in the early New England colonies.

Historical Backgrounds

*P*uritan primitivism was a selective continuation of patterns deeply rooted in historical Western culture. The Western peoples have indeed, "throughout a great part of [their] historic march, walked with face turned backward" toward the first, the ancient, the golden, the exemplary.[11] Many characteristic features of the Christian Middle Ages, which provide so many lines of continuity with Protestantism, were shaped by the belief that the first is best.

To restrict our view to religious belief and practice, we may recall the importance attached by medieval churchmen to agreement with antiquity, with the apostolic *depositum*, with the early Fathers. In the quest for truth, theology faced backward rather than forward; redeeming knowledge was a recovery and loyal representation of the

11. Lois Whitney, *Primitivism and the Idea of Progress in English Popular Literature of the Eighteenth Century* (Baltimore, 1934), xi.

"faith once delivered," not an advance. Beginning with the Cluniac agitations of the tenth century, successive waves of monastic reform were inspired by ideals of return to an uncorrupted primitive monasticism. Thus the reforming interest in the investiture controversy of the eleventh century aimed at the restoration of ancient discipline; and Waldensians, Spiritual Franciscans, Lollards, Hussites, and other proponents of radical reform and heresy were strongly restitutionist in outlook, as was the more restrained Catholic Reformation of the late fifteenth through the sixteenth centuries. Such advocates of reform "always saw themselves as belonging to the apostolic church of earlier Christian tradition . . . ; their aim was to restore it to that tradition."[12]

Many popular genres of religious literature—the Fathers of the desert, the acts of the martyrs, the lives of the saints—and the myriad admonitions to an imitatio Christi reflected the typical exemplarist pattern of primitivist thinking. Medieval religious art and architecture—painting, statuary, and the sculptural programs of the cathedrals—continually re-presented characters and events of the biblical primordium, as did, in some measure, liturgical pageants, the reverence for relics, the quest of the crusaders to regain the Holy Land, and recommended topics for meditation. Medieval primitivism is a vast subject, far beyond the scope of this study, but it is important for understanding Puritan devotion to first times and exemplary patterns as a conserving impulse that itself faced backward to a long-established reflex.

Yet within the mainstream of ecclesiastical development, medieval esteem for the first was shaped by the church's transference to itself of attributes and prerogatives of the Great Time. Through apostolic succession and continual sacramental re-presentation, the church was believed to maintain unbroken continuity with the first era and thus to partake fully of its power and esteem. The church was Holy Mother, a supernatural institution indwelt, informed and guarded from essential error by the Holy Spirit; it enjoyed special exemption from the normal limitations of postapostolic time. Through its

12. Gordon Leff, *The Dissolution of the Medieval Outlook: An Essay on Intellectual and Spiritual Change in the Fourteenth Century* (New York, 1976), 119, 130–144.

hierarchy, law, courts, formularies, sacraments, theological doctors, and episcopal *magisterium* (or teaching authority), it functioned as the immediate source and medium of Redemption. It could formulate and impose laws upon its membership, forgive sins, dispense indulgences, declare the meaning of the Bible. Scripture might be viewed as the sole and exclusive basis of ecclesiastical doctrine and authority, or as coordinate in some degree with extrascriptural tradition, but in either case it was Scripture as mediated by the church, Scripture as understood by the succession of Fathers, Doctors, canonists, bishops, and councils of the superhuman church that came to expression.[13] Hence the sacred Book, with its report of the normative period, could not offer a vantage point from which to criticize the existing church. There was no degeneration from primitive excellence, but only the perpetuation of a faithful continuity.

To the generation of Christian humanists who came to the fore about 1500, such claims of harmony with the first rang hollow. Influenced both by the apostolic ideal of late medieval reform and by the Renaissance humanists' promotion of classical antiquity as the standard for all cultural activities, proponents of the new Christian learning too wished "to go backward in time." Finding the theological and moral standards of the primary (that is, the apostolic and patristic) age debased beyond recognition in the contemporary church, they announced a program of "renovatio, restitutio, restauratio." Thus in an early stage of his career, Erasmus was a classicist and his primordium, not Christian, but pagan antiquity. It was probably a meeting with John Colet in 1499 that convinced him of the superiority of the Christian philosophy and turned him into a new path as restorer of biblical and patristic texts and teachings. In his subsequent career in Christian humanism, his characteristic appeal was to "that ancient and genuine theology, now overgrown with thorny subtleties," and to the much simpler and more pastoral order of the earliest Christian church. That was now to be reclaimed in all "its pristine splendor and dignity." In the early years of the sixteenth century, the Erasmian call *ad fontes* provided the basis of an impressive Christian-humanist episode in English religious and

13. Heiko Oberman, *The Harvest of Medieval Theology: Gabriel Biel and Late Medieval Nominalism* (Grand Rapids, Mich., 1967), 365–373.

intellectual life. It also supplied a vital supporting context and many of the keynote themes of the Henrician Reformation.[14]

The Magisterial Reformation was "characteristically medieval in looking backwards for its model and its standard," but, in heavy reliance upon late medieval restorationist currents and upon Christian humanism, it rejected the Roman claim that biblical and apostolic norms were sustained in the present ecclesiastical system. The reformers viewed Catholic history, not as a preserving continuity, but as a progressive fall from the purity of primitive times. While not proceeding to the extreme restitutionist conclusions of the Anabaptists, they were agreed that Catholic Christianity had moved far out of harmony with early Christian teaching and example, that the church's doctrine and at least the essential forms of practice must be conformed anew to the biblical presentation. In restoring the service of Communion, for instance, Luther urged: "We must . . . begin by setting aside all the later additions to the first, simple institution." "The closer our Mass resembles that first mass of all, which Christ celebrated at the Last Supper, the more Christian it will be." "All we have attempted," agreed Calvin, "is to restore the native purity from which [the Christian ordinances] had degenerated," indeed, to bring every key issue and practice of faith "back to its [biblical] fountainhead."[15]

Probably influenced by Lollard devotion to "the condition of the church when it enjoyed direct conversation with Christ, the estate of the Primitive Church," and certainly influenced by Erasmian humanism, pre-Puritan English reformers shared completely the Protestant determination that doctrine and ordinances "should be renovated and

14. Johan Huizinga, *Men and Ideas: History, the Middle Ages, the Renaissance,* trans. James S. Holmes and Hans van Marle (London, 1960), 277; Hans J. Hillerbrand, ed., *Erasmus and His Age: Selected Letters of Desiderius Erasmus* (New York, 1970), 31. See also Abraham Friesen, "The Impulse toward Restitutionist Thought in Christian Humanism," *Journal of the American Academy of Religion,* XLIV (1976), 29–45. Connections with the English Reformation are discussed in James Kelsey McConica, *English Humanists and Reformation Politics under Henry VIII and Edward VI* (Oxford, 1965).

15. Owen Chadwick, *The Reformation* (Baltimore, 1964), 19; Martin Luther, *Martin Luther,* ed. John Dillenberger (Chicago, 1961), 271, 286; John C. Olin, ed., *John Calvin and Jacopo Sadoleto: A Reformation Debate: Sadoleto's Letter to the Genevans and Calvin's Reply* (New York, 1966), 64, 88.

restored according to the institutions of our Saviour Christ."[16] In the legion of similar texts that occur in Reformation literature, the historian of ideas does well to observe carefully the primitivist intent. Reformation biblicism, in England as elsewhere, grounded biblical jurisdiction in part upon the assumption that Scripture manifests a "first, original and most perfect" state of things which in the "corruption of [Catholic] time" became "deformed and corrupted."[17] It was in the context of Protestant calls for a "retrograde movement" to biblical originals that the preparation and gradual popularization of a vernacular English Bible became the "supreme event" of the English Reformation.[18]

The Patristic Primordium

If indeed the English Puritans were people of the Book, and if their "religious and theological framework was of the golden age variety," the question arises, How distinctive was their outlook?[19] Did Puritan biblicism basically recapitulate the primitivist themes of earlier Protestant tradition, or perhaps intensify them, or did it adapt them to a recognizably Puritan orientation? What, exactly, did the reformers have in mind when they appealed to the first, original state that preceded the Catholic betrayal?

16. Howard Kaminsky, "Wyclifism as Ideology of Revolution," *CH*, XXXII (1963), 68; Thomas Cranmer, *The Work of Thomas Cranmer*, ed. G. E. Duffield (Philadelphia, 1965), 52. See also John Edmund Cox, ed., *Miscellaneous Writings and Letters of Thomas Cranmer* (Cambridge, 1846), 344, vol. II of *The Works of Thomas Cranmer* . . . ; George Joye, *The Unite and Schisme of the Olde Chirche* (n.p., 1543), sig. A8; Stephen Gardiner, *The Oration of True Obedience* (1535), in Pierre Janelle, ed. and trans., *Obedience in Church and State: Three Political Tracts by Stephen Gardiner* (London, 1930), 69; John Hooper, *The Early Writings of John Hooper*, ed. Samuel Carr (Cambridge, 1843), 83.

17. Hooper, *Early Writings*, 83; Cranmer, *Writings and Letters*, 528; Joye, *Unite and Schisme*, sig. A5. See also *WT*, I, 15–17.

18. John N. King, *English Reformation Literature: The Tudor Origins of the Protestant Tradition* (Princeton, N.J., 1982), 151; E. G. Rupp, *Studies in the Making of the English Protestant Tradition (Mainly in the Reign of Henry VIII)* (Cambridge, 1966), 48.

19. Marshall M. Knappen, *Tudor Puritanism: A Chapter in the History of Idealism* (1939; Gloucester, Mass., 1963), 351.

That primitive church so often invoked in early Protestant literature was not, in fact, identified exclusively with the church of the
New Testament. In partial retention of centuries of veneration of
the immediately postbiblical age of the Fathers, but reflecting as well
the Christian humanist program of patristic revival, the reformers
tended to revere the ancient church of the centuries immediately following the close of the New Testament narrative. There had been,
in short, no sharp break in the church's teaching and practice at the
close of the New Testament era, but a substantial historical interim,
usually held to encompass the second through the fifth centuries
A.D., which predated the fatal descent into Roman error. In espousing
this concept the reformers had no wish to compromise the principle
of *sola scriptura:* the New Testament remained the norm. What distinguished the intervening epoch of holy antiquity was explicitly its
fidelity to the apostolic way. If the patristic sources sometimes con-
tradicted each other, or if they departed from biblical doctrine, they
were subject to critical scrutiny and censure. But with few exceptions they were to be regarded as a loyal, if secondary, extension
of the Great Time and thus remained a vital resource for Christian
reformation. Hence in early Protestant preaching and polemic, biblical appeal frequently was combined with patristic citations, and the
reformers felt themselves "armed not only with the energy of the
Divine Word, but with the aid of the holy Fathers also." [20]

As on the Continent, the Reformation in England may be understood partly as a struggle to reclaim the patristic heritage from Roman
misinterpretation. Thomas Cranmer, archbishop of the Henrician and
Edwardian church, and George Joye, an exiled radical, might be at
variance upon many points of doctrine, but they were in complete
agreement that Protestant teaching and practice were not only "confirmed with the testimonies of the holy scriptures" but also "approved
with the whole consent of the old holy doctors of the church im-

20. John Calvin, *Institutes of the Christian Religion,* ed. John T. McNeill,
2 vols. (Philadelphia, 1960), II, 1171–1172; Olin, ed., *Reformation Debate,* 73.
See also John M. Headley, *Luther's View of Church History* (New Haven,
Conn., 1963), 83. Relatively resistant to humanist influence, Luther was less
inclined than the other major reformers to identify any past period of the church
as normative (Headley, *Luther's View,* 160–161, 163–164, 170–171, 235–236,
261).

mediately after the Apostles."[21] Yet, clearly, the more convinced proponents of the official and semi-Catholic English church stood to gain the most from appeal to a secondary primordium. Support for the liturgical forms and milieu of the Book of Common Prayer as well as the church's episcopal polity often could be marshaled more readily from the "old ecclesiastical writers" than directly from the New Testament.

So long as no apparent discord with biblical teaching was in question, the presumption that the biblical primordium was extended in a fashion through the first centuries after Christ lent needed authority in many cases where clear biblical directive was lacking. In consequence, representatives of the official Reformation, making the most of the Erasmian heritage at this point, oriented themselves with peculiar intensity to the patristic era. We may note that Cranmer, whose library was packed with the early Fathers, had no intention of deriving the liturgical structures of the Prayer Book exclusively from Scripture. His formulation of "the true and Catholic doctrine of the Sacrament," for instance, was "grounded . . . upon God's holy word" but also "approved by the consent of the most ancient Doctors of the Church." The patristic content of his several drafts and discussions of the English liturgy is extensive.[22]

When, later in the sixteenth century, there arose a forceful Puritan opposition to the standing order, dissenters and apologists for the church began to part ways in their respective attitudes toward the ancient postbiblical church. A definitive element in the slowly emerging Anglican tendency of these and later years was the claim that the authorized religious forms loyally restored "the custom of the primitive church," that is, "the order most generally used in the

21. George Joye, *A Present Consolacion for the Sufferers of Persecucion* . . . (London, 1544), sig. F6; Cranmer, *Work of Cranmer*, xii. See also S. L. Greenslade, *The English Reformers and the Fathers of the Church* (Oxford, 1960), 3–9.

22. Hugh Latimer, *Sermons and Remains of Hugh Latimer*, ed. George Elwes Corrie (Cambridge, 1845), 319, 333, 340; Henry Christmas, ed., *The Works of Nicholas Ridley* (Cambridge, 1841), 28, 94, 248. Note Cranmer's title, *A Defence of the True and Catholic Doctrine of the Sacrament . . . Grounded . . . upon God's Holy Word, and Approved by the Consent of the Most Ancient Doctors of the Church* (1550), in Cranmer, *Work of Cranmer*, 45–231 (see also 341–365; and *WT*, I, 11, 15–17).

church for the space of five hundred years after Christ."[23] Official spokesmen from Matthew Parker to William Laud increasingly were convinced that, to strengthen their position in the face of Puritan criticism, Anglican "*Divines* must become [more] studious, of [that] *pious and venerable antiquitie*," upon which a substantial part of the church's legitimacy must rest.[24]

Yet apologists for the Elizabethan Settlement who did now tend to defend and expand patristic appeal were alarmed to note that critics of the church seemed ever readier to depreciate "the *testimony, and tradition of the Ancient Catholicke Church*." With voice and pen they moved to censure those who "would fain find a difference between the Apostles' times, and the next ages ensuing" or would "deny credit to all antiquity in matter[s] not gainsaid by Scripture." Such procedure not only left "the aunctient Fathers sclandered"; it narrowed unacceptably the church's anchorage in ancient precedent. But protestation in this vein swayed few advocates of reform; they saw and meant to pursue the obvious logic of their position. Faced with an intransigent monarch and perceiving a design to entrench the established structure further by exploiting reverence for the Fathers— "They that be against us in this cause *will* appeal to the Fathers," complained a dissenter of the 1560s—they could only loft the biblical standard higher. They were driven to radicalize the traditional Protestant commitment to biblical supremacy.[25]

23. Gilbert Burnet, *The History of the Reformation of the Church of England*, 7 vols. (Oxford, 1865), V, 507. See also John Jewel, *An Apology of the Church of England*, ed. John E. Booty (Ithaca, N.Y., 1963), 64–65; John Overal, dedication to King James I, in John Ayre, ed., *The Works of John Jewel*, 4 vols. (Cambridge, 1846), IV, appendix 4, 1306–1307; William Scott and James Bliss, eds., *The Works of William Laud*, 7 vols. (Oxford, 1847–1860), II, 361. For identification of the primitive church with the church of the first five centuries, see *WT*, I, 11; and John Kenneth Reynold Luoma, "The Primitive Church as a Normative Principle in the Theology of the Sixteenth Century . . ." (Ph.D. diss., Hartford Seminary Foundation, 1974), 77–78.

24. Francis White, *A Treatise of the Sabbath Day* (London, 1635), dedication to William Laud. See also Hastings Robinson, ed. and trans., *Zurich Letters . . .* , 3 vols. (Cambridge, 1842–1847), III, 389; [Matthew Parker], *A Briefe Examination for the Tyme, of a Certaine Declaration . . .* (n.p., [ca. 1566]), sigs. **3–**4, ***1–***4; [Roger Hacket], *A Sermon Principally Entreating of the Crosse in Baptisme* (London, 1606), 1–2; *WT*, II, 227–228.

25. White, *Sabbath Day*, dedication; Anthony Gilby, *To My Lovynge Breth-*

In an age in which churchmen, especially those touched by Erasmian influence, ascribed normative status to classical antiquity and
the first Catholic Fathers as well as to the Old and New Testament
histories, at no time were the Puritans to stand alone in their devotion to a historical strong time. Their peculiar mission within the
Church of England was to confine primitivist appeal to the world of
the Protestant Book. Thus now and throughout the Puritan era part
of the burden of dissenting rhetoric would be to insist that the church
had "remayned a chaste virgin" only in the apostolic era and that
immediately "in the next ages it began to waxe wanton." In short,
the traditionally vaunted patristic time, although relatively pure by
the standard of later ages, was relatively impure when compared to
the standard of the first and best; thence it became necessary so to
stress the sacred text's superiority to "all authority . . . of the church
also, of councils, Fathers, or others whatsoever" as to make a proportional shift from the older, patristic ground. Thus Anthony Gilby,
speaking for the London dissenting ministers in the first decade of
Puritan activity, deliberately minimized reference to the "old Doctors, . . . [because] Gods truthe nedyth not mans auctoryte." Similarly, Thomas Sampson, "the puritan conscience of early Elizabethan
England," was prepared to employ the "ancient Catholic doctors" in
anti-Catholic debate; but he also urged the New Testament as the
all-essential standard by which the present English church should be
measured.[26]

Yet a more emphatic drift from patristic authority was registered by the Presbyterians, who presented their antiepiscopal plan of
church polity as a transcript of "the perfectest church that ever was,

---

ren That Is Troublyd about the Popishe Aparrel (n.p., [ca. 1566]), sig. Biii
(emphasis mine); Thomas Bilson, *The Perpetuall Government of Christs Church*
(London, 1610), "To the Christian Reader," sig. **2; George Downame, *A
Defence of the Sermon Preached at the Consecration of the L. Bishop of Bath
and Welles* (London, 1611), 23; John Bridges, *A Defence of the Government
Established in the Church of Englande for Ecclesiasticall Matters* (London, 1587),
169.

26. Thomas Brightman, *A Revelation of the Apocalyps* (Amsterdam, 1611),
45; John Strype, *Annals of the Reformation*, 4 vols. in 7 (1824; New York,
1968), I, pt. 2, 139; Gilby, *Popishe Aparrel*, sig. Biii; Thomas Sampson, *A
Warning to Take Heede of Fowlers Psalter* (London, 1578), 29; [Thomas Samp-
son], "Certain Humble Petitions . . . ," in Strype, *Annals*, III, pt. 2, 293–294.

which was that in the apostles' times." In a strongly worded *Admonition to the Parliament* (1572), a document organized about the hope of "restitution" of "the purity of the primitive church," John Field (Patrick Collinson dubs him "the Lenin of Elizabethan puritanism") and Thomas Wilcox defined the archetypal "old time" exclusively in New Testament terms and drew a program of vigorous local pastoral care and discipline wholly from "the prescript of God's word." Elsewhere Wilcox explained that, although he honored "the fathers rightly understood," in deciding religious matters he did "not greatly delight in allegation of humane [that is, extrabiblical] authorities." Similarly, in Thomas Cartwright's work, the formula, "That is true, whatsoever is first," was applied almost exclusively to Scripture; "whatsoever is later" than the New Testament was in his opinion of little and infrequent use in directing reform of English religion. As Francis Bacon complained about 1590, "embasing the authority of the Fathers" had become an open tactic of the Presbyterian agitation.[27]

Following the Presbyterian lead, Puritan thought from the 1580s onward tended to minimize patristic jurisdiction. An imposing contrast appears if comparable works of partisans of the standing order and of dissenting spokesmen are juxtaposed. While the former, ever more conscious of the apologetic possibilities of the patristic primordium, remained within the Erasmian and Cranmerian heritage and freely extended and amplified the authority of first and sacred times through the fifth century A.D. or later, members of the emerging Spiritual Brotherhood of Puritan clergy preferred to assume that "the Word of God is the touchstone of everything."[28] As is well

27. Thomas Cartwright, *A Replye to an Answere Made of M. Doctor Whitgifte* (n.p., 1573), 104; *AP*, 8, 9, 13; Thomas Wilcox, *A Discourse touching the Doctrine of Doubting* (Cambridge, 1598), 153, 179; Cartwright, *Replye*, 104; Basil Montagu, ed., *The Works of Francis Bacon*, new ed., 3 vols. (Philadelphia, 1851), II, 419. Cartwright recommended critical use of the early church's conciliar documents by the rule that "the elder they are, the further they are from corruption" (in Albert Peel and Leland H. Carlson, eds., *Cartwrightiana* [London, 1951], 114). See also Cartwright, *Replye*, 31, 142, 154, 170. For further discussion of patristic authority in the thought of Cartwright, see Luoma, "The Primitive Church," 71–84. The comments on Sampson and Field are from Patrick Collinson, *Archbishop Grindal, 1519–1583: The Struggle for a Reformed Church* (Berkeley, Calif., 1979), 71, 169.

28. Henry Smith, *The Sermons of Master Henry Smith . . .* (London, 1628), 145. One might compare, for instance, White, *Sabbath Day*, with Thomas Shepard, *Theses Sabbaticae*, in *Works*, III, 9–271.

known, displays of patristic erudition in preaching became a prime object of contempt among advocates of the Puritan plain style of edifying rhetoric. From his post in exile William Ames announced in 1630 that it was not *"lawfull to allege the sentences of Fathers in Sermons,"* because "they were men subject to errours" and "their authority causeth not a certaine and Divine Faith." They might be cited for special polemical purposes, but then so "that it may plainely appeare, that the Minister is compelled to goe out of the bounds of the Scripture, and that he doth this onely for . . . [unavoidable] causes . . . , the edification of Beleevers requiring no such thing." Ames probably had in mind the frequent invocation of the Fathers in the Church of England's two official books of homilies, and certainly the sermons of men like Lancelot Andrewes and Richard Senhouse.[29]

Here, in any case, was a first distinctive note in Puritan biblicism: antagonism to the formula of Bible *and* Fathers that had been organic to the original English Reformation and that continued to hold sway among proponents of the established church. At no time did this entail total repudiation of the Fathers. Many Puritans would cling to the belief that "those that came nearest unto the apostles times, because they were nearest the light, did see best"; but their retreat from the older standard was clear. Dudley Fenner and John Rainolds were willing to ascribe some weight to the first two centuries A.D., but thereafter lay "corrupter times" deserving "neither imitation nor approbation." In early New England, occasional appeals could be heard to what "had been in use in the purest churches for 300 years after Christ," but these took the strictly secondary place dictated by the immigrants' enthusiastic biblicism.[30]

29. William Ames, *Conscience with the Power and Cases Thereof* (n.p., 1639), book 4, 74.

30. Cartwright, *Replye*, 103; Dudley Fenner, *A Brief and Plain Declaration Containing the Desires of All These Faithful Ministers, That Have and Do Seek for the Discipline and Reformation of the Church of England* (London, 1584), 125; [John Rainolds?], *An Answere to a Sermon Preached the 17 of April Anno D. 1608, by George Downame* (n.p., 1609), 88, 95; John Winthrop, *The History of New England from 1630 to 1649,* ed. James Savage (1853; New York, 1972), I, 203. See also Samuel Hieron, *The Workes of Mr. Samuel Hieron,* 2 vols. (London, 1635), 531–532; Robert Bolton, *Mr. Boltons Last and Learned Worke of the Foure Last Things . . . ,* 3d ed. (London, 1635), 147; John Cotton, *A Practical Commentary . . . upon the First Epistle Generall of John* (London, 1656), 77; Cotton, *The Way of Congregational Churches Cleared* (1648), in Larzer Ziff, ed., *John Cotton on the Churches of New England* (Cambridge,

A second distinctive note appears in the organization of the apostolic churches extolled by Puritan writers, and again it is best seen in relief against competing Anglican perspectives. After the initial controversies over vestments and before the Caroline divines had forced liturgical concerns to the fore, dissenting complaint about the religious settlement tended to focus upon "the government established in the Church of Englande." In response to Presbyterian criticism, full-scale defenses of episcopal polity had begun to appear in the later 1580s, in which we can see at once the generous appeal to patristic precedents that rapidly was becoming a keystone of Anglican utterance. But joined thereto is the second note, ringing equally clear through the literature and serving perhaps equally well to typify it. What alarmed episcopal advocates the most in Presbyterian theory was its challenge to unilateral, hierarchical authority, and they hastened to attest the "disorder," the "confusion," the "pestilent perturbations" that must ensue should pyramidal rule be overthrown.[31]

Accordingly, in the advocates' rendering of the early Christian experience, the principle of "fatherly superiority" became a major structuring device.[32] To neutralize Presbyterian appeal, they strove to find an episcopal function in the ministry of the twelve apostles, and the patristic evidence permitted this to be amplified in a "continuous succession" through the first five centuries and beyond. For these writers, the ancient congregations of the apostolic-patristic age formed a *primordium of "orders, and degrees."* Its general welfare and cohesion in the face of persecution and heresy had been secured precisely by an inequality of roles, and particularly by the supervisory and disciplinary functions of the episcopal officer ruling in each diocese.[33]

Mass., 1968), 301; [John Davenport], *An Apology of the Churches in New-England for Church-Government* (London, 1643), 33; Thomas Hooker, *A Survey of the Summe of Church-Discipline* (London, 1648), 232. For scholarly comment, see Perry Miller, *The New England Mind: The Seventeenth Century* (1939; Cambridge, Mass., 1954), 467; *WT*, I, 310; Knott, *Sword*, 108.

31. Bridges, *Defence of the Government Established in the Church of Englande*; Bilson, *Perpetuall Government*, "To the Reader," sig. *8.

32. The "fatherly superiority" is from Bilson's subtitle; Thomas Bell, *The Regiment of the Church* (London, 1606), sig. A4, 16–17.

33. Richard Field, *Of the Church, Five Bookes* (London, 1606), "The Fifth Book," 128; Adrian Saravia, *Of the Diverse Degrees of the Ministers of the Gospell* (London, 1591), 41; Bilson, *Perpetuall Government*, 1–2, "To the Reader," sig. *3.

Dissenting accounts of first-age polity and discipline, drawn largely and often exclusively from New Testament sources, breathed a more democratic spirit, one closely connected to hopes for structural reform of the church. The Presbyterian program first fully articulated by Thomas Cartwright in the early 1570s provided through the decades a large commonality of Puritan opinion on the subject of ecclesiastical government, and on most of the essential points it was to be adopted without major change by Congregational theorists. In two ways in particular the proposed platform for ecclesiastical reorganization flouted the hierarchical rationale underlying the episcopate. First, to the adult male members of a parish church was ascribed the right to screen and select their pastoral officer, or at least to approve the choice of patron or bishop. Second, the body of clergy thus selected was to form a brotherhood whose members stood in a relation of parity one to another.

These proposals, which called for a profound reversal of initiative at the parish level, arose from a more democratic vision of primitive Christianity than what took form in Anglican apologetics. There was agreement that a figure designated "bishop" stood within the leadership described in the apostolic reports, but he was a local pastor, a type of the parish-based "presbyter" of Cartwright's doctrine. That presbyter offered no first instance of the lordly role claimed by English bishops. For "then," in the normative age, "the congregation had authority to call ministers"; and the men so chosen and tied to their single flocks knew nothing of the diocesan autocracy shortly to arise. They assembled from time to time in elected "classes" and synods, but there they interacted as "equal among themselves" in the larger business of the church universal.[34] Contrasted with the Anglican emphasis upon vertical orders and degrees, the Puritan construction thus emerges as a *primordium of consent and parity,* stressing lateral relationships between Christian believers and officers.

Considering that veneration for the first was constituent to English Protestantism from the earliest years, inability to agree upon the constitution of primitive times was painfully symptomatic of the opening rift between proponents and assailants of the Elizabethan compromise. It should also alert one that the Puritan primordium

---

34. Walter Travers, *A Full and Plaine Declaration of Ecclesiastical Discipline* . . . (Leiden, 1617), 40; *AP,* 9–10; Leonard J. Trinterud, ed., *Elizabethan Puritanism* (New York, 1971), 273–276.

no less than the Anglican was a selective, highly interpretive construct. This was equally evident in the handling of the two Testaments. Minimization of patristic authority went hand in hand with the assignment of greater weight and attention to New Testament precedents, and yet this was not accompanied, as in the older Lollard or newer radical Protestant circles, by deemphasis of the Old Testament. "Primitive" and "apostolic" might be virtually synonymous in Anabaptist thought, but Puritan concepts remained congruent with the larger biblical scenario of Reformed Protestantism and its special regard for the ancient Hebrew books.

In particular, the Reformed ideal—which contrasted vividly with both Anabaptist and Lutheran views—of an official religious and moral reformation embracing the whole of society necessitated inclusion of Old Testament precedents within the domain of the first. It would be a grave error, for instance, to infer from the Presbyterians' concentration upon apostolic discipline that the older Testament played but a small role in their scriptural program. On the contrary, their various and often enthusiastic adaptations of the covenantal ideal bespoke a reliance upon the Old Testament materials that perhaps exceeded the Reformed average. In particular, all essential elements of the National Covenant—the conception of England (or New England) as a covenanted people husbanded by godly magistrates and subject to a Deuteronomic arrangement of judgments and mercies— were derived primarily from the Pentateuch and from the books of Kings and Chronicles. Restriction of the Fathers' importance thus was the gesture of a full-orbed biblicism in which the Old Testament served as necessary and in many respects equal partner to the New in the constitution of the first-time drama.

Sacred Writ as Precedential Drama

Englishmen thus turned to ancient story were no strangers to the representative powers of imagination. William Perkins, we may be sure, would have been astonished to hear his outlook derided as "totally imageless, totally devoid of visual content or sensual appeal, an abstraction made up of concepts and words." As a species of Reformed Protestants, Puritans participated wholeheartedly in detraction—and occasionally physical destruction—of Roman

Catholic statuary, painting, stained glass images, gorgeous liturgical vestiture, and the like. They repudiated the older liturgical pageants, processionals, and stations of the cross. They resented the retention of ornate elements in the liturgies of the Prayer Book and, in the later Stuart years, feared the liturgical ambitions of William Laud and the Caroline divines as a virtual return to Catholicism. Puritans wanted worship to be "simple," dissociated from holy objects and buildings and returned to the plainness of New Testament assembly, preaching, and Eucharist. Yet none of this justifies the conclusion that Puritan worship was imageless or abstract or that its well-known emphases upon the preached word promoted an essentially "cerebral" or "cognitive" outlook, with the denaturing rationalism that these terms imply. Such emphases were present, but they did not stand alone. For the simple fact is that, if Puritans did wish to jettison the colorful, sensual panoplies of traditional worship, the intention was to return Christians more completely to the intense, richly imagined world of the biblical primordium.[35]

To the eyes of the Puritan faithful, Scripture presented a dramatic panorama which moved from Creation to Redemption to Resurrection and Last Things, a panorama that sprang into present life in preaching, biblical study, and meditation. Identification with the biblical world ever had played a role in historic Christian devotion, and certainly it was an element in the religious practice of contemporary English Protestants who felt little or no estrangement from the received forms of the English church. But in dissenting quarters, among both the pastor-theologians and the laity of whose views we have record, the drive toward absorption in the sacred histories tended to go well beyond Anglican standards. Probably it owed much to Christian humanist efforts to take "a historical approach to the 'prescribed texts' of the Christian religion," to the summons of John Colet and Desiderius Erasmus to "revisit first-century Palestine, to go back in time to the birthplace of Christianity." It surely reflected the ready availability since the 1550s of vernacular translations of the

35. Theodore Roszak, *Where the Wasteland Ends: Politics and Transcendence in Postindustrial Society* (Garden City, N.Y., 1973), 116; Henry Warner Bowden, *American Indians and Christian Missions: Studies in Cultural Conflict* (Chicago, 1981), 124. See also *AP*, 9–15; *WT*, I, 258–293, 325–345; and the discussion of "image" and "word" in Peter Burke, *Popular Culture in Early Modern Europe* (New York, 1978), 228–229.

Bible and several decades of aggressively biblical preaching by Reformed divines.[36] Judged by later standards, the outlook was anachronistic. It registered an inability to perceive the enormous cultural and intellectual contrasts between the biblical ages and Elizabethan and Stuart England and knew nothing of the historical diversities reflected in the biblical narratives themselves. Sacred antiquity was not to be conceived historically as a distant, alien, and heterogeneous world. It was to be reentered and experienced.

Approached thus, the biblical text became a kind of lens projecting an entire realm of experience over against the everyday. Protestant iconophobia might deny the external representation of sacred event in statue and mural, but its other side was the compulsion to realize within memory and imagination an intensely event-full world that was nothing if not visual and that drew heavily upon the human propensity for dramatic identification. When the authors of the dissenting tract *Lamentable Complaint* set forth to propound the duty of Christian magistrates in reforming the church, they did not cite abstract principle or textbook lore; they chanted, "Oh that *worthie Prince Nehemiah*, whose praises can never be sounded sufficiently, for the valure that he shewed in repairing the walles of Ierusalem." The basic appeal was to a closely imagined domain in which the reader or auditor, in this precritical age, simply found him- or herself. Occasionally, specific instruction in imaginative identification was provided, as when William Ames, clarifying the place of psalmody in Reformed worship, urged, "We ought in our thoughts to put on . . . the person, either of them, of whom those Psalmes were composed, or of them who composed them, that what ever is spoken there, we may . . . take it as spoken to ourselves."[37]

36. Mircea Eliade, *Myths, Dreams, and Mysteries: The Encounter between Contemporary Faiths and Archaic Realities*, trans. Philip Mairet (New York, 1960), 30; A. G. Dickens, *Reformation and Society in Sixteenth-Century Europe* (London, 1966), 32; E. Harris Harbison, *The Christian Scholar in the Age of Reformation* (New York, 1956), 59–60, 92, 112. William Tyndale called readers of his biblical translations to "go . . . read the stories of the Bible for your learning and comfort, and see everything practised before your eyes" (*Doctrinal Treatises* . . . , ed. Henry Walter [Cambridge, 1848], 404). The pattern here described exemplifies Eliade's thesis that "one is always contemporary with a myth" when one imagines or recites it (*Mysteries*, 30).

37. In *A Parte of a Register* . . . (n.p., [1593]), 259; Ames, *Conscience*, book 4, 44.

But most often the projection of self into the visualized primordium was spontaneous and taken for granted. Struggling through the disciplines of "preparation for conversion," Thomas Shepard provided a standard example of biblical re-presentation: he "did see God like a consuming fire . . . [and] myself like a poor prisoner leading to that fire, and . . . I knew not what to do . . . , [then] it came to my mind that I should do as Christ; when he was in an agony he prayed earnestly. And so I fell down to prayer." John Rogers of Dedham once so entered into the spirit of scriptural imagery that in one high moment during preaching he seized "hold with both hands at one time of the supporters of the Canopy over the Pulpit, . . . roaring hideously, to represent the torments of the damned."[38] With few exceptions Puritan sermons—and a great majority of Puritan treatises and commentaries also consist of material originally preached—provide copious documentation that the Puritan primordium was a real, dramatically engaging, unquestioned world of scene, society, characters, action, and moral atmosphere.

Aptly, then, it can be argued that "much of the special character of the Puritan approach to experience" stems from the "simple fact" that the Bible was approached as "neither a codification nor a credo," but a dramatic narrative. But this insight, which captures nicely the element of living spectacle, does not reveal the supereminent grandeur with which that spectacle was invested in Puritan perspective. As in Eliade's mythical time of origins, so in the Puritan primordium the action did not belong to everyday history, but was transfigured by the active presence and power of the supernatural. While the Bible disclosed an essentially human world, it was a world in which the three transcendent persons of the Trinity intervened at will. The principal human actors were lifted beyond the ordinary by divine election and favor (or disfavor). Their lives, deeds, and destinies were of unexampled force and significance. In this time of times, "the giftes of the spirite of wisedome, discretion, knowledge . . . were poured forth more plentifully than ever they were, eyther before, or shall be after." The apostolic "master

38. Thomas Shepard, *The Autobiography*, in Michael McGiffert, ed., *God's Plot: The Paradoxes of Puritan Piety, Being the Autobiography and Journal of Thomas Shepard* (n.p., 1972), 43. The Rogers incident is cited in David D. Hall, *The Faithful Shepherd: A History of the New England Ministry in the Seventeenth Century* (Chapel Hill, N.C., 1972), 65.

builders," for example, created "the fairest and beautifullest image [of the church] that ever was, . . . buildings of golde and silver and precious stones." Through its course the Great Time was studded with miracle, prophecy, angelic visitation, ecstatic experience, and open communications with divinity.[39]

Biblical narrative, then, did not dwell upon commonplaces; it told of "extraordinary persons" and "extraordinary times" suffused with unearthly insight and power. Through them were manifest the source, shape, and end of human life. The narratives themselves were written by participants and eyewitnesses, by persons, moreover, "immediately called to be the clerks or secretaries of the Holy Ghost." Since the Holy Ghost thus controlled "both . . . their tongue and style," their words were "even as gold," not only infallibly accurate in detail but also expressly adapted to convey the power of sacred events. In sum, scriptural history was more than a diverting drama. Its ability to elicit identification was heightened immeasurably by the superhuman aura and the momentousness of primordial acts related in inspired narrative. Dedicated to a moralist, pragmatic conception of Christian life, Puritans could not permit primordial engrossment to become an end in itself. The aim of Scripture was, not entertainment, but edification. They thus tended to concentrate "on the process by which individuals experience [biblical] scenes" and, especially, the impact of them upon Christian obedience, "rather than upon the scenes themselves." Nevertheless, the achievement of a vividly imagined contemporaneity with scenes fraught with personal meaning was a cornerstone of Puritan approaches to Scripture.[40]

To focus for a moment upon preaching, nothing could be more misleading than to think of the Bible, in this context, as a compendium of facts, laws, doctrines, truths, texts, decrees, or "divine axioms" or to maintain that the sermonic agenda was established first by the schematic requirements of Ramist logic. In preparing

39. Daniel J. Boorstin, *The Americans: The Colonial Experience* (New York, 1958), 18, 19, 29; Cartwright, *Replye*, 51, 54, 178.

40. Thomas Hooker, *Survey*, pt. 1, 222; David D. Hall, ed., *The Antinomian Controversy, 1636–1638* (Middletown, Conn., 1968), 268; William Perkins, *The Work of William Perkins*, ed. Ian Breward (Appleford, England, 1970), 334; Dudley Fenner, quoted in Knappen, *Tudor Puritanism*, 356; John Dod, *A Plaine and Familiar Exposition on the Lords Prayer*, 2d ed. (London, 1635), 123; Knott, *Sword*, 79.

their pulpit exhortations, few of the preachers assumed that "the first work . . . was . . . to translate the Bible into doctrines" or that "the Bible should be approached . . . as a welter of raw material [or "axioms" or "arguments"] out of which the propositions of art were to be refined by the [logical] processes of invention and disposition."[41] Any broad sampling of sermons from the time of the Vestiarian Controversy to the civil war will reveal that the Scripture was approached, in the first instance, not as a logical structure, but as dramatic event and that the "first work" of the preacher thus was to engage the imagination with "lively representations." The foundational task was to call a portion of the drama into convincing life. If doctrines, uses, laws, or propositions of art were indeed specified, or inferable, their root in dramatic occurrence seldom was forgotten.[42]

Hence, it went without saying, a peculiarly expressive homiletical language was required. Several scholars have highlighted that imagistic richness of Puritan rhetoric and shown that its evocative qualities depended basically upon biblical imagery. The rhetoric was sown thick, for example, with depictions of "wayfaring and warfaring" common to the Old Testament and with verbal pictures of the apostolic churches. By no means was the famous plain style intended to eliminate dramatic qualities from sermonic language. Puritans hated the "painted eloquence" of some Anglican preaching, not for its use of color and image, but for its employment of nonbiblical

41. Miller and Johnson, eds., *The Puritans*, I, 42; Miller, *Seventeenth Century*, 341. Following Miller, Harry Stout contends that "Puritan methods of biblical analysis and preaching were derived chiefly from Ramus" and that Puritan preachers strove essentially to "diagra[m] the logical structure of Scripture with geometric precision" ("Puritanism Considered as a Profane Movement," *Christian Scholar's Review*, X [1980], 15). For a corrective, see Knott, *Sword*, 6, 46.

42. Alexander Grosart, ed., *The Complete Works of Richard Sibbes, D.D.*, 7 vols. (Edinburgh, 1862–1864), I, ci. See Richard Bernard's accent upon the dramatic in his instruction on preaching in *The Faithfull Shephard* (London, 1607), 22–24. According to William Haller, "The Puritan sermon commonly labored to escape from abstract to imagistic methods of presenting doctrine" (*The Rise of Puritanism* . . . [1938; Philadelphia, 1972], 143).

The Decalogue, to take one example, was not construed as an abstract code, but as a personal and contractual communication at a tremendous moment in a long-developing sequence of events related in hundreds of pages of Old Testament history. See, for example, Dod, *Ten Commandements*, 2–3.

"proverbs, similitudes and stories" that captured neither the unique inspiration nor the simple vividness of Scripture.[43] If the preachers often devised similes or tropes of their own, they "typically cit[ed] the Bible as a warrant for such practices," holding closely in mind the archetypal simplicity of scriptural imagery. Judging from the evidence of preaching, what constituted the people of the Book was not so much a bent toward logical precision or a taste for "exact, legalistic interpretations of Scripture"—although these were present—as a more fundamental act of visualization and entry into the primordial world.[44]

The world that came thus to life in Puritan discourse was irresistible. Since it established nothing less than reality itself, it exercised a virtually tyrannical claim upon imagination and belief. No other imagined scenes, whether from history or fictive fancy, could be granted independent status or authority beside it.[45] Both its characterization of the human scene and its right to compel belief were absolute, ultimately placing in question the very right of other drama to exist. Puritans might approve and enjoy the Protestant theater of John Bale, John Foxe, Bernard Ochino, or Theodore Beza; with Foxe, Richard Bernard, John Reynolds, or Anne Bradstreet, they might themselves turn playwrights, allegorists, or poets. Such activities were admitted so far as they remained obeisant extensions of the sacred drama and its all-definitive concerns, as did Foxe's *Christus Triumphans* (1556) or Reynolds's *Triumph of God's Revenge against the Sin of Murder* (1621). But beyond this limited realm Puritans would tend either to ignore or to assail works of the imagination.

Their well-known antagonism toward popular ballads, romances, poems, interludes, and courtly masques of the day, and above all toward stage plays and players, had many grounds. Erotic dalliance, the parade of vice for amusement, the use of materials from pagan antiquity, waste of time, diversion from more godly pursuits, com-

43. John Udall, *Amendment of Life* (London, 1588), sig. B3; Laurence Chaderton, *An Excellent and Godly Sermon . . . Preached at Paules Crosse . . .* (London, 1580), sig. Fvii.

44. Knott, *Sword*, 48; T. H. Breen, *The Character of the Good Ruler: A Study of Puritan Political Ideas in New England, 1630–1700* (New Haven, Conn., 1970), 14.

45. Erich Auerbach, *Mimesis: The Representation of Reality in Western Literature*, trans. Willard R. Trask (Garden City, N.Y., 1957), 12.

petition for Sabbath audiences, and confusion of sexes in the theater (males assuming female roles) usually headed the list of objections. But underlying them was the deeper complaint of a people absorbed in a total myth. They were convinced that the life of the Christian community from start to finish was founded in drama. It lived from the power of scriptural story to enthrall, to convey an overwhelming sense of reality, and to influence. Hence the high scandal of un-Christian poetry, song, or theater lay not simply in immoral or idle content but in its wish, as it were, to create an alternative primordium. Implicitly at issue was its dangerously competitive capacity to suspend disbelief, to engross the imagination, to shape a view of the world, to affect behavior. For these were alone the prerogatives of the two Christian Testaments. So long as they were drawn into that world and its definition of the real and the good, England's forward Protestants would not join Scripture to Jonson or Shakespeare as sources of vision and inspiration.

Perhaps the dramatically compelling character of primordial event was nowhere clearer than in the exemplary obligations it imposed. One did not become a part of biblical occurrence and then stand away from it untouched. The beholder was moved to an actual imitation of selected actions. Primordial event became archetypal.

In their perception of Scripture as a treasury of archetypes, Puritans drew again upon ancient Christian assumption. To take only the most obvious example, the apostolic ideal that figured so prominently in Catholic reform and in the Reformation was of course a paradigmatic construction; restoration of primitive purity was to be achieved by massive imitation of New Testament pattern. In keeping with his emphasis upon Christian liberty, Martin Luther recognized the imperative force of biblical models only in matters integral to the gospel of divine forgiveness, such as the Eucharist. On the whole he attached relatively little importance to scripturally reported details of ecclesiastical organization or liturgical practices. But in the more moralist ethos of Reformed Protestantism it well could be said that "the characters, events, and propositions contained in the Scriptures function as types, which serve to categorize all human experience"; and more, the types were paradigms controlling many of the more specific details of civil and ecclesiastical life. Biblical mimesis was a vital element in the Genevan experience. It was stronger yet in the Zwinglian Reformation, "based on using the Bible as a book of precedents." Heinrich Bullinger could argue, for instance, that a sitting position was preferred at the Eucharist because "the Lord sat at table with his disciples."[46]

In the English Reformation, the range of biblical paradigms extended from personal minutiae to matters of broad national concern. The radical, Little Bilney, "reckoned himself bounden so straitly to keep . . . the words of Christ after the very letter, that because our Lord biddeth us when we will pray to enter into our chamber and shut the door, he thought it therefore sin to say his service abroad and always would be sure to have his chamber door shut unto him while he said mattins." On a larger scale, a salient and distinctive English motif was the portrayal of Henry VIII and Edward VI as exemplifications of Old Testament models of godly kingship. In particular the "good kings" of 1 and 2 Kings and 1 and 2 Chronicles seemed to provide a pattern relevant to the English undertaking: a monarch, sovereign in his own dominions, who by assuming supreme headship of the church and "weed[ing] out all false worshippings of God and all wicked doctrine" established right religion in the realm and thereby elicited divine favor.[47] Thus the right form of English kingship was to be discovered through identification with the primordial monarchs. Their reigns and deeds were not merely pleasant or suggestive examples but prescriptive models requiring continual reiteration.

In conformity with this earlier development, a standard feature of Puritan dissent was the wish "that both prince and people may openly and religiously enter into an holy league with the living God, after the godly examples of king Asa, of king Josiah, and other [biblical] rulers."[48] But Puritans were far from content simply to repeat

46. William Hunt, *The Puritan Moment: The Coming of Revolution in an English County* (Cambridge, Mass., 1983), 117; George Yule, "Continental Patterns and the Reformation in England and Scotland," *Scottish Journal of Theology*, XXII (1969), 308; John T. McNeill, *The History and Character of Calvinism* (London, 1967), 87.

47. Rupp, *Studies*, 25; Thomas Becon, *The Catechism of Thomas Becon*, ed. John Ayre (Cambridge, 1844), 303–304. For other examples, see Cranmer, *Writings and Letters*, 127. See also Gardiner, *Oration*, 109; Myles Coverdale, *Remains of Myles Coverdale . . .* , ed. George Pearson (Cambridge, 1846), 5–7, 18; John Strype, *The Life of the Learned Sir John Cheke . . .* (Oxford, 1821), 192.

48. [Sampson], "Petitions," in Strype, *Annals*, III, pt. 2, 286. See also Edward Dering, *A Sermon Preached before the Queenes Majestie . . . 1569*, in *M[aster Edward] Derings Workes* (London, 1597), 11–12, 18–19; Thomas

established exemplarist routines. Confronted with regal and episcopal authority which not only stymied further reform but strove to
consolidate the standing order by appeals to the Fathers and to the
theologically indifferent character of many areas of ecclesiastical government and practice, they resorted to a much closer scanning of the
biblical narrative. This meant not only a recession of interest in the
patristic epoch but a much more detailed elaboration of the exemplary force of biblical event. It was axiomatic to "the original Puritan
party," formed in the mid-1560s in opposition to the government's
new vestiarian demands, that "all reformations ought to be framed
after the first sincere state"; therefore, they directed attention to the
"holy men" of the primordium, to "Samuel and other prophetes, [to]
Peter, [and] Paul," all of whom wore "simple apparell." And when
the authorities insisted that impressive clerical vesture was necessary
to establish the proper distance between clergy and laity, the reply
was that "neither the New Testament decreed, [nor] the primitive
church appointed any [such] distinction."[49]

In the further development of such themes, the Presbyterian movement of the 1570s and 1580s was a landmark. Field and Wilcox's
Admonition to the Parliament (1572) outlined church reform as a
detailed imitation of apostolic patterns:

> In those [primordial] days, . . . election was made by the com-
> mon consent of the whole church. . . . Then every pastor had
> his flock. . . . Then the ministers were preachers. . . . Then
> ministers were not tied to any form of prayers invented by man,
> but [prayed] as the spirit moved them. . . . Then nothing [was]
> taught but God's word.

And so on.[50] As is the case with Presbyterian texts generally, with
Cartwright's debates with Archbishop Whitgift or Dudley Fenner's
summarizing *Declaration of Ecclesiastical Discipline*, so the *Admo-*

Cartwright, *A Treatise of Christian Religion* (London, 1616), 131; Dod, *Ten Commandements*, 242–243.

49. *EPM*, 75; Strype, *Annals*, I, pt. 2, 149; [Robert Crowley], *A Brief Discourse against the Outwarde Apparell* . . . (n.p., 1566), sigs. Biv–v; [Robert Crowley], *An Answere for the Tyme, to the Examination* . . . (n.p., [ca. 1566]), 21; John Strype, *The Life and Acts of Matthew Parker* . . . , 3 vols. (Oxford, 1821), I, 331–332.

50. *AP*, 9–12. See also Eusebius Pagit, *A Godly Sermon: Preached at Detford in Kent* . . . *1572* (London, 1586), sigs. A6–A7.

nition mirrored a much-expanded interest in scriptural precedents. Picturing the early Presbyterian Puritans as pioneer modernizers, one interpretation suggestively accents the "radical functionalism" of their proposed polity of active preachers and lay officers; but it exaggerates that modern proclivity by neglecting the profoundly archaic exemplarism upon which, in conscious theory, that polity fundamentally was based. So long as their program remained unrealized, Presbyterians would continue to sigh for the sacred past. They would risk and suffer much to advance the thesis that "the further a man goes from the first institution, the more he offends." It was mythic situations and deeds, not abstract precepts or, in the first instance, considerations of improved function that imparted the "orders which Christ has prescribed, in his word, for the ruling of the church."[51]

From the time of the original Presbyterian movement to the 1630s, much of the theological development within Puritanism arose from the assumption that the history of the Old and New Testament peoples was precedential. This assumption, although held with varying degrees of programmatic intent, does much indeed to "locate Puritanism within the distinctive Reformed tradition of international Calvinism." While defenders of the established church busied themselves qualifying and supplementing biblical authority, Puritan thinkers moved into an ever more resolute biblicism with special focus upon the archetypes of the Great Time. This was a selective affair, of course. Many Old Testament patterns—temple worship, the "eye for an eye"—had been repealed in the Christian dispensation, and no calls ever would appear for emulation of Cain or Judas or for a pentecostal speaking in tongues. Yet Cartwright's insistence that "the word of God contayneth the direction of . . . what soever

---

51. David Little, *Religion, Order, and Law: A Study in Pre-Revolutionary England* (New York, 1969), 94 (and see 70); [Walter Travers], *A Defence of the Ecclesiastical Discipline Ordayned of God to Be Used in His Church, against a Replie of Maister Bridges* . . . (n.p., 1588), 101; John Udall, *A Demonstration of the Truth of That Discipline, Which Christ Has Prescribed in His Word, for the Government of His Church, in All Times and Places, until the End of the World* (1588), ed. Edward Arber (London, 1880), 11. A. F. Scott Pearson finds that the "guiding principle" of Cartwright's pathbreaking Presbyterian lectures at Cambridge in 1570 was the notion that "the Church should be modelled on that of Apostolic times" (*Thomas Cartwright and Elizabethan Puritanism, 1535–1603* [Cambridge, 1925], 29).

things can fall into any part of mans life," or Perkins's that "the word of God must be our rule and square whereby we are to frame and fashion all our actions," when seen in the light of their common and intense interest in scriptural paradigms, pointed the way to a large expansion of archetypal jurisdiction over the Christian life.[52] Moving well beyond the Presbyterian focus upon church government, members of the emerging Spiritual Brotherhood in the late sixteenth and early seventeenth centuries worked out programs for the "domestical duties" of the Christian family, the good magistrate, the conduct of the Christian Sabbath, public and private fasts, the Christian's "daily rule" (or schedule), the plain style of preaching and writing, all heavily dependent upon biblical pattern and example. Numerous lesser matters, such as the "government of the tongue," the use of lots, and military training were handled similarly.[53]

52. John F. Wilson, *Pulpit in Parliament: Puritanism during the English Civil Wars, 1640–1648* (Princeton, N.J., 1969), 144 (and see 143); Cartwright, *Replye*, 26; Perkins, *Work of Perkins*, 464. See also Shepard, *Works*, III, 346; Miller and Johnson, *The Puritans*, I, 43, 209. Wilson and George Yule stand virtually alone among historians of Puritanism in pinpointing the central "precedential" element (Yule, "Continental Patterns," *Scottish Journal of Theology*, XXII [1969], 317–323).

53. On "domestical duties," see, for example, Perkins, *Work of Perkins*, 411–440; Robert Cleaver, *A Godly Form of Householde Governement* (London, 1612). On the good magistrate, see Breen, *Good Ruler*, 278–279, and the sources cited there. On the Sabbath, see, for example, Nicholas Bownde, *The Doctrine of the Sabbath* (London, 1595); Thomas Shepard, *Theses Sabbaticae*, in *Works*, III. On fasts, see, for example, Richard Greenham, *The Works of the Reverend . . . M[aster] Richard Greenham . . .* , 3d ed. (London, 1601), 504–508; Arthur Hildersam, *The Doctrine of Fasting and Praier . . .* (London, 1633), 3. On the daily rule, see, for example, Richard Rogers, *Seven Treatises . . .* (London, 1603), 294–403; Paul Baynes, *Briefe Directions unto a Godly Life* (London, 1637), 166–187. The avoidance of "human wisdom" and imitation of the "simplicity of holy scripture" were crucial concerns of the dissenters' "plain style" (for example, Perkins, *Work of Perkins*, 345; Cotton, *Epistle of John*, 47; Ames, *Conscience*, book 4, 71, 75, 78; Hieron, *Workes*, 534; Haller, *Rise*, 130–132; Knott, *Sword*, 50).

On those lesser matters, see, for example, William Perkins, *A Direction for the Government of the Tongue*, in *The Workes of that Famous and Worthy Minister of Christ, Mr. William Perkins*, 3 vols. (London, 1635), I, 439–452; William Ames, *The Marrow of Theology* (1629), trans. and ed. John D. Eusden (Boston, 1968), 272–273; John Davenport, *A Royall Edict for Military Exercises . . .* (London, 1629), 6.

In Puritan teaching, two primordial qualities that the saint or the church was obliged especially to capture in the repetition of scriptural paradigms were purity and simplicity. For centuries both traits had been associated with the apostolic norm of reformist primitivism. More recently, Christian humanists and Protestant reformers had joined in celebration of the "pristine purity and simplicity" of the early church. Drawing upon these heritages and sensitized further by the English church's many Catholic retentions, Puritan dissenters advertised aggressively the plainness of primitive ways. Their concern is not illuminated by associating the primitive with a rude, undeveloped condition. Movement toward the simpler was, not a careless relaxation, but an act of organized discipline and self-denial. Moreover, it was taken for granted that for most practical purposes and for all religious purposes the biblical primordium showed mankind in its highest and best estate, an estate that Protestants were still struggling to regain. Puritan intellectuals, for example, were at home with the traditional views that Hebrew was the mother and ultimate norm of languages, that Moses was the wisest of all men as well as a master scientist, and that the Bible was a virtual compendium of all arts and sciences. Measured by such standards, simplicity was a quality, not of the childhood, but of the fullest years and centuries of the Judaeo-Christian career, a time of humbler tastes.

It was this element of their theory that lured dissenters, in the manner of the "cultural primitivism" described by Arthur O. Lovejoy, toward a life far "simpler" and less sophisticated and "less burdened with apparatus." Its partial realization in practice led John T. McNeill to propose that the "one universal principle in Puritanism" was "the principle of 'economy,'" defined as a movement toward "great simplification of worship and life." Advocacy of a plain style in preaching, of a homiletical speech stripped of witty and erudite adornment, is perhaps the most familiar example, although it is clear that a Catholic or an Anglican devoted to the Prayer Book entering a Puritan meetinghouse in the Dutch Netherlands or New England would have been struck first by "the bareness and simplicity of the architecture and furnishings." A suspicion of adornment and artificial complexity, indeed, forms a kind of center about which much Puritan teaching and practice in the areas of diet, dress, speech, worship, preaching, and the like might be organized suggestively. No accidental philistinism, such taste for the unadorned was a studied imitation of the "simplicitie and wonderfull plainese" of scriptural models.[54]

From the time of the Vestiarian Controversy, Puritan spokesmen liked to remind their countrymen that, as the stream of history flowed out "distant from the [apostolic] fountain," the "less pure and clear" it became. So too they practically made a career of appeal to the time of "the beginning when [the church] was purest," to "the Apostells' time, when all thinges wer puer," and "before th[e] white came to be speckled and spotted with blacke errours, and staines." Thus purity denoted the freshly minted, unalloyed quality of biblical-era teachings and institutions before the great postapostolic vitiation, and it joined simplicity as an ardently and constantly recommended trait in Puritan circles. Laurence Humphrey and Thomas Sampson, the two most prominent among the original antivestment men, joined voices in 1566 to set the mark for every generation of Puritan opinion to follow, including the future New Englanders': "These things are our principal object,—the authority of the scriptures,—the [primitive] simplicity of the ministry of Christ,—the purity of the earliest and best churches."[55]

By about 1590, the essential failure of a quarter-century of struggle for ecclesiastical reformation had been borne in upon much of the Puritan leadership. Retreat from structural reform and concentration upon the arts of inward, self-disciplining piety were an identifying feature of the Spiritual Brotherhood of Puritan clergy that arose during this time. The result was the first major pietist episode within magisterial Protestantism. Since an enhanced and somewhat

---

54. Arthur O. Lovejoy and George Boas, *Primitivism and Related Ideas in Antiquity* (Baltimore, 1935), 8–9; John T. McNeill, *Modern Christian Movements* (Philadelphia, 1954), 19; Horton Davies, *The Worship of the English Puritans* (Westminster, 1948), 246; Haller, *Rise*, 130. For comments upon the "extreme simplicity" of Puritan worship, see *WT*, I, 286, II, 187–188, 200–211, 253–281. For references to the plain style as imitative of biblical language, see *A Christian Letter of Certaine English Protestants* . . . (Middelburg, 1599), 45; Ames, *Conscience*, book 4, 71–75; Hieron, *Workes*, 534; Knott, *Sword*, 50.

55. Brightman, *Apocalyps*, 47 (and see 114); John Cotton, *Singing of Psalmes a Gospel-Ordinance* (London, 1647), 62; Gilby, *Popishe Aparrel*, sig. Civ; Crowley, *Answere*, 21; Thomas Taylor, *Christs Victorie over the Dragon* (London, 1633), 141; Robinson, ed., *Zurich Letters*, I, 161. See also Trinterud, ed., *Puritanism*, 4–8.

systematized interest in devotional meditation was an important feature of this newer spirituality, the pietist turn of the late sixteenth century led to some remarkable expansion of the dramatic, participatory possibilities of the biblical primordium. The forms of pietist meditation that now arose accent "feeling theological issues as part of a concrete, dramatic scene," and they evidence how the people of the Book now were induced to go *within* the drama, periodically to enter and dwell within the charmed primordial world.[56]

By the 1590s pietist spokesmen were urging their charges to meditate regularly upon a great variety of topics. The "matter" of a good meditation, according to Richard Rogers, "may be of any part of Gods word[,] on God himselfe . . . or . . . the infinite varietie of good things which wee receive of his free bountie; also of his workes and judgements[,] or on our estate, as our sinnes, . . . our mortalitie" and the like. Yet it was "God's word" that had priority in meditative practice; the biblical text supplied the primary and most abundant and frequently recommended subject matter.[57] And the key to the biblical role in this context is that Scripture invoked a world of absorbing action. Like the vivid exegesis of a biblical sermon or the eucharistic reenactment of the Last Supper, a formal meditation represented an immediate and concretely imagined return to the primitive time. Commentators who believe that the Puritans' "interest in the Bible was rational and practical rather than imaginative and devotional" or that a "predisposition to exalt abstract mentality" led to neglect of "the sensuous imagination" might consider profitably the imaginative and certainly sensuous content of the brotherhood's meditative enterprise.[58]

56. Louis L. Martz, *The Poetry of Meditation: A Study in English Religious Literature of the Seventeenth Century* (New Haven, Conn., 1954), 156–157. Martz, however, finds little interest in meditation among Puritans before Richard Baxter's full discussion of the subject in *The Saints' Everlasting Rest* of 1650. To the contrary, Baxter's work should be considered a summary and fruition of more than half a century of devotional fervor in the Puritan vein.

57. Rogers, *Treatises*, 236. For the biblical emphasis, see Greenham, *Works*, 22; Bownde, *Sabbath*, 203; Perkins, *Workes*, I, 187; *WP*, I, 191. See also Barbara Kiefer Lewalski, *Protestant Poetics and the Seventeenth-Century Religious Lyric* (Princeton, N.J., 1979), 148.

58. Larzer Ziff, *Puritanism in America: New Culture in a New World* (New York, 1973), 14; E. Brooks Holifield, *The Covenant Sealed: The Development*

Richard Baxter's exhortation—to "get the liveliest Picture of them [the objects of meditation] in thy minde that possibly thou canst; meditate of them, as if thou were all the while beholding them"— sums up the meditator's desire to achieve imaginative contemporaneity with primordial event. A saint "meditates on the word," according to Richard Greenham, when he "so remembereth it and museth on it, that he goeth from poynt to poynt," scanning every detail. Meditation, agreed Thomas Hooker, "dwells and staies" upon its topic and "lookes on every side." If the sacred scene be sufficiently reinvoked, the meditator should become raptly absorbed in the action, achieving a state of complete dramatic identification: "When a man is deepe in meditation . . . , he neither seeth nor heareth any other thing." This might happen when, dwelling upon Christ's Passion, the saint "conceive[d he] saw those streames of bloud trickling downe his cheekes" or "his hands thrust through with nailes," or envisioned, while concentrating upon an apocalyptic text, that "the heavens opened, and the fire melting round about . . . and the Lord Christ comming in flaming fire."[59]

Particularly gripping were the scenes of love portrayed in the Song of Songs. Seen in their traditional symbolic signification, the poem's evocation of reciprocally wooing, embracing love, of "paps plump, round, [and] fair," and of lovesick desire afforded material for many a self-forgetful pietist revery. Long before taking thought of emigration to Massachusetts, John Winthrop was virtually reliving memorable passages: "O my Lord, my love, how wholly delectable art thou! lett him kisse me with the kisses of his mouthe, for his love is sweeter than wine . . . how pleasant are thy embracings!"[60] In all of these examples, the scriptural text was seen as a door through which the saint might return to the enthralling primordium.

Meditation itself, as should be expected, was viewed as an imi-

---

of *Puritan Sacramental Theology in Old and New England, 1570–1720* (New Haven, Conn., 1974), 38.

59. Baxter, quoted in Martz, *Meditation,* 172–173; Greenham, *Works,* 22; Thomas Hooker, *The Soules Preparation for Christ* . . . (London, 1632), 83–84; Thomas Hooker, *The Soules Implantation* . . . (London, 1637), 53, 244. See also Bownde, *Sabbath,* 203.

60. [Henry Finch], *An Exposition of the Song of Solomon: Called Canticles* (London, 1615), 30; WP, I, 204. See also Knott, *Sword,* 53–54.

tation of primordial archetype. Nicholas Bownde, for one, found warrant for meditative exercises in Joshua's speech to the Israelite people after the death of Moses: reminding them of the Mosaic law and its functions within the National Covenant, Joshua urged all to "meditate therein day and night." Christians, Bownde concluded, were to go and do likewise. More distinctly in the imitative mode, however, was Puritan eucharistic devotion. The brotherhood bore a sharp hostility toward "sensuous," corporeal elements in Catholic, Anglican, and Lutheran eucharistic doctrine and tended to concentrate upon the "mental states" attending sacramental experience. It is clear that these were shaped in part by the "vivid spectacle" of recreated primordial action: "When he broke the bread and poured the wine, the minister silently though graphically described the passion of Christ." From the earliest years of the English Reformation, intense debate had focused upon the transformation of the Catholic Mass into a form more in keeping with biblical intention. Gestures suggesting the now-abhorred notions of re-presented sacrifice and transubstantiation were eliminated early. But it was not until the early 1550s, with bishops Ridley and Hooper successfully exhorting the magistrates "to turn the altars into tables, according to the first institution of Christ," that the English Eucharist began to approximate "the Lord's Board," a sacramental supper served from a table located centrally in nave or chancel.[61]

From the start, a principal motif in Puritan views of the supper was the need to achieve closer correspondence with the New Testament original. Whereas the Elizabethan Prayer Book, rejecting Ridley and Hooper's more radical arrangement, provided for Communion taken singly, successively, and in kneeling posture and employed the traditional wafer and several verbal formulas suggestive of Catholic practice, Puritans called for a genuine imitation of the Last Supper. They wished a rite with communicants seated at table, "common and usual bread," and the use of "no other words but such as Christ left." When they had the opportunity to conduct their own service apart from the forms of the Prayer Book, as in late-sixteenth-century Emmanuel College or in New England, they strove to recreate the spirit

61. Bownde, *Sabbath*, 206; Holifield, *Covenant Sealed*, 54; *WT*, I, 364. I am indebted here to E. Brooks Holifield's authoritative study of Puritan sacramentalism.

and gestures of the biblical archetype. The aim was to invoke through reiteration the sacred event.[62]

When, then, the brotherhood expounded the mental states befitting eucharistic participation, it was to be expected that they should have partly in mind the spectacle of the primordial Communion, with its doubled portrayal of a personal communion with the Lord and of his bloody, sacrificial atonement. It was all the more fitting, therefore, that the clergy should insist upon the imaginative-visual aspect of the eucharist, that they should stress, as Gordon Wakefield puts it, "the *visibility* of the rites" and, after 1625, resist the Laudian relocation of the Communion tables in the altar position, where the clerical operation upon the elements would not be visible to all communicants. It was of the very essence of Puritan conceptions of the communion that it should generate visualization, that it "present to the eye," that it should display "before our eyes a visible crucifying of Christ" and an image of its conveyance to mankind.[63] Thus in the Puritan eucharist we may see an especially clear instance of reinvocation and reenactment of sacred event. And by no means was the quality of "sensuousness" eliminated; it was, rather, in keeping with the pietist interest in subjective states, transmuted into imaginative experience.[64]

With this tentative sketch of the primitivist dimension, it should now be apparent how the ancient histories, poems, letters, and laws collected in the Protestant Bible came to function in the Puritan setting as a living word, a recapturable mythic drama, an avenue of return to a sacred past. Such themes, at the very center of the Puritan orientation, suggest severe limitations upon the conception of Puritanism as a new force straining toward modernity. What would

---

62. *WT*, I, 63; *AP*, 13–14; Thomas Lechford, *Plain Dealing . . .* , ed. J. Hammond Trumbull (Boston, 1867), 46; James Bass Mullinger, *The University of Cambridge*, 3 vols. (Cambridge, 1873–1911), II, 314 n. 1.

63. Gordon Stevens Wakefield, *Puritan Devotion: Its Place in the Development of Christian Piety* (London, 1957), 38; Holifield, *Covenant Sealed*, 54; John Preston, *The Breast-Plate of Faith and Love*, 5th ed. (London, 1634), 73; Greenham, *Works*, 479. See also Cartwright, *Treatise*, 232; and John Rogers, *The Doctrine of Faith . . .* , 3d ed. (London, 1629), 385.

64. Cf. Knott's discussion of appeal to the physical senses in Puritan preaching (*Sword*, 48).

a Puritan meditator, inwardly focused upon the Passion, or members of John Wilson and John Cotton's Massachusetts congregation, "stand[ing] up and mak[ing] a narrow shift" to "see the minister consecrating" the eucharistic elements, make of the assertion that "Puritanism was in fact the reflex of the increasing rationalization of Western life, and had little room in its orthodox formulations for embodiments of the particularistic and irrational"? [65]

Here, as in many another modernizing interpretation, the argument distorts the actual place and function of selected elements within the total complex of Puritan thought and practice. Puritanism may well have chanced to contribute to the "rationalization of Western life," but, through its engagement with the decidedly particularistic world of the biblical primordium, it also preserved and reinforced ancient ways of thinking and doing. One need only observe that terms like *imitation, pattern, model, example, primitive, old, ancient, first, purity,* and *simplicity* are historically first among those through which a distinctively Puritan rendition of the Christian Redemption came to expression. They mark out a hitherto little-explored glacier of meaning, a coherent and major configuration that contains many indexes to a fuller understanding of Puritan belief and action.

It would, moreover, be a grave mistake to suppose that Puritan rationality was not itself extensively conditioned by biblical primitivism. The next step is to examine how Puritans, hardly in a rationalizing mood, restrained the intellectual capacity in their pursuit of a greater reclamation of the first.

65. Peter W. Williams, *Popular Religion in America: Symbolic Change and the Modernization Process in Historical Perspective* (Englewood Cliffs, N.J., 1980), 71; Lechford, *Plain Dealing,* 46.

TWO

THE PROTESTANT

EPISTEMOLOGY

*B*elligerent, untiring opposition to "human invention" was a cardinal feature of the Puritan movement in all its phases. No other technical term, not "covenant," not "sanctification," not "discipline" or "purity," is more revealing of the distinctively Puritan phenomenon within the English church. Resistance to the inventive propensity of the mind underscores the immense value placed by precise Protestants upon acts of self-control. To restraint of impulse in the moral sphere now was joined restraint of intellect as a directive for the right use of reason and imagination in the religious. Sacred writ opened a world able sublimely to exercise the mental powers, but it also made peremptory claims upon them. By supplying in fullness all instruction empowered to guide mankind to a happy end, it established obvious boundaries for intellection. Beyond the range of the biblical data, no theological inquiry safely could rove, nor might ecclesiastical arrangements be devised to alter or supplement those of apostolic times. The presumed right to contrive new structural or theological forms not found among the first was the opening wedge which had admitted the myriad errors of popish religion; and although reduced in scale, such license continued as the major obstacle to true restitution within the English church. Against this error, compounded with the hubris of prelatical officers within an episcopal system, the most concentrated rounds of Puritan polemic would be flung.

Historical Backgrounds

The Puritans' care to restrict the mind takes its place in a long history of protest against speculative excess in theology. Much medieval philosophy, informed by the allegorical techniques of the early Alexandrian Fathers as well as the traditional Platonic tenet that "the principles of being and of knowing are the same" and that rigorously correct deduction therefore yields reliable knowledge, was carried on in a speculative, rationalistic spirit.[1] Those whose agenda was "faith seeking understanding" began with the data of biblical revelation and the church's articles of faith, but they were not strictly bounded by them. They probed for the unapparent "reasons" of belief, for additional rational knowledge of the Trinity, the angelic world, the Incarnation, and the like. The reintroduction of Aristotle in the twelfth and thirteenth centuries focused attention upon the sensory origin of knowledge and thereby posed a challenge to the speculative quest of Christian Platonic theologians, but the great Thomist tradition that Aristotle inspired was dedicated to upholding the harmony of faith and reason, and it conceived theology as a deductive science of ambitious operations upon and beyond revealed data.

Against such trends, many voices were raised. Peter Damian, for instance, an eleventh-century opponent of dialectic, "distrusted all reason [and] . . . restricted all intellectual activity to the study of the Bible and its commentaries"; and the attacks of Bernard of Clairvaux upon Peter Abelard are well known. A key element in the *devotio moderna* of the fourteenth and fifteenth centuries was a protest against the "wild speculation" and much "reasoning and disputing" of scholastic theology. Intellectually the most powerful protest against deductive rationalism was that of the nominalist movement of the late Middle Ages, which "reversed the [speculative] direction of scholasticism" by critically reexamining traditional epistemology, sharply abridging the functions of reason, and taking a "restricted, non-speculative" approach to most theological issues.[2] On the eve of

1. Eugene R. Fairweather, ed. and trans., *A Scholastic Miscellany: Anselm to Ockham* (New York, 1970), 390.
2. Gordon Leff, *Medieval Thought: St. Augustine to Ockham* (Baltimore, 1958), 97; R. R. Post, *The Modern Devotion: Confrontation with Reformation and Humanism* (Leiden, 1968), 320; Gordon Leff, *William of Ockham: The*

the Reformation, the humanist movement and, particularly, Christian humanism took up the cry against scholastic rationalism. The view of Erasmus that "metaphysical speculation in religious matters was useless," his attacks upon the "brazen" habit of seeking "logical explanations . . . of God's mysteries," and his limitation of theological activity to explication of the simple "philosophy of Christ" handed down in the New Testament and the patristic literature suggested a comparatively humble role for the Christian intellectual.[3]

In Reformation thought, antirationalist influences from nominalist, humanist, and other sources joined with a conviction of the radically fallen character of the human faculties, the central authority of the Bible, and the primitive church to produce a distinctive set of emphases which here will be called the "Protestant epistemology." It assumed that, from any rational standpoint, the essentials of Redemption are "foolish, absurd, and impossible." Here the cognitive faculties could perform no autonomous function; of themselves they could neither find the needed direction of inquiry nor obtain the desired knowledge. No disclosures of Christian belief or practice were to be made through an inherent necessity of thinking or through the "wild adventure . . . without any certain rule" of allegorical interpretation; but all was given objectively in Holy Writ. The proper nexus between faith and understanding, therefore, could be found only through acts of intellectual self-denial: one must "cast away his own imagination and reason" and center the mental faculties "teachably" upon the "object" of Scripture.[4]

In order adequately to appreciate the importance Puritans were to attach to the Protestant epistemology and its careful confinement of rational and imaginative activity, it is necessary to recall the impact

Metamorphosis of Scholarly Discourse (Manchester, 1975), xxi–xxiv; Heiko Oberman, "The Shape of Medieval Thought: The Birthpangs of the Modern Era," *Archiv für Reformationsgeschichte*, II (1973), 22–23.

3. James Kelsey McConica, *English Humanists and Reformation Politics under Henry VIII and Edward VI* (Oxford, 1965), 25–26; Hans J. Hillerbrand, ed., *Erasmus and His Age: Selected Letters of Desiderius Erasmus* (New York, 1970), 30–31.

4. Martin Luther, *Martin Luther*, ed. John Dillenberger (Chicago, 1961), 128; William Tyndale, *The Work of William Tyndale*, ed. G. E. Duffield (Philadelphia, 1965), 63; William Tyndale, *The Beginning of the New Testament Translated by William Tyndale* (1525), ed. A. W. Pollard (Oxford, 1926), sig. Bii; Joachim Staedtke, *Die Theologie des jungen Bullinger* (Zurich, 1962), 89.

of primitivist ideas upon Protestant, and especially upon Reformed, scriptural usage. When the religious role of the intellect was viewed from this angle, additional constraints appeared. Then the mental faculties found their proper role within a dialectic of return to the primordial time and imitation of original acts and qualities. Submission of the faculties to Scripture was but due acknowledgment of the jurisdiction of sacred times and paradigms over all significant human activities in postprimordial time. Nevertheless, just as the passions continually threatened to drive behavior beyond the bounds of biblical precept, so the elaborate discursive, logical, speculative, and fanciful capacities of the mind were prone to unfurl out of all proportion to the simple cognitive tasks that led to Redemption.

Specifically, the career of Roman Catholicism since the patristic epoch had illustrated how experience of the mind's inventive facilities, combined with motives of power and greed, could generate the illusion that Christian authorities might modify or improve revealed patterns and even create new, extrabiblical doctrines, laws, or forms of worship. For hundreds of years Catholic leaders had engaged in wholesale invention in every area of Christian thought and practice. The result was a vast sprawl of ecclesiastical paraphernalia—

> as of beads, of lady psalters, and rosaries, of fifteen Oos, of St Barnard's verses, of St Agathe's letters, of purgatory, of masses satisfactory, of stations and jubilees, of feigned relics, of hallowed beads, bells, bread, water, palms, candles, fire, and such other; of superstitious fastings, of fraternities, of pardons, with such like merchandise

—and theological confusions—

> an infinite table of sophisters and school-doctors, of reals and nominals, of sententioners and summists, . . . [of] sophisms, problems, elenches, corollaries, quiddities, subtilties, 2d intentions, intrinsical moods, with other prodigious sorceries

—all grossly out of harmony with simple, primordial worship and teaching and therefore devoid of religious value.[5] The Catholic case

---

5. John Edmund Cox, ed., *Miscellaneous Writings and Letters of Thomas Cranmer* (Cambridge, 1846), 148, vol. II of *The Works of Thomas Cranmer . . .*; Henry Christmas, ed., *Select Works of John Bale*, (Cambridge, 1849), 350, 381.

proved fully that, when permitted to function beyond and in excess of Scripture, the mind could only cast itself into "mist" and "dreams"; it could but summon "lewd imaginations."[6]

When salvation was at issue, it therefore was imperative that such "wanton and vain cogitations" be arrested by laying them to "the touch stone" of Scripture. Within a right Protestant perspective, the mind was thus tamed to primordially simple uses. Christians must "submit their whole intellect to Christ" by confining it strictly to the comprehension of scriptural drama and doctrine. Reason, like imagination, became an "organ . . . exercised upon matter provided by the Word," an organ, that is, of obeisant and unresisting absorption in the primordial world.[7] In contrast to the learning of the scholastics, which had "defiled the [biblical] gold with [speculative] dung," Christian theology became essentially a *biblical* theology, a summary and clarification of the sacred book and a guide to direct study of the text. Catholic doctrines of free will, which ignored biblical teaching of the will's depravity, were nothing but a "play on words"; unbiblical treatises like the Pseudo-Dionysius's *Celestial Hierarchy* were "for the most part nothing but talk." In Calvin's succinct summary: "Our wisdom ought to be nothing else than to embrace with humble teachableness . . . whatever is taught in Sacred Scripture."[8]

In denying the privilege of invention to the Christian intellect, Reformed Protestants thus demonstrated their continuing allegiance to a traditional way of thinking that was closely bound up with primitivist belief. Medieval and Renaissance thinkers moved "in a world in which the genetical principle of comprehension was not known." In theology, as, indeed, in the several areas of learning, knowledge

6. See, for example, Wilhelm Pauck, ed., *Melanchthon and Bucer* (Philadelphia, 1969), 30; Tyndale, *Work of Tyndale*, 31, 36; William Tyndale, John Frith, and Robert Barnes, *The Whole Works of W[illiam] Tyndale, John Frith, and Doct[or Robert] Barnes* (London, 1573), 257; Luther, *Martin Luther*, 174.

7. Henry Bullinger, *The Decades of Henry Bullinger*, ed. Thomas Harding, 4 vols. (Cambridge, 1849–1852), I, 66; Tyndale, Frith, and Barnes, *Whole Works*, 3; Martin Bucer, quoted in E. C. Whitaker, *Martin Bucer and the Book of Common Prayer* (Great Wakering, England, 1974), 72; Brian Gerrish, *Grace and Reason: A Study in the Theology of Luther* (Oxford, 1962), 24.

8. Luther, *Martin Luther*, 183, 186; Clyde Leonard Manschreck, *Melanchthon: The Quiet Reformer* (New York, 1958), 84; John Calvin, *Institutes of the Christian Religion*, ed. John C. McNeill, 2 vols. (Philadelphia, 1960), I, 4; book 1, chap. 14, sect. 4, 164, chap. 18, sect. 4, 237.

rarely was viewed in developmental terms. So far as it was given to mankind to know, theological truth was promulgated already. If it was old, given in ancient times and embedded in the biblical and patristic writings, it was also complete, "viewed as a finished . . . corpus," imbued with the timeless and final quality of sacred event and precept. In this spirit, the reformers celebrated the completeness and fixity of Christian doctrine: The Scripture was written "to endure for ever." God and his church were to be "the same, yesterday and forever . . . the same as they were from the beginning." The biblical gospel was "most perfect and complete in all respects." Divine law, an emanation of "eternal and unchangeable will," was "prescribed for men of all nations and times." Hence Christian doctrine, once rightly apprehended, was "never to be changed"; "to adde unto it . . . or to change it . . . is grete synne." Under these conditions, the role of the intellect was by definition conservative. It possessed no license to discern or create the new, but only the call to complete and refine a schedule of knowledge already disclosed. The "quest for truth [was] thought of as the *recovery* of what is embedded in tradition, . . . rather than the *discovery* of what is new."[9]

These, then, were the defining themes of the Protestant epistemology. The intellectual faculties, possessed of an expansive and troublesome inclination toward illicit invention, required restraint, the framework of which was the scriptural exhibition of timeless, completed truth. When confined to primordial doctrine and paradigm, the intellect was empowered to direct Christians and the Christian church upon the narrow path to Redemption. When permitted to operate apart from biblical constraint, it plunged into ruinous fantasy and dark learning. A defining theme of Puritanism, then, was to be its commitment to the preservation and intensification of these judgments over against a persistent Anglican advocacy of invention.

9. Hardin Craig, *The Enchanted Glass: The Elizabethan Mind in Literature* (Oxford, 1936), 156; George Joye, *The Subversion of Moreis False Foundacion* . . . (n.p., 1543), 54; Whitaker, *Martin Bucer*, 134; Luther, *Martin Luther*, 181; Arthur C. Cochrane, ed., *Reformed Confessions of the Sixteenth Century* (Philadelphia, 1966), 192; Calvin, *Institutes*, book 4, chap. 20, sect. 15, 1503; Samuel Carr, ed., *The Early Writings of John Hooper* (Cambridge, 1843), 26; Joye, *Subversion*, 55; E. Harris Harbison, *The Christian Scholar in the Age of Reformation* (New York, 1956), 5.

Anglican Departures: Adiaphora

"At the very center" of efforts to justify the official Reformation under Henry VIII and Edward VI, written into the Prayer Book, the Thirty-nine Articles, and other formularies of the Church of England, *adiaphora*—the notion of "things indifferent"—became, in time, "the corner-stone of Anglicanism."[10] Of continental origin, adiaphorism apparently was first popularized in England in the 1530s.

As formulated by Cranmer and other apologists for the official Reformation, it grew from a distinction between "the realm of faith and morals and that of church order and ceremonies." Matters of faith and morals were necessary to salvation and therefore under explicit biblical jurisdiction; here the church could only receive and obey. But in the realm of government and ritual, much was merely incidental to salvation and therefore not biblically prescribed. Performance of the Eucharist, conveying the person and benefits of Christ, was clearly essential to Redemption and thus biblically determined; yet many details of that performance, like the choice of kneeling, standing, or sitting while receiving the elements, were not. Such matters were "indifferent" and thereby determinable by church officials responsive to reason, expedience, and decency. There was no obligation to ground them in biblical paradigm.[11]

By thus sponsoring a partial removal of church structure and rite from biblical control and placing their determination in human

10. Bernard J. Verkamp, *The Indifferent Mean: Adiaphorism in the English Reformation to 1554* (Athens, Ohio, 1977), xvi; *EPM*, 27. Patrick Collinson labels Grindal's "acceptance of the need to be conformable in things of themselves indifferent" as "the hallmark of an incipient Anglicanism" in the 1560s (*Archbishop Grindal, 1519–1583: The Struggle for a Reformed Church* [Berkeley, Calif., 1979], 171).

11. Thomas Cranmer, *The Work of Thomas Cranmer*, ed. G. E. Duffield (Philadelphia, 1965), xxii–xxiii. See also Thomas Starkey, *An Exhortation to the People . . .* (London, [1540?]), 4–11, 41–43; *LB*, xviii–xix; Brian Gerrish, ed., *The Faith of Christendom: A Source Book of Creeds and Confessions* (Cleveland, Ohio, 1963), 192, 196–197. The issue of "things [that] of themselves be indifferent" was also the crux of the Vestiarian Controversy involving Bishop John Hooper in the early 1550s (Aubrey Townsend, ed., *The Writings of John Bradford* [Cambridge, 1853], 375–395).

hands, the concept of things indifferent provided full warrant to King-in-Parliament and episcopacy to settle an external religious establishment; but, portentously, it also asserted the capability of the human faculties in religious affairs. The privileges of ecclesiastical invention were, indeed, customarily stated in modest terms. Inessential affairs of government and worship never were to be determined in disharmony with biblical teaching and archetype, and suitable adiaphoristic arrangements were to be adopted from the patristic primordium where available.[12] More important, proponents before Richard Hooker clearly wished adiaphorism to be understood as a legitimate interpretation, and in no sense a violation, of the Protestant epistemology. Cranmer, the arch-adiaphorist of English ritual, yielded to none in his castigation of the "rules, traditions, and professions" that Catholics, neglecting Scripture, "have studied out of their own brain."[13]

But, with these qualifications stated, there yet remained a specific emphasis upon the ability of the human faculties to contrive a right order for the domain of inessentials. Thus the Convocation of Canterbury of 1539 could propose a "Book of Ceremonies" which was to affirm the use of adiaphoristic "rites and ceremonies *devised by men* . . . upon causes reasonable," and the preface as well as the introductory statement "Of Ceremonies" attached to all sixteenth- and early seventeenth-century editions of the Prayer Book declared the validity of ceremonial procedures "by the wit of man . . . devised."[14] In addition, a general agreement upon the criteria of proper devisement afforded much opportunity for sophisticated calculation. The oft-cited rule was that the fashioning of adiaphora must conduce efficiently to "decent order" in Christian practice; but it also was essential that decency and order be estimated relative to the "diversity of times, places, or conditions of the people," a thought that also suggested the need periodically to review and perhaps to "alter and change" adiaphoristic arrangements.[15] The inventive "wit of man," in

12. Cranmer, *Work of Cranmer*, xxii–xxiii; Gerrish, ed., *Faith of Christendom*, 192, 196; *LB*, xii–xv, xix.

13. Cranmer, *Writings and Letters*, I, 146, 148.

14. John Strype, *Ecclesiastical Memorials* . . . , 6 vols. (Oxford, 1822), II, 412; *LB*, xii, xviii (emphasis mine).

15. Strype, *Memorials*, II, 412–413; John Strype, *Annals of the Reformation*, 4 vols. in 7 (1824; New York, 1968), I, pt. 2, 466, III, pt. 2, 67; *LB*, xviii,

short, was to find a generous and continuing occupation in fashioning ritual and polity.

This entire pattern, with its candid delimitation of scriptural authority, was taken over by the Elizabethan church. Some of those who contributed to the settlement in religion hoped that Catholic liturgical retentions soon would be set aside, but the authorized attitude toward such aims was evidenced by the unmitigated adiaphorism of the Thirty-nine Articles of 1563. These "decreed" episcopal government "rightly . . . ordered" and proclaimed the right of the authorities to "ordain, change, and abolish" ceremonial adiaphora "only by man's authority," so long as Scripture not be opposed and the issues of decency and order and "diversities of countries, times, and men's manners" be duly considered. Elizabeth's wide-ranging ecclesiastical *Injunctions* of 1559, setting forth a uniform order of church government and worship, had reflected a full assertion of such privilege, as had the issue of a revised Prayer Book in the same year with the older preface and the rubric "Of Ceremonies" retained without essential change and with an explicit ornaments rubric inserted before Morning and Evening Prayer. Since from the 1560s church spokesmen continually had to reckon with an aggressive, disturbingly articulate, and at times politically powerful Puritan determination to affix "the infamous title of the invention of man" upon established ecclesiastical forms, an important part of the Anglican story during Elizabethan and Stuart times consisted of a dogged defense under fire of the right "to institute, to change, clean to put away . . . and to constitute other" religiously neutral arrangements.[16]

During the major confrontations of the 1560s and the following two decades—the Vestiarian Controversy, the Whitgift-Cartwright debates, and the classis movement—Anglican respondents did little more than rehearse, perhaps in more imperious tones, the now-

---

xix; Townsend, ed., *Writings of Bradford*, 389; Hugh Frederic Woodhouse, *The Doctrine of the Church in Anglican Theology, 1507–1603* (London, 1954), 119–120; Edward Cardwell, ed., *Documentary Annals of the Reformed Church of England*, 2 vols. (Oxford, 1844), I, 264.

16. Gerrish, ed., *Faith of Christendom*, 192, 196–198; Henry Gee and William John Hardy, eds., *Documents Illustrative of English Church History* (London, 1896), 417–442; *LB*, xii–xix; [Matthew Parker], *A Briefe Examination for the Tyme, of a Certaine Declaration* . . . (n.p., [ca. 1566]), sig. ***3; Cardwell, ed., *Annals*, I, 264.

conventional adiaphoristic wisdom. In other areas, new ground was broken. Most notable were the efforts of Richard Bancroft and Adrian Saravia around 1590 to drive beyond an adiaphoristic to a more clearly restorationist rationale for episcopacy, but this strategy added nothing to the case for invention.[17] The man who stepped forth to meet the need for a fuller rationalization of the role of inventive reason and imagination in religion was Richard Hooker. Stimulated by a deep, conservative reverence for the religious establishment, alarmed by the Presbyterian campaigns of the 1580s, and convinced of the inadequacy of existing Anglican apologetics, Hooker began in 1591 to prepare his full and ingenious anti-Puritan monument, *Of the Laws of Ecclesiastical Polity*.

Aiming at a full vindication of ecclesiastical invention, this first "specifically Anglican" theology concentrated heavily upon the issue of reason and its prerogatives in religion. Hooker found the ramifying assault upon what "the brain of man has devised . . . in things divine" dangerously cogent. To counter it he undertook a comprehensive reappraisal of the "power and authority of the Word of God" in relation to the "force [of] man's reason." Greatly moderating both the traditional Protestant understanding of the fallen and wayward character of the human faculties and the hostility to Catholicism that had given the Protestant epistemology much of its original bite, and citing classical and Catholic sources almost as readily as biblical texts, Hooker ventured upon a major departure from the Reformed tradition. He proposed a definition of reason, neither fundamentally impaired by the Fall nor requiring a religious conversion for proper orientation, that might adequately discern and apply the "Divine law" grounding the existing orders of nature, society, and the church. The segment of God's law that instructs men in the Atonement through Christ's "death and merit," which Hooker identified as the essential matter "necessary to Salvation," is conveyed uniquely in Scripture. Because the divine program of redemption from sin stands above the reach of rational inference, it had to be revealed supernaturally; and in this domain, God "precisely forbids men to use their own inventions." But—and here is Hooker's great point—against the Puritan

17. Richard Bancroft, *A Sermon Preached at Paules Crosse* (London, 1588); Tadataka Maruyama, *The Ecclesiology of Theodore Beza* (Geneva, 1978), 179–184.

contention that adiaphorism "pinned" the word of God in an impossibly "narrow roume," he now could reply that Scripture embraces but a small domain within the great concourse of divine wisdom and rule.[18]

Beyond the few suprarational essentials, which Hooker took trouble to restrict as much as possible, there extend large additional reaches of providential government whose principles, though they too may be presumed or taught in sacred writ, are imparted to mankind through a variety of extrascriptural sources. The "greatest part of the Law moral," for example, is "easy for all men to know" by reliance upon the "Law of Nature and Reason." The Bible, in a word, was not the sovereign repository of Christian teaching imagined in Puritan circles; it was not "the only law whereby God has opened his will." Contrary to the Presbyterian claim, it supplied only fragmentary guidance for the affairs of ecclesiastical polity and worship. When the church is confronted with the need to develop fitting "ceremonies, order and . . . kind of church government," it is not primarily to Scripture, but to complementary sources of general revelation that it must turn.[19]

The particular media through which divine law is to inform the church's institutional and liturgical life are innate moral and aesthetic inclination, venerable usage, "experience and practice," and the obvious requirements in a given society of order, propriety, and the general good. And yet, unlike Scripture, these do not convey a formulated scheme. They yield, as it were, the raw suggestions and clues from which man's intellect, itself an emanation of higher reason, must infer and fashion an appropriate platform for the visible church. Considering the paucity of scriptural direction for the church's form, an institutionally viable Church of England never could have emerged without extensive rational and practical invention. By defining such activity as an authentic and essential application of the divine government, Hooker aimed to retrieve "human capacity, judgment and wit," together with the myriad inventions of

18. H. G. Alexander, *Religion in England, 1558–1662* (London, 1968), 128; John Keble, ed., *The Works of Richard Hooker*, 7th ed., 3 vols. (London, 1888), I, 182–183, III, 213; Richard Hooker, *Of the Laws of Ecclesiastical Polity*, 2 vols. (London, 1907), I, 206, 208–209, 214, 298–299, 310; Thomas Cartwright, *A Replye to an Answere Made of M. Doctor Whitgift* (n.p., 1573), 26.

19. R. Hooker, *Laws*, I, 238, 298–299.

the Church of England, from the reproaches of the Protestant epistemology.[20]

A key feature of Hooker's work comes to light in his attitudes
toward Presbyterian primitivism. For his frank minimization of scriptural jurisdiction clearly aimed partially to release the intellect from
the restrictive duty of return to primordial instruction and paradigm.
Protesting the Puritan ambition ever more to "enlarge the necessary
use of the Word of God," he wished rather to stress the many areas
of the church's life—including many undeniably significant areas—
that were not subject to archetypal rule. He was careful to expand
upon those "many things" for which no sacred pattern was given.
He deemed it absurd to claim that practices of the New Testament
church, which must include the use of "common brooks or rivers" in
baptism or the secret conduct of worship, were all paradigmatic for
the church in later eras; and he stressed the evident harm that would
be done to English Christianity if such clearly useful features as the
parish system or the collection of tithes were abolished for presumed
"conformity's sake with the . . . first times." In all such areas, laws
for the government of English Christianity had been determined,
and rightly, not by slavish conformity to primitive incidentals, but
by active rational analysis of present needs in the light of general
revelation.[21]

Nowhere was Hooker's attenuation of biblical rule more clearly
expressed than in his expansion of the traditional adiaphorist stress
upon the "diversity of times, places or conditions of the people" into
a broad statement of historical relativism. The few and "necessary"
laws of Redemption might remain fixed and timeless, in the style of
sacred event and precept; but, for the most part, directives ordering
the church's "regiment" and worship do not compose a finished, perfect corpus. To the contrary, they are plainly addressed to mankind
in their peculiar historical and social circumstances. Such factors as
experience, propriety, the people's general good, or reasonableness—

20. R. Hooker, *Works*, III, 213.

21. R. Hooker, *Laws*, I, 111, 234, 254–255, 365. John Kenneth Reynold
Luoma has argued that biblical restorationism is "the logical structure to
[Thomas] Cartwright's work" and that Hooker's *Laws*, addressed primarily to
the Presbyterian challenge, was intended essentially as a counter-restorationist
statement ("The Primitive Church as a Normative Principle in the Theology
of the Sixteenth Century . . ." [Ph.D. diss., Hartford Seminary Foundation,
1974], 14).

these were not frozen directives, but modes of adaptation to "the nature of things changeable according to the difference of times, places, persons and other . . . circumstances." Regarded from this angle, even the church discipline devised by the Genevans, so extravagantly doted upon by Presbyterian Puritans, could be appraised as a wise harmonization of divine will with that city's "present estate," with a turbulent democracy on hand and the episcopal office inoperative.

But more, Hooker was prepared openly to assert the historically conditioned and ephemeral character of many biblical patterns. Numerous scriptural laws and practices, including "laws of [that is, enacted by] God himself," plainly were relative to "temporary" ends and circumstances. To that degree themselves impermanent, they were susceptible of alteration or abrogation as changing times should require. The practices of supporting the Christian pastorate by voluntary contribution, for instance, or of receiving Communion after a meal, far from being "immutable" archetypes, were an accommodation to the ruder and socially simpler circumstances of the New Testament church. Therefore, it was not necessary to choose between the simplicity of earliest Christian days and the variegated, affluent, and vast thing that England's official Christianity had become by the sixteenth century. Such qualities, so far as they apply to adiaphora, were strictly relative. And indeed—offense of offenses, from any Puritan standpoint—the quality of simplicity itself, which Hooker readily acknowledged as a feature of biblical Christianity, thus could be seen as an accommodation to rude times! To insist, then, with the Presbyterian party, that the main features of New Testament Christianity were immutable designs binding the church in all ages to supine imitation was "to urge the state of one only age as a pattern for all to follow." It was completely to misunderstand the dynamically historical tasks of those who must frame, sustain, and periodically revise the "laws of ecclesiastical polity."[22]

Contemplated as a theological treatise written within a Reformed

22. R. Hooker, *Laws*, I, 83–84, 221–222, 328–329, 332–333, 349, 364–367, II, 47–50. Part of Hooker's argument concerning the abrogation of the ceremonial and judicial laws was drawn from standard Reformed theology. What was new was his expansion of the theme into a more explicit relativism and his application of it to New Testament materials. For comments on Hooker's "sense of perspective and [historical] process," see Luoma, "The Primitive Church," 97–98.

context, the *Laws of Ecclesiastical Polity* presents a strange spectacle indeed. The creators of Reformed theology had been concerned to *limit*, but Hooker to *extend* the reach of human wit toward the things of God. They wished greatly to *expand*, but he to *contract* biblical authority within contemporary Christianity. From the time of Cranmer, these tendencies had been implicit within the theory of adiaphorism, but never had they been carried to such length or expounded with such deliberateness or philosophical fullness. No interpretation of Puritanism as a modernizing force should fail to observe that here, in the most exhaustive and profound of all *anti*-Puritan formulations, a well-coordinated complex of modernizing themes emerges: a greater confidence in the congruence of human and divine wisdom, a substantial freeing of the rational judgment from the confinements of timeless mimesis, an assignment of priority to "experience" (with a limited recognition of historical change and relativity), and, not incidentally, a much freer use of extrabiblical sources in theological construction. These themes reflect precisely the direction in which Anglican thought was being impelled under successive waves of primitivist criticism. They were to figure heavily, if diversely, in Stuart Anglicanism and provide an ever sharper contrast with the thought of the Spiritual Brotherhood.

The *Laws*, with its abrupt rationalism and difficult style, was a worst seller for several years after its appearance in the 1590s, but gradually it came to "initiate a new phase in English religious thought."[23] Hooker's first and splendid mustering of "that characteristically Anglican thing, a defence of Reason," buttressed with appeal to "the ancient Fathers in their times," placed before the theological public a greatly broadened option in theological method. During the decades after his death, with a growing number of apologists for the Church of England helping to consolidate its anti-Puritan cast and strengthen its conceptual foundations, frequent, open, and major departures from the strict tradition of Reformed biblicism appeared within Anglican quarters. Thomas Jackson's elaborate disquisitions upon the divine essence and attributes, Joseph Hall's half-Senecan rendition of Christian piety, Robert Sanderson's moral philosophy

23. Gerald R. Cragg, *Freedom and Authority: A Study of English Thought in the Early Seventeenth Century* (Philadelphia, 1975), 98, 118–121. Books 1 through 4 of the *Laws* appeared in 1593, and book 5 in 1597. The remaining sections remained in manuscript for more than half a century.

premising that "the holy Scripture is not the Adequate Rule of conscience," Jeremy Taylor's rehearsal in his huge *Ductor Dubitantium* (1660) of the familiar Hookerian positions upon nature, reason, and Scripture—all were joined to an acrid impatience with critics of the official church and an entire unwillingness longer to endure the restrictions imposed by those who would leash reason to Holy Writ.[24]

Puritan thinkers, in sharp contrast, sustained and at times intensified the older Protestant suspicion of the untrammeled mind. Their thesis was that men proceed aright when they *"confine . . . Reason to the compass of the Wisdom of the Scripture."*[25] Here, in a parting of ways over issues drawn in the Protestant epistemology, no less than in the oft-remarked Arminian trends of Stuart times, the deepest distinctions between Puritan and (if in a less homogeneous sense) Anglican perspectives are to be sought.

The Puritan Case against Human Invention

While Hooker and, in time, many an Anglican apologist for the seventeenth-century church specifically minimized the impact of the Fall upon the cognitive faculties, Puritan spokesmen set themselves to uphold the sobering perspectives of the Protestant epistemology. They remained convinced, in the purview of "total depravity," that *"every* faculty of soul and body" was disordered equally by original sin and directly "prone . . . to evil"—a contention that must qualify the widely promulgated idea that Puritanism accepted from Renaissance humanism "an emphasis upon human reason and an optimistic view of man's capacity."[26]

24. Cragg, *Freedom and Authority,* 145; [Roger Hacket], *A Sermon Principally Entreating of the Crosse in Baptisme . . .* (London, 1606), 1–2; Thomas Jackson, *The Works of Thomas Jackson,* 12 vols. (Oxford, 1844), V, 3–558; Josiah Pratt, ed., *The Works of Joseph Hall,* 10 vols. (London, 1808), VII, 5–40; Sanderson, quoted in Norman K. Clifford, "Casuistical Divinity in English Puritanism during the Seventeenth Century: Its Origins, Development, and Significance" (Ph.D. diss., University of London, 1957), 315–316; Reginald Heber, ed., *The Whole Works of the Right Reverend Jeremy Taylor,* 15 vols. (London, 1822), XI, 342, 356, 381, 434–465, XII, 191–280, XIII, 68–96.

25. Thomas Hooker, *The Application of Redemption . . .* (London, 1657), 303.

26. See R. Hooker, *Laws,* I, 266–268; Jackson, *Works,* IX, 238; William

Yet the failure of the intellect described here was not restricted to that rationalization of sinful impulse discovered and explored by Puritan pietist introspection. It amounted to a fundamental collapse of cognitive function. Man's mind might "somewhat" be able "to wade into worldly things" not directly contingent upon revelation, but "in matters of faith and religion" different rules applied. Here Puritans stood squarely with earlier Reformed Protestants, declaring the mind utterly unable "to pierce anything," its great capacities without fruitful application. Incapable of forming valid concepts or reasoning accurately, it could but wander, wayward. Here was ground sufficient to damn "philosophy," as instanced by Platonic metaphysics or Aristotelian ethics, since aside from a few faint perceptions of natural law its deliverances all flow "from the braines and invention of men." Again, the "abstracted notions of a deity" promulgated in Catholic mystical theology are "cobwebs" that "any man's wit can easily invent." Such constructions simply scatter mental energy in "vaine and curious searching" without credible result.[27]

How might this futility be overcome? At this point too, Puritan leaders sustained the older Reformed conviction that in all significant matters of faith, if the mind is to be restored to good function, it must submit to a tight focus upon Scripture. The whole errant course of evil and nonsense issuing from "the vanitie and weakenes

---

Perkins, *The Work of William Perkins*, ed. Ian Breward (Appleforth, England, 1970), 192 (emphasis mine); Clifford, "Casuistical Divinity," 109. See also J. Sears McGee, *The Godly Man in Stuart England: Anglicans, Puritans, and the Two Tables, 1620–1670* (New Haven, Conn., 1976), 85–86. A relevant discussion of the "limits of reason" within Puritanism is John Morgan, *Godly Learning: Puritan Attitudes towards Reason, Learning, and Education, 1560–1640* (Cambridge, 1986), 41–61.

27. In Thomas Wilcox, *The Works of that Late Reverend and Learned Divine, Mr. Thomas Wilcocks* . . . (London, 1624), 13; Thomas Cartwright, *A Commentary upon the Epistle of Saint Paule Written to the Colossians* (London, 1612), 122; Thomas Shepard, *The Works of Thomas Shepard*, 3 vols. (Boston, 1853), III, 82, 171; Edward Dering, *Certaine Godly and Comfortable Letters* . . . , in Edward Dering, *M[aster Edward] Derings Workes* (London, 1597), sig. A8. See also William Ames, *The Marrow of Theology* (1629), trans. and ed. John D. Eusden (Boston, 1968), 225–226; William Ames, *Technometry* (1643), trans. and ed. Lee W. Gibbs (Philadelphia, 1979), 101–103, 109; John Cotton, *An Exposition upon the Thirteenth Chapter of the Revelation* (London, 1655), 27; John Davenport, *The Knowledge of Christ* . . . (London, 1653), 7; William Haller, *The Rise of Puritanism* . . . (1938; Philadelphia, 1972), 304.

of mans reason" might be stopped if the mind be "reformed" by the measure of Scripture. As the clerical brotherhood increasingly concentrated after the 1580s upon the dynamics of religious conversion, so it insisted that right Christian perception was a product of the special gifts of illumination imparted through conversion—a position directly opposed to Hooker's confidence in the natural capacities of reason and specifically repudiated by him.[28] But, more to the point, the clergy labored to awe their converts' regenerated intellects into continence by the spectacle of biblical finality. In "matters religious" the mind may not proceed "*à priori* . . . but by things . . . which may be discerned, because they are described and set downe unto us in the word."[29] By its sheer wonder and cogency the Word from the ancient time imposed itself as both content and limit of ratiocination; it became the enclosing arena within which alone intellection could be true.

On this side as on many others, the new logic of Petrus Ramus proved easily conformable to the Puritan interest. At no time were all Puritans Ramists, or all Ramists Puritans, and it is a considerable mistake to see in the Ramist pattern a controlling influence upon Puritan theology.[30] Ramist logic was palatable to many Puritans pre-

28. Laurence Chaderton, *An Excellent and Godly Sermon . . . Preached at Paules Crosse . . .* (London, 1580), sig. Eiii; Wilcox, *Works*, 60; R. Hooker, *Laws*, I, 101–105. I agree with Egil Grislis that Hooker did not mean "the general capacity for thinking present in all men, but only the special kind of judicious reasoning present in all those who 'are of God' " ("The Hermeneutical Problem in Richard Hooker," in W. Speed Hill, ed., *Studies in Richard Hooker: Essays Preliminary to an Edition of His Works* [Cleveland, Ohio, 1972], 178). But this should be viewed in relation to his virtually inclusive concept of membership in the religious community and his hostility to Puritan evangelicalism. Seen from the standpoint of a Cartwright or a Perkins, his concept of the use of reason in religion did not transcend the natural.

29. Thomas Wilcox, *A Discourse touching the Doctrine of Doubting* (Cambridge, 1598), 100; T. Hooker, *Application of Redemption*, 303.

30. Ames, *Technometry*, ix. It is far too much to claim, for instance, that, for William Ames, "a true understanding of Ramism was the beginning of good religion" (Keith L. Sprunger, *The Learned Doctor William Ames: Dutch Backgrounds of English and American Puritanism* [Urbana, Ill., 1972], 15). Ames's essential understanding of "good religion" is drawn from the tradition of Reformed-Puritan soteriology that antedates substantial Ramist influence in England, and from the pietist strain that developed after about 1580. Ramism served as a cogent way of articulating parts of this theology, not as its "beginning."

cisely because of its convenient adaptability to an existing and fully formed theological outlook. Those in the forefront of the movement to broaden the hold of the Protestant Bible upon the English people and to promote a plain style of religious expression had reason to welcome the Ramists' emphasis upon simplicity and accessibility of knowledge.

But, more, when they considered the new scheme as a tool for organizing or "disposing" the "art" of theology, they could but admire its fitness for holding the mind to a body of fixed truths. Students of Puritan Ramism concur that it was an ideal handmaiden for confident dogmatists. In yet another demonstration of the premodern bent of their conscious theory, dissenters interested in the logic of Ramus understood completely that it was "not a method of inquiry but a method of organization." Logic in this acceptation was no instrument of "faith seeking understanding" through speculative or deductive means; it aimed solely to facilitate the grasp and rhetorical delivery of old and given truths. It "started with the assumption that truth exists as a single, eternal, and fully formulated essence"—a formula that applied supremely to the revealed truths of the Bible.[31]

"Invention" in Ramist logic was not the contrivance of something new, but a signification from Latin meaning to find or discover something already existent. Invention in this context meant retrieval of the requisite "arguments" needed for construction of a logical discourse from their locations within existing literatures. Just as Ramus himself had drawn primarily upon the "storehouse of ancient wisdom" in classical sources, Puritan Ramists like William Ames believed "that the Bible provides the 'places' . . . from which all the arguments needed to relate God and man can be taken."[32] For them the new logic was primarily another lens to train on the body of drama and teaching disclosed forever and in its entirety in the sacred narratives. For theological and pastoral purposes the aim of logical procedure was thus to discern the elements of biblical teaching, to reveal their larger patterns, and to cast the result of inquiry into easily communicable form. This scheme would permit no reach of the intellect beyond the biblically given and fixed.

31. Wilbur Samuel Howell, *Logic and Rhetoric in England, 1500–1700* (Princeton, N.J., 1956), 348; Perry Miller, *The New England Mind: The Seventeenth Century* (1939; Cambridge, Mass., 1954), 144, 166.
32. John D. Eusden, introduction to Ames, *Marrow*, 40–43.

Given their agreement upon such points, it is understandable that the theology of the Puritans in all periods was fervently antitheoretic. Whether one looks at the major systematic productions, works like Perkins's *Golden Chain* (1590), Ames's *Marrow of Theology* (1629), or Samuel Stone's unpublished "Whole Body of Divinity" (written in Connecticut around 1650), or at the myriad of more focused exegetical and homiletical efforts, one discovers a pervasive concentration upon the concrete and determinable. This derives in part from the moralist element in Puritan and, indeed, in all Reformed soteriology, with its insistence upon practical results in the realm of behavior; and to this may be added the peculiarly experiential, conversionist interests that came to the fore late in the Elizabethan period. But it derives as well from the empiricist values of the Protestant epistemology, from the desire to mesh intellectual action with solid, unfailing, complete "Prime Truth as its Prime Object."[33] Richard Hooker, who regarded Presbyterian ecclesiology as a fanciful deduction that went far beyond scriptural data, might doubt such claims. But Puritan thinkers clearly possessed not only a "supreme confidence in the ability of reason"—if illuminated in the context of a personal conversion—to find the truth plainly exhibited in Scripture but also a conviction that the restoration of cognitive function essential to theology emerged through renunciation of "theory and speculation" across biblical boundaries. In their scorn for productions of "the mere wit of man," a team of Puritan respondents to the *Laws* thus could show how Hooker, lacking a proper understanding of the mind's needed "foundation in holie writt," had retained no adequate criterion for distinguishing truth from nonsense. They merely compiled a short catalog of the cognitively empty assertions—that "tenne [is] the number of natures perfections," that angels turn the heavenly spheres, and the like—that they found strewn in Hooker's work. The reader was to draw the obvious conclusion.[34]

Puritan disdain for intellectual excess should not be confused with the Protestant anti-intellectualism of then or of later times. The

33. Richard Baxter, quoted in William Haller, *Liberty and Reformation in the Puritan Revolution* (New York, 1955), 195.

34. Edmund S. Morgan, *The Puritan Dilemma: The Story of John Winthrop*, ed. Oscar Handlin (Boston, 1958), 81; John Downame, quoted in Haller, *Rise*, 85; *A Christian Letter of Certaine English Protestants* (Middelburg, Neth., 1599), 35–36.

well-known vital connection with Cambridge University, the ardent struggle against the left-leaning critics of an educated ministry of the 1640s and 1650s, the learned cast of the bulk of Puritan utterance, the founding of Harvard College—these and many other signs argue a continued loyalty to the Reformed tradition of intellectual responsibility. Once submissively centered on the scriptural material, the mind had much, often sophisticated work to perform. Biblical interpretation and application provided a wide field within which the faculties of conception and inference might profitably work.

In the face of persistent misrepresentation by their opponents within the English church, critics of the religious establishment denied that they "ever wrote, said, or thought" that every religious form must be "expressly commanded" in Scripture. They acknowledged countless cases in which biblical instruction was "not set down in precise words," but conveyed through implication. William Perkins, for example, argued in his *Treatise of the Vocations or Callings of Men* that every approved human calling was prescribed and commanded in the sacred text, yet not all were "particularly prescribed." In such cases it was necessary to consider the congruence of a proposed vocation with biblical teaching and law generally, and by this measure traveling players or operators of gaming houses, though not mentioned in Scripture, could be judged to have "no calling at all." Again, John Cotton could acknowledge the lack of biblical command or example "for women to partake of the Lord's Supper," yet insist that "the proportion of the Lord's supper with the Passover, and deduction from Scriptures as put no difference between male and female, make it to be received as the just will and ordinance of God." Proceeding thus, Perkins, Cotton, and their colleagues were but specifying assent to an exegetical principle acknowledged throughout the international community of Reformed churches. Like their Scottish and continental cousins, they insisted that what was drawn from Scripture by clear "proportion, or deduction, by consequence, . . . is as well the Word of God, as that which is an express commandment or example."[35] Yet this was no formula for ambitious thinking. If it

---

35. Edward Dering, *The Praelections . . . upon . . . Hebrews*, in Dering, *Workes*, sig. C; Perkins, *Work of Perkins*, 447–448; John Cotton, *The Grounds and Ends of Baptisme of the Children of the Faithfull* (London, 1647), 4. This position was in keeping with the international consensus of Reformed theology

allowed a measure of analytical scope, it was merely another corollary of biblical exegesis; and it required a more, not a less, intensive examination of sacred texts.

In some cases, the power of deduction legitimately might be increased, and a dividend of extra cogency be attained, through syllogistic argument. Syllogisms appear occasionally in the literature, especially that of a polemical turn:

> Where there is not true discipline, Christ does not reign,
> But the Church of England has not true discipline.
> Therefore it is not part of Christ's kingdom.[36]

But even here, in a relatively extreme statement, the thrust of intellect was leashed firmly back to a biblical baseline: New Testament "discipline." And so it was in Puritan usage generally. Syllogistic argument was but another calculation of text-centered meanings, and one seldom at variance with the limiting rule of "proportion, or deduction."

Poised in relief, then, against freer Anglican ways, stood the Puritan ideals of restraint of intellect and the preemption of it by scriptural content, and again one sees how largely the dissenting case turned upon "appeal to that which was first." Every primordial quality of Scripture was pertinent: its dramatic, absorbing presentation, its display of unique "first times," its supernatural aura, its affecting purity and simplicity, its vivid exempla. These were credentials that fitted Christian writ to captivate the mind, to be "the only lodestar to follow," to give "the rule, the line, the square . . . whereby to . . . try all judgments . . . of men." When thoroughly drilled in imaginative reenactment of sacred event through meditation, sacrament, or evocative sermonizing, Christians most readily could be compelled to discount their own "judgement and wisdom," to become "marvellous . . . tractable," and "willingly content to take every truth that is revealed, without quarrelling." One might even

---

(Heinrich Heppe and Ernst Bizer, *Die Dogmatik der evangelisch-reformierten Kirche* [Neukirchen, 1958], 13).

36. Albert Peel, ed., *The Seconde Parte of a Register . . .* , 2 vols. (Cambridge, 1915), II, 65. For other examples, see Perkins, *Work of Perkins*, 334–335; John Preston, *The Breast-Plate of Faith and Love*, 5th ed. (London, 1634), 8; Jeremiah Chaplin, *The Life of Henry Dunster: First President of Harvard College* (Boston, 1872), 293.

consent, as required by William Perkins, not "to conceive a thought in his mind, unless he have counsel or warrant from the Word of God so to think."[37]

If, by its power of dramatic enthrallment, the Christian Book was thus able to curb excessive ventures of the mind, so it imposed a crucial extra measure of restraint by its display of the perfect and timeless. Countenancing no dissent on this point from Reformation teaching, dissenters established as a rule of thumb in all biblical interpretation "that the word of God . . . is of absolute perfection," a finished and closed order of truth that admitted of no additions, modifications, or embellishments. In partial retention of the older Protestant position, Richard Hooker did maintain that scriptural instruction in matters essential to salvation was immutable. But through his open avowal of the historically relative character of the church's inventive activities in the much more extensive domain of inessentials, he greatly compromised primitivist attunement to the perfect and unchanging.[38]

The Puritan remains, in contrast, are distinguished by unyielding devotion to the biblical primordium in all its sacred finality. In pointed repudiation of the Anglican regard for "diversity of times, places or conditions," dissenting publicists rang changes without end upon the "perpetual" status of scriptural norms: "Wee are taught not by daies and times to measure [God's] commandments, but to hold them without change, . . . for ever." To seize and "hold them . . . without change," that was the function of the intellect engaged with unvarying truths. Since divine law was not "subject to alteration or chaunge as mens lawes . . . are," there was no question of inventive accommodation to changing circumstances. A biblical original was "no commandement belonging to any certain time, but perpetuall, and pertaining to all times and states of the Church." Therefore, the

37. Cartwright, Replye, 163; Leonard J. Trinterud, ed., Elizabethan Puritanism (New York, 1971), 28; Cartwright, A Treatise of Christian Religion (London, 1616), 78; Dudley Fenner, Certain Godly and Learned Treatises (Edinburgh, 1592), 92; Thomas Hooker, The Soules Preparation for Christ . . . (London, 1632), 39; William Perkins, The Workes of That Famous and Worthy Minister of Christ, Mr. William Perkins, 3 vols. (London, 1635), II, 477.

38. Bradshaw quoted in Perry Miller, "Errand into the Wilderness," in Miller, Errand into the Wilderness (New York, 1956), 20 (see also Wilcox, Works, 42); R. Hooker, Works, III, 212–213.

orders of worship and polity imposed through biblical event, once correctly assimilated, should "stand firme and inviolable, without alteration . . . whilst the world standeth."[39]

Presumably, such emphasis had much to offer in a period of English history marked by rapid socioeconomic change, but creative adaptation to a shifting society was no part of its proponents' conscious purpose. Pointedly, the major Puritan proposals for reform of polity, worship, and discipline avoid any claim to adaptive ingenuity or originality. The Presbyterian program of church discipline, for example, rooted in a perception of fixed New Testament archetype, certainly was not understood as a variable response to moral need or, in any sense, as an act of positive creation. Presbyterian spokesmen might point out that the local selection of pastors or the elders' disciplinary watch would lead to the more effective cure of souls or would better order a morally turpid population, but they did not intend thereby to ground the pastoral forms, first, in function.

For the biblical forms were universals. In their very character as archetypes they came adapted to every exigency of pastoral and disciplinary function, irrespective of time, place, and society. Likewise, the Sabbatarian movement that arose in the 1580s, coupled as it was with a crusade against holidays lacking scriptural warrant, probably helped to meet the need of an early capitalist society for a more regular work force, but Sabbatarian theorists did not conceive the Lord's Day as an adjustment to the times.[40] To the contrary, for them the Sabbath denoted deliberate reversion to a fixed order of precept and form that must shape human society and development, not the other way around. So, too, did the many pietist descriptions of the Chris-

39. Dering, Praelections, in Dering, Workes, sig. D3; Wilcox, Works, 37; Walter Travers, A Full and Plaine Declaration of Ecclesiastical Discipline . . . (Leiden, 1617), 7; John Davenport, The Knowledge of Christ . . . (London, 1653), 85. Note also John Udall's title, A Demonstration of the Truth of That Discipline, Which Christ Has Prescribed in His Word, for the Government of His Church, in All Times and Places, until the End of the World (1588), ed. Edward Arber (London, 1880). Puritan theory did, of course, admit that incidental features of religious practice, like the time or length of the worship service, were "indifferent" and modifiable to circumstance. See, for example, Cartwright, Replye, 27; Ames, Marrow, 285–286.

40. Cf. David Little, Religion, Order, and Law: A Study in Pre-Revolutionary England (New York, 1969), 94, 128; Christopher Hill, Society and Puritanism in Pre-Revolutionary England, 2d ed. (New York, 1967), 145–218.

tian family as a "little church," on the assumption that "the only rule of ordering the family" is the "perfect way" plotted in Scripture. The Daily Rule adopted by many pietist dissenters demonstrated how "a Christian is tied to measure and square out his . . . affairs after the rules of Scripture," which direct all Christians everywhere and uniformly "how to begin the day, how to proceed in the severall actions of the same, and how to end it." The exercise of fasting was not an adaptable "humane constitution, but an ordinance of God." And so on.[41] To understand the Puritan movement in its own terms: these and the many other elements of the dissenting program display, not creative, but conformist intent. If the Reformation was thus to be "advanced," it was not through human art or the "march of mind" of a later era, but through a curbing of human capacities by the scripturally incarnated body of prime, fixed truth.

A similar tale of bristling contempt for the new often surfaces in the literature. For centuries a pejorative contrast of new to old had been a commonplace of Catholic thinking. It played varying but important roles both in the thought of defenders of established tradition and in the appeal of critics to eclipsed apostolic norms. It was adapted by England's earliest Protestants in their warfare against Catholic innovations upon the biblical heritage. Cranmer, Tyndale, and their reforming colleagues also repudiated hotly "the opprobrious epithet 'new'" hurled back by Catholic defenders.[42] Puritan debaters, with their case for reform resting so heavily upon the biblically first and ancient, hastened to affix the label of "novelty" to objectionable elements retained or devised by the established church. From the Anglican standpoint, of course, with its primitivist admixture and its strong sense of continuity with patristic ways, bearers of the "Puritan humour" were the true purveyors of "new fangled" devices. It seemed a sufficient stroke against the Presbyterians to show how Thomas Cartwright "first invented [his] . . . innovation" of rule by presbyters. From the 1580s defenders of traditional Sun-

41. Perkins, *Work of Perkins*, 416, 418; Fenner, *Treatises*, 1; Robert Cleaver, *A Godly Form of Householde Governement* . . . (London, 1612), sig. A1; Richard Rogers, *Seven Treatises* . . . (London, 1603), 303; Nicholas Bownde, *The Holy Exercise of Fasting* (Cambridge, 1604), 1.

42. George Boas, *Essays on Primitivism and Related Ideas in the Middle Ages* (Baltimore, 1948), 175; Maurice Powicke, *The Reformation in England* (1941; London, 1961), 16.

day observance against the growing crusade for a renovated Sabbath strove to "put the visor of novelty" upon "our Novell Sabbatarians." Archbishop William Laud accused those who "accuse us of innovation" of being themselves "the chief innovators of the Christian world." Since Presbyterian and Congregational elders, for instance, were "never heard of" until the sixteenth century, he deemed their advocates patently "guilty of innovation."[43]

But it was the Puritans, with their more narrowly drawn conception of mythic antiquity, who made the most of the charge. It could even be directed against other Puritans, as the New England Congregationalists discovered when they found themselves in the 1630s and 1640s accused by Presbyterian writers of promoting a "novel invention . . . newly sprung up," "but of yesterday." Since it was transparently true, to all men and women properly shepherded by God's word, that "true Antiquity . . . is that which fetches its originall from the beginning," then newness was a telltale and damning quality adhering inevitably to all inventive "additions" to the ancient charter of polity and worship. All "ecclesiasticall Constitutions or customes," whether Catholic or Anglican, which lacked "warrant from the . . . word . . . are but *new formes*." For, once refusing to "be swayed by [the] old [biblical] rule," the mind could but "innovate" a depraved product. Scripturally blueprinted forms, on the other hand, though they "may seeme new" from the standpoint of Hooker's or Laud's attenuated biblicism, were "not new." Even the early Fathers, insisted John Cotton, were "too young" to guide the church, for "no other writings besides the Scripture can plead true Antiquity."[44]

43. A. F. Scott Pearson, *Thomas Cartwright and Elizabethan Puritanism, 1535–1603* (Cambridge, 1925), 285; Shepard, *Works*, III, 11; Francis White, *A Treatise of the Sabbath Day* (London, 1635), 256; "Laud's Speech at the Censure," in Stuart E. Prall, ed., *The Puritan Revolution: A Documentary History* (Garden City, N.Y., 1968), 82–83. See also Hugh Frederic Woodhouse, *Doctrine of the Church*, 123. For comments on the term "innovation" in the 16th and 17th centuries, see Peter Gay, *A Loss of Mastery: Puritan Historians in Colonial America* (Berkeley, Calif., 1966), 10–11, 130–131.

44. John Cotton, *The Way of Congregational Churches Cleared* (1648), in Larzer Ziff, ed., *John Cotton on the Churches of New England* (Cambridge, Mass., 1968), 293, 301; John Cotton, *A Practical Commentary . . . upon the First Epistle Generall of John* (London, 1656), 77, 78; John Davenport, *An Apologeticall Reply to a Booke Called: An Answer to the Unjust Complaint of W.B.* (Rotterdam, 1636), 13. See also Miller, *Seventeenth Century*, 365–366.

As they struggled thus to expurgate novelty from English Protestantism, Puritan reformers unwittingly may have hastened the coming of modern times, but the student of their literature continually will be reminded how little their outlook conforms to later esteemed notions of mankind's ever new march into the future. The purpose they saw in reformation was, not to release Christian saints for secular adventure or uplift, but to confine them to the reign of originals. They were facing backward toward the sacred and ancient and in flight from contemptible newness. "Novelty" served them no less as a term of abhorrence than idleness, fornication, or Sabbath-breaking.[45]

All of the ideas we have examined under the rubric of the Protestant epistemology come, perhaps, to their most recurrent expression in the strictures against human invention that punctuated and in many ways typified Puritan utterance. A mainstay of the early reformers' polemic, the assault upon religious forms and concepts "devised by men" was one of the key gestures through which the Protestant movement defined itself against Catholic Christianity.[46] In context of the English church's official adiaphorism, defenders of the religious establishment were obliged to adopt a softer stance on the issue, and this shift was not lost upon Puritan critics. A large part of the Puritan story, therefore, is the adaptation of an already familiar

45. David Little's study of Puritan concepts of order and law depicts Cartwright and Perkins as exponents of an "inbreaking *new* order of God" imposing "a decision between the *old* order and the *new*" and commitment to "a radically *new* conception of social life and authority" (emphasis added). He contrasts this with the Stoic perspective in which "the individual's obedience always refers *back* to the old structure of things, never *forward* to something . . . transforming." *Religion, Order, and Law,* 36, 86, 106, 111. This is a valid point. Much in Cartwright and Perkins was directed against the traditional and the established and to transforming ends. But Little's way of putting the case imparts an erroneous impression. In Puritan thought the "new" carries a consistently pejorative charge; the avowed criterion of order is the "ancient" and primitive; the Elizabethan Settlement was damned precisely because it perpetuated "new" additions to the first and pure. The thrust was not simply forward but also dialectically backward to the standards of the Great Time.

46. For English examples, see Cranmer, *Writings and Letters,* 146; Tyndale, Frith, and Barnes, *Whole Works,* 61; Hugh Latimer, *Sermons and Remains of Hugh Latimer,* ed. George E. Corrie (Cambridge, 1845), 354.

animus against invention to the peculiar needs of polemic against a half-reformed church.

Human invention! What twentieth-century expositor of Puritan intent has seen the theme as a key to the task of definition? And yet the term "invention" is one of the half-dozen or so key terms in the dissidents' technical vocabulary, occurring with seldom-failing frequency and emotional bite in all classes of the literature and in all periods. Arrayed in deadly hostility against the paradigmatic "ordinances of Christ" was, again and again, the "wickedness of [man's] inventions." Any way one formulated it—"human ordinances and the inventions of men," forms or ideas "framed in the shop of human policy," products of "the braines and invention of men," "mens devices," "that which man's brains hath devised"—few solid bursts of Puritan complaint were complete without it. It may well be difficult for a modern audience to feel the full measure of opprobrium normally associated with the act and fact of invention, as in a description of the office of bishop as "a meere humain creature, invented meerly to lift that man of sinne [the pope] into his chaire," or in New Englander Peter Bulkeley's rendition of the Fall of Man as the tale of an "inventer."[47]

So far as the Puritan movement may be defined in terms of dissatisfaction with the official religion of the Elizabethan and Stuart church, "invention" may be considered its most eloquently terse diagnosis of the Anglican error. The church's failure to regenerate and morally order the greatest part of the population came back largely to this: to an attachment to man-made forms with no power to convert and hold a people. Richard Hooker saw to the heart of the

47. Udall, *Demonstration*, 6; Shepard, *Works*, III, 314–315; John Udall, "The Epistle" to Dudley, *The True Remedie against Famine and Warres* . . . (London, n.d.), 3; Cartwright, *Colossians*, 122; Richard Greenham, *The Works of the Reverend . . . M[aster] Richard Greenham . . .* , 3d ed. (London, 1601), 23; Strype, *Annals*, II, pt. 1, 297; Thomas Hooker, *A Survey of the Summe of Church-Discipline* (London, 1648), sig. Kkk3; Peter Bulkeley, *The Gospel-Covenant; or, The Covenant of Grace Opened* (London, 1651), 248. According to Bulkeley, the Adamic forefather "would be finding out many inventions of his own, and if he could not invent them in the shop of his own mind, then he would take them out of the shop of the devil; by those inventions thinking to make himself more excellent than God had made him; and so . . . [he] defaced the Image of God which was stamped upon him."

matter when he identified the charge, "The brain of man has devised it," as the dissenters' prime taunt against misliked patterns of worship, discipline, and polity.[48] And when one attempts to understand the precise reprimand in the accusation, one is brought forthwith to the primitivist dimension. For a people pledged to the Book, the rise and progress of an adiaphorist orthodoxy put in jeopardy the biblical center of Protestantism; but, more specifically, it meant erosion of the prestige of the beginnings. It meant that from Cranmer to Laud the claimed right to invent and mandate religious forms obliterated necessary distinctions between "whatsoever is first" and "whatsoever is later," weighted unduly the patristic centuries, and equated the profane apparatus of modern English religion with the supereminent ordinances of the Great Time. Much of the energy of Puritan teaching went into the effort to reclaim supremacy for the ancient, pure, simple, and fixed estate of the Christian dispensation. Somehow the nation must be persuaded that the Lord had clothed his church with all necessary form in the elevated, mythic time and that the great duty of man, most especially in an age of reformation, was remembrance and imitation. Only this could secure the requisite taming of the intellect and stop the flow of "men's devices." Thus considered, the clamor against invention is no less revealing of bedrock assumptions than the covenantal demand for repentance and amendment or, after the 1580s, the pietist admonition, "Examine yourself."

This and the foregoing chapter have offered one reading of the Puritan strain in English religious dissent. The drive toward greater purity embraced desires and concerns that did not reduce to a dynamic of loss and restoration, although in every case the charisma of the Book was fundamental. Yet we have tried to demonstrate that the ferment that gave rise in the 1560s to a restive opposition and sustained it for many decades was fed by devotion to an ancient but historically eclipsed order of Judaeo-Christian observance. In an age of wholesale appeals to the patristic primordium, the Graeco-Roman classics, and (somewhat later) to an "ancient constitution" of English common law, at no time did Puritans stand alone as champions of a special past. But they were unmatched in acclaiming the order of

48. William Ames, *A Fresh Suit against Human Ceremonies in God's Worship* (n.p., 1633), pt. 1, 99; R. Hooker, *Works*, IV, 213.

life both covenantal and apostolic that they made of the two Testaments. They did not always agree upon the details of this order or to what degree it already was recaptured in the church and nation, but they did share a conviction of its paramount authority. They did contend that it was best and purest because it was "first" in the scheme of things redemptive. Albeit with varying stress and inclusiveness, they did believe that the prescriptive forms of Christian community had been made manifest in mythic times and that additional and man-made contributions were anathema. They united in abhorring "degeneracy from the primitive." And they tended to equate reformation (re-formation) with repristination.[49] These conceptions had been present in Christian thought for centuries, but within the stream of English magisterial Protestantism it was the distinctive Puritan role to exalt the virtues of the first, pure times and patterns and to achieve their closer identification with the world unfolded in the canonical writings. Within the Puritan spectrum, the Presbyterian and Congregational movements show that these emphases, when pushed to the fullest, could generate a truly radical alternative both to the form and ethos of the official church.

Current theses that impute to Puritanism a reorientation toward the future misread the distinctive content of the campaign for further re-formation in early modern English culture. Citizens embarked upon that venture had a clear sense of their station and direction within time, and they took their primary cues and bearings from a sacred past. Indeed, the belief that Christians must "always be making progress, and never retreating" in the work of reformation was essential to their search, as was a view of the Elizabethan compromise as the arrest of a once-dynamic process. Again, to prize first things above all was to subvert loyalty to authorized structures and repudiate the traditionalist concepts upon which they in part were built. In this way a harvest of latent consequences unrelated to idealization of a long-lost time unwittingly was prepared. And certainly a real reform along Presbyterian or Congregational lines would have created a church and society unlike anything in the English past.

But the future tense cannot be said to dominate in a movement to build a better future by enlarging the hold of timeless myth upon the

49. Hastings Robinson., ed. and trans., *The Zurich Letters* . . . , 3 vols. (Cambridge, 1842–1847), I, 2.

citizenry, by summoning them *back* to reenter the primordial world and reiterate its sacred gestures. This brand of dissent conceived the truths and forms of Christianity as complete and fixed, not as plastic and improvable; it generated antagonism toward the "new"; it sponsored an ascetic approach to the uses of reason. To study these issues in finer detail, it is fitting to pursue primitivist aspiration in the context in which it was freest to unfold. Therefore the inquiry turns next to early Congregational New England, where the magic of firstness could be experienced at first hand. There the proclamation, "Wee fled from mens inventions," was a far more accurate disclosure of the aims of its founding leaders than the routinely alleged "errand into the wilderness." [50]

50. *Ibid.*, I, 161; Thomas Hutchinson, *A Collection of Original Papers . . .* (1769), *The Hutchinson Papers*, 2 vols., Prince Society Publications (1865; New York, 1967), II, 132.

THREE

THE ERRAND

INTO THE

WILDERNESS

RECONSIDERED

S ince the first sympathetic investigations of the 1930s, students of American Puritanism often have chosen to accent transitional themes. Presuming some version of the proposition, "Without [an] understanding of Puritanism . . . there is no understanding of America," they have seen in the settlers' outlook an index of progress toward coming conditions. The world that was Stuart English and Congregational, it would seem, was not so very different from our own; it pointed already to familiar American conventions. In the continued pursuit of this interest, one particularly transfixing thesis has emerged: the founders themselves, and to a marked degree, were preoccupied with time forward. They were "radically new" in outlook, possessed of a virtually modern sense of direction in time. Bursting medieval constraints, they had "a Whitmanesque sense of looking into the future, a view of a greater civilization for which they were laying the foundations"; they were the original carriers of the nation's hopeful and individualistic "culture core"; they forged the futuristic standpoint that was to become the "sacred drama of American nationhood."[1]

1. Perry Miller and Thomas H. Johnson, eds., *The Puritans*, 2 vols. (New York, 1963), I, 1; Loren Baritz, *City on a Hill: A History of Ideas and Myths*

While varied in approach, such depictions of American Puritanism most often proceed upon a common premise: They take for granted that the first founders of Massachusetts were bent upon an errand to revolutionize the world. We take up the inquiry at this point. In terms of our special theme, the issue may then be posed, Had the founders so far involved themselves in a mission dedicated to the future of man as to override the classic Puritan priorities?

Perry Miller's "Errand into the Wilderness" and What Historians Have Made of It

No essay upon the colonial American experience has been more admired and influential than Perry Miller's "Errand into the Wilderness" (1952). There Miller presented an arresting explanation of the migration of the 1630s. The founders of Massachusetts, he had come to believe, were an "organized task force" embarked upon a world-saving mission. They had voyaged to America to create a model of Christian reformation that all England and Europe were to imitate.[2] This was a strikingly new proposal. Earlier historians of the

---

in America (New York, 1964), 31; A. W. Plumstead, ed., The Wall and the Garden: Selected Massachusetts Election Sermons, 1670–1775 (Minneapolis, Minn., 1968), 28; William G. McLoughlin, Revivals, Awakenings, and Reform: An Essay on Religion and Social Change in America (Chicago, 1978), xiv, 1, 25; Sacvan Bercovitch, The American Jeremiad (Madison, Wis., 1978), 132. These themes receive special billing within the growing body of consensus scholarship that emerged in the seventies and early eighties and that tends to an interest in "civil religion," in millennial ideas, and in historic America as "God's New Israel" and as a "redeemer nation." For a contrary point of view stressing the alien and disjunctive, see, for example, Darrett B. Rutman, American Puritanism: Faith and Practice (Philadelphia, 1970), 52–88; Kenneth A. Lockridge, A New England Town, the First Hundred Years: Dedham, Massachusetts, 1636–1736 (New York, 1970), 56, 76, 162, 174.

2. Perry Miller, "Errand into the Wilderness," in Miller, Errand into the Wilderness (New York, 1956), 11. For earlier occurrences, see Miller, The New England Mind: The Seventeenth Century (Cambridge, Mass., 1954), 470, 477; Miller, "Declension in a Bible Commonwealth," in Miller, Nature's Nation (Cambridge, Mass., 1967), 22. In 1932 Nellis M. Crouse rang every current change upon the thesis that "religion was the mainspring of the migration to New England" with no mention of an "errand" ("Causes of the Great Migration, 1630–1640," NEQ, V [1932], 32).

Great Migration knew nothing of a Puritan exemplary mission. Its rapid acceptance therefore marks a watershed in the scholarship. By the 1960s the founding Errand had made its way into the textbooks, and there it reigns today. Yet just here, in the virtually axiomatic authority this conception has attained, may be ample ground for re-opening inquiry into the founders' intent.

As Sacvan Bercovitch has perceived, Miller's Errand into the Wilderness has "become influential in the wrong way"; its brilliantly devised argument has commanded such passive acceptance that little inquiry into the documentary basis has occurred. Yet scholars have not always understood the Errand in the same way. A reexamination of the issue properly begins with a look at the original formulation.[3]

If Miller's essay is scrutinized for its statement and documentation of the Puritan Errand, some little-remarked features of the argument appear. First, Miller's main business was not to expound or substantiate the concept of a founding Errand, but, rather, to interpret the psychology of the second and third generations as manifested in the jeremiads. A brief exposition of the aims of the first generation was offered merely as required by the larger concern. Second, in defining the Errand, Miller made a seldom-appreciated distinction. The founders' aspiration, he held, is not reducible to a single statement of purpose; it embraced two distinct levels of meaning. In the first sense it meant the will to construct a covenanted community based, in John Winthrop's words, upon a due form of civil and ecclesiastical government. In this signification, the Errand meant the colonists' "actual business," their "conscious intention." Furthermore, it designated that intention as "an end in itself"; the founders were running the Errand on their own behalf, serving their own religious welfare. But, Miller proceeded, behind the explicit intention appeared a second, an "aim behind [the] aim" by which the colonists were seen "despatched for a further purpose."

That purpose was the creation of a "working model" of fully reformed Christendom "so that ultimately all Europe would imitate New England." It also entailed the training of a civil and ecclesiastical leadership that eventually, following an anticipated Puritan

3. Sacvan Bercovitch, "New England's Errand Reappraised," in John Higham and Paul K. Conkin, eds., *New Directions in American Intellectual History* (Baltimore, 1979), 85. The argument of this section and the following appeared in an earlier form in Theodore Dwight Bozeman, "The Puritans' 'Errand into the Wilderness' Reconsidered," *NEQ*, LIX (1986), 231–251.

triumph in the mother country, would return to govern England. And what was the status of this headier ambition in the colonists' consciousness? To this question Miller gave ambiguous answer. On the one hand he could suggest that the second meaning of Errand was fully conscious, collective, and overt: thus "Winthrop and his colleagues . . . went in order to work out that complete reformation which was not accomplished in England, but which would quickly be accomplished if only the saints back there had a working model to guide them." On the other hand, Miller deliberately contrasted this "aim behind the aim" with the "conscious intention," the "definite" aim, the "avowed end" of the Errand in the first sense. He identified only Winthrop, in his well-known invocation of a "Citty upon a Hill," as "fully conscious" of the further purpose. Neither in the essay of 1952 nor elsewhere did Miller cite other texts from the period 1629–1640 affirming a higher Errand. He described the expectation of a completed reformation and a return to England as an "unspoken assumption" entertained by the settlers only in their "heart of hearts."[4] Clearly, at this level, we are left in uncertainty. Even should we grant Miller's interpretation of it, Winthrop's single text does not a grandiose theory make. We are here presented, not with a convincing demonstration that the founders were moved by world-redeeming purpose, but with an ambiguously formulated proposal obviously best regarded as a hypothesis in need of testing.

Both the subtlety and the ambiguity of Miller's formulation of the Errand are emphasized when we look at what others have made of it. Briefly, it is a story of how a minimally developed proposal, without substantial additional research, has been hardened into fact and then inflated well out of proportion to the original statement. Of the many existing scholarly discussions of the reputed original Errand, the great majority that cite sources rely exclusively upon the argument of Miller's "Errand," often quoting as well Winthrop's reference to a "Citty upon a Hill."[5] Miller's careful distinction between

---

4. Miller, "Errand," in Miller, *Errand*, 3–5, 11–12. Miller probably adopted the distinction between the two meanings of *errand* from the *Oxford English Dictionary*, s.v. "Errand."

5. For example, Baritz, *City on a Hill*, 17 (and see 8, 31–32); Lawrence A. Cremin, *American Education: The Colonial Experience, 1607–1783* (New York, 1970), 15; Richard S. Dunn, *Puritans and Yankees: The Winthrop Dynasty of New England, 1630–1717* (1962; New York, 1971), 11; Kai T. Erikson, *Wayward*

the two meanings of the Errand is all but universally disregarded, and the homelier themes of what he designated the "conscious intention" largely are ignored. The more sensational note, the obligation to create a model or "beacon" to guide England or Europe (or, often, "the entire world"), dominates attention, although the accompanying idea—the return to England—is forgotten. Invariably, those discussions either explicitly or implicitly equate the Errand with a *single* element of Miller's *second* sense, with a "mission to establish a model city."[6]

Further, none of the commentators appears to be troubled by—or even to have noted—Miller's partially developed contrast between the colonists' open and "actual business" and the vaguer, partly implicit, and unstated character of the "aim behind that aim." Creation of "a Bible state of such compelling virtue that it would reform all Christianity by example" regularly is rendered as an *avowed, conscious* goal. All writers accept without a quaver Miller's identification of the Errand, however defined, as the firm *collective* aspiration of "*the* original Puritan settlers." In most cases, the drive to redeem by example is also construed as the founders' *preponderant* aim: "filled with a sense of their own historic mission," they are said to have regarded the construction of a "society which would shine as a beacon" as "the chief aim of the undertaking," as its "primary concern" or "overriding objective."[7]

Puritans: A Study in the Sociology of Deviance (New York, 1966), v–vi. Some 80-odd books and articles in several disciplines were consulted; a number are cited in nn. 11–18 below.

6. Baritz, *City on a Hill*, 17; Harry S. Stout, "University Men in New England, 1620–1660: A Demographic Analysis," *Journal of Interdisciplinary History*, IV (1973–1974), 396–397. Francis J. Bremer explicitly argues that Miller offered the exemplary theme as "the central explanation of the Great Migration" (*The Puritan Experiment: New England Society from Bradford to Edwards* [New York, 1976], 37). An exception to the general disregard of the theme of triumphant return is David E. Stannard, *The Puritan Way of Death: A Study in Religion, Culture, and Social Change* (New York, 1977), 96.

7. On conscious agenda, see Erikson, *Wayward Puritans*, v–vi. Oscar Handlin's comment is typical: The "New England Puritans thought of themselves as led . . . to a new Canaan where they were to create a new kind of society that would be a model for the whole world" ("The Significance of the Seventeenth Century," in James Morton Smith, ed., *Seventeenth-Century America: Essays in Colonial History* [Chapel Hill, N.C., 1959], 11).

On collective aspiration, see Wesley Frank Craven, *The Colonies in Transi-*

Reflecting a sharpened interest in historical eschatology, several later writers magnify the Errand motif, construed as always in Miller's second sense, by associating it with the "deep-rooted expectation . . . for Christ's imminent Second Coming" or, yet more spectacularly, with the founding of the millennium. What in Miller was a wish to spur the Reformation to completion now becomes an ambition to serve as "vanguard of the movement . . . to bring God's kingdom home." Boston's founding thus can be described as the "cosmic climax" to which "the entire history of the real world" pointed.[8]

In accord with such emphases, William Haller's analysis of Elizabethan and early Stuart religious nationalism has been integrated

---

tion, 1660–1713 (New York, 1968), 3. Dunn's phrasing is typical: "They were setting up a model" (Puritans and Yankees, 11 [emphasis mine]). That Miller conceived the Errand as fully conscious and collective may seem an obvious inference from his oft-cited comment: "The migration was no retreat from Europe: it was a flank attack. We are to be a city set upon a hill, the eyes of all the world upon us; what we succeed in demonstrating, Europe will be bound to imitate" (The New England Mind: From Colony to Province [Cambridge, Mass., 1953], 5). Yet it is only reasonable to insist that this statement, probably written within months of the "Errand into the Wilderness," be interpreted in terms of the fuller account.

On preponderant aim, see Edmund S. Morgan, "The Historians of Early New England," in Ray Allen Billington, ed., The Reinterpretation of Early American History (New York, 1968), 42; George D. Langdon, Jr., Pilgrim Colony: A History of New Plymouth, 1620–1691 (New Haven, Conn., 1966), 80; George Lee Haskins, Law and Authority in Early Massachusetts: A Study in Tradition and Design (New York, 1960), 26; William Kellaway, The New England Company, 1649–1776: Missionary Society to the American Indians (New York, 1961), 4; Charles M. Segal and David C. Stineback, eds., Puritans, Indians, and Manifest Destiny (New York, 1977), 105.

8. Stannard, Way of Death, 39–40; Baritz, City on a Hill, 31. Baritz appears to have drawn upon Miller and Johnson, eds., The Puritans, I, 86. See also Jesper Rosenmeier, "Veritas: The Sealing of the Promise," Harvard Library Bulletin, XVI (1968), 33; Bercovitch, Jeremiad, 8–9, 25; John F. Berens, Providence and Patriotism in Early America, 1640–1815 (Charlottesville, Va., 1978), 23; Segal and Stineback, eds., Manifest Destiny, 105; Cecelia Tichi, New World, New Earth: Environmental Reform in American Literature from the Puritans through Whitman (New Haven, Conn., 1979), 17; Emory Elliott, Power and the Pulpit in Puritan New England (Princeton, N.J., 1975), 4; Mason I. Lowance, Jr., The Language of Canaan: Metaphor and Symbol in New England from the Puritans to the Transcendentalists (Cambridge, Mass., 1980), 117.

into several later accounts of the New England Errand. Briefly, Haller described the rise of a conception of England as an "elect" nation historically chosen and favored by Providence and now called to an eschatological world leadership in the final Protestant struggles against the Catholic (and Turkish) Antichrist. The major contribution to this outlook was made by John Foxe; its fullest embodiment was his *Acts and Monuments*, accepted by "Englishmen in general in the reign of Elizabeth . . . as an expression of the national faith second in authority only to the Bible." Haller himself suggested the obvious link between assumptions of an English national mission and the founding ideals of New Englanders. Thereafter, the alleged English assumption of a singular election repeatedly has been invoked as a natural and supporting background for the New England Errand.[9]

To an extraordinary degree, modern Puritan studies have been mired in definitional confusion and disagreement. It would be difficult to find anywhere a steadier flow of complaints that "the chief difficulty in writing about the Puritans . . . is one of definitions." In the absence of a broadly accepted concept of their Puritan differentia, it is comforting to believe that one can comprehend the motives driving the first immigrants to a far colony; and surely nothing has seemed more certain than their peculiar pretense to be embarked upon a conscious, explicit, collective, and overridingly important world mission. Such a mission, moreover, then can serve as the premise to a larger interpretation of the national past: The settlers' vision of an exemplary community "struck the keynote of American history."[10]

9. William Haller, *The Elect Nation: The Meaning and Relevance of Foxe's Book of Martyrs* (New York, 1963), 14. For adaptations, see David D. Hall, "Understanding the Puritans," in Herbert J. Bass, ed., *The State of American History* (Chicago, 1970), 341, 348 n. 45; Bercovitch, *Jeremiad*, 35, 215 n. 9; Bremer, *Puritan Experiment*, 33–34.

10. Emil Oberholzer, "Puritanism Revisited," in Alden T. Vaughan and George Athan Billias, eds., *Perspectives on Early American History: Essays in Honor of Richard B. Morris* (New York, 1973), 214; Daniel J. Boorstin, *The Americans: The Colonial Experience* (New York, 1964), 3. See also John William Ward, *Andrew Jackson: Symbol for an Age* (New York, 1962), 138; Segal and Stineback, eds., *Manifest Destiny*, 29–30; David W. Noble, *Historians against History: The Frontier Thesis and the National Covenant in American Historical Writing since 1870* (Minneapolis, Minn., 1965), 3, 6, 13. Edmund S. Morgan's influential treatment of late-century New England "tribalism" rests in part upon

About 1970, however, a restiveness with the conception of a founding mission became apparent. Researchers touching upon the migration and settlement often failed to discover evidence of a founding Errand, and in a few cases alternative hypotheses have been suggested: the settlers were primarily persecuted dissidents seeking sanctuary; they were social conservatives concerned primarily to rescue local liberties from the encroaching absolutism of Charles I; or they were in flight from an eschatological catastrophe soon to befall England. These studies do not converge upon a single line of attack, although most stress an exilic theme, but they do register a rising undercurrent of dissent from the ascription of a grandiose redemptive mission to Winthrop-era migrants.[11]

a comparison with the period of migration in which, he argues, the founders "strove to make New England a beacon to the world, not a refuge from it" (*The Puritan Family: Religion and Domestic Relations in Seventeenth-Century New England*, rev. ed. [New York, 1966], 173).

11. For the three cited hypotheses, see Richard Waterhouse, "Reluctant Emigrants: The English Background of the First Generation of the New England Puritan Clergy," *Historical Magazine of the Protestant Episcopal Church*, XLIV (1975), 479, 485; T. H. Breen, *Puritans and Adventurers: Change and Persistence in Early America* (New York, 1980), 6–19; Avihu Zakai, "Exile and Kingdom: Reformation, Separation, and the Millennial Quest in the Formation of Massachusetts and Its Relationship with England, 1628–1660" (Ph.D. diss., Johns Hopkins University, 1983), 384–387. Two modern interpreters of the life and thought of Richard Mather agree that he "saw migration to Massachusetts Bay as an escape rather than as a bold initiative" (B. R. Burg, *Richard Mather of Dorchester* [Lexington, Ky., 1976], 19; Robert Middlekauff, *The Mathers: Three Generations of Puritan Intellectuals, 1596–1728* [London, 1971], 32–33). A variety of studies comment on the motives of selected groups of migrants. None reports evidence pointing to an "errand." John J. Waters, "Hingham, Massachusetts, 1631–1661," *Journal of Social History*, I (1968), 355–356, 358–360; T. H. Breen and Stephen Foster, "Moving to the New World: The Character of Early Massachusetts Immigration," *WMQ*, 3d Ser., XXX (1973), 199–207; Peter Clark, *English Provincial Society from the Reformation to the Revolution: Religion, Politics, and Society in Kent, 1500–1640* (London, 1977), 372; David Grayson Allen, *In English Ways: The Movement of Societies and the Transferal of English Local Law and Custom to Massachusetts Bay in the Seventeenth Century* (Chapel Hill, N.C., 1981), 163–204; William Hunt, *The Puritan Moment: The Coming of Revolution in an English County* (Cambridge, Mass., 1983), 253–260 (esp. 259); Norman C. P. Tyack, "The Humbler Puritans of East Anglia and the New England Movement: Evidence from the Court Records of the 1630s," *NEHGR*, CXXXVIII (1984), 79–106; Virginia DeJohn Anderson, "Migrants and Motives: Religion and the Settlement of New England, 1630–

Among students of Elizabethan religious thought as well, reevaluation of the Haller thesis was undertaken. Major studies of the theology of John Foxe and his contemporaries concluded that the apocalyptic conception of England as the elect nation, attributed by Haller to Foxe and his Protestant colleagues, is erroneous. Haller and his followers are found "guilty of reading . . . into Elizabethan authors meanings that not only were not intended but also were flatly denied." A thorough canvass of Elizabethan materials reveals that "no such interpretation existed either before Foxe, . . . or in Foxe's own work, or in the work of his contemporaries or immediate successors." Foxe's conception of the struggle against Antichrist was genuinely international. In an extensive commentary on the Book of Revelation ignored by Haller, Foxe insisted upon the universality of biblical prophecies and denied to England as a nation a favored place.[12]

Thus a tide of scholarly opinion has risen against Haller's thesis. At some points the attack may have been pressed too vigorously. In certain respects, as in his obvious assertions of a national covenant, Foxe certainly did assign "a special place" to England.[13]

1640," *NEQ*, LVIII (1985), 374–381. The most sweeping denial of a founding Errand of all is Andrew Delbanco, "The Puritan Errand Re-Viewed," *Journal of American Studies*, XVIII (1984), 343–360.

12. Katharine R. Firth, *The Apocalyptic Tradition in Reformation Britain, 1530–1645* (Oxford, 1979), 107–108 (see also 252); V. Norskov Olsen, *John Foxe and the Elizabethan Church* (Berkeley, Calif., 1973), 36–47; Richard Bauckham, *Tudor Apocalypse* (Oxford, 1978), 13, 71–72, 85–87, 90 n. 61, 126, 128, 235. The critiques offered by Firth, Bauckham, and Olsen are corroborated by Paul Christianson, *Reformers and Babylon: English Apocalyptic Visions from the Reformation to the Eve of the Civil War* (Toronto, 1978), 41, 100, 102. See also T.H.L. Parker, ed., *English Reformers* (Philadelphia, 1966), 68.

Firth, Bauckham, and Christianson agree that a genuine elect-nation motif did emerge in the 17th century and that its first appearance in the context of an interpretation of the Book of Revelation was in a Latin commentary published by Thomas Brightman in 1609 (Firth, *Apocalyptic Tradition*, 167; Bauckham, *Tudor Apocalypse*, 223; Christianson, *Reformers and Babylon*, 102). To this it should be added that Brightman's statement was ambiguous and that definite assignment of a special apocalyptic role to England probably was rare before 1640. The earliest clear assertion that I have found is Richard Bernard, *A Key of Knowledge for the Opening of the Secret Mysteries of St. Johns Mysticall Revelation* (London, 1617), sigs. C3–C7.

13. Haller also notes "a special place in the designs of providence" for England. In the *Acts and Monuments*, greatly overproportionate attention is given

But for present purposes it is sufficient to observe that this did not include the climactic leadership of the Protestant cause. Haller's contention that Foxe and other Elizabethan authorities saw England as "appointed . . . to consummate the reformation" "to lead mankind . . . to ultimate redemption" is completely without warrant.[14]

Undisturbed by these newer developments, the interpretive prestige of the Errand into the Wilderness continued to run high among students of the Great Migration. It is, indeed, time to bring this construct under closer scrutiny: What and how numerous are the extant sources expressive of "reasons for settling"? Do they document a collective consecration to the fabulous, world-historical mission customarily assigned to the immigration of the 1630s?

A City upon a Hill? The Founders' Agenda Reappraised

Students of American Puritanism readily will agree that the "most-quoted phrases of Puritan literature" are those of John Win-

---

to England; a direct and independent national link to primitive apostolic Christianity is affirmed through the legend of Joseph of Arimathea as the founder of the English church; the English birth of the Emperor Constantine is asserted; the account of Wyclif's career—even if Foxe does not stress that Wyclif was English—claims an English origin for the Reformation; the account of the pouring out of the seven vials identifies the Elizabethan succession and the later prosecution of Jesuit invaders as two of the three crucial acts in the unfolding apocalyptic sequence to 1600; and Foxe's entire narrative presupposes English election to the special trials and favors of a national covenant (Haller, *Elect Nation*, 20; *AM*, I, 306, II, 791–796). For Foxe's view of Constantine's English birth, see Olsen, *John Foxe*, 184.

14. Haller, *Elect Nation*, 18, 109 (and see 80). Haller claimed that England's call to "lead the world to its redemption" was proclaimed by the dedicatory preface to the Geneva Bible, which in fact merely describes England as "an example to all that believe." He cited texts from Foxe and others demonstrating their belief that "England was entering upon a new day" with the succession of Elizabeth to the throne, but none documents an assumption as to world leadership (pp. 80, 87–88, 94–95). I have discovered no supporting texts in *Acts and Monuments*; the famous prefaces make no reference to an English vanguard (I, 502–523). In a sermon published in 1578 Foxe made an ardent appeal for further worldwide reformation, but he assigned no leadership role to England (*A Sermon Preached at the Christening of a Certaine Jew, at London* [London, 1578], sigs. Mvii–Nii).

throp's lay sermon, "A Model of Christian Charity": "Men shall say of succeeding plantacions: the lord make it like that of New England: for . . . wee shall be as a Citty upon a Hill, the eies of all people are uppon us." This text, ritually cited in evidence for the Errand, is an obvious point of departure. What does this famed text signify, if considered in the whole context of the sermon? The argument of the "Model of Christian Charity" is clear enough; it is directed throughout to the presentation of a single and urgent thesis. Having pondered the difficulties of establishing a colony in unfamiliar, unsettled territory, Winthrop foresaw a time of deprivation and hardship. Necessities were apt to be in short supply for a time, and this circumstance would bear hard, perhaps intolerably, upon those of modest means. They, in turn, could scarcely then be held within the unity of purpose and effort required for the project's success; they might become sources of dangerous unrest. The purpose of Winthrop's sermon, therefore, was to urge "Christian charity"; his repeated theme was that a "community of perills calls for extraordinary liberallity." As in the primitive times, Christians now must subdue their possessive instincts and freely lend or share their goods, "abridg[ing them]selves of . . . superfluities, for the supply of others necessities." In this way, the community could go forward "knitt together" in pursuit of its chosen goals. It could develop a "due forme of Government both civill and ecclesiasticall" to the end that authentic Christianity might be realized "under the power and purity of . . . holy Ordinances."[15]

If a thesis about sharing love, together with a reminder of common ends, comprehends the essential message of the sermon, what are we to make of the author's proclamation that "wee shall be as a Citty upon a Hill, the eies of all people are uppon us"? As a preliminary it should be noted that the "Model" is only a single entry in a substantial corpus of writings. From the period of its first conception in 1629 to his death in 1649, the revered first governor of the Bay recorded his hopes for the Massachusetts project in a series of letters and more formal documents, including his extensive *History of New England*. Had his perception of the colony's mission actually revolved

15. Richard Schlatter, "The Puritan Strain," in John Higham, ed., *The Reconstruction of American History* (New York, 1962), 42; John Winthrop, "A Model of Christian Charity," in Edmund S. Morgan, ed., *Puritan Political Ideas, 1558–1794* (Indianapolis, Ind., 1965), 78, 90, 92, 93.

around the wish to create a beacon for the nations, as is routinely maintained, it is reasonable to expect that this ideal frequently and forcefully would come to expression in his written remains. What could be more disconcerting, therefore, than to find that the Bay project, except in the passing reference in the "Model," nowhere in the entire corpus is pictured as a redemptive city upon a hill, a light to the nations, or a decisive pattern for English, European, or world-wide reform?

If, however, for the purpose of the moment one concentrates upon the sermon itself, it will be perplexing to recall that Winthrop's reflections upon the "Citty upon a Hill" have become the "most quoted phrases of Puritan literature." They do not stand as climax or conclusion to Winthrop's principal arguments. They occur, instead, in passing, in the midst of a paragraph that commences with and proceeds to other and thematically more central matters. Judging from the evidence of the sermon itself, the famed text is nothing more than a momentary embellishment of the argument, a touch of rhetorical hyperbole rephrasing a popular biblical text (Matthew 5:14).

To construe it as a charge to the settlers to function as a model to the nations, as "the hub of the universe, whose light and wisdom would radiate out in all directions" and change the course of history, ignores the plain meaning of Winthrop's formulation. He predicted that, if the covenant should be kept, God would "make us a prayse and glory, that men shall say of succeeding plantacions: the lord make it like that of New England." Of succeeding plantations! Significantly, the appeal is not to England, Europe, or "the world."[16] He then continued: "Wee shall be as a Citty upon a Hill, the eies of all people are uppon us; soe that if wee shall deale falsely with our god in this worke . . . wee shall be made a story and a by-word through the world," to the discredit of the continuing Reformation. The projected impact upon "all people," in other words, presupposed the *failure* of New England's enterprise. Winthrop knew too well,

16. Perry Miller's treatment of this point is unconvincing: "Winthrop [referred to] subsequent plantations, yet what was England itself but one of God's plantations?" ("Errand," in Miller, *Errand*, 12). The reference to the "hub of the universe" is in Baritz, *City on a Hill*, 17. In a typical handling of the "City" text, Conrad Cherry reflexively renders it as "a light to the nations" (*God's New Israel: Religious Interpretations of American Destiny* [Englewood Cliffs, N. J., 1971], vii).

in the words of a sympathetic English observer in 1632, that there were "a thousand eyes watchinge over you to pick a hole in your coats."[17] There is, in sum, little in the "Model of Christian Charity" to support the conventional interpretation of Winthrop's most famous words. They would appear to be not only the most quoted but also the least understood in the Puritan literature.

But, it may be objected, did Miller not, and properly, intend his reading of the "Model" to be seen in the context of a larger body of literature produced by several apologists for the colonial project? And may not Winthrop's "Citty upon a Hill," if read accordingly, be seen as a play upon higher purposes generally assumed? In truth, at this point the hypothesis of an Errand becomes easiest to test. To a far greater extent than usually is recognized, the New England founders expounded, debated, clarified, and committed to paper their consciously held reasons for venturing to the New World. Perhaps the most commonly cited sources, after Winthrop's "Model," are John Cotton's farewell sermon to the first departing body of settlers for the Bay and two much later writings by Edward Johnson and Peter Bulkeley.[18] But there are a host of other extant testimonies from members of the first New England generation and their close English associates, including at least eight laypersons, of "the reasons moving [them] to transplant themselves." In addition, there are no

17. Winthrop, "Model," in Morgan, ed., *Puritan Political Ideas*, 93; *WP*, III, 76. Loren Baritz, Edmund S. Morgan, and many others unaccountably see the "Citty" passage as the culmination of the sermon (Baritz, *City on a Hill*, 17; Morgan, *The Puritan Dilemma: The Story of John Winthrop*, ed. Oscar Handlin [Boston, 1958], 70). Note that Morgan does not describe "the establishment of churches organized precisely as God commanded" *as* the colonists' "commission," as did Winthrop, but as a "requirement of" a larger "commission to create a model," as Winthrop did not (70, 76). For a more accurate reading, see Middlekauff, *The Mathers*, 26; and David Leverenz, *The Language of Puritan Feeling: An Exploration in Literature, Psychology, and Social History* (New Brunswick, N.J., 1980), 265. Writing in 1641, Cotton also stressed the negative impact of a New England failure: this would "force all whose eyes are on you, throughout the Christian world to think, these [Congregationalist institutions] are but the inventions of men" (*The Powring out of the Seven Vials* [London, 1642], 24).

18. John Cotton, *Gods Promise to His Plantations* (1630), 3, in *Old South Leaflets* (Boston, n.d.), III, no. 53; *WWP*; Peter Bulkeley, *The Gospel-Covenant; or, The Covenant of Grace Opened* (London, 1646) (the revised edition of Bulkeley's work [London, 1651] is as often cited).

fewer than six more detailed tabulations of "reasons" compiled by
John Winthrop, several pastors, and the anonymous author of *Good
News from New-England*.[19] A review of these data ought to yield

19. The quote is a section title in *Good News from New-England* (1648),
MHSC, 4th Ser., I (Boston, 1852), 197–198. "Reasons" are tabulated there;
and in "General Observations for the Plantation of New England" and "General
Conclusions and Particular Considerations," in *WP*, II, 106–127 (both date from
1629 and appear to be the work primarily of John Winthrop); Thomas Shepard,
The Autobiography, in Michael McGiffert, ed., *God's Plot: The Paradoxes of
Piety, Being the Autobiography and Journal of Thomas Shepard* (n.p., 1972),
55–57; John Cotton, "Cotton's Reasons for His Removal to New England"
(1634), in Alexander Young, ed., *Chronicles of the First Planters of the Colony
of Massachusetts Bay, from 1623 to 1636* (Boston, 1846), 438–444; Richard
Mather, "Arguments Tending to Prove the Removing from Old England to New
. . . to Be Not Onley Lawful, but Also Necessary . . . " (1635), in Increase
Mather, *The Life and Death . . . of Richard Mather . . .* (Cambridge, Mass.,
1670), 12–19; Samuel Symonds to John Winthrop, Jan. 11, 1646/7, in *WP*, V,
126. Cotton also gathered reasons for removal in *Gods Promise*, 8–9, *Old South
Leaflets*, III, no. 53.
  Some texts that reveal original purposes but are not cited below are: Matthew
Cradock and Thomas Goffe to John Endicott, Apr. 1629, in *RMB*, I, 386; *A True
Relation of the Last Voyage to New-England, 1629*, in Young, ed., *Chronicles*,
215; John White, *The Planters Plea; or, The Grounds of Plantations Examined
. . .* (1630), 6, 12, in Peter Force, ed., *Tracts and Other Papers, Relating Princi-
pally to the Origin, Settlement, and Progress of the Colonies in North America
. . .*, 4 vols. (Washington, D.C., 1836–1847), II; *MCCP* (1634 or 1635), 279;
Nathaniel Ward to John Winthrop, Jr., Dec. 24, 1635, in *WP*, III, 216; minute
entry for Sept. 9, 1644, in *Records of the United Colonies of New-England*,
in Ebenezer Hazard, *Historical Collections . . .*, 2 vols. (Philadelphia, 1744),
II, 17; T.H., "To the Reader," in *WWP*, 21–22; Nicholas Streeter, quoted in
Isabel MacBeath Calder, *The New Haven Colony* (Hamden, Conn., 1970), 103;
Thomas Goodwin *et al.*, "Preface" to John Davenport, *Another Essay . . .*
(Cambridge, Mass., 1663), sig. A3; John Wilson *et al.*, *A Copy of the Letter . . .
to Mr. John Dury . . .* (Cambridge, Mass., 1664), 2, 11; Roger Clap, *Memoirs
of Capt[ain] Roger Clap . . .*, in Young, ed., *Chronicles*, 356, 364; an anony-
mously cited testimony in Cotton Mather, *Magnalia Christi Americana*, ed.
Thomas Robbins, 2 vols. (New York, 1853), I, 308. John Winthrop described
the motive of Henry Vane, Jr., for emigration in *The History of New England
from 1630 to 1649*, ed. James Savage (1853; New York, 1972), I, 170. Comment
upon Anne Hutchinson's reasons for removal appeared during her trial before
the General Court in 1637 (David D. Hall, ed., *The Antinomian Controversy,
1636–1638* [Middletown, Conn., 1968], 338–339). Thomas Shepard reported
his wife's motives in his *Autobiography*, In McGiffert, ed., *God's Plot*, 64.

the evidence for a conscious, explicit, collective, overriding, world-redeeming Errand.

Descriptions of the Great Migration as impelled by a bold vision of the future tend to obscure the wavering, undecided attitude of many contemplating flight. The decision to depart from home and country often was taken, if at all, only after anxious and sometimes protracted debate. There were not only the expostulations of friendly critics to meet; of greater importance were the doubts and scruples of prospective emigrants themselves. Would it, for example, not be "a greate wronge to our owne country and church to take away the godly people" and thus increase the likelihood of covenantal judgment? Should not Christians "stay and suffer for Christ" in the teeth of worsening conditions?[20] In the course of coping with such issues, men like Winthrop, Thomas Shepard, and Richard Mather were formulating what one historian has called a "casuistry of emigration," a body of often carefully wrought argument in which a wide variety of "arguments" and "considerations" found their place. It embodied the considerable effort of reflection and persuasion that would be expected of men who, so far from being seized by a high and clear sense of mission abroad, were tossed and restrained by a genuine ambivalence.[21] And yet it also inventoried the conscious purposes of those who fought through ambivalence and elected, albeit in most cases reluctantly, to depart their homeland.

20. *WP*, II, 112, 115, 119, 141; Shepard, *Autobiography*, in McGiffert, ed., *God's Plot*, 56. It was also important to find warrant in biblical examples of flight to escape persecution. See John Allin and Thomas Shepard, *A Defence of the Answer Made unto the Nine Questions or Positions Sent from New-England, against the Reply Thereto by . . . John Ball* (London, 1648), 5; Richard Mather, "Arguments," in Increase Mather, *Richard Mather*, 12–19; Cotton, *Gods Promise*, 5–10, in *Old South Leaflets*, III, no. 53; John Davenport, *An Apologeticall Reply to a Booke Called: An Answer to the Unjust Complaint of W.B.* (Rotterdam, 1636), 103; Cotton, "Reasons," in Young, ed., *Chronicles*, 440.

21. The casuistry was aimed in part to parry the charge of separatism. Keith L. Sprunger has argued that two sections of William Ames's *Conscience* were directed to this task. In the cited texts, Ames refers exclusively to motives of flight; no hint of an Errand appears (Sprunger, "William Ames and the Settlement of Massachusetts Bay," *NEQ*, XXXIX [1966], 72–77; Ames, *Conscience with the Power and Cases Thereof* [n.p., 1639], book 4, chap. 12, 61–64, book 5, chap. 12, 140–142).

The absence of explicit appeal to an Errand in Winthrop's larger body of writing is the more telling, since he appears to have been the prime mover of an extensive effort by those initially engaged in the project to define, weigh, and refine "arguments for the plantation of New England." These were elaborated in several drafts of two distinct documents, "General Observations for the Plantation of New England" and "General Conclusions and Particular Considerations." Nowhere in all the literature of the Great Migration is there to be found a more detailed and considered justification of the removal from England. This material provides a perfectly clear profile of the mission visualized by Winthrop and his immediate colleagues.

Six major and repeated arguments readily may be identified. Four of these posit negative ends, of flight and escape from onerous conditions in England: overpopulation, economic distress, the corruption by anti-Puritan influences of schools and universities, and the hanging threat of God's covenantal punishment upon an unreformed land. Such considerations point plainly to New England as a *refuge* from adversity. There remain, however, two arguments delineating a positive function. First, the colony was to provide a Protestant "bullwarke" against the "kingdom of Antichrist which the Jesuites labour to reare" in North America; this would entail the Christianization of the native peoples. Second, the colony was to perform the additional service of "raysinge and upholdinge a particular Churche." These latter functions point to a conception of New England as a missionary enterprise dedicated—Winthrop says "chiefly"—to the "propagation of religion." Then, solely in the "General Conclusions and Particular Considerations," a seventh point appears: in light of God's impending judgment upon England, removal to a safe site would preserve covenantally faithful church members, that "they may be of better use to their mother Churche" later. They were to "returne after the storme" and presumably contribute to the restoration of true religion. "Refuge," then, and the "propagation of religion" in an unclaimed corner of the world as well as the preservation of saints to aid the eventual recovery of English Protestantism—these were the specific aims debated, refined, and affirmed by Winthrop and his associates as they pondered their dangerous undertaking, quelled doubts, and strove to rally enthusiasm. Other early statements of policy by officers of the Massachusetts Bay Company underscored the priority assigned to the establishment of right religion and to conversion of the natives, but otherwise added nothing new to Winthrop's seven points.[22] The customarily alleged "overriding objective" is nowhere to be discerned.

A broad field of evidence is yet to be scanned. The remaining revelations of original purpose include reports of debates by clergy interested in the venture but concerned about biblical authorization, and numerous summaries of motives both before and after the fact. The record they furnish of the colonial mission as conceived by several founders readily can be inventoried under a few heads. Economic reasons were cited occasionally but not frequently, as were the "planting of the Gospel" in vacant parts, conversion of the Indians, and the desire to remain with emigrating "friends." John Dane's recollection, that he "bent [him]self to cum to nu ingland, thinking that I should be more fre here than thare [England]" from a young man's characteristic temptations, reminds us also of the presence of miscellaneous individual aspirations.[23] Yet none of the above looms large in the total

22. The negative ends are delineated, respectively, in *WP*: II, 111, 114, 118, 123, 139; II, 111–112, 114–115, 118, 122, 139; II, 112, 115, 118, 139; II, 111, 114, 118, 121–122, 138–139, 142. Positive ends, respectively: II, 114, 117, 138; II, 112, 115, 118, 124, 132, 140. "Return after the storm" is discussed in II, 125; for varying formulations, see II, 128, 133. For other early statements of policy see *RMB*, I, 37–38, 384, 386, 390.

In a passing moment, Winthrop suggested that "it is likely that [God] has some great work in hand" in the colonial scheme. The probable meaning of this phrase is given in the same paragraph: "a worke of God for the good of his Church," that is, through the specified contributions of the "propagation of religion" and the preservation of saints from the English storm. Cf. Bercovitch's interpretation of the passage in light of the assumption that the Great Migration was "a historic mission for mankind." *WP*, II, 140; Bercovitch, *Jeremiad*, 38–39.

23. For economic reasons, see Cotton, *Gods Promise*, 8–9, *Old South Leaflets*, III, no. 53; *Good News from New-England, MHSC*, 4th Ser., I (1852), 197–198; and cf. Hunt, *Puritan Moment*, 238–239. For the "planting of the Gospel," see Thomas Dudley, "Governor Thomas Dudley's Letter to the Countess of Lincoln, March, 1631," 7, in Peter Force, *Tracts and Other Papers, Relating Principally to the Origin, Settlement, and Progress of the Colonies in North America . . . ,* 4 vols. (Washington, D.C., 1836–1847), II; Francis Higginson, *A True Relation of the Last Voyage to New-England, 1629,* in Young, ed., *Chronicles,* 215. For interest in conversion of the Indians, see *WP*, V, 126; Higginson, *True Relation,* 215; Clap, *Memoirs,* in Young, ed., *Chronicles,* 364. For the desire to remain with friends, see John Cotton, *The Way of Congregational Churches Cleared* (1648), in Larzer Ziff, ed., *John Cotton on the Churches of New England* (Cambridge, Mass., 1968), 304; Thomas Shepard, *The Works of Thomas Shepard,* 3

body of testimony. With overwhelming frequency, the data fall into two categories: the wish to secure a refuge and the determination to win "liberty of the Ordinances."

If the immigrants to New England were in fact a bold "vanguard" aggressively intent upon their exemplary Errand, it would be remarkable that a very large portion of their apologetic for the venture concentrated upon exilic themes. Ezekiel Rogers, a first-generation Massachusetts pastor and son-in-law of the great Richard Rogers, struck the forlorn note clearly: they had chosen, he wrote in 1646, to become "poor Exiles of Christ, . . . God's Exiles."[24] Not only Winthrop, as we have seen, and Ezekiel Rogers but also Thomas Hooker, Thomas Shepard, John Cotton, Richard Mather, John Allin, and others were prepared without a trace of reserve to describe their voyage as a flight from adversity. They identified, moreover, two separable incentives to flight: the imminent prospect of a divine judgment upon England and persecution for nonconformity.

Fear of national catastrophe gripped many English dissenters on the eve of the Great Migration. Long before the 1620s, men had begun to think of England as joined in a covenantal relation with the Lord. In this conception the nation was found subject to a Deuteronomic arrangement: obedience to divine law guaranteed favor and prosperity, while disobedience ensured affliction. Puritan interests understandably found the National Covenant a useful weapon in their struggle for religious reform. Fidelity to the covenant came to be defined in terms of the biblicist program for completing the English Reformation. From this perspective, the trend of events under the Stuarts, especially after 1625, pointed to a willful flouting of the covenant. Continuing failure of magistracy and church to bring the English people under evangelical care and discipline, explicit royal and episcopal hostility to Puritan aspirations, promulgation of the anti-Sabbatarian *Book of Sports* in 1618 and again in

---

vols. (Boston, 1853), II, 243. Dane's account is in Dane, "John Dane's Narrative, 1682," *NEHGR*, VIII (1854), 154.

24. Ezekiel Rogers to William Sykes, Dec. 2, 1646, in *HCEI*, LIII (July 1917), 220. The "Preface" to the Cambridge Platform of 1648 referred to the Bay immigrants as "poor outcasts"; and Edward Johnson, who arrived in 1636, explained that he and his fellow immigrants had chosen "to take up a perpetuall banishment." Williston Walker, *The Creeds and Platforms of Congregationalism* (1893; Boston, 1960), 196; *WWP*, 53.

1633, the project of James I for a Catholic marriage and the marriage of Charles I to Henrietta Maria of France in 1625, lenient treatment of Catholics, failure strongly to support the Protestant cause in the Thirty Years' War, the rise of an Arminian and high church party within the church, Laud's crackdown on nonconformity—given this stream of provocations, how long would divine wrath be restrained?

On the Continent, the means of a catastrophic punishment seemed at hand. After the outbreak of the Thirty Years' War in 1618, the Protestant cause stumbled through years of defeat on all fronts. With the Catholic recovery of Bohemia (1620) and the Palatinate (1623), the fall of the last Huguenot stronghold (La Rochelle, 1627), and Geneva in standing jeopardy, the very survival of Protestantism was placed in question. When the bloody march of Catholic armies through much of Protestant Europe was pondered in the light of covenantal failure at home, a terrifying probability emerged: England was next. Here was a prospect to lend urgency to thoughts of emigration. In 1626 Thomas Hooker was reflecting anxiously upon the conflict that had "flamed and consumed all the country round about us, Bohemia, and the Palatinate and Denmark" and wondering whether "this little England," in view of her continuing intransigence in religious reformation and her many retrograde tendencies under Stuart rule, "should not [also] be searched." Then, in 1631, in the course of a personal "meditation in God's word," Hooker became convinced that a Catholic invasion was imminent: "God told me . . . that he would destroy England." Although Hooker at this time was planning flight to Protestant Holland, he explicitly identified New England as an alternative haven.[25]

Shortly before John Winthrop committed himself to the Bay Company project, he too was reading the signs of the times against the background of covenantal defection and European disaster. On the Continent, "all the other Churches" had been "smitten . . . before our eyes," and at home "the increasinge of our sinnes gives us [likewise] great cause to looke for some heavye Scquorge and Judgment." The same concern, as we have noted, appeared prominently in his

---

25. Thomas Hooker, "The Church's Deliverances," in George H. Williams *et al.*, eds., *Thomas Hooker: Writings in England and Holland, 1626–1633*, Harvard Theological Studies, XXVIII (Cambridge, Mass., 1975), 67; Thomas Hooker, "The Danger of Desertion," *ibid.*, 244.

lists of "Particular Considerations" rationalizing the colonial project; there he took the position that "all other churches of Europe beinge brought to desolation it cannot be but that the like judgement is comminge upon us." In each case, Winthrop's focus turned immediately to the need for "a shelter and a hidinge place," a "place for a refuge for many whome he meaneth to save in the general distruction."[26]

This was probably what Hugh Peter had in mind when he claimed that "many" decided to leave for New England upon learning of the king's reissue of the *Book of Sports* in 1633. Such open promoting of recreational frivolity on the Sabbath surely would be the final and intolerable challenge to the Lord's patience. Not all prospective immigrants were prepared to be as specific as Charles Chauncy, who told a congregation in 1630 that "there was a great army, a great fleet and a great many of flatt bottome boates pre[p]ared in France for the Invadinge of this kingdome . . . and that [therefore] some Familyes are pre[p]aringe to goe for New England"; but the conception of a safely distant asylum for devout Protestants anticipating bloody conquest occupied a high place among the purposes of many a founder.[27]

Notwithstanding the defeat of political Puritanism in the 1580s, semiconformity persisted on a broad scale and probably also extended its influence in later Elizabethan and early Stuart England. At the very time when John Whitgift and Richard Bancroft were routing the politically active Presbyterian movement, reformist impulses were marking out another path. In the decades after 1590 a clerical Spiritual Brotherhood emerged to provide a deeply pietistic reformulation of dissenters' faith. Conversionist, meditative, and interested in introspection, spiritual diaries, charting "geographies of consciousness," adapting the Sabbath to disciplined devotion, and the

26. *WP*, II, 91, 111, 119.

27. Hugh Peter, *A Dying Fathers Last Legacy to an Only Child . . .* (Boston, 1717), 77; "Articles Objected . . . against Charles Chauncy . . ." (1630), Massachusetts Historical Society, *Proceedings*, 1st Ser., XIII (Boston, 1875), 340. For additional documentation, see Shepard, *Works*, I, 331; Increase Mather, *Richard Mather*, 17–18; Cotton, *Gods Promise*, 9, *Old South Leaflets*, III, no. 53; Cotton Mather, *Magnalia*, I, 361; Michael Metcalfe, "To All the True Professors . . . ," *NEHGR*, XVI (1862), 281–283. See also James Fulton Maclear, "The Influence of the Puritan Clergy on the House of Commons, 1625–1629," *CH*, XIV (1945), 276.

formation of small devotional groups, the Brotherhood with a growing body of laity created an "impressively homogeneous" milieu of thought and praxis in dozens of parishes that stood largely outside the formal diocesan machinery sanctioned by the monarch.

Generally moderate, relatively apolitical, and ably led, pietistic Puritanism was thence promulgated by growing numbers of sympathetic university graduates, Puritan lectureships, Sabbath exercises, muted forms of the prophesyings, fast days and days of thanksgiving, the formation of covenanted elites within Anglican parishes, and an astonishingly overproportionate command of the public press. A few moderate Puritan voices were to be found in the episcopate, and these often were able "to apply a generously protestant interpretation" to the monarch's ecclesiastical policy.[28] Nonseparating Puritans in many parts of England thus were enabled, by variously evading or compromising the formal requirements of ecclesiastical conformity, to sustain their position within the church.

With the accession of James I, the circumstances permitting semi-conformity began to tighten. The meager results of the Hampton Court Conference between Puritan leaders and the king were followed by enactment of the Canons of 1604, designed to bring all disputed details of church life under strict regulation. Most notable was canon 36, which required clerical attestation of loyalty to the established liturgy and polity. The more systematic screening of clerical applicants by this test made painful inroads into areas of dissent that had survived under Elizabeth. If opportunities for dissenters were narrowed, however, they were not foreclosed. Some men of Puritan sympathies still held political and ecclesiastical power under James I, and the highest-ranking enforcer of official ecclesiastical policy, the archbishop of Canterbury, fell into royal disfavor early in the reign. Access to the public press remained relatively open. Puritan prophesyings and lectureships abounded, as did conventicles, and dissenting influences at Cambridge University remained strong. As shown by the Jacobean career of John Cotton at Boston or Thomas Hooker at Chelmsford, future New England clergy who came of age during

28. Patrick Collinson, "Towards a Broader Understanding of the Early Dissenting Tradition," in C. Robert Cole and Michael E. Moody, eds., *The Dissenting Tradition: Essays for Leland H. Carlson* (Athens, Ohio, 1975), 12; *EPM*, 59.

these years managed to enter the ministry and sustain themselves there by taking discreetly evasive action.

But the latitude upon which they depended soon was to be curtailed. During the 1620s churchmen of a militantly anti-Puritan stamp, sponsoring a traditionalist and catholicizing conception of the English church and, in some instances, an offensively Arminian revision of Reformed theology, were advancing to ecclesiastical power. Their fervid aim was to uproot dissent, to secure "thorough" accord with the established ritual, government, and canons. When Charles I, who strongly supported such aims, succeeded to the throne in 1625, the new men gained extensive control over religious policy. Pastors like Richard Mather, who reportedly never wore the surplice in his English ministry, now were driven to a fundamental reappraisal of their "balance of conformity and conscience." Now they found it necessary to choose between substantially greater compliance and silencing, deprivation of office, and other penalties.[29]

These details are reasonably well known. What has not received due notice is the central role played by ceremonies in the thought of future clerical emigrants. If Puritan pietism had the effect of withdrawing emphasis from the political arena, it did not in the least abate the biblicist primitivism that played so crucial a role in the earlier vestiarian and Presbyterian agitations. This was particularly true in discussions of worship, in which Puritan publicists continued to demand the original and pure and to denounce the human inven-

---

29. A brief account of events is in H. G. Alexander, *Religion in England* (London, 1968), 129–156. See also Hunt, *Puritan Moment*, 253–257; and David D. Hall, *The Faithful Shepherd: A History of the New England Ministry in the Seventeenth Century* (Chapel Hill, N.C., 1972), 72–75 (quote, 73). The fullest account of the Canons of 1604 is in S. B. Babbage, *Puritanism and Richard Bancroft* (London, 1962), 74–102; they are reprinted in Edward Cardwell, ed., *Synodalia*, 2 vols. (Oxford, 1842), I, 164–329. On the subject of conventicles, see, for example, Stephen Foster, *Notes from the Caroline Underground: Alexander Leighton, the Puritan Triumvirate, and the Laudian Reaction to Nonconformity* (Hamden, Conn., 1978), 3–11. It is also worth noting that English commentators upon the Great Migration consistently focused upon the need to "preserve conscience" and find refuge. See, for example, Stuart E. Prall, ed., *The Puritan Revolution: A Documentary History* (Garden City, N.Y., 1968), 57–58; John Milton, *Of Reformation touching Church Discipline in England*, ed. Harry Morgan Ayres, in *The Works of John Milton*, 18 vols. (New York, 1931–1938), III, pt. 1, 50; below, chap. 8, n. 18.

tions littering the official liturgy. The Canons of 1604 assured that the forms of worship would be a source of heightened friction by singling out for special attention the most frequently assailed ceremonial requirements: the use of the surplice and other vestments, bowing at the name of Jesus, kneeling during eucharistic reception, and making the sign of the cross during baptism.[30]

But it remained for the Laudians of the 1620s and 1630s to press "ceremonyes and gestures" beyond the point of endurance for many nonseparating members of the Spiritual Brotherhood. Men who saw in elaborate and beautiful liturgy the truest and most elevated expression of Christian piety brought a much-heightened imperative to the enforcement of ritual requirements. In radical antithesis to biblical primitivism and to the restrictive ideal of the Protestant epistemology, their liturgical program looked not simply to the maintenance but to the substantial enrichment of the forms of worship outlined in the Book of Common Prayer. They wished to add further ornament and to make the whole more imposing, complex, colorful, and magnificent. Their activities, therefore, bearing down irreconcilably upon Puritan sensitivity to the entire problematic of "human additions," did much to prepare key minds for the decision to separate and depart.

Within the span of a few years, while John Winthrop was drawing up a list of Puritan "grevances," including "the suspension and silenceing of many . . . ministers for not conformitie in some poynts of ceremonies and refuseinge subscription [as] directed by the late canons," a number of key clergy found themselves driven beyond the stance of semiconformity on precisely these issues.[31] There was John Cotton, for one, who presumably performed the required subscrip-

30. For the canonical requirements concerning vestments, see Cardwell, ed., *Synodalia*, I, 254, 258, 280, 288–289; for requirements on bowing, kneeling, and the sign of the cross, see 255, 257, 260–264. See also the "Millenary Petition," in Henry Gee and William John Hardy, eds., *Documents Illustrative of English Church History* (London, 1896), 509.

31. *WP*, I, 305. At the same time, John White, another prime mover in the Massachusetts Bay Company, was urging a covenanted elite within his Dorchester congregation to "vow" to "cleave unto the true and pure worship of God established according to his own ordinances, opposing . . . all ways of Innovation" (Frances Rose-Troup, *John White, the Patriarch of Dorchester . . .* [New York, 1930], 22).

tion to the Prayer Book upon his ordination to the ministry in 1610. But Cotton was a product of Emmanuel College, the foremost Puritan "seminary" at Cambridge University. By the beginning of the seventeenth century, the college had become noted for its ceremonial deviations and had developed an abridged rite from which sacramental kneeling and the surplice had been excised.[32] During his tenure at Emmanuel, Cotton appears to have identified himself squarely with the anticeremonial position and to have viewed subscription as obnoxious but unavoidable.

Serving since 1612 as vicar of Saint Botolph's Church in Boston, Lincolnshire, he was much troubled by his new liturgical obligations, and about 1615 he came to the decision that he could no longer "digest the ceremonies." He was prepared, as he later reported, to use "the ceremonies of the ring in marriage, and standing at the creed," but "surplices, [the] cross in Baptism, [and] kneeling at the Communion" were intolerable. The better to square performance with principle, he now organized like-minded parishioners into a covenanted subgroup and developed a specialized ministry to them that made no use of the offensive rites. After 1618, when an auxiliary minister was appointed to preside over parts of the service to which Cotton objected, he was able to evade them altogether. Avoidance of extra-biblical ceremonies was not the sole purpose of his specialized ministry, but it appears to have been the dominant one. The "covenant with the Lord" that his elite group devised was designed specifically for "godly persons" wishing "to follow after the Lord in the purity of his Worship."[33]

As Cotton himself repeatedly emphasized, it was his unbending persistence in ceremonial irregularity that eventually forced his dislodgment from old Boston. Despite an occasional brush with

32. Larzer Ziff, *The Career of John Cotton: Puritanism and the American Experience* (Princeton, N.J., 1962), 24. The Emmanuel practice was squelched in part in 1604 (John Bass Mullinger, *The University of Cambridge*, 3 vols. [Cambridge, 1873–1911], II, 456). For persisting irregularities thereafter, see T. Hooker, *Writings in England and Holland*, 3.

33. Samuel Whiting, *John Cotton's Life and Letters*, in Young, ed., *Chronicles*, 423; Cotton, *Congregational Churches*, in Ziff, ed., *John Cotton*, 198; Ziff, *Career of Cotton*, 46–51, 56. For a probable reflection of Cotton's old Boston conventicle, see Cotton, *A Practical Commentary . . . upon the First Epistle Generall of John* (London, 1656), 283.

authority over his privileged arrangement, he preserved his position for nearly a decade and a half after 1618. But in 1632, he received a peremptory summons to appear before William Laud and the feared Court of High Commission to answer for his practices. Unwilling to return to conformity, Cotton was certain that his appearance would lead not only to suspension from the ministry but also to a severe fine and perhaps imprisonment. He went at once into hiding and began to weigh his options. His "Reasons for . . . Removal to New England," written in 1634, in which he claimed the complete concurrence of "my brother [Thomas] Hooker," reconstructs the basic terms of his eventual decision to emigrate. For Cotton as for Winthrop, Hooker, Shepard and several others, such a terrific personal undertaking required extensive rationalization. Numerous "reasons" could be formulated, but the ultimate issue was clear. As a Christian dedicated to "bear witness against Levitical ceremonies" during the Laudian ascendancy, he had faced a straight and stark choice between "imprisonment" and "banishment" and had chosen the latter. He had withdrawn "from the present storm" to a safe sanctuary. God had indicated the way by "opening a door" to survival and a new ministry abroad.[34] In Cotton's view, before she was anything else, New England was a sanctuary from liturgical tyranny.

A comparable preoccupation with the offense of ceremonies emerges from a review of the careers of several figures who found temporary asylum in Holland before their turn to New England. One may instance John Davenport, whose refusal "to use the ceremonies" was the outstanding affront leading Laudian authorities to remove him from his clerical living in the early 1630s. Half a decade earlier, despite misgivings, Davenport declared that he had "never" refused the cross in baptism or the surplice or administered the Eucharist "to any but those that kneeled." He also agreed in a debate with Alexander Leighton that sacramental kneeling was a "thing indifferent," not in conflict with Scripture. But by the early 1630s his resistance had stiffened. In 1632, by then convinced that sacramental kneel-

34. Cotton, "Reasons," in Young, ed., *Chronicles*, 438–444. See also Cotton, *Congregational Churches*, in Ziff, ed., *John Cotton*, 199; and Cotton, "An Apologetical Preface" to John Norton, *The Answer to the Whole Set of Questions of William . . . Apollonius . . .* (1648), trans. Douglas Horton (Cambridge, Mass., 1958), 10. See also Stephen Goffe to William Boswell, June 1633, Additional Ms. 6384, I, fol. 137, British Library, London.

ing was inadmissable, he began to absent himself from eucharistic celebrations in his London parish.[35]

Upon Laud's elevation to the archbishopric the following year, Davenport anticipated swift reprisal, possibly including imprisonment. He abandoned his charge, went into hiding, and shortly sailed for the Dutch Netherlands. Other issues, most notably his work as one of the Puritan feofees for impropriations, also figured in his fear of persecution, and his growing interest in Congregational polity also testified to a wide range of dissatisfactions with the established church. But by his own testimony the matter of ceremonies was uppermost in determining his decision to withdraw. "The onely cause of all my present sufferings," he explained before his departure, "is the alteracion of my judgm[en]t in matters of conformity to the ceremonies established whereby I cannot practise them as formerly I have done." Both during his troubled interim in the Netherlands and after his transfer to New England, he stressed his "alteration" of mind in explanation of his forced flight from England. First among the train of forces driving him ultimately to the New World was his painful realization that he "durst not continue" in the use of rites at variance with biblical direction.[36] There is no evidence that he—or Hooker or Davenport, whose experiences were similar—had at any time become concerned with an Errand.

The Thomas Hooker story, too, centered on the ceremonial crisis and the search for a refuge. For more than half a decade before his departure in 1631, Hooker held a lectureship at Chelmsford, Essex— an arrangement that exempted him from the regular performance of the established liturgy normally required of clergy. For circumvention of the Prayer Book, emphasis on "awakening" preaching, and leadership in an unauthorized conference of like-minded ministers, he was cited upon a charge of "licentious irregularities" before

35. John Davenport, *Letters of John Davenport, Puritan Divine*, ed. Isabel MacBeath Calder (New Haven, Conn., 1937), 13, 24–25, 33–38; Calder, *New Haven*, 4–6, 16, 21; Perry Miller, *Orthodoxy in Massachusetts, 1630–1650* (Boston, 1959), 114 n. 4.

36. Davenport, *Letters*, 39. See also Davenport, *Apologeticall Reply*, 107; Davenport, *An Answer of the Elders of the Severall Churches in New-England unto Nine Positions Sent over to Them* (London, 1643), 51. For Davenport's participation in the impropriations scheme, see William Haller, *The Rise of Puritanism . . .* (1938; Philadelphia, 1972), 80–81.

the Court of High Commission in mid-1629. His removal from the lectureship followed swiftly. Continuing to preach in private houses and to participate in the conference, he received an ominous second summons from the court a year later.

His state of mind shortly after the summons, when he had decided to flee the country rather than face probable imprisonment, is reflected in his "farewell sermon," "The Danger of Desertion" (1631). There Hooker focused upon his expectation that God shortly would take vengeance upon the erring nation, but he as clearly identified the Laudians' rising effrontery to "the purity of God's worship" as the most critical cause of divine displeasure. Although he had chosen to fly to the Netherlands, he described "New England [as] . . . a refuge . . . a rock and a shelter . . . to run unto." His later transfer from Holland to "the last remaining haven" for true religion was motivated by his disillusionment with the Dutch situation, by the increasing pressure of the English government upon the congregationalist movement there, and the aggravation of his ague in the cold and wet climate.[37]

It is now evident that any accounting of the founders' aims, any effort to view the Great Migration in their terms, must address a highly principled and obstinate resistance to hardening liturgical policy and the resulting threat of persecution. As with Cotton, Davenport, and Hooker, so with Charles Chauncy, Richard Mather, and Hugh Peter: animus against the increasingly ceremonial cast of English worship provided the ultimate motivation for flight to Massachusetts.[38] By no means was that animus always the first pre-

37. The relevant details are covered in Frank Shuffelton, *Thomas Hooker, 1586–1647* (Princeton, N.J., 1977), 121–158; T. Hooker, *Writings in England and Holland*, 4–24; and Hunt, *Puritan Moment*, 196–201, 253–256, 259–260. Citations from the "Danger of Desertion," in *Writings in England and Holland*, are on 236, 246, 249. Hooker chose removal to Holland for reasons of convenience and uncertainty about the Massachusetts venture when compared with the comparative success of nonseparating Congregationalism in the Dutch context. Shortly before leaving the Netherlands, he prepared a "Preface" to William Ames, *A Fresh Suit against Human Ceremonies in God's Worship* (n.p., 1633). There, in the context of a polemic centered upon the surplice, sacramental kneeling, the cross in baptism, and other "human additions" to worship, he lamented the state of the "many poore Ministers" being forced "to flye even unto the [American] Indians for safety" (sigs. i3, k).

38. For data on Chauncy, see *Dictionary of American Biography*, s.v.

cipitant, but it is a recurrent theme in the literature of the Great Migration. During a controversy in earliest Salem, Francis Higginson and Samuel Skelton declared that "they came away from the Common-Prayer and Ceremonies, and had suffered much for their Non-Conformity" on these points. About 1640 John Cotton reminded his Boston parishioners, "You have left your Trades, friends, Country, and have put your self upon a changeable and hazardous Journey because your Consciences could not submit to Ceremonies." Thomas Shepard and John Allin recollected vividly in the late 1640s the "time when humane Worship and inventions were growne to such an intolerable height, that the consciences of Gods saints . . . could no longer bear them"; since the immediate alternative was persecution, they chose "to fly into the Wildernesse from the face of the Dragon." About a decade later, John Eliot agreed: "The cause of our coming into New-England . . . [was] that we might be freed from the ceremonies and have liberty to enjoy all the pure ordinances of Christ . . . without . . . human additions and novelties.³⁹

"Chauncy, Charles"; Great Britain, *Calendar of State Papers, Domestic Series, of the Reign of Charles I, 1629–1631*, 233, 240–241, 266, 1635–1636, 123–124, 152, 483, 490, 495; "Articles Objected against Charles Chauncy," MHS, *Proceedings*, 1st Ser., XIII (Boston, 1875), 338; Cotton Mather, *Magnalia*, I, 467. For Mather, see Kenneth Ballard Murdock, *Increase Mather: The Foremost American Puritan* (Cambridge, Mass., 1925), 16; Miller and Johnson, eds., *The Puritans*, II, 491; Increase Mather, *Richard Mather*, 12–20. For Peters, see Raymond Phineas Stearns, ed., "Letters and Documents by or Relating to Hugh Peter," *HCEI*, LXXI (1935), 305, 310, 317.

39. Nathaniel Morton, *New England's Memorial* . . . (Cambridge, 1669), 76–77; Helle M. Alpert, "Robert Keayne: Notes of Sermons by John Cotton and Proceedings of the First Church of Boston from 23 November 1639 to 1 June 1640" (Ph.D. diss., Tufts University, 1974), 195; Allin and Shepard, *Defence*, 3–4 (and see 58, 61); John Eliot, "The Learned Conjectures of Reverend Mr. John Eliot," preface to Thomas Thorowgood, *Jews in America; or, Probabilities That Those Indians Are Judaical* . . . (London, 1660), 20–22. For Shepard's transition to an anticeremonial militance sometime between 1627 and 1633, see Shepard, *Autobiography*, in McGiffert, ed., *God's Plot*, 48, 55. Ezekiel Rogers recorded in his will that, "being inlightened concerning the evell and snare of subscriptions and cerrimonies" and "other sad signes of the times," he had been harassed by church authorities and was eventually "driven . . . into New England" ("Ezekiel Rogers's Will," in *Documents from the Harvard University Archives, 1638–1750*, IV, *Documents, 1638–1722* [Colonial Society of Massachusetts, *Publications, Collections*, XLIX (Boston, 1975)], 98–99). The Reverend Samuel Collins of Braintree, Essex, wrote to William Laud in 1632

The picture that emerges from a review of such materials is again one of flight from adversity, cast against a background of disaffection in which the issue of ceremonies occupied the most prominent place.[40] Indisputably, the clergy held and pursued positive goals as well, but it cannot be sustained that "the migration was no retreat from Europe" or that "these were not . . . refugees seeking a promised land." "This was the situation," Cotton recalled in 1645, "that we [nonconforming clergy] either had to perish uselessly in prison or leave the country."[41]

Why were Cotton, Davenport, Hooker, and many of their colleagues in the period of migration so stubbornly antagonistic toward Laudian initiatives? Why were they prepared to defy authority, risk persecution, and uproot themselves from their mother country on behalf of a handful of reportedly "indifferent" practices? Again, we are confronted with the biblicist premises of the Puritan agitation and its restorationist schema. It was not ceremonies in general that had excited the emigrants' hostility, but, in Allin and Shepard's revealing phrase, "humane Worship and inventions." "Vile human inventions," as Chauncy spat it out, principally sparked their revulsion.

---

that "many of his congregation were prepared to emigrate to New England at the first sign of a change in their habitual forms of worship" (Hunt, *Puritan Moment*, 258). In a deposition of 1643 against a Laudian cleric of Cambridgeshire, one Henry Reader recalled that, when faced with the Laudian innovations, "divers of the inhabitants . . . were forced, the better to enjoy the peace of a good conscience and for their ease, to remove . . . , some beyond sea" (Margaret Spufford, *Contrasting Communities: English Villagers in the Sixteenth and Seventeenth Centuries* [Cambridge, 1774], 236).

40. Many later documents also represented the original "depart[ure] from our country . . . into this Pathmos" as a forced alternative to "conforming to the ceremonies then pressed upon . . . consciences" ("To the High and Mighty Prince Charles the Second" [1660], in *RMB*, IV, pt. 1, 452). "A Petition to the Parliament in 1651," in Thomas Hutchinson, *The History of the Colony and Province of Massachusetts-Bay*, ed. Lawrence Shaw Mayo, 3 vols. (Cambridge, Mass., 1936), I, 429. See also "An Humble Proposal, for the Inlargement of University Learning . . ." (1659), in Samuel Eliot Morison, *Harvard College in the Seventeenth Century*, 2 vols. (Cambridge, Mass., 1936), II, facing 368.

41. Miller, *Colony to Province*, 5; Cotton, "Apologetical Preface" to Norton, *The Answer*, 10. See also Eliot, "Learned Conjectures," in Thorowgood, *Jews in America, Indians*, 22. Cotton, Allin, Shepard, Davenport, and perhaps others specifically identified with the earlier plight of the Marian refugees (Cotton, *Gods Promise*, 9, *Old South Leaflets*, III, no. 53; Davenport, *Apologeticall Reply*, 106; Allin and Shepard, *Defence*, 5).

The Protestant epistemology, with its full esteem for biblical originals and its demand, "You shall not make [forms of worship] for yourself, i.e. by your own cogitation," manifestly furnished much of the framework within which the liturgical crisis was comprehended.[42]

Consider the case, again, of John Cotton. As he saw it, the head and front of the Prayer Book's offense lay explicitly in its "Alteration from Primitive Patterns," and his engagement with select parishioners in old Boston to evade the prescribed liturgy was grounded in his often-expressed contempt for "impure mixtures of humane invention." When under episcopal discipline in 1621 for refusal to kneel at the Eucharist, he presented his bishop with the following audacious syllogism:

> Cultus non institutus, non est acceptus:
> Genuflexio in perceptione Eucharistae est
>   cultus non institutus;
> Ergo, non est acceptus.

"Non institutus" was the wrong. For Cotton it was a rule of thumb that all significant Christian activity, and certainly the patterns of worship, must be brought under biblical jurisdiction. But the Bible, which gave explicit archetypal direction for performance of the supper, did not "institute" the practice of kneeling. On this point, as on many others, what the Book of Common Prayer had to offer was, not submissive report of the primitive pattern, but the admixture of an element invented in postprimordial time and therefore impure. A grasp of these themes is absolutely essential to an adequate understanding of Cotton's outlook as a principal founder of Massachusetts.[43]

Repeatedly, the Protestant epistemology provided him the basic vocabulary for expressing the aims of religiously motivated migrants. "Wee believe," he wrote some time after his transfer to new Boston,

---

42. Allin and Shepard, *Defence*, 3–4; Cotton Mather, *Magnalia*, I, 467; William Ames, *The Marrow of Theology* (1629), trans. and ed. John D. Eusden (Boston, 1968), 279.

43. John Cotton, *Some Treasure Fetched out of Rubbish* (London, 1660), 7; Cotton, *Christ the Fountaine of Life* (London, 1651), 23; Cotton, *Congregational Churches*, in Ziff, ed., *John Cotton*, 197. Identification of the ceremonies with the "graven idols" of the Second Commandment was an element of Cotton's concern, but it was scarcely the "crux" suggested by Ziff, *Career of Cotton*, 68.

that "there is a vast difference betweene mens inventions and God's institutions; *we fled from mens inventions.*" On another occasion he reported that "the body of the members" in First Church, Boston, "do in generall professe, the reason of their comming over to us was, that they might be freed from the bondage of . . . human inventions." Such statements, with their unequivocal report of intentions, bespeak a state of mind that might seem hard to reconcile with the assumption of an affirmative, forward-looking, and perhaps millennially fired Errand into the Wilderness. They point to an exilic choice whose foremost watchword was not City upon a Hill, but "abrenunciation . . . of inventions." [44]

If there is abundant evidence that the colonial venture was conceived negatively, as avoidance, flight, and asylum, even more evidence points to a positive conception, to a goal whose vividness and frequency of appearance in both clerical and lay testimony readily qualifies it as the overriding positive objective of the founders. "What was your end of coming hither?" Thomas Shepard asked his Newtown congregation sometime in the late 1630s. Shepard now wished to review with his auditors, including several of his former parishioners, their primary religious end within the colonial enterprise. It was, in a word, unobstructed use of the primitively instituted ordinances of Christian practice. In the many reports of original, explicit, and positive purpose left by articulate founders, including most of the prominent clergy, this—the "liberty of the ordinances"—was the incessantly repeated motif: "What came you into this Wilderness for? . . . You came . . . that you might have the Ordinances of God in his Churches rightly gathered." [45] "Liberty" and "ordinances"— those interested in the purpose of the Puritan founders will find less in an elusive Errand and more in these two indubitable slogans of the early literature.

44. John Cotton, "Mr. Cotton's Answer to a Letter from Sir Richard Saltonstall," in Thomas Hutchinson, *A Collection of Original Papers . . .* (1769), *The Hutchinson Papers*, 2 vols., Prince Society Publications (1865; New York, 1967), II, 132 (emphasis mine); John Cotton, *A Letter of Mr. John Cottons . . . to Mr. [Roger] Williams*, 20, in *The Complete Writings of Roger Williams*, 7 vols. (New York, 1963), I; Cotton, *An Exposition upon the Thirteenth Chapter of the Revelation* (London, 1655), 258.

45. Shepard, *Works*, II, 376; John Wilson, *A Seasonable Watch-word unto Christians against the Dreams and Dreamers of This Generation . . .* (Cambridge, Mass., 1677), 6.

Historians in search of a lineage for the libertarian theme in eighteenth-century American rhetoric might also wish to note the frequent appeal to liberty by the New England founders. It was a crucial moment for Thomas Shepard, as he pondered the wisdom of joining Winthrop's colony, when "the Lord let me see the glory of those liberties in New England." And John Norton, who arrived in 1636, believed, "The sole cause of our transplanting ourselves . . . over the Atlantic ocean, . . . was liberty, to walk peaceably in the Faith of the Gospel." The attainment of "liberties of the Gospel" quickly was established as a basic meaning of the Massachusetts undertaking.[46] But "liberty" in this context had a specific denotation. In the newcomers' religious goals, freedom, rightly understood, consisted in "opportunity to administer . . . all the holy ordinances of God, according to the pattern set before us in the Scripture." Above everything else, the ordinances gave justifiable content to new-won liberty; hence in the view of an agent of the United Colonies in 1644, "the most considerable persons in these Colonies came into these parts of America that they might enjoy Christ in his ordinances without disturbance."[47] The question, then, is whether the immigrants' special passion for "Christ in his ordinances" came to focus in an Errand. Did they intend to use New World liberty to drive history forward, reform England and perhaps the world by creating an exemplary society built upon true ordinances?

First, the term "ordinance." Early New Englanders might well dispute the form or status of particular ordinances, as of baptism or church eldership, but commitment to "ordained" things was shared by all save the Antinomians. On one level, "ordinance" invoked the moralist strain in Puritan-Reformed theology, with its emphasis upon law and command. The term commonly was used in Puritan literature from the 1560s through the 1630s as an equivalent of

46. Shepard, *Autobiography*, in McGiffert, ed., *God's Plot*, 56; John Norton, *The Heart of N—— England Rent at the Blasphemies of the Present Generation* . . . (London, 1660), 82; WWP, 140. See also Cotton, "Reasons," in Young, ed., *Chronicles*, 441; Cotton, *Gods Promise*, 9, *Old South Leaflets*, III, no. 53; Davenport, *Answer*, 51; Thomas Tillam, "Uppon the First Sight of New-England, June 29, 1638," in Harrison T. Meserole, ed., *Seventeenth-Century American Poetry* (Garden City, N.Y., 1968), 398.

47. Davenport, *Answer*, 51; *Records of the United Colonies*, in Hazard, *Historical Collections*, II, 17.

"statute," "law," or "commandment." But Puritan moralism itself was tied to a primitivist outlook. Biblical ordinances were not simply promulgated at large; they emerged in the unique, supernatural, and precedential time of the beginnings.

In the setting of early New England—itself eventually to be viewed as a first and golden age—just this primitivist-archetypal sense of Christian ordinances was uppermost. What most immediately concerned the founders were not the statutes of the Decalogue, but archetypally enacted patterns of ecclesiastical polity and worship. These were the "ordinances" that Edward Johnson had in mind when he rhapsodized upon "the chief end of their coming hither, namely, to be made partakers of the blessed Ordinances of Christ." These were what the clerical authors of the "Modell of Church and Civill Power" intended when they described "the end of our planting in this part of the World, which was not only to enjoy the pure Ordinances, but to enjoy them in all purity." In a phrase from the anonymous preface to Johnson's *Wonder-Working Providence*, "Christ and his ordinances in their primitive purity": this was what pious immigrants had sought liberty to enjoy. And these ordinances, including both a simplified liturgy divested of the English ceremonies and the congregational scheme of church polity, were to be enjoyed in "purity," dissected from postprimordial accretions. In 1634, this was the burden of layman James Cudworth's exhilarated report of what New England meant to him. It meant, not a world-redeeming mission, but the unrestricted relishing of "the purity of . . . ordinances," of "that which my forefathers desired to see but could not," of a radical reformation of English Protestant Christianity by the measure of the first and true.[48]

Insofar as the "chief end" of the founders was expressed in such

48. *WWP*, 235; "A Modell of Church and Civill Power . . . ," segmentally entered in Roger Williams, *The Bloudy Tenent of Persecution*, in *Writings of Williams*, III, 279; "To the Reader," *WWP*, 22; James Cudworth to Dr. [John] Stoughton, in *HCEI*, 2d Ser., IX (1868), 82–83. For additional references to purity, see Allin and Shepard, *Defence*, 58; *WWP*, 196, 219; Winthrop, *History*, I, 170. My analysis connects with David M. Scobey's suggestion that the founders "did not claim to forge a revolutionary new order but to revive an earlier past." Theirs, he concludes, was an "errand of recovery" ("Revising the Errand: New England's Ways and the Puritan Sense of the Past," *WMQ*, 3d Ser., XLI [1984], 3–15).

terms, this migration to Massachusetts takes on the dimension of a restorationist campaign. Thus, to give the biblical ordinances full play in the "free air of the new world" was indeed to fulfill at last the thwarted promise of the English Reformation, but this was not cast into the larger formula of an Errand to save the world or inaugurate the millennium. As in the texts cited above, the express wish is to have and to hold biblically certified practices. They were inestimably valuable in themselves, but their greater function within the history of Redemption was not immediately at issue. Further, the very context of thought within which the ordinances were understood focused attention *backward* toward the reinvoked drama of primitive Christianity. Before there could be any question of historical advance, there had to be a secure recovery of origins. Appreciation of that recovery, then, is vital to comprehending the first immigrants' religious purposes. Emigration meant freedom to come to terms with long-lost originals. The impulse was *revival*, directed to restoration and fulfilling enjoyment of forms ordained in the primal age.

Arrogant Apprehensions Disavowed

*H*ad the founders of Massachusetts actually intended an overarching Errand, surely it would have been a persistent theme in their many explicit statements of purpose, and especially in the tabulations of "arguments" by Winthrop, Cotton, Thomas Shepard and Richard Mather, and others. But it was not. There is, to be sure, a handful of early texts that do attribute an exemplary role to New England. Given the powerful exemplarist element in Puritan biblicism, such a role would seem predictable enough, and sufficient models were already on hand.

Some New Englanders might have noted that the English edition of the *Lawes and Statutes of Geneva* (1562) held up that Protestant city to Englishmen "that they may behold as in a glass, a Christian Reformation, and employ themselves [in] imitation." They more likely were aware that the Geneva Bible urged upon England the role of "an example to all" other nations, so that the "eyes of all that feare God" would then be trained upon her. And, indeed, the imagery of the exemplary city, the beacon or mirror, and the watching eyes abounded in the period. If a Presbyterian radical could imagine a painful preaching clergy established as a "City set on a hill . . . and looked unto far and near," so could Francis Bacon praise the English episcopate as a "city upon a hill." In Puritan sermons before the Long Parliament of 1640–1648, "the international . . . significance of the reformation of English life was . . . repeatedly emphasized," as in Thomas Hill's admonition that "the eyes of . . . the Protestant world are now upon you." And when we find the Council for Virginia proclaiming in 1610 that "the eyes of all Europe are looking upon our endevors to spread the Gospell among the Heathen people of Virginia, [and] to plant our English nation there," or discover William Bradford lauding the pathetically unimportant Plymouth church as a "small candle" whose "light here kindled hath shone . . . in some sort to our whole nation," one reasonably may surmise an English rhetorical routine whose occasional appearance in New England does not necessarily entail a grand and singular Errand.[49]

Consider the few texts in which founding figures style their colony as an exemplary "city," "light," or the like. At least two of these, from Johnson's *Wonder-Working Providence* and Peter Bulkeley's *Gospel-Covenant*, have been adduced as evidence for the Errand, but this construal suffers under critical examination.[50] Edward Johnson,

49. Robert Fills, trans., *The Lawes and Statutes of Geneva* (London, 1562), iv; "To the Most Vertuous and Noble Queen . . . ," in *The Geneva Bible: A Facsimile of the 1560 Edition*, ed. Lloyd E. Berry (Madison, Wis., 1969), iv; John Udall, *The True Remedie against Famine and Warres* . . . (London, n.d.), 73; Basil Montagu, ed. *The Works of Francis Bacon*, new ed., 3 vols. (Philadelphia, 1851), II, 414; John F. Wilson, *Pulpit in Parliament: Puritanism during the English Civil Wars, 1640–1648* (Princeton, N.J., 1969), 204; Alexander Brown, *The Genesis of the United States*, 2 vols. (Boston, 1890), 463; William Bradford, *Of Plymouth Plantation, 1620–1647*, ed. Samuel Eliot Morison (New York, 1952), 236. Other examples are found in John Brinsley, *The Third Part of the True Watch* (London, 1622), 504; Jer[emiah] Dyke, *A Sermon Preached at the Publicke Fast* . . . (London, 1628), 36; Henry Wilkinson, *Babylons Ruine, Jerusalems Rising* (London, 1643), 19; John Milton, quoted in Bercovitch, *Jeremiad*, 39; Patrick Collinson, *Archbishop Grindal, 1519–1583: The Struggle for a Reformed Church* (Berkeley, Calif., 1979), 115; H. R. Trevor-Roper, *Religion, the Reformation, and Social Change, and Other Essays* (London, 1967), 271. In a preface to Bulkeley's *Gospel-Covenant* (1646) Thomas Shepard called the work a "light . . . set upon a hill" ("To the Reader," sig. B3).

50. Bremer, *Puritan Experiment*, 37, cites Johnson, as does Miller, *Seventeenth Century*, 470. Alan Heimert, "Puritanism, the Wilderness, and the Frontier," *NEQ*, XXVI (1953), 361, cites Bulkeley. David Minter, *The Inter-*

for instance, told the colonists they were "to be set as lights upon a Hill more obvious than the highest Mountaine." They were to "make choyce of the right, that all . . . Nations . . . who are soonly to submit to Christs Kingdome, may be followers of you." God "purposely pickt out this People for a patterne of purity and soundnesse." Yet, contrary to first impression, there is no persuasive evidence here for a founding Errand. *Wonder-Working Providence* was written in 1650–1651, a full decade after the Great Migration had come to an end. It interpreted the role of New England in light of the English Revolution and under the influence of the copious millennial speculation which that event had evoked. From this much altered standpoint, Johnson was ready to maintain that New England's Congregational establishments presented an influential spectacle of reformation to other nations as they were beginning to be marshaled into the millennial kingdom.[51]

But as to the aims of the founders, the reader of Johnson's work will note the retrospective, contrived, and highly colored character of his introductory "Commission of the People of Christ shipped for New England"; for here alone he appears to suggest that the imagery of "lights upon a Hill" was ingredient to the first settlers' intention. In the more factual narratives that compose the bulk of the work, Johnson consistently portrays first intentions in other terms. He describes the immigrants' sober choice to flee fear and persecution and "take up a perpetuall banishment." While they proposed from afar to "pray without ceasing for England," their "chiefe errand," their "end of . . . coming hither," was to recover first forms. They would "worship the Lord in the purity of his Ordinances"; "purity in Religion" was what they had "spent their whole travel for." By 1650, working within a much-altered climate of opinion, Johnson moved to supplement the primitivist foundation with millennial concerns and to assign an undeniably historic mission to the Puritan colonies; but this revision cannot reasonably be taken as an account of original purpose.[52]

---

preted *Design as a Structural Principle in American Prose* (New Haven, Conn., 1969), 45–48, cites both. For similar texts see, *WP*, V, 126; Cotton, *Congregational Churches*, in Ziff, ed., *John Cotton*, 304–305; Norton, *The Heart of N—— England Rent*, 82.

51. *WWP*, 29, 32, 35.

52. For the aims of the founders, see *WWP*, 53, 179, 196, 219, 235.

In *Gospel-Covenant* (1646), Bulkeley warned his countrymen to "take heed . . . lest being now as a City upon an hill, which many seek unto, you be left like a Beacon upon the top of a mountain, desolate and forsaken." "Which many seek unto," however, suggests, not a center of radiating influence, but an attractive enterprise leading the way to itself. And note the flatly negative import of the "Beacon" imagery. The passage may reflect concern about the disturbing decline in immigration to New England after 1640. In a later passage Bulkeley again described the colonies as "a City set upon an hill," but now the point was, as in Winthrop's "Model," that "men . . . will cry shame upon us, if we walk contrary to the Covenant"—not their conversion by New England example. He did urge his hearers "so to walk, that this [covenantal obedience] may be our excellency and dignity among the Nations"; but nowhere did he describe New England's purpose as the creation of an exemplary city that would convert the world, or ascribe such an aim to the settlers of the previous decade.[53]

If it were otherwise, if indeed it was a sense of their catalytic role in the schedule of world redemption that had brought these Puritans across four thousand miles of ocean, we would not find them speaking with humility, even skepticism, about the exemplary function of their society. And yet at least six of the founders, including eminent clergy, openly discounted the world-redeeming pretension ascribed to them three centuries later. Roger Ludlow, describing in

53. Bulkeley, *Gospel-Covenant* (1646), 15, 383. Similarly, in 1647 the Ipswich magistrate Samuel Symonds described New England's accomplishments as "an occasion to stirr up the zeale of the two nations [England and Scotland] to sett upon reformacion of religion," and her church-state arrangements as "matter of conviccion to the episcopacy and others that this way of church government and civill government may stand together." This, however, was not an outline of founding purpose, but a statement of "what seemes [ex post facto] to be gods ends in bringing his people hether" (*WP*, V, 126). The same is true of Cotton's remark in 1647 that New England had "enlightened" "many thousands in England . . . to desire an utter subversion of episcopacy, and conformity," of Edward Johnson's announcement in 1650 that New England's impact "begins to be left upon many parts of the World," and of John Norton's claim in 1660 that "New England has now shined twenty years and more like a light upon a hill" (Cotton, *Congregational Churches*, in Ziff, ed., *John Cotton*, 304–305; *WWP*, 49; Norton, *The Heart of N—— England Rent*, 79). Norton also maintained that "the sole cause of our transplanting ourselves . . . was liberty, to walk peaceably in the Faith of the Gospel" (82).

1638 the "establish[ment of] the lord Jesus in his Kingly Throne" as "the en[d] of our Comminge into these westerne partes," also added a telling note: "Wee knowe that our profession will finde fewe frends upon the face of the earth." Only if one assumes the Errand will this appear a passing aberration. Seven years later, Richard Mather and William Tompson wrote a common letter of counsel to their old congregations in England. Pleased to offer advice as able, they yet wished to deny that they saw themselves "to be the only Prophets . . . able to give a word of counsel . . . such arrogant apprehensions are far from us." In Robert Middlekauff's apt commentary, "They did not want to be understood as posing as the representatives of a morally superior culture."[54]

Even more interesting is a flat disclaimer issued by John Cotton about 1650. In one of his several debates with Roger Williams, Cotton denied that Bay Congregationalism was an immediately binding model for reform abroad: "It is an insolent phrase that savoureth of more arrogancy, then either we dare use, or allow in our selves or others, to seeme to make our [mode of] calling to the Ministry in New-England, a Rule, and patterne, and precedent to all the Churches of Christ throughout the world." About the same time, he was telling his Boston parishioners that for the foreseeable future it was unreasonable to expect England to adopt the Congregational way: "For [the] present, it is certaine [that] the Body of the Nation of England, is not Capable of Fellowship in Independent churches." Therefore, he advocated a flexible establishment providing Presbyterian (!) nurture for the larger portion of the citizenry.[55]

Proceeding with similar reserve in 1648, John Allin and Thomas

54. "Roger Ludlow, in Behalf of the General Assembly of Connecticut, to the Governor and Assistants of Massachusetts," WP, IV, 36; Middlekauff, The Mathers, 32–33. In his preface to Norton, The Answer (1648), Cotton specifically discussed New England's potential contribution to ecclesiastical reform in England. He argued that the New World churches had vital insights to offer, but he did not present them as the decisive element for England or otherwise place his commentary in the context of a presumed Errand. New England's offering was rather to be "put . . . as once the widow put her mites, into the treasury" ("Apologetical Preface," 12).

55. John Cotton, Master John Cotton's Answer to Master Roger Williams (1647), in Writings of Williams, II, 219–220; Francis J. Bremer, "In Defense of Regicide: John Cotton on the Execution of Charles I," WMQ, 3d Ser., XXXVII (1980), 122.

Shepard addressed the charge that New England had contributed to the stalling of ecclesiastical reform in the mother country by strengthening the hand of Independency: "If any through weaknesse, or zeale without knowledge, have been too clamorous to cry up *New-England* way, with reproach to others; wee desire the world to take notice, that they have neither patent nor patterne from us so to doe." In fact, they argued, the New England way of attaining reformation through the creation of new covenanted churches clearly was unsuited to England; there the problem was the reform of existing churches. Hence the conclusion, "Neither our Doctrine nor practice do prescribe and limit the way of attaining . . . reformation" in the mother country.[56]

None of these assertions is incompatible with the conviction that Congregational Protestantism as worked out in New England was in fullest accord with New Testament direction or that, ideally, it should be universal practice. Cotton, for example, would allow variations on the point of "calling" only within the framework of the "consent of the Church," and he surely hoped that in due course England would submit to Congregationalism in all its details. Allin and Shepard merely recapitulated nonseparatist doctrine that established English churches were implicitly true churches and therefore not subject to the New England device of a new "gathering." But it is of greatest significance that, as if with one voice, these prominent figures insisted that they had come "not hither proudly to censure others, but to reforme our owne."[57] Their state of mind corresponds to the Errand as defined in Miller's *first* sense; it is distinctly inhospitable to the crusading exemplarism usually associated with an Errand into the Wilderness. Least of all does it provide the originating instance of claims to an American national mission on behalf of the world. Such claims were to loom large in later history, but to find their progenitor in a Massachusetts City upon a Hill is to mistake the purposes of the 1630s.

56. Allin and Shepard, *Defence*, 10, 33.
57. Cotton, *Answer to Roger Williams*, in *Writings of Williams*, II, 220; Allin and Shepard, *Defence*, 33.

FOUR

ECCLESIASTICAL

RE-FORMATION IN

EARLIEST NEW

ENGLAND

*C*onstrued as a summons to a grand and fateful Errand, John Winthrop's "Model" has served in many accounts as a draft of ideals for a self-sacrificing, model community whose aspirations pointed dramatically toward the future. In the more aggressive versions, Winthrop's allegedly consummating portrait of a City upon a Hill, impelling the world ahead by demonstration of higher possibilities, first "struck the keynote of American history."[1] Yet when the "Model" is read without the mesmeric surmise of an Errand, when, in particular, the normally highlighted passage is recognized as a rhetorical commonplace, the sermon's significance as a preliminary statement of the settlers' religious ideals is not in the least reduced. For those were the ideals of a people bent upon restoration. Consistently, their conceptions of the "propagation of religion," which Winthrop identified as the colony's "chief" end, focused upon the self-contained value of *return* to the primitively certified structure of Christian belief, discipline, and worship.

Approached in this way, as a strategic briefing for a community in quest of reconnection with originals, the "Model" presents an unfa-

1. Daniel Boorstin, *The Americans: The Colonial Experience* (New York, 1964), 3.

miliar aspect, one unaccommodated to modern preconceptions. Here was no first installment upon an American plan of restless progress, for the basic horizon moved to and from the primal time of special, sacred beginnings. Prerequisite to understanding the "Model" is a recognition that final authority and direction for human affairs is conveyed through the ancient and best primitive times of the Old and New Testament. Winthrop presumed and reinforced intimate personal commerce with living, mythic drama, with events, deeds, laws, personages, and emotions. He remarked, for instance, the satisfaction of lonely "Adam when Eve was [first] brought to him" and Jonathan's sacrificial care for his companion David. He dwelt undisturbedly upon supernatural characteristics, upon the appearance of angels or the enlivening operation of the "Spirit upon the drie bones [in] Ezek[iel]"; and he stressed at virtually every stage of the exhortation the binding force of originative "patterns," as in the "patterns . . . wee have . . . of our Saviour whoe . . . [sacrificed himself] to ease the infirmities of the rest of his body [that is, members of the church]" and thereby provided a vivid, imitable model of Christian charity.[2]

Like all his colleagues in the Great Migration, Winthrop believed that biblical occurrence delineated a fixed and ageless order of life, and so the community he proposed to found upon it would incorporate no expectations of fundamental change. In mythic instruction every important contingency in human affairs was foreseen, including all the "times and occasions extraordinary" of a foundling colony. As prescribed by the "articles" of the colonists' covenant with the Lord, grounded in standard fashion upon the exemplary compact of ancient Israel, the round of religious and moral life in a reformed Protestant colony was to be designated in a few formulas of perennial standing. Within the context of a scripturally shaped "forme of Government both civill and ecclesiasticall" and a social order whose graded structure would "hold conformity" with the changelessly hierarchical chain of living creatures, Christians were to live together in mutual support, to attend closely to the great business of "salvation under the power and purity of . . . holy Ordinances," and to

2. John Winthrop, "A Model of Christian Charity," in Edmund S. Morgan, ed., *Puritan Political Ideas, 1558–1794* (Indianapolis, Ind., 1965), 80, 85, 86, 87, 88.

keep the divine laws. Fluctuations in execution of those duties—the cycles of disobedience and repentant return and the corresponding manifestations of divine favor and anger—of course were embraced within the covenantal scheme. But the framework of life, the people's outlook and duty, and the covenantal pact itself would remain ever the same.[3]

By advocating civil and ecclesiastical structures that would overleap and discard established elements of English tradition found astray from the primal norms, the "Model" provides a convincing demonstration of the antitraditionalist element in any primitivist theology. No less clearly, it reveals a mind pressing forward to fresh opportunities and, from our standpoint, to historically new and venturesome departures in human community. Well and good: this is an important part of the historical record. But it must not be allowed to distract attention from the disconcertingly archaic and regressive foundations upon which Winthrop's vision of a Puritan colony so undeniably was built. Only in this way, by full recognition of elements alien to the experience of most twentieth-century students, can the "Model" be appraised accurately as a prolegomenon to any understanding of the three Puritan colonies, for their early religious and political leaders were pledged to begin again at a pure beginning.

Further Light: A Summons to the Future?

The famed "Puritan experiment" in seventeenth-century New England was, in fact, nothing so conveniently familiar as the expression may suggest. To a twentieth-century audience, the term "experiment" points to scientific procedure; it denotes the subjection of an uncertain proposition to a trial that might either verify or falsify it. Historians who speak of the "experiment in democratic government" or the "lively experiment" with religious toleration conducted by the young American nation use the term in this sense. The same meaning is intended in modern descriptions of early New England as "a proving ground" where persons went to "test their ideas," as the scene of a "radically experimental" approach to church polity, or as a "sort of laboratory in which experiments were tried

3. *Ibid.*, esp. 76, 79, 83, 90.

out for subsequent use in England."[4] Now New Englanders occasionally expressed a wish that their institutions might demonstrate the
viability of biblically formed community to an incredulous public, as
when Samuel Symonds hoped in 1646 that the New World venture
might "hold forth matter of conviction to the episcopacy and others
that this way of church government and civil government may stand
together." But the possibility of disproof, crucial to the modern conception of experiment, was not therewith implied.[5] Today it seems
clear that the early settlers did not arrive with a fully worked-out
scheme for reform in either church or state. The patterns exhibited
in *A Platform of Discipline Gathered out of the Word of God* (the
Cambridge Platform) and the *Laws and Liberties of Massachusetts* of
1648 reflect considerable adaptation and development. Yet from the
standpoint of the Puritans themselves, the venture was not under-

4. Experiments: John William Ward, *Andrew Jackson: Symbol for an Age*
(New York, 1962), 113; Sidney E. Mead, *The Lively Experiment: The Shaping
of Christianity in America* (New York, 1963).

Modern descriptions: William Haller, Jr., *The Puritan Frontier: Town-Plant-
ing in New England Colonial Development, 1630–1660* (1951; New York, 1972),
17; David D. Hall, ed., *The Antinomian Controversy, 1636–1638* (Middletown,
Conn., 1968), 20; Christopher Hill, *The Century of Revolution, 1603–1714*
(New York, 1961), 84. See also Edmund S. Morgan, *The Puritan Dilemma:
The Story of John Winthrop*, ed. Oscar Handlin (Boston, 1958), x; Richard D.
Brown, *Modernization: The Transformation of American Life, 1600–1865* (New
York, 1976), 37; John Cotton, *John Cotton on the Churches of New England*, ed.
Larzer Ziff (Cambridge, Mass., 1968), 25; Samuel Eliot Morison, *The Intellec-
tual Life of Colonial New England*, 2d ed. (New York, 1956), 6–7; Boorstin, *The
Americans*, 6; and note the title of Francis J. Bremer, *The Puritan Experiment:
New England Society from Bradford to Edwards* (New York, 1976).

5. WP, V, 126. See also John Norton, quoted in Bremer, *Puritan Experiment*,
37; Kai T. Erikson, *Wayward Puritans: A Study in the Sociology of Deviance*
(New York, 1966), 57; Perry Miller, *Orthodoxy in Massachusetts, 1630–1650*
(Boston, 1959), 149–150.

In Puritan vocabulary the term *experimental* meant "felt," "experienced."
See, for example, Paul Baynes, *A Commentarie upon the First Chapter of the
Epistle of Saint Paul, Written to the Ephesians* (London, 1618), 71; John Cotton,
An Exposition upon the Thirteenth Chapter of Revelation (London, 1655), 139;
Thomas Shepard, "To the Reader," in Peter Bulkeley, *The Gospel-Covenant;
or, The Covenant of Grace Opened* (London, 1646), sig. A8; Don Gleason Hill,
ed., *The Record of Baptisms, Marriages and Deaths, and Admissions to the
Church and Dismissals Therefrom . . . in the Town of Dedham, Massachusetts,
1638–1845* (Dedham, Mass., 1888), 3.

stood as a test of potentially unsound forms of ecclesiastical polity or discipline or—so far as these were subject to biblical direction—civil magistracy and law. Proper procedures for the gathering of a church might, at first, be unclear, as records of the first foundings plainly show; but the road to clarity lay essentially in discerning and realizing sacred forms whose veracity and completeness were never in question. As touching "things divine," whether in church or state, the founders' aim was to clarify concepts and put them into practice, not to audit, adapt, and perhaps discard them.

What is most dubious in the ascription of experimental aims to the first New Englanders is the implied easy congruity with twentieth-century states of mind, with a pragmatic attitude to truth, with an innovative bias, and with the forward slant of scientific research. To deny that Puritan thought embraced a hope for a better future and an interest in the progressive discovery of truth would be equally false to the evidence. But these elements require cautious analysis. Reserving discussion of millennial themes to a later chapter, we may instance the well-known claims of Congregational Puritans to be upon a course of *"progress in Reformation."* [6] Congregational doctrine undeniably directed attention to the "new light" that seemed to be marking the path of Christian reformation in the early seventeenth century. But just as certainly, the resulting notion of progress bears but sharply limited resemblance to the modern concept.

Congregational Puritans, conscious of having pressed far and decisively beyond Anglican positions in their grasp of ecclesiastical polity, were inclined to believe that the Reformation was a "cumulative and still expanding force" in the seventeenth century. They admired the Presbyterians, who had refused to be contained by the prematurely arrested reformation of the Elizabethan Settlement, and pushed on (or back) to truer comprehension of the divine plan for the church. Presbyterians, however, now seemed determined to repeat the Anglican error, and to cling uncritically to their transitional scheme.

Congregationalists, New Englanders among them, were too impressed by the spectacle of continuing reformation to settle for the claim that the Reformation had risen to completion in the Presbyterian polity. Too many more recent insights had been garnered by

6. CG, 13.

Protestant seekers of God's will to permit passive acquiescence in this claim. When men like John Cotton foresaw a "farre greater light then yet shineth," they were likely to have emergent Congregationalism in mind, but their vision was not restricted to ecclesiastical polity. Speaking from early Cambridge, Massachusetts, Thomas Shepard remarked the deficiency of Protestant piety before the recent and uplifting "discovery," distinctively a work of the Elizabethan Puritans, of the authentic biblical Sabbath. Thus with the aim of accommodating possible additional discoveries, Congregational thinkers preferred to espouse a concept of continuing reformation, one that gave high honor to "the first Reformers in Germany" and to "the Calvinian Reformed churches of the first reformation," but that refused to regard them as givers of the definitive "rule[s] for restorations."[7] Beyond Luther and Calvin, beyond all sixteenth-century Protestant polities and credos, stretched higher but attainable reaches of "further light."

An impressive number of early spokesmen, musing upon their Congregational establishment, specifically resisted the "conceit of having allready attained a perfect reformation." As they understood the matter, the colonies' arrangements in church and state took their place in a still "continuing . . . course of reformation." In the early 1640s, for example, Richard Mather objected to calls for a standard doctrinal platform for the Massachusetts churches. He felt that such a step would make the saints unreceptive to "further 'light' which God might provide at a future date." In the same spirit, John Fiske's congregation at Chelmsford, Massachusetts, urged that the Cambridge

7. Perry Miller, *The New England Mind: The Seventeenth Century* (Boston, 1954), 469–470; John Cotton, *A Letter of Mr. John Cotton's . . . to Mr. [Roger] Williams . . .* (1646), 28, in *The Complete Writings of Roger Williams*, 7 vols. (New York, 1963), I. Thomas Shepard, *The Works of Thomas Shepard*, 3 vols. (Boston, 1853), III, 12–14, 267; Thomas Goodwin et al., *An Apologeticall Narration* (1643), ed. Robert S. Paul (Philadelphia, 1963), sig. 2w; John Norton, *The Answer to the Whole Set of Questions of . . . William Apollonius*, trans. Douglas Horton (Cambridge, Mass., 1958), 5. Defending his Presbyterian scheme in the early 1570s, Thomas Cartwright had argued that Luther and a number of other first-generation reformers "were excellent personages, yet their knowledge was in part, and though they brought many things to our light, yet they being sent out in the morning, [before] ever the sun of the gospel was risen so high, [did] oversee many things" (*A Replye to an Answere Made of M. Doctor Whitgifte . . .* [London, 1573], 196).

Platform of 1648 be accepted with the reserve befitting churches open to "any further light which it may please God to cause to break forth unto us." A year or two later Edward Johnson agreed. He declared that "the churches of Christ in N[ew] E[ngland]" were ready "to make confession . . . to all the world, and are yet ready to receive any further light," and it may have been at his behest that the first pillars of the Woburn congregation chose to write the further light formula directly into their church covenant.[8]

"Further light"—the recurrence of this phrase in the literature of early New England points to a genuinely progressive element within the Congregational movement. But one should pause before translating it into the modern lingo of boundless possibility and openness to the future; as a "belief in the evolution of truth, continuous revelation," it is surely misrepresented.[9] The theological context and aim of New England's "continuing Reformation" may suggest reasons to guard against such hasty modernization. For New Englanders, as for all Congregational theorists, it was a first principle that any advance in theological comprehension must be achieved in compliance with the Protestant epistemology. "Further light" was a slogan for biblicists. It presupposed that the total body of "Fundamental truths" had been manifested in primitive times and remained "the same in all generations" without a hint of change or development. Not truth, but men's apprehension of it was subject to a measure of progression, to be accomplished exclusively by a deeper penetration of the sacred writings through which truth was conveyed. "The greatest light that I expect," Cotton told Roger Williams, "is . . . instructive [solely] . . . in the way of the word."[10] Hence the way forward to added light was

8. *CG*, 13; Norton, *The Answer*, 6–7; David Kobrin, "The Expansion of the Visible Church in New England, 1629–1650," *CH*, XXXVI (1967), 207; John Fiske, *The Notebook of the Reverend John Fiske, 1644–1675*, ed. Robert Pope (Colonial Society of Massachusetts, *Publications*, XLVII [Boston, 1974]), 97; *WWP*, 216, 242.

9. Christopher Hill, *The World Turned Upside Down: Radical Ideas during the English Revolution* (New York, 1972), 296. See also Clifford K. Shipton, "The Locus of Authority in Colonial Massachusetts," in George Athan Billias, ed., *Law and Authority in Colonial America: Selected Essays* (Barre, Mass., 1965), 143–144.

10. John Norton, *The Orthodox Evangelist* (London, 1654), "Epistle Dedicatory," unpag.; Thomas Hooker, *A Survey of the Summe of Church Discipline* (London, 1648), sig. A2; Cotton, *Letter to Mr. Williams*, 28, in *Writings of Williams*, I.

simultaneously the way backward into a structure of mythic drama and teaching that, unlike a modern constitution, possessed no inherent capacity to be amended or augmented. As George H. Williams rightly has stressed, the Puritan concept of continuing reformation did not mean "a new revelation or a new covenantal dispensation." What it did mean was a movement of "restitution and return" that, in Edward Johnson's words, despised and rejected every addition of "New Light to the Old [biblical] Word" and upheld to the full the traditional Puritan contempt for "innovation."[11]

Of the several early formulations of New England Congregational theory, the fullest and most authoritative were probably the "Modell of Church and Civill Power" (1634 or 1635), John Cotton's *Keys of the Kingdom of Heaven* (1644), John Norton's *Answer* (written ca. 1645; published 1648), Thomas Hooker's *Survey of the Summe of Church-Discipline* (1648), and *A Platform of Discipline Gathered out of the Word of God* (the Cambridge Platform, 1648).[12] These documents reveal an outlook that is determined fundamentally by a primitivist idealism. Negatively expressed, the governing aim in every case was to make the fullest possible withdrawal from the Catholic and Anglican error of human invention, addition, and novelty. In positive terms, the end was to regain the "*form* and pattern of [church] Government" exemplarily displayed in scriptural narrative. Citation of the early Fathers, natural law, or other extrabiblical sources was secondary and for the most part negligible; it was "the counsell and

11. George H. Williams, "The Idea of the Wilderness of the New World in Cotton Mather's *Magnalia Christi Americana*," in Cotton Mather, *Magnalia Christi Americana, Books I and II*, ed. Kenneth B. Murdock (Cambridge, Mass., 1977), 52; *WWP*, 172. For comments on "innovation," see Fiske, *Notebook* (Colonial Society of Massachusetts, *Publications*, XLVIII [1974]), 20; Thomas Shepard, "Thomas Shepard's Election Sermon, in 1638," *NEHGR*, XXIV (1870), 363. "Novelties" were cited by the Massachusetts General Court as one cause for declaration of a Day of Humiliation in March 1638 (*RMB*, I, 253).

12. See also Richard Mather, *Church-Government and Church-Covenant Discussed . . .* (London, 1643 [written 1639]); Richard Mather, "A Letter of Richard Mather to a Cleric in Old England," ed. B. Richard Burg, *WMQ*, 3d Ser., XXIX (1972), 81–98; John Davenport, *An Answer of the Elders of the Severall Churches in New-England unto Nine Positions Sent over to Them* (London, 1643); John Allin and Thomas Shepard, *A Defence of the Answer Made unto the Nine Questions or Positions Sent from New-England, against the Reply Thereto by . . . John Ball* (London, 1648); John Cotton, *The Way of Congregational Churches Cleared* (1648), in Ziff, ed., *John Cotton*, 165–364.

will of God in his Word" that filled in the schedule of ecclesiastical knowledge, answered every question, met every objection, settled every issue.[13]

But here as elsewhere in New England literature, no routine acknowledgment of the Bible as the Puritans' sourcebook and final authority will disclose the underlying conception. However they might employ the abstractive techniques of logic and argument, Cotton, Hooker, and their colleagues did not cite Scripture as a canon lawyer might cite Gratian; they first entered it as a living field of action. For them the sacred writ invoked into life at once a vividly real world of the "primitive times." Only as this panorama of primitive event became alive, familiar, and compelling in the believers' imagination was it able to prescribe "form and pattern" to a modern Christian church. The "partes of Church-Government," as the authors of the Cambridge Platform expressed it, "are all . . . exactly described in the word of God"; but they were described in the context of mythic event, through enactment, through dramatic exhibition. And so a first task of the Congregational expositor was to summon to life the acts of "*Paul* in matters of Christian libertie," the examples of "Moses, Joshua, David, Solom[on], Asa, Jehoshaphat, Hezekiah, Josiah . . . putting forth their authority in matters of religion," the lament of Jeremiah against "False devices of men" in worship, or the authority of "Peter considered not only as an apostle, but an elder also, yea, and a believer too."[14] If the edifice of polity that finally emerged from these authors' deliberations was cast into a formal schema, it was nevertheless understood as founded in drama. It arose, not from the undifferentiated flow of events per se, but from the peculiarly arresting spectacle of mythic precedent.

To the intellectual historian, perhaps the singular feature of the five documents is their underlying assumption that every defining feature of a properly ordered church is delineated in an ancient and sacred "express example."[15] Everything else—the schematization, the swirls of polemic, the occasionally heavy reliance upon traditional

13. PCD, 203; MCCP, 261.

14. PCD, 203, 236; MCCP, 260; Hooker, *Survey*, 6; John Cotton, *The Keys of the Kingdom of Heaven* (1644), in Ziff, ed., *John Cotton*, 91.

15. PCD, 198. As the cited passage indicates, it was in some cases necessary to appeal to "just consequence" from express texts. See also above, chap. 2, n. 39.

forms of logical dispute, even the obtrusive Ramism of Hooker's *Survey of the Summe*—is secondary to "rightly proceeding according to the [biblical] pattern." With a true radical's instinct for the vulnerable premise, Roger Williams bore down hard upon mimetic appeals; his "disjunctive typology" and his Seeker's tenet that the Catholic apostasy had "interrupted" the apostolic succession of "ministry and order" were explicit challenges to the precedential basis of Puritan ecclesiology. But in the Congregational colonies, "examples" charted all. Each defining feature of the church was "taken from the pattern set before us" in the covering biblical "case[s]." The proposition that the "church of brethren have the *power*" to choose their officers was grounded upon the use of "vote and suffrage" in the selection of Judas's successor in the apostolic band (Acts 1:15), upon the election of elders in the earliest church in Antioch "by the lifting up of the hands" (Acts 14:23), upon the apostles' instruction to the saints gathered in Jerusalem to elect a staff of seven deacons, and upon similar instances (Acts 6:3, 5, 6).[16]

By the same token, the "Church covenant" by which a Christian congregation was to be formed found its original in "the Covenant . . . which made the Family of Abraham and the children of Israel to be a church and people unto God." "Synods" were to echo "the pattern of that precedent of synods" (Acts 15:18), in which a dispute concerning the Christian use of Mosaic law was "sent up to the apostles and elders at Jerusalem." And when candidates for church membership stood to make the required public testimony of their faith, they reiterated the deeds recorded in Acts 2; for it was clear that those men and women who at the apostolic Pentecost sought membership in the church, "before they were admitted by the Apostles," mourned their sins before all and claimed pardon through Christ.[17]

16. *PCD*, 233; *Writings of Williams*, VII, 155; Cotton, *Keys*, in Ziff, ed., *John Cotton*, 102, 150; Norton, *The Answer*, 115. See also Richard Mather and William Tompson, *A Modest and Brotherly Answer to Mr. Charles Herle . . .* (London, 1644), 8. (Tompson's coauthorship is argued by B. R. Burg, *Richard Mather of Dorchester* [Lexington, Ky., 1976], 59.) In the cited passage the authors ask, if "in the Primitive Apostolic times . . . pastors were chosen by the congregations, what warrant can there be to take another course in these days, since the ancient pattern . . . ought to be kept until the appearing of Jesus Christ." See also *PCD*, 214.

17. Church covenant: *PCD*, 208; T. Hooker, *Survey*, pt. 1, 69. Thomas Weld presented Nehemiah 9:38 and 10:29 as the paradigm of an express, written

While reviewing such instances, the point to hold in mind is their evocative character, their re-presentation of mythic action. It would be a grave distortion to portray them as mere grist for the systematizer's mill, as fragmented proof texts or abstract imperatives shorn of original narrative character. They required of the beholder a dramatic identification. If in many instances, most obviously in the margins of the Cambridge Platform, archetypal episodes were not narrated, but simply cited in chapter and verse, they yet provide no evidence of exegetical abstraction. For Congregational theorists to have narrated and commented upon every applicable scriptural pattern would have been impossibly cumbrous; the Cambridge Platform then would have swollen to three or four times its present size.

But more important, we should remember the tacit mental resources of a constituency for whom the Bible was the Book of overwhelming and primary significance, continually to be read, reviewed, pondered, heard in sermonic recital, and in varying degrees committed to memory. A bare reference to Matthew 3:6, for instance, would suffice to summon to imagination John the Baptist's baptism of confessed sinners in the Jordan River.[18] Again, if we find our authors occasionally citing rules in addition to acted paradigms, it should be remembered that biblical precepts, too, were comprehended within a dramatic context. Thus, reference to the rule outlining disciplinary procedure (Matthew 18:15–17) was intended to invoke not merely a formal set of instructions but also the imposing and eventful oration of Jesus to the disciples in which the instructions were imparted. Puritan exegetes, moreover, obviously understood rules and precepts as a description of procedures thereafter carried out in the New Testament churches. In these terms, the further light of the New England way must be comprehended within a setting of continual reentry and indwelling in what Thomas Shepard called the "golden age" of primal event. Always, the step *back* into the time of sacred beginnings provided the resources for a step *forward* into fuller vision and practice.[19]

church covenant (*An Answer to W.R. His Narration . . .* [London, 1644], 31). Synods: Cotton, *Keys,* in Ziff, ed., *John Cotton,* 105, 121; *PCD,* 233; *MCCP,* 390; Norton, *The Answer,* 128, 133; T. Hooker, *Survey,* pt. 4, 1. Church membership: *PCD,* 222–223; see also Allin and Shepard, *Defence,* 190–192.

18. *PCD,* 205.

19. Cotton, *Keys,* in Ziff, ed., *John Cotton,* 103; T. Hooker, *Survey,* pt. 3, 33–40; *PCD,* 218; *MCCP,* 406, 407; Shepard, *Works,* II, 144.

Church-gathering at Dedham, 1637–1638

An important event in early New England that brought the very issue of beginnings to the fore was the formal "gathering into Churches" "such as were in the Primitive Times." Well before the Great Migration, Congregational theorists had worked out a distinctive approach to the formation of Christian churches. Churches were to be founded by the device of a "church covenant," a voluntary agreement entered upon by a select group of adult men. In Salem, with probable reliance upon prior and varied practical implementations of the device in England, Holland, and perhaps Plymouth, the first covenanted congregation in Massachusetts was instituted in 1629. Records of this and subsequent gatherings in earliest New England are for the most part either sketchy or nonexistent, although enough remains to suggest that a rough uniformity of procedure soon was attained, but by happy circumstance we do possess one reasonably full account.[20] In the newly settled town of Dedham, late in 1637, the townsmen began a lengthy "prepar[ation] for spiritual communion in a church society." A year later, they enacted the covenant and elected officers. John Allin, selected as pastor, prepared a brief history of these events. In the pages of his narrative we are able to glimpse the prospective "pillars" of the Dedham congregation at work upon the actual rites of ecclesiastical beginning.[21]

The gathering at Dedham illustrates again the ambiguous, dialectical relation between old and new that historically had marked the Puritan agitation. Seen from any regular standpoint within the Church of England, it was an act of high-handed innovation, rudely dispensing with ties to the historic, institutional church. Allin and his colleagues clearly thought of themselves as founders. They knew

20. *WWP*, 25. A summary of the procedures of a church-gathering may be found in Robert Pope's introduction to Fiske, *Notebook*, xi–xiv. In 1635 the culminating rite of covenant formation was subjected by the Massachusetts General Court to the supervision of magistrates and neighboring ministers (*RMB*, I, 168). For contemporary accounts of the gathering process, see Nathaniel Morton, *New England's Memorial . . .* (Cambridge, Mass., 1669), 75–76; *WWP*, 214–215; Charles J. Hoadly, ed., *Records of the Colony and Plantation of New Haven, from 1638 to 1649* (Hartford, Conn., 1857), 14–16; Fiske, *Notebook* (Colonial Society of Massachusetts, *Publications*, XLVIII [1974]), xii–xiii.

21. Hill, ed., *Dedham*, 1; Fiske, *Notebook* (Colonial Society of Massachusetts, *Publications*, XLVIII [1974]), xi.

that the founding of their church community was in some measure a datable product of rational calculation and decision. Presuming upon the high measure of autonomy assigned by Congregational theory to locally gathered lay Christians, they consciously were accepting responsibility for themselves and their "holy fellowship" and anticipating the spiritual welfare of generations to come. The structures of community and office that they were to bring into being were in some degree marked by the voluntarism and the "radical functionalism" that David Little has associated with Genevan and early English Presbyterian polity at the congregational level. Moreover, the founders understood their work in relation to the Congregational affirmation of further light: of all the lately vouchsafed insights into the "liberty of God's people" and the nature of the visible church. In these several ways, at least, Dedham's ceremonies of gathering bespeak a transition out of traditionalist modes. They bring to expression that portentous activation and dignification of lay peoples of modest social rank that was such a widespread characteristic of the Puritan movement as well as the sense of fresh undertakings and expanding opportunities imparted by immigration and settlement in new territory.[22]

Yet such observations open only a fraction of the event to view. Although Allin's report offers but a skeletal résumé of a process lasting more than a year, it reveals that the Dedhamites associated a peculiar, ceremonial gravity with "the first beginnings of the church" in their township. In part because "few of them [were] known to one another before," it was judged necessary for "all the inhabitants who affected church communion" to participate in a long series of weekly "disputes or conferences" for purposes of mutual acquaintance. They must also settle some thirteen issues pertaining to the formation and conduct of a "particular visible congregation." In the early spring of 1638, after nearly six months of doctrinal debate, ten men of whom there were "best hopes of soundness" began to meet separately to identify among themselves a core of prospective first members. After nearly half a year of mutual exploration, eight men at last achieved consensus and received approval by "a meeting or conference of the

---

22. Hill, ed., *Dedham*, 9, 10. For the Dedhamites' social rank, see Kenneth A. Lockridge, *A New England Town, the First Hundred Years: Dedham, Massachusetts, 1636–1736* (New York, 1970), 4, 11–12.

whole town." They then entered a final round of "trial of ourselves," spent "one day in special manner to declare our judgment upon all the heads of the Christian religion," and proceeded to the covenanting ceremony. This in turn opened the way to additional weighty procedures, including special meetings designed for the selection of officers and the institution of proper "ordinances."[23]

The extraordinary amount of time, energy, and care that many citizens of Dedham poured into these activities indicates their sense of "the great weight of the work" of foundations. Their activities confirmed fully the Congregational tenet that, where opportunity for the "new constituting of Churches" was presented, the decisive act of church "reformation [was] to be sought in the first Constitution." Ritual elements, with their peculiar gravity, abounded. They were evident in the several times of special "humiliation," fasting, and prayer that punctuated the year of preparation and, of course, in the formal acts of entry into covenant and the selection and ordination of officers.[24]

Further, the prolonged series of meetings directed to doctrinal discussion and mutual examination reveals the exalted value assigned for the occasion to the harmonization of individual variances. Since a people undertaking such a work must proceed "according [to the] rule of the gospel in everything," and since their ecclesiastical forms must be founded "only in the order instituted by Christ," ideological unity was a clear prerequisite. Allin's account emphasized the "sweet consent of judgment . . . in all points" upon which every stage of the process necessarily depended; and this, in turn, was to be generated by self-abridging identification with the relevant biblical narratives.[25] Allin, who participated directly in all events reported in his summary, recorded no trace either of interest in an Errand or of millennial zeal. If he portrayed an impassioned people, so he defined their behavior as a restorationist revival. Their special commission was to draw form *"immediately"* from the mythic source.

A. W. Plumstead's observation that the New England Puritans "had a lively, daily sense of penetrating to the very center . . . of a

23. Hill, ed., *Dedham*, 1, 2, 5, 7, 8, 9, 12, 13. Six of the original 10 men, plus 2 newcomers, were chosen for the final group of "pillars."

24. Hill, ed., *Dedham*, 2, 5, 6, 7, 10, 15, 18; Allin and Shepard, *Defence*, 10.

25. Hill, ed., *Dedham*, 2, 3, 9.

compelling mythology" is corroborated fully by the Allin account. And, as Plumstead recognizes, the essentially primitivist character of that "mythology," its summons to "re-enact[ment of] the days of Moses and the early Christians" must be recognized if the Dedhamites' concept of biblical rule and order is adequately to be understood. Notwithstanding the sketchy, heavily condensed form of Allin's narrative, it makes sufficiently evident that the participants in the town's church gathering had no conception of their endeavor as an absolute beginning. They strove to make a clean break with "all the superstitions . . . [and] commands of [the papal] Antichrist" as well as with catholicizing elements retained in the Church of England. But the error of these things lay in their "not agreeing with [the] holy word," in their discordance with primordial story and paradigm, wherefore a genuine foundational work for the seventeenth century would consist in recovery of a broken bond back to the originative times of Israel and the New Testament church. What the colonists now demanded of themselves was a procedure of renewal through return and conformity to a pure source and, only by this means, an advance toward fresh understanding and practice.[26]

Accordingly, their "disputes or conferences" were conducted within a horizon of re-presented mythic event. They turned their thoughts to the vividly remembered "stories of Abraham and his family constituted a church by covenant Gen[esis] 15 and 17 [and] the people of Israel coming out of Egypt Exod[us] 10 etc.," or of "Revel[ation] 1 the 7 [Congregational] churches of Asia." They assumed unquestioningly that authorization to gather a church flowed from a personal "union" with Christ, the prime biblical personage, the towering Redeemer and the "priest, prophet, and king of his church." And, like Congregationalists everywhere, they envisioned the founding of their church as a conscious emulation of biblical story, precept, and "example." So the very "distribution" of Christ's New Testament church into "particular visible congregations enjoying their distinct officers" was to be derived from cited episodes in Acts, Matthew, 1 Corinthians, Philippians, Revelation, and else-

26. A. W. Plumstead, ed., *The Wall and the Garden: Selected Massachusetts Election Sermons, 1670–1775* (Minneapolis, Minn., 1968), 27; Hill, ed., *Dedham*, 12.

where. The solemn Sabbath observation was to issue from "god[']s institution [the seventh day of rest] in Paradise renewed in the 4th commandment."[27]

This, then, was what Dedham's founders appear to have made of their opportunity to experience "first beginnings of the church" in their wilderness town. That much of their specific program rested upon misconstruction of the alleged primitive church, or that in numerous unanticipated ways it pointed beyond the immediate theological or communal framework, few would deny today. But so far as Allin's narrative may reflect accurately the Dedhamites' outlook, they were simply binding themselves back to biblical beginnings. The only "beginning" they countenanced was a renaissance of biblical forms and of primordial "purity." Here, in their view, was no laboratory or proving ground for ideas in need of a test, but a unique reconstitution of the church as it stood forth in the sacred time with converted membership, local organization, firm discipline, and uncorrupted sacraments. In accord with the usual expectations of covenantal theology, the Dedhamites anticipated that laxity and disobedience would periodically jeopardize the restored state of the church. But then, as always, the curative formula was "restor[ation] . . . in [a] way of solemn reformation . . . by renewing this covenant" according to the relevant scriptural examples. Even after their gathering, Dedhamites within the church covenant would always be beginning again, returning to originals.[28]

For the present, it was enough to relish the benefits of reconnection with the primal stories and their power to impart convictions of order and well-being. Allin paused to note that the church's first celebration of the communion, performed "as near as could be" in form to the original Lord's Supper, was unspeakably "sweet." The uplifting sensation of proximity to first things seemed, in particular, to have calmed "one sister . . . long . . . full of Doubtings" and otherwise to have "confirmed" all newly received members in the "brotherly love" ingredient both to biblical community and to its presumed recovery in Dedham of the 1630s.[29]

27. Hill, ed., *Dedham*, 2, 3, 4, 12.
28. *Ibid.*, 3, 13.
29. *Ibid.*, 20.

Human Invention: The Deepest Grievance

Whether looking at theory or practice, at the Cambridge Platform or a church-gathering, it also is necessary to recognize the long-cumulating expectations engendered by the Protestant epistemology. Those expectations centered upon the wish to expurgate "humane crea[tions], meer Inventions." In this way the New England case confirms Arthur O. Lovejoy's claim that primitivist belief, converted into a practical program, works through "elimination," that its purpose is not "to add . . . but to undo." The effect of fresh insight into the nature and shape of the Christian life was not, in design, to augment and enrich, but to prune and contract the inherited body of doctrine and liturgy. It was not, in the first instance, to construct an imposing religious establishment that would convert the world by example, exhibit new levels of human achievement or devotion, or ring in the millennium. What, according to then-reigning theory, New England had to offer was not an expansion, but a contraction of Christian tradition. Here was a new opportunity to attend to first essentials, to separate the "bright Gold" of the Great Time from man-made "Brasse," to have divine "Institutions . . . in their native simplicity without any humane dressings." The eight laymen who subscribed Dedham's church covenant therewith pledged themselves not only to honor Scripture as "the only rule" for Christian life but also to abhor and avoid added "devices . . . of men."[30] They saw their gathering as an opportunity to expunge those countless uninstituted forms that yet lay encrusted upon the English church. Thus one would have difficulty finding a more expressive phrase in the vocabulary of New World Puritans than "human invention" and its various synonyms.

Aside from the sheer frequency and fervor with which invention is castigated in the founders' remains, the most telling clue to its significance is the tone of understatement in which it usually appears, as in Anne Bradstreet's profession that "no humane Invention can

30. Arthur O. Lovejoy and George Boas, *Primitivism and Related Ideas in Antiquity* (Baltimore, 1935), 17; *WWP*, 89; *PCD*, 213; *New Englands First Fruits* (London, 1643), reprinted as appendix D in Samuel Eliot Morison, *The Founding of Harvard College* (Cambridge, Mass., 1935), 443; Hill, ed., *Dedham*, 12.

work upon the Soul." The assumed self-evidence of the proposition that "invention" confounds true purposes reveals the most. Hence one finds the New England saints debating, not the validity or significance of the concept itself, but only the fitness of specific applications. For the tacit and unquestioned presupposition of the entire procedure is the Protestant epistemology, with its primitivist background, its assurance of the supremacy of first times and examples, its supposition, *"That which is not in the Word, is a device of man,"* and its hostility to "brain-imagery." This was, simply, a fundamental context of thought in early New England.[31]

Not only did it guide and bind spokesmen for Congregational polity whose expositions of the biblical polity were developed in explicit contrast with "meer inve[n]tions . . . of men," but it also provided a potent language for defense and subversion of many aspects of the New England way. In the late 1630s an outspoken layman was fined by the Massachusetts General Court "for calling the church covenant a stinking carryon and a humane invention." Roger Williams, too, branded the program of religious establishment marked out in the Massachusetts elders' "Modell of Church and Civill Power" of 1634 or 1635 "a meere humane invention." The antinomian leader John Wheelwright, in his controversial Fast Day Sermon of 1636, lashed out at the ministers' peddling of "their own inventions" in the form of an unbiblical covenant of works. And from their first appearance in New England, Baptist voices were raised sharp against the Congregational rite of infant baptism and also the practice of sprinkling as "an invention of men." In this world of discourse, no combatant's thrust could gouge a deeper wound.[32]

For their part, leaders of the established order in church and state

31. John Harvard Ellis, ed., *The Works of Anne Bradstreet in Prose and Verse* (New York, 1932), 9; Thomas Hooker, *Survey*, pt. 4, 10 (note that Hooker and his antagonist are in complete agreement on this point); Shepard, *Works*, III, 82.

32. PCD, 236; RMB, I, 252; *Writings of Williams*, III, 393; Hall, ed., *Antinomian Controversy*, 161; Ebenezer Hazard, ed., *Historical Collections . . .*, 2 vols. (Philadelphia, 1744), II, 73–74; William Bradford, *Of Plymouth Plantation, 1620–1647*, ed. Samuel Eliot Morison (New York, 1952), 313. In a dispute with Henry Dunster on the baptismal issue, Jonathan Mitchel at mid-century also was led momentarily to wonder "whether the other way might not be right, and infant-baptism [be] an invention of men" (quoted in Jeremiah Chaplin, *The Life of Henry Dunster: First President of Harvard College* [Boston, 1872], 106).

knew well how to employ the powerful tacit threat of the terminology, as in Cotton's attack upon Roger Williams's notion of "separated" churches as a patent "invention," or his final confrontation
with Anne Hutchinson, in which he designated her late revelations as
"your own inventions." Early in the Antinomian Controversy, John
Winthrop asked John Wheelwright to cease using "some words and
phrases," such as "person of the Holy Ghost" and "real union" with
the Holy Ghost, "which were of human invention" and thereby stop
the spreading "variances." Sometime later, Winthrop, joined by his
pastor John Wilson "and diverse others," conducted a search "and
could not find the person of the Holy Ghost in scripture." They
thereupon "desired, that the Word person might be foreborn, being
a term of human invention." And so it went in countless cases, in
the Watertown congregation's "covenant . . . to renounce all . . .
human traditions and inventions whatsoever, in the worship of God,"
in Thomas Hooker's attacks upon the Presbyterian concept of an authoritarian elder as "a *human creature* of mans devising," in John
Davenport's characterization of the Halfway Covenant as a "human
invention." In every instance, the crucial assumption, deeply embedded in the Protestant epistemology, was that Christian "knowledge hath its being, and is *bounded in its operations*" by the one,
complete, and immutable structure of scriptural instruction.[33]

While the much imputed "millennial enthusiasm" will be found a
relatively rare and fluctuating commodity in earliest New England,
signs of restorationist ardor meet the eye at every turn. The dramatic and mimetic components of Puritan biblicism, often joined to
the antagonism to the "folly and froth of mans brains" imbedded
in the Protestant epistemology, do much to shape the entire literature outlining and defending Congregational polity.[34] Nor can any
survey of the large sermonic remains, of the various collections of
professions of faith made by candidates for church membership, or of
spiritual diaries fail to observe how extensively the laity and clergy

33. Cotton, *Letter to Mr. Williams*, 55, in *Writings of Williams*, I; Hall,
ed., *Antinomian Controversy*, 359; John Winthrop, *The History of New England from 1630 to 1649*, ed. James Savage (1853; New York, 1972), I, 203,
206–207; T. Hooker, *Survey*, pt. 1, 2, 119 (emphasis mine); John Davenport,
Another Essay . . . (Cambridge, Mass., 1663), 15; Cotton Mather, *Magnalia
Christi Americana*, ed. Thomas Robbins, 2 vols. (New York, 1853), I, 377.

34. T. Hooker, *Survey*, pt. 2, 44.

were drawn into the web of mythic story and inspired by retrieval of the simple and pure. Like the church gathering at Dedham, so recorded examples of Congregational discipline, of the formation of Indian praying towns, of baptismal controversies are scarcely intelligible without discernment of the underlying drive to return, recover, simplify, and eliminate. These themes, moreover, determine the solution of a recognized puzzle of the period: the decision to prepare a new metrical translation of the Book of Psalms.

Singing Primordial Song: The Bay Psalm Book of 1640

We have no direct record of the proceedings, but in the late 1630s the informal consociation of the Massachusetts clergy became concerned about the singing of Psalms in Congregational worship. After some deliberation, several "chief Divines in the Country," including Thomas Weld, John Eliot, Richard Mather, and perhaps John Cotton were assigned portions of the Psalter for fresh translation from the Hebrew. The fruit of their labors, rhymed for singing and with a preface supplied by Cotton, was issued from the Cambridge press in 1640 as *The Whole Booke of Psalmes Faithfully Translated into English Metre.* A work of some three hundred pages, this was the first book prepared and printed in English America. Eventually known as the Bay Psalm Book, it was to become in a later edition the standard of psalmody in the New England churches.[35] Now it is reasonable to wonder what moved the consociation to press this laborious project. Other rhymed translations lay ready to hand. The long-standard Sternhold-Hopkins collection was available in a variety of editions, including a series of Anglo-Genevan versions originating in the work of advanced reformers among the Marian exiles of the 1550s. So too for more literal tastes in translating there was the Ainsworth Psalter in use among the Plymouth Separatists. These, obviously, were unacceptable. But why? Scholarly comment on the Bay Psalm project either disregards the question, remarks the Puritan interest in a "literal rendering," or judges it "not clear why

---

35. Zoltán Haraszti, *The Enigma of the Bay Psalm Book* (Chicago, 1956), 12–13, 19–27, 56.

a new metrical version and so large a printing venture was under-taken." Thus, partly in reference to this question, Zoltán Haraszti has spoken of the "enigma of the Bay Psalm Book."[36]

Yet the difficulty vanishes if we view the Bay hymnal against the background of English psalmody. A major innovation of the reformers was the introduction into worship of vernacular songs to be sung by the entire congregation. From the early sixteenth century, congregational singing of Psalms in metrical translation had been a characteristic feature of Reformed orders of worship. Within Lutheranism, the emphasis upon "christian liberty" was coupled with resistance to treatment of the Bible as a book of precedents. Luther enthusiastically encouraged the development of a tradition in church song embracing both paraphrastic renditions of the Psalms and nonbiblical hymns. But Reformed leaders like Calvin tended to reject the use of extrabiblical elements in congregational praise and to emphasize the Psalter as the exclusive pattern of Christian song; it was to be translated as literally as possible, subject only to the exigencies of rhyme and meter.[37]

At the congregational level, English Protestantism tended clearly to the Reformed approach. The reign of Edward VI inspired a "great simplification in church music," which limited singing in the official liturgy to a Gloria in Excelsis and a prescribed Psalm, and from 1550 to 1553 London's several "churches of the strangers" for Protestant exiles presented models of continental Reformed worship in which

36. On disregarding question, see Morison, *Intellectual Life*, 115–116; Benjamin Brawley, *A History of the English Hymn* (New York, 1932), 43–44. On literal rendering, see Perry Miller and Thomas H. Johnson, eds., *The Puritans*, rev. ed. (New York, 1963), II, 555–556; Haraszti, *Enigma*, 7–8. On uncertainty, see Sydney E. Ahlstrom, *A Religious History of the American People* (New Haven, Conn., 1972), 150. Speculative suggestions are offered by Ahlstrom (150), and Haraszti (8–9). Charles E. Hambrick-Stowe's suggestion that the ministers deemed earlier translations "linguistically inadequate" stops short of the essential insight (*The Practice of Piety: Puritan Devotional Disciplines in Seventeenth-Century New England* [Chapel Hill, N.C., 1982], 111).

37. Owen Chadwick, *The Reformation* (Baltimore, 1964), 78, 91; J. A. Lamb, *The Psalms in Christian Worship* (London, 1962), 133–136; *WT*, I, 380. Zwingli apparently did not permit congregational singing (John Calvin, *Institutes of the Christian Religion*, ed. John T. McNeill, 2 vols. [Philadelphia, 1960], book 3, chap. 20, sect. 31, 894 n. 65).

the singing of Psalms played an integral role.[38] A trend toward popular psalmody was reflected in the early evolution of the Sternhold-Hopkins Psalter from 1548 to 1553, but the decisive influence appears to have been exercised by Marian exiles who returned after Elizabeth's succession enthusiastic about the vigorous Psalm singing at Geneva and other Reformed centers. One of the notable developments in Elizabethan church history was the rapid rise of congregational psalmody "after the Geneva Fashion, all the congregation —men, women and boys, singing together."[39] Metrical Psalms, according to the title page of the standard Sternhold-Hopkins Psalter, were "allowed to be soong . . . in churches, . . . before and after morning and evening prayer, as also before and after Sermons"; but the practice quickly spread to other uses, to religious lectures, prophesyings, and days of thanksgiving and humiliation as well as to private and domestic gatherings and individual devotion. Psalm singing, as a direct recovery of biblical song, became a defining mark of Puritan interests in worship and was particularly stressed by members of the Spiritual Brotherhood.[40]

Genevan influence also was felt in the further development of the metrical Psalter. An early edition of the Sternhold-Hopkins had become the basis of song in the English church at Geneva in the mid-1550s. Yet John Knox, William Whittingham, and other exilic leaders were not satisfied with the received text, whose translations often were loose and inaccurate. Desiring better to imitate

38. *WT*, I, 382–383; *LB*, 11, 225; Nicholas Temperley, *The Music of the English Parish Church*, 2 vols. (Cambridge, 1979), I, 17–18.

39. Quoted in Henry W. Foote, *Three Centuries of American Hymnody* (Cambridge, Mass., 1967), 23 (and see 24). See also Peter Le Huray, *Music and the Reformation in England, 1549–1660* (New York, 1967), 372–374.

40. *WT*, I, 278, 285–286, 290, II, 123, 253, 269, 278; Ronald A. Marchant, *The Puritans and the Church Courts in the Diocese of York, 1560–1642* (London, 1960), 37–38; Marshall M. Knappen, *Tudor Puritanism: A Chapter in the History of Idealism* (1939; Gloucester, Mass., 1966), 388–389, 431. For the views of the ranking Puritan clergy, see, for example, Thomas Cartwright, *A Commentary upon the Epistle of Saint Paule Written to the Colossians* (London, 1612), 199; John Dod, *A Plaine and Familiar Exposition on the Lords Prayer*, 2d ed. (London, 1635), 87; Richard Rogers, *Seven Treatises* . . . (London, 1603), 162; Nicholas Bownde, *The Doctrine of the Sabbath* (London, 1595), 235; Lewis Bayly, *The Practice of Pietie* . . . (London, 1630), 364.

the New Testament practice of "edif[ying] one an other with" "the Psalmes of the Prophet David," they modified the text more fully to regain original effect, attempted to "frame the ryme to the Hebrew [words and] sense," and added for the first time a simple and, in their judgment, congruent musical notation.[41] This stricter Anglo-Genevan Psalter was carried back to England by returning exiles and became an influence upon further development of the Sternhold-Hopkins. Whittingham himself was listed as a contributor to ensuing editions, whose title pages also announced that the text had been more carefully "conferred with the Hebreue." Yet this standard of Elizabethan and Stuart times, which early acquired "almost canonical authority" (often bound together with the Book of Common Prayer) and had appeared in some two hundred editions by 1630, was not fully conformed to strict biblicist ideals. In generous accommodation to English rhyme and meter, many of the translations remained paraphrastic. Further, a small selection of extrascriptural songs were included, like "The Song of St. Ambrose, called the Te Deum," and Robert Wisdom's hymn, "Reserve us Lord, by thy clear word, / from Turk and Pope, defend us Lord."[42]

In the stricter context of Puritan Separatism, dissatisfaction with these features led eventually to the preparation of an alternative Psalter. Henry Ainsworth, a Cambridge-trained Hebraist and refugee in Amsterdam after 1593, published his *Book of Psalmes* in 1612. Yet more closely measured by "the Original [Hebrew] text" and purged of hymns, it nevertheless made freer use of verse forms than Sternhold-Hopkins and in some cases employed tunes of greater variety and complexity. It was adopted by Ainsworth's Separatist congregation in Amsterdam and by John Robinson's in Leiden. The Pilgrim fraction of Robinson's congregation naturally carried it with them to New Plymouth, where it remained in use until the colony's end in 1691. In probable reflection of Plymouth influence, the church

41. *The Forme of Prayers and Ministration of the Sacraments . . .* , in David Laing, ed., *The Works of John Knox*, 6 vols. (Edinburgh, 1895), IV, 164–167; *WT*, I, 386–389.

42. Foote, *American Hymnody*, 11, 13, 26; *WT*, I, 386–387, 390; [Thomas Sternhold *et al.*], *The Whole Book of Psalms Collected into English Meter* (London, 1575), 11, (London, 1607), 102, 114, (London, 1638), 102, 113.

at Salem also adopted the Ainsworth Psalter and apparently retained it until 1667.[43]

For the most part these developments stood in contrast to the ways with song promoted by royal and episcopal authority in the English church. Although it was a loosely worded ecclesiastical injunction permitting "an hymn, or suchlike song" in Morning and Evening Prayer that from 1559 allowed the introduction of "Geneva jigs" into Prayer Book services, the practice never was endorsed enthusiastically by the church hierarchy. Only in its direction for Morning Prayer did the Book of Common Prayer provide for a Psalm to be "said or sung."[44] By virtue of its association with Puritan dissent and its activation of the laity in worship, congregational psalmody seemed increasingly ill advised from the more distinctly Anglican perspectives that began to emerge in the late sixteenth century. John Cosin, Matthew Wren, and other high churchmen of the Stuart reign found the general "bawling" of Psalms tainted by Puritan associations and incongruous with the liturgical serenity and formality they wished to foster.[45] While they might find it impossible to reverse the popular attachment to Psalm singing, their preference and support was for the verse anthems, motets, and other choral productions performed in the specialized liturgical settings of cathedrals, collegiate chapels, and the royal court. That many of the texts so employed were not of biblical composition was of little concern, since in these quarters Puritan applications of the Protestant epistemology were regarded as fanatically excessive. Likewise, the few English hymns that appeared in the late sixteenth and early seventeenth centuries were almost exclusively the compositions of anti-Puritan churchmen.[46]

43. Henry Ainsworth, *The Book of Psalms* . . . (Amsterdam, 1612), sig. **2. Ainsworth provided both a new prose translation and a metrical rendering of each Psalm. Henry Barrow, an earlier Separatist, had complained of "the rhyming and paraphrasing of the Psalms" (Haraszti, *Enigma*, 123 n. 1).

44. Henry Gee and William John Hardy, eds., *Documents Illustrative of English Church History* (London, 1896), 435; *LB*, 11. The provision for a Psalm "said or sung" in Morning Prayer appeared in the 1549, 1552, and 1559 versions of the Prayer Book.

45. *WT*, II, 280–281.

46. Le Huray, *Music*, 386–387; *WT*, I, 383, 389–391, 403–404, II, 259, 282–283; Frank Ll. Harrison, "Church Music in England," in *The New Oxford*

This, then, was roughly how matters stood when the Massachusetts elders ventured to prepare a new Psalter late in the 1630s. Despite a royal and Laudian inclination toward choral song, often based upon nonbiblical texts, metrical psalmody had been dominant for decades. Its familiar standard, Sternhold-Hopkins, was touched by influences from the Anglo-Genevan Psalter but retained a number of hymns and a tendency to paraphrasis. A few other collections of hymns were also available. The Ainsworth translation corresponded in part to a severer ideal of translation and was already in use at Plymouth and Salem. Given these circumstances, and the explanations provided by the Massachusetts translators in their preface to the *Whole Booke of Psalmes*, the enigma dissolves.

Neither the failure of hymnody to develop as a popular form in England (or New England) during the period covered, the English Genevans' or Henry Ainsworth's efforts to recover more of the psalmic "Original," nor the Bay Psalm Book itself is accounted for sufficiently as a fruit of "narrow biblicism" or as a result of belief in the "plenary inspiration of the Bible." Such judgments, even though they may be combined with passing recognition of a widespread hostility to the "human composure" of musical texts, do not report adequately the pertinent concepts of Reformed biblicism.[47] Both the translations and the original explanatory preface of the Bay Psalm Book make clear that the New Englanders saw themselves as standing within a tradition of restitutionist achievement. They took their place within a long-standing debate over congregational song. Is the whole congregation to be engaged in worshipful song? Were biblical Psalms, or "invented" hymns to be sung? What concessions to metrical need were to be made in the translation of biblical songs? According to the preface, these were questions that, by 1640, required discussion and a better resolution. Richard Mather, Thomas Weld, John Eliot, and John Cotton now were ready to presume upon the achievements of the past, to discern their imperfections, and to press on and back to a fuller recovery of primordial singing.

History of Music, IV, *The Age of Humanism, 1540–1630* (London, 1968), 470, 505.

47. WT, I, 396; Foote, *American Hymnody*, 34. The issue of "human composure" is mentioned but not pursued by WT, II, 255; Foote, *American Hymnody*, 34; Percy A. Scholes, *Oxford Companion to Music*, 10th ed., ed. John Owen Ward (London, 1970), 502.

Should the full congregation sing, and should Psalms be sung, or hymns? In the preface to the first Bay Psalter, these issues were addressed through the now familiar recourse to first times and patterns. Accounts of ecclesiastical song were to be found in the scriptural narratives of the Mosaic and Davidic eras, of "Solomons time," "Jehosaphats time," "Ezra his time," "Hezekiahs time," the "ocasions, [of] Isaiah and Micah etc.," and "in the dayes of the New Testament." A review of the relevant stories and "testimonies" yielded the desired archetypal guidance: no priestly soloists or "order of singing Choristers" was to be found, for in worship during the ancient times songs were "sung by a joynt consent and harmony of all the Church in heart and voyce." Though various biblical figures both before and after David produced "spirituall songs," the standard of congregational singing clearly was the book of the Psalms of David. Conceived and penned by "an extraordinary gift of the Spirit" and employed repeatedly in scriptural scenes of worship, the Davidic Psalter stood forth as the plenary model of liturgical song for "Gods Spirituall Israell" under the New as well as the Old Testament.[48]

The Davidic Psalter possessed, further, the required qualities of completeness and fixity, containing a "compleat . . . System" of praise and adapted by "the Holy-Ghost himself . . . to suit all the conditions [and] necessityes . . . of men." Those who might claim that the historical circumstances of the church in the seventeenth century were "new" and therefore required composition of fresh Psalms simply had misunderstood the range of an archetype bearing "universall, and perpetuall authority in all nations and ages." Hymns, then, even those "invented by the gifts of godly men in every age of the church," were ruled out of order as the contrivances of "mans conceived gift" and as clashing additions to primal perfection. A new edition of the Psalms therefore was required, standing more emphatically outside the framework of Anglican worship and purged of the hymns that wrongly had been included in Sternhold-Hopkins.[49]

As pressing as were these concerns, they were but background to the main issue, and the principal labor, of metrical translation.

48. *The Whole Booke of Psalmes Faithfully Translated into English Metre* (Cambridge, Mass., 1640), sigs. *2–**3.
49. *Ibid.*

Here the guiding aim of the assigned translators, in the words of the preface, was to eliminate the many "alterations of the sacred text" to be found in previous translations. Yet it does not follow that the new project fairly can be understood as a "literalist" desire for "strict adherence to the literal text of inspired Scripture."[50] What is lacking in such designations is an awareness of the restorationist implication of exact translation. Influenced by the Erasmian humanist ideal of translation as the bringing forth of an "ancient and genuine theology" in "its pristine splendor and dignity," English Bible translators from Tyndale to the refugees who prepared the Geneva Bible envisioned their assignment as a momentous act, excising translative corruptions and regaining the purity, brevity, and perfect inflection of sacred story and teaching—and song. If, to that end, it was necessary to discover and comply with the "integrity" and "propriety of the words," this was no mechanical conformation to an embalmed and one-dimensional text. The search for close accuracy was, rather, a means to facilitate more authentic access to the redemptive deeds, ordinances, and prescriptions of the primordial ages. This was certainly the case with the Massachusetts project, whose authors spoke with feeling of the "holy harmony, and melody" of the ancient accounts of praise and strove explicitly for retrieval of "this ordinance . . . in its native purity."[51]

A particular difficulty arose, however, in respect to a metrical translation, and here was the core of the whole matter. No hint of dissatisfaction appears in the *Whole Booke of Psalmes* with established translations of the Davidic Psalms as rendered in "our english Bibles," presumably in the first instance the Geneva and the King James versions. What caused offense were "the corruptions in our common psalme books" cast in rhyme and meter for singing. Here the antitraditionalist element in primitivist thinking was to smite accepted practice the hardest. From the New England standpoint, the

50. Foote, *American Hymnody*, 34; Percy A. Scholes, *The Puritans and Music in England and New England: A Contribution to the Cultural History of Two Nations* (London, 1934), 259.

51. Hans J. Hillerbrand, ed., *Erasmus and His Age: Selected Letters of Desiderius Erasmus* (New York, 1970), 31, and see 36, 95, 129; *The Geneva Bible: A Facsimile of the 1560 Edition*, ed. Lloyd E. Berry (Madison, Wis., 1969), iv; *Whole Booke of Psalmes Translated*, sigs. *2, **3.

popular Psalm books, however underwritten by age and use, were beset by cross-purposes. Now it was possible to see how the translators' will closely to render the Hebrew meaning had been swayed by regard for musical regularities. Sternhold-Hopkins, with its use of seventeen distinct metrical patterns, was the apparent chief target of this complaint; yet the professedly strict Ainsworth version, which sustained much of the metrical variation of the English standard and in a few cases exceeded it in musical complexity, must also have been in view. Such catering to meter greatly enriched the repertoire of usable melodies, but it did so at high cost. Translators bending thus to indulge tune inevitably had been lured into "poeticall licence." They had presented "rather . . . a paraphrase then the words of David" and condoned "addition to the words" and "variations of the sense." On these grounds Mather and his colleagues now moved to contain the temptations of meter. Simply put, they abandoned outright eleven of Sternhold-Hopkins's seventeen verse patterns. If the number of adaptable tunes therewith was much reduced, that was a price gladly borne for a more authentic text.[52]

The Ainsworth Psalter, furthermore, like the Sternhold-Hopkins, presumed a concord of text with tune and printed the metrical translation together with the corresponding musical notes. Now in their determination to re-present the intended exemplary form of primitive psalmody, the Bay elders carefully noted, "The Lord hath hid from us the hebrew tunes, lest wee should think our selves bound to imitate them." The original tunes, that is, purposefully had been excluded from the psalmic archetypes. Since musical performance was undeniably a part of original psalmody, appropriate melodies might be provided—a relatively rare example of legitimate human invention—but these never could be permitted to suggest modification of the Hebrew sense. Apparently the better to assure this, the

---

52. *Whole Booke of Psalmes Translated,* sigs. **2–**3. Paraphrasing violated "the rule: 2 Chron. 29:30": "Then Hezekiah and the king and the princes commanded the Levites to praise the Lord with the words of David. . . . So they praised" (sig. **3). I give the text in the Geneva Bible rendering. The 17 metrical patterns of Sternhold-Hopkins are discussed in Irving Lowens, *Music and Musicians in Early America* (New York, 1964), 29. The "difficulty of Ainsworth's tunes" specifically was censured in the New Englander's preface (*Whole Booke of Psalmes Translated,* **2).

Bay Psalm Book was printed entirely without musical notation. A terse afterword simply informed the user that fitting melodies were available in other English psalters.[53]

With the musical problem thus set in safer perspective, the Bay translators were free to concentrate on restoring fidelity to the English rendition. Each Psalm must, of course, be set in "english rithmes" suited to available tunes, but this now would be done with studied avoidance of paraphrase: "[We] have not soe much as presumed to . . . give the sense of [David's] meaning in other words." No knowing "additions" or "detraction" from the original had been countenanced. The result of this effort was another clear signal of the force of primitivist ideals in early New England: a spare, stripped-down text that made but minimal concession to the demand for meter and was separated physically from the adiaphoristic element of tune. This was the way back to native purity and to primitively plain style. Those who should wish for a more "smooth and elegant" effect were reminded that "Gods [primally simple] Altar needs not our pollishings."[54]

The Bay Psalm Book of 1640, then, was shaped primarily by restitutionist aims, and it dramatizes again the distinctively premodern expectations that Massachusetts Puritans associated with "progress in Reformation." Their endeavor embraced an ideal of perfectibility, of a fuller practice of worship that would move the Bay a step closer to Christian preciseness. The preface to the new Psalter specifically defined the reform of psalmody in light of the special opportunities attained through immigration. Already colonial freedom had made possible extensive reforms in church formation, structure, discipline, and worship; now "this ordinance also" was to be set forth in a "new edition."[55]

But by what measure was it *new*? Can it be taken as an advanced

53. For discussion of the Ainsworth Psalter, see Waldo S. Pratt, *The Music of the Pilgrims: A Description of the Psalm-Book Brought to Plymouth in 1620* (Boston, 1921), 13. The quotation is from *Whole Booke of Psalmes Translated*, sig. **2; cf. John Cotton, *Singing of Psalmes a Gospel-Ordinance* (London, 1647), 56. The restriction to six metrical patterns is noted in Lowens, *Music*, 29. For the afterword, see sig. L14. It also seems unlikely that the earliest Cambridge press possessed musical type.

54. *Whole Booke of Psalmes Translated*, sigs. **3–**4.

55. *Ibid.*, sig. **3.

pointer along a path of linear development or as a builder of zeal for the future? If these questions be entertained seriously, it is striking that the Psalm Book reflects no trace of thinking *ahead*. Millennial or world-reforming gestures are absent altogether. The project is explicable entirely as an act of primitivist refugees seeking a better imaginative and practical correspondence with primordial singing. John Cotton, in a separate treatment in *Singing of Psalmes* (1647), expanded upon the themes of the preface, denying the church's right to "invent . . . spiritual songs" and explaining that "as water near the fountain may fall out to be troubled, and so become less pure and clear," so the essential task of Protestant reform in this as in all areas was a return to "the purest times." [56] Within a decade, apparent dissatisfaction with the 1640 version did stimulate the preparation of another edition, one that included a small number of "hymns." But that revision was entrusted to Henry Dunster, then president of Harvard College, a noted Hebraist and a primitivist zealot who later repudiated the Congregational practice of infant baptism as lacking a clear scriptural model. Dunster's hymns, in fact, were extracted literally from Scripture; and his "refined" translation, which smoothed the often rough versification of the first edition, revealed no desire to take license with the original. The Psalms, Cotton Mather was later to comment, had "never yet seen a *translation* . . . nearer to the Hebrew *original*." [57]

A larger canvass of the ecclesiastical scene in earliest New England would disclose more fully the fundamental hold of restorationist ideals upon the founders. Indeed, students of their disciplinary, sacramental, or Sabbatarian ideas will want to pursue further that pull toward fuller reconnection with beginnings that shaped every effort toward "further reformation" during the early years. Yet for present purposes the basic pattern stands sufficiently revealed. In this survey of Congregational further light, of church-gathering, and of psalmody, four closely linked elements are prominent: an absorp-

56. Cotton, *Singing of Psalmes*, 19, 62, 64. The desire to "indicate the Bay Colony's ecclesiastical self-sufficiency" may also have played a role, but I know of no evidence that it was "paramount" (Ahlstrom, *Religious History*, 150; and see Haraszti, *Enigma*, 7–10; and Ola Elizabeth Winslow, *John Eliot: "Apostle to the Indians"* [Boston, 1968], 66–67).

57. Chaplin, *Henry Dunster*, 122, 130–131; Cotton Mather, *Magnalia*, ed. Robbins, I, 407.

tion in mythic story, a drive to recover divine rule and pattern, an accompanying determination to abrogate additions to the primitive and assure containment of man's dangerously independent wit, and a will by these means to purify and simplify the forms of religious community. For many New Englanders, however, it was not enough to be assured that the churches of Christ were being brought to the biblical measure. As Winthrop instructed his hearers on the *Arbella* in 1630, the work in hand entailed a coordinated revision in both the ecclesiastical and the civil domains. A mythically guided "due form" of civil order was to be constituted also.

FIVE

POLITICAL MIMESIS:

THE GOOD RULER

AND "MOSES HIS

JUDICIALS"

*I*n point of the relation between religion and civil concerns, it was of major consequence that Puritanism—which remained by and large within the magisterial mainstream of the Protestant movement—was an expression of Reformed, not Lutheran, outlook. The Wittenbergers' conception of the "two kingdoms" of church and civil estate defined the Christian Redemption as an inward and invisible reality. Christianity was a separate spiritual kingdom embracing the small number of justified believers —"few and far between," Luther said—within the larger community. Persons animated by Christian love might perform public tasks in order to maintain peace and order and thus serve the welfare of their neighbors, but the civil realm itself stood neutral, outside the sphere of radical renewal. This was all the more true in light of Luther's belief in the imminent end of the world.[1]

In contrast, Swiss, South German, English, and Dutch Protestants

---

1. Martin Luther, *Martin Luther*, ed. John Dillenberger (Chicago, 1961), 371. Ties between "the Puritan social ideal" and the distinctive Reformed pattern within Protestantism often are overlooked, as in, for example, Kenneth A. Lockridge, *A New England Town, the First Hundred Years: Dedham, Massachusetts, 1636–1736* (New York, 1970), 16–18.

of Reformed persuasion beheld in the Protestant gospel a mandate
for the moral reformation of the larger society. Their redemptive
programs integrated personal with social renewal and charged both
clergy and magistracy with parts of the task of claiming public life for
the kingdom. In England, the Reformed claim upon society at large
prevailed, although in time Puritan and Anglican interests developed
it in sharply divergent directions. It achieved peculiarly forceful expression in the idea of a privileged National Covenant with the Lord.
Puritan dissidents held no monopoly upon that doctrine, but from
the 1560s through the civil war and interregnum the most frequent
invocations of the covenant emerged in the context of Puritan preaching and polemic. There obedience to covenantal demand often was
tied to the cause of further reformation. In the American context,
the continuing hold of Reformed ideals was revealed in a generous
adaptation of the National Covenant to the New England enterprise.

At this key nexus in Puritan thought we come again upon the
primitivist dimension. James C. Spalding has shown that in the
Admonition to Parliament of 1572, the "first open manifesto of the
puritan party," "restitution and restoration" provided the central formula for avoidance of God's covenantal wrath. These stresses, of
course, were no peculiarity of English dissent in the early 1570s.
Puritan reform prospectuses in any period, with the various millennial renditions after 1640 forming an only partial exception, were
basically *retrospective* and sought to impose a biblical ascendancy
upon the nation. Key spokesmen like Thomas Cartwright, Thomas
Wilcox, William Perkins, and Robert Cleaver articulated the Reformed claim upon society in just these terms: "The word of God
contayneth the direction . . . of what soever things can fall into any
part of mans life," of "all our actions, either public or private." In
addition to the church, it embraced the family and all "the public
societies of men."[2] Covenantal safety finally was to be won only by

2. James C. Spalding, "Restitution as a Normative Factor for Puritan Dissent," *Journal of the American Academy of Religion*, XLIV (1976), 47–63;
Thomas Cartwright, *A Replye to an Answere Made of M. Doctor Whitgifte*
. . . (n.p., 1573), 26; Thomas Wilcox, *The Works of That Late Reverend and
Learned Divine, Mr. Thomas Wilcocks* . . . (London, 1624), 7; Robert Cleaver,
A Godly Form of Householde Governement . . . (London, 1612), sig. A1. See
also William Perkins, *The Work of William Perkins*, ed. Ian Breward (Appleford, England, 1970), 464; Thomas Shepard, *The Works of Thomas Shepard*, 3
vols. (Boston, 1853), III, 346.

drawing men back to a comprehension of their social existence in the matrix of ancient myth.

Patterns for Imitation: The Political Sphere

*I*n New England, it was self-evident that zeal for the normative age should beget a sense of social responsibility. The founders' concept of a Deuteronomic covenant was closely related to their ambition to encompass "civil as well as . . . religious matters," so far as they bore upon the Christian destiny of men and women, within biblical rule and pattern. Thomas Shepard assured citizens of New-town and students at early Harvard College in the late 1630s that all humanly significant activities were grounded in biblical warrant: "The whole Scriptures contain the perfect rule of all moral actions." In Boston, John Cotton applauded Perkins's view that "the word, and scriptures of God doe conteyne a . . . platforme . . . [of] ethicks, eoconomicks, politicks, [and] academy" as well as "theology . . . , church-government, [and] prophecy." A striking example is to be found in the missionary career of John Eliot, who intended his Indian praying towns to "be wholly governed by the Scriptures in all things both in Church and State."[3]

In the effort to imbue civil life with redemptive aim, the biblical example, in its full primitivist context, was a pervasive tool of thought. Assuming without question that scriptural "Examples" were "patternes for imitation," colonists who believed that archetypal instruction necessarily comprehended "all the actions . . . of life," even descending at times to precise employments of eyes, feet, and speech, found mythic precedents an indispensable source of legitimacy in public practice. It was normal that the Massachusetts General Court should summon a prominent citizen and "deman[d] a rule" (a biblical precept or archetype) for his attack upon a recent sentence of the Court, and then find itself pondering the allegation of "*Joab* his rough speech to *David*." Likewise, when, in a military cam-

3. Shepard, *Works*, III, 44, 346; John Cotton, *A Copy of a Letter from Mr. Cotton to Lord Say and Seal in the Year 1636*, in Edmund S. Morgan, ed., *Puritan Political Ideas, 1558–1794* (Indianapolis, Ind., 1965), 168; Henry Whitfield *et al.*, *The Light Appearing More and More towards the Perfect Day* (1651), MHSC, 3d Ser., IV (Boston, 1834), 127.

paign against the Pequots, Captain John Underhill adapted to Indian tactics by dividing his command of one hundred men into "small bodies" with separate officers, he took "the ground from the old and ancient practice [Exodus 18:21, 25; Deuteronomy 1:15], when they chose captains . . . of fifties and captains of tens." Again, in explaining the "fury" with which, in a later action, his forces destroyed native women and children together with male combatants, he recalled the bloody scenes of "David's war" with the Geshurites and other enemies of Israel. In this and other divinely sanctioned accounts of quarterless warfare, "no respect of persons" was shown. "We had," Underhill concluded, "sufficient light from the word of God for our proceedings."[4]

At times in early New England, important political decisions were taken in deliberate imitation of sacred pattern. It was so when the first assembly of New Haven planters acted to restrict the political franchise to church members through consideration of "such [political officials] as were describ[ed] in Exod. 18:2, Deut. 1:13, with Deut. 17:15 and I Cor. 6:1 to 7"; or when the Massachusetts General Court in 1637 presented its sentence of banishment upon prominent antinomians as an imitation of Abraham's expulsion of Hagar and Ishmael for "disturbance."[5] Yet more impressive in this connection is the record of a tense affair arising in 1643 from the Bay's involvement in a feud between two French adventurers, Charles de Saint Étienne de La Tour and Charles de Menon, sieur d'Aulnay de Charnise, engaged in violent competition for control of New Brunswick and Nova Scotia. D'Aulnay, the stronger and more ag-

4. John Cotton, *A Brief Exposition with Practical Observations upon the Whole Book of Canticles* (London, 1655), 27; Shepard, *Works*, III, 346 (see also John Eliot, *Indian Dialogues* . . . [Cambridge, Mass., 1671], 59); David D. Hall, ed., *The Antinomian Controversy, 1636–1638* (Middletown, Conn., 1968), 276; John Underhill, *News from America* . . . (1638), MHSC, 3d Ser., VI (Boston, 1837), 4, 25.

5. Charles J. Hoadly, ed., *Records of the Colony and Plantation of New Haven, from 1638 to 1649* (Hartford, Conn., 1857), 12–15; Hall, ed., *Antinomian Controversy*, 261. In Hoadly (13) the reference to Exodus 18:2 appears to be an error. For similar evidence from Massachusetts, see, for example, MCCP, 412–413. In his account of the antinomians' expulsion from the colony, John Winthrop added "the example of Lot in Abraham's family" (*The History of New England from 1630 to 1649*, ed. James Savage [1853; New York, 1972], I, 250).

gressive party, frequently had raided English settlements on the coast of Maine, and there was reason to fear eventual strikes upon Massachusetts territory. Faced in June 1643 with a request by La Tour for aid against his rival, Governor Winthrop and several other magistrates saw a chance to counter d'Aulnay's growing power. They decided to let La Tour and his men remain for a short time in Boston in order to hire additional ships and manpower.

The government's admission of some 140 armed Roman Catholics into Protestant territory caused an immediate uproar. Winthrop received several letters of protest as well as a formal remonstrance signed by three magistrates and four of the clergy, whereupon a full-scale debate of the matter was arranged. According to Winthrop's report of the "ensuing arguments," in which "all the [available] magistrates and deputies, and the elders also" participated, the debate's most prominent feature was a lengthy wrangle over biblical precedent. Issues of security, the deceitfulness of papists, and the likelihood of precipitating war with France also were aired. But the question of legitimacy, of the "lawfulness" of aid to La Tour, clearly was to be decided only in a thorough review of applicable biblical texts. Numerous episodes were rehearsed in detail: Jehoshaphat's alliance with Ahab, his "joining . . . with Ahaziah in making ships," his assistance to Jehorim, Josiah's aid to the king of Babylon, Amaziah's "hiring an army out of Israel," the "example" of Abraham's aid to Lot, the generosity of the Good Samaritan, Solomon's entertainment of the Queen of Sheba, and Joshua's aid to the Gibeonites. Behind the thrust and parry of argument, as the gathered leadership of the Bay pondered the wisdom of an important political decision, was an imaginative absorption back in paradigmatic narratives. Disagreement upon proper interpretation of biblical story there was, but none as to its archetypal authority. The proceedings reflect quiet accord that the right course, whatever factors of interest and security it might entail, would be disclosed as an imitative indwelling in sacred precedents.[6]

As T. H. Breen has noted, Puritan conceptions of the "character of the good ruler" were distinguished in part by a perfectionist ele-

---

6. Winthrop, *History*, II, 107–114. A succinct account of the La Tour–d'Aulnay affair is in Edmund S. Morgan, *The Puritan Dilemma: The Story of John Winthrop*, ed. Oscar Handlin (Boston, 1958), 190–193.

ment. Favoring "mediocrity [the golden mean]" over "preciseness" as the acceptable standard of Protestant practice, Anglican writers berated "political perfectionists" who made "extreme and unrealistic demands." But Puritans associated magisterial behavior with the dire necessities of the National Covenant and assigned political officers a crucial responsibility for pressing the citizenry to the standard of covenantal obedience. Rulers were to enforce the commandments, wipe out immorality, purify the church, uphold the Sabbath, and suppress heresy. Ecclesiastical and moral superintendence—this was the highest ideal of political thought and practice in early New England, and awareness of its mythic, mimetic dimensions is essential.[7] The conception of a covenanted, morally policed commonwealth obviously was rooted in English experience, in circumstances of struggle against a hostile religious establishment and a life-and-death political and military conflict between Catholic and Protestant interests; but it was articulated largely in terms drawn from the primal Book. Continually, magistrates were urged to press for recovery of the Christian estate as it was in ancient days, in times of reform and rectitude, and therewith to avoid the wrath that befell the Hebrew church and people.

Moreover, in taking up this charge, they were but executing a biblically configured office. Both in Old and New England, Puritan spokesmen insisted upon this again and again. The "lawful and . . . godly Seignorie" envisioned in Puritan theory was to function as "did the godly and Christian Kings in former times: as *Hezechiah* and *Josiah*."[8] Ever eloquent in his Rhode Island exile, Roger Williams might inveigh without ceasing against such claims. He found no paradigm for a Christian commonwealth and magistracy in the old Josiahs and their church-state. The coming of the Messiah and a new and spiritual dispensation had relegated them to mere history

7. T. H. Breen, *The Character of the Good Ruler: A Study of Puritan Political Ideas in New England, 1630–1670* (New Haven, Conn., 1970), 1–4, 14–16, 35–47.

8. *AP*, 13; John Dod, *A Plaine and Familiar Exposition of the Ten Commandements*, 2d ed. (London, 1618), 242–243. See also Edward Dering, *M[aster] Edward] Derings Workes* (London, 1597), 11, 18–19; Richard Greenham, *The Works of the Reverend . . . M[aster] Richard Greenham . . .* , 3d. ed. (London, 1601), 78; Nicholas Bownde, *The Doctrine of the Sabbath* (London, 1595), 274–275.

without precedential force. But commentators on political office in New England were emphatic in calling attention to the "excellent precedents" public officials had "set before them for patterns in the Scripture." The early "Modell of Church and Civill Power," the Cambridge Platform, and book-length treatises on "civil government" by John Cotton and Thomas Cobbett were unanimous on the grounding of civil authority partly in the recorded acts of those political officers from Moses to Josiah who were "commended in the book of God" for their aggressive attention to the people's covenantal status and were therefore "exemplary to all Christians."[9] "Thus did *Josiah*" was considered by the clerical authors of the "Modell of Church and Civill Power" as irrefutable warrant to New England officers performing their office as nursing fathers of the churches. When in time of war, pestilence, or other public calamity the magistrate proclaimed a fast day, he acted "*as Jehoshaphat did,* 2 Chron. xx : 3"; or, in taking coercive action against Baptists and Quakers, he was imitating not only David and other "good kings" of the Old Testament but also Christ, who in driving the money changers from the temple "laid on his bodily hand in such sort" and was "herein imitable . . . by men of [political] place."[10]

Except in the case of John Winthrop, evidence for the political perspectives of Massachusetts' first "men of place" is fragmentary. Nonetheless, their devotion to mimesis is well represented, as in the vigorous dissent of Governor Henry Vane, Jr., from an act passed by the General Court in 1637 to prevent further immigration of persons infected with antinomian ideas. Vane argued that the legislation not only ignored biblical examples but also stood flagrantly in accord with negative ones—like the rough treatment meted out to the unwelcome prophet Elijah by King Ahab (1 Kings 16:29–18:17). And in opposition to the magistrates' claim to form a standing council

9. John Davenport, *An Apologeticall Reply to a Booke Called: An Answer to the Unjust Complaint of W.B.* (Rotterdam, 1636), xiii–xiv; *PCD*, 236; *MCCP*, 312, and see 391. See also Thomas Cobbet, *The Civil Magistrates' Power in Matters of Religion Modestly Debated* (London, 1653), "Epistle Dedicatory," unpag., and 34; [John Cotton?], *A Discourse about Civil Government in a New Plantation Whose Design Is Religion* (Cambridge, Mass., 1663), 9.

10. *MCCP*, 390; Cotton, *The Keys of the Kingdom of Heaven* (1644), in Larzer Ziff, ed., *John Cotton on the Churches of New England* (Cambridge, Mass., 1968), 154; Cobbet, *Civil Magistrates' Power*, 10.

empowered to act apart from regular sessions of the General Court, Deputy Richard Saltonstall in 1642 presented the view that, "in a commonwealth, rightly and religiously constituted, there is no power, office, or administration, or authority, but such as are commanded and ordained of God." He found, of course, no model of a standing council ordained in Scripture.[11]

By far the fullest record of political thought from the period was left by John Winthrop. His writings testify to the assumption that the official prerogatives and acts of political officers in many instances were preenacted in biblical story. The dominant figure in Bay politics to his death in 1649 and a highly literate and able theorist in his own right, Winthrop clearly regarded conformance to scriptural exemplars as a defining term of political duty. This was evident, for instance, in his contributions to the dispute within Massachusetts during the 1630s and 1640s over the limits of magisterial authority. One group, with Winthrop as its leading spokesman, held a high view of political office and ascribed considerable "discretionary" power to the colony's magistrates. An opposing group, which included Richard Saltonstall, beheld in this a potential for arbitrary government and strove to limit magisterial power. Appeals to natural law, to common sense, and the inevitable considerations of interest and power all entered into Winthrop's polemic on behalf of discretionary privileges, but he labored as well to establish their archetypal foundation. Thus when Nathaniel Ward advised in a sermon before the General Court in 1641 that the people should "keep all their magistrates in an equal rank, and not give more honor or power to one than to another," Winthrop's first thought was that "it is against the prac-

11. [Henry Vane, Jr.], "A Brief Answer to a Certain Declaration," in Thomas Hutchinson, A Collection of Original Papers . . . (1769), The Hutchinson Papers, 2 vols., Prince Society Publications (1865; New York, 1967), I, 84–96; Winthrop, History, II, 89. As shown by the example from Saltonstall, occasionally the finer details of political structure were discussed in biblical perspective, but there was no general demand that the particulars of governmental structure or procedure evolved from Massachusetts' patent be grounded specifically in Old Testament precedent. Like arrangements concerning the frequency, size, or order of the Congregational worship service, they were for the most part adiaphora auxiliary to the central conception: the office and duty of the "good ruler." Vane's position reflected a radical political theology in which "whatsoever is done in word or deed . . . in [a Christian] commonwealth, must be done in the name of the Lord Jesus (Colossians 3:17)" (84, 87–88).

tice of Israel (where some were rulers of thousands, and some but of tens)." And when, two years later, an effort was underway to strip the magistrates of the right of legislative veto they held in the General Court, Winthrop declared that the action would debase the government to a "meere Democratie" lacking "warrant in scripture . . . [for] there was no such Government in Israell." [12]

Perhaps the most vivid demonstration of Winthrop's precedential commitments appears in the context of the popular party's drive to impose a specific body of codified criminal laws and penalties. Since the magistrates were also the colony's judicial officers, the imposition of a code of law would eliminate the latitude previously exercised in apportioning sentences to the unique circumstances of individual crimes. In the lengthy debate that boiled around this issue, Winthrop assigned strategic importance to mythic models. To rebut the popular call for a body of laws defining all criminal cases, he argued that it was "by discretion," in the absence of a specific covering law, that king "Solomon judge[d] betweene the harlots." To confute the demand for precise "prescript penalties" in every category of criminal instance, he cited several laws from Exodus and Deuteronomy proving that the Hebrew judicial system had provided judges with discretion in fitting penalties to individual cases. He also pointed out that biblical judges often varied penalties for the same offense, as when "Bathsheba was not putt to deathe for her Adulterye, because the Kinges desire, had with her, the force of a Lawe," and added that rigid prescription of penalties "take[s] away the use of Admonition, which is allso a divine sentence and an Ordinance of God, . . . as appeares in Solomons Admonition to Adonijah and Nehemiahs to those that brake the Sabbaoth." [13]

12. Winthrop, *History*, II, 36; John Winthrop, "John Winthrop's Defense of the Negative Vote," in *WP*, IV, 383. A good account of the dispute is in Breen, *Good Ruler*, 35–86; Winthrop also faulted Ward for "grounding his propositions much upon the old Roman and Grecian governments" rather than biblical models (*History*, II, 35). Similarly, at a General Court session in 1636, with Winthrop presiding as governor, it was ordered "that a certain number of the magistrates should be chosen for life." The "reason was," Winthrop wrote, "that it was showed from the word of God etc. that the principal magistrates ought to be for life" (*History*, I, 184). See also Winthrop's arguments in the case of La Tour and d'Aulnay (*WP*, IV, 402–410).

13. John Winthrop, "A Reply in Further Defense of an Order," in *WP*, III, 467; and "On Arbitrary Government," in *WP*, IV, 474–476. Summoned to

By recognizing the fundamental status of such appeals to mythic pattern, one may better comprehend the tendency of early New Englanders to discuss the political order, as a modern expositor puts it, in "spiritual language." Then one shall see more readily that for Winthrop and other spokesmen, at least in intention, the Reformed claim to civil life basically was conceived as an extension of scriptural jurisdiction. This, in turn, imposed upon political officers the duty, when possible, to discover the covering relationship between ancient pattern and corresponding modern problems and cases. Again the distinguishing Puritan factor is disclosed as an *imitation* of biblical event.

According to Their Equity: The Mosaic Laws and Legal Reform

The dramatized example was not the only, or even the major, conceptual device employed by Puritans set to· draw the political realm more tautly under biblical rule. Scriptural "precept" was another, with an importance gauged to the intense moral and legal tendencies of Reformed Protestantism. From the 1530s, the English Reformation had embraced a legalist and covenantal element which laid distinctively heavy emphasis upon obedience to scriptural law and accordingly granted the Old Testament a large place in the constitution of the Christian primordium. In keeping with this stress, and drawing at the same time upon medieval tradition, figures like William Tyndale, Myles Coverdale, John Bale, and Thomas Becon stressed that "God's [scriptural] law" was the guiding norm of "all civil and man's laws." The prince or magistrate was "commanded of God to be learned himself in the laws and ordinances of God, that he may do all things according to God's book."[14]

---

mediate the dispute, the ministers agreed with Winthrop that "the penulties of great crimes may sometimes be mitigated by such as are in chiefe power" and cited the example of "Solomon mittigat[ing] the punishment of Abiathar, for his service done to his father formerly" (*RMB*, II, 94); the reference is to 1 Kings 2:26–27. Winthrop also found an archetype of the magistrate's "negative vote" in Jeremiah 26 ("Defense," in *WP*, IV, 389).

14. William Tyndale, *Expositions and Notes on Sundry Portions of the Holy*

All of these thinkers, with magisterial Protestants generally, accepted the traditional distinction between "ceremonial," "judicial," and "moral" law within Scripture. In the Christian dispensation, judicial legislation covering the everyday life of ancient Israelites and ceremonial law prescribing their ritual practice were superseded; only the moral law epitomized in the Decalogue remained in force.[15] Hence the management of legal affairs "according to God's book" did not require a literal adoption of the large corpus of statutory material in the Old Testament, but a general regard for congruence with the Ten Commandments and other expressions of the divine and unchanging will.

The enthusiastic biblicism of the Protestant movement also generated more radical claims for the scriptural laws. In view of John Wyclif's demonstrable impact upon many of the English reformers, his demand that the biblical "law of Christ" be made the prime rule "in every human contract and case" is perhaps a clue to following sixteenth-century English developments, as is Martin Bucer's argument in *De Regno Christi* (written at Cambridge University in the early 1550s and dedicated to Edward VI) that criminal penalties in the envisioned English kingdom of Christ be drawn directly from biblical statutes. By mid-century and thereafter, voices were heard demanding the revision of English law to accord with biblical standards. In 1550, Thomas Lever published an attack upon "the customes and lawes of Englande" pertaining to "wages, tythes and fees" as "cleane contrarye" to divine command. About the same time, John Hooper was urging English lawyers broadly to "conform their law to

---

Scriptures, together with "The Practice of Prelates," ed. Henry Walter (Cambridge, 1849), 323–334; Thomas Becon, *The Catechism of Thomas Becon*, ed. John Ayre (Cambridge, 1844), 303. See also John Ayre, ed., *The Early Works of Thomas Becon* (Cambridge, 1843), 4; Myles Coverdale, *Remains of Myles Coverdale . . .* , ed. George Pearson (Cambridge, 1846), 11; John Bale, *King Johan*, ed. Barry B. Adams (San Marino, Calif., 1969), 109; John Bale, *The Laboryouse Journey and Search of Johan Leplande* (London, 1549), sig. Aiv.

15. The distinction was not "specifically Puritan," as claimed by George Lee Haskins, *Law and Authority in Early Massachusetts: A Study in Tradition and Design* (New York, 1960), 158. It was a commonplace of medieval and Reformation theology. For background, see P.D.L. Avis, "Moses and the Magistrate: A Study in the Rise of Protestant Legalism," *Journal of Ecclesiastical History*, XXVI (1975), 149–172.

God's law, and such laws as be contrary to God's laws abrogate."[16] It is significant that both Hooper and Lever were aggressive exponents of positions that in time would become a part of the early Puritan opposition to the Elizabethan Settlement. From the 1570s, if not earlier, some Puritan critics of an unreformed England would comment critically upon the state of English law, and their remarks would center on the authority of "the judicial laws of Moses" in a covenanted Christian state.

As A. F. Scott Pearson has shown, the contemporary status of "Mosaic" legislation was a prominent question in the literary disputations of the early 1570s between Thomas Cartwright (the principal early theorist of English Presbyterianism) and Archbishop John Whitgift. As an integral part of his general program for a full biblical and covenantal reformation, Cartwright had identified and called for the elimination of several discrepancies between English law and judicial practice and the plain requirements of the laws of Moses. In Whitgift's response the characteristic lineaments of an Anglican position came into view. Whereas Cartwright wished to extend, his opponent wished to restrict biblical jurisdiction. Cartwright's demand, as Whitgift understood (or caricatured) it, was that "all the judicial laws of Moses," excepting only those obviously relative to passing local conditions, remained in effect in the Christian age. This view would strip prince and magistrate of time-honored discretionary privileges and compel lawyers to discard their "huge volumes and multitudes of cases" in favor of an absurdly direct adoption of biblical codes. This Whitgift rejected. He appealed to John Calvin and other Reformed authorities in defense of the position that the Judicials, the codes of nomadic and agrarian biblical societies, had been "abrogated." "We have nothing to do," he said on another occasion, "with Moses' . . . judicial laws." Like the general patterns of Christian worship, so the legal management of criminal actions

16. Howard Kaminsky, "Wyclifism as Ideology of Revolution," *CH*, XXXII (1963), 68, and see 66; Martin Bucer, *De Regno Christi* (1550), in Wilhelm Pauck, ed., *Melanchthon and Bucer* (Philadelphia, 1969), 378–384; Thomas Lever, *Sermons*, ed. Edward Arber (London, 1871), 84–85; Samuel Carr, ed., *The Early Writings of John Hooper* (Cambridge, 1843), 469–470. Some background is supplied by Julius Goebel, Jr., "King's Law and Local Custom in Seventeenth Century New England," in David H. Flaherty, ed., *Essays in the History of Early American Law* (Chapel Hill, N.C., 1969), 92 n. 14.

was a realm of adiaphora, covered only in broad principle by biblical prescription; and thus, like the Prayer Book, the "huge volumes" of English law legitimately had been invented by authorities enjoying a generous privilege of situational "discretion." They might, moreover, readily "add to it or . . . take from it, or . . . alter and change it" in accord with "the [changing] time, manner of the country, and condition of the people." [17]

The Whitgift-Cartwright dispute about the relevance of the Judicials reveals again the more "precise" biblicist direction in which Puritan thinkers tended to take their Reformed heritage. Calvin and Henry Bullinger, the preeminent continental Reformed influences upon sixteenth-century English theology, represented mainstream Reformed thinking about the Mosaic civil law. Agreeing that the body of Judicials had lost its jurisdiction as a binding national code with the coming of Christ, both were eager to refute those of the Radical Reformation "who deny that a commonwealth is duly framed which neglects the political system of Moses." [18] Drawing like all the reformers upon the tradition of natural law, they would have the laws of Christian states founded upon the principles of natural right engraved upon the human conscience and, since man's conscience was darkened by the Fall, restated with objective clarity in the Decalogue. Both Calvin and Bullinger inclined to use the term "equity" (*aequitas*) to describe the unique cogency of civil laws grounded in natural right. The achievement of equity, not conformity to the judicial law, was to be the Christian magistrate's first aim in lawmaking; and while he might well take guidance from those of the Judicials

17. John Ayre, ed., *The Works of John Whitgift*, 3 vols. (Cambridge, 1851), I, 272–278; John Strype, *The Life and Acts of John Whitgift . . .* , 3 vols. (Oxford, 1822), I, 152. See also Whitgift, *Works*, III, 576. A. F. Scott Pearson's account is in his *Thomas Cartwright and Elizabethan Puritanism, 1535–1603* (Cambridge, 1925), 90–91. Attention also is given to this element by David Little, *Religion, Order, and Law: A Study in Pre-Revolutionary England* (New York, 1969), 101–104.

18. John Calvin, *Institutes of the Christian Religion*, ed. John T. McNeill, 2 vols. (Philadelphia, 1960), book 4, chap. 20, sect. 14, 1502; Henry Bullinger, *The Decades of Henry Bullinger*, ed. Thomas Harding, 4 vols. (Cambridge, 1849–1852), I, 341. See also Zacharius Ursinus, *Commentary on the Heidelberg Catechism* (1616), trans. G. W. Williard (Grand Rapids, Mich., 1950), 491–492, 497; Wolfgangus Musculus, *Common Places of Christian Religion* (London, 1563), 112–113, 119.

that retained contemporary relevance, he was at liberty to dispense with them altogether in favor of other laws either old or new that sufficiently served the ends of equity in their historical situation.[19]

Whitgift's emphasis upon freedom from the Judicials was flavored by the typically Anglican compulsion to defend existing forms and procedures, but it was recognizably aligned with the position of Calvin, Bullinger, and other major Reformed spokesmen. To a greater degree than acknowledged by Whitgift, Cartwright's standpoint too was rooted in Reformed teaching. What he had in view as the norm of law was not, as Whitgift charged, the whole, literal formulas of the Mosaic rules, but their inner moral principle, their "substance and . . . marrow." He conceded the historical contingence of many, perhaps most, of the statutes; undeniably, they reflected in countless details the unique "disposition of the [Hebrew] people, and state off that country" and hardly were transferable en bloc to sixteenth-century England.[20]

But there was another side to the Judicials, which Cartwright wished to stress. For, unlike other bodies of law, they had been instituted in the Great Time of the Old Testament and were therefore uniquely shaped to the norms of right. They partook, if in varying degree, of the "constant and everlasting equity" that continued in force in the Christian era. If many were patently irrelevant to the modern English scene, others were of abiding value either directly or by way of analogy. Indeed, the very lawyers to whose "huge volumes" Whitgift referred could tell him that, in fact, English law stood and must stand in part directly upon "the plain words of the law of Moses." There was no denying that matters not scripturally defined and involving no great moral principle might be handled sufficiently by the resources of human reason and wisdom, yet these composed but a fraction of the realm of law. And in the array of weightier and more complex matters with which magistrates must contend, the instinct of natural justice, even where clarified by the Decalogue, was a demonstrably fallible guide. Therefore, it was folly

---

19. Calvin, *Institutes*, book 4, chap. 20, sects. 14–16, 1502–1505; Bullinger, *Decades*, I, 341–342, II, 280–282. Bullinger's position was somewhat closer to Cartwright's.

20. Thomas Cartwright, *The Second Replie of Thomas Cartwright: Agaynst Master Doctor Whitgiftes Second Answer touching the Churche Discipline* ([Zurich], 1675), 95–97. See also Whitgift, *Works*, I, 270.

to grant the formulation or application of law "so generally" to the "discretion of the prince and magistrate" as Whitgift required. When formulating laws of ethical weight, Christian legislators should have the sacred writ at hand; they "ought [first] to propound unto themselves [the pertinent biblical] laws, and in light of their equity, by a just proportion of circumstances of places, etc., frame them."[21] In this way, by agreeing to the formula of equity but also making it the great pivot upon which his defense of the Judicials would turn, Cartwright proposed both to restrict the discretionary latitude claimed by Whitgift and to compel English law and justice into a closer biblical accord.

Although his theoretical position implied a broad critique of English law both civil and criminal, Cartwright's immediate concern was sharply limited. Primarily he wished to establish that "there are certen lawes amongest the Judicialles, which can not be chaunged," namely those stipulating the death penalty for the high transgressions of blasphemy, idolatry, murder, adultery, incest, "and suche like."[22] He would show that, alike in England and ancient Israel, such crimes struck bluntly against natural and moral law; they endangered the moral well-being of the commonwealth; they jeopardized the general safety under the National Covenant and its demands for strict policing of the people's sins. And in just these instances, in which the Mosaic penalties evidenced a full and unalterable equity, English law fell short. Adultery, for instance, normally was punished in the ecclesiastical courts with fines and penances; and if, as for murder, the law normally required death, it also provided the possibility of a pardon by the monarch or Privy Council.[23] Such were

21. Cartwright, *Second Replie*, 97, 104; Whitgift, *Works*, I, 270. See also Little, *Religion, Order, and Law*, 101–104; Cartwright, *Replye*, 28.

22. Cartwright, *Second Replie*, 95. See also Eusebius Pagit, *A Godly Sermon: Preached at Detford in Kent . . . 1572* (London, 1586), sigs. B4–B7; and Cartwright, *Replye*, 36. Bucer is a possible source for this emphasis; see *De Regno Christi*, in Pauck, ed., *Melanchthon and Bucer*, 378–383.

23. On the issue of adultery, see Haskins, *Law and Authority*, 149, 184, 271 n. 55. The pardoning prerogative is discussed in Whitgift, *Works*, I, 273; Michael Dalton, *The Countrey Justice . . .* , 5th ed. (London, 1635), 243; J. H. Baker, "Criminal Courts and Procedure at Common Law, 1550–1800," in J. S. Cockburn, ed., *Crime in England, 1550–1800* (Princeton, N. J., 1977), 44–45. Edward Dering, in the early 1570s, and John Penry, in the later 1580s, joined with Cartwright in objecting to the practice of the monarch, who through the

the usages Cartwright would have reformed by a better calculation of the Judicials' bearing upon England.

If Whitgift did misrepresent Cartwright's outlook upon the Judicials, he understood clearly that his opponent's arguments opened a door to more extreme positions. Demands of a more sweeping character came to light in 1573 when Bishop Edwin Sandys complained in a letter to Bullinger of an emerging contention that Mosaic law bound Christian authorities and that "they ought not in the slightest degree to depart from them." Such views came to light again in 1578 when now Archbishop Sandys's archepiscopal visitation discovered *"precise folks . . .* binding us to observe the *judicials* of Moses," and they appeared once more a decade later in the thought of the Separatist Henry Barrow.[24] His dependence upon Cartwright or other sources of legal criticism is unclear, but he censured those who "abrogate all God's judicial laws," insisted that the Bible contained the "perfect, and necessary laws for . . . [the] commonwealth" and that the Judicials "were not made for the Jews' state only," asserted the obligation of "King and magistrate to see these laws executed, and not to make new," and declared that a general failure to follow biblical law had "perverted . . . the whole order and course of judgment and justice."[25] With these words, Barrow marked out a radical bibli-

---

pardoning prerogative "alter[ed] the penalties of the judicial law of Moses" (*A (Parte of a Register . . .* [n.p., 1592], 80; John Strype, *Annals of the Reformation*, 4 vols. in 7 [1824; New York, 1968], IV, 249). Decades before, Thomas Becon had sounded a similar note in his *Catechism*, 310. Among continental Reformed theologians, the position that "it is not lawfull for a prince to forgive the punishment of offenders" had been propounded by Peter Martyr Vermigli in a work appearing in English translation in 1583 (*The Common Places of the Most Famous and Renowmed Divine Doctor Peter Martyr . . .* [London, 1583], pt. 4, 263). The same position was attributed (erroneously) to Calvin in Johannes Piscator's abridgment, *Aphorismi doctrinae Christianae maximam partem ex Institutione Calvini excerpti* (n.p., 1592), which appeared in English translation in 1596 as *Aphorismes of Christian Religion; or, A Verie Compendious Abridgement of M. I[ohn] Calvins Institutions* (London, 1596), 38–39, 185.

24. Hastings Robinson, ed. and trans., *The Zurich Letters . . .* , 3 vols. (Cambridge, 1842–1847), I, 295–296; Strype, *Annals*, II, pt. 2, 165. Sandys became archbishop of York in 1575.

25. Strype, *Annals*, IV, 249; Leland Carlson, ed., *The Writings of Henry Barrow, 1587–1590* (London, 1962), 414, 602, and see 198–199. Similar ideas, often tied to millennial aspirations, were much in evidence after 1640: Haskins, *Law and Authority*, 125; B. S. Capp, *The Fifth-Monarchy Men: A Study in*

cist legalism that eclipsed the normal Protestant distinction between moral law and the rescinded judicial law, and vindicated Whitgift's fears of an attack upon the whole legal system.

But it was Cartwright's approach to legal reform, joining scriptural bias to the comparatively flexible concepts of equity and proportion, that would commend itself to a number of nonseparating Puritan leaders and that would be influential in New England. Edward Dering, a close associate of Cartwright, took essentially the same position in the early 1570s, as did the barrister and legal writer Henry Finch a decade later. Similarly, William Perkins, whose high standing with the New Englanders is well known, recognized with Cartwright that some areas of necessary legislation were not directly encompassed by Old Testament law and therefore were "put into the hand of the magistrate by God himself, to be ordered according to his discretion." Yet Perkins also wished to assure the Judicials a revered place in English lawmaking and judicial practice. He denounced both the opinion (held by Whitgift) "that the whole judicial law is wholly abolished" and the "other extreme" (likely in reference to Barrow), that "judicial laws bind Christians as straightly as Jews." Hewing to "the mean between both," he gave particular attention to formulating the criteria—conformity to the Decalogue and to the natural law as expressed in the general consent of nations—that would enable magistrates better to identify and apply the "common [permanent] equity" diversely embodied in the Mosaic statutes.[26]

Seventeenth-Century English Millenarianism (London, 1972), 163–171. See also *Examen Legum Angliae* (1656), in Mark DeWolfe Howe, ed., *Readings in American Legal History* (Cambridge, Mass., 1949), 87–88. John Calvin earlier had repudiated the position to be taken up by Barrow and was in turn attacked by Barrow (Calvin, *Institutes*, book 4, chap. 20, sects. 14, 15, 1502, 1505; Barrow, *Writings*, 414).

26. *A Parte of a Register*, 80; Wilfred R. Prest, "The Art of Law and the Law of God: Sir Henry Finch (1558–1625)," in Donald Pennington and Keith Thomas, eds., *Puritans and Revolutionaries: Essays in Seventeenth-Century History Presented to Christopher Hill* (Oxford, 1978), 98, 101; Perkins, *Work of Perkins*, ed. Breward, 484–485; William Perkins, *William Perkins, 1558–1602, English Puritanist; His Pioneer Works on Casuistry: "A Discourse of Conscience" and "The Whole Treatise of Cases of Conscience,"* ed. Thomas F. Merrill (Nieuwkoop, 1966), 12–13. The subject is also discussed in William Perkins, *A Commentarie or Exposition upon the Five First Chapters of the Epistle to the Galatians . . .* (Cambridge, 1604), 230–234. See also John Paget, *A*

Yet for men like Perkins or the great William Ames of a generation later (who propounded a similar position), the reform of English law by the standard of Mosaic equity remained perforce largely a matter of theory.[27] The case was otherwise in New England, most clearly in Massachusetts. There John Cotton's compilation "Moses His Judicials" (1636) could provide a point of departure for the colony's eventual collection of *Laws and Liberties of Massachusetts* (1648), and there the dominant magistrate kept a journal preserving many details of legal history.

No longer is it thought that Massachusetts law in the original period was drawn more or less wholesale from biblical texts.[28] This older view has given way to recognition of the Bible as "only one influence among many" in a larger process of borrowing and adaptation from a rich legal heritage, and as the most successful manifestation of a widespread striving for legal reform in contemporary English society. Many areas of law—land law and maritime law, for example—had relatively little to do with the great moral concerns of Reformed Protestantism and thus were not targets of biblical reform. The case was otherwise in the area of criminal law, and historians often have remarked the Old Testament component in the colonists' early criminal legislation and legal discussion.[29] Yet in most appraisals

---

Defence of Church-Government . . . (London, 1641), 54. In 1585 the Anglican apologist Thomas Rogers distinguished between the "Brownist" position that Christian states are "necessarily tied unto all the judicials of Moses" and the more moderate position "that we are bound, though not unto all, yet unto some of the judicials." He associated the former view with Henry Barrow and the latter with Cartwright and Philip Stubbes (*The Catholic Doctrine of the Church of England* . . . , ed. J.J.S. Perowne [Cambridge, 1854], 90). For Stubbes's position, see *The Anatomy of Abuses* (London, 1583), rpt. in New Shakespeare Society, *Publications*, 6th Ser., VI (1879), 134.

27. William Ames, *Conscience with the Power and Cases Thereof* (n.p., 1639), book 5, 99 [91]–109, 169–172, 192–196, 263–268.

28. Paul Samuel Reinsch, "The English Common Law in the Early American Colonies," in Association of American Law Schools, *Select Essays in Anglo-American Legal History*, I (Boston, 1907), 375; Charles J. Hilkey, *Legal Development in Colonial Massachusetts, 1630–1680* (1910; New York, 1967), 68–69, 93, 142; Haskins, *Law and Authority*, 7, 142. The change in thinking owes much, of course, to Haskins.

29. Haskins, *Law and Authority*, 162. Bradley Chapin estimates that up to 1660 nearly 40% of substantive criminal law in the Bay derived directly from Scripture (*Criminal Justice in Colonial America, 1606–1660* [Athens, Ga.,

Puritan concerns for legal reform are not given their due. In order to discover the role of Mosaic law in this historic setting, it is essential to see it in relation to an already-established tradition of advocacy for the Judicials understood "according to equity" and sagely "proportioned" to current circumstances. "Equity" and "proportion"—these were crucial mediating terms through which Bay colonists would strive to expand biblical rule in their seventeenth-century settlements.

Evidence points to a near consensus among the first New England ministers on the relevance of the Judicials. This can be seen most conveniently in the "Modell of Church and Civill Power," that "first example of a collective ministerial view" drawn up about 1634 or 1635 by the informal consociation of Bay ministers, and in a transcript of a formal clerical debate upon the question "How Far Moses Judicials Bind Mass[achusetts]" of uncertain date.[30] The latter document almost certainly is related to the Bay colony's attempt, beginning in May 1636, to formulate a code of law. This, in turn, was part of the broader effort during the later 1630s and 1640s to trim the magistrates' discretionary power. John Cotton, who with Hugh Peter and Thomas Shepard had been assigned to a committee in that year to "make a draught of lawes agreeable to the word of God," was ready in 1636 with a "model of Moses his Judicials."[31] Not then accepted,

---

1984], 5). G. B. Warden notes that in the area of law "almost all of the major reforms proposed during the Puritan Revolution" but not accomplished in England were carried out in New England ("Law Reform in England and New England, 1620 to 1660," *WMQ*, 3d Ser., XXXV [1978], 688).

30. Robert Francis Scholz, " 'The Reverend Elders,' Faith, Fellowship, and Politics in the Ministerial Community of Massachusetts Bay, 1630–1710" (Ph.D. diss., University of Minnesota, 1966), 61; "How Far Moses' Judicials Bind Mass[achusetts]," Massachusetts Historical Society, *Proceedings*, 2d Ser., XVI (Boston, 1902), 274–284. Richard B. Morris's commentary on the latter does not represent accurately the meaning and mediating role of "equity" (*Studies in the History of American Law, with Special Reference to the Seventeenth and Eighteenth Centuries*, 2d ed. [Philadelphia, 1958], 34).

31. *RMB*, I, 174–175; Max Farrand, ed., *The Laws and Liberties of Massachusetts* (1648) (Cambridge, Mass., 1929), sig. A2. Hugh Peter, who returned to England in 1641 to aid the revolution, urged a thorough legal reform based upon the Decalogue, "to which Moses' Judicials added, with Solomon's rules and experiments, will be complete" (*Good Work for a Good Magistrate* . . . [London, 1651], 32–33).

the Cotton draft was presented again in 1639 and contributed elements to the famous *Body of Liberties* of 1641. These events supply the probable context for the formal debate upon the Judicials.

Views of the three recorded participants in that debate substantially agree among themselves and with the doctrine of the "Modell of Church and Civill Power." In both documents, issues bearing upon "the Magistrates power in the making of Laws" were construed in terms of the Reformed claim upon civil society. It was appreciated that New England afforded unprecedented opportunity to bring disposition of "the bodies, goods, lands, [and] liberties of the people" adequately under biblical direction. These and the other great matters of political existence were not secular adiaphora. They were not subject to the magistrate's pretension to leave mythic ground and "make what laws he please," but were comprehended within "the Laws and Rules of the word of God," including the Mosaic legislation. Far from "antiquated," the "Civil Laws . . . expressed in the Word of God in *Moses* Judicials" were to provide the starting point and model for the modern magistrate. The clerical spokesmen recognized, as had Cartwright, Perkins, Ames, and others before them, that Moses' precise formulations often were partly or wholly relative to time and place and to that degree "temporary" in standing. What was merely relative might be set aside. Yet many of the Judicials, in whole or in part, bore a permanent "general and moral equity."[32]

---

32. *MCCP*, 254–255; "How Far Moses' Judicials Bind Mass[achusetts]," MHS, *Proceedings*, 2d Ser., XVI (Boston, 1902), 281. The record of Zechariah Symmes's contributions to "How Far Moses' Judicials" is scanty but includes a clear denial that the Judicials were "antiquated" (284). See also Shepard, *Works*, III, 54: "The learned generally doubt not to affirm that Moses' judicials bind all nations, so far forth as they contain moral equity." In New Haven, John Davenport agreed that "whatsoever Ordinance of the Old Testament is not repealed in the New Testament . . . , but was of moral and perpetual equity, the same binds us in these days" (*An Apology of the Churches in New-England for Church Government* [London, 1643], 8). These texts do not support John D. Eusden's conclusion that "early New England leaders were as receptive to arguments drawn from nature and reason as they were to those of the Pentateuch and a moral code." The assumption that natural law was an independent and coordinate source alongside biblical law misrepresents the Puritan conception. As in the rule stated by Perkins, appeal to natural law in early New England was a subordinate tactic for validating biblical precept. Of course, it is correct to view, with Eusden, the "long Western tradition of natural law" as an objectively

Here, if always strictly within the biblical context, a sizable field opened within which magisterial—and clerical—interpretation was required. For now in the welter of biblical legislation covering civil and criminal matters great and small, those laws whose "grounds [or] ends or effects" were tied to special historical circumstances must be identified. Further, should the magistrate confront a case of fundamental right or offense not covered by a specific and perpetual rule, he was not thereby freed from biblical demand. He now must seek the appropriate rule and penalty by reasoning from the Mosaic Judicials' "general consequence and proportion." He must be conscious "not only [of] those [laws and penalties] which are literally expressed, but also [of] all such necessary consequences and deduct[ions], that may be justly drawn from them." Thus approached and adapted, Mosaic law became an obligatory basis of the magisterial function. There were, in George Phillipps's words, "no other Lawes but these" to stand as a finally regulative pattern of positive law for Christian communities. They were designed for the ages, and for New England.[33]

Men debating "How Far Moses' Judicials Bind Mass[achusetts]" obviously felt a spur of practical urgency. John Cotton, one of the debaters, and likely the preeminent biblical exegete in the English New World, was to be the first Puritan leader with sufficient practical incentive to endeavor a comprehensive application of Mosaic law according to its equity and proportion. His outline of "Moses His Judicials" was not an isolated monument to the biblicist extremism of New England theocrats, nor was it a product of "millennial enthusiasm." It stood within and realized in tentatively systematic form the tradition of Puritan thinking upon the Judicials that commenced in the 1570s, if not earlier, and had been carried forward in moderate form by Dering, Perkins, Ames, and others.

Throughout his New England career, Cotton maintained "a tender respect in all lawes to the judicials of *Moses* . . . that are built upon moral equity" and contended that "it lyes on every Common-

---

coordinate source of New England law; but this should not be confused with the Puritans' view of the matter. See John D. Eusden, "Natural Law and Covenant Theology in New England, 1620–1670," *Natural Law Forum*, V (1960), 1–2.

33. "How Far Moses' Judicials Bind Mass[achusetts]," MHS, *Proceedings*, 2d Ser., XVI (Boston, 1902), 281; MCCP, 254.

wealth to establish the same."[34] According to the preface to the *Laws and Liberties of Massachusetts*, the committee to which Cotton was appointed in 1636 had been directed to "compose a modell of the Judiciall lawes of Moses [together] with such other cases as might be referred." In addition, the antidiscretionary interests, whose demands for limitation of magisterial power were the real force behind the codifying project, were interested in preventing the growth of arbitrary government. They wished that the committee's work might be cast "in resemblance to a Magna charta."[35] Cotton therefore had a difficult assignment. A "model" of relevant Old Testament laws must be assembled, yet there were also the "other cases" to incorporate, as well as the assertion of liberties expected of a Magna Charta, and already-existing laws must be taken into account. Thus the draft never was intended as a mere transcription of biblical statutes. And as the "Modell of Church and Civill Power," in which Cotton almost surely had a hand, specifically recognized a restricted area of legislation about "civill and indifferent things about the Commonweale" not embraced in Mosaic law, so Cotton was free to develop a number of items, as ordinances establishing the "protection and provision

34. John Cotton, *The Powring out of the Seven Vials* (London, 1642), "The Third Vial," 20–21; "How Far Moses' Judicials Bind Mass[achusetts]," MHS, *Proceedings*, 2d Ser., XVI (Boston, 1902), 282–284. Cotton's compilation of "Moses His Judicials" was published in London in 1641 as *An Abstract; or, The Lawes of New England*. . . . It is interpreted in millennial terms by J. F. Maclear, "New England and the Fifth Monarchy: The Quest for the Millennium in Early American Puritanism," *WMQ*, 3d Ser., XXXII (1975), 238–239; Philip F. Gura, *A Glimpse of Sion's Glory: Puritan Radicalism in New England, 1620–1660* (Middletown, Conn., 1984), 133.

35. Farrand, ed., *Laws and Liberties*, sig. A2; Winthrop, *History*, I, 160. The role of Hugh Peter, Thomas Shepard, and the other members in the draft's formulation is unclear. It is commonly assumed that Cotton was the author, but Winthrop's note on the presentation of the "model" to the General Court in October 1636 states only that Cotton "present[ed]" the draft compiled by himself and "some other ministers." Winthrop's note on Cotton's resubmission of the draft to the Court in 1639 does point to Cotton as the author; yet the preface to the *Laws and Liberties* refers authorship to "some of the Elders of our Churches." See Winthrop, *History*, I, 202, 322; Farrand, ed., *Laws and Liberties*, sig. A2. Charles M. Andrews assumed that a new and different document was involved in 1639 (*The Colonial Period of American History*, 4 vols. [New Haven, Conn., 1934–1938], I, 455). I follow Haskins, *Law and Authority*, 127.

of the Countrey," without reliance upon biblical codes. He was also free to draw upon the charter and existing Bay laws and practices for several details.[36]

And yet his main intent clearly was to press the biblical connections. Marginalia of references to Mosaic legislation and, in some cases, to archetypes accompanied a majority of the proposed laws. Those governing crime, the functions of magistrates, commercial behavior, and matters of inheritance were documented heavily, and the compilation concluded in a short doxology to "the Lord . . . our Judge [and] . . . Law-giver." In a few instances, as in those not directly referable to specific judicials and involving calculations of general "proportion," marginalia were not provided, but the biblical background, we may presume, was sufficiently clear to members of Cotton's committee and of the General Court. Even a certainly indifferent provision for an agricultural storehouse in each town was grounded upon a Deuteronomic rule.[37]

Of greatest importance was Cotton's section on capital crimes, since the properly severe control of high offenses against the divine will and the National Covenant had been the cardinal issue in Cartwright's and Perkins and Ames's advocacy of "certein lawes amongest the Judicialles, which can not be chaunged."[38] Here at last, beyond

36. *MCCP*, 255; Cotton, *Abstract*, 4. For use of existing laws and practices, see Andrews, *Colonial Period*, I, 455; John E. Pomfret and Floyd M. Shumway, *Founding the American Colonies, 1583–1660* (New York, 1971), 262.

37. Cotton, *Abstract*, 5, 15. For Cotton's appeal to archetypes, see, for example, 3. To support life tenure for members of the Standing Council, he there cited 1 Kings 12:6. The biblical text reports King Rehoboam taking counsel with "the old men that had stood before Solomon his father." Cotton's proposed laws regulating taxation appear to reflect calculation of "proportion" (5–6). General grounds for taxation can be found, for example, in 1 Kings 4:7 and 2 Chronicles 17:5. The biblical background is also manifest in Cotton's rule against "prophane swearing and cursing" and in his adoption of the law already in force tying freemanship to church membership (3, 12). The *MCCP* had derived the rule respecting freemanship "from the patterne of Israel, where none had power to choose but only Israel" (413). Cotton drew without citation upon biblical rules governing sodomy and buggery, willful perjury, and flogging (*Abstract*, 11; and cf. with the biblical texts cited in Farrand, ed., *Laws and Liberties*, 5; *Abstract*, 13, and see Deuteronomy 19:16–21; *Abstract*, 16, and see Deuteronomy 25:3).

38. Cartwright, *Second Replie*, 95–96, 98–102; Merrill, ed., *William Perkins*, 13–14; Perkins, *Work of Perkins*, ed. Breward, 599; Ames, *Conscience*, book 5, 169–171, 192–196.

the reach of pardons, bribes, half-secularized ecclesiastical courts, and corruptly inadequate capital laws, the manifest equity of the ancient measures against blasphemy, murder, adultery, and the like could be given free expression. On the other hand, and again following Perkins and Ames, Cotton rejected the English practice of hanging thieves and drew a more moderate penalty from biblical statutes requiring restitution.[39] Other "less heinous" crimes, too, like fornication, were placed in proper perspective with penalties derived, literally or by the rule of proportion, from the Judicials. In short, Cotton had gone far to translate the theory of the "Modell of Church and Civill Power" into a practical program of legal reform.

In the event, the Cotton code was not adopted. After many delays, the General Court enacted into law a very different document, the *Body of Liberties* (1641). This proving unsatisfactory, the definitive *Laws and Liberties of Massachusetts*, the "first modern code of the Western world," was promulgated in 1648. Save in their presentation of capital laws, neither code resembled Cotton's in its overt and extensive biblical documentation; both drew heavily upon English law.[40]

Yet one may not conclude that the colonial lawmakers, "with only minor exceptions, actually followed English example."[41] First, it should be remembered that "Moses His Judicials" was a *draft* intended for further discussion and debate prior to approval. The preface to the *Laws and Liberties* reported that the "modell of the Judi-

39. Haskins, *Law and Authority*, 153. See also Ames, *Conscience*, book 5, 263–266. Perkins accepted the death penalty only for hardened, unreformable thieves; Cartwright spoke ambiguously on the subject, but appears to have upheld a uniform capital penalty (Perkins, *Work of Perkins*, ed. Breward, 487; Cartwright, *Second Replie*, 103, 109–110, 117). See also Bucer, *De Regno Christi*, in Pauck, ed., *Melanchthon and Bucer*, 382.

40. Haskins, *Law and Authority*, 120. Bradley Chapin has estimated that about 41% of Massachusetts law before 1660 was drawn from English sources, and another 39% from the Old Testament; yet such figures can only be crude approximations (*Criminal Justice*, 5). Cf. the Bay codes with New Haven's, many of which are biblically annotated (Hoadly, ed., *New Haven*, II, 571–615). Roman civil law was a possible additional influence upon the New England codes (Warden, "Law Reform in England and New England," *WMQ*, 3d Ser., XXXV [1975], 686–687).

41. Daniel J. Boorstin, *The Americans: The Colonial Experience* (New York, 1964), 21.

ciall lawes of Moses" had been commissioned by the General Court "with intent to make use of them in composing our lawes"; and it is possible, perhaps likely, that Cotton's copious marginalia were intended to supply a full documentation required only at this stage to secure approval of his formulations.[42] Second, and in any case, a comparison of Cotton's code with the *Body of Liberties* suggests that the Cotton draft failed of acceptance, not because of excessive biblicism, but because it fell short of meeting the demands of the popular party bent upon abridging the magistracy's discretionary privileges. Not only had Cotton upheld a prime element of the discretionary party's program—that "Counsellors [were] to be chosen for life"— and proven far more adept in discovering scriptural grounds for the magistrates' than for the freemen's prerogatives, but he had shown little disposition to frame his material in true resemblance to a Magna Charta. The *Body of Liberties*, in contrast, was concerned primarily, not with the legal articulation of governmental power, but with its limitation, with assertion of "rites, freedomes, [and] Immunities"; and the author(s) pointed out that its provisions were "expressed . . . under the name . . . of Liberties, and not in the exact form of Laws or Statutes."[43]

And if, third, one does find a substantial reception of the parent law both in the *Body of Liberties* and the *Laws and Liberties*, it should not be conceived as a separate and exclusive alternative to biblical law.[44] English judges and legal writers of the late sixteenth and early seventeenth centuries made "habitual" appeal to the Judicials as a source and sanction of law, and this was predictably the more so among men of Puritan persuasion. In fact, much of English law, as the New Englanders knew, either directly or through the more circuitous formulas of natural law, equity, or proportion could be construed, with Edward Coke, as "grounded upon the [Judicial] Law

42. Farrand, ed., *Laws and Liberties*, sig. A2. Pomfret and Shumway argue that the *Body of Liberties* was the joint product of Ward and Cotton; Howe interprets Cotton's compilation as a "thoughtful draft of a code which was taken into account as such by those who did frame the first code" (Pomfret and Shumway, *Founding*, 180; Howe, ed., *Readings*, 182).

43. Cotton, *Abstract*, 2; Nathaniel Ward, *The Massachusetts Body of Liberties*, in Morgan, ed., *Political Ideas*, 202.

44. This seems to be the assumption, for example, of Jules Zanger, "Crime and Punishment in Early Massachusetts," *WMQ*, 3d Ser., XXII (1965), 471.

of God."[45] And as to the alleged meagerness of biblical reference in Massachusetts codes of the 1640s, a different appraisal is indicated in light of the tacit resources of a biblically drilled constituency, as evidenced by cases even in Cotton's compilation where an obvious biblical reference was not identified or where a fitting report of "deductions" based upon consequence and proportion could not be made in the tiny confines of a margin.

Nathaniel Ward prepared the draft that in revised form became the *Body of Liberties*. For about a decade before 1618 Ward had served as "practiser in the . . . common law," but then he joined the ranks of Puritan clergymen and activists who were to run afoul of the Laudian program after 1625. Before his excommunication and deprivation by Laud (1633) he served as the enthusiastic editor of a treatise that urged English magistrates "to renew government to the primitive beauty of it" by recourse to the "originall . . . , Archetype or first draught of Magistracie." That was to be found in the career of Moses, "the greatest Law-giver that ever was," and in the corpus of Mosaic statutes. Hence the good ruler would have "always . . . a Copie of the law of his God before him" and be guided by its "substance" or equity.[46] Later, as minister at Ipswich from 1634 to 1636, Ward presumably took part with the other elders in formulation of the "Modell of Church and Civill Power," with its strong invocation of Mosaic jurisdiction. Then, four years after the adoption of the *Body of Liberties*, we find him insisting that "Popular Liberties," too, are "not of Mans making or giving, but Gods: Man is but to measure them out by Gods Rule."[47]

45. Haskins, *Law and Authority*, 144–145; Goebel, "King's Law," in Flaherty, ed., *Essays*, 92n; Thorp L. Wolford, "The Laws and Liberties of 1648," in Flaherty, ed., *Essays*, 152. Wolford observes that Michael Dalton's *Countrey Justice*, "one of the English treatises ordered by the General Court [to aid in preparation of the *Laws and Liberties*], was typical, citing Biblical authority throughout" (152). John Dykstra Eusden is fully aware of the biblical connections in *Puritans, Lawyers, and Politics in Early Seventeenth-Century New England* (1958; Hamden, Conn., 1968), 123–124. Coke is quoted in Haskins, *Law and Authority*, 144.

46. Samuel Eliot Morison, *Builders of the Bay Colony*, rev. ed. (Boston, 1958), 231; Winthrop, *History*, II, 55; Samuel Ward, *Jethro's Justice of Peace* (London, 1627), 2–4, 37, 63. For Nathaniel Ward's affirmative comments, see the "Epistle Dedicatory" and the brief afterword in *Jethro's Justice*, 71–72.

47. Nathaniel Ward, *The Simple Cobler of Aggawam in America* (1647), ed. P. M. Zall (Lincoln, Nebr., 1969), 48.

If these particulars may be taken as an index of Ward's outlook, and if the General Court's revision of his draft before final passage retained its general character, then the paucity of biblical documentation in the *Body of Liberties* and its many obvious debts to common law should not be taken for evidence of a secular trend in lawmaking. And, indeed, it is biblical law and biblical law alone that is invoked in the *Body of Liberties* as an authoritative source and check. No "custome or prescription" was to be permitted which could be "proved to bee morallie sinfull by the word of god," and in the absence of an "expresse law" covering any criminal case the "defect" was to be remedied by immediate resort to "the word of god." Usury was to be prohibited as "contrarie to the law of god," and the lot of slaves was to be eased by the humane requirements of "the law of god established in Israell."[48]

The Judicials actually are granted an imposing role in the *Body of Liberties*. To begin with, some of its provisions were likely informed by the roundabout deductions from specific statutes that Puritan theory allowed. It is impossible to reconstruct such calculations, but many possible deductive paths from biblical law and equity to Ward's injunctions against deeds and promises "gotten by Illegal violence," against judicial misbehavior, and the like are obvious.[49] Beyond this uncertain realm, however, one encounters readily identifiable formulas taken directly from Mosaic sources. There is, for example, the call for equal standing under law for inhabitants and "forreiners," the limitation of terms of servitude to seven years, and the provision that in intestate cases eldest sons receive a double portion of inheritance.[50] In keeping with the traditional intent of Puritan theory, by far the heaviest draft is drawn upon biblical laws governing serious crime. In this category belong the rule against usury, the provision for mandatory emancipation and compensation of a servant maimed by a master, and, on the side of "liberties," the requirement of two

48. Ward, *Body of Liberties*, in Morgan, ed., *Puritan Political Ideas*, 179, 183, 191, 196. See Deuteronomy 23:19 for the usually cited rule on usury.

49. See, for example, Ward, *Body of Liberties*, in Morgan, ed., *Puritan Political Ideas*, 187, 195, and cf. Deuteronomy 16:18–20 and Deuteronomy 23:15–16, respectively.

50. Ward, *Body of Liberties*, in Morgan, ed., *Puritan Political Ideas*, 179, 194, 196; and cf. Exodus 12:49, Deuteronomy 15:12–13, and Deuteronomy 21:17, respectively. The *Body of Liberties* required double inheritance for eldest sons only in intestate cases.

or more witnesses for conviction under a capital charge and the restriction of flogging to forty stripes.[51]

Yet the Mosaic centerpiece was the list of capital laws. That the list
is shorter than Cotton's, excluding several laws designated capital in
the Old Testament, may arise from the assumption that "no divine
warrant was needed for the infliction of penalties that were *less* severe
than those prescribed in the Bible." But their omission as likely reflected the judgment that those laws lacked a permanent equity, that
is, were tied to the historical circumstances of ancient Israel.[52] Ward's
capital laws, in any case—cast in succinct propositions that were to
be carried over almost verbatim into the code of 1648—included all
those insisted upon by Cartwright, drawn from identified texts in
Exodus, Leviticus, Deuteronomy, and Numbers. Even were they to
provide the sole demonstrable biblical influence in the *Body of Liberties*, the capital laws could not be construed as residual or token in
effect. Their inclusion in a legally enacted code probably marks the
first concrete fruition of Cartwright's original crusade in behalf of the
unchangeable status of those Mosaic penalties whose manifest equity
was not restricted by historical circumstances.[53] Theft, as Perkins,

51. Ward, *Body of Liberties*, in Morgan, ed., *Puritan Political Ideas*, 183, 187,
188, 195–196; and cf. with Deuteronomy 23:19, Exodus 21:26–27, Deuteronomy 19:15, and Deuteronomy 25:3, respectively. The two-witness rule also
was instituted at New Haven (Hoadly, ed., *New Haven*, II, 572). "In England
there were no clear rules as to how many witnesses were needed to prove a
crime," and no standard limit upon the number of lashes to be inflicted for
crimes punishable by whipping (Chapin, *Criminal Justice*, 44–45, 53).

52. Haskins, *Law and Authority*, 151.

53. Isabel MacBeath Calder's widely accepted argument that Cotton's "Moses
His Judicials" was adopted at New Haven in 1639 is unconvincing (*The New
Haven Colony* [Hamden, Conn., 1970], 51, 106; Morgan, ed., *Puritan Political
Ideas*, 178; Haskins, *Law and Authority*, 125). She maintains that Winthrop
sent a transcript of the Cotton code to New Haven in 1638 and that the settlers
promptly adopted it as their "frame of government and code of laws." The New
Haven records state that Winthrop sent a "copy" of "such fundamentals as
were established in Massachusetts by allowance of their patent." It is not clear
that this is a reference to Cotton's code, which was never "established" in the
Bay. But, more important, the records of the initial steps in the formation of
a government for New Haven state simply that "in all publique offices w[hi]ch
concerne C[i]vill order . . . we would all of us be ordered by those rules w[hi]ch
the scripture holds forth to us." This may well reflect Cotton's influence, but
Calder's inference that "this statement could mean only the adoption of the

Ames, and Cotton all had recommended, was not rendered punishable by death; but adultery, unnatural vice, blasphemy, and perjury endangering life—none of them a capital offense in England—now became so.[54]

Turning from the *Body of Liberties*, with its partial embodiment of the antidiscretionary party's drive to define and stabilize colony law, to the main spokesman for magisterial latitude, one discovers no shift away from the Judicials. John Winthrop, whose several contributions to the case for discretion constitute the earliest notable New World exercise in political and legal theory, would show how to reconcile judicial discretion with a vigorous loyalty to the laws of Moses. He offered no dissent from the general position on Mosaic law laid down, for instance, in the "Modell of Church and Civill Power." He openly affirmed "the rules of God's laws" as an essential platform of Christian government. A legal structure for the new colony, strongly rooted in the Judicials, there obviously had to be; but the discretionary interests for whom he spoke—in his words, "most of the magistrates and some of the elders"—wished to coordinate it with a conception of discretionary justice drawn at large from the Old Testament.[55]

That the obligation to appraise the equity of biblical statutes and deduce contemporary applications implied a generous view of magisterial authority was clear to Winthrop from the start. But a more elaborate justification was required than Puritan theorists had as yet

---

frame of government and code of laws drafted by John Cotton" is too confidently stated (Calder, *New Haven*, 51; Hoadly, *New Haven*, I, 12, II, 518, and see I, 130). More specific legislation shaping a frame of government was passed by the New Haven General Court in 1643. It appears to reflect some borrowings from the Cotton code, but, again, Calder's conclusion that it reflected merely a more entire application of the previously adopted "Moses His Judicials" is not justified by the similarities and slights the many differences (Hoadly, *New Haven*, I, 112–116; Calder, *New Haven*, 118–119).

54. Morison, *Builders*, 232. Ward's selection of capital crimes omits 11 included in Cotton's code, a difference which suggests the wide interpretive margin afforded by the formula "according to equity." The *Laws and Liberties* added 3 to Ward's, making 2 separate crimes of Cotton's provision against rebellious children, and adding rape (Ward, *Body of Liberties*, in Morgan, ed., *Puritan Political Ideas*, 197–199; Farrand, ed., *Laws and Liberties*, 5–6).

55. Winthrop, *History*, I, 322–323, II, 57, 229; Winthrop, "On Arbitrary Government," in *WP*, IV, 473, 480.

supplied. For one thing, it was plain that magistracy, as it was instituted in sacred times, required uncommon personal "parts and
gifts." This was written plainly in the careers of Solomon and other
archetypal figures. But to lend this office greater weight, God had
complemented their natural gifts with an extra and supernatural
grace, a "wisdom . . . to do justice." To be sure, biblical judges were
bound by the Judicials, but Winthrop observed that these stated precise penalties only for capital crimes and a few others and that in
some noncapital cases alternative penalties were provided. Also relevant were several extraordinary instances in which capital offenders,
whether through judicial process or otherwise, were not punished
with death, as when "David his life was not taken away for his Adulterye and murder." In fine, Old Testament law and magistracy were
mutually flexible, the one leaving many sentences undefined or variable, the other apportioning penalties to the ever-varying magnitude
and circumstances of individual crimes. Upon occasion an offender's
genuine repentance might also be taken into account. And throughout, the magistrate could attain the unique satisfaction of imitating
the virtuosic "wisdome and mercye of God."[56]

If these conceptions provided a coherent and scripturally validated
alternative to the deputies' legal demands, they were in part directed
to eliciting a fuller and more sophisticated comprehension of the
Judicials. Since Winthrop granted out of hand that Christian magistrates were obliged "to square all their proceedings by the rule
of Gods word," which included all "the Fundamentalls which God
gave, to the Com[mon]w[ealth] of Israel" and certainly the Mosaic
laws, he could assure his opponents that adequate safeguards against
magisterial "tyranny" already were in place. These lay, as Thomas
Hooker disapprovingly expressed it, in the judge's "breast." Judges
were and would be restrained not only by their sense of obligation
to a mythically rooted ordinance but also by their personal intimacy
with biblical law, by their total grasp of its "ground and equity," and
by their sense of the range and "proportion" of punishment embraced
in its many sets of variable penalties.[57]

56. Winthrop, *History*, II, 56–57, 228; Winthrop, "On Arbitrary Government," in *WP*, IV, 474–477 (reference to David, 476).
57. Winthrop, "Further Defense," in *WP*, III, 474; Winthrop, "On Arbitrary
Government," in *WP*, IV, 473; Winthrop, *History*, II, 56, 57; *WP*, IV, 81.

Where some of the deputies clamored for a uniform system of penalties and professed dissatisfaction with the *Body of Liberties* for its failure to fix penalties for all noncapital offenses, Winthrop could warn of the dangerous presumption "to prescribe penaltyes, where God prescribes none."[58] And where, before and even after 1641, anti-discretionary voices called for a more complete enactment of laws covering the usual categories of offense, he could object that, pursuant to a suitable translation of Mosaic standards for the Bay, the needed legal structure should be developed gradually and by instance of actual judicial decisions. In a few pressing cases, as seen in the Bay's adultery law of 1631, these decisions might lead to passage of a covering statute; but ordinarily, as in common law, they simply would be recorded as a point of reference for future cases.[59] In that way, the proper discretionary handling of cases, where the judge followed ways of biblical justice and achieved a relevant and thus wise adaptation of biblical laws, would itself provide the colony's operative criminal law. The two biblical institutions of flexible law and discretionary magistracy simultaneously would then be honored.[60] But if a comprehensive body of laws were enacted, exact penalties affixed to every crime, and judicial latitude thus largely eliminated, the result would be a painful departure from scriptural legality. No magistrate then could achieve a fitting expression of his high office and endowments. Mechanical sentencing would replace the consultation of the relevant Judicials, the calculation of their equity, and the thoughtful search for the "Just Sentence," and the ensuing "contempt and violation" of divine ordinances would bring down covenantal vengeance upon the colony.[61]

58. Winthrop, "On Arbitrary Government," in *WP*, IV, 477.

59. For the adultery statute, see *RMB*, I, 91–92. In the case leading to adoption of the statute, the convicted adulterer was flogged; but further consideration led the General Court, which at this time consisted only of the governor (Winthrop), his deputy, and assistants, to enact a law based squarely on Mosaic statutes defining adultery as a capital offense.

60. Winthrop, *History*, I, 322–323. See also Morgan, *Puritan Dilemma*, 168. This procedure, Winthrop noted, also would avoid putting laws on the books "repugnant to the laws of England" and therefore in violation of the charter (*History*, I, 323).

61. Winthrop, "On Arbitrary Government," in *WP*, IV, 477; Winthrop, *History*, II, 228.

To what degree did actual criminal justice in early Massachusetts embrace the allegiance to Mosaic law and equity variously expressed by Winthrop, the *Body of Liberties*, and the ministers? Records of court actions from the period seldom provide data beyond a brief statement of charge and sentence. But we have seen how Winthrop, whose preeminence in the early Bay magistracy is a matter of record, viewed the pondering of biblical law as integral to the judicial task; and collateral report in his journal upon actions of special interest or seriousness gives us a glimpse into a background of intense and direct biblicist concern.

Since 1636, Bay magistrates had been pledged by action of the General Court to "proceede in the courts . . . according to the lawes nowe established, and where there is noe law, then as neere the lawe of God as they can." On several occasions the Court called upon the clergy to perform the approximate function of a state's attorney in disputed cases, and in their opinions they cited biblical laws and precedents, not English law.[62] Certainly there are scattered signs in the records of direct reliance upon the Judicials, a reliance that at times contributed to striking departures from English practice.[63] Massachusetts' handling of theft, which is regulated in Mosaic law but did not come under statutory rule in the Bay until 1646, is an instructive example. In English justice, "grand larceny" involving property more than twelve pennies in value was a hanging offense in the early seventeenth century; pilferage of goods less than twelve pennies in value was punishable by flogging. But as the General Court explained in 1646 in response to a group of petitioners demanding wholesale

62. *RMB*, I, 174–175; Edwin Powers, *Crime and Punishment in Early Massachusetts, 1620–1692: A Documentary History* (Boston, 1966), 512. For an example, see *RMB*, II, 90–95. Taking a stronger position, the General Court of New Haven in 1644 "ordered that the judicial laws of God . . . shall be accounted . . . a rule to all the courts in this jurisdiction . . . till they be branched out into particulars hereafter" (Hoadly, ed., *New Haven*, I, 130).

63. Haskins presents an excellent general analysis of the trend in *Law and Authority*, 137, 141–162. In 1647, the General Court cited Exodus 21:36 and 22:5 in support of a law regulating fencing and branding of livestock (*RMB*, II, 190). For discussion of the Court's probable use of texts from Numbers, Deuteronomy, and 1 Chronicles in devising rules for the descent of lands to all children, see George L. Haskins, "The Beginnings of Partible Inheritance in the American Colonies," *Yale Law Journal*, LI (1941–1942), 1309–1311. Common law required descent of land to the eldest son.

adoption of English law, theft was not and would not be punished in the English manner in the Puritan colony "because we read otherwise in the Scripture."[64] Presumably what most of the magistrates had read in Scripture on the subject of theft corroborated Winthrop's general analysis of Mosaic penalties. The pertinent judicials express no uniform punishment. Two statutes state no penalty, while at least three others require varying degrees of multiple restitution ranging from one and one-fifth to fivefold; and one empowers the judge to order offenders unable to pay to be sold into slavery, the sale price providing restitution to the injured party.[65]

These provisions, interpreted in the tradition of Cartwright and in the light of discretionary theory, mark out approximately the penal range within which the colonial magistrates actually operated. A review of the records of the Court of Assistants (Boston) and the Quarterly Courts of Essex County (Salem) for the earliest period reveals the magistrates' imposing diverse punishments upon persons convicted of stealing, including time in the stocks and bilbos, whipping, and fines. The public wearing of a "paper" descriptive of the crime and degradation from the rank of gentleman were also imposed.[66]

Yet these measures were secondary to the standard biblical punishment: restitution. English law required restitution in a limited set of property crimes, like willful destruction, but in Massachusetts during the first two decades it functioned as the normative penalty for theft.

---

64. Michael Dalton, *The Countrey Justice . . .* , 5th ed. (London, 1635), 252–259; Hutchinson, *Papers,* I, 233. Massachusetts laws of 1642 and 1647 mandated the death penalty for a third conviction of theft (Farrand, ed., *Laws and Liberties,* 4–5). The Bay also limited flogging to 40 stripes, a rule "of biblical origin, not present in the common law" (Wolford, "Laws and Liberties," in Flaherty, ed., *Essays,* 167). Elimination of the death penalty for petty theft probably owed something as well to the contemporary English effort to make law more rational and humane and to concern about scarcity of labor in the colony (Chapin, *Criminal Justice,* 9).

65. Leviticus 6:1–5, 19:13; Deuteronomy 24:14–15; Exodus 22:1–4; Numbers 5:5–8. Restitution through sale of the offender is required by Exodus 22:1–4.

66. John Noble and John F. Cronin, eds., *Records of the Court of Assistants of the Colony of the Massachusetts Bay, 1630–1692,* 3 vols. (Boston, 1901–1928), II, 9, 13, 19, 53; George Francis Dow, ed., *Records and Files of the Quarterly Courts of Essex County, Massachusetts,* 8 vols. (Salem, Mass., 1911–1921), I, 18, 51, 59.

It was the most frequent punishment assigned. The other penalties mentioned above often were combined with restitution. Whipping generally was imposed as a substitute when the thief was unable to make restitution, and in an evident adaptation of the judicial directing destitute thieves to be sold for compensation, theft by a servant from his master occasionally was punished by restitution in the form of an extension of term of service.[67] Taken collectively, this wide array of sentences reveals that the magistrates adapted penal decisions to the nature and measure of the fault in the manner espoused by Winthrop. But it also shows that the magistrates turned to the Judicials for fitting modes of punishment. In their break with the long-established definition of theft as a capital "felony" and in their employment of graded variations upon restitution, they exhibited an immediacy of recourse to sacred rules that had infrequent precedent in English practice.[68]

Overt Mosaic priorities as well as a demonstration of the difficulties of adapting Moses to Massachusetts also were evident in the response of the General Court to an extraordinary series of sexual offenses that came to light in 1641. Several instances of "uncleanness" were discovered and brought to trial in rapid succession, causing some alarm among political and clerical leaders ever mindful of threats to their community's safety under the terms of the National Covenant. In four cases involving fornication, child rape, and bestiality, supplemental comment in Winthrop's History enables us again to appreciate the primary role assigned in Massachusetts to the permanent Judicials. Winthrop's synopses, if we may assume their accuracy, reveal the courts carrying out literally the directive of 1636. Since none of the present crimes was as yet covered by colony statute, they were without exception decided in deference to "express law in the word of God." Thus a servant witnessed by a citizen of Salem "in

67. On restitutions, see Noble and Cronin, eds., *Court of Assistants*, II, 19, 32, 83, 118, for example; Dow, ed., *Records and Files*, I, 25, 38, 57, 84, among others; and see Haskins, *Law and Authority*, 153. On alternatives to and variants on restitution, see Haskins, *Law and Authority*, 153–154 and the sources cited there. For a New Haven case of theft in which the magistrates imposed double restitution "according to the law of God, in that case," see Hoadly, ed., *New Haven*, I, 51.

68. The magistrates' power to vary penalties for common theft was reduced by an ordinance enacted in 1646 that prescribed treble restitution for most offenses (*RMB*, II, 100; Farrand, ed., *Laws and Liberties*, 5).

buggery with a cow" was dealt with in accord with Leviticus 20:15. He was to hang, and the cow to be "brought forth and slain before him" moments before the execution.[69] Yet equally revealing is the regularity with which "there arose a question" or "a difficulty arose" as circumstantial variations from express law were encountered. Not even the buggery case could be settled on a straightforward basis, for although Old Testament law clearly defines bestiality as a capital offense, it also requires, as noted above, more than one witness for a capital conviction. Only after much debate was the Court able to agree that the accused's own confession fulfilled the requirement of a second witness and thus met the biblical standard.[70]

Problems of yet greater moment surfaced in the two cases of child rape. At common law, rape of a female under ten years of age was a felony punishable by death, but rape is nowhere defined as a capital offense in the Old Testament.[71] Yet when outraged opinion on the Court leaned toward the death penalty, it was articulated in entire keeping with existing Puritan theory. In order to establish a credible "proportion" that would sustain the extreme penalty, proponents argued that "by the equity of the law against sodomy [Leviticus 20:13] . . . it should be death, for a man to have carnal copulation with a girl so young, as there can be no possibility of generation, for it is against nature as well as sodomy." Child rape, that is, being as much against nature as sodomy, reasonably could be drawn under the same rule. Again, in the more aggravated of the cases, which involved the abuse of two girls seven and nine years of age by three men over an extended period of time, members of the Court debated whether sexual contact short of penetration but producing ejaculation could be brought under the judicial on sodomy. They also considered whether a sin not capital under biblical statutes, yet committed in flagrant and continuous disregard of established law and authority, might not be construed as "presumptious capital si[n], as Deut. 17:12," and thereby be punishable by death.[72]

---

69. Winthrop, *History*, II, 46, 48–50; *RMB*, I, 339, 344. For a New Haven case of bestiality described in appeal to the "everlasting equity" of Leviticus 20:15, see Hoadly, ed., *New Haven*, I, 69.

70. Winthrop, *History*, II, 37, 48–50. For another case of buggery not punished by death, see Noble, ed., *Court of Assistants*, II, 121. The reduced penalty apparently resulted from failure to prove penetration.

71. Haskins, *Law and Authority*, 150.

72. Winthrop, *History*, II, 38, 47.

For assistance in deciding these issues the Court conducted a survey of clerical opinions in the Bay, New Haven, New Plymouth, and Connecticut. The three surviving responses, including one by Charles Chauncy, are formulated in reference to "the judicials of Moses that are appendances to the moral law, and grounded on the law of nature, or the Decalogue," as well as to estimation of their relevance to "cases . . . which are not in so many words extant in Holy Writ, yet the substance of the matter . . . may be drawn . . . out of the Scripture by good consequence."[73] In an independent statement Thomas Shepard agreed "that we are to proportion out the punishment . . . from the Judicialls of Moses." By Winthrop's report a majority of the ministers opposed the death penalty, and for the moment it was concluded that the death sentence probably exceeded the measure of scriptural punishment in cases of rape; hence the offenders were sentenced to flogging, fines, and other punishments. Yet later in the year the Court passed a law declaring rape of a female under ten years (the common law formula) a capital offense. Presumably this reflected further consideration of the "equity of the laws against sodomy" and perhaps of the nature of "presumptious capital si[n]" as defined by Deuteronomy.[74]

As they pondered adjustments of the two-witness rule, the equity of the judicial against sodomy and its proportion to child rape, or the dimensions of "presumptious capital si[n]," the colonists were taking their place among the first Puritans practically to endeavor to apply the circuitous procedures of deduction outlined by Cartwright, Perkins, and others. It was a pioneering effort, attended with many uncertainties. John Winthrop was moved to prepare "a discourse . . . concerning Fornication, Rape etc."; extensive consultations with the

73. Charles Chauncy, in "Opinions of Three Ministers on Unnatural Vice, 1642," appendix 10 of William Bradford, *Of Plymouth Plantation, 1620–1647*, ed. Samuel Eliot Morison (New York, 1952), 408, 411; [Thomas Shepard?], "A Breefe Answer to a Breefe Discourse concerning the Punishment of Theft, Single Fornication, Rape, etc. . . ." [1642?], 263, Shepard Family Papers, Massachusetts Historical Society, Boston. Chauncy claimed that "all orthodox divines" acknowledged that some of the Judicials were "immutable and perpetual." Yet the claim is not supported by the passage from Calvin's *Institutes* that Chauncy cites as evidence (408).

74. *RMB*, II, 214; see Haskins, *Law and Authority*, 151, for commentary. For the Court's adaptation of the judicial upon fornication to a varying situation, see Winthrop, *History*, II, 37; see also 249–250.

clerical synod were held.[75] The fact was, as Thomas Shepard explained, that by following biblical direction in part beyond the range of established English law and practice, the colonists had entered upon "untroden paths [because] . . . the whole Christian woorld hath hitherto not attended to Moses Judicialls as th[eir] rule, and therefore have bin wanting to cleare up th[eir] proportions."[76] To clear up the proportions, to plot the reach of equity, to make the sometimes fine calculations and inferences necessary to bring covenant-jeopardizing crime more firmly within Mosaic regulation—these were the challenges taken up in earnest by magisterial authority in early Massachusetts.

The materials surveyed above reflect a common assumption that removal to a far-flung colony had cleared the way to a more complete recovery of Mosaic legality as interpreted in the tradition of Cartwright. This assumption set Massachusetts and the other Puritan colonies clearly apart from Rhode Island, whose sundry Seekers, Gortonists, and antinomians rejected the precedential authority of the Old Testament and adapted their colony's code of 1647 largely from English digests and statutes. At no time did Bay officials repudiate the constraints placed upon lawmaking by their charter. No more than Cartwright did they repudiate the traditional belief that biblical law was the moral anchor of most existing law. Hence, in response to criticism from abroad, they hastened to attest allegiance to English law, and while preparing the *Laws and Liberties* they procured and consulted legal texts in current use in England. Throughout they drew both instinctively and extensively upon their legal heritage.

But often enough—if largely in the area of criminal law—they felt free to modify it where Mosaic issues seemed at stake. They could not, with Sir Edward Coke, maintain the inviolable sanctity of common law. At least in some particulars, it too was to be brought to the biblical touchstone. The colony's growing legal corpus thus can

75. Winthrop, *History*, II, 46. See also his reference to "the advice of the elders" in the former case (48). Winthrop's discourse apparently is not extant.

76. *WP*, IV, 345. The position taken in "A Breefe Answer," apparently a contemporary critique of Winthrop's discourse, was that "the moral equity of all Moses' Judicials, compared one with another do best proportion out punishment for all commonwealths to walk by" ([Shepard?], "A Breefe Answer," 263, Shepard Family Papers, MHS).

be seen as a new and distinct creation that made generous use of legal tradition but brought to bear upon it the characteristic Puritan "zeal to reform every aspect of human activity." In the eyes of Thomas Lechford, a lawyer and devotee of common law who resided uneasily in the Bay from 1638 to 1641, the colonists' reformist approach to English law understandably seemed radical. He was disconcerted at their readiness "to flight all former laws . . . to go hammer out new, according to several exigencies; upon pretense that the Word of God is sufficient to rule us."[77] "New," however, is exactly what the legal venture was not, if seen from the perspective of a Cotton, Ward, or Winthrop. Neither Haskins nor Lechford fully appreciated the special value Puritans attached to acts of recovery. The appeal to "Moses His Judicials" in fact bespoke a desire to revolve the legal order back to harmony with ancient norms.

Predictably, the ideal of re-form dominated Massachusetts' definitive statement upon the subject of law, the eloquent preface to the final synthesis achieved by the codification movement. In this wonderfully succinct summary of colony principles attached to the *Laws and Liberties* and in closely worded formulations reflecting compromise of delegative and discretionary interests, the need for a detailed compilation of laws was affirmed. Many of these laws, like those regulating the weights of bread or the fixing of town boundaries, stood outside the range of biblical concern. Many were drafted in large or entire reliance upon the parent law, and most bore the mark of American experience. And yet the aim of the preface was to direct the reader back to the legal forms of ancient Israel. Users of the code were to understand that behind and lending resonance to the entire enterprise was the body of laws given by Moses. The principles of right embodied in those laws "were . . . so full and comprehensive as out of them clear deductions were to be drawne to all particular cases in future times." For this reason the General Court had called upon Cotton and others of the clergy to prepare "a modell of the Judiciall lawes of Moses." Their assignment had been to make apparent the tenets of biblical legality that the English settlers, in close identification with the first chosen nation, were to have in mind as they

---

77. Haskins, *Law and Authority*, 191 (see also Eusden, "Natural Law," *Natural Law Forum*, V [1960], 13–16); Thomas Lechford, *Plain Dealing . . .* , ed. J. Hammond Trumbull (Boston, 1867), 68.

managed their own medley of "particular cases."[78] Thus the present collection included many an adaptive deduction from Mosaic principle, and thus it was a display of ingenuity deployed in adjustment to the historical present and the foreseeable future.

Here too, then, was a formula for progress in reformation, for a resilient response to shifting community needs. But that response was bounded by the primitive ordinance of magistracy; it was securely anchored in the ageless and wide-reaching equity of the laws of Moses. In this sense the future was comprehended already in the primitive statutes; it was to be secured only as it might be "drawn out of" and hence continually tied back to the first matrix of human law. These ideas, of course, merely recapitulated positions long since taken by Protestants from Bucer to Winthrop (whose thought has been reviewed); but it is important to grasp that the makers of the compilation of 1648 consciously worked "to the end that [the colony's code] might be most agreeable with the rule of Scripture."[79]

Again, then, one finds the Puritan element in early New England bound up with orientations to the scriptural primordium. It is only fair to observe that the resort to "equity" was a more roundabout transaction with the first than was the direct, wholesale imitation endeavored by the authors of the Cambridge Platform. But does one, then, only discover a present-minded legal pragmatism that did more to dilute than to honor the larger program of restitution? Such a conclusion would slight the greater context of concerns within which "Moses His Judicials" became a keynote of reform. The ferment of interest in moral and primitive purity did give rise

78. Farrand, ed., *Laws and Liberties*, sig. A2. The meaning of the preface is made clearer by Cotton's commentary in *WP*,V, 193. For a similar presentation, see the foreword to the 1658 revision of the laws of New Plymouth: David Pulsifer, ed., *Records of the Colony of New Plymouth*, 12 vols. (Boston, 1861), XI, 72–73. The Massachusetts compilers' reliance upon English law is discussed in Haskins, *Law and Authority*, 134–135.

79. Farrand, ed., *Laws and Liberties*, sig. A2; *WWP*, 244. For an excellent analysis of the *Laws and Liberties*, see Haskins, *Law and Authority*, 132–162. Yet Haskins's assertions that "the Bible . . . was an indispensable touchstone, but not the cornerstone" of distinctively "Puritan legal thinking," or that in the realm of law and politics as understood by "the Puritan mind" it was "not . . . the fountainhead and authority which it was for theology, but . . . the confirmation . . . of rational conclusions drawn from natural premises," do not report accurately the settlers' conscious outlook (162).

to radical spirits like Henry Barrow. But with the overwhelming majority of nonseparating dissenters through the Elizabethan and Tudor decades, Cartwright and Perkins, Cotton, and Winthrop were realistic reformers in the spirit of magisterial Protestantism. In their role as Presbyterian or Congregational advocates, they would allow no conscious alteration of apostolic forms in order to fit sixteenth- or seventeenth-century circumstances, but in fact they intended no disruption of English life. Their ecclesiastical programs were not impossibly alien to existing society. Of this, New England stood forth as proof.

But the Mosaic legislation presented a different case. It included countless obsolete and inapplicable elements: "cities of refuge," polygamy, cancellation of debts every seventh year, allowance of defecation "outside the camp," permission to forage in a neighbor's vineyard or grain field. The wholesale adoption of such statutes was a blatantly absurd prospect and one associated with the Protestant lunatic fringe. In this perspective, the appeal to equity was a tactical boon to the aims of restoration. By proclaiming a profounder grasp of their intent, it neutralized the literal irrelevance of most of the Hebrew laws. It made it possible to remain within the magisterial mainstream, to accept the broad lineaments of present society and law, and yet to expand the biblical claim.

Further, the tying of concern for legal reform specifically to the Judicials was a strong move to the left within Reformed divinity. Going beyond the position of Calvin, Bullinger, and Whitgift, it affirmed a definite, urgent role for the Judicials in the shaping and management of a Christian state. If, with few exceptions, equity was an elusive quality of the scriptural statutes, it was written much clearer there than in the natural law dimly intelligible to human reason; and it remained a gift of the primordium, of covenanted Israel and the towering figure of Moses.

Hence the repeated avowal, "All good laws and order enacted in any place by men are either expressly mentioned in the word, or are to be collected and deducted from the word," however imperfectly realized, was a genuine carrier of the Puritan impulse. It did encourage Winthrop and his colleagues to order their legislative and judicial responsibilities in reference to first times. Furthermore, through its appeal to originative pattern, it enjoined as well the familiar restraints of the Protestant epistemology. New Englanders were no proponents of a Lutheran "Christian liberty" pursuing "bold new lawmaking" beyond the framework of biblical statutes.[80] Mosaic equity, an emanation of unchanging divine order, must overrule the frail and mutable exercises of the human mind. Upon this point, definers of the Puritan way like Cartwright and Perkins had been explicit: the equity of the Judicials was "constant, and everlasting . . . perfecter . . . then [anything] the forge off mans reason . . . is able to devise." This was a note often sounded in Massachusetts, in Winthrop's blast against fixed penalties grounded only upon "human Aut[hority] or Invention," in Shepard's reminder to his Cambridge congregation that the minds of men can be trusted to frame laws only through strict collection and application of "the general rules, recorded in Scripture," and in Cotton's oft-quoted assertion, made during the clerical debate over the Judicials, that "the more any law smells of man the more unprofitable."[81] In all these utterances the Reformed claim upon society at large is in evidence, but their strategic standard is primitivist, summoning the colonists back to accord with the first, the perfect, and unalterable.

Those familiar with medieval legal concepts will recognize here a harking back to the "declaratory" concept of lawmaking. If the "essential characteristic of medieval government was that it discovered the law" (given in Scripture and the natural law) "and then administered it, while modern government first makes and then administers laws," the difficulty of a too hasty modernization of the New England pioneers again becomes apparent.[82] Indeed, one may see a progressive element in their break with any mere traditionary or authoritarian appeal to established law. Stretching their charter's prohibition of legislation contrary to the laws and statutes of En-

---

80. Shepard, *Works*, III, 346 (see also *CC*, 142); *WP*, V, 192–193; Eusden, "Natural Law," *Natural Law Forum*, V (1960), 8. Eusden's presentation overlooks the moralist and conditionalist features of English Protestant theology from the time of Tyndale and imputes a Lutheran conception of "christian liberty" to Reformed-Puritan theology.

81. Cartwright, *Second Replie*, 97, and see Perkins, *Work of Perkins*, ed. Breward, 489. *WP*, IV, 475; Shepard, *Works*, III, 346–347; "How Far Moses' Judicials Bind Mass[achusetts]," MHS, *Proceedings*, 2d Ser., XVI (Boston, 1902), 284.

82. G. R. Elton, *England under the Tudors* (London, 1955), 168. See also Haskins, *Law and Authority*, 123; and Christopher Morris, *Political Thought in England: Tyndale to Hooker* (London, 1953), 77.

gland beyond fair limits, at times the colonists treated English law as plastic and modifiable to their distinct social and religious program. Perhaps a modern note obtrudes as well in the magistracy's concept of the adaptive potential of judicial office, although it continued therein a trend already established in English law.[83] But none of this was cast in simple future tense. More than one motive may have impelled Winthrop to urge a discretionary role for his colony's judiciary, but his professed wish was to hew the nearer to Hebrew example. Reform, as always, was re-form. From the time of Cartwright to the founding two decades of New England, Puritan concepts of legal reform were organized around a consistent principal aim—to retrieve and apply the legal standards unfolded in Old Testament narrative—for in those standards every modern exigency, through the measure of equity, already was embraced.

83. Haskins, *Law and Authority*, 122.

SIX

FIRST

PHASES OF

PURITAN

MILLENNIALISM

*D*uring the latter 1970s and the 1980s the American Puritans' Errand into the Wilderness was remodeled along eschatological lines. Scholarly agreement mushroomed upon the proposition that the Massachusetts Bay project presented yet another chapter in Western Christianity's periodic pursuit of the millennium. In particular, it was argued that anticipation of both an "apocalyptic firestorm" in England and a New World millennium formed a principal motive of the Great Migration of the 1630s and that the notable trends in early American Congregational practice were millennially inspired. And with the attention of the founders now found riveted upon a revolutionary future, their Errand can be described as the critically important first embodiment of the millennial role that, in one handy summary, "was progressively attributed to the Puritan gathered church, to New England as the land of promise, . . . to American Protestantism, and finally to the American nation."[1]

1. Michael Eugene Mooney, "Millennialism and Antichrist in New England, 1630–1760" (Ph.D. diss., Syracuse University, 1982), 94; Leonard I. Sweet, "Millennialism in America: Recent Studies," *Theological Studies*, XL (1979), 528.

Given the discussion thus far of classic Puritan thought, it is worth considering whether such theses reveal as much as they obscure. This and the following two chapters will extend the argument of Chapter 4 into the eschatological future. They will present evidence, first, that millennial hope was a far more modest factor in early American Puritan theology than usually assumed and, second, that Puritan millennialism in its formative phases generated hope for the future primarily by refocusing *retro*spective priorities.

In the earlier inventory of reasons underlying the Great Migration, no evidence appeared that the migrants were in flight from an expected eschatological calamity. It is clear that events in England and on the Continent during the later 1620s provoked prominent Puritans, including John Winthrop, Thomas Hooker, Francis Higginson, Charles Chauncy, Richard Mather, and other future New Englanders to dire prediction that England soon was to be scourged: the country probably would be subjected to "the calamities of a war" with Catholic invaders and likely "destroyed" in the issue.[2] What is questionable is, not that these beliefs were held and expressed by many Puritan leaders or that they helped motivate the transit to a far colony, but that they were basically and consistently eschatological in type and envisioned the current turmoil of the Thirty Years' War and the coming devastation of England as constituting or immediately portending the apocalyptic prelude to a millennial age.

A review of the texts commonly cited in this connection yields a different picture. In the first place, their conceptual starting point is not eschatology, but, rather, the traditional Deuteronomic patterns of the National Covenant.[3] That England, by her persistent failure to accomplish thorough reformation, was "tempting" Providence to inflict punishment had been a favorite theme of Puritan publicists for decades. Now with a cumulative series of additional apostasies adding

2. Francis Higginson, quoted in Cotton Mather, *Magnalia Christi Americana*, ed. Thomas Robbins, 2 vols. (New York, 1853), I, 361.

3. See, for example, Richard Mather, "Arguments Tending to Prove the Removing from Old England to New . . . to Be Not Onley Lawful, but Also Necessary . . . ," in Increase Mather, *The Life and Death . . . of Richard Mather* (Cambridge, 1670), 17–18; Thomas Hooker, "The Danger of Desertion," in George H. Williams *et al.*, eds., *Thomas Hooker: Writings in England and Holland, 1626–1633*, Harvard Theological Studies, XXVIII (Cambridge, Mass., 1975), 228–252; John Cotton, *Gods Promise to His Plantations* (1630), 9, in *Old South Leaflets* (Boston, n.d.), III, no. 53; WP, II, 91, 138.

to covenantal anxiety, the striking success of anti-Protestant forces in the first phases of the Thirty Years' War made apparent the probable immediate agency of providential ire. Clearly, what most Puritan commentators of the 1620s expected was a Catholic military invasion. This was the "plague" that already had visited La Rochelle, the Palatinate, and other continental Protestant strongholds.[4] Since reconquest invariably was followed by forcible re-Catholicization, one well might speak of a "desolation." But to equate this forecast simply with eschatology, whether millennial or not, stretches the evidence unacceptably.

Richard Mather, for one, announced about 1635 his resolve to "remove from a place where [there] are fearful signs of Desolation" to the New England sanctuary. Several historians have construed this in straight apocalyptic terms, but it is difficult to see why. Mather's amplification of the point appealed fundamentally to the Deuteronomic pattern that stood at the heart of the National Covenant. An "abundance of sin and sinners," a "general security," and the like were certain to bring upon England, as already upon other nations and principalities, "God's wrathful Judgments." Mather obviously had in mind a Catholic invasion, an event that he thought might bring about a state of affairs comparable to the captivity of Judah in ancient Babylonia or perhaps the destruction of Sodom. Throughout, Mather's interpretive orientation pointed *back* to biblical event and cited mythic examples of flight to avoid adversity. There was no impulse forward to focus upon the impending desolation and its possible function within a final eschatological schedule.[5]

The same is true of John Winthrop, who spoke of a nearing "scourge" of convenantal retribution. He, too, obviously had in

4. For decades Protestant reverses on the Continent had been understood in covenantal terms by English churchmen. See, for example, *AM*, IV, 23; John Foxe, *A Sermon of Christ Crucified* (London, 1570), sig. Aiii.

5. Richard Mather, "Arguments," in Increase Mather, *Richard Mather*, 12–19. J. F. Maclear, "New England and the Fifth Monarchy: The Quest for the Millennium in Early American Puritanism," *WMQ*, 3d Ser., XXXII (1975), 230; Robert Middlekauff, *The Mathers: Three Generations of Puritan Intellectuals, 1596–1728* (London, 1971), 22–23; and Stephen J. Stein, "Transatlantic Extension: Apocalyptic in Early New England," in C. A. Patrides and Joseph Wittreich, eds., *The Apocalypse in English Renaissance Thought and Literature: Patterns, Antecedents, and Repercussions* (Manchester, 1984), 267, all assume that Mather's concern was eschatological.

view an extension of Catholic military successes to England, which now stood before the "like judgement" that already had befallen many European Protestants. Obviously, the subjugation of England would mean the "general destruction" of English Protestantism. But Winthrop, like Mather, did not load the anticipated event with eschatological meaning. The vials, the scrolls, the trumpets, the beasts of prophetic speculation do not appear, and the relation of covenantal punishment to the final events of history is left undetermined. His tentative suggestion that a colony of refugees withdrawn to New England might be able to "returne after the storme" and perform some "future service" is ambiguous, but it was consistent with covenantal doctrine for Winthrop to expect that the Catholic conquest would be but a finite interval (the captivity of Judah, as he noted, had lasted seventy years) followed by Protestant resurgence.[6] If Mather, Winthrop, and certain other founding emigrants were driven to New England partly by fear of Catholic invasion, their concern is referable primarily to a belief in the Deuteronomic structure of England's National Covenant, and much less evidently to an alleged "preoccupation with the Last Things" of apocalyptic prophecy.[7]

6. *WP*, II, 91, 111–112, 125. A "return after the storm" would be a plausible development within a millennial context, of course; but there is no additional evidence known to me showing that Winthrop by 1629–1630 had become a convert to millennial doctrine. No trace of it appears in the "Model." He once expressed hope that the Bay project would "helpe on the comminge of the fullnesse of the Gentiles"; but, as shown below, this motif is no automatic index of millennial belief (*WP*, II, 138).

7. Maclear, "Fifth Monarchy," *WMQ*, 3d Ser., XXXII (1975), 230. For a general survey of Puritan commentary upon the contemporary Catholic threat, see Marvin A. Breslow, *A Mirror of England: English Puritan Views of Foreign Nations, 1618–1640* (Cambridge, Mass., 1970). The author finds that the "fundamental historical metaphor" employed was the covenantal "image of England as Israel." The leading aim was to provoke a return to covenantal obedience, thus securing England's "restoration to God's favor." Breslow also shows that the severity of the European conflict and of the anticipated assault upon England led to an "*almost* apocalyptic vision" of events. In the dark hours of Protestant defeat, Puritan writers drew consolation from prophetic predictions of the ultimate overthrow of Antichrist at Armageddon, but they did not identify the present struggle *as* Armageddon. In his treatment of future New Englanders, Breslow makes no claim that they placed a literally apocalyptic interpretation upon the European war. *Mirror of England*, 140, 142, 146–152 (italics are mine); for comment on future New Englanders, see 41, 114. Cotton's simple asser-

A second popular contention plays upon the positive dimension of early seventeenth-century millennialism. Here the fearful prospect of national setback or ruin is held to be counterpoised by the hope of a subsequent earthly transformation. Assuming outright that "millenarian fervor" is a generically Puritan trait and was peculiarly concentrated among Puritan emigrants to New England, a number of writers have identified millennial aspiration as a chief cause of the Great Migration. The Puritan settlers now are found purposing to "anticipate the coming era when the saints would reign." One prominent scholar even insists that a note of "millenarianism rang through Winthrop's image of New England as 'a City upon a Hill.' " The line of interpretation climaxes in the thesis that the New Englanders perceived themselves as founders of the millennium. They now are depicted as setting forth to "build a New Jerusalem . . . on the shores of North America." A theme so striking hardly could be lost upon the journalists. In a 1982 article summarizing the newer scholarship, *Newsweek* maintained flatly that "John Winthrop and his fellow Puritans . . . saw themselves as . . . destined . . . to found a 'city upon a hill' which, come the millennium, would see the historical Boston transformed into the eschatological 'New Jerusalem.' " The discussion here will provide little support for such claims. There is no question that millennial ideas were in vogue about 1640 and thereafter, but what of their role as a "selective factor drawing many eschatologically sensitive Puritans to the New World" and flavoring events and ideas during the earlier period?[8] The approach to an

---

tion that Christians may take flight "when some grievous sinnes overspread a Country that threaten desolation" likewise derives from standard Deuteronomic conviction, as does Shepard's concern for "national sins, which shortly bring national, and most heavy plagues" (Cotton, *Gods Promise*, 9; Thomas Shepard, *The Works of Thomas Shepard*, 3 vols. [Boston, 1853], I, 331). In his *Parable of the Ten Virgins*, Shepard referred to the already accomplished "desolation" of many continental Protestant centers as plain examples of covenantal punishment (*Works*, II, 244, 435–436).

8. David D. Hall, "Understanding the Puritans," in Herbert J. Bass, ed., *The State of American History* (Chicago, 1970), 341; Maclear, "Fifth Monarchy," *WMQ*, 3d Ser., XXXII (1975), 230; David D. Hall, *The Faithful Shepherd: A History of the New England Ministry in the Seventeenth Century* (Chapel Hill, N.C., 1972), 150; Paul Christianson, *Reformers and Babylon: English Apocalyptic Visions from the Reformation to the Eve of the Civil War* (Toronto, 1978), 135; Kenneth L. Woodward and David Gates, "How the Bible Made

answer properly begins with an overview of backgrounds in English eschatological thought.

Thomas Brightman, the Middle Advent, and the Rise of Puritan Millennialism

Within English Puritan circles, the "seminal influence" in the seventeenth-century shift toward the millennial concept was exerted by Thomas Brightman (1562–1607), whose innovative interpretation first appeared in commentaries on Revelation, Daniel, and Canticles between 1609 and 1616. Much misunderstanding of New England ideas has grown from the failure to appreciate the full novelty of Brightman's position among English Protestants of the early seventeenth century. Terminological looseness is partly to blame; consumers of research in the field virtually find it necessary to develop a private glossary of discrepant usages of the term "millennial" (or "millenarian").[9] Here, the term *millennial* will signify an

America," *Newsweek*, Dec. 27, 1982, 46. See also Charles L. Sanford, *The Quest for Paradise: Europe and the American Moral Imagination* (Urbana, Ill., 1961), 73, 81; J. A. de Jong, *As the Waters Cover the Sea: Millennial Expectations in the Rise of Anglo-American Missions, 1640–1810* (Kampen, 1970), 29–30; Robert G. Clouse, "The Rebirth of Millenarianism," in Peter Toon, ed., *Puritans, the Millennium, and the Future of Israel: Puritan Eschatology, 1600 to 1660* (Cambridge, 1970), 55; Mason I. Lowance, Jr., *The Language of Canaan: Metaphor and Symbol in New England from the Puritans to the Transcendentalists* (Cambridge, Mass., 1980), 117–118, 130, 134; Cecelia Tichi, *New World, New Earth: Environmental Reform in American Literature from the Puritans through Whitman* (New Haven, Conn., 1979), 15–18; Charles M. Segal and David C. Stineback, eds. *Puritans, Indians, and Manifest Destiny* (New York, 1977), 105; Avihu Zakai, " 'Epiphany at Matadi': Perry Miller's *Orthodoxy in Massachusetts* and the Meaning of American History," *Reviews in American History*, XIII (1985), 638–639. The idea that "in early New England . . . the orthodoxy . . . [was] anticipating [the millennium's] advent in America itself " is a staple of the writings of Sacvan Bercovitch (see "Typology in Puritan New England: The Williams-Cotton Controversy Reassessed," *American Quarterly*, XIX [1967], 180; and *The American Jeremiad* [Madison, Wis., 1978], 42).

9. Maclear, "Fifth Monarchy," *WMQ*, 3d Ser., XXXII (1975), 227. See also William M. Lamont, *Godly Rule: Politics and Religion, 1603–60* (London, 1969), 94–96. On terminological confusion, see Richard Bauckham, *Tudor Apocalypse* (Oxford, 1978), 208; Christianson, *Reformers and Babylon*, 7. See also Bryan W. Ball, *A Great Expectation: Eschatological Thought in English*

imminent, collective, enduring transformation of the human condition within history. Temporal agencies (preachers and theologians, princes and armies) might be enlisted, but only as auxiliary to a massive intrusion of supernatural power. No mere improvement on the present, there was to be a partial transcendence of the normal imperfections of man's estate.[10] Brightman inherited from John Bale, John Foxe, and other prophetic theorists of the preceding era the assumption that the book of Revelation supplies an inclusive calendar of redemptive history from the primitive church to the Second Coming. But the pivotal and distinctively *millennial* inference toward which he directed this older dispensationalism, in sharp contrast with dominant sixteenth-century concepts, was that for an extended interval before the end of history the world was partially to realize the Heavenly Kingdom.[11]

Novel as it was from predominant earlier standpoints within Reformed divinity, Brightman's conception of a transfigured historical life built upon trends in English thought already evident by the turn of the century. Traditional prophetic commentary projected a pessimistic prospectus of the end times, in which inimical forces unceasingly were to challenge Protestant fortunes until an abrupt and all-destroying display of divine power (the Second Coming) should bring history to its violent conclusion. Virtually all Elizabethan Puritans shared this view, as did Reformed Protestants generally through-

Protestantism to 1660 (Leiden, 1975), 160 n. 21; and Bernard Capp, *"Godly Rule and English Millenarianism," Past and Present*, no. 52 (Aug. 1970), 107–108.

10. The definition is adapted in part from Norman Cohn, "Medieval Millenarianism: Its Bearing on the Comparative Study of Millenarian Movements," in Sylvia A. Thrupp, ed., *Millennial Dreams in Action: Studies in Revolutionary Religious Movements* (New York, 1970), 31. In the present study, *imminence* means that the transfigurative event or events—even if several decades distant—are sufficiently near to undercut the usual sense of linear time and business as usual.

11. While, strictly speaking, the term *millennium* denotes an interval of 1,000 years, the length of the "millennial" era itself was in dispute in the period. Thus Brightman expected the "millenary reign" to last approximately 600 years; in the 1640s Ephraim Huit and Thomas Parker forecast transfigured eras of 1,335 and 45 years, respectively. Huit, *The Whole Prophecie of Daniel Explained . . .* (London, 1644), 348–356; Parker, *The Visions and Prophecies of Daniel Expounded . . .* (London, 1646), 34–35. For Brightman's view, see Peter Toon, "The Latter-Day Glory," in Toon, ed., *Puritans*, 28–30.

out the sixteenth and seventeenth centuries. After the accession of Elizabeth I to the throne in 1558, new prospects seemed to open for the Protestant movement. A more expansive optimism about divine purposes within history now came to the fore in some quarters.[12] In part this rested upon the assumption, nurtured by the experience of Protestant consolidation under Elizabeth, that the Antichrist's power was being abridged and that, despite Catholic interference, the Reformation now would proceed toward higher levels of historical achievement. Carrying forward and in some instances amplifying a widely held theme, a few writers predicted the conversion of the Jews to Christianity shortly before the world's end.[13] And, in any case, the final doom of Antichristian forces was sure and imminent.

12. Bauckham, *Tudor Apocalypse*, 146–147. Yet William Perkins, the most prominent Puritan intellectual of the day, openly opposed this trend (171–173, 210, 226). For the unequivocally amillennial stance of Elizabethan Puritan eschatology, see also, for example, John Dod, *A Methodical Short Catechisme* . . . , appended to Dod, *A Plaine and Familiar Exposition of the Ten Commandements* (London, 1618), sig. Bb7; and George Gifford, *Sermons upon the Whole Booke of the Revelation* (London, 1596), sigs. A6–B, 385–427. The confession of faith adopted in 1596 by the Amsterdam Separatist congregation under Henry Ainsworth also espoused an amillennial outlook (Williston Walker, ed., *The Creeds and Platforms of Congregationalism* [1893; Boston, 1960], 64). For the amillennial position of the great majority of continental Reformed theologians during the period of our study, see Heinrich Heppe and Ernst Bizer, *Die Dogmatik der evangelisch-reformierten Kirche* (Neukirchen, 1958), 557–561; and Erhard Kunz, *Protestantische Eschatologie: Von der Reformation bis zur Aufklärung* (Freiburg, 1980), 23–67.

13. The expectation of Jewish conversion probably had not "entered Puritanism" by means of "the Geneva Bible's gloss on Romans 11:26" or by the "enthusiastic advocacy" of William Perkins, as suggested by Maclear, "Fifth Monarchy," *WMQ*, 3d Ser., XXXII (1975), 229. Other research has established that the doctrine was "a common medieval theme" that received particular attention in Joachimist speculation and was favored in the 16th century by such Protestant leaders as Martin Bucer and Peter Martyr Vermigli, both of whom served for a time in academic appointments in England (Marjorie Reeves, *The Influence of Prophecy in the Later Middle Ages: A Study in Joachimism* [Oxford, 1969], 6, 222, 237, 307, 322, 427, 460, 482; Bauckham, *Tudor Apocalypse*, 225; de Jong, *Millennial Expectations*, 9). The theme also had appeared in John Bale, *The Image of both Churches* (1545–1547), in Henry Christmas, ed., *Select Works of John Bale* (Cambridge, 1849), 341, 370. For more on Perkins, see above, n. 12, and below, n. 44. For the views of Leo Jud, George Gifford, Arthur Dent, Andrew Willet, and others, see Bauckham, *Tudor Apocalypse*, 225.

John Foxe gave major voice to these interests, with their limited adumbration of Brightman's "millenary reign," in his *Acts and Monuments*, established by the late sixteenth century as "an expression of the [English] national faith second in authority only to the Bible."[14] Foxe's views, however, require a careful sorting out. Frankly adapting traditional ideas to Elizabethan Protestant nationalism, Foxe propounded a dispensationalist calendar according to which primal apostolic Christianity gradually had been eclipsed by Roman apostasy through the early Middle Ages, was "utterly almost extinguished" during the era of highest papal pretension, but was set upon a course of recovery again by the rise of John Wyclif about 1371.[15]

From that point forward, according to Foxe, redemptive history had been dominated by two contrary but similar processes. First was the violent and increasing persecution of the restorationist movement by Satan, "loosed" for this purpose in the fourteenth century and embodied, respectively, in papal Catholicism and the Turkish menace. Second, however, was the continuing work of recovery itself. Since Wyclif "sprang up . . . to waken and raise up again the world," the great Reformation had been on the advance. "By little and little" the "antichristian" bent of papal religion had been exposed, the "number of [the pope's] church [had been] decreasing." Above all, the work of recovery, "the renewing of the old ancient church" of primitive times begun by Wyclif and decisively advanced by the sixteenth-century reformers, had proceeded apace, with "the number of the true church [steadily] increasing." It was, Foxe believed, destined to "fructifie and increase" indefinitely.[16]

Foxe was genuinely uncertain how and to what degree this process would continue and how it was to be linked to the eventual cataclysms of the Second Coming. Nowhere did he invoke "the triumph of the true church under the leadership of an Elizabethan New Israel," but he did clearly urge and envision further advance on an

14. Thomas Brightman, *A Revelation of the Apocalyps* (Amsterdam, 1611), 657; William Haller, *The Elect Nation: The Meaning and Relevance of Foxe's Book of Martyrs* (New York, 1963), 14. The first English edition of the *Acts and Monuments* appeared in 1563; it was followed in 1570 by a much-expanded version and by two slightly revised editions in 1576 and 1583.

15. *AM*, I, 5; for reference to Wyclif, see I, 4–7, II, 726–727; and Haller, *Elect Nation*, 136–137.

16. *AM*, I, 5, 9, II, 796, IV, 121.

international scale. In a lengthy and passionate sermon delivered three years before his death, he spoke tentatively of a coming time when "the Gentiles shall mount to their fulnes, and the Jewes also [thereupon] . . . shall returne unto the faith." By "fulnes" Foxe meant completion of the Protestant drive against representations of the divine in picture, statue, and sacrament; for it was, he thought, the ancient aversion to "graven images" that largely sustained Jewish alienation from Christianity. In some indeterminate sense these historical developments worked toward and heralded the eternal state of heaven itself, and in this respect Foxe's late outlook incorporated what fairly may be termed a protomillennial element. His specific, if ambiguous, expectation of a fuller degree of reformation and Jewish conversion before "the day of the Lord's coming" unmistakably anticipated Brightman's formulations.[17]

But it would be easy to overemphasize this side of Foxe's eschatology. Protestant "fulnes" might be dimly proleptic of heaven, but heaven was not a continuation of worldly events. In particular, a careful analysis of Foxe's position—or that of many another late-sixteenth- and early seventeenth-century prophetic commentator—can only confute the widespread assumption that expectation of Jewish conversion was an automatic index of genuinely millennial belief.[18] Foxe knew nothing of a protracted period of terrestrial bliss following the end-time destruction. If he was uncertain what exactly the future would bring and when the apocalyptic climax would break upon the world, he was perfectly assured that the great objects of Christian hope were but dully anticipated within history. "Though we would call it a world," he insisted, the historical order of things was "now . . . fading away, but as a thing past a way already." In this Foxe expressed not only his personal view but the "consensus of Tudor theology."[19]

17. Bauckham, *Tudor Apocalypse*, 157; John Foxe, *A Sermon Preached at the Christening of a Certaine Jew, at London* (London, 1578), sig. Mvii; *AM*, IV, 95.

18. Bauckham points out that the doctrine of Jewish conversion was held by many like Perkins and Foxe who saw it as "the last event before the End, rather than as inaugurating a golden age" (*Tudor Apocalypse*, 225). It was not therefore a necessarily "*millenarian* conviction that the Last Days were approaching in which the Jews would be converted to Christianity" (W. Clark Gilpin, *The Millenarian Piety of Roger Williams* [Chicago, 1979], 19, emphasis mine).

19. Foxe, *Christ Crucified*, 26; Bauckham, *Tudor Apocalypse*, 209, 224.

The overriding Christian aim was, not to build an earthly kingdom, but "to pass . . . through . . . this desolate world," plagued
to the end with papal and Turkish malice and cruelty, en route to
heavenly paradise. If the signs of the times, read with the aid of
careful exegesis of Revelation, indeed supplied grounds for an "expectation of higher things, of better things" soon to come, these
were to be attained only in meager foretaste this side of the Resurrection. Only the destruction of history, an event Foxe estimated
"not to be far off," could end the ambiguity of human affairs.[20] The
critical distance between Foxe's and Brightman's versions of Last
Things is nowhere displayed more clearly than in their respective interpretations of "new Jerusalem," a prime apocalyptic symbol whose
association with the millennialist debacle at Münster was not readily
forgotten. Whereas Brightman, pressing ahead to a new position,
was to insist that "new Jerusalem . . . is *not* that city which the saints
shall enjoy in heaven after this life, but a [transfigured] Church to
be expected on earth," Foxe maintained, to the contrary, that "new
Jerusalem the . . . Citie of God all garnished with glory" was descriptive exclusively of the heavenly state.[21]

The claim that Foxe "made the pursuit of the Millennium . . .
orthodox," so that the transition to Brightman was but "a tiny shuf-
fle forward," is therefore without foundation. Fuller analysis reveals "a great gulf" between Foxe's and Brightman's views of the
end times.[22] However Foxe may have expanded the boundaries of

20. Foxe, *Christ Crucified*, 27; *AM*, IV, 95. See also Katharine R. Firth, *The
Apocalyptic Tradition in Reformation Britain, 1530–1645* (Oxford, 1979), 252.
Bauckham notes that Foxe at various times predicted 1564, 1570, 1586, and 1594
as the time of the Second Coming, but understood these as "general hints"
rather than hard and fast calculations (*Tudor Apocalypse*, 164–165).

21. Brightman, *Apocalyps*, 101, emphasis mine; Foxe, *Christ Crucified*, 28.
Similarly, Thomas Cartwright insisted that the "city on a hill full of precious
stones" of Revelation 21 was "impossible to be found in this world" (*A Commentary upon the Epistle of Saint Paule Written to the Colossians* [London,
1612], 167).

22. Lamont, *Godly Rule*, 33, 95. See also William Lamont, "Puritanism as
History and Historiography: Some Further Thoughts," *Past and Present*, no.
44 (Aug. 1969), 137. V. Norskov Olsen, *John Foxe and the Elizabethan Church*
(Berkeley, Calif., 1973), 83, and see 100. To counter frequent misrepresentation,
Olsen insists that the amillennial cast of Foxe's theology "cannot be emphasized
strongly enough" (36). See also Capp, "*Godly Rule*," *Past and Present*, no.
52 (Aug. 1971), 106–117; and Marjorie Reeves, "History and Eschatology:

traditional eschatology, he remained an amillennialist. Within his frame of reference neither New England pioneers nor Puritan activists in the English Civil War could have found latitude to conceive of themselves as founders of a this-worldly New Jerusalem. And what was true for Foxe was true for English eschatology generally before Brightman lifted the discussion to a new conceptual level. Since the early sixteenth century, Reformed Protestants not only had ignored millennial possibilities, they positively had scorned them. Millenary hopes bore a double stigma. They were associated both with the "Luxury and Sensuality" thought to have been embraced in the chiliasm of the patristic era and with the errors and excesses of the Radical Reformation. Anticipation of a "golden age on earth before the Day of Judgment" was condemned as heretical by the Second Helvetic Confession of 1565, the most widely received among Reformed confessions of the sixteenth century.[23] In theological works translated into English during the century, Heinrich Bullinger, Peter Martyr Vermigli, John Calvin, Wolfgang Musculus, and many others had held "the opinion of the thousand years" up to contempt. It had been repudiated by Myles Coverdale, John Hooper, John Jewel, John Whitgift, and other prominent leaders and intellectuals of the English church, and specific condemnation was included in the English liturgy of 1552 and in the Forty-two Articles of 1553.[24]

Medieval and Early Protestant Thought in Some English and Scottish Writers," *Medievalia et Humanistica*, N.S., IV (1973), 107–108.

23. For 16th-century treatments of patristic chiliasm, see Henry Bullinger, *A Hundred Sermons upon the Apocalipse of Jesu Christ* (London, 1573), 273. See also Bauckham, *Tudor Apocalypse*, 211, and the sources cited there, and below, n. 44. On the association with Münster see B. S. Capp, *The Fifth-Monarchy Men: A Study in English Millenarianism* (London, 1972), 229; and Toon, *Puritans*, 19. Arthur C. Cochrane, ed., *Reformed Confessions of the Sixteenth Century* (Philadelphia, 1966), 245–246.

24. Wolfgangus Musculus, *Common Places of Christian Religion* (London, 1563), 452; Peter Martyr Vermigli, *The Common Places of the Most Famous and Renowned Divine Doctor Peter Martyr* . . . (London, 1583), 386; Bullinger, *Apocalipse*, 273; John Calvin, *Institution of Christian Religion*, trans. Thomas Norton (London, 1562), book 3, chap. 25, sect. 5, 328–329; Myles Coverdale, *Remains of Myles Coverdale* . . . ., ed. George Pearson (Cambridge, 1846), 184; Samuel Carr, ed., *The Early Writings of John Hooper* (Cambridge, 1843), 161; John Jewel, *An Apology of the Church of England*, ed. John E. Booty (Ithaca, N.Y., 1963), 606; John Ayre, ed., *The Works of John Whitgift*, 3 vols. (Cambridge, 1851–1853), II, 434. For additional references, see Henry Gough,

After the death of Foxe in 1587, a variety of commentators continued to explore and press his twin assurances that the Protestant cause would advance until the end and that Antichrist's power was receding.[25] In the wake of the "wonderful year" of 1588 and the exhilarating rout of the Spanish Armada, prophetic discussion inevitably turned in a more optimistic direction. Several writers now were moved to suggest that Antichrist's power would be broken within history immediately before the end. The trend was augmented further by a "noticeably increasing" inclination to assign Protestant princes and military forces a temporal role in bringing the Antichristian beast to its doom. Carrying all of these tendencies to perhaps their highest development in the sixteenth century, the Scottish mathematician John Napier contributed to prophetic debate in the early 1590s the calculation of a forty-nine year interval of Protestant expansion between the fall of Rome and the Last Judgment.[26] But however such instances, in retrospect, may anticipate a millennial position, they are far from embracing the key conceptions. As in Foxe, all expectations yet were subordinated to concern for a nearing apocalyptic annihilation of pope and Turk. The focus throughout was upon last-minute events before the final cataclysm, not upon the rise within history of an age of triumph and fulfillment.

Hence, while paying full regard to Elizabethan developments, it would be an error to construe the eventual emergence of a millennial outlook as a straight and necessary progression from previous concepts. Brightman articulated his vision of the last age in space

---

ed., *A General Index to the Publications of the Parker Society* (Oxford, 1855), 536. On condemnation, see Capp, *Fifth-Monarchy Men*, 32; Bryan W. Ball, *A Great Expectation: Eschatological Thought in English Protestantism to 1660* (Leiden, 1975), 244–245.

25. See, for example, Arthur Dent, *The Ruine of Rome* . . . (London, 1607), 142, 239; John Napier, *A Plaine Discovery of the Whole Revelation of St. John* . . . (Edinburgh, 1593), 179. For the views of William Fulke, see Bauckham, *Tudor Apocalypse*, 146, and the sources cited there; the general development is discussed there in chap. 9.

26. Prominent in this trend were George Gifford, Arthur Dent, and James VI of Scotland (Bauckham, *Tudor Apocalypse*, 174–176; and Ernest Lee Tuveson, *Millennium and Utopia: A Study in the Background of the Idea of Progress* [New York, 1964], 53). Napier, *Plaine Discovery*, 12–16, 179–186. Napier sustained the Augustinian view of the "thousand of years" of Revelation 20 as an interval in the past (62).

opened up by optimistic trends within late Elizabethan commentary, yet his conceptual transition was abrupt. He was probably the first Englishman otherwise in the mainstream of Reformed thought to break categorically with the long-reigning conviction that "the world will bee alwaies like it selfe," incapable of utopia.[27] What seems to have made the difference was his study of themes in the still-living tradition of prophetic interpretation that had originated with Joachim of Fiore some four centuries before.

Through its integration of Joachimist elements with the historicist exegesis of Revelation already established by Bale, Foxe, and other English predecessors, Brightman's *Revelation of the Apocalyps* became the eschatological magnum opus in which the "full force of an optimistic expectation concerning history [was] first felt." Brightman himself was painfully aware that his presentation, although not affirming a literal chiliad, would be perceived as a departure from a long-standing Reformed consensus. He pleaded with his readers not to "think it . . . strange . . . that a new interpretation of the Apocalyps [herewith] is presented," and attempted to distance it from patristic chiliasm.[28] The editors of his part commentaries on Daniel and Canticles recognized that he had expounded a "new way," which went "beyond the streine and against the streame" of established exegesis. Thus when an early advocate like Robert Parker hailed Brightman as a "great . . . light in the Church of God," he was acknowledging discovery of a fundamentally altered way of construing the eschatological hope.[29]

There was, in fact, little in Brightman that was absolutely new in Protestant theology. What *was* new was the serious and extended re-

27. Dent, *Ruine of Rome*, 240, and see 142. At the time he began work upon *The Image of Both Churches* (ca. 1540), his major eschatological work, John Bale apparently had subscribed to a millennial interpretation of the "thousand years" of Revelation 20, but in course of the project he changed his mind and reverted to the traditional view (Bauckham, *Tudor Apocalypse*, 27–28, 216–217).

28. Reeves, "History and Eschatology," *Medievalia et Humanistica*, N.S., IV (1973), 109. Reeves also analyzes the Joachimist influence upon Brightman (109–111). See also Bauckham, *Tudor Apocalypse*, 212–221. Brightman, *Apocalyps*, sig. A2 (see also 664), 657–658.

29. Thomas Brightman, *A Commentary on the Canticles* (London, 1644), 975; Brightman, *A Most Comfortable Exposition of the Last and Most Difficult Part of the Prophecie of Daniel* (n.p., 1635), 111; Robert Parker, *An Exposition of the Powring out of the Fourth Vial . . .* (London, 1650), sig. A3.

statement of previously rejected or marginal ideas by a respected and otherwise orthodox member of the Puritan brotherhood. A notable element of his prophetic program, a centuries-old theme of Joachimist eschatology, was the doctrine of the Middle Advent of Christ. By the late sixteenth century, a number of commentators had adapted this traditional idea of the Spiritual Franciscans to Protestant use. Thus in a commentary on Revelation published in English translation in 1582, the Italian Protestant Joachimist Giacopo Brocardo propounded a "threefold coming" of Christ. Between the traditional first coming in the flesh and the last coming to judgment he located a "second comminge . . . in spyrite" through which Christ would destroy papal Christianity and "renew the church and world."[30]

Brightman too was an exponent of further light yet to break forth from the Word, and a critical stage in his "new interpretation" of biblical eschatology was the discovery, demonstrably under the influence of Joachimist sources, that the Second Coming of Christ was not the all-dominating event of the last times. At least in part he came to this realization through reflection upon a previously uncomprehended reference in 2 Thessalonians 2 : 8 to the "Brightness of his [Christ's] coming."[31] Pondering this passage in the light of clear promises in Revelation of the destruction of Antichristian forces and the rise of a new world order, Brightman became convinced that Bale, Foxe, and Reformed commentators generally had misconstrued the ultimate sequence of events. Taking an audaciously new tack, he now found forecast an intermediate future advent of Christ that was to precede the final Second Coming by hundreds of years. This was not premillennialism in the modern acceptation. There was not to be a personal appearance of the Lord, but an efflux of his "brightness," and this Brightman understood as a terrific exertion of supernatural power that would revolutionize the course of world history. In part, as in the calling of the Jews, Christ was to act by sheer miracle and "perform all wholly by himself"; in part he would facilitate and hasten human agency, as in the defeat of the popish and Turkish armies

---

30. Jiacopo Brocardo, *The Revelation of S. Jhon Revealed*, trans. James Sanford (London, 1582), 133, 136. Brocardo visited England in 1577 (Bauckham, *Tudor Apocalypse*, 218). For the Joachimist Middle Advent, see Reeves, *Influence of Prophecy*, 198, 291–292, 468 n. 9, 475, 482–483, 494–495, 501; Bauckham, *Tudor Apocalypse*, 213–220, 229, 272–276.

31. For the Joachimist influence, see Bauckham, *Tudor Apocalypse*, 212–226.

in the final battle of Armageddon.[32] But once these deeds were accomplished, a very long aeon then must pass before his appearance in person to roll up the world like a scroll and preside at the Last Judgment.

In his considerable expansion of these points, Brightman made it clear that the Middle Coming was the means to an earthly transfiguration of prolonged and drastic effect. With all the traditional vehemence he disclaimed "novelty," but his proposals leaped beyond established Reformed models of the penultimate stage of history.[33] To focus expectation upon an intermediate advent placed the Second Coming and, indeed, the whole problematic of the latter days in profoundly altered perspective. Christ's final coming, therewith removed to a point "600 yeers at least" beyond the imminent revolution, no longer immediately commanded the eschatological horizon. There now would intervene a full and engrossing act of redemptive history before the final curtain would drop. It was not the fleeting prelude of Napier's scheme, but an epoch of long duration. Moreover, as the fruit of a supernatural intervention, it stood forth as a veritable "apotheosis of history" and became itself a major object of the Christian hope.[34]

The measure of the conception is not taken by defining the millennial condition as "a period of earthly felicity." No longer was the glory of the elect upon their worldly pilgrimage to be forever "concealed from the world . . . by a life of humiliation and suffering."[35] Where the earlier visions of Jewish conversion and the Gentiles' fullness had depicted a dramatically improved but essentially untransfigured earthly estate, now it could be proclaimed that later in the seventeenth century (apparently Brightman expected a period of rapid transition to commence about 1650) the Christian peoples would take a preliminary step beyond finitude, a step that

32. Brightman, *Apocalyps*, 626–627, 634–637, 678; for other references to a distinct Middle Advent, see 13–15, 444, 634, 644, 710.

33. *Ibid.*, 48, 78, 395, 664.

34. Brightman, *Canticles*, 1077; Reeves, "History and Eschatology," *Medievalia et Humanistica*, N.S., IV (1973), 111.

35. John F. Wilson, *Pulpit in Parliament: Puritanism during the English Civil Wars, 1640–1648* (Princeton, N.J., 1969), 194; Bauckham, *Tudor Apocalypse*, 116 (see also 130–131).

would, not abrogate the historical estate, but strain it to the limits of possibility.[36]

Then they should enjoy a full retrieval of biblical religion, a "face to face" meeting with the Lord in worship, instantaneous acquisition of knowledge, unbroken peace, perpetual spring, an "abundance of all good things" (perhaps including miraculous medicaments for the cure of bodily wounds and ills)—in short, a victory over all enemies to Christian truth and felicity save physical mortality. At least thirty generations would enjoy a "golden age, and highest top of holy felicity, and happiness, which mortall men may expect, yea or thinke of in this earthly and base habitation." Without hesitation, therefore, Brightman applied the imagery of the New Jerusalem, with its associations of heavenly sublimity, to the age of earthly wonder soon to dawn. The Kingdom of Christ there so refulgently begun would not be "interrupted" by the Second Coming and Last Judgment, but after the six hundred years would be "translated from earth into heaven." Thus was the story to be told about the earth's last days transformed from tragedy to full-scale "Comedy."[37]

Appreciation of the conceptual distance between amillennial and millennial perspective, between Foxe and Brightman, is necessary for two reasons. First, the erroneous ascription of millennial idealism to the New England founders has been encouraged by the assumption that Puritan eschatology developed in a straight continuum from Foxe (if not earlier) to Brightman and beyond and that the millennial label therefore can be applied with little regard to chronology. Thus we encounter assertions that "millenarian fervor" is a generic trait that "runs through Puritanism" in all periods, that a "millennial fervor spread steadily from the period of the Marian exile," and the like.[38] Unless we wish to treat "anyone who was interested in

36. Brightman speculated that the destruction of Rome and the conversion of the Jews would occur about 1650 (*Apocalyps*, 626; *Canticles*, 1051).

37. Brightman, *Apocalyps*, 447, 626, 680, 704–705, sig. A3; Brightman, *Daniel*, 104.

38. Hall, "Understanding the Puritans," in Bass, ed., *The State of American History*, 341; Bercovitch, *Jeremiad*, 35. William G. McLoughlin also describes "a millennium of peace and plenty" as an integral of the Puritans' Calvinistic world view, in *Revivals, Awakenings, and Reform: An Essay on Religion and Social Change in America* (Chicago, 1978), 43, and see 34. See also Sanford,

the contemporary relevance of the Apocalypse as a 'millenarian,' " it is time to recognize that such claims misrepresent the development of English eschatological thought in general and of Puritan ideas in particular. Although eventually adapted to Puritan aims, millennialism was not an original feature of the Puritan movement. It probably played no part in the formative half-century of Puritan development beginning about 1560. An authentically millennial formula first entered Puritanism through the bold speculations of Brightman, chiefly his commentary on Revelation; this, in turn, was not available to the public until 1609 at the earliest.[39]

This leads to the second reason. For if Brightman's *Apocalyps* was published in 1609, did it then instantly become the "common property" of the English reading public?[40] And were its new proposals rapidly taken up by Puritan thinkers? Much modern discussion of Brightman's influence assumes yes, to both questions, and thus lends plausibility to the view that a full millennial belief was widely diffused in Puritan circles by the time of the Great Migration.[41] Yet there are substantial reasons to doubt both the ready availability and the quick assimilation of Brightman's ideas within England. Unlike John Foxe of the previous or Joseph Mede of the next generation, Brightman wrote from a position of stringent opposition to the religious establishment. He intertwined prophetic commentary with a vigorous attack upon the Church of England from a Presbyterian standpoint. In an ambitious extension of covenantal doctrine, he de-

---

Quest, 80; Mooney, "Millennialism," 90; Lamont, *Godly Rule*, 24–25, 33–35; Lamont, "Puritanism," *Past and Present*, no. 44 (Aug. 1969), 137–140.

39. Thomas Cartwright, for instance, dubbed "Chilias[m]" an exercise in "ignorance" (*The Second Replie of Thomas Cartwright: Agaynst Master Doctor Whitgiftes Second Answer touching the Churche Discipline* [(Zurich), 1675], 6). Brightman's works existed in manuscript for several years before their posthumous publication. I have discovered no evidence that copies were in circulation, or that his work was otherwise being explored, at an earlier date.

40. Christianson, *Reformers and Babylon*, 129. See also Avihu Zakai, "Exile and Kingdom: Reformation, Separation, and the Millennial Quest in the Formation of Massachusetts and Its Relationship with England, 1628–1660" (Ph.D. diss., Johns Hopkins University, 1983), 120.

41. See, for example, Firth, *Apocalyptic Tradition*, 164–179; Ball, *Great Expectation*, 60; Christianson, *Reformers and Babylon*, 129; Maclear, "Fifth Monarchy," *WMQ*, 3d Ser., XXXII (1975), 229–230.

clared that, unless primitive "church discipline" were at once established and the English liturgy purged of its Catholic cast, the present hierarchy would be caught up in the "sea of troubles" soon to engulf the enemies of Christ. Understandably, Brightman became a figure "persecuted when alive, and pursuivanted when dead." [42] There could be no question of an approved English printing of the *Apocalyps* before the collapse of Anglican censorship in 1641. When Brightman died in 1607, the Latin manuscript of his major work remained unpublished. It was printed in Latin editions in 1609 and 1612 and in English translation in 1611, 1615, and 1616; all were published abroad. An occasional reference to the *Apocalyps* in works published in England before 1641 proves that copies had been smuggled in from the Netherlands and circulated among interested parties, but this was clandestine, restricted activity. No approved English editions of any of Brightman's apocalyptic writings appeared before the 1640s. [43]

While it would be a mistake to underestimate Puritan capacity for clandestine procedure, there is little reason to assume a generalized readiness to embrace the heady doctrine of Christ's Middle Advent and an earthly New Jerusalem. After 1600 as before, the time-honored aversion to chiliasm ran strong within the Spiritual Brotherhood, and their "great Rabbi," William Perkins, was on

42. Brightman, *Apocalyps*, sigs. A3–A4, 103–129, 154; Anthony Tuckney, "To the Reader," in John Cotton, *A Brief Exposition with Practical Observations upon the Whole Book of Canticles* (London, 1655), sig. A6. For more on Brightman's Puritan bent, see Peter Lake, *Moderate Puritans and the Elizabethan Church* (Cambridge, 1982), 252–254. Francis Osborne remembered disapprovingly in 1658 that his family had harbored him for some years at serious risk (*The Works of Francis Osborn* . . . , 8th ed. [London, 1682], 436).

43. Ball, *Great Expectation*, 60. References to the *Apocalyps* may be found in Richard Bernard, *A Key of Knowledge for the Opening of the Secret Mysteries of St. Johns Mysticall Revelation* (London, 1617), sig. C8; Robert Bolton, *Mr. Boltons Last and Learned Worke of the Foure Last Things* . . . , 3d ed. (London, 1635), 54; George Hakewill, cited in Firth, *Apocalyptic Tradition*, 201; Joseph Mede, *The Key of the Revelation* . . . , 2d ed. (London, 1650), 13; Henry Burton, *The Seven Vials* (London, 1628), 140. After the lifting of censorship, the first items from Brightman to be made available were two short digests: *Reverend Mr. Brightmans Judgement; or, Prophecies* (London, 1641), and *Brightmans Predictions; or, Prophecies* (London, 1641). The earliest London edition of the *Apocalyps* appeared in 1644 in *The Workes of that Famous, Reverend, and Learned Divine, Mr. Thomas Brightman* (London, 1644).

record in opposition to freewheeling prophetic calculation.[44] In 1618 David Pareus, a continental Reformed theologian admired and often cited by Puritan writers, published a full commentary upon Revelation that repudiated Brightman's view and insisted that "storms of afflictions" would remain the Christian lot until the Second Coming.[45] This was not an eccentric response, for it reflected the dominantly amillennial cast of Reformed thought abroad. It is also probable that Brightman's construction, which reflected the immediate "post-Armada mood of optimism about God's purposes in history," seemed less cogent in the period of Protestant catastrophe following the outbreak of the Thirty Years' War.[46] In any case, it is unreasonable to suppose that Brightman's abrupt reconfiguration of eschatological belief would be accepted rapidly and without substantial resistance within a Puritan leadership steeped in traditional amillennial views.

With an eye cocked to one of the most potent of Puritan prejudices, Brightman himself had foreseen that the odium of the new would be attached to his interpretation, and labored to counter it. He

44. Perkins does not appear as the exemplar of a "new and optimistic strain in Puritan prophetic commentary." His primary intention was to dampen, not to encourage, eschatological fervor; he found no reason to believe that Jewish conversion was imminent; he specifically characterized conjecture as to the "yeere or the age wherein the second comming of Christ and the last judgement shall be" as "the devices of men." This must have been meant to include the copious conjecture along such lines in Foxe's *Acts and Monuments*. Maclear, "Fifth Monarchy," *WMQ*, 3d Ser., XXXII (1975), 227; Perkins, *Workes*, I, 259–268, III, 470. See also Bauckham, *Tudor Apocalypse*, 172–173, 210. "Great Rabbi" was a slur by Richard Montagu in 1624. John Cosin, *The Correspondence of John Cosin*, ed. George Ornsby, I (Publications of the Surtees Society, LII [Durham, 1869]), 51, 54. For attacks on chiliasm, see, for example, Dent, *Ruine of Rome*, 268–269; Thomas Taylor, *Christs Victorie over the Dragon . . .* (London, 1633), 231.

45. David Pareus, *In Divinam Apocalypsin S. Apostoli et Evangelistae Johannis Commentarius* (Heidelberg, 1618); the first English edition was *A Commentary upon the Divine Revelation . . .* , trans. Elias Arnold (London, 1644). Other Latin editions appeared in 1622 and 1642. So far as I can determine, only a tiny minority of 17th-century European Reformed thinkers adopted a millennial view; see Kunz, *Protestantische Eschatologie*, 43–67, esp. 47, 59, and 59 n. 120.

46. Bauckham, *Tudor Apocalypse*, 227. See also Capp, "Godly Rule," *Past and Present*, no. 52 (Aug. 1971), 114–115. Capp, however, overestimates the gradualist element in Brightman.

sought to do so in part by stressing the restorationist heart of his critique of the Church of England and in part by claiming special inspiration.[47] Nevertheless, his influence was slow to diffuse. Inquiries into early seventeenth-century English eschatology show, at most, a spotty and limited millennial influence in Puritan quarters before the late 1630s.[48] Puritan unwillingness to affirm an earthly transfiguration is emphasized in texts where Brightman is cited but approval of the millennial concept withheld.[49]

At least four clear cases of Puritan conversion to a millennial position, probably under Brightman's influence, can be identified before 1629, and the writings of these men undoubtedly became additional vehicles for the spread of the millennial idea.[50] They offer,

47. Brightman's claim to special inspiration has been noticed by Toon, *Puritans*, 27. See also Brightman, *Apocalyps*, sig. A2, 711.

48. See Capp, *Fifth-Monarchy Men*, 23–50; Christianson, *Reformers and Babylon*, 100–131; de Jong, *Millennial Expectations*, esp. 13–29; Ball, *Great Expectation*, 157–192. Capp claims that Thomas Goodwin had been a millennialist since the 1620s. In the text cited in evidence, however, Goodwin, writing in the early 1640s, says that "for this twenty years I have not known how to answer" key questions about the mechanics of a millennial transformation. That is, his conceptual breakthrough had just then occurred. Capp, *Fifth-Monarchy Men*, 30; Goodwin, *The World to Come* . . . (London, 1655), 30. David H. Watters declares outright that "the vast majority of Englishmen and Americans in the seventeenth century" were millennialists (*"With Bodilie Eyes": Eschatological Themes in Puritan Literature and Gravestone Art* [Ann Arbor, Mich., 1981], 4).

49. See, for example, Bolton, *Foure Last Things*, 54. For a fuller view of Bolton's eschatology, see 3, 21, and his *Two Sermons Preached at Northampton at Two Severall Assises There* (London, 1635), 67. See also Burton, *Seven Vials*, sig. g3, 3, 129, 140, 141. At this time (1628) Burton did affirm the destruction of Antichrist within history but saw this as an immediate "forerunner" of "the great day [of Judgment] of God Almighty." Cf. Henry Burton, *The Grounds of Christian Religion* (London, 1635), 44. Only later did Burton move to a full millennial position. See also Taylor, *Christs Victorie*, 14, 46, 716–718, 722, 790.

50. Genuinely millennial positions appear in Cotton, *A Brief Exposition of the Whole Book of Canticles, or, Song of Solomon* (London, 1642). Everett H. Emerson dates the composition of this work between 1624 and 1632. Emerson, *John Cotton* (New York, 1965), 163; Bernard, *Key*; [Henry Finch], *The Worlds Great Restauration* (London, 1621); and Huit, *Daniel*. Huit composed his work before emigrating to Massachusetts in 1639 (sigs. A2–A3). Robert Parker, an early exponent of nonseparating Congregationalism, spoke in passing of "the brightnesse of Christs coming to call the Jews" in a tract prepared but not published before his death in 1614. Brightman's influence is manifest in the tract,

however, but the first hints of a widespread millennial movement. Early seventeenth-century Puritan eschatology has not been charted fully, but there is every reason to believe that for three decades and more after Brightman's death the overwhelming majority of Puritan spokesmen expected a nearing end to history at Judgment Day. Proponents of the Brightman thesis would not easily overturn the tenacious conviction that the discussion of New Jerusalem in Revelation 20 forecast, not a worldly state of affairs, but "the Church triumphant in heaven, after the resurrection of the last day." This was also the view of New Englanders like Thomas Weld, who remained certain as of the early 1630s that the tears of human suffering "never on earth" would be wiped away "yet in the [heavenly] New Jerusalem." Several men gestured beyond apocalyptic, coupling the traditional view to an interest in the latter-day "fulness of the Gentiles" or Jewish conversion, but they did not break through to the essential millennial theme. They continued to see the gospel's coming surge among Jews and Gentiles as a transitory moment before the cataclysm that would end history, not as the opening of a new chapter in human affairs that both would alter the essential human condition and postpone the Second Coming for many centuries.[51]

The Mystery of the Vialls Opened . . . (London, 1650), 11, 3. A Scottish expositor also published a millennialist commentary in the period: Patrick Forbes, *An Exquisite Commentary upon the Revelation of St. John* (Edinburgh, 1613).

51. Bernard, *Key*, 336; Everett Emerson, ed., *Letters from New England: The Massachusetts Bay Colony, 1629–38* (Amherst, Mass., 1976), 95. Dent, *Ruine* (1607), approached but did not embrace unequivocally the full transfigurationist position (123–125, 239–240, 278–279). Thomas Draxe, *The Worldes Resurrection; or, The Generall Calling of the Jewes* . . . (London, 1608), placed the Gentiles' fullness and Jews' conversion "a little before Christ his second coming," and stated that they "shall not be generall, much lesse universall" (50, 90). In his *Brides Longing for Her Bride-Groomes Second Comming* (London, 1638), Richard Sibbes spoke of Jewish conversion and of "a glorious estate of the Church to be here upon Earth" but did not develop a full millennial conception. His dominant interest was in the imminent Second Coming, to which the special coming time was but a prelude and apparently not a protracted one. He also insisted that hypocrites would remain a fundamental problem within the church "to the end of the World" and saw no hope that the lion and lamb would lie down together within history (4, 23, 64, 66).

For plainly amillennial constructions by leading members of the Spiritual Brotherhood, see, for example, Nicholas Byfield, *The Rule of Faith* (London, 1626), 498, 504–514; Bolton, *Two Sermons*, 67; Thomas Taylor, *A Commen-*

After the publication of Brightman's *Apocalyps*, the next major development in millennial theory was the near-simultaneous publication, in 1627, of John Henry Alsted's *Diatribe de Milleannis Apocalypticis* and Joseph Mede's *Clavis Apocalyptica*.[52] These works presented an updated millennialism more in keeping with the current dismal state of the international Protestant movement. Mede unmistakably had Brightman in mind as he repudiated the identification of "the brightness of [Christ's] coming" with anything short of the full Second Coming, bringing a "great day of universal revenge and judgment." But he also transformed the traditional concept by identifying the last coming of Christ to perform the Last Judgment and to found his kingdom as an event within the time process commencing a thousand years before the end of history. Alsted, to the contrary, placed "the Majesty of Christ coming to Judgment" after the thousand years and cited favorably the Joachimist teaching of "a certain middle coming." Both men projected a totally future, literal millennium more credibly attuned than Brightman's version to the one-thousand-year concept of Revelation 20.[53] Mede, in addition, strove to remove the sensualist stigma from patristic chiliasm. Although not themselves Puritans—Alsted was a German theologian who never visited England, and Mede was outspokenly hostile to critics of the established church—these two figures were joined with Brightman to form a triumvirate of eschatological authorities often and respectfully cited by later Puritan thinkers. Their influence, however, was not felt quickly. It has not been shown, in terms of the specifically millennial concept,

tarie upon the Epistle of St. Paul Written to Titus (Cambridge, 1612), 480–490; Taylor, *Christs Victorie*, 231, 335, 716–718, 722; John Ball, *A Short Treatise Contayning All the Principall Grounds of Christian Religion* (London, 1629), 235–242.

52. Alsted's work was published in Frankfurt, Mede's in Cambridge. English editions appeared only after 1640: Mede, *The Key of the Revelation* (London, 1643); and Alsted, *The Beloved City* . . . (London, 1643).

53. Clouse, "Millenarianism," in Toon, ed., *Puritans*, 49; and Capp, *Fifth-Monarchy Men*, 28–29, call attention to the impact of current events. For Mede's comments upon the "brightness of his coming," see *Key* (1650), pt. 2, 123–124. See also Mede, *The Works of . . . Joseph Mede*, 3d ed. (London, 1672), 772. For Mede the inner-historical "Secundus Adventus Christi" did entail initially "a miraculous apparition of Christ from heaven," but not his departure from heaven to rule personally upon earth (*Works*, 603–604, 772). The best general account of his teaching is in Firth, *Apocalyptic Tradition*, 214–225.

that they influenced any broad English constituency for a decade or more after 1627. Mede himself acknowledged that his view of the future would seem "almost incredible in respect of inveterate [amillennial] prejudices."[54]

The first clearly collective instance of millennial zeal within Puritanism was to await yet another turn in English history. Many details of the development are irrecoverable, but a flurry of overtly millennial speculation has been identified with one and possibly more groups of English Puritan expatriates in the Low Countries in the late 1630s and early 1640s. Notable participants were Thomas Goodwin, Philip Nye, John Archer, and the author (possibly Goodwin) of *A Glimpse of Sion's Glory* (1641).[55] These men were of Congregational persuasion. Goodwin and Nye later belonged to the small group of "dissenting brethren" that stymied the Presbyterian majority in the Westminster Assembly. Their early belief in a coming transformation probably imparted the millennial bent that was to become a hallmark of English Independency after 1641.[56] From their station in exile they enjoyed free access to Brightman's works as well as to Alsted's and Mede's, and they were amply motivated to reconsider eschatological conventions. Their activities mirrored the frustrations with the standing order accumulated by Puritan activists during more than a decade of experience under Charles I and his high church and often Arminian favorites within the Church of England. They may have registered relief at the rise in Protestant fortunes in the Thirty

54. See Ball, *Great Expectation*, 176; Mede, *Key* (1650) pt. 2, 121. Clouse's claim that the publication of Alsted's work caused English Puritans after 1627 "to begin to forget their inhibitions" against millennialism is unsupported by any evidence drawn from the period 1627–1640 (Clouse, "Millenarianism," in Toon, ed., *Puritans*, 42, 44).

55. Christianson, *Reformers and Babylon*, 209–218; Geoffrey F. Nuttall, *Visible Saints: The Congregational Way* (Oxford, 1957), 148; John F. Wilson, "A Glimpse of Sion's Glory," *CH*, XXXI (1962), 70. Goodwin, *An Exposition of the Revelation*, which affirms both the Middle Advent and a literal chiliad, was said by his son to have been composed in 1639 (John C. Miller, ed., *The Works of Thomas Goodwin*, 12 vols. [Edinburgh, 1861], III, xxviii, 20, 22).

56. Nuttall, *Visible Saints*, 143–155; Wilson, *Pulpit in Parliament*, 223–230; Tai Liu, *Discord in Zion: Puritan Divines and the Puritan Revolution, 1640–1660* (The Hague, 1973), 78. Jeremiah Burroughs, also a possible author of *A Glimpse of Sion's Glory*, was another of the "dissenting brethren." His authorship of the tract is argued by Christianson, *Reformers and Babylon*, 251–252.

Years' War during the 1630s. They certainly reflected an awareness of the historic crisis generated by the king's troubles with Scotland beginning in 1637.

In any event, that crisis and its mounting into civil war and revolution subsequently provided the context for a flowering of genuinely millennial ideas in both Old and New England, a development in which Goodwin and other exiles were to be influential. It is only with the arrival of that extraordinary period that Brightman's views, as well as Alsted's and Mede's, were able to circulate freely.[57] And it is only then that one discovers ample evidence of widespread and sustained Puritan inquisitiveness about the end state and a desire to explore in detail the millennial concept. Rapidly after 1640, so large a segment of the Spiritual Brotherhood, including many non-Independents, discovered the pertinence of millennial belief to the new historical dispensation unfolding in the parliamentary struggle that it well may be called "that classical 'heresy' which most threatened the orthodoxy of Puritan piety during the Civil War period."[58] Here, at last, under the stimulus of a national crisis a full seventy years after the Elizabethan Settlement began to evoke opposition—indeed, a full decade after the arrival of the Winthrop fleet in Massachusetts Bay—one finds a basic and sustained departure from traditional canons of Protestant judgment respecting the realization of divine aims in history. Only now may we begin to speak meaningfully of a *pervasive* eschatological *fervor* of a *millennial* type.

Chiliastic Zeal in Earliest New England: The Evidence

If the American immigrants indeed were motivated by a wholesale millennial fervor, they stood astonishingly far in advance of their associates both in England and in continental exile. Their Great Migration then would represent a first and certainly major collective episode in the rise of English millennialism that predated by several

---

57. See Capp, *Fifth-Monarchy Men*, 28; Christopher Hill, *Antichrist in Seventeenth-Century England* (London, 1971), 27.

58. Wilson, *Pulpit in Parliament*, 194, and see 192–195, 212–230. See also Capp, *Fifth-Monarchy Men*, 38.

years either the activity at Arnheim or the surge of the 1640s. Was it so? So far as the evidence allows one to ascertain, was there indeed a dramatic millennial hope drawing Puritans to the New World and shaping New England's thought and life during the formative period?

To begin with, claims that the Massachusetts founders hoped to "inaugurate" the millennium in their plantation rest upon a probable misreading of then-current prophetic theory. Within the end-time scheme of Brightman and his followers, it is hard to see how such a conception could arise. Indeed, the great last epoch required a proper inauguration, one both anticipating and catalyzing world-wide transformation; but this was not scheduled to occur in the early 1630s (Brightman and Cotton both expected the turning point in the 1650s), and not in Massachusetts. It was the Jewish Christians, rising to greatness in the last age, that some forecasters expected to build a Redeemer Nation with an errand to run on behalf of mankind. For Brightman, the Jews' calling was both integral and crucial to the global diffusion of millennial glory, but he left it to others to explore the causal and exemplary roles of that event.

A decade after Brightman's death, Richard Bernard, drawing upon his admired forebear, reminded his countrymen that the "most happy condition" of the church was not to be attained until *after* the "conversion of the Jewes." But now he foresaw in that very occurrence the fount of "life and riches to the Christian world." Specifically, he predicted that the end-time Christian-Jewish nation would so bedazzle the as-yet-unconverted "Gentiles and their Kings" that they should "come to her . . . and that with earnest desire and high estimation of her . . . and be joyned to the Lord, and become his people also with her."[59]

Here, already, was the full conception that was to recur in numerous variations in prophetic writing through the period of this study. The Jewish "return," as Cotton later was to say, now was construed as an "instrumental cause" bringing "a great concourse of many Nations" into the New Jerusalem. Probably the most emphatic statement of the theme emerged in the Puritan barrister Henry Finch's *Great Restauration* of 1621. Drawing again upon Brightman but going well beyond him, Finch described the millennial kingdom as a worldwide reign in which Christianized Jews would be the

59. Bernard, *Key*, 336, 339.

"Kings and chiefe Monarches of the earth." From them "the Gospell shall go out to all Nations," not only in force of spiritual example but also by military conquest. They were in the end to "subdue and bring under [Christ's] yoke, all nations that doe oppose" Christianization. This was an extreme position, and its suggestion of English subordination within a future Jewish empire angered James I and led to Finch's arrest and professional decline. But it illustrates nicely the impulse in prophecy then to hail the Jews' eventual resumption of their biblical role as elect nation. Joseph Mede lent to the theme his weighty approval: it was to be through "their [the Jews'] restitution," in his judgment, that "the whole world shall come unto Christ."[60]

Contemporary theory thus allowed scant place for a New England inauguration of the new age, and there is little evidence that millennial expectation fostered the Massachusetts Bay project. The commonly cited texts are John Winthrop's reference to the creation of a "bullwarke against the kingdom of Antichrist which the Jesuites labour to reare up" in the New World, his "Model of Christian Charity," and Cotton's farewell sermon to the Winthrop group of 1629. Winthrop's "bullwarke," we learn, divulged an explicit and vast project for "advancing history toward the day of Armageddon"; specific anticipation of a "cosmic climax" and a New England "Mount Zion of the Apocalypse" is discovered in the "Model"; and Cotton is found (in 1629) suggesting to Winthrop's flock "that their plantation would become the scene of . . . New Jerusalem."[61]

60. Cotton, *Canticles* (1655), 180, 212, 220, and see 221–222; [Finch], *Great Restauration*, 7, 10, 71; Mede, *Key* (1650), sig. a2. See also Thomas Parker, *Daniel*, 155; Draxe, *Resurrection*, 39, 49–53; Peter Bulkeley, *The Gospel-Covenant; or, The Covenant of Grace Opened* (London, 1646), 20–21; Thomas Tillam, *The Two Witnesses . . .* (London, 1651), 149–150; J. C. Davis, *Utopia and the Ideal Society: A Study of English Utopian Writing, 1516–1700* (Cambridge, 1981), 146–147. Middlekauff, Maclear, and Bloch agree that the "first-generation New England Puritans saw themselves primarily as exiles and still viewed England, not America, as the spearhead of apocalyptic developments" (Middlekauff, *The Mathers*, 33–34; Maclear, "Fifth Monarchy," *WMQ*, 3d Ser., XXXII [1975], 248; Ruth H. Bloch, *The Visionary Republic: Millennial Themes in American Thought, 1756–1800* [Cambridge, 1985], 11).

61. *WP*, II, 114, 117, 138; Maclear, "Fifth Monarchy," *WMQ*, 3d Ser., XXXII (1975), 230 (see also Sanford, *Quest*, 89; and Zakai, "Exile and Kingdom," 108); Loren Baritz, *City on a Hill: A History of Ideas and Myths in America* (New York, 1964), 31; Bercovitch, *Jeremiad*, 8–9; Jesper Rosenmeier, "Veritas: The

These renderings do not persuade. That Winthrop, struggling late in 1629 to assemble promotional arguments for the Bay project, struck upon the obvious consideration of providing a counterforce to Catholic missionary advances in North America tells us nothing of the type or intensity of his eschatological belief. He refers neither to "advancing history" nor to Armageddon and provides no millennial connection for the otherwise routine reference to Antichrist.[62] Like claims for a world-saving Errand and the ascription of an eschatological agenda to either Winthrop's "Model" or Cotton's *Gods Promise to His Plantations* lose sight completely of their manifest content. In view of Winthrop's and Cotton's common insistence upon accord with "the first Plantation of the Primitive Church," there is far more reason to construe the two documents as displays of restorationist than of millennial interest. The governing ideas of the "Model" have been examined above. *Gods Promise* is built upon a similar grid: it envisions the New England plantation, in imitation of biblical precedents, as a providentially commissioned place for a company of refugees and pioneers whose greatest good will be "liberty and purity of . . . [primitively instituted] Ordinances."[63] There, subject to standard Deuteronomic terms and conditions, the people may expect to "prosper . . . and increase" an indefinite time. Restoration and covenant, not eschatology and the millennium, provide the conceptual basis of Cotton's famous farewell.[64]

Sealing of the Promise," *Harvard Library Bulletin*, XVI (1968), 33, and see 34. Bercovitch, *Jeremiad*, 8–9, follows Rosenmeier. See also Emory Elliott, ed., *Puritan Influences in American Literature* (Urbana, Ill., 1979), xiv; de Jong, *Millennial Expectations*, 29–30; Zakai, "Exile and Kingdom," 2, 350, 481; and Philip F. Gura, *A Glimpse of Sion's Glory: Puritan Radicalism in New England, 1620–1660* (Middletown, Conn., 1984), 13, 127.

62. The wish to compete with Catholic missionary work among American natives had been a theme of the earlier Virginia colonization (Alexander Brown, *The Genesis of the United States*, 2 vols. [Boston, 1890], 291, 352). For a general discussion of the Antichrist theme in early 17th-century England, and one which finds no general millennial connections before the 1640s, see Hill, *Antichrist*, 1–40.

63. Cotton, *Gods Promise*, 7, 14. Cotton unequivocally presented the unnamed plantation site as "*a place*," "*a Country*," "*a land of promise.*" There is no warrant to render this as "*the site*" or "*the scene*" for unique eschatological developments, as do Rosenmeier, "Veritas," *Harvard Library Bulletin*, XVI (1968), 33; and Bercovitch, *Jeremiad*, 8–9.

64. Cotton, *Gods Promise*, 12. The two major published analyses of Cotton's

Moving to a smaller and presumably more manageable focus, a number of modern interpreters have argued that the unique Congregational pattern that developed in New England in the 1630s was "inspired" by a frequently overlooked "chiliastic zeal." Seen thus, the New England way in its emergent period pointed far beyond traditional issues of church polity. Its marked preoccupation with the church's purity, its mandatory public testimony of personal regeneration, and its gathering of the elect into "objective holy communities" were conscious, strategic anticipations of the approaching millennial era.[65]

Since John Cotton was second to none in praise of purity and probably played the key role in introducing the unprecedented requirement of a public testimony, it has been necessary to claim that he was inspired to these actions fundamentally by eschatological conviction. No evidence, however, supports the claim. The first known instance in which Cotton associated the idea of a visibly pure church with millennial expectation is a set of sermons dating from 1639, three or four years after the procedures of church-gathering had been regularized.[66] Furthermore, Cotton did prepare commentary on

---

life and work both provide an analytical summary of *Gods Promise*; neither detected a millennial element (Emerson, *John Cotton*, 52–53; Larzer Ziff, *The Career of John Cotton: Puritanism and the American Experience* [Princeton, N.J., 1962], 60–62).

65. Hall, "Understanding the Puritans," in Bass, ed., *The State of American History*, 341; Maclear, "Fifth Monarchy," *WMQ*, 3d Ser., XXXII (1975), 229. This line of argument first was worked out in 1965 in Aletha Joy Bourne Gilsdorf, "The Puritan Apocalypse: New England Eschatology in the Seventeenth Century" (Ph.D. diss., University of Chicago, 1968). See also Hall, *Faithful Shepherd*, 60, 86, 97; and Nuttall, *Visible Saints*, 143–155. In support of his argument that a "fervent millennial ideology" was associated with Congregationalism "by the 1630s," Maclear cites the view of the Arnheim theorists "that Independency is a beginning of Christs temporal kingdom here on earth." Yet there is no evidence known to me that such views developed at Arnheim before 1639 at the earliest. Maclear's source is Nuttall, who cited no earlier source (Maclear, "Fifth Monarchy," *WMQ*, 3d Ser., XXXII [1975], 229; Nuttall, *Visible Saints*, 148).

66. Cotton's earliest and inchoate statement of the theme was *An Exposition upon the Thirteenth Chapter of the Revelation* (London, 1655 [composed 1639–1641]), 9, 123, 230; he drew the connections more clearly in *The Churches Resurrection . . .* (London, 1642), 10–11, 20–21, and in *The Powring out of the Seven Vials* (London, 1642), "The Seventh Vial," 16–17, both probably composed in 1641. Gilsdorf recognized the lack of evidence before 1639, acknowl-

issues in Congregational theory on six separate occasions in 1634 and 1635 and in no case identified millennial hope as the governing motive or issue behind any component of the New England system.[67]

But the most serious difficulty appears when one recalls the concerns from which the Congregationalism of men like Cotton demonstrably arose. For as in Puritan theology generally, so in Congregational theory in particular the quest for purity had a lineage and content that stood in no necessary affiliation with eschatology. One crucial dimension was the drive for restored connections with the faith and way of primitive times. Another emerged from the Puritan stress upon personal conversion to a sanctified mode of life. Long before the 1630s, in fact long before Brightman had showed Cotton and others the way to a genuinely millennial outlook, these yoked commitments had more than sufficed to nurture hunger for greater purity in the church. Since the 1570s they had generated "presby-

---

edging that "whether Cotton actually reasoned in this way [in 1636 and earlier] we shall probably never know" ("Puritan Apocalypse," 76–77). Arguing for the other founders' millennial stance as of about 1635, Gilsdorf also cited Thomas Parker, Edward Johnson, John Eliot, William Hooke, and John Davenport. Yet Parker not only was inclined to Presbyterianism and opposed to the test of a public relation, he also specifically challenged millennial interpretations of the New Jerusalem of Revelation 20. In the last earthly stage he saw a mere 45-year "inchoation" of heaven (Perry Miller, *Orthodoxy in Massachusetts, 1630–1650* [Boston, 1959], 122; Parker, *Daniel*, 147–155). Johnson and Eliot are not known to have addressed the subject before mid-century. Hooke's apocalyptic writings date from after the fall of the Protectorate. And Davenport's only notable utterance on the millennium dates—"unfortunately," says Gilsdorf—from 1669 (Gilsdorf, "Puritan Apocalypse," 101n). Davenport's statement appears in his preface to Increase Mather, *The Mystery of Israel's Salvation . . .* (London, 1669).

67. John Cotton, "Questions and Answers upon Church-Government," pt. 4 of Cotton, *A Treatise* (Boston, 1713); Cotton, *A Sermon Delivered at Salem* (1636), in Larzer Ziff, ed., *John Cotton on the Churches of New England* (Cambridge, Mass., 1968); Cotton, *A Copy of a Letter of Mr. Cotton of Boston* ([London], 1641; written ca. 1636); Cotton, *The True Constitution of a Particular Visible Church . . .* (London, 1642; written ca. 1636); Cotton, *The Way of the Churches of Christ in New-England . . .* (London, 1645; written ca. 1642); Cotton, *The Keys of the Kingdom of Heaven* (1644), in Ziff, ed., *John Cotton.* Emerson, *John Cotton*, 163–165, supplies the probable dates of composition. *The True Constitution of a Particular Visible Church* is a slightly revised edition of "Questions and Answers upon Church Government" with an added section dealing with issues of church discipline and the authority of the presbytery.

terian" calls for a more stringent system of church discipline, for a rigorous screening of eucharistic communicants, and for many other correctives to an indiscriminate parish Christianity.[68] In a number of ways early Congregationalism intensified this tradition of concern, but it sought no leap beyond it into eschatology.

As Perry Miller long ago observed, protagonists of Congregational polity in early New England depended heavily upon theory already worked out by a small group of dissenters active during the quarter-century before the Great Migration. Though few, and not in agreement on all points, they were the founding theorists of the nonseparating species of Congregational polity that was to establish itself in early Massachusetts, Connecticut, and New Haven. Most often invoked in New England were Paul Baynes, Robert Parker, and—the preeminent figure—William Ames; Henry Jacob and William Bradshaw were also names to reckon with. Cotton, Hooker, Davenport, John Norton, Richard Mather, and others who ruled the New England clerical roost in the 1630s and 1640s acknowledged Baynes, Parker, and Ames as inspiring their own conversions to the Congregational position.[69] They were cited repeatedly in the polemical documents through which New England apologists strove to explain their ecclesiastical forms to English and Scottish critics.[70] No inventory of

68. For Puritan insistence upon the "holiness of the [sacramental] communicant," see E. Brooks Holifield, *The Covenant Sealed: The Development of Puritan Sacramental Theology in Old and New England, 1570–1720* (New Haven, Conn., 1974), 28, 55–56. For English Congregational applications, see Nuttall, *Visible Saints*, 136–137.

69. Only in the loosest sense can these men be described as a "school." See Miller, *Orthodoxy*, 80; and cf. Nuttall, *Visible Saints*, 9–11; see also Keith L. Sprunger, *The Learned Doctor William Ames: Dutch Backgrounds of English and American Puritanism* (Urbana, Ill., 1972), 37. On the conversions, see Miller, *Orthodoxy*, 73–101, 108–120.

70. See John Allin and Thomas Shepard, *A Defence of the Answer Made unto the Nine Questions or Positions Sent from New-England, against the Reply Thereto by . . . John Ball* (London, 1648), 73, 110, 124, 129, 149, 150; [Richard Mather?], *An Apologie of the Churches in New-England for Church-Covenant* (London, 1643), 35, 36, 41, 42, 46; John Norton, *The Answer to the Whole Set of Questions of . . . William Apollonius . . .* (1648), trans. Douglas Horton (Cambridge, Mass., 1958), 7, 46, 51, 53, 80; Cotton, *Congregational Churches*, in Ziff, ed., *John Cotton*, 189, 198. [Richard Mather], *Church-Government and Church-Covenant Discussed . . .* (London, 1643), contains more than 30 such references.

the "grounds" of the New England way can neglect the authoritative background provided by the "learned Dr. Ames" and his early Congregational colleagues. For their published writings reveal that an intensified stress upon the purity of gathered churches, coupled with rejection of "the profane and scandalous mixtures of people in the [average English] Congregation," was from the first central to the nonseparating Congregational enterprise and that their defining associations were restorationist and moralist, not eschatological.[71]

With the possible exception of Robert Parker, these men left behind no evidence that English Congregationalists, in some special manner, "anxiously awaited the apocalypse."[72] They infrequently and routinely gestured toward the Second Coming and Judgment Day and saw no unusual bearing of these ideas upon ecclesiastical polity. At no time did they adopt a millennial view.[73] In light of the widely held judgment that William Ames was the preeminent individual influence upon New England theology, it is of particular interest that his eschatological position was both clearly amillennial and decidedly lacking in anxious expectancy or zeal.[74] As for church polity,

71. Henry Jacob, *A Confession and Protestation of the Faith of Certaine Christians* . . . (Middelburg, Neth., 1616), sig. B8. The same was true of the two separating Congregationalists whose works were most valued by New Englanders: John Robinson and Henry Ainsworth.

72. Bercovitch, *Jeremiad*, 37. Parker, whose *Mystery of the Vialls Opened* draws at a number of points upon Brightman's interpretation of Revelation, may present a partial exception, but this should not be granted too hastily. Parker's millennial turn, and the composition of the *Mystery*, may date from a later period in his career when he had moved to a more Presbyterian outlook. In any case, he leaves no trace in that work or in *A Scholasticall Discourse against Symbolizing with Antichrist in Ceremonies* . . . (n.p., 1607) that he had come to perceive Congregational practice in any respect as a specialized anticipation of an earthly New Jerusalem. (I have been unable to consult his *De Politeia Ecclesiastica Christi* [Frankfurt, 1616].)

73. See, for example, Henry Jacob, *The Divine Beginning . . . of Christs True . . . Church* (Leiden, 1610), sigs. F, F2, F4, G4; William Bradshaw, *A Plaine and Pithy Exposition of the Second Epistle of Paul to the Thessalonians* (London, 1620), 27, 28, 35–53, 87–88, 108–109; Paul Baynes, *A Commentarie upon the First Chapter of the Epistle of Saint Paul, Written to the Ephesians* (London, 1618), 59–61, 237–243; Baynes, *A Commentarie upon the First and Second Chapters of Saint Paul to the Colossians* . . . (London, 1635), 18–20, 59, 62; Baynes, *Two Godly and Fruitfull Treatises* (London, 1619), 256–260.

74. See the section entitled "The End of the World" in William Ames, *The Marrow of Theology* (1629), trans. and ed. John D. Eusden (Boston, 1968),

all members of the group agreed that, insofar as possible, restriction of church membership to the pure (that is, to the "proved elect" and regenerate) was a sine qua non of authentic churches, although they did not prescribe the formal test of a public relation and interrogation that was later to appear in New England. Finally, they left their audiences in little doubt about the theological priorities that mandated narrower criteria of church membership. Their overriding concerns were two: first, the fuller sanctification and disciplinary control of the elect within their churchly fellowship; second, a fuller loyalty to the "holy native simplicity" of what "Christ did institute or the Apostles frame" within the apostolic communities.[75]

Those, exactly, were the priorities affirmed in New England of the 1630s.[76] From that decade at least seven notable ecclesiological for-

214–216. See also Sprunger, *William Ames*, 185. Ames does appear to have pondered the prophetic ideas of Joseph Mede (Mede, *Works*, 782–783).

75. Miller, *Orthodoxy*, 77–78; Baynes, *Colossians*, 217; Paul Baynes, *The Diocesans Tryall* (n.p., 1621), 1. For the immense stress upon sanctification in these materials, see, for example, Jacob, *Confession*, sig. B8; Ames, *Marrow*, 167–171, 178–179, 199–202. Baynes's *Diocesans Tryall* does not dwell upon the gathering or composition of churches, and I have not found a fuller elaboration of these themes elsewhere in his published work, but there is no doubt as to his passion for sanctification (Baynes, *Briefe Directions unto a Godly Life* [London, 1637], 26–50, 71–76). For Bradshaw's views on sanctification, see *A Direction for the Weaker Sort of Christians* (London, 1609), 86–109. For primitivist themes, see Henry Jacob, *Reasons Taken out of Gods Word* . . . (Middelburg, Neth., 1604), sig. A3, 1–5; Ames, *Marrow*, 179–181. The bulk of Bradshaw's published work was devoted to the issue of "ceremonies." See the eight tracts collected as *Several Treatises of Worship and Ceremonies* (Cambridge, 1660). These texts are almost devoid of eschatological reference.

76. Material remaining from the Congregationalist episode in the Dutch Netherlands during the 1620s and early 1630s entirely corroborates the present account. See, for example, John Davenport, *An Apologeticall Reply to a Booke Called: An Answer to the Unjust Complaint of W.B.* (Rotterdam, 1636), 1, 13, 31–32, 125–140, 259; William Ames, *A Fresh Suit against Human Ceremonies in God's Worship* (n.p., 1633), 7–8, 12, 44, 130–131; John Paget, "Mr. [John] Paget's Twenty Propositions to Mr. [Thomas] Hooker with His Answer Thereto," in Raymond Phineas Stearns, ed., *Congregationalism in the Dutch Netherlands: The Rise and Fall of the English Congregational Classis, 1621–1635* (Chicago, 1940), 105–113; Hugh Peter, "The Fifteen Articles and *Covenant* of Mr. Hugh Peter, Minister of Rhotterdam," in Champlin Burrage, *The Early English Dissenters in the Light of Recent Research (1550–1641)*, 2 vols. (Cambridge, 1912), I, 302–303. For the theme of "holiness" in Congregationalist thought, see Nuttall, *Visible Saints*, 131–155. Nuttall, however, largely ignores the primitivist dimension.

mulations remain: the "Modell of Church and Civill Power"; Cotton's "Questions and Answers upon Church Government" (1634), *A Copy of a Letter from Mr. Cotton* (1636), and *The True Constitution of a Particular Visible Church* (1636); Richard Mather's *Apologie of the Churches in New-England for Church-Covenant* (1639); John Davenport's(?) *Answer of the Elders of the Severall Churches in New-England unto Nine Positions Sent over to Them* (1639); and Mather's *Church-Government and Church-Covenant Discussed* (1639).[77] These documents make it clear that the quest for purity was a principal theme of the clerical founders, but they also disclose that the envisioned state of New World congregations—kept "pure from hypocrites" and returned to "first purity"—was associated primarily with ideals of conversion, sanctification, and apostolicity.[78] None reflects the "fervent millennial ideology" that has been ascribed unhesitatingly to the immigrants. Whether upholding their case for exclusionary sacraments, church discipline, or the narrow covenanting of individual churches, the authors' allegiance was to biblical institution and to the visible enactment of the Covenant of Grace within the lives of the converted.[79]

This allegiance was unequivocal in discussions of restriction of

77. The dates given are probable dates of composition. Richard Mather's probable authorship of *An Apologie* and *Church-Government and Church-Covenant Discussed* is established by B. R. Burg, *Richard Mather of Dorchester* (Lexington, Ky., 1976), 176 n. 14; Davenport's authorship of *An Answer of the Elders* is claimed without documentation by Isabel MacBeath Calder in her preface to *Letters of John Davenport, Puritan Divine* (New Haven, Conn., 1937), 6. For another outline of church polity, see Richard Mather, "A Letter of Richard Mather to a Cleric in Old England," ed. B. Richard Burg, *WMQ*, 3d Ser., XXIX (1972), 81–98.

78. Richard Mather, "A Letter," *WMQ*, 3d Ser., XXIX (1972), 90; John Davenport, *An Answer of the Elders of the Severall Churches in New-England unto Nine Positions Sent over to Them* (London, 1643), 56 (the "purity" motif recurs here, 56, 67).

79. MCCP, 248, 260–261, 390, 406–407; Richard Mather, *Church-Government*, 7–24; Richard Mather, *Apologie*, 6; Cotton, *Keys*, in Ziff, ed., *John Cotton*, 87–164. In his *Canticles* (1655), Cotton situated a discussion of Congregational exclusiveness within the context of a paean to the "Primitive Apostolic Church" (105, 107, and see 79–118 for the general context). For the moral theme, it is also profitable to survey the various available reprints of the earliest New England church covenants; see Walker, *Creeds and Platforms*, 116–117, 121, 131, 154–156; Woburn's covenant is reprinted in *WWP*, 216.

membership to visible saints and of the required public testimony. The clergy consistently viewed this measure in light of New England's new-won "opportunity to administer . . . all the ordinances of God, according to the pattern set before us in Scripture," and laid equal stress upon its elevated moral intent.[80] Mather went so far as to explain the new requirement as a reaction to perceived decline in moral zeal. Removed from the stimulus of episcopal surveillance and repression and standing under the benevolent protection of friendly colony governments, New Englanders had found it increasingly difficult to sustain the tense disciplines of the Puritan way. For this reason a greater need had emerged "to be . . . studious in the examination of mens estates" as they proceeded toward membership in their communities.[81]

Purity's dual associations with restoration and disciplined holiness —with "pure ordinances [and] pure people," in Shepard's phrase— originated partly in differing concerns and were of course capable of separate treatment. But immigrant spokesmen never doubted and continually affirmed their close conjunction within the plan of Christian Redemption. And as they strove to display the close and ultimate harmony of moralist and primitivist doctrine, at least one of the foremost founders found John Foxe an important guide. What Richard Mather retrieved from Foxe was not, let it be emphasized, a notion of millennial-national mission, but a compelling legend establishing an apostolic source for Britain's first Christianity. Joseph of Arimathea,

80. Davenport, *Answer*, 51. See also Richard Mather, *Church-Government*, 21, and Richard Mather, "A Letter," *WMQ*, 3d Ser., XXIX (1972), 90–91. In their somewhat later *Defence* (1648), Allin and Shepard also presented the public testimony as a device "ever required in the purest [that is, apostolic] times" and as essential in the present for ridding the church of those "heaps of prophane persons" included in English parish churches (188, 190–191; and see 10, 20, 120, 188–201). Even here, in a polemic composed during the period of millennial excitement, little eschatological concern is discoverable. For other post-1640 expressions in the same vein, see Norton, *The Answer*, 25–43; Thomas Hooker, *A Survey of the Summe of Church-Discipline* (London, 1648), pt. 1, chap. 2, 14–33; PCD, 205–209, 212–213, 221–224, 227–229.

81. Mather, *Apologie*, 30. See also Davenport, *Answer*, 62–64, 69–70. The New England evidence is entirely consistent with Nuttall's thesis that "what the Congregational men had in mind in limiting church membership to visible saints was to be assured of those whose regeneration was real . . . and whose holiness . . . would be effectual" (*Visible Saints*, 161).

the story's central figure, was the man who had recovered, garbed, and entombed the dead body of Christ (Mark 15:43–46). Subsequently he became the first missionary to Britain and successfully planted Christianity there within the lifetime of the Apostles.

For Mather, Joseph's direct link to Christianity's first and transcendentally important period guaranteed England's founding churches a full share in both dimensions of apostolic purity. As a Congregationalist, he drew the obvious conclusion: England's earliest Christian communities had been organized in total conformity to Christ's "appointments." They were independent, covenanted, disciplined congregations of professed saints, saints who had made public profession of their faith and repentance upon entry into the church. Their churches were, in short, Congregational in type, like those of New England in the 1630s. This was, however, but background to the high claim that Mather now advanced. The New England way, he inferred, inclusive of the practice of public testimony, *was* primitive Arimathean-British Christianity at last regained. Through their close screening of prospective members, the New England congregations had retrieved an ancient apostolicity rooted in sacred appointment and in an ideal of converted, sanctified sainthood, both drawn from the fountainhead of the Christian dispensation.[82] Rising to this lofty train of thought, Mather provided a far more representative index of the norms governing the first immigrants' quest for a higher ecclesiastical purity than scantily documented hypotheses of "millennial fervor."

To recur, then, to the earlier question: Was there an initial and crucially inspiring millennial consensus among the first New Englanders? The evidence points unmistakably to the negative. Interest in a millennial errand has arisen from serious concerns: from a wish to remedy long-standing neglect of prophetic themes and, in some authors, from the conviction that a consensual and linear view of American history must be anchored in comprehensive appeal to the early and decisive experience of Puritan America. Again, the first settlers' alleged hope for an American millennium has proven useful to Americanists in search of parentage for themes as diverse as environmental reform and prophetic typology.[83] Here is an estimation

82. Shepard, *Works*, II, 65; Richard Mather, *Church-Government*, 24–25; Richard Mather, *Apologie*, 36–37.
83. Tichi, *New World*, vii–x, 15–36; Lowance, *Language of Canaan*, vii–ix.

of the importance of beginnings that Puritans well might envy. Yet, in the final analysis, the notion of a pervasive millennialism rooted in "the start" of the Puritan enterprise has tended to function more as an unduly powerful presupposition than as a cautiously derived result of research in the Puritan materials.

Those materials show that a true and reasonably influential millennial doctrine in New England emerged in rough chronological parallel with the comparable development in the Dutch Netherlands and in England. Probably the first founder to expound an unequivocally millennial outlook was John Cotton, who did so in a series of Thursday lectures in Boston between 1639 and 1641. In these lectures Cotton presented a full commentary upon the Revelation, of which three published segments are extant: *An Exposition upon the Thirteenth Chapter of the Revelation, The Powring out of the Seven Vials*, and *The Churches Resurrection*.

It is indeed significant, as J. F. Maclear has suggested, that these works were a product of the critical time around 1640 when the great English conflict, which New Englanders followed with deep concern, was beginning to unfold.[84] Cotton's lectures were composed in full sensitivity to the growing crisis in Scotland that so greatly was to alter the terms of England's national existence for two decades. In an early lecture he remarked the portentous "stirs in Scotland" and later depicted the Scottish revolt as the "pouring out of the fifth vial" in the prophetic timetable of Revelation 16. Thus even in the remote New England colonies, it was the great upsurge in the mother country that caused the millennial heresy of Brightman and Mede to climb the agenda of Puritan faith.[85]

84. Maclear, "Fifth Monarchy," *WMQ*, 3d Ser., XXXII (1975), 232. For probable dating of Cotton's lectures, see the preface of the *Exposition upon Revelation*. The three segments were published in London in 1655, 1642, and 1642 respectively.

85. Cotton, *Exposition upon Revelation*, 96 (and see 259 for reference to the calling of the Long Parliament); Cotton, *Seven Vials*, "The Fifth Vial," 7–8. Cotton had delivered an earlier set of lectures upon Canticles before his departure from old Boston, and there, obviously under the influence of Brightman's commentary on the work, he treated it as a "prophetical history." But compared with his views of the 1640s, and with the exception of a reasonably specific discussion of the coming "Church of the Jews," the millennial concept remained inchoate in this early work (*Canticles* [1642], 221–223, 228, 230, 246). I have found no evidence that Cotton stressed or even expressed these concepts in Massachusetts before 1639. Considered as an unmistakably protomillennial

Joining Brightman's concepts of a Middle Coming and a millennial church to Mede's greater stress upon the political transformation of all "kingdoms," Cotton regaled his Thursday audiences with the image of a coming world order that likely far exceeded their expectations. Edward Johnson later was to claim that Cotton had opened the meaning of Revelation "as nere was of old." Leaving the sketchy glimpses of the 1630s far behind and repeatedly acknowledging the pivotal influence of "holy Brightman," Cotton amplified the themes of Catholic destruction and Jewish conversion into a vision of protracted and worldwide millennial reign. While he did not with Brightman employ the symbolism of Revelation 21 as the organizing theme for his end-time prospectus, he did now accept the fateful transferal of New Jerusalem from heaven to earth.[86]

New Jerusalem, of course, was not New England. Cotton did not hold that New England had inaugurated, was called to inaugurate, or conceivably could inaugurate the millennium. Nowhere did he affirm that "the great American migration had taken place so that the Lord could have a laboratory model of ecclesiastical polity ready for mass production" when the great hour arrived. Nor did he or any other New Englander of the 1630s or 1640s identify the Puritan colonies as *the* scene or headquarters of the New Jerusalem.[87] Cotton applauded the "great Reformation of churches" that the migrants had wrought. In their covenanted, relatively purified congregations he

---

statement, Cotton's first treatment of Canticles had no counterpart among the English works of Shepard, Thomas Hooker, Davenport, Richard Mather, or any other notable emigrant theologian known to me. A partial exception is Huit's *Daniel*; see below, n. 98.

86. *WWP*, 89; Cotton, *Exposition upon Revelation*, 87; Cotton, *Resurrection*, 13. See also the comments on Brightman in Anthony Tuckney's preface to Cotton, *Canticles* (1655), sig. A8. Cotton's version of the millennium is discussed more fully below in Chapter 8.

87. Larzer Ziff, *Puritanism in America: New Culture in a New World* (New York, 1973), 177; Lowance, *Language of Canaan*, 134. John F. Wilson's argument that in these tracts "Cotton portrayed the Bay Colony experiment as a proleptical participation in the millennial reign" is truer to Cotton's intent, but the point should not be exaggerated (*Pulpit in Parliament*, 226). In a few other texts of the period, a concept of New England as in some special sense adumbrating the millennium does appear, but none presents this as a—or the—conscious purpose of the Great Migration. See *WP*, V, 126; T. Hooker, *Survey*, sig. c; *WWP*, 49, 60.

saw the foremost achievement in Protestant reformation, and this he deemed "fair preparation" for the new age. Having uprooted every discernible remnant of popery and achieved an advanced state of biblical recovery, the settlements stood in singular readiness for the great transition, and by implication they should be spared some of the upheavals that elsewhere must accompany it.[88]

But Cotton was too aware of lapses and imperfections, and too alert to the larger eschatological schedule, to see in any of this the dynamic of world renewal. Hypocrisy, economic oppression, carnal self-love, formality, and mounting evidence that some of the settlers were growing weary of religious rigors—precisely these New England failings stood as reminders that "the thousand years are not yet begun." If repentance were forthcoming and if the churches held to their course of reformation, then the colonies would have full share in the millennial pleasures when they arrived, but they possessed no power to inaugurate the decisive changes. New Jerusalem could not appear until the ruin of Rome and the rise of a Jewish church. Those were the inaugural events, and they would occur far from American shores, probably about 1655.[89]

Indeed, in one specific "corner of the world" the preliminary commotions already had begun. They commenced in the Scottish popular protest against the Prayer Book, which Charles I had sought to impose in 1637, and had grown into a national movement against episcopacy and human inventions in worship in both Scotland and England. From there it would "goe on from our native countrey to all the Catholickes Countries . . . untill it come unto the very gates of *Rome* itself." Cotton did not deny to New England a role in this activity. "Our work," he suggested, was to wrestle in prayer from afar that Protestant forces might succeed and that they might pass beyond the halfway house of Presbyterianism. Moreover, the "bright and cleare knowledge" soon to spread worldwide would "bring in all nations" to the Congregational way: "We should not be wanting on our parts to help with what light we have."[90] Perhaps Cotton meant

88. Cotton, *Resurrection*, 20–21.

89. *Ibid.*; Cotton, *Seven Vials*, "The Seventh Vial," 16, "The Fifth Vial," 7.

90. Cotton, *Seven Vials*, "The Fifth Vial," 7, "The Seventh Vial," 5, 15–17. Cotton also urged, "Let us help them what we can by Prayer," in *Exposition upon Revelation*, 262; he suggested 1655 as the date of a "great blow" against

that letters and polemical tracts addressing issues of church government might be of service and even that the settlements themselves
might supply needed evidence that churches of visible saints did not
undermine effective, orderly society; but this was not the stuff of a
"millennial errand." New World colonies were neither to precipitate,
nor to provide the central site for, the wondrous times to come.

We should not confuse this emerging millennialism with expectations of the Second Coming.[91] At times, millennial (or protomillennial) and amillennial themes might appear inconsistently juxtaposed,
as in Shepard's *Ten Virgins*; but paramount in Puritan quarters at
mid-century was the Joachimist-Brightman teaching that "Christ has
three commings" and that "the latter commings are two distinct commings, not one (as it hath beene thought)." Hence it was absolutely
necessary to distinguish between Christ's "second comming unto
Judgement" and his earlier and entirely distinct "comming in the
brightnesse of the Gospell."[92] What was expected—or read already

---

Rome (93). Joseph Mede, as James W. Davidson has pointed out, also specifically
envisioned America as "a place remote from the central drama" (*The Logic of
Millennial Thought: Eighteenth-Century New England* [New Haven, Conn.,
1978], 54).

91. Thus in one article Jesper Rosenmeier associates the American Puritans'
hope for "New Jerusalem" with "Christ's triumphant descent"; in another,
he finds them envisioning the millennium as "the first step in the Second
Coming . . . after which he would reappear at the resurrection of the body
and the day of judgment" ("Veritas," *Harvard Library Bulletin*, XVI [1968], 33;
"New England's Perfection: The Image of Adam and the Image of Christ in the
Antinomian Crisis, 1634 to 1638," *WMQ*, 3d Ser., XXVII [1970], 457). With
slight variations the error is widely repeated.

92. John Archer, quoted in Reeves, "History and Eschatology," *Medievalia
et Humanistica*, N.S., IV (1973), 117; [Finch], *Great Restauration*, 48. Archer
was among the few, however, to identify the Middle Coming as a personal
coming of Christ to earth. For New England expressions, see, for example,
[John Davenport], *An Apology of the Churches in New-England for Church
Government* (London, 1643), 46; Davenport, *Answer*, 54; Cotton, *Exposition
upon Revelation*, 217; Cotton, *Seven Vials*, "Third Part of the Sixth Vial," 2–5,
and "The Seventh Vial," 5; *WWP*, 34–35, 159; Henry Whitfield *et al.*, *The Light
Appearing More and More towards the Perfect Day* (1651), in *MHSC*, 3d Ser.,
IV (Boston, 1834), 120. See also Shepard's distinction between the "brightness
of his coming" and the "Second Coming" in *Works*, II, 24–25, and Johnson's
identical distinction between "brightness of his Gospel" and "last coming" in
WWP, 34–35. The distinction is implicit in Cotton, *Canticles* (1655), 219.

in current events—was the penultimate coming, the Middle Advent and its effect upon world history for a privileged interval long before the Second Coming. This was the view which now came to the fore and enjoyed, in rough synchrony with theological developments in the mother country, a period of vitality and significance during the 1640s and early 1650s.

During the first decade of turmoil, the appearance of Anne Bradstreet's "Dialogue between New and Old England" (1642), Thomas Parker's *Visions and Prophecies of Daniel Expounded* (1646), Thomas Hooker's preface to his *Survey of the Summe of Church-Discipline* (1648), John Eliot's *Christian Commonwealth* (1650 or 1651), and Edward Johnson's *Wonder-Working Providence* (1650) demonstrate that the traditional abhorrence of chiliasm was much diminished and that a broad interest had been generated in the promise of a "brighter day" for Protestant mankind of Brightman, Mede, Alsted, and Cotton.[93] Even at this point, however, it is well to avoid excessive claims. At no time did the new eschatological fashion come broadly to "dominate religious writing" in New England. We might see this, for example, by placing Cotton's Boston lectures on Revelation and Canticles, his only American productions with sizable eschatological content, in the much larger context of his published output from his arrival in 1633 to his death in 1652. No reader would infer from the several other writings—on Congregational theory and practice, on the Covenant of Grace and the holiness of church members, on baptism, on the singing of Psalms, on church and state—that their author was in the grip of a constant and determinative millennial enthusiasm.[94]

93. A fuller inventory of millennial utterances would include Cotton, *Canticles* (1655; written ca. 1645); Samuel Symond to John Winthrop, Feb. 1646, *WP*, V, 126; Bulkeley, *Gospel-Covenant* (1646), 15–21; various expressions by John Eliot in the Indian tracts of 1647–1653, *MHSC*, 3d Ser., IV (Boston, 1834), 119–121, 127, 131, 212–216; John Davenport to Mary, Lady Vere, Dec. 1647, in Davenport, *Letters*, 81–82; Richard Mather, "To the Christian Reader," in John Eliot and Jonathan Mayhew, *Tears of Repentance . . .* (1653), *MHSC*, 3d Ser., IV (Boston, 1834), 217–225; and possibly William Aspinwall, *A Brief Description of the Fifth Monarchy . . .* (London, 1653). In "Fifth Monarchy," *WMQ*, 3d Ser., XXXII (1975), 252 n. 65, Maclear argues the possibility that the last tract was composed in New England.

94. Lowance, *Language of Canaan*, 118. For a bibliography of Cotton's works, see Emerson, *John Cotton*, 164–166. In works composed in the early

Like Cotton, Eliot and Johnson exuberantly pursued the new theme, but others remained cautious. There are few eschatological references of any sort in the writings of John Winthrop (d. 1649). Shepard and Hooker, after Cotton the two most prolific orthodox writers in New England of the 1640s, had far less than he to say upon millennial topics. Hesitant millennial notes creep into Shepard's *Ten Virgins*, but its dominating concern is, not the Middle Advent, but the traditional Second Coming. In 1648 Shepard hoped that the developing mission to the Indians was "preparative" to a Protestant golden age, but disclaimed certainty of what the future would bring.[95] In the preface to his *Survey of the Summe of Church-Discipline*, drawing upon Brightman and Mede, Hooker identified the 1640s as "*the season*, when all the kingdomes of the world, are becoming the Lords and his Christs," yet the thesis applied in the text is that "Ecclesiastical Policy is a skill of ordering the affairs of Christs house, according to the [primitive] pattern." Similarly, in his preface to *The Answer*, John Norton hoped for "the ruin of Rome, the coming in

---

1640s, Davenport and Richard Mather reflected briefly upon the "consumption" of Antichrist, the "brightness of [Christ's] coming," the growth in Christian understanding "especially touching the ordering of [Christ's] house" near the end of history (Davenport, *Answer*, 54; Mather, *Apology*, 46). Here is a point of connection between Congregational polity and eschatology. Yet both statements are hurried, undeveloped, and completely innocent of any special associations with New England.

95. Thomas Shepard's disclaimer of 1648 is in *The Clear Sun-shine of the Gospel Breaking Forth upon the Indians in New-England*, MHSC, 3d Ser., III (Boston, 1834), 60: "I have no skill in prophecies, . . . nor do I believe every man's interpretation of such scripture" (see also 64). Shepard's earlier *Parable of the Ten Virgins*, composed between 1636 and 1640, propounded briefly the "brightness of Christ's coming," the destruction of Catholicism, and Jewish conversion (*Works*, II, 24–25, 410, 448, 508; see also *Works*, I, 40). These ideas, however, remain marginal. They are not expanded into a specifically millennial vision. Significantly, Shepard cited Pareus's rebuttal of Brightman. His real concentration was upon the *Second* Coming, the "terror of the Lord and the wrath to come, and the heavenly state" (*Works*, II, 145–146, 404, 410, 528–534, 634). He had nothing to say of New England's inaugurating a millennial age and explicitly rejected Brightman's conception of the New Jerusalem. He rather saw the colonial enterprise in the later 1630s as lapsing into the "carnal security" that he believed to be the predicted general state of "virgin churches" in the interval before the Second Coming and the end of time (*Works*, II, 13–16, 25–26, 184, 370–378, 441–443, 527).

of the fullness of the Gentiles, [and] the calling of the Jews"; but these themes play little if any part in the some two hundred pages of Norton's text.[96]

Thomas Parker's *Daniel* explicitly repudiates the Brightman-Cotton rendition of New Jerusalem, positing instead a mere forty-five year interval of millennial "inchoation" as prelude to the imminent Second Coming.[97] To this it might be added that Ephraim Huit's *Daniel* (1644), lately commended as a showpiece of "the millennium in America," was in all probability written before Huit emigrated to New England in 1639, and that Michael Wigglesworth's *Day of Doom* (1662), by far the single most popular eschatological statement written by a New Englander in the seventeenth century, was without trace of the millennial concept in any form.[98]

While it stands beyond doubt that a rich and long-neglected vein of millennial discussion runs through New England theology beginning

96. T. Hooker, *Survey*, sig. a3 (see also sig. a), 1–11; Norton, *The Answer*, 7. Elsewhere Norton identified New Jerusalem with heaven (*The Orthodox Evangelist* [London, 1654], 343–344, and see 353–354). Sargent Bush, Jr., also finds little millennial interest in Hooker's writings (*The Writings of Thomas Hooker: Spiritual Adventure in Two Worlds* [Madison, Wis., 1980], 24).

97. Thomas Parker, *Daniel*, 34–35, 147–148, 154–155. Parker also believed, with Brightman, that the final age would be preceded by a general "inundation of the Reformed Churches" (62). Tending to a Presbyterian understanding of church polity, he also drew no special associations with New England.

98. Sacvan Bercovitch describes Huit's tract as "the first comprehensive commentary on Daniel written in America," but Huit's dedication indicates an English origin (Bercovitch, *The Millennium in America*, brochure, AMS Press series [New York, 1980], 4; Huit, *Daniel*, sigs. A2–A3). Virtually all scholars interested in Huit's *Daniel* have assumed unquestioningly its American authorship. See Le Roy Edwin Froom, *The Prophetic Faith of Our Fathers: The Historical Development of Prophetic Interpretation*, 4 vols. (Washington, D.C., 1946–1954), II, 60; Ira V. Brown, "Watchers for the Second Coming: The Millenarian Tradition in America," *Mississippi Valley Historical Review*, XXXIX (1952–1953), 445; Maclear, "Fifth Monarchy," *WMQ*, 3d Ser., XXXII (1975), 235; Gilpin, *Roger Williams*, 62; Gura, *Sion's Glory*, 132.

Michael Wigglesworth, *The Day of Doom . . .* , ed. Kenneth B. Murdock (New York, 1966). The few eschatological references in Wigglesworth's *Diary* likewise concentrate upon "the great and dreadful day of Judgment" and "the saints' future [heavenly] glory" (*The Diary of Michael Wigglesworth, 1653–1657: The Conscience of a Puritan*, ed. Edmund S. Morgan [New York, 1965], 51, 97).

about 1640, it easily can be exaggerated. The useful role now for historians is to avoid promotion of this element beyond its original importance and with too little regard for the hesitant, inchoate form in which it often was propounded, and to discover its place within a far larger ensemble of concerns.

SEVEN

JOHN COTTON

AND END-TIME

PROGRESS

With the Puritan engagement with the millennium in sharper focus, it is time to inquire more closely into ties to the primitivist dimension. Specifically, the question is whether early New England millennialism was a progressive adventure in ideas. To what degree was the eschatology of Cotton, Eliot, and their millennially aroused colleagues governed by the category of the future? As they now moved to alter Reformed concepts of the Christian career in time, they unwittingly contributed to the complex development that was to give rise to the dogma of linear progress. Yet in this instance the lines of intellectual history do not run straight and clear. Many a Congregational settler, reappraising the prophetic outlook in light of the English crisis, learned to attach greater value to time future, but no one on record envisioned present history as an essentially linear procession into the greater age. In the new eschatology the future meant eclipse of the ordinary past, of the past that was human invention and loss of primal integrity, but it also meant fulfillment of the *retro*spective hope that had inspired the Great Migration.

The increased potency of that hope, once transposed into prophecy, can be discerned in two documents of the period that anticipate and describe most fully the coming transformation: Cotton's *Churches Resurrection* and Eliot's *Christian Commonwealth*. Taken together, they provide an inclusive sketch of the new age, with Cotton outlining its ecclesiastical structure and Eliot projecting "Civil Policy." To recapture their understanding of the last-time epic at the most basic level, one does well to consider their common and emphatic exclusion of the category "human" from any part in a theology of the Last Things. Unitedly, they proclaimed that the Lord was about "to shake all the Earth" free of "all *humane* Powers, Polities, Dominions, and Governments." The contemplated divine action would accomplish what more than a century of reformation and three-quarters of a century of Puritan crusading had been unable to realize: the general routing of *man's* "institutions" by God's. Here was the tie to the larger program of Puritan thought. So framed, millennial doctrine became a final impeachment of Richard Hooker's *Laws of Ecclesiastical Polity* and of the fatal doctrine of adiaphora open to man's maneuver. As Cotton put it, the great church to come would be one in which the saints, now joyously immersed in the world of sacred writ, "shall execute not their owne Government but the government of Christ." In Eliot's phrasing, the coming order was to be a biblical commonwealth in which "no Humane . . . Policy or Wisdom doth guide any thing, but all is done by Divine direction."[1]

Here, in the uniform vision of mankind rendered resistless to scriptural rule, is a quintessential marker of the Puritan complexion of the newer eschatology of the 1640s and 1650s. For now it became evident that the necessary catalyst of man's imminent and *progressive* venture into a newness beyond profane history was precisely the removal of novelty, of all long-hated invention, from the face of the earth. Thus the mature eschatology of Cotton and Eliot signals again the premodern side of the Puritan attitude. For them the great leap forward into a brighter day was to be simultaneously a magnificent recession from history's corruptions, back toward the purity of sacred originals. How is this striking dependence of last upon first things best to be understood?

Primordium and Millennium in Puritan Perspective

Mircea Eliade's approach to "Judaeo-Christian apocalypses" is relevant here. His basic suggestion is that historical Western

1. CC, 130, 131, 141, emphasis mine; John Cotton, *The Churches Resurrection* . . . (London, 1642), 11.

eschatologies can be comprehended as modified instances of mythic thinking generally. Distinguished by their focus upon a future state, and thus as uniquely "granting . . . value to the future," Christian myths of the end of the world nevertheless do not understand time as forward transit. They do not supersede, but redirect mythic concentration upon sacred and privileged beginnings. It is the highest ideals of myth, the devotion to first times and the concern for their recovery, that now are associated with a future estate. Although the relation is not one of simple repetition, eschatology may be said to recapitulate cosmogony. The future era, whether heaven or the millennium, will "rebegin"; it will recapture Edenic conditions. Thus the future that awaits expectant saints involves a "restoration of Paradise," a state of things that, far from sweeping their gaze forward in a unilinear sense, promises a climactic "return to primordial time."[2] Students of Western eschatology, then, must cope with a dizzying, unmodern logic that insists upon connecting the end with the beginning of history and that discerns *first* things restored in the *final* earthly estate.[3]

By placing sacred past and transfigured future in polar relationship, this eschatological model embodies many helps to better understanding the hope for a new world in mid-seventeenth-century New England. For this hope, trained as it was upon a future condition, nevertheless sustained an immeasurably potent inner concern to recover primordial content.

Given the insatiable Puritan taste for recovery of the primitive, it is no surprise that Brightman, Cotton, and others may have incorporated motifs of return into their concepts of the future. Yet we should note also that Eliade's analysis tends to stress the paradisiacal element, thus conjuring associations with the exotic abundance and

2. Mircea Eliade, *Cosmos and History: The Myth of the Eternal Return*, trans. Willard R. Trask (New York, 1959), 107; Mircea Eliade, *Myth and Reality*, trans. Willard R. Trask (New York, 1963), 65, 76; Robert A. Segal, "Eliade's Theory of Millenarianism," *Religious Studies*, XIV (1978), 159. See also *International Encyclopedia of the Social Sciences* (1968), s.v. "Millenarism," by Yonina Talmon, 353, 360.

3. Eliade, *Myth and Reality*, 54–74; Mircea Eliade, *Mephistopheles and the Androgyne: Studies in Religious Myth and Symbol*, trans. J. M. Cohen (New York, 1965), 125–159; Mircea Eliade, " 'Cargo Cults' and Cosmic Regeneration," in Sylvia A. Thrupp, ed., *Millennial Dreams in Action: Studies in Revolutionary Religious Movements* (New York, 1970), 139–143.

delight and the absence of ills in the unspoiled Garden of Eden. A sensuous, pleasureful note clearly is implied. That Protestant eschatology of the sixteenth and seventeenth century dwelt upon such associations has been maintained as well by others, who join Eliade in detecting a large enthusiasm for "restoration of the Edenic paradise" in contemporary Protestant sources, both Puritan and non-Puritan.[4] Now, motifs of paradise certainly played a role in Protestant eschatology. Looking only at Puritan sectors, we find that Brightman's "millenary reign" embraced an "abundance of all good things," including everbearing fruit trees. Similar notes occur in the prophetic contributions of Richard Bernard, Henry Finch, John Archer, and others, and Cotton connected the state of a fully renewed church with Adam's "estate . . . in the garden of Paradise."[5] But have we then discovered the characteristic content of the last-time restoration visualized by the first American millennialists? Was the main anticipated effect of Christ's bright coming the recovery of a fruited garden and "sylvan felicity"?[6]

To these questions the answer is firmly negative. As their restorationist emphasis demonstrates, Puritan dreams of an approaching better world were an extension of Reformed and biblicist ideals; and these ideals, as the most casual student of the Puritan movement will know, were neither sylvan nor paradisiac and were disposed to

4. Mircea Eliade, "Paradise and Utopia," in Frank E. Manuel, ed., *Utopias and Utopian Thought* (Boston, 1965), 261, 264–266, 269 (see also Eliade, *Myth and Reality*, 65–66); Charles L. Sanford, *The Quest for Paradise: Europe and the American Moral Imagination* (Urbana, Ill., 1961), 82–85; Robert Middlekauff, *The Mathers: Three Generations of Puritan Intellectuals, 1596–1728* (London, 1971), 23; Mason I. Lowance, Jr., *The Language of Canaan: Metaphor and Symbol in New England from the Puritans to the Transcendentalists* (Cambridge, Mass., 1980), 119–120. Eliade's own venture into American Puritan eschatology is little more than a paraphrase of material from Sanford (Eliade, "Paradise," 261–270; Sanford, *Quest*, 80, 82).

5. Thomas Brightman, *A Revelation of the Apocalyps* (Amsterdam, 1611), 704–705; Richard Bernard, *A Key of Knowledge for the Opening of the Secret Mysteries of St. Johns Mysticall Revelation* (London, 1617), 334–335; [Henry Finch], *The Worlds Great Restauration* (London, 1621), 233; John Cotton, *A Brief Exposition of the Whole Book of Canticles, or, Song of Solomon* (London, 1642), 130. Archer's invocation of a "fulness of all temporal blessings" is quoted in Ernest Lee Tuveson, *Millennium and Utopia: A Study in the Background of the Idea of Progress* (New York, 1964), 86.

6. Sanford, *Quest*, viii.

suspect, not to favor, sensuous delights. So extraordinary, indeed, was its preoccupation with methods of self-control as to lead Michael Walzer, in *The Revolution of the Saints,* virtually to *define* Puritanism as the needed ordering agent in a context of social breakdown and early modernization. While hardly sufficient as a comprehensive explanation, his account brings into focus the unrelenting, almost unbearably grave accents upon control and denial that pervade Puritan utterance. Others may have dreamed of a green paradise or of beds of Arcadian ease, and such notes were sounded by apocalyptic extremists in the middle years of the seventeenth century, but that was not the precisionist way.

Both in England and New England much of the vast effort in Puritan preaching and cure of souls had been lavished upon the arts of sanctification, upon the "Great Warfare" of the individual with wayward impulse and temptation; and if this meant anything distinctive within the broad Protestant movement, it meant a comparatively radical commitment to an ascetic style of life. The short list of pleasures these Christians allowed themselves was carefully contained, like sober marital love within a properly sanctified family or the ecstatic but cautiously restricted enlargements that might be imparted occasionally in prayer or meditation. Those Puritans who anticipated a transfigured life did not expect thereupon to relax their antagonism to carnal pleasure and their hard-won virtuosity in self-denial. To stress the Edenic element in Puritan millennialism is therefore to flirt with a serious misrepresentation.

Puritan objection to the sensuously self-indulgent elements in patristic chiliasm went far to explain the long resistance within the Spiritual Brotherhood to the millennial concept. Brightman himself had labored to clear his New Jerusalem from association with the excesses of patristic thinkers who "leaned too much in their opinions to the delights of the body"; and if, indeed, he was receptive to the prospect of physical abundance, of "continual spring and harvest," he simultaneously made clear that this was a minor aspect of the total experience. It was largely a matter of speculation upon obscure texts with which he would prefer "not [to] meddle any whit at all." As for Brightman, so for Bernard, Finch, Cotton, Eliot, Edward Johnson, and many others the admittedly "unmeasurable pleasantness" of the coming era was a function, not of relaxed indulgence, but of finally secured and rigorous conformity to biblical rule. Uniformly they believed that the world would become "the Kingdome of Christ, when by the Scepter of his word he ruleth among [the] people."[7]

New Englanders portrayed the kingdom as a panoramic display of ascetic holiness whose absolute center was the Christian church remodeled along Congregational lines. They looked for the day when churches in every nation would be found swollen with genuinely regenerate men and women sincerely clamoring for "full and exact conformity to heavenly rules." A generalized system of church discipline was to extend everywhere an all-seeing "watch" upon behavior. Scorning the sumptuous liturgy of Mass and Prayer Book, all Christian citizens would rally to the lean simplicity of primal ordinances.[8] By Congregational lights, that was a restorationist's paradise indeed, but it was not patterned upon prelapsarian Eden. It was an intense visualization of the long-urged further reformation of English Christianity now carried through, by force of the Middle Advent, to ecstatic completion and to ecumenical dominance. Its programmatic aspect was the enclosure of church, state, and by implication all the "moral actions of man" within the jurisdiction of biblical precept and archetype as those were construed, in 1640, by men and women of Congregational bent.[9]

Enclosure—this appears as a fundamental feature of the future dreamed of in mid-seventeenth-century New England. With its ap-

7. Brightman, *Apocalyps*, 657, 658, 704. B. S. Capp, *The Fifth-Monarchy Men: A Study in Seventeenth-Century English Millenarianism* (London, 1972), 28, notes that for Brightman "the millennium was the purified Presbyterian church."

8. Isabel MacBeath Calder, ed., *Letters of John Davenport, Puritan Divine* (New Haven, Conn., 1937), 82. For a reference to millennial church discipline, see Cotton, *Resurrection*, 10. On Mass and Prayer Book, see also, for example, John Cotton, *A Brief Exposition with Practical Observations upon the Whole Book of Canticles* (London, 1655), 179–283; WWP, 137–138. See also Brightman, *Apocalyps*, 637, 679, 684.

9. CC, 163. In his study of Roger Williams's millennial doctrine, W. Clark Gilpin argues that the primitivist element "cannot be overemphasized; when he spoke of the millennial rule of Christ, he referred quite specifically to a restoration of the church to what he conceived to be its apostolic form" (*The Millenarian Piety of Roger Williams* [Chicago, 1979], 61). Both Sanford and Eliade note that the restored primitive church figured prominently in Puritan millennial visions, but neither appears to recognize the critical distinctions between this element and Edenic paradise (Sanford, *Quest*, 104–105; Eliade, "Paradise," in Manuel, ed., *Utopias and Utopian Thought*, 266–267).

pearance we cross the threshold into the millennium proper, to that state which was to see Congregational-Puritan ideals brought to their fullest actualization in history. Pursuing this theme further will enable one to grasp what New England eschatologists of the period finally understood and affirmed as "progress." To do this we turn again to Cotton and will attempt to reconstruct and set in context his view of the course of events during the climactic era of mankind's historical *progression*: the era of kingdom building to commence with the fall of the Catholic adversary.

Progress through Regress in the Last Times

Already in his lectures on Revelation Cotton evinced an interest, and one probably unprecedented in New England, in charting and celebrating the millennial experience itself. Now was the time to impress upon Christian audiences the full transfigurative implication of the Middle Advent. In his emerging concept, there remained many signs that the finite state of human history was not to be transcended until the Second Coming. Although many would, many individuals and nations would not be converted so to share in the promised epoch. Death would cease to evoke terror, but the condition of mortality would remain; and while "restrained" for the duration, Satan would retain the capacity to "tempt."[10] And yet Christ's "coming in . . . brightness" was to bring a great extension of the ordinary limits upon Christian belief, performance, and felicity within history. How far the millennium was to surpass the normal historical condition of mankind could be seen, to begin with, in the circumstances of its origin. For Cotton now publicized the idea advanced by Brightman and taken up by Bernard, Finch, and others, that centuries before the traditionally expected Second Coming there was to be a preliminary intrusion of divine power, that this would facilitate a mass mobilization of Protestant armies, and that in the ensuing battle of

10. Cotton, *Resurrection*, 5, 7, 12–13, 14, 16. For the Middle Coming, see also John Cotton, *The Powring out of the Seven Vials* (London, 1642), "Third Part of the Sixth Vial," 2; Cotton, *An Exposition upon the Thirteenth Chapter of the Revelation* (London, 1655), 217; and the discussion of the "brightening" of the world with a "bright and clear knowledge" in *Seven Vials*, "The Seventh Vial," 4–5.

Armageddon every military and political force opposed to the Reformation would be crushed. Perhaps borrowing from Foxe, Cotton assured his audience how, with Catholicism's graven images expelled and hence the "greatest impediments of [Jewish] conversion" eliminated, that people would enter the Christian fold. And with every effective agent of resistance destroyed, the now-expanded Christian enterprise could develop freely for the first time and establish itself worldwide in "great . . . felicity and tranquillity."[11]

But however exhilarating such prospects must have seemed, the full measure of the Middle Advent remained to be taken. For if, in the formula popularized by Mede, "all the kingdoms of the world" were hence to pass into Reformed Protestant jurisdiction, the new-won "reign . . . both in Church and Commonwealth" was not to be grasped as a straight extension of current Protestant conditions anywhere, New England included. When the new epoch commenced, Christian comprehension, sensibility, and power of accomplishment were to be heightened far beyond any previous historical experience from the end of New Testament times to the seventeenth-century present. The supernatural power released by the Bright Coming was to flow more abundantly through the age and work a "general change" in the human condition. Every Christian soul was to brim with redeeming "knowledge." The great access of transforming grace would cause Christians to "Shine as Stars" and allure others to conversion by sheer example. Satan, that historic agency of mankind's ills and corruptions, was to be imprisoned in a deep pit and his power to "deceive the nations" curtailed. The halting achievements of Protestant reform of individual and ecclesiastical life at last would be brought to fulfillment. Congregationalism would prevail everywhere.[12]

Few if any theorists of the 1640s and 1650s saw the millennial order as the creation of an instant. It was the way of the Middle Coming both to build upon previous beginnings and to propel events toward completion through a process of gradual development. This was a point much stressed in both of Cotton's prophetic surveys of

11. Cotton, *Exposition on Revelation*, 120, 217; Cotton, *Seven Vials*, "The Fourth Part of the Sixth Vial," 1–5; Cotton, *Resurrection*, 16.

12. Cotton, *Exposition upon Revelation*, 122; Cotton, *Resurrection*, 5, 7, 14. For the theme of "knowledge," see Cotton, *Seven Vials*, "Seventh Vial," 5, 12. See also Cotton, *Canticles* (1642), 230.

Canticles. The calling of the Jews, as an example, was to "begin at first . . . with some of the lowest people, and so ascend higher . . . to more eminent persons." Right doctrine and regard for the ordinances was to "spread" but slowly through the nations. Withal, the church's emergence toward "full stature and beauty" was a matter of "gradual increase" from height to height, and no wonder that Cotton, following the unfolding spectacle through the chapters of Solomon's song, could proclaim that "Growth is . . . Glorious."[13] But what was here celebrated? In this special context, within a vision of humanity being swept ahead into the last age and its wonders, what is to be understood by growth, by increase, by ascent? The answer involves turning back to view again the representation of reality which underlay and imparted shape to Cotton's and his millennialist colleagues' picture of redemptive history.

Cotton spoke for generations of Puritan reformers as he declared that "Prime Antiquity . . . is the image of God," both source and measure of the Christian way, and that authentic "Antiquity . . . is that which fetches its originall from the [biblical] beginning." And the principle here articulated—the prestige of the beginnings—was not forgotten when Puritan thinkers came to visualize the place of their struggle within the history of the Christian movement.[14] Freely adopting a historical periodization shared in broad outline by magisterial and radical reformers alike, these English dissenters connected the primacy of scriptural origins with a vision of the church's history unfolding in three stages. There were, first, primitive antiquity, embracing selectively the Jewish church of the Old Testament but more especially the apostolic and immediate postapostolic eras to the time of Constantine or later; second, the centuries of decline and eclipse by Catholic apostasy; and, third, the time of recovery, adumbrated by medieval restorationists like Peter Waldo and John Wyclif, expanding through much of Christendom in the sixteenth century and continuing to the end of the world. In Cotton's succinct summary: the "Churches . . . had a time to be established by the Apostles. . . . Afterward they grew to . . . a time . . . of deformation, . . . [and] so afterward they came to a new Reformation."[15]

13. Cotton, *Canticles* (1642), 221–222; Cotton, *Canticles* (1655), 181.
14. John Cotton, *A Practical Commentary . . . upon the First Epistle Generall of John* (London, 1656), 77, 108.
15. The broadly tripartite pattern was subject to innumerable variations of

Here indeed was an interest in the church's historical experience, but one not to be confused with the modern devotion to historicity. The given objective was, not study of an institution in time, subject to causality and change, but demonstration of linkage to the time of times. Strictly speaking, the subject matter of this history was not temporal at all. The true church of the present was not a historical product and in that sense to be understood in terms of its history. Analogy and correspondence were the appropriate analytical categories, not causality and intrinsic development, for the church was true only so far as it incorporated the timeless doctrine and forms of Scripture. And by the same token its march through history was not a simple *pro*cession to be captured in a straight narrative flow from beginning to the present and toward the Second Coming. The narrative would be sequential, of course, but not guided alone by chronology. Primitive antiquity must stand forth as the unmoved center from which that narrative was comprehended and as the absolute historical good whose alternating loss and retrieval structures the flow of events.

Puritan eschatology in the Brightman tradition was in several senses an extension and enlargement of this very historiographical conception. Brightman inherited from Foxe and other sixteenth-century prophetic writers a "historicist" understanding of biblical apocalyptic that correlated prophecy and history on a grand scale. Briefly, historicist analysis discovered in the biblical material, especially in Revelation, a "continuous prophecy of the course of church and world history from the Incarnation [or earlier] to the End."[16] Apocalyptic exegesis was therefore integrated with a narration of the inclusive Christian story, and this story inevitably was shaped in accord with primitivist convention. From Bale to Foxe, therefore, eschatology in England was wedded to an elaborate restorationist historiography. To this tradition, and to the conception of the church's historical future that took form within it, Brightman and, through him, Cotton were to fall heir.

What was that conception? In the context just described, the age

---

detail, some embracing seven or more "ages" or dispensations. See, for example, Katharine R. Firth, *The Apocalyptic Tradition in Reformation Britain, 1530–1645* (Oxford, 1979), 41; *AM*, I, 4–5. Cotton, *Resurrection*, 17.

16. Richard Bauckham, *Tudor Apocalypse* (Oxford, 1978), 15, 71.

of reformation encompassed the entire interval from Luther to the world's end. Hence the earthly future of Christianity, in point of the agenda before the church, was but a continuation of the immediate past. Some Puritan writers were more sanguine than others about the advance of reform beyond the stage of the present, Richard Bernard more than Arthur Dent, but they all were agreed that the first reformers' great struggle for reform and recovery must be waged by their successors and theirs to the end of time. Re-form remained the ideal. If on the one hand the saints were to be moved by the exciting hope of Catholic ruin and the Lord's coming, no less were they to be inspired by zeal for the long-lost "primitive spring" of the church and by their wish to cleanse her from "corruption of human fantasies."[17] By the same token, if the story of the future extracted from the prophetic books did assume progressive sequence, its meaning scarcely could be gathered in simple linear terms. It was, in Foxe's words, always essential that the "course of times" be related in order, with "what went before, and what followed after" carefully distinguished.[18]

But for what reason? The answer does not square with the modern expectation of successive changes emerging genetically one from another and establishing directionality forward and perhaps upward. To "go upward," as Foxe specifically declared, was to curve backward "to the Apostles' time"; and, accordingly, the right sequence of "before" and "after" was necessary in order that "the things that be first" duly might "be *preferred before* those that be later." Thus again the sovereignty of the first was affirmed. Antiquity's primacy, which Foxe once called the "one general rule" for interpreting the Christian condition within history, ever would continue to complicate the directional character of the church's career.[19] In this world of thought, the sense of fundamental serial time prerequisite to a doctrine of progress was but fractionally present.

Brightman's essential contribution to the heritage of primitivist historiography was to add a fourth state, the period of millennial

17. John Bale, *The Image of Both Churches* (1545–1547), in Henry Christmas, ed., *Select Works of John Bale* (Cambridge, 1849), 253, 300.

18. *AM*, I, 515.

19. John Foxe, *Actes and Monuments of These Latter and Perillous Dayes* (London, 1563), 6; *AM*, I, 515.

transfiguration, to the customary sequence. That is, to the recognized interval of continuing but indecisive reformation he joined a term of reformation carried and completed to "that fulnesse, than which nothing can be farther expected on earth." But if Brightman in this particular did pass well beyond the limits of an amillennial outlook, he adhered otherwise strictly to historicist convention. He saw a finely apt depiction of the prophetic theologian, and indeed of the Christian theologian per se, in the symbolic creatures of Revelation 4 "full of eyes both before and behind" and able thus to envision the interrelatedness of first and last things.[20] His mammoth commentary on Revelation was conceived broadly upon the premise that "*whatsoever is first, that is true; and whatsoever is later, that is false,*" and this remained the touchstone for his entire account of Christian reformation both before and after the pivotal year of 1650. For this was an activity that did "go forward constantly" until that "pleasantness" which "belong[ed] to the first beginning" had been regained and the end-time "perfection" thus secured.[21]

Within this larger vision, the millennial age provided a fine spectacle of progress. Thus, for instance, the forthcoming conversion and Christianization of the Jews was to exhibit an orderly progression through three stages. There was to be a "first conversion . . . like the morning; [a] first growing age [which Brightman estimated would begin about 1700], *faire as the Moone;* [and a] stronger age, *cleer as the Sunne.*"[22] But the modern expositor, warned by Brightman's many firm strictures against "novelty" and "invention" and his persistent celebration of "ancient truth" and "first purity," should be careful not to confuse the notion of development demonstrated here with the very different ideals of later times. Brightman did not understand the millennial experience as incremental development. While his concept no doubt had a power exceeding its intent to awaken a sense of open possibility, he formally espoused no such idea, and only the grossest misunderstanding could result were one

20. Thomas Brightman, *A Commentary on the Canticles* (London, 1644), 1071; Brightman, *Apocalyps*, 148.

21. Brightman, *Apocalyps*, 101, 113, 114. The italicized text was quoted also by Cartwright and Foxe (Thomas Cartwright, *A Replye to an Answere Made of M. Doctor Whitgifte* . . . [n.p., 1573], 104; Foxe, *AM*, I, 515).

22. Brightman, *Canticles*, 1051. For his dating of the second stage, see 1065.

to compare the process involved with evolution and its implication of limitless development.

As should be evident, the millennium as here understood operates upon different principles entirely. End-time progress was to work toward a state in which "the end shall be answerable to the beginning." The period of procession, in fact, was but a short phase, perhaps a century, whose procedures and sequences were predetermined from the outset and schematically foretold in biblical narrative. Just as the "farther [the church] proceedeth [from her] first beginnings the more filth she gathereth," so now in the last age her "forward" motion must describe an arc back toward full reconnection with the primitive "integrity and purenes of God his institution[s]." New Jerusalem was a "restoration," and its form was that of an all-encompassing, monopolistic Presbyterian establishment "every severall part of which was described once most exactly" in sacred writ and thus enclosed within the finality of archetypal rules and examples. The church, once thus "recalled . . . into the exact rule of God's will," would enter a blessed stasis. The "peace" of the New Jerusalem was to be in part the peace of the complete, fixed, and undisturbed, "prepared against al alteration."[23]

Once the underlying dialectic of pro- and regressive movement is grasped, this final and static conception will be found the natural culmination, not the contradiction, of the dynamic, change-oriented process by which it was to be realized. The operative concept, in a phrase suggested by Leonard Sweet, was "progress through regress." Eschatological change as Brightman visualized it was history straining to complete its circle of movement toward an original repose.[24]

23. Brightman, *Apocalyps*, 101, 114, 290, 688–689, 694 (I have altered the sequence of the material cited from 114). In his *Key*, 243, Bernard found in Revelation a comparison of the millennial New Jerusalem to "a square number of equall sides . . . to shew [its] stable and unmoveable state." Avihu Zakai finds in Puritan thought a "cyclical interpretation of time [that] . . . did not contradict millennial expectations, for in the millennium the whole circular movement of time and history was to come to its finale" ("Exile and Kingdom: Reformation, Separation, and the Millennial Quest in the Formation of Massachusetts and Its Relationship with England, 1628–1660" [Ph.D. diss., Johns Hopkins University, 1983], 455–556).

24. Leonard I. Sweet, "Millennialism in America: Recent Studies," *Theological Studies*, XL (1979), 520. This last point has reference to John F. Wilson's

When, in the mid-1640s, Cotton assures his Boston audiences that millennial "growth is glorious," his defining associations lie in the primitivist-historicist tradition and its development toward a concept of the future as an enclosing canopy. Since his intellectual career is charted in a steady flow of publications for more than three decades, it is possible to follow his changes and fluctuations from the early pastorate at Saint Botolph's in old Boston to his death in Massachusetts in 1652. Thus one can trace his drift from a more conventional soteriology into the semi-antinomianism that so attracted Anne Hutchinson, or his move from an amillennial position to the partially developed speculations of the earlier study of Canticles (about 1624–1632). But upon the key issues of primitivist belief, he persistently adheres to the position generally upheld within the Spiritual Brotherhood and assimilated into millennial speculation by Brightman. Cotton's lifelong conviction was that Christian life is anchorage in the Great Time. His belief that "all errors . . . are aberrations from the first [and fixed] way of truth" and his early and harsh censures against the English church's "Alterates [deviations] from Primitive Patterns" were more than matched, to take but one example, by his later presentation of the Congregational way as an exact incorporation of what Christ "primitively did bequeath" or by his indignant response to the charge—one of the severest conceivable vituperations in any seventeenth-century Reformed vocabulary—of "novel invention."[25] Through the years of his increasing interest in

---

observation that in historical millennial thought "the framework of meaning is one in which the process of realizing a goal contradicts the content of that goal" (*Public Religion in American Culture* [Philadelphia, 1979], 108–109). It should be added that for Brightman the end-time restoration was more than a simple reiteration of the first. He apparently envisioned millennial Christianity as embodying a "more ample glory . . . than ever before" and thus as a more elevated state than the biblical primordium. But it was precisely the *primitive* qualities that were to be enjoyed in yet greater fullness (*Apocalyps*, 634, 685).

25. John Cotton, *Epistle of John*, 189; and see Cotton, *The Way of Congregational Churches Cleared* (1648), in Larzer Ziff, ed., *John Cotton on the Churches of New England* (Cambridge, Mass., 1968), 293; Cotton, *Some Treasure Fetched out of Rubbish* (London, 1660), 7; Cotton, *The Keys of the Kingdom of Heaven* (1644), in Ziff, ed., *John Cotton*, 71. Cotton replied to the charge of "invention" in *Congregational Churches*, 293–301; and *A Letter of Mr. John Cottons . . . to Mr. [Roger] Williams*, 55, in *The Complete Writings of Roger Williams*, 7 vols. (New York, 1963), I.

Brightman's work, through the years of his outspoken predictions of New Jerusalem on earth, one detects not the least abatement of dedication to the first and fixed.

From his earliest work on Canticles through the second round of lectures on the same text dating from about 1645, Cotton's eschatological works were virtual compendiums of primitivist clichés. Their themes were so handled as to stress in maximum degree "the difference between God's institutions, and mens inventions." Consider, as an example, Cotton's careful delimitation of the preliminary destructive impact of the Bright Coming. That fabulous violence was not to be poured out promiscuously upon human civilization as a whole. "Inventions" were its prime target, and so too the men, women, churches, and nations that bred and sponsored them. Cotton's excited discussions of the coming ruin of Catholicism yield but a fraction of their meaning to the reader not alert to their underlying dichotomy between the sacred original and the humanly devised additional. In Cotton's view, the divine ire poised to pour upon Catholic error had been evoked largely by the papist church's long history of obtrusion beyond scriptural rule. It was precisely the vast resulting corpus of additions, idolatrously claiming sacred prestige but altogether "savoring of human inventions and wisdom," that now, already weakening under Protestant attack, was being targeted for the final stroke.[26] Further, it was this explicit roster of destruction that set the stage for the Middle Advent's constructive work. For now, Cotton thought, even while the devastation was underway, an international order of churches would begin to arise, premised upon the final stilling of man's untrustable wit and the compliance of his every faculty to the perfect and unalterable of biblical revelation.

A primitivist design was evident, too, in Cotton's larger format of ideas. No more than Bale, Foxe, or Brightman did he conceive of eschatology as an isolated analysis of the future, and it is significant that his important millennial statements all occur in the context of lengthy commentaries on Revelation and Canticles, which largely were occupied with interpretation of the past. These commentaries are a fruitage of the historicist tradition, with its attention to the church's history from the Incarnation (or earlier) to the Second

---

26. Cotton, *Canticles* (1655), 64; Cotton, *Seven Vials*, "The Fourth Vial," 10, "The Seventh Vial," 7.

Coming and with its commitment to a painstaking, step-by-step trek through each packed verse of the sacred text in which Last Things and their significance were brought finally to light. Only small fragments of Cotton's study of Revelation remain, but we have the complete text of his two full commentaries on Canticles. Again the decisive inspiration was supplied by Brightman, probably the first English Protestant to set Canticles, traditionally not regarded as apocalyptic, in the historicist-eschatological format.[27]

For some time Cotton "thought somewhat strange" of Brightman's approach, but by the mid-1620s he had gone over to the new view. He now believed that Canticles contained a "prophetical history" outlining "the Estate of the Church in all the Ages" from the time of King Solomon to the Last Judgment. According to the best available estimate, Cotton had built upon Brightman's foundation to prepare and preach a comprehensive set of lectures on Canticles sometime between 1624 and 1632. During the mid-1640s he revised, expanded, and presumably preached again the entire cycle of lectures. This revision, published in 1655 as *A Brief Exposition with Practical Observations upon the Whole Book of Canticles*, embodies the fullest statement of Cotton's mature and considered eschatological position.[28]

27. See Anthony Tuckney's "To the Reader," in Cotton, *Canticles* (1655), sig. A6. There is a possibility of influence by Theodore Beza's *Sermon sur le Cantique* of 1586; see Tadataka Maruyama, *The Ecclesiology of Theodore Beza* (Geneva, 1978), 148–153. For a brief introduction to the eschatological turn in commentary upon Canticles, see Bryan W. Ball, *A Great Expectation: Eschatological Thought in English Protestantism to 1660* (Leiden, 1975), 239–242. See also Lowance, *Language of Canaan*, 41–54. For Puritan examples of the traditional approach, see Dudley Fenner's preface to his *The Song of Songs* (London, 1587); and George Gifford, *Fifteene Sermons upon the Song of Salomon* (London, 1600), 1–18. Likewise, the Puritan Separatist Henry Ainsworth's *Solomon's Song of Songs* (n.p., 1623) upheld a noneschatological reading; it was untouched by Brightman's views, did not treat Canticles as a prophetic work, and clearly taught an amillennial position (sig. N1). A transitional work was [Henry Finch], *An Exposition of the Song of Solomon: Called Canticles . . .* (London, 1615), which for the most part pursued traditional paths but introduced themes from Brightman at the end (1–4, 125).

28. Tuckney, "To the Reader," in Cotton, *Canticles* (1655), sig. A6, 2; Cotton, *Canticles* (1642), 5, 10 (and see Ball, *Great Expectation*, 239). For probable dates of composition, see Everett H. Emerson, *John Cotton* (New York, 1965), 163–164.

A full three-quarters of the revised *Canticles* treats the period from Solomon to the present. Only in the last section, corresponding to the final two and one-half of Canticles' eight chapters, did Cotton pass to "Prophetical description" of the future. To hasten through the first three-quarters of the commentary, however, would thwart his historicist purposes. The lengthy historical sections are no mere preliminary exercise subserving the presumedly weightier matter of the future. Beyond question, Cotton valued the predictive element in biblical prophecy. Here, as throughout his writings, he recognized the power of "types" (such as Jerusalem) to point ahead and foreshadow their "antitypes" (such as New Jerusalem). Again, the historicist scheme clearly conveys a sense of foreordained movement from stage to stage and toward the Middle Advent. Should these elements be allowed to determine our conception of Cotton's intent, it would be tempting to cite Canticles as evidence to impute an unqualifiedly "developmental" conception of history to "the whole American Puritan colony."[29] But a closer examination of Cotton's handling of the historical material suggests a different conclusion. It shows that he imposed consistently a single organizational technique: the cycle of return to origins. Most fundamentally, this determined his conception of the millennial church.

Puritan Protestants—who employed the doctrine of the Covenant of Grace first forged with Abraham to accomplish a close integration of Old Testament history, doctrine, and law into their total conception of Christian faith—did not hesitate to apply the term "church" to the covenanted peoples of the Old Testament. Cotton was no exception. His general account began with "the estate of a pure Church . . . in the former holy times of *Solomon*" and reviewed its course through the monarchic period in biblical history.[30] By examining Cotton's structuring of this sequence, one can see how completely he had assimilated primitivist tradition. Familiar elements of

29. Cotton, *Canticles* (1655), 179; Sacvan Bercovitch, "The Historiography of Johnson's Wonder-Working Providence," in Alden T. Vaughan and Francis J. Bremer, eds., *Puritan New England: Essays on Religion, Society, and Culture* (New York, 1977), 271–272. Little of the current scholarship alleging a distinctive "Puritan typology" will be upheld once the subject is placed within the larger context of international Protestant divinity.

30. Cotton, *Canticles* (1655), 15. This corresponds roughly to the interval covered in 1 and 2 Kings and 2 Chronicles.

the National Covenant appear, linking the church and nation's prosperity or adversity to covenantal performance, but clearly this was not the chief concern shaping the narrative.[31]

As Cotton pursued the thread of his story through successive reigns, he portrayed the church and its fortunes falling, then rising, and falling again; but he conceptualized this fluctuation in terms both of covenantal reward and punishment and of a prime estate enjoyed, lost, and regained. The covenantal and restorationist patterns interlock throughout. Thus we commence with Solomon's early reign, its covenantal harmony, its "pure Church" composed of converted saints and graced "by the presence and purity of Gods Ordinances." But Cotton's audience was, even now, being prepared to recognize that, until the Transfiguration, first "purity . . . may soon degenerate"— a fact that seemed intensely relevant to New England in the mid-1640s. Cotton tells us that through Solomon's breach of covenant and allowance of pagan rites, the Jewish church began a course of "sad change" that deepened in the next reign into outright apostasy. Characteristically, Cotton interpreted this change with special reference to corruption of original and duly instituted ordinances.[32]

Yet the age of decline, Cotton tells us, was succeeded by an age of recovery. Under King Asa, covenantal law was reaffirmed and the "Ordinances of God [again] set and kept in right order," "purity," and "beauty"—qualities already explicitly identified with "the estate of a pure Church . . . in . . . former holy times."[33] Thus the basic cycle is established. After its era of "splendor," the primitive (early Solomonic) church declined; a term of eclipse and loss was endured; then appeared "*Asa* his reformation." Cotton thus located the prototype of "reformation" some two millennia before Tyndale, Cranmer, Luther, and Calvin, and found in this first of reforming monarchs a type of the "godly magistrate" of Puritan preaching. Asa, thus, a "pattern for imitation," is depicted as a restorer of the church to prime integrity. He was dedicated to "reforming religion," "renewing" and "restoring" the ordinances, and in all to regain the "comelinesse of concord" linked to primitive things.

31. For example, *ibid.*, 22: "*Rehoboam* forsook the Law of the Lord, and all Israel with him; whereupon God sent *Shishak* King of *AEgypt* . . . who subdued them."

32. *Ibid.*, 15, 17, 22 (this passage obviously reflects upon New England), 23.

33. *Ibid.*, 15 (cf. 92–93, 208), 24–26.

In Cotton's chronicle of succeeding reigns, the cycle recurs many times. The prime and static order of law and rite, forever threatened by forces of corruption, periodically is recaptured through an activity of restitution. Had the church forsaken its first ways? Then emerged upright King Jehoshaphat, that active "emblem of Magistrates," who labored to "restor[e] the people from corruption . . . and went about through all the country, to bring them back againe to the purity of Gods worship"; then arose Hezekiah, or Josiah, who proclaimed a new covenant and law, pursued "zealous Reformation," and "restore[d] the Ordinances" to their first "greennesse, and purity." Was Israel overrun, was the Temple destroyed, and were the people led into captivity? Then, when Babylonian power was broken, came a season of "return to [the] Native Countrey," where "Christ [was] waiting . . . in his Ordinances," and the covenant was to be renewed under the reforming ministrations of "Magistrates, noursing-fathers." These analyses stand forth to the reader with obvious weight and seriousness of their own. The Jewish church, standing within the Covenant of Grace, participated in the Christian Redemption. Its experiences were of immediate relevance to the seventeenth century, and from them Cotton continually extracted the familiar uses and doctrines of Puritan preaching through which the New England churches might be tied back to the primal source. Yet, ultimately, the reader was to understand that here, in the story of the Hebrew church in decline and restoration, is given the very context of values and procedures that in days of "greater light" to come was to guide the Christian enterprise through its last historical age.[34]

Only now, after a lengthy course of historical exposition, was Cotton ready to introduce his audience to the familiar world of the primitive apostolic church, its time of flourishing, the lengthy epoch of decline and eclipse, and the eventual emergence of "instruments of Christ tending and turning towards purity of reformation." His treatment, which occupies roughly the second half of the commentary, is sufficiently full and so conformed to convention as to constitute a *locus classicus* of primitivist historiography. Reviewing this material, one begins to see the significance for this inquiry of Cotton's gradually developed historical schema. Of course, it is true that

34. *Ibid.*, 25–29, 32–34, 47–53, 59.

after the Incarnation everything operated upon a higher plane: the applicable depositum of sacred originals was modified and enriched; the shadows of temple rite and sacrifice were dispersed; Old Testament prefigurations of the Christian Redemption gave way to the real thing. Nonetheless, within that framework the Old Testament rules applied. As he traced its course through time, Cotton found the Christian church standing in perfect alignment with the long-range contour of biblical history. He presented the church of the Christian age as a continuing exemplification of the restitutionist dynamic underlying the church's career "from Solomons time (inclusively)." [35]

"Inclusively," Cotton explained, meant the entire span of time "to the last Judgement" and thus embraced as well the forthcoming career of the church toward and through the millennium. For this reason it is doubly important that *Canticles*, considered as a historicist exercise, be grasped as a unity. Bostonians, who had followed Cotton's exegesis through its long course toward consideration of the final age and were then taken through his thrilled preview of the rising New Jerusalem, were able fully to appreciate its magnitude. For by tracing the church's fluctuating antemillennial course Cotton also had mapped the *limits* of religious reformation within history untransformed. There were always the standing threat and the frequent depredations imposed by militarily powerful enemies of the truth: Assyrians, Catholics, Turks. But the more distressing lesson of history was that the church itself, in its human foundation, was fallible; its impulse toward first times wavered; its grasp on originals was imperfect and insecure. The deterioriation of first purity was, not an occasional aberration, but an unvarying rule of the church's life in history, one that vitiated the highest achievements of reform; and to its insidious operation New England too was prey. [36]

Once one had grasped the precarious status of "purity" within normal history, one was then well equipped to follow the strategy of the millennial transformation. For the power of the Bright Coming was to be exerted explicitly against the limits theretofore imposed upon reform. Obviously the Roman and, eventually, the Turkish menaces

35. *Ibid.*, 2, 154.
36. *Ibid.*, 2. Cotton never attributed to New England, in the commentary on Canticles or elsewhere, a complete and stable restoration of faith and polity (see *ibid.*, 213).

were to be destroyed, together with the Anglican episcopacy; but, more, miraculous conversions and a great access of new graces and knowledge were much to increase the number, capacity, vigor, and staying power of end-time Christians. From this point of view, the Middle Advent was an act of liberation, freeing the impulse toward originals from both outer resistance and inner weakness and breaking the iron succession of purity and decay. Therewith were given all the conditions necessary for the spectacular season of "growth" that now was to emerge.

The portal into the millennium, then, was to be a last, unfettered crusade toward restoration. As Cotton developed the sequence, he stood in the line of prophetic writers taught by Brightman to envision the rise of New Jerusalem as a "renovation," a "great restoration," and here the peculiar complexity of primitivist thinking about past and future stood out as in no other context. When he described the ecclesiastical project of the Bright Coming, he had in mind no mere apostolic afterglow. The "arising of [a] . . . New Church" was not an anticlimax. It stood forth and drove forward in its own right as a distinct and gigantic work. It stood within the economy of Redemption, perhaps, on a par with the Creation or the Ascension. A dazzling, elevated, and *processive* course of action it was, and even as it neared completion, it pointed ahead to the greater consummations of Second Coming, Resurrection, and heavenly beatitude. But it also was to be viewed synoptically within the full historicist sequence. Cotton promised his audience that, great as it was, the millennial transition should be accomplished free from "all affectation of innovation," because the church of the future, in its supernaturally empowered ascent to "grown stature," at the same time was tied back through the ages.[37] It was linked by the precedential authority of Josiah and Nehemiah, Wyclif and Calvin, and the churches of their epochs to the fundamental perception they had all shared and obeyed: the perception that the very life of the true church within time is exhibited through acts of memory and loyalty directed toward a prime beginning.

As a disciple of Brightman, Cotton affirmed that the order of sacred originals associated with apostolicity and with the godly magistracy

37. Bernard, *Key*, 336; [Finch], *Great Restauration*; Cotton, *Canticles* (1655), 179, 217.

of ancient Israel maintained full jurisdiction throughout millennial time. To the corpus of first-age precept and pattern, Christ's coming in brightness was to add not a jot or a tittle. Its effect was, rather, to implement and impose them in the last age. This explains the striking symmetry in Cotton's respective accounts of the primitive and the millennial churches:[38]

The Church in Christs time [was] commended . . . By her beauty . . . [and] superlative Fairnesse. . . . This . . . Beauty . . . May all be referred [to] . . . the comelinesse of the several parts. . . . [In those days the church's] fairnesse or beauty lyeth. . . . In the integrity of all the parts, none lacking . . . The symmetry or fit proportion of al the members to one another . . . fitly . . . joyned together . . . By the Ordinances of Christ	[The church of New Jerusalem is to be] admirably beautifull in all the parts of it. . . . The Fairnesse and beauty of the Church implyeth suitably to what is found in the beauty of the body. 1. A complete integrity of all the members. . . . 2. A fit proportion all of the members . . . one to another; each one set in his place . . . And all the Ordinances fitly dispensed

The paraphrastic character of the latter text suggests that Cotton saw the millennial church as a kind of mirror trained back upon the apostolic primordium. To the church seen taking form in Canticles' final chapters he would ascribe excellences unsurpassable within history, but he also believed that in manifesting them it was to shine with a reflected light. The preeminence of first times never was more forcefully displayed than here, and there is some evidence that Cotton's bias in the matter became more pronounced even as he was fully engaged in the eschatological speculation of the 1640s. Thus, in the Canticles of 1624–1632 he conceded that "the Church was never

38. Cotton, Canticles (1655), 79, 92, 187, 208.

so compleatly beautifull in all her parts, as it shallbe when the Jewes are called." In the revised commentary of the 1640s this qualification vanishes, and we find him stating that "the primitive Apostolick Church was . . . the most completely and obundantly fair, of all that ever have been before it, or shall be after it, upon the face of the earth."[39]

At all events, the immense hold of prime antiquity was clear. Unlike the churches of the Reformation, with their partial and precarious restitution "much what like" to the primitive church, the millennial institution was to be capable of a full, clear reflection of the ethos and pattern of the normative time.[40] It was a New Jerusalem, but Jerusalem all the same; and during its inaugural period, the reality of the image this church represented to the world would emerge proportional to its representation of the "superlative Fairness" of archetypes.

Even yet, however, we are a step away from understanding adequately the events to be set in motion by the Middle Advent. To begin with, in the texts just cited, "beauty" is a property of the primitive and millennial churches. Canticles, after all, is a collection of love poetry. To an exegete like Cotton, who found ecclesiastical structures prefigured in the enticing bride with doves' eyes and scarlet lips of Canticles 4, "comeliness" took a natural place among the church's charms. Canticles' vocabulary of beauty, love, and desire, which Cotton found apt to his topic and handled with enthusiasm, provided a useful additional means of celebrating the prized status of first things.

Here, if anywhere, was a context in which eschatology might take an Edenic turn and come to dwell upon states of indulgent pleasure. Indeed, given the openly physical and erotic content of much of the work, the most determined interpreter might well feel pressed to neutralize the sensuous interest entirely; and Cotton, drawing upon an ancient tradition of exegesis, did make the most of it as a depiction of "conjugal love" between Christ and his church. And yet in the end he achieved a remarkably thorough translation of the erotic into

39. Cotton, *Canticles* (1642), 221; Cotton, *Canticles* (1655), 92.

40. Cotton, *Canticles* (1655), 174–175. In the earlier text Cotton specifically mentioned the want, in apostolic times, of "a Christian Magistrate, . . . and some purity of the Sacrament."

acceptably Puritan doctrine. A wooed maiden's "navel like a round goblet," for example, he found "fitly [to] resemble Baptism," on the grounds that the navel is an infant's link with saving nourishment during its immaturity. Yet more to the point, and referring to the parallel texts given above, one notes the defining characteristics there associated with beauty. "Fairness," we are told, lies in qualities of order and completeness and in obeisant linkage, as Cotton expressed it elsewhere in the work, to "the whole row of Ordinances," including the New Testament mechanisms of church discipline.[41] Millennial beauty, then, for all the sensuous revel of the Song of Songs, was to be closely tied to order. It was far more suggestive of structure and limitation than of release and enjoyment, and this recognition brings us to the summum bonum of Cotton's total conception as well as to the fullest understanding of its Puritan cast.

Tirelessly clamoring for moral as well as primitive purity, the Spiritual Brotherhood prized and took joy in order. The saints were to be known by the imposition of controls upon themselves, their families, and their communities. That, in turn, made the traditional chiliasm so distasteful to Puritan thinkers and reduced the paradisiac element within their millennial speculation to a marginal role. And if, within the Brightman heritage, the millennial transition was perceived as a progressive (or regressive) recovery of primitive content, that content also embraced one fixed, complete, and tightly wrought scheme for the conversion and ordering of mankind. Puritan-Congregational "patterns" were the measure of its "growth up from one measure of light to another," and so it came as well bearing an unconditional demand for self-denial and subjection. Seen in this light, the Middle Advent becomes a massive, forced incorporation of human wills and institutions back into the uniform "reign of Sovereign Authority" long associated by English Puritans with biblical command and example.[42]

Considered as a process, the dramatic "increase of beauty" that Cotton foresaw in the millennial dawn is difficult to render in twentieth-century terminology. Seen as a linear movement through time, it marked a great turn forward of history's cycle to a state genuinely future and genuinely climactic, but its core was the "recovery of

41. Cotton, *Canticles* (1642), 2–5, 27, 191.
42. *Ibid.*, 181; Cotton, *Exposition upon Revelation*, 122.

[the Jews'] lost inheritance" and a general return to the rigors of first times. Here we recognize the complementarity of *Urzeit* and *Endzeit*, the dialectical play of *pro-* and *re*gression, the profound qualification of serial time remarked at several earlier points. But now there is a difference. Now the limits upon recovery were to be lifted. Now events were to be driven on by the irresistible force of miracle. Now, therefore, the cycle of return to origins could achieve closure and finality. The procedure resembled involution, which describes exhaustive development curved back within a narrow and closed field of possibilities. Advance was to continue through a limited interval until sacred design ruled all. The prospect that enthralled Cotton and his audiences was a radically efficient enclosure of mankind's future estate within primordial and timeless "chains of gold."[43]

Hence if Cotton thus foresaw a scene of growth and ascent in the early millennium, he also located that scene within a severe and limiting horizon. It would be a majestic spectacle, that time of rapid movement toward perfection, and all the more so when one recognized within it a tide of progress reaching the outer limits of historical possibility. There could be no mistake. In that final surge ahead the ultimate rationale and value of progress itself would be disclosed. And what now met the gaze of the forecaster who turned his eyes to that nearing time was a spectacle of rapid enclosure in given, fixed forms. Nor was this a peculiarity of Cotton's vision of the "church's resurrection." The theme of enclosure was basic to the tradition of prophetic exegesis emanating from Brightman's commentaries. That the New Jerusalem would be founded upon "full and exact conformity to heavenly rules" was an unchallenged article of faith among New England commentators of Cotton's period. To recognize its fundamental role in the body of prophecy they produced requires some qualification of the thesis that finds in English millennialism of the period a dominant "progressivism" paving the way for the later "dogma of unilinear progress."[44]

But if this be so, another question now arises. For the millennial

43. Cotton, *Canticles* (1655), 25, 180, 188.

44. Tuveson, *Millennium*, vi, viii, 75–112. James W. Davidson and Avihu Zakai argue that treatment of millennialism as transitional to the idea of progress tends to misrepresent the aims of millennial theorists (Davidson, *The Logic of Millennial Thought: Eighteenth-Century New England* [New Haven, Conn., 1978], 34–35; Zakai, "Exile and Kingdom," 453–456).

story as told by Cotton and his colleagues compassed not only an idealized picture of Christianity's last drive toward perfection; it also rendered some account of that end-time perfection itself as a state to be enjoyed by countless generations during the several centuries remaining before the Second Coming and the end of history. With fixed "rules" fully in place and "exact conformity" assured, what was the future of humanity to be?[45] When the brief era of dynamic ascent was succeeded by the millennium proper, what would the privilege of living in those days entail? Would Christian thought and practice then consist in frozen repetition? What was to become of choice, of error, and of social change? Answers to such questions are pointed to by John Eliot, who among New England thinkers at mid-century gave the most attention to understanding the millennial epoch itself.

45. Davenport, *Letters*, 82.

EIGHT

JOHN ELIOT AND

THE CIVIL PART

OF THE KINGDOM

OF CHRIST

*I*n Cotton's portrayal of the New Jerusalem, as in the portrayals of the great majority of Puritan millennialists in both old and New England, the ecclesiastical interest predominated. It was the church—its membership, structure, doctrine, rise to beauty and perfection—that remained steadily in the center of the account, just as it had stood ever in the center of the Puritan agitation since the 1560s. More than once, however, one finds Cotton positing a close bond between the ecclesiastical and the political. Again, this was entirely consistent with Puritan tradition. Standing equally aloof from Lutheran notions of the two kingdoms and from Richard Hooker's indiscriminate equation of church and nationality, the Spiritual Brotherhood drew the closest associations between church reform, England's collective and Deuteronomic covenant, and the special moral and ecclesiastical guardianship therein assigned to godly magistrate and monarch.

Within the Brightman tradition, these associations were retained and projected upon an international scale, for the impact of the Middle Advent was to be comprehensive. All political structures surviving Armageddon were to be transformed into agencies supporting the central religious reformation. Such doctrine might rankle Roger Williams. For him the imminent coming was to be a "spiritual" work that did not involve the coercive mechanisms of the state.[1] But in the Congregational colonies after 1640, those persuaded of the millennial thesis agreed that commonwealth and churches alike stood before a great change, that, in Mede's accented formula, all "Kingdoms of the world [were to become] our Lords and his Christs."[2] New Englanders were encouraged both by the parliamentary takeover in England and by their own experience with a cooperative magistracy to believe that soon "the whole civill Government of people upon Earth shall become [Christ's]" and that "godly civill government shall have a great share" in the new era. Nevertheless, as with Cotton, ecclesiastical priorities spoke the loudest: the coming "glorious church upon earth" and, especially, Congregational concern for the "ordering of [God's] house and public worship" dominated attention.[3] During the period 1640–1660, only one American commentator undertook a detailed forecast of the governmental structure of New Jerusalem: John Eliot, teacher of the church at Roxbury and the most notable of the colonial missionaries to the Indians.

Judicial Leviathan: John Eliot's Millennial Commonwealth

*I*n the spring of 1661 the Massachusetts General Court took irritated note of a volume published in England in 1659 under the

1. Thomas Brightman, *A Revelation of the Apocalyps* (Amsterdam, 1611), 637. See also [Henry Finch], *The Worlds Great Restauration* (London, 1621), 10, 14, 233; Richard Bernard, *A Key of Knowledge for the Opening of the Secret Mysteries of St. Johns Mysticall Revelation* (London, 1617), 309, 325, 329–340. *The Complete Writings of Roger Williams,* 7 vols. (New York, 1963), III, 363.

2. Joseph Mede, *The Key of the Revelation . . . ,* 2d ed. (London, 1650), 23, 26. Mede built upon a text from Revelation 11:15, but it was probably he who first headlined its millennial implications. The formula was repeated almost verbatim by Thomas Hooker, *A Survey of the Summe of Church-Discipline* (London, 1648), sig. a3; *WWP,* 138; Thomas Parker, *The Visions and Prophecies of Daniel Expounded . . .* (London, 1646), 12; Peter Bulkeley, *The Gospel-Covenant; or, The Covenant of Grace Opened* (London, 1646), 20–21; and John Eliot, contribution to Henry Whitfield *et al., The Light Appearing More and More towards the Perfect Day* (1651), *MHSC,* 3d Ser., IV (Boston, 1834), 120.

3. *WWP,* 34, 146. See also John Cotton, *A Brief Exposition with Practical Observations upon the Whole Book of Canticles* (London, 1655), 221–222, 226–228; Thomas Shepard, *The Works of Thomas Shepard,* 3 vols. (Boston, 1853), I, 40; John Davenport, *An Answer of the Elders of the Severall Churches in New-England unto Nine Positions Sent over to Them* (London, 1643), 54.

title *The Christian Commonwealth*. An order was to be drawn and posted in Boston and four neighboring towns requiring that all copies held by Massachusetts citizens be destroyed or turned in to the nearest magistrate. So far as possible, the work was to be "totally suppressed." John Eliot, its author, was to prepare and sign a formal recantation, to be incorporated into the Court's official minutes. Why were these actions taken? The Court was specific: it had found the book "justly offencive and in speciall [as] relating to kingly Government in England." Only a year before, the English revolution had come to its fitful end. Charles II was on the throne, backed by a conservative Parliament; and Massachusetts authorities had good reason to fear encroachment upon the colony's traditional liberties, perhaps even revocation of her charter. Understandably, the Court judged it an inapt moment for a prominent colonist to be identified with opinions unfriendly to monarchy and approving "the late innovators," let alone for those opinions to make their way further among the Massachusetts population. "Much is spoken of the rightful Heir of the Crown of England," Eliot had written, "but Christ is the only right Heir of the Crown of England." But by May 1661, he recognized that such words did "too manifestly scandalize" the new government. In his recantation, graceful but ignominious, he not only "cordially disoun[ed]" the offensive theses but also acknowledged "the government of England, by King, Lords, and Commons" as lawful, "eminent," and reconcilable with Scripture.[4]

The Court's action and Eliot's recantation were events of the early Restoration. But the text of *Christian Commonwealth*, though published in 1659, had been written about 1651.[5] Then millennial speculation was rampant and had in some quarters begun to expand beyond the primarily ecclesiastical focus of a Brightman, Cotton, or Thomas Goodwin to an explicit concern with social and political reconstitution. Many of those who sketched secularized programs for "True Magistracy Restored" or for a "levelled" social order stood outside the Reformed-Puritan brotherhood, but in more orthodox minds as well the mid-century upheavals were to increase interest in the New Jerusalem considered as a comprehensive social system.[6] In New En-

4. *RMB*, IV, pt. 2, 5–6; *CC*, 133.
5. For dating and discussion of the delay in publication, see J. F. Maclear, "New England and the Fifth Monarchy: The Quest for the Millennium in Early American Puritanism," *WMQ*, 3d Ser., XXXII (1975), 253–254.
6. For the former, see, for example, Gerrard Winstanley, *The Law of Free-*

gland, John Eliot alone presumed to detail a latter-day agenda within which king, Lords, and Commons found no place and the science and form of political rule were fashioned anew.

By about 1650 it was clear to Eliot that the Middle Advent had begun its intrusion upon history through the events of the English Civil War. Probably he was disappointed with the standoff between Presbyterians and Independents, and he found the rise of radical sects alarming, but now he wished to concentrate upon the governmental situation. Simply put, the traditional political world was being "dashed in pieces," clearing a path for fresh departures. What would arise in its stead? Those upon whose shoulders political responsibility now fell could not be trusted to contrive a new polity—"human invention" was out of the question—nor might they passively await divine initiative. In Eliot's judgment the hour demanded an aggressive continuation of the "great business of changing the Government," and that in turn required a reasonably explicit blueprint of the future body politic. He appears to have known that various "Polities and Platformes" had been offered already, but these he disqualified as "contrived by the wisdom of man," and the writings of soundly biblical men like Cotton and Goodwin revealed but sketchy interest in the new age considered as a political phenomenon. For these reasons the English leadership stood "perplexed, sighing . . . for direction." To that situation Eliot felt he could speak, and he ascribed a large role to himself in spurring political reform through its next steps. This he would do by supplying the badly needed "Platforme of Government" and, if he could, persuading the English authorities to adopt it.[7] *The Christian Commonwealth* aimed to accomplish both, and it was likely against his wish that the manuscript (sent to England about 1651) was withheld from publication for eight years.

To what extent was Eliot's entire and remarkable sketch of millennial polity dependent upon the premises of Cotton's Last Times ecclesiology? With the shift from ecclesiastical to political terrain, is there a corresponding move to more mundane values, to a concern for human development, or perhaps even a turn toward the progressivist

---

dom in a Platform; or, True Magistracy Restored (London, 1652). The latter was expressed, for instance, in the widespread citation of Mede's slogan: "The Kingdoms of the world are [to] become our Lord's."

7. CC, 132–134, 138.

ideology of the modern world? Certainly such trends were evident through the 1640s and 1650s, in some sectors of English millennial thought; and, to recall Eliot's starting point, one reasonably might expect him to follow suit. He believed no less devoutly than Gerrard Winstanley or John Lilburne that inherited political structures had lost authority and were on the way out. The limits hitherto imposed upon thought and activity were removed, and for the moment the future stood open and undefined. If a cogent program were offered, men stood ready to cooperate in building a higher and more grati- fying form of political life. Attack upon tradition, the removal of limits, the opening of the future, seizure of opportunity—already one is in danger of misunderstanding the author entirely.

Eliot, in fact, was a Cotton protégé who consulted periodically with his Boston mentor and whose eschatological attitudes corresponded closely with those of the older man.[8] Both in devotion to the primi- tively fixed and in enmity toward novelty and invention he was fully Cotton's equal, and these concerns were much to the fore in the younger man's mind as he began to emerge around mid-century as a millennial enthusiast in his own right. If the future was, in a sense, undefined, this was but the result of a passing failure in scriptural exegesis; and if Eliot did now advocate constructive human endeavor on a great scale, its mode, as ever before in Puritan thought, was imitation of given and total pattern. His *Christian Commonwealth* is as ingenuous and thoroughgoing a document of millennial primi- tivism, with its drive toward closure and fixity, as Cotton's writings on Revelation or Canticles.

Eliot's first reflections upon ultimate government arose within the context of his missionary work among the Algonkian peoples of eastern Massachusetts. Arriving in the colony in 1631 and set- tling as teacher of the church at Roxbury the following year, by the mid-1640s he had begun to learn the Algonkian language and had

8. For Eliot's dependence upon Cotton, see Whitfield *et al.*, *Light Appearing, MHSC*, 3d Ser., IV (1834), 127, 137, 140; John Owen *et al.*, *Strength out of Weaknesse* . . . , *MHSC*, 3d Ser., IV (1834), 173. In "John Eliot's Description of New England in 1650," Massachusetts Historical Society, *Proceedings*, 2d Ser., II (Boston, 1885), 50, Eliot reported that he did "weekly communicate counsels" with Cotton. Cotton is described as Eliot's special "patron" in Cotton Mather, *Magnalia Christi Americana*, ed. Thomas Robbins, 2 vols. (New York, 1853), I, 538.

mounted a personal campaign to bring the Indians to the joined standards of "Christianity and civilization." By the decade's end a few converts had been made and the interest of others gained, but they remained for the most part widely dispersed geographically. Further, the natives' tribal life, in which Eliot could discern no decent form of "Government and Order," clashed with every Puritan instinct for strict rule and regular labor. This Eliot proposed to remedy by founding special "praying towns," where Christianized Indians could be assembled and helped to build a common and disciplined life apart from their heathen tribespeople.[9]

For this great project Eliot bore the primary responsibility; and as he laid plans for the first of the towns (Natick, founded 1651), he became intensely aware, as did the settlers of Dedham and many other New Englanders before him, of the importance of beginnings. A political foundation properly conceived and executed would become "a patterne and Copie before them, to imitate in all the Countrey, . . . in civilizing them in their Order, Government, [and] Law." Pattern and copy—here was a thought to cause a Puritan clergyman instinctively to "fly to the Scriptures."[10] Furthermore, the special circumstances of the Indian work gave Eliot a greater freedom to develop and apply a personal version of restorationist politics than he would have enjoyed in Roxbury or elsewhere in the Bay. Massachusetts officials would not expect a praying town to conform too closely to the existing models, and freshly converted natives would not bring with them to Natick the political traditions and demands for "liberties" of the English. Further, as a people in transition, partly freed from their ancestral identity, they had been brought to a primary, receptive state. Eliot viewed his charges as an *"abrasa tabula scraped board"* upon which he might "write and imprint" an altogether fresh set of principles. In this way, in the spirit of the Congregational quest for further light, and after consultation with "Mr. Cotton and others," he "this vow did solemnly make. . . . [to] instruct them to

9. CC, 135. For general discussion of the praying towns, see Alden T. Vaughan, *New England Frontier: Puritans and Indians, 1620–1675* (Boston, 1965), 235–266; James Axtell, *The Invasion Within: The Contest of Cultures in Colonial North America* (New York, 1985), 139–143.

10. Owen et al., *Strength out of Weaknesse, MHSC*, 3d Ser., IV (1834), 171; Whitfield et al., *Light Appearing, MHSC*, 3d Ser., IV (1834), 131.

imbrace [only] such Government . . . as the Lord hath commanded in the holy Scriptures."[11]

Almost a century before, in his famous sketch for an English "Kingdom of Christ," Martin Bucer had recommended to Edward VI a complete redesign of English magistracy. It should conform, he argued, to Mosaic practice as recorded in Exodus 18: "Moses chose able men out of all Israel, and made them heads over the people, rulers of thousands, rulers of hundreds, of fifties, and of tens." The magistrates thus chosen should administer a national body of civil and criminal law thoroughly revised to conform to "divine Law" and especially to the Decalogue. Captain John Underhill actually put Exodus 18 into practice during the Pequot War of 1637, assigning "captains . . . of fifties and captains of tens" to the military forces under his command.[12]

Whether Eliot knew of Bucer's plan or was reminded of Underhill's procedure, we do not know, but it was principally from Exodus 18 that he now "collected" a political model for Natick. In his summary: "The particular form of Government, which is approved of God [and] instituted by Moses . . . is this; that they chuse . . . unto themselves Rulers of thousands . . . , of hundreds, of fifties, and of tens, who shall govern according to the . . . Law of God . . . , written in the Scriptures."[13] By implementing this plan at Natick, Eliot would assure to the town's political foundation the mythic dimension needful for a right beginning. By the same token, that foundation would be invested with the precedential authority which Eliot saw as key to bringing the remaining Indian population under a bibli-

11. John Eliot, "The Learned Conjectures of Reverend Mr. Eliot," preface to Thomas Thorowgood, *Jewes in America; or, Probabilities, That Those Indians are Judaical . . .* (London, 1660), 27 (irreg. pag.); Whitfield *et al.*, *Light Appearing, MHSC,* 3d Ser., IV (1834), 127; *CC,* 135.

12. Martin Bucer, *De Regno Christi* (1550), in Wilhelm Pauck, ed., *Melanchthon and Bucer* (Philadelphia, 1969), 357–361, 362, 378–384; John Underhill, *News from America . . .* , *MHSC,* 3d Ser., VI (Boston, 1837), 4. Bucer also cited auxiliary texts, especially Deuteronomy 1:15 and 16:18.

13. *CC,* 144–145. For secondary accounts, see Ola Elizabeth Winslow, *John Eliot, "Apostle to the Indians"* (Boston, 1968), 127–129; and Vaughan, *Frontier,* 265–266. It went without saying that these figures referred to numbers of adult men. Women and children, as in standard English theory, were "comprehended" in their husbands and fathers (*CC,* 144).

cal government. Hence, in the late summer of 1651, he fixed a date for an assembly of natives interested in forming a Christian government. On August 6 the "great meeting" took place at Natick, then under construction. We know but few details of the occasion: after prayer, Eliot read and expounded Exodus 18; the Indian men then proceeded to enact the "Divine Pattern." With roughly one hundred male adults in attendance, "rulers of thousands" were omitted; but one ruler of a hundred, two rulers of fifties, and ten rulers of ten were selected, and the government was begun.[14]

Thus far, Eliot's venture in fuller Christian government remains within familiar primitivist precincts. Yet unlike Martin Bucer, or John Underhill, or, in all probability, the founders of Dedham, Eliot came to the issue of governance in a state of profound millennial excitement. In no way did this shunt to the margin his many other concerns as a Puritan pastor-theologian and missionary, but it could lead him to glimpse higher possibilities in an otherwise routine account of biblicist restoration. In his earliest missionary report, *The Day-Breaking, If Not the Sun-Rising of the Gospell with the Indians in New-England* (1647), Eliot in passing drew a connection between the Indian mission and the millennium. The New England activity he saw as a harbinger of the rule of Christ, which in the coming Great Time would expand to "the utmost ends of the earth."[15] The *Day-Breaking*, however, like Eliot's subsequent reports from 1647 to 1648, is hardly a document of eschatological intensity, and the point remained undeveloped. Indeed, in the last report for 1648 and the

14. Owen *et al.*, *Strength out of Weaknesse*, MHSC, 3d Ser., IV (1834), 171. The process actually was completed a month later, when another assembly of natives under Eliot's guidance made a covenant to "ent[er] into this Government" and accept its disciplines (172–173). No study is available of how this scheme worked in practice, or how it related to legislation of the General Court in 1647 and 1656 providing a judiciary for "Indians submitted to our Government." RMB, II, 188; Daniel Gookin, *Historical Collections of the Indians in New England . . .* (1674), MHSC, 1st Ser., I (Boston, 1792), 177; Vaughan, *Frontier*, 294–295. See also John W. Ford, ed., *Some Correspondence between the Governor and Treasurers of the New England Company in London and the Commissioners of the United Colonies in America . . .* (New York, 1970), 28.

15. John Eliot, *The Day-Breaking, If Not the Sun-Rising of the Gospell with the Indians in New-England*, MHSC, 3d Ser., III (Boston, 1834), 14. First published in 1647, the *Day-Breaking* had been written the previous year.

first report for 1649 we find the proposal for a separately organized praying town taking form in Eliot's mind entirely without reference to thoughts of a new world order. It was a purely practical response to circumstances of distant location and tainting tribal influence that threatened to arrest missionary progress.[16] By mid-1649, however, the situation had changed dramatically.

The abrupt heightening of eschatological interest that appeared in Eliot's later reports for 1649 mirrored the explosion of such expectations in England and New England during the later 1640s. With many others he now became convinced that the sensational military and political events then unfolding in England marked the first episode of the Bright Coming. He appeared particularly impressed with news of the trial and execution of Charles I in late January and by July was proclaiming that the "Antichristian principle" embodied in monarchy, that "man [is] . . . above God," had been "thrown to the ground."[17] He had also begun seriously to ponder the possibility that the American natives were descendants of the biblical Hebrews. Such an identification, if it could be confirmed, not only would supply a gratifying tie to the Old Testament primordium; it also would mean that the New England mission was a step in the conversion of world Jewry, which prophetic commentators long had depicted as an—or the—inaugural step in the construction of New Jerusalem.

Just two years earlier a group of millennially enthusiastic English clergy had suggested, in a volume to which Eliot himself had contributed, that through the conversion of the Indian-Jews at this deci-

16. Thomas Shepard, *The Clear Sun-shine of the Gospel Breaking Forth upon the Indians in New-England*, MHSC, 3d Ser., IV (1834), 49–59; Edward Winslow, ed., *The Glorious Progress of the Gospel, amongst the Indians in New England* . . . (1649), *ibid.*, 69–99; see also CC, 135. Thomas Mayhew's published reports on the Martha's Vineyard mission, which span the years from 1649 to 1653, are entirely devoid of millennial reference. Winslow, *Glorious Progress*, 77–79; Whitfield *et al.*, *Light Appearing*, MHSC, 3d Ser., IV (1834), 109–118, 125–129; Owen *et al.*, *Strength out of Weaknesse*, MHSC, 3d Ser., IV (1834), 185–189; John Eliot and Thomas Mayhew, *Tears of Repentance* . . . (1653), MHSC, 3d Ser., IV (1834), 201–211.

17. Whitfield *et al.*, *Light Appearing*, MHSC, 3d Ser., IV (1834), 120, and see 119–121, 127, 131. Also in 1649 Eliot first recorded a sign of millennial interest among the Indians. One wished to know, "What meaneth a new heaven and a new earth?" (*ibid.*, 130).

sive juncture the New Englanders could perform a true "farther Errand" in their wilderness sanctuary.[18] Significantly, it was at this time, with his mind turned as never before to the millennium, that Eliot vowed to go directly and exclusively to biblical precedent for a governmental form. The two concerns, precedential and final, were so closely connected that, even while discussing concrete details of the Indian plan, Eliot could not restrain his enthusiasm for the coming era. An intensified devotion to first things pointed directly to New Jerusalem. The natives "shall be wholly governed by the Scriptures in all things both in Church and State; . . . and when it is so the Lord reigneth, and unto that frame the Lord will bring all the world ere he hath done." The temptation to indulge in end-time revery was so strong that Eliot found it necessary for the time being to bridle his imagination—"But I forget myself[!]"—in order to attend realistically to the practical demand and tiny scale of the task before him at Natick.[19]

18. *Ibid.*, 119–120, 126–128, 131; Shepard, *Clear Sun-shine, MHSC*, 3d Ser., IV (1834), 29. The English spokesmen, most of whom were Independent clergy well informed about the New England enterprise, knew nothing of an original millennial errand to Massachusetts. "Indeed *a long time* it was," they observed, "before God let them see any *farther* end of their comming over, then to *preserve* their consciences, *cherish* their Graces, *provide* for their sustenance." The "farther Errand" was an insight well after the fact of immigration; it came to light only in the context of developments after 1640 (*Clear Sun-shine*, 28–29). A similar idea appears in Winslow, ed., *Glorious Progress*, 95–96; and in Whitfield *et al.*, *Light Appearing, MHSC*, 3d Ser., IV (1834), 145. For the identification of Indians as Jews in New England, see Maclear, "Fifth Monarchy," *WMQ*, 3d Ser., XXXII (1975), 243–244; and Vaughan, *Frontier*, 19–20. Vaughan's imputation of this view to 17th-century Puritans "almost without exception" and without respect to chronology is an exaggeration (9). For a corrective, see Bercovitch, *Jeremiad*, 75n. In 1646 Eliot subscribed to the view that the natives were descendants of "Tartars" (*Day-Breaking*, 14). His statements in 1649 about the Hebrew connection were tentative and conditional; they are inaccurately reported by Maclear as expressing a clear conviction ("Fifth Monarchy," 245). It was Thomas Thorowgood's *Jewes in America; or, Probabilities That the Americans Are of That Race* (London, 1650) which led him to a more thorough investigation of the subject. In a preface prepared for Thorowgood's sequel to that work, Eliot announced hesitantly that he now had found "some ground to conceive, that some of the Ten Tribes might be scattered even . . . into these parts of America" ("Learned Conjectures," in Thorowgood, *Jewes in America* [1660], 1).

19. Whitfield *et al.*, *Light Appearing, MHSC*, 3d Ser., IV (1834), 127, and

After July of 1649, the chronological development of Eliot's reflections upon Natick cannot be traced with certainty. The first datable reference to the Exodus scheme appeared in a report from mid-1651, but there Eliot also observed that he had expounded it to the Indians on several earlier occasions.[20] Presumably, the general aim of scriptural rule was identified with Exodus 18 sometime between late 1649 and early 1651. But once this was accomplished, the very exhilaration at discovering "a forme of Civil Government instituted by God himself" led Eliot irresistibly forward again to the millennial theme. This time, he was not to be denied the most extravagant inferences. The leap from Natick to New Jerusalem was obvious enough. Eliot quickly convinced himself that in Exodus 18 he had discovered the governing structure soon to be imposed internationally by the "brightness of . . . [Christ's] coming." But now he came upon a practical difficulty. For the schema of Exodus 18, with its maximum provision for the government of one thousand men and their families, could not comprehend the larger citizenries of most nations. But more inclusive forms could not, in a biblicist order, be devised upon human authority; all must rest upon "Divine Pattern." Therefore, Eliot set himself to sift and probe more fully the relevant biblical material.

In short order the needed additions appeared. First, he discovered an extension of the Exodus model. From texts in Deuteronomy and Numbers he inferred a "Superiour order of Rulers" of ten, fifty, and one hundred thousand and, at the highest level, of one million. This higher structure, having been "practised by Moses in Israel," possessed every archetypal credential, but the biblical evidence for its existence was admittedly scanty, whereupon Eliot proceeded to discover a corroboration of the entire scheme in biblical angelology. As the saints should discover upon their entry into heaven, Exodus 18 was but a partial formulation of a comprehensive divine government that from eternity had regulated the angelic population. Beginning with units of tens, fifties, hundreds, and thousands, the ranks of angelic magistracy rose up, in complete accordance with the Mosaic

---

see 131. I know of no evidence to support Richard William Cogley's claim that Eliot intended "inaugurating" the millennium at Natick ("The Millenarianism of John Eliot, 'Apostle' to the Indians" [Ph.D. diss., Princeton University, 1983], 82–85).

20. Owen *et al.*, *Strength out of Weaknesse*, MHSC, 3d Ser., IV (1834), 171.

system, from "myriads" (tens of thousands) to millions. Therewith the difficulty was resolved. Eliot now had a whole vision of end-time politics: a simple hierarchy of elected rulers extending from orders of ten to orders of one million, all zealous to rule and judge according to Mosaic law. This he would now propound as "that form of Government, by which Christ means to rule all the Nations on earth," commencing with England.[21]

Starting thus with the needs of a small band of natives, Eliot made the discovery needed to guide England—and eventually mankind—toward political transfiguration. It should not be inferred that his turn from American experience to world redemption reflected an interest in enacting a New England Errand. Like Cotton's analyses of Revelation, *The Christian Commonwealth* was dedicated to "making *England* first in that blessed work of setting up the Kingdom."[22] With its comparatively democratic institutions and its biblically informed body of *Laws and Liberties*, Massachusetts stood closer than traditional England to the ultimate commonwealth, in which rulers were to be elected and valued as administrators of biblical law. But the colony remained far too widely at variance with biblical pattern to provide a world-inspiring model of the future.

Eliot's proposal not only ignored New England institutions, but it also implied a severe critique. Not only monarchs and houses of lords but, in their present form, general courts and governorships must be swept away if Christ were to rule; and this inference was likely drawn by those who demanded recantation in 1661. To the further discounting of New England institutions, Eliot's plan actually assumed that a more adequate government was taking form in Natick than in Boston, among natives distrusted and feared by many of the English and begrudged their farming land by adjacent settlers. Yet, if he saw the first praying town as a "pattern and copy" assuring the spread of biblical polity among the Indians and as a preparation

21. CC, 130–137, 159–160. The reference to Christ's coming in "brightness" is in Whitfield *et al.*, *Light Appearing*, MHSC, 3d Ser., IV (1834), 127. Cogley's argument that Eliot meant Natick to function as the exemplary model guiding England toward millennial transformation appears to hinge on his assumption of a New England errand ("John Eliot," 84). Eliot himself never claimed as much.

22. CC, 133, emphasis mine. Eliot made the same point in Whitfield *et al.*, *Light Appearing*, MHSC, 3d Ser., IV (1834), 120–121.

for the spread of Christ's government to a remote part of the earth, nowhere in *The Christian Commonwealth* did he advance Natick as such as the model for European imitation. His missionary responsibilities, he recounted, had "first put [him] upon th[e] Study" of millennial politics, but only to this degree did he wish to style the tract as a word from the New World.

What Eliot had to offer was a model rooted entirely in mythic event. It needed no prior validation in a New England experiment. All was to be drawn immediately from the biblical template. That was, always, Eliot's great point. He would allow that his chart of the future was a product of the dim "morning twilight" of coming fulfillment. At many points it might be incomplete, even vitiated by unintentional human additions. But, he was confident, the broad outline was sound. Above all, with the breakthrough to recognition of Scripture as the "onely *Magna Charta*" of Christian commonwealth, the unfailing premise of all future government was secured once and for all. And what was this, indeed, but the organic complement to the ecclesiastical programs of Brightman and Cotton? As the church was to be merged tightly with apostolic design, so now political society was to be "proportioned" rigorously to the fixed, all-sufficient, unvarying "Standard" of a polity both Mosaic and angelic.[23]

At the time of writing *The Christian Commonwealth*, so strong was Eliot's sense of an impending and rapid turn toward divine government that he was disinclined to dwell upon the mechanics of transition. True, he recognized that responsible Englishmen first must be brought to adopt the proffered polity, but his general conception, like Brightman's and Cotton's, provided for no real intermediate zone of planning, diplomacy, and instrumentation. He was "no Statesman, nor acquainted with matters of that nature," but felt this no hindrance to political theory for an age of miracle. The need of the hour was to display the sheer convincing spectacle of a *"Divine Institution, sprung from heavenly wisdom."* His countrymen, indeed, would be engaged for an interim in "setting up" and "bringing about" the new order, but in this great juncture they were to become as selfless "nobodies," agents of the "irresistible . . . force and power" of the Lord's spreading rule. Their whole duty was to "humble themselves to embrace" the commanded forms and to cooperate in their imposition—

23. CC, 135, 140–141, 151.

immediate, unilateral, and unchecked—upon the English-speaking nations and then the world. Throughout, the process corresponded to the involutional "growth" foreseen in Cotton's *Canticles*. Politically as ecclesiastically, the transitional period filled in a fixed schedule. Its aim was the "fulfilling of [primordial] design," and in quick order there would arrive the day of "Kingdom . . . come when . . . all is done by Divine direction." Then, with the political life of every nation drawn within the closed uniformity of Mosaic government, *pro*gress would be stilled.[24]

But all of this Eliot fairly took for granted. Absorbing most of his attention were the governmental operations of the millennium proper. More than any other work written in New England from 1640 to 1660, *The Christian Commonwealth* enabled the reader to imagine the course of everyday events in the transfigured state. There, for instance, one could discover that rulers of ten were to enforce "God's government" in a weekly magistrate's court or that, when warranted, appeals from this level were to be permitted to the higher courts formed at each rank of rulership.[25]

But such details taken alone do not reveal readily the consummated impact of the Middle Advent. First, the described forms and procedures must be seen within Eliot's carefully integrated scheme; next, the whole must be viewed within the continuum of centuries remaining until the Second Coming. Only then, but then with striking effect, can the extraordinary privilege of millennial citizenship be appreciated. The last age then would appear not only as a completed restitution but as a total mobilization of government to preserve the fixed harmony of Mosaic institutions against disruptive forces. Minor fluctuations would remain, but no longer the dread possibility of fundamental declension long envisaged by English doctrines of the National Covenant; thence the "Government and Administration of affairs in the [eschatological] Kingdom of Christ" was to be a vast exercise in repetition and sameness through centuries of time.[26]

Not by the wildest stretch of imagination could Eliot's Christian commonwealth be described as a political Eden, if by that be meant a return to Adamic tameness before the Fall. He supposed that the

24. *Ibid.*, 130–139.
25. *Ibid.*, 146, 149–152.
26. *Ibid.*, 130.

depravity of man, and hence the need for strict government, was an indelible mark of human history beyond the power of the Bright Coming to remove. Ever would it remain that "sin will grow apace . . . if it be not always watched, and often weeded out." Thereby the familiar moral disciplines of Reformed and Puritan faith must be sustained to the last earthly day. If the political institutions of Israel were to be reconstituted, their dominating purpose was the enforcement of biblical law, including the Judicials of Moses reckoned according to their equity.[27] Millennial citizens, in fact, would take their place within the most thoroughly governed society ever known, a society whose every tenth male was a "Ruler" granted within his small domain approximately the authority of a Massachusetts assistant or an English justice of the peace. At various levels rulership entailed responsibility for education, trade, and other concerns of the public welfare, but the prime office lay elsewhere. It was "to look that all the Commandments of God be observed, as to compel men to their . . . duty, and punish them for their . . . transgressions." In practice this meant that the "proceeding of Justice" was to be the main business of the realm. Of course, judicial functions were integral to political office in seventeenth-century English life, but in Eliot's world to come they virtually would define it. Above all else, rulers would be judges, each the president of a court with jurisdiction appropriate to his level.[28]

Thus would the general government consist largely of a pyramid of eight "Assembl[ies] of Judges," with ultimate decision in the most difficult cases passing to a yet higher supreme court in which an elite of civil judges would be joined by selected members of the clergy. All participants in this system were to be filled with the tide of biblical knowledge filling the earth in the last days. Upon the sacred writ they were to meditate daily and at length, thereby obtaining a full technical competency in biblical law and a zeal for its total application to human affairs. Court schedules were so to be coordinated and procedures streamlined as to place a premium upon speed and

27. *Ibid.,* 141–142, 144–145, 149.
28. *Ibid.,* 154, 155, 158. The ruler of ten was to sit as a court of one, but at other levels the ruler would be joined by his immediate subordinates sitting as associate judges. The ruler of fifty, for instance, would hold a court of six consisting of himself and his five subordinate rulers of ten. *Ibid.,* 149–151, 156–158, 160–161.

efficiency of judgment. Thus in a domain of one million citizens, with the system completed to the last degree, there would range over each individual citizen an active hierarchy of rulers and courts nine deep. English juries, which answered to no biblical archetype, would not appear. Having bowed the knee to this judicial Leviathan, quickly enough men would forget what it had meant in a half-reformed England to be "remissly governed."[29]

Given a continued high incidence of infractions against divine law and the rulers' swift pursuit of the resulting cases, public life in the millennium was to be anything but uneventful. Commotions of error, detection, trial, and punishment would remain to perturb the general peace and alter the lot of individuals. To this degree Eliot's depiction of the last state did incorporate an element of the dynamic and conflictual. But was it potentially disruptive of the given order of things? Could it produce true and abiding change? All evidence points to a negative answer; indeed, the more we study Eliot's work, the more essential we find his sense of changeless pattern to be.

By no coincidence, in *The Christian Commonwealth* he used the term "change" solely to describe the transition *into* the New Jerusalem, for, once that transition was complete, every possibility of further and fundamental alteration of the human estate was foreclosed.[30] This was so, in the first place, because of the swiftness, rigor, and efficiency with which any deviation from biblical precept would then be met. Eliot hardly needed to stress that millennial justice, with its grinding "wheels" and its tremendous authority, was "certain" in its effect. And considering its immediate penetration into every local group of one hundred, fifty, and even ten men and their families, whom Eliot expected to dwell together close to their respective rulers, there were to remain no secret enclaves in which conspiracy, revolt, or major crime could be pondered.[31] But in the second place, and more important, stability, as integral to the very conception, was guaranteed. In the world Eliot foresaw, the discrepancy within history between Mosaic archetype and political reality was overcome to the maximum degree. Now, for the first time in the Christian era, the ends of government were to be pursued through detailed imita-

29. *Ibid.*, 148–151, 155.
30. *Ibid.*, 140. There are three occurrences.
31. *Ibid.*, 135–136.

tion of a sacred pattern. And that pattern was a mirror of the divine completeness. It stood beyond change.

So concerned was Eliot to secure this point that the "form of 10s, 50s, 100s, and 1000s" took on an unusual significance in his mind. Both in *The Christian Commonwealth* and in his later millennial tract, *The Communion of Churches* (1665), he revealed an interest in the religious significance of numbers that suggested medieval sources and that ventured beyond the normal precincts of Puritan theology. It was, of course, biblical numbers that interested him. Numbers stressed in the sacred text, like the number twelve, were a fully certified part of revelation; but what was their special function? Eliot shunned the idea that they were arbitrary or without significance. Somehow and with singular fitness they correlated with divine "harmony." One might, for instance, examine the miracle of the loaves and fishes in Mark 6: had not Christ there conspicuously "set [the people] down by hundreds, and by fifties"? The inference was clear. Plainly, he "delighted in that order." [32]

That *order*! Here was the cutting point. For it is perfectly clear that, in Eliot's usage, "order" signified a fixed estate, a pure transcript of sacred and changeless form; and how might this better be propounded than through the fixity of numbers? Eliot strove, therefore, to impress upon his readers the numerical exactitude of the Mosaic "form"; its identical recurrence in several biblical texts; its inclusion of the fifties and hundreds in which Christ from eternity delighted; its repetition in perfect symmetry at a multiple of one thousand in the "superior order" of ten, fifty, and one hundred thousands and one million; and, withal, its manifestation of "excellent harmony and order." [33]

To imagine this government in long-range operation was thus to envision repetition. Through the millennial centuries a steady criminal traffic would emerge within society, would be drawn ineluctably into the system of justice, and always would find "final determination according to the [fixed law of the] Scriptures." Eliot even urged that records of court proceedings be kept and published so that judges

32. *Ibid.*, 135 (see also 162), 136, 137n.
33. *Ibid.*, 135. The symmetry of proportion between the higher and lower orders extended as well to the composition and relative jurisdiction of the court to be held at each level. Eliot also calculated the exact maximum constituencies of each order of rulership. *Ibid.*, 147, 159–161.

in like future cases would be able "alway[s] so to judge," that is, to maintain uniform penalties through all remaining time. Hence the last age, viewed as a political phenomenon, might well exhibit constant activity, even bustle, but this activity was not linked to change. Until the Second Coming, human society should be ruled, and ruled vigorously, by a government totally conservative, totally powerful, and totally bent to the maintenance of laws and institutions much "beautified" in their very finality.[34] In the long view the millennium meant sameness. It meant a triumphal keeping of restitution once achieved. It meant that any year, any century, was to be much like any other. It meant, in truth, that a passage had occurred beyond all vicissitudes into a state of programmed corporateness in which time passes but nothing essential changes. And this picture, as reflected through the prism of Eliot's mind, fairly represents the ideal of reformed Christian society dreamed of in Puritan philosophy since the early Elizabethan period.

Sociological Connections: Roxbury and the Millennium

*H*aving followed Eliot to the highest level of abstraction beyond contemporary history, one should recall that since 1632 his actual earthly estate had been the small agrarian village of Roxbury, Massachusetts. Are there noteworthy correlations between his experience of life in a pioneer colony and the exalted perspectives of *The Christian Commonwealth*? Such a notion may seem improbable at first reflection. His projection of a drastically reordered world to come may seem irrecoverably far removed from rural New England. The sensational Middle Advent, the transformation of government into biblicist judiciaries, the pure rule of archetypes—may not these plausibly be construed as a pipe dream offering relief from pioneer humdrum, or as a vicarious enjoyment of the excitements and hopes of revolution in the mother country? To a degree this may be true, but specific ties to the immediate social world ought also to be taken into account.

Eliot's themes of order and sameness were not applied to political

34. *Ibid.*, 136, 155, 163.

establishment alone; he also indicated an underlying socioeconomic life fully aligned with millennial rule. No less than church or state, the social order of the future was to be well ordered, uniform, and massively resistant to change. Little emphasis was placed upon urban or business characteristics. Drawing upon decades of Puritan instruction in "domestical duties," Eliot predicted that all men, women, and children were to assume their place within the strong bonds of the patriarchal family. Families, in turn, were tied covenantally to the uniform scriptural program of Redemption and law. Since adult men normally would qualify for the political franchise through marriage and the assumption of patriarchal functions, rulerships of ten, fifty, and so on were to be, in effect, federations of families joined through the male heads; and these were to "cohabit together" in permanent localities. "Neighborhood" was important. Geographical mobility was not encouraged and was associated in part with "unstable changes" through which "unruly persons" might seek to "slip out from under . . . Government." Always the citizenry should abide within "their several places" in the general society and bend themselves compliantly to "walking in their [occupational] callings." Woman's role, scarcely mentioned by Eliot, was self-evidently in the household, while, for the men, agriculture, fishing, and trade were the "necessary and useful" activities that came first to Eliot's mind. These were the most obvious features of the society—oriented to biblical rule, to family government, to established location, to a hierarchy of "places," to regular vocational performance, and to a simple economy in which trade was important but did not loom as the predominant or privileged element—that Eliot held harmonious with the "certain and peaceable order" of the world to come.[35]

As we review these glimpses of social and economic life, not forgetting their larger millennial setting, a number of possible connections with conditions in the Bay Colony to 1650 appear. The earliest New England towns have been studied intensively, with many variations in emphasis, and much of the scholarship converges in a portrayal of conservative, well-ordered, stable communities threatened later in the century by problems of land availability and by the rise of a commercial economy. Reflecting the inclinations of a largely agrarian society but responding as well to the cohesive ideals of Puri-

35. *Ibid.*, 136, 144–158.

tan social teaching, on the whole the first towns promoted the common good, discouraged selfish individualism, minimized conflict, and resisted change. With successive generations, an increasing scarcity of land and the movement of settlers away from the town centers led to serious divisions.

But the more fundamental threat to the first colonists' cohesive aims arose from another quarter. When the Massachusetts economy collapsed in conjunction with the crisis in English affairs in 1640, the second and third decades of permanent settlement became the formative era of a long-lived commercial system tied to overseas trade. By 1650–1651, when Eliot was composing *The Christian Commonwealth*, the outlines of a new mercantile order were becoming visible, especially in Boston and the other port towns. One of the most firmly established findings of modern scholarship is that the progress of business enterprise and the rise of a merchant class crystallized interests and practices that ultimately disrupted Puritan society. The new developments enhanced the social strength of the mercantile sector, engaged the merchants with English and other commercial interests unfriendly or indifferent to Puritan ideals, engendered economic individualism and absorption in worldly enterprise, and bred support for religious toleration. The shift from Puritan communalism to a more heterogeneous, change-oriented society based upon a commercial economy became the dominant trend in seventeenth-century history.[36]

Some key details of this general portrait have been challenged. Students of the port towns have found a shift to mercantile dominance before mid-century, and speculation in land and other forms of "economic individualism" appear to have been crucial to the founding and development of many towns.[37] "Diversity" and "conflict" are

36. See, for example, Kenneth A. Lockridge, *A New England Town, the First Hundred Years: Dedham, Massachusetts, 1636–1736* (New York, 1970); Philip J. Greven, Jr., *Four Generations: Population, Land, and Family in Colonial Andover, Massachusetts* (Ithaca, N.Y., 1970); John M. Murrin, "Review Essay," *History and Theory*, XI (1972), 226–275; John J. McCusker and Russell R. Menard, *The Economy of British America, 1607–1789* (Chapel Hill, N.C., 1985), 94–105.

37. On mercantile dominance, see Darrett B. Rutman, *Winthrop's Boston: Portrait of A Puritan Town, 1630–1649* (Chapel Hill, N.C., 1965); Chris-

favorite stresses of a newer body of scholarship. Among inland towns the quiet, consensual experience of subsistence agricultural communities like Dedham, Andover, or Rowley now appears in contrast to the faster-paced, commercial ways of Ipswich or Springfield. Springfield, Newbury, Gloucester, and Marblehead, we learn, were "born in contention." Boston, Salem, Newbury, Springfield, and probably other towns appear to have embraced substantial social and economic diversity from an early date. In addition, several students have argued that religious dissensus and dispute were the rule even in the early decades.[38] All of these claims will remain under debate, but it seems increasingly likely that the communal impulse was less dominant in the early Bay colony and the commercial trend of the later decades less innovative than hitherto often supposed.

With Roxbury, however, such studies that might define Eliot's immediate milieu in detail are not available. Evidence points to a small but prosperous agricultural town with an exceptionally high

---

tine Alice Young, *From "Good Order" to Glorious Revolution: Salem, Massachusetts, 1628–1689* (Ann Arbor, Mich., 1978), 7, 33, 46. On economic individualism, see David Grayson Allen, *In English Ways: The Movement of Societies and the Transferal of English Local Law and Custom to Massachusetts Bay in the Seventeenth Century* (Chapel Hill, N.C., 1981), 96, 102, 105–116, 119, 121–122, 127–133; Stephen Innes, *Labor in a New Land: Economy and Society in Seventeenth-Century Springfield* (Princeton, N.J., 1983), xvii–xviii, 3, 78. To firm my grasp of this issue, Fred Martin kindly allowed me to read a draft of his forthcoming study, "Entrepreneurship and the Founding of New England Towns: The Seventeenth Century." In a study of Gloucester and Marblehead after 1690, Christine Leigh Heyrman rejects entirely the thesis that the rise of a trading economy undermined Puritan values (*Commerce and Culture: The Maritime Communities of Colonial Massachusetts, 1690–1750* [New York, 1984]).

38. Innes, *Labor in a New Land*, xvii–xviii; Allen, *In English Ways*, 82; Heyrman, *Commerce and Culture*, 29–51, 209–224. Allen helpfully compares and contrasts Newbury, Rowley, Ipswich, Hingham, and Watertown. On diversity, see Rutman, *Boston*, 3–163; Young, *Salem*, 9–11; Allen, *In English Ways*, 82; Innes, *Labor in a New Land*, xv–xxi. On dissensus, see Philip F. Gura, *A Glimpse of Sion's Glory: Puritan Radicalism in New England, 1620–1660* (Middletown, Conn., 1984), who presents a comprehensive argument to this effect. A comparable study focused upon Connecticut is Paul R. Lucas, *Valley of Discord: Church and Society along the Connecticut River, 1636–1725* (Hanover, N.H., 1976).

percentage of church members. A property table from about 1640 reveals the usual land-based social hierarchy.[39] At the same time, leading Roxbury citizens were engaged in speculative transactions in land. They also were aware of commercial developments in the Bay. The town had been founded by the enterprising William Pynchon, who for a short period in the 1640s made it the capital of the colony's fur trade. More important, it was one of the closest towns to Boston, some two miles distant, and thus in far closer touch with life in that business center than were isolated townships like Dedham or Rowley. At least one "merchant of large transactions," Joshua Hewes, also made his home in early Roxbury and maintained a store there supplied directly from his warehouse at the town dock in Boston.[40]

Thus as teacher of the church in Roxbury, Eliot's first affiliation was with a small agricultural parish that probably reflected alike a strong drive toward consensus and stability and the potentially disruptive stirrings of business. Eliot in fact commented little upon Roxbury society, but when he discussed developments in greater New England, his premise was always the necessary unanimity and cohesion of the New World venture. *The Christian Commonwealth* aside, his entire literary output bespeaks identification with a society grounded in religious and social consensus. None offered severer strictures than he against disturbers of social unison, against the "schism" of the antinomians or the "pretense of conscience" leading to new doctrines of religious toleration. And when in 1646 Robert Child and his associate "petitioners" challenged current arrangements in church and state, Eliot hastened to damn the "trouble raised by Jesuited agents to molest the peace of the churches and Com[mon]w[ealth]."[41]

39. William Wood, *New Englands Prospect* (London, 1634), 41; Rutman, *Boston*, 178. For statistics of freemanship (presupposing church membership) in early Roxbury, see Robert Emmet Wall, Jr., *Massachusetts Bay: The Crucial Decade, 1640–1650* (New Haven, Conn., 1972), 39. The property table is in *Roxbury Land and Church Records: A Report*, 2d ed. (Boston, 1884), 4–5.

40. Francis S. Drake, *The Town of Roxbury* . . . (Roxbury, Mass., 1878), 162; Bernard Bailyn, *The New England Merchants in the Seventeenth Century* (New York, 1964), 27, 35; Eben Putnam, ed. and comp., *Lieutenant Joshua Hewes: A New England Pioneer, and Some of His Descendants* (n.p., 1913), 56–69.

41. John Eliot, "Rev. John Eliot's Records of the First Church in Roxbury, Mass.," *NEHGR*, XXXIII (1879), 62, 65; Whitfield *et al.*, *Light Appearing*, *MHSC*, 3d Ser., IV (1834), 120. Robert Dudley was assigned to the committee

At the same time, he must have had knowledge of business developments both in Roxbury and in nearby Boston and the other port towns. He made frequent visits to participate in the Boston-area consociation of elders. There he no doubt had many discussions with Cotton and other clergy of the mercantile towns and joined with them in providing political counseling and arbitration services to the General Court. It is not known to what extent Eliot by 1650–1651 realized the implications of the new commercial developments of the 1640s, but *The Christian Commonwealth* suggests a commentary upon the future in which trade, as we have noted, would play a positive role. Millennial society was to remain within finite history and subject to material want; it too must be founded upon a solid economic base. But Eliot had no idea of opening the door to commercial revolution. Trade must take a subordinate and merely functional place within the millennial commonwealth, an enterprise whose splendor and greatness was defined essentially by biblical restoration, by the Christian Redemption and Mosaic precepts.

Regarded as a product of Massachusetts experience, Eliot's prospectus of the future was, therefore, one in which communal aspirations in the early society were to be vindicated on a massive scale. And so would be the aims of Bay officials who "knew the value of trade but who believed it served the community best when subordinated to the goals of religion."[42] Consensus, order, the subservience of all parts and functions to a common religious good—these were the desiderata of the new society. And where deviations might appear, the swift instrumentalities of church and state were poised to check them at the source. In this world commerce might proceed, but no mercantile takeoff, no redirection of values toward private economic gain, no rise to influence by an entrepreneurial class with separate interests, no drift toward social heterogeneity would be countenanced for a moment.

Considered in these terms, *The Christian Commonwealth* accords fully with Cotton's map of the millennial church. Eliot's first high exercise in millennial speculation was, in short, only in the most

---

designated by the General Court to respond to the Child petition (Wall, *Massachusetts Bay*, 176). Eliot also attacked "Gorton and his [ac]complices" ("Rev. Eliot's Records," 238).

42. Bailyn, *New England Merchants*, 103.

qualified sense a progressive venture in ideas. Despite its limited approval of trade, it was much more evidently a fossilization of consensual themes in the colonists' outlook than a forecast or first manifestation of an open, individualistic, forward-striving American future. It embodied a passionate concern for the future of social institutions, but it envisioned stability, not change, as the style of the ultimate social process. It conveyed but a truncated sense of the present as a linear process eclipsing the whole human past. It ran oblique to a later America's "unquestioning assumption that the new is the better—that 'forward' is better than 'backward.'"[43] And it retained and subordinated all to the definitively Puritan element: the encompassing claim of the Great Time to order the actions of men.

43. Robin Murphy Williams, *American Society: A Sociological Interpretation*, 2d ed. (New York, 1960), 432.

NINE

THE JEREMIAD:

SHIFTING IDEALS OF

COVENANTAL MAINTENANCE,

1630–1663

Whether affirming or denying ties to modernity and progress, virtually all students of American Puritanism assume that the founders were committed to an essentially linear concept of redemptive history and their place within it. It is seldom-questioned doctrine that by the time of Augustine the Christian movement had replaced the cyclical perspectives of the Greco-Roman world with a genuinely historical vision of humanity's movement through time. Henceforward, in this view, the human career would be construed as a flow of unrepeatable events moving always forward from singular beginning to singular ending, from Creation to Second Coming.[1] In more specific terms, we are reminded periodically that Puritanism was a branch of Reformed Protestantism, with its distinctively dynamic sense of history and its urge to hasten the Reformed community toward eschatological goals. These generalizations, if they are to illuminate the worldview of Congregational New Englanders, require qualification.

Since the Puritan orientation to a scriptural strong time meant that the past—the sacred past—was never indeed past, but perpetually

---

1. See, for example, Carl L. Becker, *The Heavenly City of the Eighteenth-Century Philosophers* (New Haven, Conn., 1932), 128.

recoverable, it was hardly possible to see the historical continuum as a simple, successive movement through a flow of unrepeatable events. Sacred paradigms, in fact, clamored for repetition again and again through all remaining time. By the same token, the Puritan disposition to conceive goals—and in millennial contexts this included eschatological goals—as reclamation of the first suggests that time also took on a curved dimension of motion back to mythic origins. From a more modern standpoint, these features of Puritan thought might seem to cancel or contradict perception of Christianity as a historical procession and development from Creation to Christ's Coming, but viewed in context they do nothing of the kind. Puritan thinkers, in fact, entertained the two conceptions, the linear and the cyclical, simultaneously and experienced no disturbing tension between them. As they conceived it, the relation between time forward and (sacred) time past was dialectical, with each supplying a crucial element of a considerably more complex worldview than that to be designated as "the idea of progress."

In point of fact, to the Massachusetts founders, the "cycle" was very much a working tool of thought. Consider the terms in which Thomas Shepard in the later 1630s proclaimed the significance of the Sabbath to his Cambridge auditory, one that probably included the student body at earliest Harvard College. Reaching beyond normal primitivist appeals to draw upon the symbol system of Christian Neoplatonism, he first described the characteristic itinerary of Protestant men and women in their course from birth to final Redemption. Their "motion," he told his hearers, should assume the shape of a circle and culminate in a perfecting "reflux and return" to the Creator: "Man, being made . . . for God, has therefore his motion so toward God as that he . . . is not led in a straight line, but led . . . about in a circular motion." When "man has run his race . . . and passed through the . . . circle of his life, he then returns unto his eternal rest." Just so it was, on a smaller scale, in the course of a week spent in a remote Congregational colony and culminating in the practice of the newly restored Sabbath. Shepard directed the Cambridge saints, in imitation of the larger redemptive circuit, to revolve again and again "within the lesser . . . circle of every week," curving back each time toward the primal Sabbath rites. They in their turn were a perpetually recurring participation in the fixed Sabbath "rest" of heaven. Efflux and reflux, circles and cycles, imitation and participation, weekly renewed correspondence to a changeless good—Shepard assumed these as self-evident points on the intellectual compass and passed on to a general commendation of Sabbath discipline and duty.[2]

Yet by so defining the colonists' relation to their Sabbath, by showing that their weekly passage forward embraced an enriching cycle back to that ordinance, Shepard unknowingly foreshadowed the later strategy of covenantal maintenance that the next generation of clergy, his own son among them, would find themselves compelled to adopt. For it was a presupposition of his argument that the Sabbath, and indeed all the biblical ordinances, were practiced in New England with unique fidelity to originals. There was no need to inform his audience that in their colony a restorationist campaign was going forward as nowhere else within Christendom or to teach them that loyalty to biblical rule and pattern was the essential formula for safety within their covenant with the Lord. So long as the immigrants could retain the fresh thrill of liberty of the ordinances, they would continue in their appointed "circular motion" back to communion with the sacred and thus would remain in good covenantal standing.

But after mid-century there would come a time of change. A newer generation of religious exhorters then would confront congregations for whom the ordinances had become routine, a larger community that seemed in many ways to have declined from biblical rule, and a corresponding threat of divine vengeance. Yet, having gone to school to Shepard as well as to the other great lights among the founders, they would not stand resourceless before their age. They would insist upon comprehending current changes in mythic terms. They would remind their charges that New England's time forward into the later century must, lest it fall into mere linear drift, continue to embrace a cycle of repristination. And as they pursued this conviction in the light of New England's special history of engagement with originals, they assigned the founders' age an importance that

2. Thomas Shepard, *The Works of Thomas Shepard*, 3 vols. (Boston, 1853), III, 25–26. In this passage Shepard establishes a deliberately pejorative contrast with the merely "linear" motion of living things below the human level. Unable to enter the cycle of return to origins, they pass their mortal course and simply "cease to be." For similar texts, see Perry Miller, *The New England Mind: The Seventeenth Century* (1939; Cambridge, Mass., 1954), 180; and John Norton, *The Orthodox Evangelist* (London, 1654), 13.

went beyond all precedents in English Reformed thought. How they did so and thereby created a distinctively New World variation upon the covenantal sermon is the essential story of the American Puritan jeremiad.

Deuteronomy and Restoration: Cycles of Covenanted Community

*L*ong laboring to clarify and restore first forms of church and society, New Englanders altered many of the received ways of English community. Church covenants, utopian town covenants, the closer coordination of law and "equity" with biblical sources, the reworked Psalter—these and many other restitutionist accomplishments bespoke a society so unprecedentedly keyed to biblical pattern as to remind a number of participants of the new heavens and new earth of eschatological teaching.[3] But even as they celebrated feats of recovery, New World Puritans were concerned to preserve their hard-won gains. Retaining a strong element of traditional Christian Platonism, the Reformed theology of Cotton and Shepard, Winthrop and Edward Johnson reflected a sharp awareness of the mutability of all things historical. It also embodied deep regard for the sinful waywardness of men, women, and their institutions.

Further, veterans of religious dissent in Caroline England and of the risks and hardships of the Great Migration had uncommonly close experience of fluctuations in personal and social life. They might well wonder about the fate of their reforms through future cycles of time and change. And yet the maintenance of restored institutions did not immediately present itself as a fresh intellectual problem. Happily, the concern for the reformed community's stability amid flux had been addressed long before within English quarters and, at least in conceptual terms, been resolved to the general satisfaction of the Spiritual Brotherhood. Many theological devices spoke to the issue, but the foremost tool to the purpose cultivated within advanced English Protestantism was the covenant, that most protean construct of Puritan thinking; and it was the covenant, interwoven with restitutionist themes and buttressed with ritual supports, that

3. Miller, *Seventeenth Century*, 470; *WP*, V, 126.

was to yield New Englanders the needed confidence that reform, once achieved, could be sustained.

English dissent by the 1630s embraced an impressive inventory of covenantal rubrics, each exhibiting a partially distinct rationale and purpose.[4] Of these, the National Covenant related most directly to the task of sustaining reformation in early New England. One may recall briefly its basic elements. In identification with biblical Israel, England was pledged to a Deuteronomic pact with God. The pact obligated England to conform national life to the standards of biblical law. To the extent this was accomplished and sustained, England would enjoy divine favor and material prosperity, while defection from scriptural demands would evoke God's disfavor in the form of fire, plague, military defeat, or other disasters. Repentance and amendment would restore the people to positive standing. All elements of the general conception long predated the English Reformation, but they were taken up, worked into a more systematic statement, and applied specifically to England by William Tyndale around 1530 and thus implanted as a staple of English thought for more than a century to come. Not all proponents of the doctrine, Puritan or otherwise, presumed an always unfailing proportionality of earthly behavior to divine response, but on the whole the spotlight fell upon the reprisals and favors of a morally vigilant Lord. Probably the most programmatic statement appears in the several prefaces of the Geneva Bible (1560).[5]

Puritans were not the first in sixteenth-century England to connect covenantal obedience with the cause of further reformation, but it was inevitable that in their hands covenantal doctrine should

4. These included the covenants of Works, Grace, and Redemption, the church (or conventicular) covenant, the personal covenant, and the National (or "external") Covenant.

5. For a good summary of the doctrine of the National Covenant, see Winthrop S. Hudson, "Fast Days and Civil Religion," in *Theology in Sixteenth- and Seventeenth-Century England* . . . (Los Angeles, 1971), 14. Michael McGiffert may be right that a full-scale "contract theory of the commonwealth" did not emerge until after 1600, but the conception of England's standing in Deuteronomic relation to God, with its implicit (and at times explicit) premise of a covenanted relationship, was an Edwardian and Elizabethan commonplace. The Deuteronomic theme thus understood defines National Covenant in the present discussion. McGiffert, "Covenant, Crown, and Commons in Elizabethan Puritanism," *Journal of British Studies*, XX, no. 1 (Fall 1980), 33.

be turned toward primitivist agendas. Even if narrowly defined in terms of the Decalogue, in which Puritan exegetes saw "the whole perfection of . . . dutie to God and man," what was God's law but the moral crux of the biblical primordium and hence a necessary component in any program of reformation?[6] But further, the category of "law," as interpreted within the heavily moralist context of Puritan theology, was an expansive one that readily embraced the "originals" and "institutions" of primitivist doctrine. A much-enhanced correlation between covenantal demand and the recovery of prime content already was evident in the "first open manifesto of the Puritan party," the *Admonition to Parliament* of 1572, for there a "self-consciously restitutionist" argument was "based upon [a Deuteronomic] understanding of England existing under the judgment and mercy of God."[7] In the following decades, the Deuteronomic-restorationist connection became a keystone of Puritan dissent. Return to the biblical ordinances, as to a "holy preaching ministry" or "church discipline," regularly was portrayed as a sine qua non for achieving the level of moral control and repentance necessary to avert the Lord's "heavy judgment."[8]

In the common conception the national contract was held to rest upon a reciprocal formula promising "horrible plagues to them that transgress [God's] commandments, and . . . blessings and felicity to such as observe and obey them."[9] To observe and obey the law was

6. John Dod, *A Plaine and Familiar Exposition of the Ten Commandements* (London, 1618), 3.

7. *A Parte of a Register . . .* (n.p., [1593]), 270; W. H. Frere and C. E. Douglas, eds., *Puritan Manifestoes . . .* (1907; New York, 1972), vii; James C. Spalding, "Restitution as a Normative Factor for Puritan Dissent," *Journal of the American Academy of Religion*, XLIV (1976), 61. For another example, see [Thomas Sampson], "Certain Humble Petitions . . . ," in John Strype, *Annals of the Reformation*, 4 vols. in 7 (1824; New York, 1968), III, pt. 2, 286–288; for the attribution of this item to Sampson, see III, pt. 1, 320.

8. See, for example, *Parte of a Register*, 413, 418; Walter Travers, *A Full and Plaine Declaration of Ecclesiastical Discipline . . .* (Leiden, 1617), sig. A3; John Udall, *Demonstration of the Truth of That Discipline, Which Christ Has Prescribed in His Word, for the Government of His Church, in All Times and Places, until the End of the World* (1588), ed. Edward Arber (London, 1880), 6. The Puritan connection of "Christian primordium" and National Covenant is discussed in Richard T. Hughes, "From Civil Dissent to Civil Religion—and Beyond," *Religion in Life*, XLIX (1980), 275.

9. Quoted in Spalding, "Restitution," *Journal of the American Academy of Religion*, XLIV (1976), 53.

well and good, but that mankind seemed but seldom inclined to do so was an observation that came naturally to men and women of Reformed faith. Through the sixteenth and seventeenth centuries, English Protestants were outspoken against the varied tendencies to religious perfectionism that from time to time emerged; and as denouncers of Familism and other left-wing heresies, Puritans were second to none. Fervent conversionists that they were, at least after the pietist turn of the 1580s, they knew nevertheless that saints sporting every visible sign of regeneration must be expected to fail in their duty; and Puritan piety, the piety, for instance, of William Perkins, Richard Rogers, or Thomas Shepard, embraced cycles without end—in this life—of sin, repentance, and recovery. Hence there was little temptation to forget that the covenant was designed to conjoin two radically disparate parties, the divine and human, the perfect and imperfect. And this was a thought all the more pressing when applied to the motley, semi-Christianized citizenry of the realm as a whole and when contemplated in the light of Elizabeth's and the Stuarts' unbending refusal to open the English church to real disciplinary reform.

The necessary conclusion was that the covenant, ever and again, would be breached and that the price of national safety was a steady moral vigilance. Partly in response to these concerns, English expositors adopted the special hortatory form that has come to be termed the "jeremiad." It provided the structure of many a sermon and of many a passing admonition within sermons directed to other ends. In outline a jeremiad canvassed and lamented violations of the pact that were held to be responsible for present or imminent disaster and, no less important, provided remedial instruction. This was recognizably an "ancient formulaic refrain" common in medieval and Renaissance preaching, but in sixteenth- and seventeenth-century England it was more.[10] For the very idea of an explicit National Covenant entailed a systematization of the Deuteronomic ideal that went beyond anything in English theology before Tyndale. Accordingly, the jeremiad now assumed new prominence in English thought. Puritan clergy had no monopoly upon the form, but for them it held a special attraction. They were moved both by their high legalist rigor and their close association of covenantal obedience with the cause of further reformation to style themselves England's "watchmen" and, in that

10. Sacvan Bercovitch, *The American Jeremiad* (Madison, Wis., 1978), 6.

stance, to elevate the jeremiad to a stock-in-trade of dissenting utterance.

No English Jeremiah was content merely to diagnose the causes of present or impending calamity. He also must stir his audience to the necessary remedial steps, for all covenantal theorists agreed that the divine anger, once aroused, was corrective, not destructive, in intent. It could be turned back through timely "humiliation" and amendment of the responsible violations. This conviction, blending with a heightening concern in the later sixteenth century for the welfare of England's Protestant enterprise, contributed to the emergence of an elaborate ritual in which the concerned citizenry of the community or some portion thereof periodically were mobilized for the necessary acts of repentance. With roots in the medieval tradition of public solemn fasts, prayers, and processionals for the appeasement of God's wrath in times of calamity, the public "day of fast and humiliation" now emerged as an eminent expression of English and, especially, of Puritan piety.

Called for by royal proclamation at least as early as 1563, the observance more commonly followed episcopal injunction or more local initiative. Most often it enlisted the adult citizens of a town, city, diocese, or afflicted region in public assembly, prayer, and preaching in the mode of the jeremiad. The practice became widespread in the 1580s. Fast days never became the exclusive forum for the jeremiad, but it would be hard to imagine a true season of humiliation without one. Above all, participants were to be led "to humble themselves by fasting, and bewaile their sinfull living before GOD."[11] Certainly the fast day rite was not a Puritan creation, but it was seized upon eagerly by dissenters quick to appreciate both its correspondence to Old Testament archetype and its strategic usefulness in the general task of religious reformation. By the 1580s, anti-Puritan churchmen were complaining of public fasts conducted under Puritan auspices as

11. *The Prayer-Book of Queen Elizabeth, 1599* . . . (London, 1890), 206–216. Fast days upon national occasions were recommended in the *Second Book of Homilies* of 1571 (*WT*, II, 224–225). Mary Ellen Rickey and Thomas B. Stroup, eds., *Certaine Sermons or Homilies* (1623), facsimile (Gainesville, Fla., 1968), 92, and see 82. Some of the fast days apparently were directed to "the supply of some great want" rather than to the processing of experienced calamity (*WT*, I, 288; Nicholas Bownde, *The Holy Exercise of Fasting* [Cambridge, 1604], 120, 192).

part of the now formidable endeavor "to trouble the present estate of the Church."[12]

Many, if not most, of the fasts as well as the sizable body of extant and recognizably Puritan expositions of the practice explicitly were directed to maintenance of the English people's covenanted status. And since that task never was complete, but extended through an apparently endless series of occasions, the fast day ritual came to reflect a distinctive understanding of England's course through time. Theorists agreed that disobedience might so increase and repentance so long be delayed as to destroy outright the contractual link and invoke unmitigated catastrophe.[13] Such fears were a factor in the Great Migration of the 1630s. But that was an extremity. In normal operation, it was of the essence of the covenant that national stability could be guaranteed over the long run through timely and repeated repair of the endangered bond. And if this course were pursued, if clerical Jeremiahs regularly and sufficiently could move the erring community to "amend the things that are amisse, Repent and Amend, [so that the Lord] . . . will return from his fierce wrath," then England's course through time would describe an indefinite series of fluctuations as the covenant was breached, now healed, and breached again.[14]

Horton Davies rightly has stressed the present-mindedness of the fast days, their ties to current grievance and tribulation, but the restorationist elements should not be overlooked. As the fast day was a communal affair, so the principal exercises occurred within the dramatic, biblically laden context created by preaching—the central act of Puritan worship. It scarcely required saying that fasting rituals

12. See, for example, [Thomas Cartwright?], *The Holy Exercise of a True Fast* (1580), in Albert Peel and Leland H. Carlson, eds., *Cartwrightiana* (London, 1951), 128–129; John Udall, *The True Remedie against Famine and Warres* . . . (London, n.d.), 3; Bownde, *Fasting*, 1–26. See also Hudson, "Fast Days," in *Theology in Sixteenth- and Seventeenth-Century England*, 12–13. For fast days and their Puritan connections, see *EPM*, 214–218; *WT*, I, 260, 288, II, 245–249; Stephen Foster, *Notes from the Caroline Underground: Alexander Leighton, the Puritan Triumvirate, and the Laudian Reaction to Nonconformity* (Hamden, Conn., 1978), 17–18. Richard Bancroft, quoted in *EPM*, 218; see also Patrick Collinson's discussion there.

13. See, for example, Udall, *True Remedie*, 24, 40; Bownde, *Fasting*, 320.

14. John Preston, *The Breast-Plate of Faith and Love*, 5th ed. (London, 1634), 92 (second pagin.).

were "not an humane constitution, but an ordinance of God."[15] And
as the ministers put their audiences through carefully orchestrated
paces of humiliation and repentance, they but rang the usual changes
upon themes of fidelity to the first and fixed. A crucial event of every
fast was sermonic rehearsal of the sins identified as probable causes
of imminent or present disaster, and that required a full display of
the violated commandments in all their sacred rootage and permanence. In this moment also, associations between covenantal offense
and delay of reformation could be exploited to the full. With the
high gravity of ritual, it could be brought home that the whole cause
of national security and happiness lay in conformity with sacred rule
and ordinance (such as Sabbath keeping) and that breach of covenant
(such as Sabbath breaking) consisted essentially in deviation from
the timeless and perfect.[16]

Thus again we find fixity esteemed, and now it is a quality closely
related to the broad Reformed claim upon society and, in particular, to the Puritan interest in bringing its significant structures and
activities under biblical governance. Attention in fast day sermons
was not restricted to ecclesiastical matters or to the moral behavior
of individuals. The welfare of society in its fullness was at issue. Fast
days ordinarily were to be enjoined, and the date set, by the magistrate. Classical Puritan social theory, which incorporated no conscious overtures to a progressive civilization, was assumed and often
paraded in the covenantal sermons. Men and women were addressed

15. WT, II, 245, 251; Bownde, Fasting, 1. See also Henry Burton, Israels
Fast (London, 1628), 1.
16. On delay of reformation, see, for example, Udall, True Remedie, 2, 7–
8, 24, 46, 65–66; Bownde, Fasting, 309; Thomas Wilcox, The Summe of a
Sermon, Preached at Sowthell . . . (London, 1597), sig. D5; Burton, Israels Fast,
7, 12, 24–25. Note, for example, that the key theological strategy of Puritan
Sabbatarianism was to prove that the Fourth Commandment was part of the
moral rather than the ceremonial law and was therefore binding for all time
(Winton U. Solberg, Redeem the Time: The Puritan Sabbath in Early America
[Cambridge, Mass., 1977], 56). Solberg also discusses the Sabbatarian position
that "the Sabbath existed in the Garden of Eden before the introduction of the
ceremonies, and the Patriarchs observed the day until its reinstatement at Mt.
Sinai." It was no coincidence that Nicholas Bownde, a prominent Sabbatarian
theorist, was also the author of a standard fast day manual or that he specifically
presented the fast day as "always of the nature of the Sabbath" (Fasting, 199–
206).

in "that calling, wherein the Lord hath set us."[17] Godly magistracy, social gradation, diligent work, patriarchal family government, even general modes of dress and habits of eating and drinking—these things too, when aligned with biblical instruction, partook of permanence. They stood no less than the Sabbath or the preaching ministry under covenantal protection.[18] Unquestionably, the religious enterprise, the campaign for godliness and ecclesiastical purity, focused the Puritan jeremiad; but that enterprise, as the extant fast day sermons and manuals fully confirm, was envisaged as forming and coming to fruition within a fully congruent social framework. Once that were accomplished, church and society would assume "such a settled estate as shall be unmooveable" and, but for the continuing operation of man's sin, would stand literally beyond need or desirability of further change until the Second Coming.[19]

At the same time, if England presently stood at variance with the Lord's statutes and ordinances, if adultery, cursing, and attendance at stage plays were rife, if the church remained half-restored and the better part of the populace barely touched by religious nurture and discipline, then what were the remedial tactics to pursue in the rite of humiliation? It was, of course, a time for self-examination, the ruing of misdeeds, and the mustering—in the context of the physical self-denial established by the act of fasting—of a truly ascetic resolve for "amendment"; but none of this is sufficiently intelligible if the tie to the reflex of return is overlooked. For, as all the lines of explanation of current calamity moved not toward social or economic or military analysis, but ran back to the breaking of connection with Deuteronomic law and primitive Christianity, the cure too must be discovered in the reinvoked realm of myth. It must be enacted through recession back to the broken bond, to the Lord's law in its widest sense. At one level, the intent of the fast days was to regain the covenantal status quo regnant before the present rupture occurred, but the higher aim at all times was to seek and firm the

17. See, for example, Udall, *True Remedie*, 71, 80–81; Arthur Hildersam, *The Doctrine of Fasting and Praier* . . . (London, 1633), 46; Thomas Cartwright, *Cartwrightiana*, 145–146.

18. See, for example, Udall, *True Remedie*, 13–17, 67–69, 71; Hildersam, *Fasting*, 24.

19. Udall, *True Remedie*, 67. See also *The Reformation of Religion by Josiah* . . . (n.p., [1590]), sig. C4.

saving tie back to perfect things. Seen thus, the nation's or community's course through time did not merely describe a series of fluctuations but assumed a more distinctly cyclical rhythm of declension and return within an ideally static religious and social framework.[20]

The Birth of an American Jeremiad

*P*ossibly it was in the context of a fast day on board the flagship *Arbella* that John Winthrop delivered the "Model of Christian Charity" late in 1629.[21] In his address we find the concept of a Christian commonwealth attuned to the Great Time and "indented . . . upon certaine Articles" being carried forward in the immigrants' world of thought as an unquestioned first principle. Basic to the argument was the familiar compact linked to a program of biblicist recovery and articulated in the usual Deuteronomic formulas. But in this sermon too there emerged a new and complicating element. Properly to understand it, we must recall that nowhere in England's brief history since the turn from Rome had Puritan reformers been able to find a satisfactory realization of Protestant ideals. There had been, first, the lean beginnings under Henry VIII, then a promising but short-lived burst of new measures under Edward VI, then the Marian setback, then the initially hopeful but finally frustrating Elizabethan Settlement, then the continuing and deepening aggravations of the Stuart reigns. Puritanism, after all, was nothing if not the belief that the Protestant enterprise in England had gone awry. Surely England was the recipient of special providential favors. Was she not a covenanted, chosen nation, and had she not long escaped the turmoil and devastation of continental wars of religion? But there

20. According to Perry Miller, Puritan thinkers saw Christian history as "full of pulsations but . . . essentially static" (*Seventeenth Century*, 466). In their studies of American Puritan sermons after 1660, John G. Buchanan and Nathan O. Hatch have discerned a strong cyclical element. Buchanan specifically noted the connection with covenantal doctrine. Buchanan, "Puritan Philosophy of History from Restoration to Revolution," *HCEI*, CIV (1968), 331–334, 339–342; Hatch, *The Sacred Cause of Liberty: Republican Thought and the Millennium in Revolutionary New England* (New Haven, Conn., 1977), 94–95.

21. For references to fasting exercises on board the *Arbella*, see *WP*, II, 228, 230.

was also the nation's performance under the covenant to consider, a standing disappointment; and the imminence of punishing catastrophe was a leitmotiv of the jeremiads.

Modern English history was therefore a shadowed scene. The few patches of light were activities of dissent, like John Field's underground classes of the 1570s and 1580s, the Sabbatarian movement, or the laborious creation of a "morphology of conversion." Yet these were fragmentary achievements carried on under duress and opposition. The long-hoped-for breakthrough—the heroic push through inertia and resistance into radical renewal, the attainment of a state in which Puritanism would cease to be dissent—had not occurred; nor would a hot gospeler of the later 1620s, appraising Caroline trends, see reason to anticipate that the nation soon could be roused from its untransfigured state.

Winthrop's eyes, however, now were cast ahead to the prospects of a colony founded far from the unconverted masses and hostile authorities of England. Her clergy, political leaders, and core of lay citizens were to be "regenerate" persons of Precisionist outlook and reforming ambition. A screening operation prevented the immigration of uncooperative individuals. Winthrop did not regale his audience with prospects of a world-redeeming Errand into the Wilderness, nor is there the least sign of millennial expectation, but he did propose that the colonial venture would rise into the realm of the "extraordinary." To this ambition Puritan aspiration contributed the most, and fears aroused by covenantal doctrine were especially crucial. From other sources we know of Winthrop's beliefs that the English situation in the late 1620s was all but hopeless, that a calamitous punishment soon was to descend, and that by removal to a colony a band of Christians might escape the common plight. Should that colony, however, not greatly surpass England's performance, its fate too would be swift, for the Lord would not "beare with such faileings at our hands" as he had borne with England's.

So Winthrop reasoned that in the new society the covenantal arrangement itself must be tightened. To accommodate the exalted purposes of their anticipated new England, the voyagers under his leadership already had devised a special pact. It created a "more neare bond" for a more dedicated people. It imposed "most strickt and peculiar" demands, and in truth it implied a substantial transformation of English commonwealth. It was not merely that Winthrop presumed shortly to see enacted, within a network of supportive institutions, the biblical laws of ecclesiastical polity. He also held before his audience the image of a community in which normal egotism would be tamed by the experience of "new birth" so long championed by the Spiritual Brotherhood. Thereby New World citizens would be "infused" with benevolence. They would relive the selfless spirit of the early Christian communes. They would sustain a common life in which the weak and needy were succored, the general welfare came before private gain, and the ultimate sources of cohesion were the same "ligamentes" "of love" that bound reborn men and women into church fellowship.[22] Such a community, anchored in Scripture and harmonized in Christian charity, would represent a historic surge to qualitatively higher life.

As is well known, it became a fashion in New England after 1660, after the death of most of the notable founders, to extol them and the era they dominated in exalted terms. In light of present "sad declensions," the earlier period then seemed a veritable golden age. What seemed golden to second- and third-generation colonists, however, seems rather brass to those modern scholars that stress discrepancies between the founders' aims and their achievements and consign the high claims of a later time to the realm of legend and propaganda.[23] It is indisputable that the express ideals of the founding leaders often achieved but fragmentary realization, that early screening efforts quickly broke down, that Winthrop's ideal of a unified community quickly gave way to forces of dispersal, and that many of the first colonists engaged in bitter religious and political disputes, were seized by a lust for land or profit, or abandoned the project altogether.

22. John Winthrop, "A Model of Christian Charity," in Edmund S. Morgan, ed., *Puritan Political Ideas, 1558–1794* (Indianapolis, Ind., 1965), 76, 85, 86, 90, 91. For additional uses of the term *extraordinary*, see 78, 79, 82.

23. See, for example, T. H. Breen, *The Character of the Good Ruler: A Study of Puritan Political Ideas in New England, 1630–1700* (New Haven, Conn., 1970), 101; Sacvan Bercovitch, *The Puritan Origins of the American Self* (New Haven, Conn., 1975), 122. Robert G. Pope and Emory Elliott also treat the "primitive" New England posited in the jeremiads as an insubstantial "myth." Pope, "New England versus the New England Mind: The Myth of Declension," in Alden T. Vaughan and Francis J. Bremer, eds., *Puritan New England: Essays on Religion, Society, and Culture* (New York, 1977), 323; Emory Elliott, *Power and the Pulpit in Puritan New England* (Princeton, N.J., 1975), 88–89.

But it is equally true that the founders cannot be understood apart from their high aspirations and their struggle to realize them and that, indeed, their record of accomplishments was remarkable. Whatever their failures and disappointments, they did enact a unique church order, established visible regeneration as a prerequisite of church membership, enlisted numerous citizens in the ritual excitement of Congregational "foundation work," achieved a closer recovery of the biblical Psalter, conformed law and equity more closely to biblical standards, and wielded "godly magistracy" to the more effective control of covenantally dangerous behavior. It is unlikely that Winthrop or any of the generation of Massachusetts founders ever expected their colony to rise cleanly above the cycles of disobedience, punishment, and repentant return that, as Puritans always had construed the matter, were an irremovable part of a Christian society's earthly sojourn.[24] But many were convinced that their community's safety hinged upon narrowing the allowed range of fluctuation within the covenantal relation. Perhaps none laid claim so bluntly as Winthrop to "a speciall [covenantal] Commission" explicitly heightening standards of compliance, but there was wide agreement among clergy and lay leaders that a consciously higher measure of moral and religious performance must be exacted both in the public and private arenas.[25]

The important point is that Winthrop, Cotton, Shepard, and other

24. Both Cotton and Shepard argued that "declination" was an inevitable part of the church's life in history (Cotton, *A Brief Exposition with Practical Observations upon the Whole Book of Canticles* [London, 1655], 119; Shepard, *Works*, II, 65). The theme appeared later in Increase Mather, *A Call from Heaven to the Present and Succeeding Generations* . . . (Boston, 1679), 78–83.

25. Winthrop, "Model," in Morgan, ed., *Puritan Political Ideas*, 91. A consciously higher measure was applied in *WP*, III, 216, IV, 159; Cotton, *Canticles* (1655), 213; *WWP*, 244; Ebenezer Hazard, ed., *Historical Collections* . . . , 2 vols. (Philadelphia, 1744), II, 36; Thomas Lechford, *Plain Dealing* . . . , ed. J. Hammond Trumbull (Boston, 1867), 69; *New Englands First Fruits* . . . (London, 1643), reprinted as appendix D in Samuel Eliot Morison, *The Founding of Harvard College* (Cambridge, Mass., 1935), 443; John Winthrop, *The History of New England from 1630 to 1649*, ed. James Savage (1853; New York, 1972), II, 41. See also Edmund S. Morgan, *The Puritan Dilemma: The Story of John Winthrop*, ed. Oscar Handlin (Boston, 1958), 71; Solberg, *Redeem the Time*, 111; George Lee Haskins, *Law and Authority in Early Massachusetts: A Study in Tradition and Design* (New York, 1960), 51–52.

notables of the founding generation propounded and never surren-
dered the belief that in their New England—to recur to Winthrop's
term—an "extraordinary" accomplishment was in the making. Their
fondest hope was that the foundations laid in the first years would
be sustained and perfected by their successors and theirs until the
Second Coming, wherefore they formed no conception of their own
time as a bracketed, special era of gold. All the same, they were
certain that New England was "a great worke" and that laying foundations anew in biblical archetype was to make possible a far more
elevated style of commonwealth than theretofore. In this sense, the
later celebration of primitive New England as a heroic age is not fairly
described as a legend distorting history "for the purpose of shaming
the rising generation into reform." There were many objective bases
to which it could, and did, appeal.[26]

But if the founders did see themselves as carrying the Christian
enterprise to a qualitatively higher level, so were they embarked upon
a path that was to carry them, and far more so their successors, to a
revised understanding of covenantal maintenance. One recalls that a
close interlacing of Deuteronomic and restorationist motifs long had
been a mark of Puritan dissent. Now as a fragment of the Puritan
movement was transferred to a more hospitable locale, came, in fact,
into a socially commanding position, the traditional connection lost
nothing of its cogency. Never, it seemed, had there been apter occasion to appreciate the ties binding sacred past and present welfare
than during the years in which an actual Christian-Congregational
commonwealth was taking form. As Winthrop's "Model" and many
other utterances of the first generation made clear, the heart of New
England's special calling was seen as a retrieval of perfect things.

And as the founders pursued this mandate, and pursued it with
rare intensity, as they sought to gain the Lord's protecting favor by
regaining the spirituality and ordinances of "those times," so their
labors served only to reinforce the vintage Puritan hunger for the
unchanging. The human element, the Protestant discipleship of New
World Christians, might waver; but as they created new churches,
improved Sabbath practice, or firmed the biblical anchorage of civil
law, Massachusetts' first leaders believed they were building once for
all remaining time. That had been and remained the aim of English

26. WP, II, 121; Breen, *Good Ruler*, 101.

Puritans too. "Such a settled estate as shall be unmoveable" was their very dream. But in the English setting, even during the years of advance after 1640, that estate remained elusive. Covenantal admonition must be designed as much to elicit fresh reform as to ensure the permanence of gains already secured. In the Bay colony, it no longer was so. Citizens of a community in which the major aims of Congregational reform had been attained now must reckon the implications of that success, and of accompanying claims to perpetuity, for their continued pilgrimage in covenant.

Once reasonably acclimated to their new privileges, how would Bay spokesmen move to conserve them? The evidence of their response, of course, is less than full. During the first years after the Winthrop fleet's arrival, both religious and political authorities turned to the established devices for upholding the National Covenant. Fast day assemblies called by public authority and highlighted by penitential preaching frequently punctuated the early decades of Massachusetts history. Countless local seasons of humiliation were held in the several congregations, although little record survives of the proceedings or the forms of admonition employed.[27] Fortunately, collateral sources exist, which suggest current trends.

One set of indications may be found in the practice of "covenant renewal." This device, with some modifications, gained its greatest popularity after 1675 and traditionally has been treated in that context, but it had been for decades a widely subscribed feature of Congregational theory and practice.[28] Its pre-1630 backgrounds are shadowy, but the first generation of New England clergy seems to have taken the rite for granted.[29] The procedure was simple: in response

27. For a short account, see Perry Miller, "Declension in a Bible Commonwealth," in Miller, *Nature's Nation* (Cambridge, Mass., 1967), 14–16; Miller, *The New England Mind: From Colony to Province* (Cambridge, Mass., 1953), 19–21. At least two fast day sermons from the early period survive: Thomas Shepard, *Wine for Gospel Wantons . . .* (Cambridge, Mass., 1668); and William Hooke, *New Englands Teares, for Old Englands Feares* (London, 1641).

28. Miller, *Colony to Province*, 116–117; Robert G. Pope, *The Half-Way Covenant: Church Membership in Puritan New England* (Princeton, N.J., 1969), 240–241; David D. Hall, *The Faithful Shepherd: A History of the New England Ministry in the Seventeenth Century* (Chapel Hill, N.C., 1972), 243.

29. In 1679 Increase Mather claimed that covenant renewal was "a known Principle owned and avowed by the good old non-Conformists," and referred without documentation to Cartwright, Ames, and Thomas Parker. William

to perceived deficiencies in religious performance, the officers of an individual congregation would set aside a day for devotion to fasting and exercises of worship keyed to humiliation; the event climaxed in a collective reaffirmation of the original church covenant. In at least two of the cases on record, Boston and Salem in 1636, the church covenant was rewritten and enlarged; but the intent was, not to alter the pact, but to render the original terms more explicitly.[30] While it was specifically a church covenant, not the National Covenant, that was renewed in these affairs, the conceptual form remained the same: "manifold breaches of covenant" had evoked punitive "dispensations . . . of providence," wherefore the people must repent and, in Cotton's words, "repair the Church." And, just as in Congregational theory the church covenant itself was derived from a perfect archetype, so now the deed of renewal, properly set against a background of myth invoking and solemn ritual, was to restore impaired connection to a "Sacred Covenant . . . inviolable Forever."[31]

Ames discussed "renewing of the covenant" in his authoritative *Marrow of Theology*, but it is unclear whether he there affirmed the present validity of the procedure or merely noted its occurrence in biblical Israel. Mather, *A Discourse Concerning the Danger of Apostasy* . . . (Boston, 1679), 89; Ames, *The Marrow of Theology* (1629), trans. and ed. John D. Eusden (Boston, 1968), 180. In New England materials there is evidence that covenant renewal originally may have been connected to the Congregational concept of the English churches' "implicit covenant" or to the practice of some English Puritan clergy who gathered an elite covenanted subgroup within the larger parish context (John Allin and Thomas Shepard, *A Defence of the Answer Made unto the Nine Questions or Positions Sent from New-England, against the Reply Thereto by . . . John Ball* [London, 1648], 10; Williston Walker, *The Creeds and Platforms of Congregationalism* [1893; Boston, 1960], 198–199).

30. Solemn covenant renewals took place in the churches at Boston and Salem in 1636, at Chelmsford in 1656, and almost certainly elsewhere. The church at Scituate, then in New Plymouth, performed the rite in 1642, as did the church at Hartford, Connecticut, shortly after Thomas Hooker's death in 1647. WP, III, 223–225 and n. 1; John Fiske, "Extracts from the Records Kept by the Rev. John Fiske . . . ," HCEI, I, no. 2 (1859), 37–39; John Fiske, *The Notebook of the Reverend John Fiske, 1644–1675*, ed. Robert G. Pope, Colonial Society of Massachusetts, *Publications*, XLVII (Boston, 1974), 106; Pope, *Half-Way Covenant*, 241; Samuel Deane, *History of Scituate, Massachusetts, from Its First Settlement to 1831* (Boston, 1831), 60. See also Charles E. Hambrick-Stowe, *The Practice of Piety: Puritan Devotional Disciplines in Seventeenth-Century New England* (Chapel Hill, N.C., 1982), 131–132.

31. WP, III, 223–225; "Conference of the Elders of Massachusetts with the Rev. Robert Lenthal, of Weymouth . . . ," *Congregational Quarterly*, LXXIV

If this appears but a normal register of primitivist thinking, consider that those who thus chanted their grief at "looseing of [their] first aims" had more than the mythic world in mind. Their gaze in part was directed to an achievement of their own recent history, an achievement of the ritually charged time in which mythic pattern had been retrieved through a proper church "founding," a new congregation had been formed upon ground of a voluntary compact, and the same inscribed in a formal document. To that compact, peculiarly certified by its tie with beginnings in New England's Congregational Reformation, they had come to ascribe a limited primordial status in its own right. By so doing, they also availed themselves of a fresh tactic in covenantal maintenance, for to the repair of a prime good corrupted—now a specific, datable good of the New England way— could be summoned directly the special ritual and resolve of a season of restoration. Thus, when in a time of adversity members of the congregation in Boston, Salem, Chelmsford, or elsewhere turned reflexively to rituals of renewal, they proceeded without question to "renewe that Church Covenant we find this Church bound unto *at theire first beginning.*"[32]

A parallel trend appears in scattered reflections upon covenantal themes from early sources. There we find a number of spokesmen, specifically in execution of their responsibility for maintaining the community in covenantally safe estate, also beginning to alter traditional priorities. They inclined, when they perceived their fellow or sister Christians failing to keep to the way so carefully charted, to measure their failure by the yardstick of distinctive New England accomplishment. They were becoming accustomed, with John Cotton, to admonish by reminder that "time was when it was thus [that is, the people's faith had risen to "ripe stature"] with New English churches: but now we [grow corrupt]," or with John Pratt, to complain of "decayeing here in o[u]r first love."[33] An admirable "time" succeeded by corruption, a "first" love soon decayed—these formu-

---

(Apr. 1877), 244. John Fiske, who recorded the Chelmsford renewal of 1656, did not supply the document (*Notebook*, Colonial Society of Massachusetts, *Publications*, XLVII [1974], 106). Writing in the early 1680s, William Hubbard specifically depicted covenant renewal as a technique to "reduce [the covenanting congregation] to that their primitive pattern" (*General History of New England from the Discovery to 1680*, MHSC, 2d Ser., VI [Boston, 1815], 622).

32. Walker, *Creeds and Platforms*, 117, emphasis mine.

33. Cotton, *Canticles* (1655), 213; *RMB*, I, 359.

lations express more than a normal disturbance over lapsed virtue. Obviously they suggest the colonists' special regard for the primal and unvarying; but, more, those cherished categories now describe a state of affairs realized, or partly so, in New England, so that the inevitable call for return and recovery now can be directed to *that* standard.

The thought recurred in 1646 as delegates from Massachusetts and her sister colonies to the United Colonies pondered various "sinful miscarriages" of the day, including the Child petition's open challenge to Congregational practices of church admittance and baptism. The delegates, among them both a past and a future governor of Massachusetts, reacted by recalling the eminent attainments of New England's time of "foundations and beginnings." Then had the Lord spectacularly "gloryfyed his Grace and mercy," and "purity of religion" had been reclaimed, whence New England had become a veritable "Emmanuell's land." Since "warping and declining" from first purity was the obvious formula for ruin, the delegates' duty was to call erring citizens back to alignment with originative "rules and patterns."[34] One is able in such statements to see movement toward a new form of covenantal address, one for which there was no counterpart in English doctrine. The full construct does not yet emerge, but in the years to come, and openly after 1660, New Englanders dissatisfied with the present state of church and society would create an image of earliest New England radiant with qualities of the primitive.[35]

That image, quickly framed and focused, offered a reverse index of social and economic change and of a faltering Puritan impulse. Shifting circumstances of New England life after mid-century worked toward checkmate of the will to impose fixed moral and religious standards. With the weakening of early screening procedures and the tapering of the Great Migration after 1640, continued immigration

34. Hazard, ed., *Collections*, II, 74–75. The past and future governors were John Haynes and John Endecott. Haynes had moved to Connecticut in 1636.

35. The appeal to a New England baseline was not to be taken for granted. The strain of complaint which runs, for instance, through Shepard's treatise, *Parable of the Ten Virgins*, appealed primarily to standards of piety and sacrificial commitment established under the spur of opposition in Stuart England. It was thus, in Shepard's view, from an *English* level that New Englanders had fallen. *Works*, II, 26, 63–64, 169–170, 257–259, 373–377, 584.

could only expand the portion of the citizenry not sharing Puritan purposes. The rise, after 1640, of an economic system keyed to foreign trade enlisted interests often indifferent or hostile to Puritan ideals, encouraged economic individualism, and generated desires for a more open society, permitting free immigration and movement of people without respect to religious qualifications. The very notion of a godly commonwealth and of political authority as the steward of Congregational monopoly began to weaken during the late 1650s and 1660s in the face of increasing demands for religious toleration. The Stuart restoration of 1660 destroyed hopes for supportive reform in the mother country, raised prospects of expanded and unsympathetic English control over colonial affairs, and placed the Bay charter itself in question.

Within the churches, resentment aroused by the Halfway Covenant decisions of 1657 and 1662 polarized opinion, undermined clerical authority, and inaugurated a period of intense bickering and schism. Most alarming of all, in the eyes of those concerned about their colony's safety and danger under covenant, was the thinning of religious tone within Puritan families. This filled the cup of disappointment. Children of the founders had not become flagrantly irreligious, but an unmistakable slackening of experience had occurred. The "impossibly intense" utopian impulse of the first years was not sustained. Congregational polity and faith, once vehicles of a crusade, had become part of the ordinary fabric of life. Americans no longer faced the bracing disciplines of persecution by a hostile religious establishment, and they had left far behind the context of spreading poverty, vagrancy, crime, and disorder within which Puritan disciplinary emphases first took form. Few of the second generation experienced conversion, and the continuance of the New England way thus seemed threatened at its root.[36]

By the 1660s most of the notable founders were dead, and a generation of native-born, Harvard-trained men was taking over the watchman's role. These men present a double visage. They were themselves products of a changing era. Less charismatic than their forebears and less absorbed in the classic arts of pietistic Puritanism,

36. Kenneth A. Lockridge, *A New England Town, the First Hundred Years: Dedham, Massachusetts, 1636–1736* (New York, 1970), 176. For a discussion of religious declension, see Appendix 1, below.

they were relatively more concerned with the status, authority, and other amenities of pastoral-theological office. Some were in touch with newer intellectual fashions.[37] Yet at other points they held firmly to the past. Their sermons and tracts reveal an unabated passion for the biblically once-given and perfect and for the restitutive feats of the first generation. And these men, drilled to approve change in church or society only as the necessary result of movement toward perfection, were now to reckon with the forces of religious, social, and economic change that by the early 1660s were a major fact of life in the Bay. Short-range episodes of covenantal disobedience were, of course, anticipated in inherited theory; and appropriate penitential procedures stood to the ready. But this was change of a type and scale foreseen by the founding leaders only as a prelude to ruin. If the colonists should "fall to embrace this present world," Winthrop had warned, their enterprise would "surely perish."[38] To reach a constituency increasingly at variance with first purposes, how, now, would the newer leaders reformulate covenantal address?

The shift of emphasis in religious publication in the 1660s suggests their approach. Notwithstanding a generous sprinkling of fast day sermons, catechisms, ecclesiological statements, and other specialized items, since the pietist turn of the late sixteenth century the great mass of materials that Puritan preachers brought to press had been dominated by psychological themes: the soul's mortification and conversion, its great warfare with sinful impulse, its evasiveness and hypocrisy, its quest for religious assurance, and the like. The pietist saga of the soul remained the distinctive material of the

---

37. Hall, *Faithful Shepherd*, 176–196; Francis J. Bremer, *The Puritan Experiment: New England Society from Bradford to Edwards* (New York, 1976), 103. Comparative analysis of the works, say, of Shepard and Increase Mather will reveal a decided shift in spirituality. A clue to changing intellectual fashions is the emergence of interest after mid-century, in Bacon's fateful phrase, in the "induction of particulars." So far as I know, its first appearance in New England is in John Norton, *The Orthodox Evangelist* (London, 1654), 167; and Norton, *The Heart of N—— England Rent at the Blasphemies of the Present Generation* . . . (London, 1660), 28. Later it appears in Thomas Shepard, Jr., *Eye-Salve* . . . (Cambridge, Mass., 1673), 8; Urian Oakes, *New-England Pleaded With* . . . (Cambridge, Mass., 1673), 12; Oakes, *The Soveraign Efficacy of Divine Providence* . . . (Boston, 1682), 3; and Increase Mather, *Some Important Truths concerning Conversion* . . . (Boston, 1684), 26.

38. Winthrop, "Model," in Morgan, ed., *Puritan Political Ideas*, 92–93.

first-generation preachers, although occasionally they turned as well to fast day castigations, defense of Congregational polity, and other special tasks. But published works of the second generation respond to the spreading conviction that "Troublesome Times" were at hand. They reveal a sharp turn toward public concern.[39] Fast day and election sermons reviewing the collective state and fate of New England now came into unprecedented dominance.

Most important for present purposes is, not the trend to collective concern reflected in these works, but the evidence they offer that a new chapter in the history of the jeremiad therewith had begun. As Americanists long have been aware, in the 1660s there emerged a stereotyped rhetorical tactic that applied Deuteronomic castigation to a society deemed out of joint and a people "grown customary, formal, superficial, lukewarm." For at least three decades it was to provide "the dominant . . . almost the exclusive" form of published religious expression.[40] Following the lead of Perry Miller, the great majority of writers in the field have applied the term "jeremiad" exclusively to the sermons and other productions of this era built upon a national-covenantal grid.

This use is objectionable for two reasons. First, it obscures the historical lineage. At most points the "jeremiads" prepared by Increase Mather, Jonathan Mitchel, Samuel Danforth, and other second-generation figures had little conceptually or structurally new to offer, but carried forward loyally a tradition of Deuteronomic oratory extending back for a century or more.[41] Second, such a use has made it

39. The title of Jonathan Mitchel's election sermon of 1668 was *Nehemiah on the Wall in Troublesom Times*. The shift to social concern is discussed in Perry Miller, "Errand into the Wilderness," in Miller, *Errand into the Wilderness* (New York, 1956), 9–10.

40. *NEPW*, 27; Miller, *Colony to Province*, 29.

41. Thus John F. Berens maintains that the second-generation ministers "fashioned a special type of sermon, one designed especially to castigate the people of New England for their sins, warn them of the wrath of God, . . . point out the marks of divine anger . . . , and urge them to repent, reform, and return to the pious ways of their ancestors" (*Providence and Patriotism in Early America, 1640–1815* [Charlottesville, Va., 1978], 20). As I will argue below, the demand for return to ancestral ways was a distinctive note in the sermons, but the other elements cited by Berens had been standard in Puritan preaching for almost a century. It also has been suggested that "the jeremiad [actually] finds initial utterance in the preaching of the first [New England] generation,"

impossible adequately to discern the one feature appearing after 1660 that *is* without counterpart in the Puritan past and that represents a genuine and striking innovation. Confronted with unforeseen scenes of change, but immovably dedicated to the original cause of Massachusetts as a "plantation of religion," clerical leaders of the second generation had even greater reasons than their forebears to stand for the "decidedly pre-modern" cause of the "maintenance of the best possible state once it has been achieved."[42] The better to promote that cause, they devised a distinctively American variation upon the jeremiad, one in which the primally golden state of New England itself provided a major point of departure.

---

but no significant effort has been made to view the American sources either early or late within the full English context (Phyllis M. Jones and Nicholas R. Jones, eds., *Salvation in New England: Selections from the Sermons of the First Preachers* [Austin, Tex., 1977], xii; Bercovitch, *Jeremiad*, 5–6).

42. CG, 11; Larzer Ziff, *Puritanism in America: New Culture in a New World* (New York, 1973), 163. On Ziff's point, see also A. W. Plumstead, ed., *The Wall and the Garden: Selected Massachusetts Election Sermons, 1670–1775* (Minneapolis, Minn., 1968), 17.

TEN

NEW ENGLAND

AS PRIMORDIUM:

THE NEW

TRADITIONALISM OF

THE AMERICAN JEREMIAD,

1663–1675

*S*hortly after 1660, advancing worries about New England's estate began to reach critical mass in the minds of prominent clergy. In the yet vital spirit of Deuteronomic foreboding, they cited their community for abdication from its covenanted status. They projected an idealized picture of an earlier New England passionately devoted to the Congregational cause, then arraigned the citizenry for betrayal of its heritage. As the covenantal formula required, they interpreted the crop losses, fires, Indian attacks, and other afflictions of those years as punitive strokes of Providence. And they warned of a greater doom to come unless the offense be removed by repentance and amendment.

So far as can be determined, the motif of declension began to move front and center in fast and election day rhetoric with John Higginson's *Cause of God and His People in New-England* (1663). In Perry Miller's useful reconstruction, Higginson's contribution "approached" the form of the jeremiad, which then (after a gap in the extant material) achieved "definitive shape" in Jonathan Mitchel's *Nehemiah on the Wall* (1671) and William Stoughton's *New-England's True Interest* (1668). From then until 1675, at least seven of the published offerings belong unequivocally to the type of the jeremiad.[1]

Miller himself made no distinction between pre- and post-1675 jeremiads, but here there is reason to do so. First, the year 1675 marked a sharp turn in New England history. The devastating Indian war of 1675–1676 introduced an era of recurrent crisis and "traumatic social upheaval" lasting a quarter of a century and more, and the unrelenting crisis of those years greatly affected the colonials' religious life. In search of solace and stability, an impressive number of men and women turned anew to the churches; general resistance to the Halfway Covenant weakened abruptly; church admittances surged. As Robert Pope has concluded, events after 1675 brought forth a "radically altered . . . religious context." All of this was reflected in the jeremiads of the later years, both in their more specific reflection upon current or imminent catastrophe and in their increasingly consolatory tone.[2] The period before 1675, then, constitutes a distinct era in the history of the jeremiads.

Second, the jeremiad was established in its full lineaments by 1675. Through the rest of the century, trends and shifts of accent would occur, but always within the basic structure formed in the earlier decades. The period 1663–1674 can thereby be regarded as formative for the American jeremiad, and its fundamental intent can be

1. Perry Miller, "Declension in a Bible Commonwealth," in Miller, *Nature's Nation* (Cambridge, Mass., 1967), 24. The seven items: Samuel Danforth, *A Brief Recognition of New-Englands Errand into the Wilderness* (1671), in A. W. Plumstead, ed., *The Wall and the Garden: Selected Massachusetts Election Sermons, 1670–1755* (Minneapolis, Minn., 1968), 53–77; Eleazar Mather, *A Serious Exhortation to the Present and Succeeding Generation in New England* . . . (Cambridge, Mass., 1671); Thomas Shepard, Jr., *Eye-Salve* . . . (Cambridge, Mass., 1673); Urian Oakes, *New-England Pleaded With* . . . (Cambridge, Mass., 1673); Increase Mather, *The Day of Trouble Is Near* (Cambridge, Mass., 1674); Samuel Willard, *Useful Instructions for a Professing People in Times of Great Security and Degeneracy* . . . (Cambridge, Mass., 1673); and Samuel Torrey, *An Exhortation unto Reformation* . . . (Cambridge, Mass., 1674).

2. Robert G. Pope, *The Half-Way Covenant: Church Membership in Puritan New England* (Princeton, N.J., 1969), 185; Sacvan Bercovitch, *The American Jeremiad* (Madison, Wis., 1978), 84; Emory Elliott, *Power and the Pulpit in Puritan New England* (Princeton, N.J., 1975), 13.

read in the specimens of that era. In the spirit, as well, of the Puritan belief that the essence of an ordinance is disclosed in its beginnings, the intent here is to examine more closely the group of ten initial documents.

To begin with, we may ask why a people (whether before or after 1675), on its most solemn and ceremonial occasions, would rally to a rhetoric of denunciation. Miller provided the classic answer: at the level of the obvious, it was a case of plain consternation in the face of a changing civilization. The ritual of excoriation joined those who found their society in departure from its original religious purpose and unity. But this could not alone explain the profound disquiet that pervaded them. Further to clarify the issue, Miller turned to the settlers' Errand, for events of the 1640s and 1650s had confounded the possibility of a Congregational takeover in England and a turn to New England models and leadership. When looked upon from this vantage point, the stricken tone of the sermons registered the colonists' tragic awareness that their highest achievements were now "sidetracked and disregarded" within the mainstream of English Christianity.[3]

But this explanation was only one side of the paradox that Miller finally made of the clergy's lament. Their express wish was to reverse the society's course of change, but key elements in their teaching, specifically its untiring promotion of the Protestant ethic, stood high among the agents of change. This reflection suggested a yet subtler insight: the jeremiads were a functional response to a change simultaneously desired and abhorred. They enabled men to "make a public expiation for sins that they could not avoid committing, freeing their energies to continue working with the forces of change." By facilitating a necessary psychological adjustment to the emerging capitalist order, they allowed movement into the future. This effect, however, was latent, "below the surface"; it worked behind the backs and contrary to the explicit intentions of the colonists themselves.[4]

3. Perry Miller, "Errand into the Wilderness," in Miller, *Errand into the Wilderness* (New York, 1956), 12, 13. Miller discussed the jeremiads also in "Declension in a Bible Commonwealth," in Miller, *Nature's Nation*, 14–49; and in *The New England Mind: From Colony to Province* (Cambridge, Mass., 1961), 3–52.

4. Miller, "Declension," in Miller, *Nature's Nation*, 48; Miller, "Errand," in Miller, *Errand*, 15.

Miller's identification of anxiety, lamentation, and threat as the jeremiads' typifying content has been challenged.[5] In the vanguard of this revision, Sacvan Bercovitch disputes emphasis upon the "dark side" of the rhetoric and points to "a *far more powerful, and distinctive*, countertheme of exultation and affirmation." Bercovitch believes that, despite all disappointments, the clergy kept faith with the founders' belief that events in their plantation would usher in the millennium. Thus they literally "could not admit of failure." They might harrow their audiences with threats of divine retribution, but in the end they "virtually guaranteed success." They did so in part by assigning affliction a curative, reforming role leading the community to certain fulfillment of its mission. But they did so more fundamentally by keying their presentation to a "developmental historiography" that saw "all of life as a passage to something greater." Even as they bemoaned decline, they celebrated New England's place within a "linear-spiritual progression" of sacred history unfolding from Adam to Christ to the (millennial) New Jerusalem.[6]

5. Thus one author finds that "in addition to the . . . 'theme of denouncement,' there is a lyrical celebration of a new civilization" in Massachusetts election sermons after 1670. Another perceives a shifting emphasis in New England preaching, from decline and doom from 1665 to 1679, to an upbeat "message of assurance and hope" by the later 1680s and the 1690s. Phyllis M. Jones and Nicholas R. Jones, eds., *Salvation in New England: Selections from the Sermons of the First Preachers* (Austin, Tex., 1977), xii; Elliott, *Power and the Pulpit*, 88, 173, and see 8–14 for a synopsis. The Joneses' argument is intended as a summary of Plumstead, ed., *The Wall and the Garden*, 28: "The Puritans had . . . a view of a greater civilization for which they were laying the foundations." In fact, Plumstead's generalization applies to American Puritan thought generally, not peculiarly to the period after 1670; his controlling premise was the Errand construed in Miller's second sense; the documentation is from Cotton Mather's much later *Magnalia*. See also James W. Jones's review of Elliott in *WMQ*, 3d Ser., XXXIII (1976), 694–696.

6. Sacvan Bercovitch, *Jeremiad*, xiv, 55; Bercovitch, "Horologicals and Chronometricals: The Rhetoric of the Jeremiad," in *Literary Monographs*, III, ed. Eric Rothstein (Madison, Wis., 1978), 6 (emphasis mine), 43, 47; Bercovitch, "Typology in Puritan New England: The Williams-Cotton Controversy Reassessed," *American Quarterly*, XIX (1967), 176. Bercovitch's case rests in part upon a misleading comparison with the "European" jeremiad; by "European" he basically means English ("Horologicals," 188 n. 5; *Jeremiad*, 6–7). But Deuteronomic lament in post-Tyndalian English preaching was more systematically shaped by the ideal of the National Covenant than theretofore and does not assimilate easily to a more generalized pattern embracing medieval materi-

"Linear," "developmental," and "progression"—the ties to a later America are clear. Miller, we recall, explicitly related the jeremiads to the growth of early capitalist society, but he associated that development with the second half of the century and contrasted it with both the ideals and the social reality of the earlier period. The commercial society and ethos that grew up after 1650 was a perverse successor to the original culture, not its organic extension. Nor did the founders' children, their gaze fixed upon past grandeur and present loss, sustain a notably hopeful view of their future.[7]

Bercovitch's dissent from this position proceeds from a deeply contrasting view of early American development. By devaluing aristocracy, espousing the Protestant ethic, and opening political, educational, and commercial opportunities to a large segment of the population, the New Englanders broke with traditional culture and committed themselves "from the start to . . . modernization." The "divine plan of progress" integral to the Errand was the theological correlate to this venture. Upholding to the full their forebears' devotion to a higher mission, the Jeremiahs projected a "progressivist" view of experience tailor-made for an enterprising society. Their castigations created the sense of insecurity and unfulfillment that

---

als. In any case, the immediate historical background of an "American Puritan jeremiad" is the form of covenantal address developed within English Puritanism. It was this sermonic form that the Puritans brought with them to the New World, and its fate in the new context can be determined only by comparison of the New England documents with their English Puritan counterparts both before and after 1630. That divine punishment was "corrective, not destructive" in intent, for example, was a self-evident point in Puritan covenantal teaching. See, for example, Marvin A. Breslow, *A Mirror of England: English Puritan Views of Foreign Nations, 1618–1640* (Cambridge, Mass., 1970), 141. For sample statements of the restorative theme in the general literature, see John Dod, *A Plaine and Familiar Exposition of the Ten Commandements* (London, 1618), 23; John Udall, *The True Remedie against Famine and Warres . . .* (London, n.d.), 24; Thomas Wilcox, *The Summe of a Sermon, Preached at Sowthell . . .* (London, 1597), sigs. E2–E4; *WP*, II, 91–92.

7. Miller argued that during the 1630s and 1640s the Puritan colonies were "medieval states, based upon the fixed will of God, dedicated to the explicit purposes of [r]evelation, . . . societies of status and subordination, . . . to be governed with a view to the religious end of mankind, not to the profit motive." The founders' theological creations "proceeded from a thoroughly European" and traditional mentality. Miller, "Declension in a Bible Commonwealth," in Miller, *Nature's Nation*, 43; Miller, "Errand," in Miller, *Errand*, 9.

would assure continued striving "forward." The sermons functioned, in other words, as the catalytic rituals of "a culture on an errand—which is to say, a culture based on a faith in process"; therefore, the second and third generations joined the first as "part of the movement toward the future." Their fast and election day sermons were a key link in an organic evolution from the emergent free enterprise patterns of earliest Puritan society to the specialized middle-class capitalism of Yankee America, and from the Puritan Errand to the American national mission.[8]

Here, then, are the main interpretions of the jeremiads. The present task is to probe beyond both viewpoints and incorporate neglected evidence. The aim is to demonstrate that the classic Puritan drive toward first things remained central to the clergy's strategies after 1660, that it made a definitive contribution to the rise of an *American* jeremiad, and that recognition of its role is essential to any resolution of the issues in dispute.

How It Was in the Beginning: Primitivist Bases of the First Conservative Campaign in American History

Pursued from the 1560s to the mid-seventeenth century, the pattern of Puritan primitivism manifests impressive continuity. Through every fluctuation of fortune, through every historical defeat or advance, even through the eventual marriage with millennialism, the basics of terminology and conceptual structure remained unaltered. In England, the failure of reform, the permanent return to power of a militantly Anglican and increasingly latitudinarian episcopacy after 1660, and the beginnings of the Presbyterian slide into Unitarianism spelled the end of the Puritan agitation and its distinctive biblicism as a culturally central force. Before the forcible

---

8. Bercovitch, *Jeremiad*, xii, 16, 20, 23, 27. The overriding consensus element in Bercovitch's approach to American history is discussed by Daniel W. Howe, "Descendents of Perry Miller," *American Quarterly*, XXXIV (1982), 88–94; and cf. Jack P. Greene and J. R. Pole, "Reconstructing British-American Colonial History: An Introduction," in Greene and Pole, eds., *Colonial British America: Essays in the New History of the Early Modern Era* (Baltimore, 1984), 3–4.

reorganization under the Dominion of New England in 1684, there was no comparable watershed in New England, and even the infamous administration of Sir Edmund Andros (1686–1689) was a far less momentous check to Puritan interests than failed revolution and the Restoration in the mother country. However certain it may be that the faith of New World Congregationalism about 1700 had on several fronts passed beyond the defining boundaries of classic Puritan pietism, however dubious, for instance, the habitual and unqualified designation of Cotton Mather (1663–1728)—or even Jonathan Edwards (1703–1758)—as representatively Puritan, it is equally clear that the demise of American Puritanism was, not a matter of sudden collapse, but an imperceptibly gradual metamorphosis.[9]

Yet not all elements within the Puritan synthesis were affected equally. The inaugural set of American jeremiads may reveal a shifting pattern of Reformed spirituality, but it also attests to wholly sustained confidence in the primitivist assumptions that so long had shaped Puritan habits of mind. The formulaic contrast between the excellence of "whatsoever is first" and abasement of "whatsoever is later," with all of its associated motifs, was just as much a presupposition of the jeremiads as of the Vestiarian Controversy of the 1560s or the pioneer Congregationalism of Jacob, Baynes, and Parker early in the seventeenth century. In the manner of the traditional Puritan jeremiads, this rhetoric diagnosed current decay as a departure from primal piety, law, and ordinance. The ten documents project an absolute consensus that avoidance of covenantal affliction and revitalization of the community were conditional upon renewed loyalty to the "more pure and primitive way" of biblical and apostolic worship, faith, and morals. Every indignant assault upon New England's decay, every urgent demand for repentance and fresh resolve was to this end: a people in "deviation" from the straight and perfect must be schooled again to take their bearings from "Scripture patterne and divine Originall[s]."[10] In these particulars, second-generation

---

9. For instance, the rising interest in a Christian natural philosophy and in the "reasonableness" of Christianity among New England thinkers of the later 17th and early 18th centuries marks the opening of a new chapter in Protestant theology. Neither theme deeply engaged the interest of a Thomas Cartwright, William Perkins, or Thomas Hooker.

10. *ER*, 12; Jonathan Mitchel, *Nehemiah on the Wall in Troublesom Times* . . . (Cambridge, Mass., 1671), 27; *CG*, 12–13.

rhetoric takes an unexceptional place within the continuing history of covenantal exhortation since Elizabethan times.

But if we indeed compare the American sermons with their Elizabethan and early Stuart ancestors as well as with their contemporary counterparts in England, and if we do find the Deuteronomic-restorationist connection sustained to the full after 1660, we also become aware of an area of major revision. For to clergy of the second generation the undimmed prestige of the first had suggested a fresh tactic in covenantal maintenance. From the perspective of a far-flung colony in the third quarter of the seventeenth century, the "good old Nonconformists" of an earlier England seemed distant figures. But in truth the prime American note in the jeremiads of 1664–1674 was directly a function of the older Puritan bias toward the first.

Important background for understanding the new tactic is provided by the famous dispute over the Halfway Covenant, into which the churches and clergy were being drawn in the 1660s. The majority decisions of the Synod of 1662, affirming liberal standards of baptismal eligibility and consociational authority, were repudiated by an articulate clerical minority and resisted by most of the congregations for nearly two decades. Since no issue, save declension itself, elicited more concern and bitter debate within the churches during the ensuing three decades, it is essential to note that a vital part of the case both for and against the synod's deliverances came to rest upon a characteristically primitivist appeal. The contending sides were of one mind that the "surest way to end Controversies, is to finde out how it was in the beginning," for "nothing can be like this, or added to this." But, more, they now would define "beginnings" partly in reference to "the Primitive Times of these [New England] Churches." With each side thus obliged to find its views ratified in the ascertainable opinions and practices of the founding clergy, argument instinctively turned to allegations of "APOSTACY from [New England's] Primitive Principles."[11]

During the synodical debate, the dissenters made the most of charges of "declining *from our first Purity,*" of "innovation" and

11. John Allin, *Animadversions upon the Antisynodalia Americana* (Cambridge, Mass., 1664), 17; [Charles Chauncy?], *Anti-Synodalia Scripta Americana,* appended to Jonathan Mitchel, *Propositions concerning the Subject of Baptism and Consociation of Churches* . . . (London, 1662), 14; Increase Mather, *The First Principles of New-England* . . . (Cambridge, Mass., 1675), 4, 11.

"alteration," and were answered in kind. Jonathan Mitchel's preface to the synod's published *Propositions* insisted that the majority's positions were taken in direct "pursuance" of "former Principles," and marshaled extensive quotation from clergy of "the first and best generation" to prove it. At every high point in the ensuing controversy, in the pamphlet war of 1662–1664, in the acrid exchanges evoked by John Davenport's move to Boston's First Church in 1670, the charge of "woeful declining from our primitive and foundation work," coupled with allegations of "invention" and "innovation," was aimed to cut the sorest—and apparently succeeded.[12] Already well formulated in these terms by the time of Higginson's *Cause of God*, the debate spilled over liberally into the jeremiads. Of the ten contributors to the genre from 1663 to 1674, all save Eleazar Mather strongly identified with the synodical positions and represented "stiffnecked" dissent and the resulting ecclesiastical turmoil as a primary evidence of declension.[13]

Earlier, it was shown that scattered voices of the 1630s and 1640s, perturbed by manifestations of decline, instinctively regarded them as a betrayal of the colony's unique beginnings and directed their call for recovery in part to a realized *New England* standard. And if previous alarms were but distantly prophetic of the present and general emergency, so the watchmen of the 1660s and 1670s—their ardor for origins spurred further by the Halfway controversy—were now boldly to enlarge their forebears' intimation that the founding of New England (an event in *post*primordial time!) was an act of

---

12. Williston Walker, ed., *Creeds and Platforms of Congregationalism* (1893; Boston, 1960), 304–312; Pope, *Half-Way Covenant*, 172. On the allegations, see, for example, Allin, *Animadversions*, 35; Thomas Shepard, Jr., preface to Thomas Shepard, *The Church-Membership of Children, and Thier Right to Baptisme* (Cambridge, Mass., 1663), sigs. B3–B4; John Davenport, *Another Essay . . .* (Cambridge, 1663), 15, 54; Richard Mather and Jonathan Mitchel, *Defence of the Answer and Arguments of the Synod Met at Boston in the Year 1662* (Cambridge, Mass., 1662), 20, 22; Pope, *Half-Way Covenant*, 172–173. Note the level of indignation in the documents collected in Hamilton A. Hill, *History of the Old South Church, Boston, 1669–1884* (Boston, 1890), 100–104; and *RMB*, IV, pt. 2, 489–493. See also *NEPW*, 40; Shepard, Jr., *Eye-Salve*, 23.

13. Eleazar Mather's antisynodalist posture is described in Pope, *Half-Way Covenant*, 45, 48, 50–52. Increase Mather sided with his brother for nearly a decade after 1662 but had converted to the majority position by the time of his *Day of Trouble*.

true beginning. This development was of some magnitude in Puritan history.

In a multitude of contemporary laments in the mother country, men struggling to preserve the Puritan inheritance against a restored and vengefully Anglican regime bewailed their nation's "general declension in religion" since 1660. They denied that the established forms of Christian expression did "in any tolerable measure answer the original pattern . . . in the Scriptures, or the first transcript . . . in the primitive believers," warned of a Deuteronomic punishment to come, and tried to uphold the now venerable hope for further reformation.[14] At times such voices reflected wistfully upon the mid-century era of reform and freedom of the ordinances, but the enterprise of those two decades was too compromised by disagreement, confusion, and eventual collapse to appear a golden age to subsequent reflection. Thus in English jeremiads of the later seventeenth century, primitive times continued exclusively to mean biblical times.

It was otherwise in New England. There the jeremiads, under the impact of uniquely American experience, would begin a separate evolution. In this development the first settlers' push toward fuller reformation would become the hinge of a new rhetorical strategy. The earlier New England would be described in the sons' perorations as Protestantism's finest hour—emphatically not by virtue of a millennial Errand, but because it so fully and exultantly had regained primitive pattern as to assume in its own right a primordial status. There was no intent thereby to compromise the jurisdiction of the scriptural Great Time; that remained plenary and irreducible. Nevertheless, the concentration upon "recovering *our* primitive beautie" that arose in the 1660s led covenantal orators increasingly to associate the excellences of first and best times with the initial three decades of Massachusetts history. Ultimately it led to treatment of the period as a kind of secondary primordium, as a "first and golden age in this new world."[15] This motif, *the founders' era as primordium*,

14. John Owen, *The Works of John Owen*, 12 vols. (Edinburgh, 1862), VII, 7, IX, 510–516. For other English jeremiads after 1660, see, for example, *ibid.*, IX, 296–307, 320–334; John Flavel, *The Whole Works of the Reverend Mr. John Flavel . . .* , 2 vols. (Edinburgh, 1701), 528–535, 593–601; Iain Murray, ed., *Sermons of the Great Ejection* (London, 1962).

15. *RMB*, pt. 2, 44, emphasis mine; Miller, *From Colony to Province*, 50. This connects as well with David M. Scobey's thesis that the Jeremiahs redefined

incorporated into covenantal address from the early 1660s, defined a distinctively American variant upon the Puritan jeremiad.

Higginson's *Cause of God,* the election sermon that by Miller's reckoning fixed the type of the jeremiad, took a definite step in this direction. Higginson, once a theological pupil of Thomas Hooker's and now pastor at Salem, cast much of his material in familiar form. In the obligatory first step, he evoked the mythic world. Like most of his successors in the Jeremiah's role, he assigned a special prefig-urative status to biblical Israel and, in the present case, to the early Solomonic kingdom. There the colonists might find their present circumstance, danger, and duty perfectly delineated. Taking a cue from King Solomon, pointing his people back to times of the Hebrew Fathers for patterns of covenantal rule and blessing, Higginson urged his election day congregation to consider the American community in its formative stage. Purity had been the goal of that "vast undertaking," of its contemptuous secession from "men's inventions" and "human ceremonies," and of its pursuit of "Scripture patterne" as "the [only] perfect rule" of Christian profession and practice. Ambiguous in utterance because of his reverence for biblical first times, Higginson yet suggested to his audience that the time of "Our Fathers," with its "dazzling" display of the pure, had towered above ordinary history. Such play upon New England's "divine Original and Native beauty" impressively strengthened his campaign to recall a lax people to their covenantal bearings.[16]

This point was not lost upon William Stoughton of Dorchester, who in the election sermon for 1668 was next to expand upon the connections between New England's "true interest" and her "first beginnings" and "primitive constitution." To the founders' era he freely granted a share in the prestige of "first ways." Adverting, like Higginson, to biblical models, he concluded that, when "God doth

the founding "as an object of historical consciousness. Their sermons were the first works to view New England from afar." Scobey, "Revising The Errand: New England's Ways and the Sense of the Past," *WMQ,* 3d Ser., XLI (1984), 23.

16. *CG,* 10, 13, 14. The Solomonic text cited by Higginson was 1 Kings 8:57–58. The phrase "divine Original and Native beauty" refers in the first instance to the biblical original of the New England Congregational program, but the context makes it clear that it also applies explicitly, if secondarily, to the founders' realization of the biblical pattern.

[establish a covenanted people], there is ever that which is eminent in the *primitive frame of things amongst them.*" So it was in ancient Israel, so in the New Testament, and so too in the young colony of Massachusetts, in the pioneer days when the churches were "newly come out of the *forming hand* of God." And thus in the course of the sermon Stoughton could direct choice words "unto you Fathers [survivors of the immigrant generation], because *you have known that which was from the beginning.*"[17] By thus featuring the "eminence" of earlier days as a function of "primitive" virtue, Stoughton moved beyond Higginson to the position that henceforth would prevail in the jeremiads: a yet cautious, secondary, but explicit admittance of the founders and their age into the domain of the mythically first and great.

After 1668, their eyes now trained upon the early decades, the clergy deployed every proven device for highlighting "primitive glory." Following the lead of Higginson and Stoughton, fast and election day orators virtually besieged their audiences with appeals to the "Primitive Spirit and Way" of the foregone era. No opportunity was passed to review and celebrate the "ancient and Primitive Interest . . . in the first and best constitution." The zest, the consciousness of achievement that filled the first years, had in the sons' account little to do either with pioneering adventure or with eschatology. They found the first settlers animated by a sense of penetration back to the mythic "FIRST."[18] "In those days" newly covenanted churches stood proud in "Crystalline purity," cleansed of centuries of corruption by "the waters of the Sanctuary, which are, as they arise and flow from the Fountain of Divine Institution, clear as Crystal." Self-evidently, simplicity prevailed, and the Congregational citizenry was imbued with aversion to human inventions.[19]

Like the great happenings of biblical history, the activities of immigration and first planting were suffused by the active presence and favor of the supernatural. The settlers knew "beauty and glory." Swept up in a spiritual revival, they felt "the kingdom of heaven brake in . . . with a holy violence," and they enjoyed a "more then

17. *NETI*, 10, 16, 26.
18. Shepard, Jr., "Preface" to *BR*, 56; *NEPW*, 58; Shepard, Jr., *Eye-Salve*, 22, 39 (and see *BR*, 65). The immediate referent is Israel under Jehoshaphat, but the identification with New England is clear.
19. Danforth, *BR*, 66–68; *ER*, 17, 18; *NEPW*, 19; *CG*, 19.

ordinary way of favour" from the Lord. Had he not, as in Old Testament times, "conducted [the planters] as with the *Pillar of Cloud and Fire*" and embellished every turn in the story "by signs, by wonders" and special providences?[20] Doubting, therefore, "whether there [ever had] been any such Thing as this great Thing" of the founding, the election speakers for 1672 (Shepard) and 1673 (Oakes) urged the commissioning of "Lord's Remembrancers" to prepare a record of the Lord's acts in the country's strong time. A proper "memorial" might resemble the compilations of actions kept by English courts, but in solemnity and stature it would assume semiscriptural status. Thomas Shepard cited "*Davids acts . . .* written in the Book of *Samuel*" as an applicable pattern and suggested that the work be titled "The Book of the Chronicles of the Governours of the *MASSACHUSETS.*"[21]

It might be stretching a point to compare the New England fathers of second-generation rhetoric with the church Fathers of the patristic primordium, but it has long been recognized that from the 1650s "ancestor worship" became a staple of New England expression. Perry Miller found in the jeremiads "such a veneration of progenitors as is hardly to be matched outside China" and was perhaps responsible for popularizing a text from Stoughton's *New-Englands True Interest* that subsequently has become one of the three or four most often quoted from the entire American Puritan literature: "God sifted a whole Nation that he might send choice Grain over into this Wilderness."[22] What Miller did not notice, or did not choose to

20. *NETI*, 28, 29 (and see *ER*, 40); *BR*, 65; *NEPW*, 22, 23, 44 (and see *SE*, 7, and Shepard, Jr., *Eye-Salve*, 12).

21. *NEPW*, 23; Shepard, Jr., *Eye-Salve*, 16. Shepard also referred to Ahasuerus's book of records as cited in Esther 6:1. Increase Mather supported the proposal in his *Apostasy* of 1679, but the project was never carried out in the form envisioned by Oakes and Shepard. The closest approach was William Hubbard's *History of New England* of 1680. This work, acknowledged by the General Court in 1682, described the period of the "primitive plantations" as "the golden age of New England" and compared the ecclesiastical scene repeatedly to "the primitive church, in the days of the apostles." These designations, however, are not convincingly structural to the work. Hubbard found a decisive decline in the colony's fortunes first in the later 1660s. He also depicted "the chiefest intentions and aims" of the founders entirely without reference to a founding Errand or to millennial hopes. *General History of New England from the Discovery to 1680*, *MHSC*, 2d Ser., VI (Boston, 1815), 181, 248, 280, 416. For the founders' aims, see 101–213, 233–248, esp. 116, 181.

22. Miller, *Colony to Province*, 135; *NETI*, 19.

stress, was that homage to ancestors was embraced explicitly within the larger primitivist rationale of late-century rhetoric. Like the towering figures of Mosaic or apostolic times, so the founders of the colonial primordium must befit in stature an age of the first and great. Thus, if the forefathers were "extraordinarily qualified," if they were gifted "to move in an higher sphear," if (as Robert Middlekauff has suggested) they "assumed the proportions of the patriarchs of the Old Testament," they had been chosen by Providence to establish the "first and great fundamental design" of Congregational theocracy. And thus, when the Jeremiahs sang the fathers' virtues, when they cataloged the laity's "*Faith, . . . Fervency, . . . Zeal . . . , affection to . . . Ordinances, . . .* [and] love to [ministers]" or when they accented the wisdom and heavenly skill of the "first Ministry" and "first Magistracy," it was primitive "pattern and example" that they wished to hail.[23]

These considerations are essential to any understanding of the motif of "choice grain" that runs through the jeremiads to and beyond 1674. Stoughton's famed text, for example, belongs unmistakably to a larger unit of thought centered upon "first ways":

> As to *New Englands first wayes* . . . O what were the open professions of the Lords people that first entered this Wilderness? How did our fathers entertain the Gospel, and all the pure institutions thereof . . . ? What was their Communion and Fellowship in the Administrations of the Kingdome of Jesus Christ? What was the pitch of their Brotherly love, of their Zeal for God and his *wayes* . . . ? What was their Humility, their Mortification, their Exemplariness? How much of Holiness to the Lord was written upon all their wayes and transactions? *God sifted a whole Nation that he might send choice Grain over into this Wilderness.*

Since the point consistently made in the sermons is that "the Lord sowed this land *at first* with . . . precious seed-corn," one may conclude that the special accord between "choice" and "first" is the sustaining thesis of second-generation ancestor worship.[24]

23. *ER*, 29, 32; Shepard, Jr., *Eye-Salve*, 12, 13, 32; Robert Middlekauff, *The Mathers: Three Generations of Puritan Intellectuals, 1596–1728* (London, 1971), 101; *NEPW*, 27; *SE*, 31. See also Increase Mather's preface to *ER*, sig. B; *NETI*, 18–21.

24. *NETI*, 18–19; Shepard, Jr., *Eye-Salve*, 12, emphasis mine.

At times they may have appeared absorbed totally in securing the concept of an unspoiled age in their community's immediate history. They may have taken every pain, in Catherine Albanese's words, to "remembranc[e] the fathers in such a way that the sons really were present with these ancestors in the golden age of the beginning." But never did the Jeremiahs lose sight of their basic objective: covenantal maintenance.[25] The "glorious" image of a New World primordium might fascinate and flatter a wayward people, but it would not work their rehabilitation unless coupled with the fuller apparatus of restorationist appeal. To this end the clergy would now exploit obvious parallels with the historic church's apostasy from the primitive; adapt to the new context venerable antagonisms to human invention, novelty, and complexity; and clamor as always for retrieval of original perfection.

By comparing scenes of the 1660s and 1670s with the wonders of primitive days, the clergy strove to draw their auditors to an exploitable realization: "O what a sad *Metamorphosis* hath there of later years passed upon us." To acknowledge loss of a good estate was serious enough, but a far more painful admission was here required. The community must be spoken guilty of the cardinal misdeed in a Puritan inventory of sins. For in painful fact the "strangely changed" mentality of the newer generation and the "strangely altered" state of things in church and society recreated the very scandal that first had necessitated a Puritan movement in English Christianity: betrayal of perfect beginnings.[26]

Only thus can one account for the full odium borne by the charge of declension in late-century rhetoric. As in the traditional jeremiads, it reflected little disposition to comprehend change in social or economic terms, although the frequent demand for "less Trading, Buying, Selling" and more religion pinpointed a major source of current secularization. The shaming taunt that rang through the jeremiads attested the worst of moral faults and the most deserving of covenantal chastisement. It held that a generation had come forth "strangers to the first intention" of the country in its great age. To this exigency the formulaic contrast "then . . . , but now," for more than a century an identifying mark of Puritan calls for

---

25. Catherine L. Albanese, *Sons of the Fathers: The Civil Religion of the American Revolution* (Philadelphia, 1976), 32.
26. *NETI*, 19; *SE*, 21; *BR*, 68.

further reformation, readily was adapted. References to the colony's lost "beauty," "youth," and freshness or to earlier proximity to the cleansing "Fountain of Divine Institution" brought with them the obvious implied contrasts. New England, which "then" had much of "Heaven," was now found worldly. Once hot, she had grown cool; her winsome plainness had degenerated into affectation; her once-pure wine had become "mixed with water"; her native gold was now "dim"; and the jewels and plate the Lord had furnished when he "first began" the colonial work had been transmuted into "*Lumber*."[27]

Moving from metaphors to specifics, the clergy poured out complaints in the rhetoric of then-and-now. "O how excellent was it" then, in the primitive time! Then conversions were frequent, now rare; then families gathered regularly for religious instruction, now seldom. Then ardor for Christ and the ordinances predominated, but now trade, and the building of estates; then apparel was plain, now fashionable and gaudy. Then prevailed peace, unity, and discipline in the churches, but now dispute, schism, and laxity; then ministry and magistracy cooperated to theocratic ends, but now magistrates had begun to skirt ecclesiastical responsibility, to fail to repress public immorality, and to flirt with toleration. Then ministers were esteemed, but now assailed for their support of the Halfway Covenant (and often underpaid). Then churches acknowledged congregational interdependence and synodical authority, but now, spurning the Halfway arrangements, they verged toward "sovereign, unsociable, rigid independency."[28]

The basic pattern, etching the emphasis upon descent from first excellence, was epitomized by Samuel Danforth in 1670:

In our first and best times the kingdom of heaven brake in upon us with a holy violence and every man pressed into it. . . . How careful were you, even all sorts, . . . to take hold of the opportunities of your spiritual good . . . , ordering your secular affairs . . . so as not to interfere with your [religious duties]. . . . [You were then] gleaning day by day in the field of God's ordinances, . . . and at night going home and beating out what you had gleaned, by meditation, repetition . . . and therewith

27. SE, 9; Shepard, Jr., "Preface" to BR, 56–57, 68, 72; CG, 12; ER, 15, 18; NETI, 21, 28, 72.
28. Shepard, Jr., Eye-Salve, 23, 27.

feeding . . . your families. . . . O what a reverent esteem had you in those days of Christ's faithful ambassadors [that is, the ministers]. . . . What searching of the holy Scriptures . . . to find out the order which Christ hath constituted . . . in his house? What fervent zeal was there then against sectaries and heretics . . . ? . . . What pious care was there of sister churches, that . . . their dissensions might be healed? . . . What reverence was there then of the sentence of a council . . . ? What holy endeavors were there in those days to propagate religion to your children? . . . But who is there left among you that saw these churches in their first glory and how do you see them now? Are they not in your eyes in comparison thereof as nothing? . . . Is not the temper, complexion . . . of the churches strangely altered? Does not a careless, remiss, flat, dry . . . frame of spirit grow in upon us . . . ? They that have ordinances are as though they had none; . . . and they that are exercised in the holy things using them by the by . . . , so as not to hinder their eager prosecution of other things which their hearts are set upon. Yea and in some particular congregations amongst us is there not instead of . . . a girdle, a rent. . . ? . . . Yea and. . . . pride, contention, worldliness, covetousness, luxury, drunkenness, and uncleanness break in like a flood upon us.[29]

Audiences still laying claim to a covenantal connection, but thus arraigned for loss of primitive fullness, now required meet counsel. Upon defectors from "first love," wrath must fall. Fires, plagues, crop losses, and untimely deaths bore witness to mounting divine anger, and the clergy dwelt long upon a tremendous catastrophe to come if the Lord's wrath be not promptly appeased. Taking up the argument at this point, they offered a succinct prescription: "Restitution . . . from Declension." All the usual formulas of repentance, amendment, and prayer were to be mustered, but they must also be shaped to the insight that the path toward covenantal safety led through ritualized remembrance *back* to the Great Time. If divine wrath were to be averted, Massachusetts must become again "as at the beginning." And so with a familiar urgency the Jeremiahs pleaded with their hearers to "return," to "repent and do your first works," to "retrieve

29. BR, 65–69. For similar sequences, see *NETI*, 17–22; Shepard, Jr., *Eye-Salve*, 15–25; *NEPW*, 17–41.

your pristine Profession and Practice," to "recover . . . primitive affection." For bringing both the American and the Puritan aspects of the jeremiads into perspective, no element is more significant than this. It is a whole restatement, now adapted to a New England basis, of the immemorial Puritan commitment to "bringing things back to their first institution."[30]

But as they toiled thus to quell the Lord's anger by marching their charges back to the first and best, the clergy were opening another chapter in the Americanization of the Puritan jeremiad. One need only recall that, in Elizabethan and Stuart England, Puritan preaching in the covenantal-restorationist vein aspired as much to elicit further reform as to protect gains already made. There the call for restitution was a caustic of dissent. It invited measurement of English Christendom against disturbing images of the not-yet, of a purified church in a commonwealth rigorously supervised by godly magistrates; and these images, as Anglican apologists well knew, at many points subverted the inherited order.

But in second-generation New England a far differing outlook had come to prevail. Greatly altered circumstances had conspired to qualify the intent of covenantal utterance and, indeed, the very meaning of the Puritan impulse in the late-century setting. In the liberty of the New World, the unrealized vision of the Spiritual Brotherhood, modified to a Congregational bias, was made a reality. A decent approximation of theocracy had been achieved. And thus the watchmen's stance vis-à-vis the established order was reversed. The problem that they saw before them now was, not the transformation, but the maintenance of an established way. Restitutionist appeal was promoted by the authorities in church and state and arose from a conserving motive. A proper recognition of this shift in emphasis, historic in magnitude, might well lead to questions about unqualified applications of the term "Puritan" to later-seventeenth-century materials. But, more to the point, it supplies a first instance (and one overlooked by Reinhold Niebuhr) of the irony of American history. For the jeremiad, once the device of restless reformers, was

---

30. *ER*, 2, 31, 32; Shepard, Jr., *Eye-Salve*, 36; *SE*, 25; *BR*, 65; John Davenport, *An Apology of the Churches in New-England for Church Government* (London, 1643), 13. See also Increase Mather, *Renewal of Covenant the Great Duty Incumbent on Decaying or Distressed Churches* (Boston, 1677), sig. A3.

to become in the 1660s the chosen weapon of the first conservative campaign in American history.[31]

To recognize this shift from reconstructing to conserving intent is the better to understand, for instance, the obvious incongruity in the concept of a New World primordium. Unlike Old Testament or apostolic times, New England's first time as presented in the jeremiads was not disjoined absolutely from the present by an age of ecclesial arrogance and human invention. It described a state of affairs with which the clergy and their anticipated audiences could feel an immediate continuity. There was no clear chronological division, no great crisis, separating primitive from present time. In many ways the power of first days still was felt. The Great Migration and the first foundings of towns and churches were past and unrepeatable, but they remained alive within the memories of surviving first immigrants.[32] Not all young citizens were lukewarm. Conversions still occurred. Congregational unity and procedure were much compromised by the baptismal conflict, but the ecclesiastical system remained largely intact. The major doctrines, the political forms, the laws, and the spiritual ideals of the first commonwealth might variously be abridged in practice, but they nonetheless carried over directly into the present.

Notwithstanding Quaker and Baptist inroads, toleration was still more a threat than a reality. Nor could the Jeremiahs know that the society whose changing character they diagnosed so fiercely was in inexorable transit to a more commercial condition. In their judgment the loss of first integrity had not proceeded to a fatal stage as yet. The process might be reversed, if caught in time. In this context, restitutionist oratory did not overleap a dividing gulf to retrieve connection with the long-lost, for New England's connection with its golden age

31. In addition to issues developed in the rest of this chapter, other themes in the jeremiads—the frequent defense of "order" and the steady stream of complaint about vanity and the neglect of class lines in choice of apparel—carry forward traditionalist emphases that for centuries had been standard in English preaching (J. W. Blench, *Preaching in England in the Late Fifteenth and Sixteenth Centuries* [Oxford, 1964], 241–243, 274–275).

32. In 1674 Increase Mather suggested that the Lord was delaying covenantal punishment for as long as "there are some . . . of the first Generation still surviving" (Mather, "To the Reader," in *ER*, sig. A3). For a variation on the theme, see *ER*, 42.

was frayed, not broken. In this sense, the aim was to preserve and reinvigorate a continuity, to "keep the Kings High way, the way that . . . our worthy *predecessors* have *travelled* in before us." To a degree, therefore, that might have brought knowing winks from a John Whitgift or a William Laud, the American clergy now would link "restitution" to a program directed "to continue and strengthen, and beautifie, and build upon that which [already] hath been laid."[33]

Yet, with the very security of their native country in the balance, the Jeremiahs were not to be troubled by mere irony, and it is difficult to see what other strategy they might have seized. As Timothy H. Breen and Stephen Foster have suggested, they and their fellow colonials shared in the "corporate constitutionalism" common to most seventeenth-century social units. Theirs was a sense of community as a "historical entity which had acquired certain distinctive characteristics with the passage of time." Their self-definition rested in part upon shared memory of historic experiences and upon a common claim to rights and liberties granted in revered written documents. But New England's historical identity, her memorable events and documents, lacked the hallowing of age. One could ill appeal to the ancient and customary when a mere three decades had elapsed since the landing of the Winthrop fleet or the first church foundings, and fifteen years since the promulgation of the Cambridge Platform or the *Laws and Liberties of Massachusetts*. Under such circumstances, tradition was a relatively weak reed upon which to lean, and it should not be forgotten that the issue of restoration versus tradition was pivotal in the earlier Puritan conflicts with the Elizabethan Settlement. With the advantages of a straight traditionalist appeal thus minimized, an alternative apologia for established ways had to be discovered, one that was not compromised by the colony's relative youth. Therein lay the beauty of a restorationist approach. How better to achieve the desired idealization of "our Founders, and the Frame of things laid by them" than to represent it as an instance royal of the primitive?[34]

33. *NEPW*, 48; *NETI*, 16.

34. Timothy H. Breen and Stephen Foster, "The Puritans' Greatest Achievement: A Study of Social Cohesion in Seventeenth-Century Massachusetts," in Alden T. Vaughan and Francis J. Bremer, eds., *Puritan New England: Essays on Religion, Society, and Culture* (New York, 1977), 114; J. H. Elliott, "Revolution and Continuity in Early Modern Europe," *Past and Present*, no. 42 (Feb. 1969), 49; *NEPW*, 49.

To begin with, an order of church and society caught up into the higher sphere of the first carried its own justification. It had less need of warrant through tradition or through custom held since time out of mind. Considerations far more salient than chronology, embodied in the traditional Puritan judgment that "True Antiquity . . . is that which fetches its originall from the beginning," imparted to first things an aura of age; and this permitted the watchmen to deem *New* England ancient, in the truest and best sense, from its very inception. Unhesitatingly, they enjoined the citizenry of a colony founded scarcely three or four decades before not to "leave the good old way," the "*good old paths*," the "ancient and good wayes" of earlier time, but to sustain the country's "ancient . . . affections" to the cause of biblical religion in a supportive commonwealth.[35]

Nor did the clergy for a moment forget that Puritan convention paired esteem of the old to acid censure of the new. Alerting their fellow colonials to "keep the *Good Old Way*" and convincing them that "God hath no need of a *NEW Cart*" to bear the ark of divine institution were two sides of the same task. If the protecting terms of the covenant were to be upheld, a line of resistance to "new notions" or pretenses to "New Light"—as among the Quakers, Baptists, and antisynodalist extremists—must be developed. With the Lord poised to strike and the need acute to recover and abide in first ways, those "ready for Innovations" and "itching after new things and ways" were to be treated as virtual incendiaries of the commonwealth. Again, as it does through a century of preaching in this tradition, the summons to hew to the ancient and "take . . . heed of Innovations" provided an indispensable index to the Puritan estimate of a society gone astray.[36]

Further, an order of church and society touched by primitive grandeur was invested ipso facto with finality. Proportional to its realization of biblical pattern, it stood in definite and fixed form. Fast and election day assemblies therefore could be warned that "*no other foundations [can be] laid then those which have been laid*" and exhorted variously to "keep and preserve" the primitive design, to "hold it without Adulterating [human] deviations," to maintain

---

35. John Cotton, *A Practical Commentary . . . upon the First Epistle Generall of John* (London, 1656), 77, 188; NEPW, 46; Shepard, Jr., *Eye-Salve*, 6, 39; BR, 65.

36. Shepard, Jr., *Eye-Salve*, 37, 45; NETI, 21, 28, 29; NEPW, 49.

"stedfastness and constancy" within it.[37] Clergy who spoke thus clearly idealized a static, not a dynamic, condition of Christian civilization. Bluntly advertising their society's "true and main interest [as] . . . a fixed unalterable thing," they worked to muster resentment against "change," "alteration," "metamorphosis."[38] To "alter" was by definition to "pervert, and corrupt"; therefore, discerning Christians were not to "meddle . . . with them that are given to change," but were to abide in "the ways fixed upon" and to remain "stedfast and unmoveable . . . in the midst of all changes that may come." When these phrases are read in historical context, one recognizes the pleading of a conservative interest, imperiled by economic and social changes of the 1660s and 1670s, speaking for a communal ideal based upon conformity, fixed order, and stability. But one also sees the result of a century of Puritan indoctrination in an ideal of fixed perfection, with the Spiritual Brotherhood's once unattainable hope for "such a settled estate as shall be unmoveable" now seen provisionally fulfilled in the New England the founders built.[39]

An appreciation of the Jeremiahs' conservative adaptation of restorationist appeal lends additional depth to Miller's account of their endeavor to uphold original purpose in the face of a changing society. It also underscores his perception that the probable purgative impact of fast and election day ritual—a discharge of guilt freeing the energies of men in a protocapitalist society to participate in modernization—was latent, and contrary to manifest intent. The approach here taken to the American jeremiad thus reveals a Protestant mentality still fundamentally dedicated to a retrospective norm. Those who created the principal jeremiads from 1663 to 1674 were capable of a generous adjustment, within their theological frame, to a world in the throes of progress, but their vision of the community's future welfare was formed in nostalgia. It arose from passion for the old, the simple, and the fixed.

Integral to Miller's argument, however, was the Puritan Errand. Focusing upon the second meaning of the Errand, the mission to

37. NETI, 14, 29; ER, 17–18; Mitchel, Nehemiah, 28. The element of fixity has been noted by David Minter, The Interpreted Design as a Structural Principle in American Prose (New Haven, Conn., 1969), 59.

38. NETI, 13, 19, 29; NEPW, 49; Shepard, Jr., Eye-Salve, 18, 19, 36.

39. NETI, 13; Shepard, Jr., Eye-Salve, 19, 36; NEPW, 45; Udall, True Remedie, 67.

build a model city, he suggested that the foiling of this aim provided a needed additional explanation of the Jeremiahs' frustration
and chagrin. What, then, have the authors of the first jeremiads to
say about a New England Errand?

In light of the conclusions above respecting the founders' motives,
this is an especially interesting question. Bercovitch has contended
that "the jeremiads attest to an unswerving faith in the errand."
Others, who doubt that a world-redeeming Errand played an important role in the immigrants' thought, have suggested that "the second
generation formulated the idea of the mission of New England."[40]
Neither claim is borne out by the first group of jeremiads. Six of
the ten specifically address what Jonathan Mitchel called "OUR END
in coming hither," and the very phrase "Errand into the Wilderness"
appears in three of the sermons and supplies the title of Danforth's
election sermon of 1670, *A Brief Recognition of New-Englands Errand
into the Wilderness*.[41] But in these instances the colonial mission is
rendered consistently within the limits of Miller's *first* sense—the
will to construct a biblically guided community—and without reference to a further Errand to be run for the sake of the Christian world.
The point is illustrated readily in Higginson's pace-setting *Cause of
God* (1663), where the theme is taken up repeatedly:

> The end of our coming hither was a reformation . . . of what was
> amiss . . . in the churches we came from: from which we made
> . . . a locall secession into this wilderness, with true desires . . .
> after a more full Reformation according to Gods word. . . . New
> Englands design in this vast undertaking, it was Reformation
> i.e. *the avoyding of some special corruptions, and the Vigorous
> profession and practise of every thing . . . according to Scripture
> pattern. . . . This was and is our Cause, that Christ alone might be
> acknowledged by us, as the onely head . . . in his Church, that his
> written word might be acknowledged as the onely Rule, that onely
> and all his Institutions might be observed . . . by us, and that with*

40. Bercovitch, *Jeremiad*, 6; Middlekauff, *The Mathers*, 99; Avihu Zakai,
"Exile and Kingdom: Reformation, Separation, and the Millennial Quest in the
Formation of Massachusetts and Its Relationship with England, 1628–1660"
(Ph.D. diss., Johns Hopkins University, 1983), 387.

41. Jonathan Mitchel *et al., Elijah's Mantle* (Boston, 1722), 4; Mitchel, *Nehemiah*, 28; *BR*, 65; *NEPW*, 33.

puritie. . . . Our Fathers fled into this Wilderness from the face
*of a Lording Episcopacie, and humane injunctions in the Worship
of God.* . . . The one true Religion according to Scripture . . .
[is] the great end for which we came into this wilderness.

Even more telling is the evidence of Danforth's celebrated sermon
of 1670. Miller described Danforth as "fully aware of the ambiguity
concealed in the word 'errand'" and drew specifically from his title
and text for "Errand into the Wilderness," but in fact Danforth's
description of the Errand is uniformly unambiguous on the point at
issue: New Englanders are urged to consider

> *what it was that drew them into the wilderness, and to consider
> that it was . . . the expectation . . . of the free and clear dispensa-
> tion of the Gospel and kingdom of God.* . . . You have solemnly
> professed . . . that the cause of your leaving your country, . . .
> and transporting yourselves . . . into this . . . wilderness, was
> your liberty to walk in the faith of the Gospel with all good
> conscience according to the order of the Gospel, and your en-
> joyment of the pure worship of God according to his institution
> without human mixtures. . . . To what purpose came we into
> the wilderness . . . ? Was it not the expectation of the pure and
> faithful dispensation of the Gospel and kingdom of God? The
> times were such that we could not enjoy it in our own land, and
> therefore . . . we left our country.[42]

Statements of the other clergy who addressed the issue are virtually interchangeable with those of Higginson and Danforth.[43] For

42. *CG*, 11–14, 17; Miller, "Errand," in Miller, *Errand*, 3; *BR*, 61, 65, 72–73.
43. Mitchel, *Nehemiah*, 28; Shepard, Jr., *Eye-Salve*, 11, 37; *NEPW*, 33; *ER*,
15. See also *RMB*, IV, pt. 1, 418, 450–453, pt. 2, 471, V, 495. The generalization also applies to the several post-1674 statements upon the original errand
that I have examined: Samuel Torrey, *Mans Extremity, Gods Opportunity*
(Boston, 1695), 49; Increase Mather, *An Earnest Exhortation to the Inhabitants
of New-England* . . . (Boston, 1676), 16–17; Increase Mather, *Great Duty*, 11;
Samuel Willard, *Covenant-Keeping the Way to Blessedness* . . . (Boston, 1682),
117; Willard, *The Sinfulness of Worshipping God with Men's Institutions* . . .
(Boston, 1691), 27. James Allen stated flatly that "the Errand into this Wilder-
ness was for Purity of Worship" (*Neglect of Supporting and Maintaining the
Pure Worship of God, by the Professing People of God: Is a God-Provoking and
Land-Wasting Sin* [Boston, 1677], 11). Danforth, Eleazar Mather, and Shepard,

the most part their display of themes—refuge, liberty, human inventions, precious institutions and ordinances, primitive purity—captures accurately the aims of the founders as represented in their many clear statements on the subject and is equally unequivocal. The truth of the matter is that, whether in the 1630s or the 1660s, New England spokesmen were not occupied with a mission to the world. Undeniably, from time to time, as did their forebears, the Jeremiahs took thought of a wider responsibility to the cause of international Reformed Christianity. Stoughton could tell the election day audience in 1668 that "the faithful precious suffering saints of God in all other places, that have heard of the Lords Providences towards us, do expect and promise great things from us"; and both the younger Shepard and Oakes invoked the imagery of a light or City upon an Hill, with Oakes allowing that the New England churches already had "enlightened" European Protestants "as to the pattern of Gods home."[44] These and similar affirmations reveal that the colonial clergy, notwithstanding their sense of removal to "the uttermost ends of the earth," saw their Congregational enterprise as participant in the international movement of Christian reformation in their time. But in no instance are they offered to explain "our end in coming hither." They serve varied rhetorical purposes quite unrelated to conviction of a distinctive duty to reform the world.

Since the ministers did not understand their society's originative task as a world-saving Errand, the extra dimension of grief Miller perceived in the jeremiads cannot have been a response to the loss of an English audience for the City upon a Hill. There is no evidence that "for New England the decisive event in the middle seventeenth century was England's official refusal to attend the New England model."[45] Furthermore, the final measure of second-generation "sickness of soul" can be otherwise accounted for. In the first place, it is known that during the 1640s and 1650s the New England leadership entertained high hopes for a Puritan and eventually a Congregational breakthrough within English-speaking Christianity and

Jr., also described the Great Migration as motivated by the settlers' regard for their children's religious welfare (BR, 73; SE, 16; Shepard, Jr., Eye-Salve, 24).

44. NETI, 17; Shepard, Jr., Eye-Salve, 45; NEPW, 21. See also Mitchel, Nehemiah, 19.

45. Minter, Interpreted Design, 52. Minter's claim is drawn from Miller without other documentation.

that many looked beyond to the Middle Advent and a Congregational millennium. The subsequent dampening of revolutionary expectations, particularly where these had embraced a millennial hope,
would seem to provide cause for ample confusion and chagrin.

In reference to overt content, however, a second element appears
the more visibly. Disqualification of Miller's alleged second sense of
New England's Errand leaves one with the first. To the eye of a student once fascinated with the spectacle of a world Errand, this might
seem a meager leaving, but it is nothing of the kind. Unanimously,
the Jeremiahs of 1663–1674 testified that the Lord had assembled a
"peculiar people" in the American wilderness and defined them in
reference to a great and distinctive end. That end, as the passages
quoted from Higginson and Danforth show conclusively, was bound
up with primitivist hopes. It is enough to note that Higginson and
Danforth's meaning scarcely can be grasped without a technical comprehension of the terms "purity," "institution," "pattern," "human
mixture," and "reformation [re-formation]." When, in addition, the
clergy identify their fathers' era as a singular embodiment of the
primitive, it is reasonable to see their turmoil of mind as a product,
to coin a phrase, of restorationist disappointment.

As the oldest and stablest impulse defining a Puritan movement
within English Protestantism, allegiance to the first stood at the core
of the basically theological identity ascribed by the clergy to their
society: those gathered in the wilderness were a people of return,
pledged to live ancient lives. This crucial differentia was threatened
by the general relaxation of earlier standards, by worldliness, immorality, and contention; but in a deeper sense, it was challenged
by the slow emergence of a commercial and liberal civilization that
assigned no honor to the fixed and simple and therefore weakened
connections between primitivist outlook and social experience. Naturally, the ministers did not conceive their situation directly in such
terms, yet in something of the sort, it is suggested, lies a source of
the distress that informs their fast and election day productions. It
is hard to imagine an apter illustration of what Miller called "a fall
from a mighty designation" than that shift of sentiment and practice through the mid-century years, perceived by the ministers as
desertion of a true "beginning."[46]

46. Miller, "Errand," in Miller, *Errand*, 3.

Concentration upon the dark side of the rhetoric, upon its castigatory mood and its disclosure of torment, appears all the more justified
when, in addition to the usual Deuteronomic considerations, one discovers in the documents a poignant depiction of a fall in process from
primordial fullness. There are, to be sure, contrasting themes. In four
of the sermons, affliction was assigned a finally curative role, guar-
anteeing positive ends beyond punishment. Higginson and Mitchel
come close to a breach with inherited principle on this point.[47] They
presume that the Lord would not destroy summarily a people so carefully chosen, commissioned (with an Errand in Miller's *first* sense),
and favored. Here is a previously neglected emphasis, although it
appears as well in English sermons in the Puritan tradition after
1660. Nonetheless, it does emerge in the American materials and
may have grown more prominent after 1674.[48]

47. Bercovitch's generalization does not hold for Torrey, Stoughton, Eleazar
Mather, Shepard, Jr., or Willard, all of whom accepted the finally conditional
character of the covenant and stopped well short of a guarantee of ultimate
mercy. See *ER*, 7, 15, 17, 39–40, 42–43; *NETI*, 10–11, 16, 25, 32; *SE*, 6, 27–28;
Shepard, Jr., *Eye-Salve*, 33–35; *UI*, 1, 3, 7, 10–11, 62. Stoughton appears to
guarantee success to "a Remnant," and in 1695 Torrey spoke of a "general work
of Conversion and Reformation" in New England at the time of the Middle
Advent (*NETI*, 15; Torrey, *Mans Extremity*, 59). In his preface to Increase
Mather's *Day of Trouble*, Oakes did agree with Mather that in the impending
"trouble" God "will not make an utter end of us"; but this is a somber optimism
("To the Christian Reader," in Mather, *Day of Trouble*, sig. A2). In his election
sermon of 1673, as Bercovitch notes, Oakes did argue that "the Lords design
in humbling and proving you . . . [is] that he may do you good at your latter
end." But a closer examination reveals that the *"Latter End"* is in reference
to the "everlasting Consolations" of heaven, not to a restored New England
(*NEPW*, 63; quoted in Bercovitch, *Jeremiad*, 56). Higginson and Mitchel assert
unequivocally that the Lord "will not kill us, . . . but save [us] in the issue"
(Mitchel, *Nehemiah*, 32, and see 17; *CG*, 5, 24). By 1673, Increase Mather
seems to have moved from a more pessimistic position expressed in his preface
to *SE*, sigs. A2, A4. In the *Day of Trouble*, he did not explicitly guarantee
triumph, but held out hope that the Lord would not destroy New England
"as yet" (27; see also Mather, "To the Reader," sig. A3). Danforth's phrasing
in *BR* is ambiguous with respect to a "guarantee," but the uppermost note is
indisputably optimistic (*BR*, 75–77).
48. On English sermons, see, for example, Murray, ed., *Sermons*, 31, 122–
125; Owen, *Works*, IX, 12–15. The theme was well established in mid-century
parliamentary sermons. See, for example, Edmund Calamy, *Englands Looking-
Glasse* (London, 1642); John Strickland, *Mercy Rejoycing against Judgement;*

Hopes for a new age also appear. The first jeremiads afford solid evidence that an "expectation of glorious times" had become by the 1660s a relatively standard doctrine, although the generalization applies as well to contemporary English jeremiads.[49] But such expectation plays a modest role in shaping the sermons. Whether or not they personally espoused millennial doctrine, Higginson, Danforth, Eleazar Mather, and Samuel Willard found little or no use for it.[50] Mitchell, Stoughton, Oakes, Increase Mather, and Torrey each turned briefly to the doctrine, but not in order to define or defend a New England Errand. Mitchel and Torrey routinely celebrated the expected "consummation of the Gospel Dispensation." Stoughton

---

or, God Waiting to Be Gracious to a Sinful Nation (London, 1645).

On American materials, see Bercovitch, Jeremiad, 84–85. See also above, n. 5.

49. Increase Mather, Day of Trouble, 20. For English examples, see Murray, ed., Sermons, 31–34, 42; Flavel, Works, 530. Apt warning against exaggeration of millennial themes in these and later materials is supplied by John G. Buchanan, "Puritan Philosophy of History from Restoration and Revolution," HCEI, CIV (1968), 331.

50. Bercovitch (Jeremiad, 12–14) finds in Danforth's BR a conception of an "errand . . . to bring history . . . to an end" and a description of Massachusetts as "a herald sent to prepare the world" for the millennium. I am unable to see how the text can bear these inferences. They rest upon a much-exaggerated estimate both of the millennial component and of "figural progression" as a key to Puritan thought. Bercovitch is prepared to allege the millennium as the understood final term in a "figural series" even when it is not specified, as it certainly is not by Danforth. I see no reason to accept an equation of Danforth's reference to the "coming and kingdom of the Messiah" with the millennium, let alone with a New England Errand. Again, commenting upon a reference in the BR to Moses' "prophetical song" of Deuteronomy 32, Bercovitch claims that "as every member of Danforth's audience knew," taking their cue from a "traditional interpretation" of the passage, it "was addressed to those who were to inherit the millennial kingdom" (Jeremiad, 16). To document the existence of an established tradition of interpretation, Bercovitch then points to a comment upon the text in Oakes's election sermon of 1673; but what actually appears in Oakes's text is a commonplace reference to "the multiplication of the church, and enlargement of the Kingdom of Christ" neither explicitly nor by context identified as the millennium (NEPW, 3). In fact, Danforth's reference to Deuteronomy 32 applies his earlier definition of a "prophet" as "one who by . . . inspiration . . . made known the mysteries of salvation" (BR, 60); no eschatological intent is indicated. All of this takes us far afield from Danforth's clear and frequently stated conception of the Errand.

and Increase Mather warned that an unreformed New England might experience the "horrible Combustions and Confusions" expected to precede the millennial time. None of these men called New England to inaugurate the eschatological finale.[51] Stoughton, for instance, was concerned to warn colonial Congregationalists that continued disobedience might cause them to "lose [their] share" in the "times of Refreshment" when they arose and began to spread worldwide. Oakes alone drew a significant connection between New England and the end-time transfiguration, envisioning "this our Common-wealth" as a proleptic "specimen, or a little model," of the millennial estate; but he did not identify the conscious creation or presentation of such a model as the defining term of a conscious Errand.[52] The colonists' "great Errand into this Wilderness," rather, was to be grasped in terms of "pure Administration of Gods Worship and Ordinances" without "mixture of humane inventions." The proleptic dimension appeared as a by-product, not as the stated aim, of their wilderness labors.[53]

In the end, it is impossible to credit the thesis that progressive aims fundamentally shaped the American jeremiad. A guarantee that beyond punishment lies renewal of favor and that a new age may lie ahead lends additional substance to Miller's contention that the

51. *ER*, 18; Mitchel, *Nehemiah*, 19. Torrey's intent remained the same in millennial references in *A Plea for the Life of Dying Religion* . . . (Boston, 1683), 44; and in *Mans Extremity*, 59. *NETI*, 32–33; Increase Mather, *Day of Trouble*, 20–21. See also James West Davidson, *The Logic of Millennial Thought: Eighteenth-Century New England* (New Haven, Conn., 1978), 54, 60–61, 67.

52. *NETI*, 32–33. The same result of obedience is expressed in Torrey, *Mans Extremity*, 59. *NEPW*, 21. A similar theme of transfiguration appeared in Mitchel, *A Discourse of the Glory to Which God Hath Called Believers* . . . , 2d ed. (Boston, 1721 [date of composition uncertain; Mitchel died in 1668]), 112, and see 120. By 1674 Increase Mather had taken up the proleptic theme, envisioning New England as "a Type or Emblem of New Jerusalem." He gave no indication, however, that New England was called to or could, in fact, inaugurate the millennium. "Europe," as the "seat of the Church in these latter ages," was to be the central scene of the transfiguration. In respect to the "events to come," New England remained a far "corner of the World" ("To the Reader," in *ER*, 2; *A Discourse concerning the Danger of Apostasy* . . . [Boston, 1679], 56, 61).

53. *NEPW*, 19, 33. Oakes also told his audience, "You have been as a City upon an hill [and] have enlightened the [world]" (21). The reader should note, however, that this is not a statement of formative purpose or mission.

Jeremiahs avoided despair and provided morale for moving with the times. At the same time, it forces qualification of his emphasis upon castigatory threat. But without the larger structure of a millennial Errand, the first jeremiads confirm only the relative inaptitude of the term "progress" (layered with the meanings of later centuries) adequately to represent Puritan habits of mind.

Writers in this tradition had occasionally used the term, although it occupied a minor place in the technical vocabulary. The belief that the Christian cause "must be making progress" in reformation beyond the terms of the Elizabethan Settlement had evoked an organized Puritan opposition to begin with, and the rigorously moral cast of Puritan theology always had engendered passion for "progress to perfection."[54] These impulses, moreover, were still very much alive in later-seventeenth-century Massachusetts. At least three of the contributing Jeremiahs—Shepard, Torrey, and Higginson—represented "progress in Reformation" as a compend of New England duty. But there should be no mistake. Barring associations with novelty or human invention, such assertion carried no reproach of the past or the old; it implied an increased, not a decreased, preference for the static, and it did not assign a categorically forward dimension to the colonials' pilgrimage. So long as a Higginson, the younger Shepard, and Torrey found re-formation the immediate and restrictive complement of progress, they would make only halting moves toward a modern standpoint.

Thus when Shepard identified "progress in the work of Reformation" as "a main design of Gods people's adventuring in to this wilderness," he had in view the immigrants' stand against human "mixtures in the worship of God" and their drive back to biblically instituted ordinances. When Torrey spoke of "progress of the Work of Reformation," he meant "not onely that we should *do our first works*, but that *our last works should be more then our first*"; yet he defined *"more then our first"* with a checklist of duties entirely in keeping with his program for *"recover[y of] our first New-England Interest."* And Higginson, who associated *"progress in Reformation"* with the continuing Congregational quest for further light, retained

---

54. Hastings Robinson, ed. and trans., *Zurich Letters . . .* , 3 vols. (Cambridge, 1842–1847), I, 161; Paul Baynes, *A Helpe to True Happinesse* (London, 1635), 301.

complete its traditional meaning as the drive toward enclosure in fixed perfection: "We are to press forward . . . that we may in all be conformable to the perfect rule of the word of God."[55]

Mythic remembrance, the perfect rule of the Word, the ancient and encompassing template of biblical pattern—this established the bearings for the Jeremiahs' doctrine of progress, if one may so speak. Or, more distinctively, it was the perfection of the first as realized in most essentials in the founders' Congregational establishment. Until the Middle Advent reached Massachusetts, there must remain a residual imperfection; and while the New England way yet fell short, by some degrees, of biblical fullness, it would be necessary to remind the overzealous that "a conceit of having allready attained a perfect reformation should be farr from us." Nevertheless, it stood beyond doubt that "all the substantials" of curvature back to apostolic Congregationalism had been accomplished. Oakes, who denied that the Fathers "were at a *Ne plus ultra,* and that nothing was left to the discovery of after-times," insisted with equal fervor that "the *Congregationalway* . . . is the highest step . . . taken towards *Reformation,* and for the substance of it is the very way that was established and practised in the *Primitive times.*"[56] Exactly this assumption—that the highest stride forward was also the fullest repossession of the original and complete—underwrote the conscious doctrine of the American jeremiad in its formative period, anchored the turn of covenantal ora-

55. Shepard, Jr., *Eye-Salve,* 37; ER, 8, 27; CG, 13. The "duties" cited by Torrey were six: "renew our Covenant with God," "recover the Worship of God from those decayes which it is, fallen into," "recove[r] . . . your first Love, Peace and Union," obey God's law, attend to the religious nurture of children, and "labour to get a new Heart and a new Spirit." The last item is defined within the context of the sermon as "restor[ation of our] first Spiritual prosperity." ER, 8, 10, 12, 15, 23, 25, 26.

56. CG, 13; NEPW, 45. Higginson argued for "a full[er] reformation in the sense of our many defects," but the "defects" he listed were the positions held "about the subjects of Baptisme, and consociation of Churches" by the antisynodalist party (CG, 13–15). Cf. Bercovitch's contention that "the New England Puritan jeremiad evokes the mythic past . . . above all to demand progress. The fathers, says Danforth [in BR] were mighty men . . . but the errand they began leads *us* toward *a higher, brighter dispensation. . . .* We have a sacred duty to go beyond them. To venerate and emulate is to supersede" (*Jeremiad,* 24). I am not persuaded that any reasonable construction either of Danforth's text or of any of the early jeremiads can yield these meanings.

tory into a conservative path, and unfitted it to function as a "ritual of progress."[57]

Thus, even more than he knew, Miller was right. The sermons through 1674 were not dominated by a future horizon. They were preoccupied with loss and recovery, with remembrance and imitation. They revealed no conscious wish to accommodate change. Had they not evinced dissatisfaction and a sense of unrealized possibility, they would have ceased altogether to be Puritan; but the early Jeremiahs tied aspiration to the assumption that the substance of Congregational reformation already had been accomplished. They portrayed declension from that height as an unforeseen emergency. The founders had planned to erect an unchanging theocracy, but, after all, the circumstances of life in the New World proved as refractory as those of the Old. Because "Foundation-work" did not hold, the American jeremiad became a pastoral necessity. Now directed to conserving ends, both covenantal threat and restorationist appeal would remain essential to the preachers' repertoire. To recover, hold, and enjoy the ways once honored and to remedy remaining defects *was* the Errand they proclaimed. Certainly, it was the straight and narrow way toward safety and prosperity. No doubt the Bright Coming would bring the crowning advances and close the circle of return, but millennialism, even were it at root a futurist affair, stood marginal to the jeremiads' design. So too, if a resumed happiness under the ordinances should follow the looming ordeal with an angered Lord, it would flow from repentance and return to what Shepard called the "Ancient Land-marks of this [New England] interest."[58]

In short, in its most essential features, the American jeremiad resists modernizing interpretation. As a product of minds that did not share our historical perspectives, it projects fully as much of the alien as of the familiar. At no time were fast or election day audiences before 1675 invited to comprehend their history basically as a serial flow eclipsing the past. Such a concept was present, but it was wound in complexly among other and competing ideals. Jeremiahs from Higginson to Torrey took key bearings from a more ancient compass, which fixed a cyclical course from restoration to lapse toward prospective recovery. It set past and future, return and advance, in

57. Bercovitch, *Jeremiad*, xv, 28.
58. Shepard, Jr., *Eye-Salve*, 25–26.

strangely positive alignment. It preferred prescription to description and valued analogical over linear-causal connections within history. It pointed the way, not toward a dynamic, changing society, but to the repose of static perfection. Clearly, a rhetoric guided by this compass was in no simple sense an agent of the modern.

ELEVEN

REFLECTIONS

UPON THE

PRIMITIVIST

DIMENSION

*T*his study has explored the primitivist dimension as an index to the historic Puritan signature in the religion of England and New England. Allegiance to the first was not the sole element of that signature, but it was fundamental to the saints' ardor for the Book and to their search for purity. Although little attention has been given here to the English development after 1630, the inquiry suggests that biblical primitivism was a generic factor inspiring and shaping dissent. It helped to unify both the range of reform opinion at any given moment and the shifts through time from the 1560s (and turning to New England after the 1630s) into the era of declension. Those who hungered for a yet purer form of Christian practice and (in later-seventeenth-century New England) those who strove to preserve a purity once attained all took for granted, if with varying degrees of commitment, the set of categories summarized in Chapter 1, with the notable exception of belief in the millennium; and these were adaptable. They could be and were turned to accommodate a diversity of purposes and schemes.

It is perfectly true that the differences, say, between the Presbyterian and the more radical Congregational concept of church polity, fomented bitter discord among dissenters united on almost everything else; but those differences were plausible variations upon a common restitutionist platform. Alike in old and New England, it was "the first Apostolic directions, patterns and examples of [the] Primitive Churches" that the respective parties invoked as the "sacred pillar of fire to guide us" toward agreement.[1] And, indeed, when their proponents turned to castigate one another, their deadliest thrust was to charge misconstruction of the Great Time and its norms. Just so, the jeremiads of New England stood in a fundamental kinship with the antivestment utterances of the mid-1560s—the most substantial early manifestation of an intellectually coherent opposition to the Elizabethan Settlement—in point of the common commitment to recovery of the primitive. In this way a shared absorption in the biblical world, a world construed as revelatory of the first and best and of all requisite examples and institutions, served to define and bond Puritans, notwithstanding their frequent lack of agreement upon specific goals and means of further re-formation.

Within this perspective, then, Puritanism was a distinct and long-lived strain of Anglo-American Protestantism dedicated to the pursuit of purity both moral and primitive. It encompassed broad internal variation and underwent an impressive evolution, but it sustained throughout a set of common concepts and assumptions that did much to define the Christian community's orientation to the sacred and its stance in time and history. These directed the saints to identify with an ancient narrative, to discover that "all pleasantness did belong to the first beginning," to find there a perfected program for living redeemed in a world that "declines" from the Great Time, to rejoice that "as [primitive teaching] is new, so it is always old," to abominate Catholic and Anglican invention, and, withal, to *live ancient lives* in conformity to the first. Such ideas, it is suggested, resist inclusion in the categories of thought that come most naturally to citizens of the twentieth century, align poorly with research attempting to "hustle the colonists down the road toward modernization," and thus have remained (with two or three notable exceptions) on the far margins of scholarly inquiry.[2]

1. Thomas Goodwin *et al.*, *An Apologeticall Narration* (1643), ed. Robert S. Paul (Philadelphia, 1963), 3.

2. Thomas Brightman, *A Revelation of the Apocalyps* (Amsterdam, 1611), 47; John Cotton, *A Practical Commentary . . . upon the First Epistle Generall of John* (London, 1656), 79; T. H. Breen, *Puritans and Adventurers: Change and Persistence in Early America* (New York, 1980), xvi.

Pursuing the issue of modernization, one does not find all the evidence pointing in one direction. Indeed, like the emphases upon work and self-denial, the Sabbatarian crusade against holidays, or the democratic bias of the Presbyterian and Congregational polities, so the passion for restoration itself facilitated passage from traditional to early modern ways. Just as the Henrician reforms had made the most of apostolic and patristic appeals in their campaign against popish religion and the claim to unbroken tradition upon which it largely depended, so the Puritan reverence for first things continued to function as an antitraditionalist force in Elizabethan, Stuart, and early New England times. Faced with such offenses as the travesty of discipline in the bishops' courts or the minimal Sunday flanked by Catholic and pagan holidays, dissenting Protestants learned less to credit custom or the hallowing of time. It did not suffice to be told that surplices or acts of kneeling were "hoary headed with antiquity and continuance."[3] They remained error, waste, for the redeeming forms of prime antiquity had been lost to view as the Christian world grew further away from the time of origins and as human invention did its encrusting work. Thus the chosen task that went far to define a distinctive Puritan way within English religion was reinstatement of the long-lost; that, too, was the largest component in the Errand of New England. Hence, although to a lesser degree than in the restitutionist sects of the Radical Reformation, the way of biblicist dissent was a force breeding irreverence for organic traditions. Its congruence at this level—as opposed, always, to conscious collusion—with other cultural processes working toward a more commercial, prospective society is apparent enough.

The connections should be drawn with caution, however. Were primitivist ideas too hastily identified as a correlate of modernization, it then would be difficult to account for Cluniac reform of the eleventh century, the emergence of Methodist holiness sects in the nineteenth, or the many other waves of protest and renewal in Christian history that sought reversion to the first. If the Puritan standpoint, subversive as it was of the sense of connected tradition,

3. [Thomas Hooker], "Preface" to William Ames, *A Fresh Suit against Human Ceremonies in God's Worship* (n.p., 1633), sig. i3. See also Thomas Cartwright's remarks upon "the false cloak of tradition," in *The Second Replie of Thomas Cartwright: Agaynst Master Doctor Whitgiftes Second Answer touching the Churche Discipline* ([Zurich], 1675), 78, 339.

contributed anything to a more modern outlook, it is important to see that it did so by the sheer fortuity of its emergence in the time of transition. Nothing better could demonstrate a lack of inherent connection with the modern than the naturalness with which citizens of Massachusetts Bay in the 1660s and 1670s could turn the concept of a New England primordium to the uses of a new traditionalism bent upon perpetuating the world of the founders.

But, in addition, and yet more important, this study has found and illustrated a dozen ways that the Puritan remains speak of the past, the *sacred* past, with an unsurrendered awe. No American Puritan founder expected to lay foundations for "a country whose golden age lies in the future." No Winthrop or Cotton of those days could have comprehended the claim that "Christianity itself, with its emphasis on the linear advance of history . . . is fundamentally modern."[4] Consistently, they designated "those [great] days" as the sovereign measure defining placement and direction in time. When Puritan writers did highlight the future, as in the laying of fond plans for further reformation, their thought centered on retrieval and enclosure within the one horizon of biblical history. One's gaze was directed back to that compelling drama, and only then forward to the tasks of the present and to hopes for a better future.

Millennialism, with its vision of a strong time yet to come, was not the native expression of Puritan hopes. It emerged against heavy resistance in the third and fourth generations, long after the death of the first antivestiarians, Presbyterians, and Separatists, as a second and late mode of envisaging unattained ideals. No longer, as in classic amillennial perspective, was it "the most obvious feature of man's life in this *saeculum* . . . that it is doomed to remain incomplete," for a substantial fulfillment of human hopes now would occur within time.[5] By thus enlarging the import of the historical future, by

---

4. Clinton Rossiter, *Conservatism in America*, 2d ed. (New York, 1962), 71; Richard D. Brown, *Modernization: The Transformation of American Life, 1600–1865* (New York, 1976), 17. I thus agree with John Morgan that modernizing "implications" of Puritanism are not to be confused with "the essentially conservative *intentions* of the puritan message" (*Godly Learning: Puritan Attitudes towards Reason, Learning, and Education, 1560–1640* [Cambridge, 1986], 304).

5. Peter Brown, "St. Augustine," in Beryl Smalley, ed., *Trends in Medieval Political Thought* (New York, 1965), 12.

promising Christians more from their historical pilgrimage than travail and endurance, it became a rare way of defining progress within mental constructs available to the seventeenth century, and hence it too probably paved approaches toward a more modern outlook.

Nonetheless, the millennial doctrines here examined are not fairly represented as the first stage in a neat succession toward later doctrines of human development, with "secularization" as a middle term. Thomas Brightman may have been, in Ernest Lee Tuveson's terms, a religious progressivist, but further connections with the dogma of unilinear progress are as much oblique as direct. He and his followers had caught the vision of an end to familiar history, but the shape of their dream of things to come was determined as well by fealty to originals. Hence there was no confusion of categories when they spoke of a "future restoring" or wished for "a new face of things in their . . . *re*novation"; and through such affirmations they became the bearers, not of a unilinear, but of a dialectical understanding of past, present, and future. In Puritan quarters millennialism qualified, but never breached, and indeed reaffirmed the priority of the first. It expressed no wish to drive into the future without reclaiming ancient good; and if it found immediate place for change and reconstruction as Antichrist was brought down and a worldly New Jerusalem "grew" to fulfillment, it revealed no intention to open history to human development, but a hunger to see it closed into tightly ordered perfection.[6]

On the whole, the conclusions of this study tally ambiguously with those of much modern research into social and economic development in seventeenth-century New England and, especially, Massachusetts. The state of scholarship does not now allow one to conclude with confidence how deeply the agrarian, conservative, corporatist, utopian features of the early towns and the larger colonial arrangements were qualified by diversity, conflict, land dealing, and other forms of selfish aggrandizement. Yet the analysis here suggests that the articulate settlers saw and idealized their society primarily in fixed, consensual terms. It demonstrates that the religiously motivated founders, certainly the overwhelming majority of those with views on record, drew most consistently upon canons of restitution, reten-

6. Brightman, *Apocalyps*, 666; [Henry Finch], *The Worlds Great Restauration* (London, 1621), 38 (emphasis added).

tion, and collective moral discipline to explain their presence in the New World.

To whatever degree Puritan migrants to the Bay looked upon their remote colony as a land of social and economic opportunity, this was much tempered by a will to implement as never before their taste for the fixed and their repugnance for the new. Their intellectual concepts reflect a flat refusal to accept change and development as normal attributes of human society. They came with lofty hopes for ecclesiastical and civil reformation, and, indeed, their theology was a potent instrument for generating expectations of reform uncharacteristic of traditional society; but they wished too that the fulfillment of those hopes would bring an essentially changeless stability. The colonists might argue over details, but they agreed that there was but one right order and that sin and disintegration lay outside it. It was essential to their conscious theory that, once the antitraditional critique had been indulged, once all inventions had been purged and replaced with biblical practices, the external history of the commonwealth should subside into the routine of the communal covenant: a rhythm of declension and return within a basically static religious and social framework.

These were the stated aims of the Bay founders, and they were aims congruent with the kind of society they tried to build. If, indeed, the inherited ideal of English culture was seen in "the repetition of past ways, rather than through original achievements," and if it was second nature to the traditional English citizenry to view "innovation and novelty . . . with suspicion," then on these key fronts the New Englanders stood squarely on the side of the traditional.[7]

The major force for modernization in New England was the ascent —rapid after mid-century—of a commercialized, money economy. No doubt this development drew by way of elective affinity upon existing attitudes and behavioral tendencies inculcated by decades of Puritan preaching, yet it also created disharmonies both with the first settlers' pious restorationism and with the style of most of the early towns. Much of the history of the Bay colony in the seventeenth century is, indeed, that of a rapidly modernizing society, but it is a grave mistake to see there an untroubled evolution from foundations built in the 1630s or 1640s.

7. Richard D. Brown, *Modernization,* 11, and see 36–38, 40–43.

At many points Perry Miller's rendering of that story has been altered or confuted by subsequent writers, but his strategic high-lighting of the oblique and unanticipated consequences of events is a contribution of permanent value. Areas of continuity there were, and it would be an equally disagreeable error to style the colony's earliest phase as the inert antithesis of modernization. The inevitability and relative rapidity of the changes traced, for instance, in Kenneth Lock-ridge's study of Dedham show how different even a comparatively conservative New England town was from the undynamic commu-nities of peasant Europe to which he (perhaps inadvisedly) compares them. But it remains true that neither the traceable motives of the founders nor the patterns of the first towns or the larger colonial society in the early period embodied any deliberate impulse toward a progressive civilization. Only in the most refractory sense was the first New England an initial phase of the modern, and hence the tran-sition from the 1630s to the 1660s and beyond eludes the smoothing phrases of consensus history. As much (if not more) an affair of dis-location as of organic development, it confronts the historian with a classically ironic misfit between intentions and consequences. It was the accompanying psychic distress and restructuring that came to primary expression in the jeremiads. They are the register of a severe discontinuity in both experience and hope.[8]

What should engage the attention in all of this is not only the refraction or loss of original content but the fact that in conscious theory the Puritan impulse described in this study characteristi-cally worked *against* the grain of those developments that twentieth-century historians most often identify as signs of modernization. One need only recall the colonists' handling of the d'Aulnay cri-sis or their modifications of law and judicial practice in the name of Mosaic equity, for the common and manifestly Puritan aim displayed in such examples was bibliocracy; it was the increase of biblical-mythic jurisdiction over public life. Here the instructive contrast is with James Harrington's recognition of economic and class factors as determinants of political behavior, or with John Wise's ground-

8. Ronald P. Dufour also calls attention to the sense of "hesitancy and con-flict" as well as the "traumatic restructuring of the human psyche" that normally accompany modernization ("Modernization in Colonial Massachusetts, 1630–1763" [Ph.D. diss., College of William and Mary, 1982], 18).

ing of constitutional authority upon reason and natural law, or with Thomas Hobbes's effort to free the political order from subservience to theology. For they held in common a secularizing spirit of revulsion against biblical programs, now deemed narrow and destructive of the public peace, and a quest for natural principles of order that should release mankind from mythic confinements and clear a way for the higher pursuits of reason, science, commerce, and property. Among the truly modern notes of the century, they shared a flat oppugnancy to classic Puritan objectives.

Again, one should be reminded of the continuing hold of Deuteronomic and restorationist ideals among those who spoke as Jeremiahs to their societies from 1663 to 1675. Undeniably, at a number of points those who decried the declension about them stood in an ambivalent, half-accepting relation to the forces reshaping their society, but their most considered contribution to the times was in the best tradition of Puritan witness. However vainly, they summoned themselves and their auditors *back* to a fixed and original simplicity, not *forward* to a dynamic commercial metropolis. If in good time a civilization did arise that "tie[d] up *past* with *bad* (in one word: *backward*), and *future* with *good* (*progressive*)"—one in which social life was held "open to change, [was] expected indeed to change of itself, or if it [did] not, to *be* changed"—it was altogether alien to their vision of American purposes.[9] Having nothing consciously new to offer and standing second to none in their hunger for stability, they belonged, to that degree, to the traditional world we have lost rather than the world yet to be gained by commercial enterprise and scientific revolution.

Yet there is a final point to pursue, and it hinges upon recognition that modernization, understood to include a shift in perspective toward the future, is not the all-encompassing story of historical American thought. We do not speak here of the many traditionalist ideas that have been a constant component in the nation's intellectual life, but of the career of specifically primitivist opinion in both secular and religious contexts. In fact, the recurrent pattern of recourse to a golden age has yet to find its historian, but a variety of preliminary findings are available.

9. Ernest Gellner, *Thought and Change* (London, 1964), 3; Peter Laslett, *The World We Have Lost*, 2d ed. (New York, 1972), 4.

Thus Edwin S. Gaustad has shown "how much the sentiment of restoration and restitution prevailed in eighteenth-century America . . . [and] balanced millennial hope with an intense . . . nostalgia." Gordon S. Wood has determined that the ideal of "a golden Anglo-Saxon age" before the Norman Conquest informed the Pennsylvania state constitution of 1776. According to Catherine L. Albanese, citizens of the early Republic understood their new Fourth of July celebration as "an annual event during which one left the profane time of ordinary activity and participated in a reality which happened *in illo tempore*. The Fourth . . . was sacred time in which the rememberers of the great proclamation [the Declaration of Independence] no longer merely recollected, but lived the event in its own moment." Richard T. Hughes has found that a number of Old South intellectuals drew Old and New Testament sources together with the American Puritan foundation into a "southern primordium," this to function as a "lodestone of the white, southern identity worked out in defense of the 'peculiar institution.'" David Noble has argued at length that "many of our historians have written . . . to demonstrate that change throughout the history of the republic is mere appearance and that ultimate reality in America resides in the immutable time of origins in 1776 or 1789." John Tipple attributes to the Populist movement the view that "the way out [of difficulty] was the way back. The American economy must be restored to a former golden time of competitive capitalism." Even that lexicographical landmark, Noah Webster's *American Dictionary* (1828), embodied the author's aim to "*purify* the American language; this he aimed to do by restoring it to the condition of the 'best' language of the 'best' period in England."[10] These and many similar observations in modern schol-

10. Edwin S. Gaustad, "Restitution, Revolution, and the American Dream," *Journal of the American Academy of Religion*, XLIV (1976), 78; Gordon S. Wood, *The Creation of the American Republic, 1776–1787* (Chapel Hill, N.C., 1972), 227; Catherine L. Albanese, *Sons of the Fathers: The Civil Religion of the American Revolution* (Philadelphia, 1976), 189–190; David W. Noble, *The Eternal Adam and the New World Garden: The Central Myth in the American Novel since 1830* (New York, 1968), ix; Richard T. Hughes, "A Civic Theology for the South: The Case of Benjamin M. Palmer," *Journal of Church and State*, XXV (1983), 450; John Tipple, "The Robber Baron in the Gilded Age: Entrepreneur or Iconoclast?" in H. Wayne Morgan, ed., *The Gilded Age: A Reappraisal* (Syracuse, N.Y., 1963), 29; Daniel Boorstin, *The Americans: The*

arly literature point to the recurrence of a protean but recognizably restorationist configuration that deserves more attention from intellectual historians.

Return and recovery, often joined to censure of human invention in the religious sphere, has been an especially powerful invocation within many American Protestant communities. Some decades ago, Sidney Mead remarked upon "the tendency chronic in Christendom but perhaps more acute among Englishmen, to support every contemporary innovation by an appeal to 'primitive Christianity.'" He also maintained that "throughout the whole period of rapid adaptation to the exigencies of the 'frontier' . . . most of the ministerial leaders continued to insist . . . that there was really nothing new but only the repristination of the apostolic and hence normative ways." These comments clearly pointed to historically powerful and neglected themes, but ones that have since received relatively scant attention.[11] In 1980, Richard T. Hughes claimed that, however varied the specific formulas, veneration of a prehistorical "primordium" had determined "the theological method . . . most dominant throughout much of the American experience." Later, two dissertations, one treating Roger Williams's preoccupation with "restauration," the other surveying the role of "Christian primitivism" among nineteenth-century Mormons, came to stand virtually alone as extended studies of the ideal of repristination in a specific context.[12]

Yet many of the themes and concerns (and much of the terminology) of the foregoing chapters have been constituent to a variety of religious communities throughout American history. They have

---

Colonial Experience (New York, 1964), 280. Webster's best age dated from the accession of Elizabeth I (1558) to the death of George II (1760) (Boorstin, 280). See also Wood, *Creation of the American Republic*, 227.

11. Sidney E. Mead, "The Rise of the Evangelical Conception of the Ministry in America (1607–1850)," in H. Richard Niebuhr and Daniel D. Williams, eds., *The Ministry in Historical Perspectives* (New York, 1956), 211. See also Richard Hofstadter, *Anti-Intellectualism in American Life* (New York, 1963), 82–83.

12. Richard T. Hughes, "From Civil Dissent to Civil Religion—and Beyond," *Religion in Life*, XLIX (1980), 268; Marvin S. Hill, "The Role of Christian Primitivism in the Origin and Development of the Mormon Kingdom, 1830–44" (Ph.D. diss., University of Chicago, 1968); Crawford Leonard Allen, " 'The Restauration of Zion': Roger Williams and the Quest for the Primitive Church" (Ph.D. diss., University of Iowa, 1984).

proved particularly useful to groups marking a fresh and purifying start in Christianity on the basis of a new dispensation or a schism from an established tradition. Thus was the Campbellite struggle to separate American Protestantism from the "accruing embarrassments of the [post-biblical] ages," thus the Mormon claim to have overcome the apostasy of centuries through restoration of biblical church and priesthood, thus the Christian Scientists' drive to reinstate primitive Christianity and its lost element of healing, or thus the variety of holiness and pentecostal schisms all centered upon a recovery of primitively certified but forgotten ecstasy.[13]

And often enough the more traditional evangelical denominations have signaled "object[ion] to all human inventions and additions" in the worship and service of God and recalled and testified to their own beginnings in the reclamation of primitive norms and forms. This was true as well of the Philadelphia Quakers who brought about a spiritual reformation of their faith community in the late eighteenth century. They were driven by awareness of "a great declension in many professing among us from the primitive Simplicity of our Forefathers." And it was true of the liberal Arminians of the same century and the Unitarians and Universalists of the age of William Ellery Channing and the Ballous, all of whom "denounced . . . creeds and dogmas as man-made corruptions" and "were attempting to get at the historical truth of the gospel, and to return to the practices of primitive Christianity." One modern authority on the dispensationalist premillennialism that has dominated American Protestant eschatology since the 1880s reminds us that even latter-day watchers for the Second Coming "[take their cues] from the first century" and strive to "restate what the Apostles taught."[14]

13. H. Shelton Smith, Robert T. Handy, and Lefferts A. Loetscher, *American Christianity: An Historical Interpretation with Representative Documents*, 2 vols. (New York, 1960–1963), I, 583.

14. Samuel Miller, *Presbyterianism the Truly Primitive and Apostolical Constitution of the Church of Christ* (Philadelphia, 1835), 66; Frederick B. Tolles, *Meeting House and Counting House: The Quaker Merchants of Philadelphia, 1682–1783* (Chapel Hill, N.C., 1948), 236; Robert J. Wilson III, *The Benevolent Deity: Ebenezer Gay and the Rise of Rational Religion in New England, 1696–1787* (Philadelphia, 1984), 128; Timothy P. Weber, *Living in the Shadow of the Second Coming: American Premillennialism, 1875–1982*, 2d ed. (Grand Rapids, Mich., 1983), 38.

A review of such instances (countless more could be supplied) reveals a remarkable fact: from the first American Arminians to today's dispensationalists, all of the examples cited reflect some measure of Puritan inheritance. That influence was not limited to the Congregational, Presbyterian, and Baptist churches that stand closest historically to sixteenth- and seventeenth-century English dissent. Figures as diverse as Alexander Campbell, Joseph Smith, William Ellery Channing, and Mary Baker Eddy were all products in some degree, even if by way of rebellion and radical revision, of the Reformed-Puritan ethos that dominated American Protestantism through the early twentieth century. It is well to recognize that this heritage has spoken with a contrapuntal voice. In many ways its adherents—and its rebels—have contributed to those features of our civilization that we deem modern. Yet, through their recurrent emphasis upon the supremacy of the first, they also have preserved an archaic reflex of thought and behavior. Further investigation of their varied primitivist loyalties will add a needed strand of complexity to future interpretations of the American Protestant past.

APPENDIX 1

PRIMITIVISM

AND MYTH

Whate were the elements of conscious theory that defined English and American Puritanism for the century and more after about 1565? An extensive sampling of English Protestant theology from the age of Cranmer and Tyndale to the end of the century yielded the hypothesis that the concerns generating Puritan dissent in the decades after Elizabeth's accession were yoked to a distinctive premise regarding the nature and authority of the Bible: that the Book drew much of its special magic from its disclosure of the first. This insight, pursued further, led to the primitivist construct dominating these pages. As the project unfolded, I found valuable conceptual assistance—and some useful terminology—in the writings of Arthur O. Lovejoy, George Boas, and Mircea Eliade. They offered ways of conceptualizing systems of thought, attentive to man's pilgrimage through time, in which the "first" is deemed normative. I will clarify here my indebtedness to them and explain more fully the relevance of their work to students of the Puritan way.

In their seminal study, *Primitivism and Related Ideas in Antiquity* (1935), Lovejoy and Boas formulated a detailed conceptual morphology of Western primitivism from classical to modern times. Of the two major types of primitivism they discerned, "chronological primitivism" rests upon the assumption that "the highest degree of excellence or happiness in man's life existed at the beginning of history." This might be linked to a theory of historical decline, "undulation," or cycles; but in association with historical phases of Christian belief, it was more often related to a "Theory of Decline and Future Restoration":

The best age of mankind hitherto was at the beginning; [but] there has been in the past . . . a progressive decline; . . . but . . . at some future time there will, or may, be a restoration of man's primeval goodness, or happiness, or both.

Chronological primitivism often was combined with "cultural primitivism," embodying "the discontent of the civilized with civilization, . . . the belief of men living in a relatively highly evolved and complex cultural condition that a life far simpler . . . is a more desirable life." Common to both chronological and cultural primitivism was the belief that the original simplicity of "nature" had been corrupted by the clumsy and superfluous additions of human "art," and that a program of social reform was desirable to return society to its primeval estate.[1]

Many points of correspondence to that typology will be recognizable to students familiar with Puritan concepts of the apostolic age, the Roman apostasy, the contemporary "restitution" of apostolic belief, and the dissenters' persistent testimony against the "highly evolved and complex" condition of Catholic and Anglican religion. Yet a close familiarity with the Puritan materials might also disclose some discrepancies. For instance, the first and best age featured in Puritan preaching and polemic is not described adequately as a best time characterized by a high degree of excellence or happiness. Lovejoy and Boas, again, give little account of the special exemplary obligations, deriving from the first age, that the English dissenters expounded endlessly. In these and other respects, the above themes require substantial supplement if they accurately are to direct us to the primitivist design of Puritan thought.

Mircea Eliade offers an alternative view of "primitive times," in the context of ancient myth, that better accords with certain features of Protestant perspective. Three aspects of his interpretation should receive our careful attention. First, a *myth* is defined as a dramatic recounting of a "sacred history," a narrative of events that took place, not in ordinary historical or "profane" time, but in the supernaturally charged "strong" or "great" "time of the beginnings" in which human history originated. Mythic actors are not everyday human figures. They are "Supernatural Beings," gods, heroes, or ancestors,

1. Arthur O. Lovejoy and George Boas, *Primitivism and Related Ideas in Antiquity* (Baltimore, 1935), 2–3, 7, 11–13, 16.

and their significant activities and the manifestation of their sacred powers are the focus of the mythic story.[2]

Second, Eliade contends that archaic men were acutely aware of mortality, the impermanent human condition in historical time. Mythic drama, with its display of pretemporal, superhuman, and immortal occurrence, invited them to a consoling "nostalgia for the perfection of beginnings." In this context nostalgia meant far more than wistful remembrance, for men and women of early societies refused to live solely in the linear present. They wished to be "seized by the sacred, exalting power of the [primal] events" and thereby to transcend transience and death. Hence they marked out a second and "circular" path, periodically leaving their historical moment behind to "travel *back*," as it were, and achieve imaginative reentry into the drama of the great time. Each retelling or reiteration of mythic story was a cycle of *return*.[3]

Third, on one level, by relating the origin of the world and "all the primordial events in consequence of which man became what he is today," myths provided a meaningful explanation of mankind's current situation. But the "foremost function of myth" was, not to explain the world, but to reveal "the exemplary model for all significant human activities." Returning to the time of origins meant more than a passive absorption in the sacred events, for myth also tied men to the first through an axis of pattern and imitation. Early peoples not only relived, they reenacted original deeds in dramatically vivid rituals. Their ritual action copied mythic "archetypes." It "exactly *repeat[ed]*" an act performed at the beginning of time by a god, a hero, or an ancestor." Thus the ancient Babylonian New Year's ceremony included a mimed re-creation of the cosmogonic battle in which chaos was ended and the present order founded. Beyond the sphere of ritual, in archaic societies the entire complex of important cultural acts echoed events of the strong time, for "everything which lacks an exemplary model is 'meaningless,' i.e., it lacks reality." Without ties to the first, there was no significance beyond the pass-

2. Mircea Eliade, *Myths, Dreams, and Mysteries: The Encounter between Contemporary Faiths and Archaic Realities*, trans. Philip Mairet (New York, 1960), 23; Eliade, *Myth and Reality*, trans. Willard R. Trask (New York, 1963), 6–11, 19.

3. Mircea Eliade, *The Sacred and the Profane: The Nature of Religion*, trans. Willard R. Trask (New York, 1959), 70, 91; Eliade, *Myth and Reality*, 19.

ing moment. Hence salmon fishing, the cultivation of yams, or any of the range of valued activities within a given culture likewise found its formative instance in mythic story.[4]

Eliade's wide-ranging application of these ideas, with many additions not touched upon here, unleashed a vigorous controversy in the history of religions and related disciplines—a debate not entered here. My contention is, simply, that the concepts of the Great Time, of periodic return to that time and imitation of its qualities and deeds, illuminate aspects of Puritan biblicism not sufficiently represented in the work of Lovejoy and Boas. It is true that Eliade's "great time" refers to a realm of prehistory. As he himself has observed, the biblical narratives historicize myth; that is, they represent sacred event as temporal occurrence; they depict first times as lying within rather than outside or before human history. Yet he also observes a substantial carryover of mythic elements in historical Christian uses of Scripture and specifically has called attention to the American Puritans' passion to "return to the Golden Age of Christianity."[5]

Undisputably, in important respects the Puritan definition of the human career in time was more historical than mythic. The very appeal to an original past, with its corollary that the church had undergone phases of development from original excellence to current corruption, suggests that primitivist conceptions are not as history-less as often claimed, and most of the time Puritan perspectives hewed close to the earthy realism of scriptural events. And yet, and with greater force than magisterial Protestants generally, they contrasted the biblical era with the succeeding degenerate ages in ways that closely parallel Eliade's distinction between an originative, repeatable primordium and the unsignifying, profane times of ordinary human history. If cautiously applied, those concepts open attractively unconventional avenues of approach to the meaning of Puritanism. The proof, of course, is in their application and the new thresholds of understanding to which they may lead, here and elsewhere.

4. Mircea Eliade, *Myth and Reality*, 6–8, 11; Eliade, *Cosmos and History: The Myth of the Eternal Return*, trans. Willard R. Trask (1954; New York, 1959), 22, 34, 35, 55 (and see 21–27).

5. Mircea Eliade, "Paradise and Utopia," in Frank E. Manuel, ed., *Utopias and Utopian Thought* (Boston, 1965), 267. For the retention of mythic "return" within Christianity, see, for example, Eliade, *Mysteries*, 29–31.

APPENDIX 2

RELIGIOUS

DECLENSION IN

SEVENTEENTH-CENTURY

NEW ENGLAND

*T*he claim that the second half of the seventeenth century was a period of decreasing religious vitality (manifest in steadily declining church membership), although a commonplace of the scholarly literature, was compromised by Robert Pope's fine *Half-Way Covenant*. Probably the most noteworthy of his findings is that 1675 marked a turning point in New England's religious history. With the outbreak in that year of a devastating Indian war, a period of intermittent crisis began that triggered fresh religious concern and an impressive revival of church membership. The discovery of a "new religiosity" after 1675 effectively qualifies the assumption of a general decline throughout the period, although Pope's data do not prove that post-1675 piety, motivated to a large degree by extraordinary psychosocial circumstances, was in quality or style like that of the founders.[1]

---

1. Robert G. Pope, *The Half-Way Covenant: Church Membership in Puritan New England* (Princeton, N.J., 1969), 185–275, esp. 236; Robert G. Pope, "New England versus the New England Mind: The Myth of Declension," in Alden T. Vaughan and Francis J. Bremer, eds., *Puritan New England: Essays on Religion, Society, and Culture* (New York, 1977), 319. See also the critiques by Stephen Foster, *Their Solitary Way: The Puritan Social Ethic in the First*

Pope's sweeping denial of declension in the period before 1675, however, is much less persuasive. He rightly complains that the term "declension" often is employed in a vague and uncritical manner, but he does not provide the comparison of the theological and devotional styles of the first and following generations upon which a more precise definition of terms, and certainly his judgment that the concept of declension "totally misconstrues" seventeenth-century religious trends, must in part depend. He acknowledges that fewer second-generation Puritans experienced a conversion, but when he insists that this signals "the maturation of a sectarian movement" *rather than* decline, he undervalues both the idealistic purposes of the earlier period and the long-standing and crucial place of "effectual calling" in the pietist soteriology of the Spiritual Brotherhood.[2] There are also the usual phenomena of routinization to consider. It is sociologically contrary to assume that the demonstrably vivid spirituality of a once-persecuted and militant people—whose marked disciplinary ethos had arisen amid overpopulation, vagabondage, and disorder in Elizabethan England—could be bequeathed intact to children of an era of ready-made religious and material privileges.[3]

A slump in church membership there was. Pope's own statistical

---

Century of Settlement in New England (New Haven, Conn., 1971), 178 n. 12; and James Hoopes, "Art as History: Perry Miller's *New England Mind*," *American Quarterly*, XXXIV (1982), 20–22. In a study of 17th-century church admissions at Milford, Connecticut, Gerald F. Moran finds "not a linear but a cyclical history of religious participation," and dates the first surge from ca. 1665 ("Religious Renewal, Puritan Tribalism, and the Family in Seventeenth-Century Milford, Connecticut," *WMQ*, 3d Ser., XXXVI [1979], 241–244).

2. Pope, "Myth," in Vaughan and Bremer, eds., *Puritan New England*, 317, 323. Cf. Stephen Foster's remark that what appeared as declension to the New Englanders must appear as "simply growth and development" to the historian ("The Godly in Transit: English Popular Protestantism and the Creation of a Puritan Establishment in America," in David D. Hall and Stephen Foster, eds., *Seventeenth-Century New England* [Colonial Society of Massachusetts, *Publications*, LXIII (Boston, 1984)], 238).

3. Connections between the Puritan "culture of discipline" and the Elizabethan and early Stuart crisis of overpopulation and vagrancy are discussed, for example, in Keith Wrightson and David Levine, *Poverty and Piety in an English Village: Terling, 1525–1700* (New York, 1979); William Hunt, *The Puritan Moment: The Coming of Revolution in an English County* (Cambridge, Mass., 1983).

study of three Boston-area churches supports the conclusion that "the middle of the century . . . marks the lowest ebb in church membership."[4] But he proposes to explain the phenomenon as an index of an actually intensified "religious scrupulosity." This theme, a speculative suggestion of Edmund S. Morgan's, also is called upon by Pope to account for another of his key findings: the refusal of a majority of Massachusetts churches to adopt the Halfway Covenant, although approved by a general synod, before the time of troubles after 1675.[5]

I can find no cogent reason to accept either this display of conservative reluctance or the refusal of many young baptized adults (presumably aware of the implications of lacking the requisite signs of a "work of grace") to seek full church membership as demonstrations of a "quality of religious scrupulosity" peculiar to the second generation. In the context of the "morphology of conversion," scrupulosity long had been a distinguishing element of Puritan piety and stood central to the entire problematic of religious assurance that had engrossed the Spiritual Brotherhood and their constituencies for three-quarters of a century before 1660. In any event, even could such a specialized hesitance be shown to have been a positive and unique trait of second-generation piety, this is not equivalent to proof that the founders' children were "equally religious," nor does it negate what Darrett Rutman aptly has called "a public and private literature of tremendous extent" bemoaning spiritual decay.[6]

Religion "is in part the human response to contingency and powerlessness"—an argument used by Pope to explain the post-1675 recovery. Then, however, the evidence that New Englanders quickly established a high level of material prosperity and social stability, enjoyed a relative absence of plague and famine, a low mortality rate, and high longevity and were spared much of the "acute anxieties and

4. Pope, "Myth," in Vaughan and Bremer, eds., *Puritan New England*, 318. A similar finding is reported in Moran, "Religious Renewal," *WMQ*, 3d Ser., XXXVI (1979), 241–243.

5. Edmund S. Morgan, "New England Puritanism: Another Approach," *WMQ*, 3d Ser., XVIII (1961), 241–242; Morgan, letter, *ibid.*, XIX (1962), 642–644.

6. Darrett B. Rutman, "God's Bridge Falling Down: 'Another Approach' to Puritanism Assayed," *ibid.*, XIX (1962), 419. The phrase "equally religious" is from Morgan, letter, *ibid.*, 643.

disruptions of experience characteristic of Puritans elsewhere" also is relevant to any interpretation of religious trends to 1675.[7]

7. Pope, "Myth," in Vaughan and Bremer, eds., *Puritan New England*, 319; Philip J. Greven, Jr., *Four Generations: Population, Land, and Family in Colonial Andover, Massachusetts* (Ithaca, N.Y., 1970), 278. See also Timothy H. Breen and Stephen Foster, "The Puritans' Greatest Achievement: A Study of Social Cohesion in Seventeenth-Century Massachusetts," in Vaughan and Bremer, eds., *Puritan New England*, 111–118; Kenneth A. Lockridge, *A New England Town, the First Hundred Years: Dedham, Massachusetts, 1636–1736* (New York, 1970), 63–75; Greven, *Four Generations*, 25–26, 109–110, 269–271. Ross W. Beales, Jr., in his study of mid-century Dorchester, concluded that "the second generation in Dorchester was not 'scrupulous' in the sense suggested by Morgan and Pope" ("The Half-Way Covenant and Religious Scrupulosity: The First Church of Dorchester, Massachusetts, as a Test Case," *WMQ*, 3d Ser., XXXI [1974], 479–480).

APPENDIX 3

SEPARATISTS

AND QUAKERS

*I*n 1938, focusing upon the period 1640–1660, A. S. P. Woodhouse provided the classic analysis of English Puritanism as a spectrum of right (Presbyterian), center (Independent), and left (sectarian) parties. In the meantime, it has become a cliché that at all times "there were right and left wings to the party and various center factions in between."[1] Yet if recognition of a spectrum of separable types has advanced understanding of Puritanism as a multiplicity within unity, it simultaneously has led to further debate over the proper terminus both to left and right. Especially for periods before 1640, a convincing case has been made for extension of Woodhouse's spectrum further to the right. Although some scholars continued to regard Presbyterianism as the conservative right, others argued cogently for inclusion of "conforming Puritans" who were dissatisfied with one or more major particulars of the Elizabethan compromise but whose taste for change did not extend to the thorough restructuring sought by the Presbyterians.[2]

1. A.S.P. Woodhouse, ed., *Puritanism and Liberty: Being the Army Debates (1647–49)*, 2d ed. (Chicago, 1951), 14–18; M. M. Knappen, *Tudor Puritanism: A Chapter in the History of Idealism* (1939; Gloucester, Mass., 1966), 339; H. G. Alexander, *Religion in England, 1559–1662* (London, 1968), 57; Jerald C. Brauer, "Reflections on the Nature of English Puritanism," *CH*, XXIII (1954), 103.

2. For the first position, see Alan Simpson, *Puritanism in Old and New England* (Chicago, 1955), 1; and David D. Hall, "Understanding the Puritans," in Herbert J. Bass, ed., *The State of American History* (Chicago, 1970), 331; for the second, see John T. McNeill, *Modern Christian Movements* (Philadelphia,

Refusal to admit this extension makes it impossible to give adequate account of the biblical-primitivist convictions of such figures as John Foxe. Guided by the belief that the first was truest, Foxe "refused throughout his life [1516–1587] to accept any office that required him to wear the vestments" required by royal injunction and the official liturgy; yet he also firmly rejected the Presbyterian positions of Thomas Cartwright, John Field, and the *Admonition to Parliament* of 1572 and suffused his huge *Acts and Monuments* with a pious royalism compliant to the monarch's supremacy in matters ecclesiastical.[3] The Puritan element in Foxe—and many others—is undeniable, even if counterbalanced by other and conflicting commitments.

Weightier issues are at stake in determination of the boundary to the left. One body of opinion, often accenting the fact that contemporaries reserved the term "Puritan" for members of the English church who sought change from within, insists that the spectrum cannot reasonably include the Separatists—those who despaired of the received church and gathered in underground or exilic congregations —and certainly not the more radical groups that sprang into prominence after 1640.[4] The opposing view portrays Puritanism as a continuum of concepts and convictions that did not stop short at the boundaries of the established church, but evolved ultimately through the whole gamut of positions leftward, including "Separatists . . . , spiritual sectarians, and miscellaneous fanatics." Much of the argument of Philip Gura's *Glimpse of Sion's Glory*, the fullest and most impressive study of "Puritan radicalism" yet to appear, is built upon the assumption that antinomian and spiritist developments in early New England retained an unequivocally Puritan character. In such

1954), 19; Alexander, *Religion in England*, 57; and Leonard J. Trinterud, ed., *Elizabethan Puritanism* (New York, 1971), 9–15.

3. This account of Foxe is drawn from Trinterud, ed., *Puritanism*, 40–45. See also *EPM*, 74, 76.

4. The principal statement here is Basil Hall, "Puritanism: The Problem of Definition," in *Studies in Church History*, II, ed. G. J. Cuming (London, 1965), 283–296. See also Michael Walzer, *The Revolution of the Saints: A Study in the Origins of Radical Politics* (New York, 1969), viii; J. Sears McGee, *The Godly Man in Stuart England: Anglicans, Puritans, and the Two Tables, 1620–1670* (New Haven, Conn., 1976), 9; Christopher Hill, *Society and Puritanism in Pre-Revolutionary England*, 2d ed. (New York, 1967), 20.

approaches the Quakers tend to receive special attention, for, as the largest and most coherent group on the far margin, they appear as the end result of a distinct evolution that served to reveal "the direction of the Puritan movement as a whole."[5]

A complete review of these issues would entail discussion of the law-covenant moralism and the conversionist, introspective pietism that was integral to the Puritan enterprise, and thus would lead us too far afield from the issues treated here. Yet the aim has been to exhibit the restorationist connections, and these too must be considered in any attempt to establish the status of Separatists, Quakers, and other groups to the left. Examined from this perspective, Separatists and Quakers are separate and largely dissimilar cases. The foregoing chapters have dealt chiefly with nonseparating positions, but they did not intend to imply a reduced commitment to the biblical strong time or the Protestant epistemology among those who took the final step of separation. As suggested, for instance, by Henry Barrow's relatively radical advocacy of legal reform as a restoration of the Mosaic Judicials, Separatist programs revealed a particularly vivid continuity of Puritan content in just this connection. Robert Browne, John Robinson, and many others represented the necessity of separation in good part by magnifying the disjuncture between the then of apostolic Christianity and the now of unrepaired declension within English Christianity. Recognition of this element affords impressive additional support for the view that the Separatists—including those who moved on to a Baptist position—retained "the greater part of those ideas and ideals which still, as hitherto, they had in common with the more conservative Puritans from among whom they came" and therefore warrant inclusion in the category "Puritan."[6]

5. McNeill, *Movements*, 19; Geoffrey F. Nuttall, *The Holy Spirit in Puritan Faith and Experience*, 2d ed. (Oxford, 1947), viii. For inclusion of the Quakers, see also Brauer, "Puritanism," *CH*, XXIII (1954), 103; Hall, "Understanding the Puritans," in Bass, ed., *The State of American History*, 331; E. Brooks Holifield, *The Covenant Sealed: The Development of Puritan Sacramental Theology in Old and New England, 1570–1720* (New Haven, Conn., 1974), x; Michael Eugene Mooney, "Millennialism and Antichrist in New England, 1630–1760" (Ph.D. diss., Syracuse University, 1982), 89; Hugh Barbour, *The Quakers in Puritan England* (New Haven, Conn., 1964), 2.

6. Nuttall, *Holy Spirit*, 9. But cf. Paul Christianson, "Reformers and the Church of England under Elizabeth I and the Early Stuarts," *Journal of Ecclesiastical History*, XXXI (1980), 474, 481.

When we turn to the Quakers, however, we are brought to a different result. Geoffrey Nuttall, in his treatise *The Holy Spirit in Puritan Faith and Experience*, assembled the largest battery of arguments to prove that Quakers "cannot be denied the name" of Puritan. He rested his case upon the assumption—impossible to sustain today— that Puritanism can be construed essentially as "a movement toward immediacy" dwelling upon experience of the Holy Spirit within. In this sense Quaker spiritism was merely its natural extension. A similar approach was adopted in Alan Simpson's elegant study *Puritanism in Old and New England*: "An enterprise which began in the sixteenth century by exhorting men to prepare themselves for a miracle of grace and ended [in Quakerism] by asserting the presence of the Holy Spirit in every individual is one movement."[7]

It is easier in retrospect, with a much larger body of detailed scholarship on hand, to appreciate the vagueness of these formulas as well as their inattention to sources of the Quaker impulse that stand altogether outside the world of magisterial Protestantism. But, more to the point, how are we to find a place for this spiritist turn of events unequivocally *within* "one movement" which for nearly a century before the Quaker era had specialized in celebration of the objective events, norms, and archetypes of the Book of Books? Parenthetically, one might add that in this as in other respects the earlier clashes in both Old and New England between Puritan and antinomian opinions strongly adumbrated the later Quaker conflicts. For in a number of antinomian patterns, and definitely among the English Grindletonians and the Massachusetts Hutchinsonians, an unmistakably spiritist element emerged; and this with much justice the orthodoxy hastened to damn as a threat to the biblical center of Reformed and Puritan faith.[8]

7. Nuttall, *Holy Spirit*, 91; Simpson, *Puritanism*, 1.

8. For comment on the Grindletonians, see Nuttall, *Holy Spirit*, 178–179. For the spiritist element in New England antinomianism, see David D. Hall, ed., *The Antinomian Controversy, 1636–1638* (Middletown, Conn., 1968), 203, 221, 230, 235, 238. Hall concludes that "the Antinomianism of Anne Hutchinson . . . prefigured the radical stance of the Quakers" (20). In all three of the crucial considerations defining "Puritanism"—law-covenant moralism, pietist inwardness focused to a large degree upon the quest for assurance, and biblicist primitivism—New England antinomianism moved decisively beyond established boundaries. If the extant reports of antinomian opinions, all from hostile sources, can be trusted, the critique of Puritan "legalism" and of false devotion

This is not to deny that Quakerism—or spiritist antinomianism—was in measure a development out of the Puritan background. It is not to deny that numerous figures of the 1640s and 1650s passed through a gamut of phases leading through Presbyterianism to Quakerism and in some cases beyond or that Quakerism incorporated sizable residues of Puritan spirituality and language together with many an invocation of biblical drama and teaching. It is to affirm that on the spiritist fringe beyond Separatism the lines of continuity with the biblicist avowals of a Thomas Cartwright or a William Perkins blur beyond recognition. There an essentially new species of religious endeavor began to emerge. It minimized the objective and historical understandings of biblical event that at all times had been integral to Reformed and Puritan perspectives. It hastened to repudiate the classic Puritan passion for recovery of primitively given forms and ordinances. All of this belonged to the realm of "outward" observance that Quakers tirelessly opposed to the spiritual source within. Early Quaker spirituality will be found to have its primitivist structures, too, although they have not been examined in detail; but in this context, reviling of human invention and appeal to "the ancient apostolic ORDER of the Church of Christ" took form relative to understandings of authority and imagination supplied by the contra-Puritan principle of the Inner Light, a principle invoked in deliberate and strident defiance of every claim to govern human reason and imagination by the Protestant epistemology.[9] While, therefore, it is vital to comprehend continuities between Puritan and Quaker content, it is necessary to insist that seventeenth-century spiritism was, not so much a bridge taking many thousands of English Protestants to a farther Puritan precinct, as a prism projecting them toward the greatly differing world of the Radical Reformation.

---

to the scriptural "letter" extended explicitly and with some venom to sacred archetypes, to the Sabbath and the "ordinances of Christ." John Winthrop, *The History of New England from 1630 to 1649*, ed. James Savage (1853; New York, 1972), I, 253; WWP, 129; Hall, ed., *Antinomian Controversy*, 234, 300.

9. Hugh Barbour and Arthur O. Roberts, eds., *Early Quaker Writings, 1650–1700* (Grand Rapids, Mich., 1973), 515.

BIBLIOGRAPHY

PRIMARY SOURCES

MANUSCRIPTS

Goffe, Stephen. To William Boswell, June 1663. Add. Ms. 6394, I, fol. 137. British Library, London.

Gouge, William. Manuscript notes of sermon. Sloane Ms. 250, fol. 203. British Library, London.

Mather Family Papers. American Antiquarian Society. Worcester, Mass.

Shepard, Thomas. "A Breefe Answer to a Breefe Discourse concerning the Punishment of Theft, Single Fornication, Rape, etc. . . ." [1642?]. Shepard Family Papers, Massachusetts Historical Society.

Shepard Family Papers. Massachusetts Historical Society. Boston.

Stone, Samuel. "The Whole Body of Divinity in a Catechetical Way Handled." Massachusetts Historical Society. Boston.

PUBLISHED WORKS

(Authors' names as they appear on the title page have been silently translated, regularized, and expanded.)

Ainsworth, Henry. *The Book of Psalmes*. . . . Amsterdam, 1612.

———. *Solomon's Song of Songs*. N.p., 1623.

Allen, James. *Neglect of Supporting and Maintaining the Pure Worship of God, by the Professing People of God: Is a God-Provoking and Land-Wasting Sin*. Boston, 1687.

Allin, John. *Animadversions upon the Antisynodalia Americana*. Cambridge, Mass., 1664.

Allin, John, and Thomas Shepard. *A Defence of the Answer Made unto the Nine Questions or Positions Sent from New-England, against the Reply Thereto by . . . John Ball*. London, 1648.

Alsted, John Henry. *The Beloved City*. . . . London, 1643.

Ames, William. *Conscience with the Power and Cases Thereof*. N.p., 1639.

———. *A Fresh Suit against Human Ceremonies in God's Worship*. N.p., 1633.

———. *The Marrow of Theology* (1629). Translated and edited by John D. Eusden. Boston, 1968.

———. *Technometry* (1643). Translated and edited by Lee W. Gibbs. Philadelphia, 1979.

"Articles Objected . . . against Charles Chauncey . . ." (1630). Massachusetts Historical Society, *Proceedings*, 1st Ser., XIII (Boston, 1875), 337–340.

Aspinwall, William. *A Brief Description of the Fifth Monarchy.* . . . London, 1653.

Bacon, Francis. *The Works of Francis Bacon.* Edited by Basil Montagu. New ed. 3 vols. Philadelphia, 1851.

Bale, John. *The Image of Both Churches* (1545–1547). In Henry Christmas, ed., *Select Works of John Bale* (Cambridge, 1849).

———. *King Johan.* Edited by Barry B. Adams. San Marino, Calif., 1969.

———. *The Laboryouse Journey and Search of Johan Leplande.* London, 1549.

Ball, John. *A Short Treatise: Contayning All the Principall Grounds of Christian Religion.* London, 1629.

Bancroft, Richard. *A Sermon Preached at Paules Crosse.* London, 1588.

Barnes, Robert. *The Whole Workes of W[illiam] Tyndall, John Frith, and Doct[or Robert] Barnes.* London, 1573.

Barrow, Henry. *The Writings of Henry Barrow, 1587–1590.* Edited by Leland H. Carlson. London, 1962.

Bayly, Lewis. *The Practice of Pietie.* London, 1630.

Baynes, Paul. *Briefe Directions unto a Godly Life.* London, 1637.

———. *A Commentarie upon the First and Second Chapters of Saint Paul to the Colossians.* . . . London, 1635.

———. *A Commentarie upon the First Chapter of the Epistle of Saint Paul, Written to the Ephesians.* London, 1618.

———. *The Diocesans Tryall.* N.p., 1621.

———. *A Helpe to True Happinesse.* 3d ed. London, 1635.

———. *Two Godly and Fruitfull Treatises.* London, 1619.

Becon, Thomas. *The Catechism of Thomas Becon.* Edited by John Ayre. Cambridge, 1844.

———. *The Early Works of Thomas Becon.* Edited by John Ayre. Cambridge, 1843.

Bell, Thomas. *The Regiment of the Church.* London, 1606.

Bernard, Richard. *The Faithfull Shephard.* London, 1607.

———. *A Key of Knowledge for the Opening of the Secret Mysteries of St. Johns Mysticall Revelation.* London, 1617.

Bilson, Thomas. *The Perpetuall Government of Christs Church.* London, 1610.

Bolton, Robert. *Mr. Boltons Last and Learned Worke of the Foure Last Things.* . . . 3d ed. London, 1635.

———. *Two Sermons Preached at Northampton at Two Severall Assises There.* London, 1635.

Bownde, Nicholas. *The Doctrine of the Sabbath.* London, 1595.

———. *The Holy Exercise of Fasting.* Cambridge, 1604.

Bradford, John. *The Writings of John Bradford.* Edited by Aubrey Townsend. Cambridge, 1853.

Bradford, William. *Of Plymouth Plantation, 1620–1647.* Edited by Samuel Eliot Morison. New York, 1952.

Bradshaw, William. *A Direction for the Weaker Sort of Christians.* London, 1609.

——— . *A Plaine and Pithy Exposition of the Second Epistle of Paul to the Thessalonians.* London, 1620.

——— . *Several Treatises of Worship and Ceremonies.* Cambridge, 1660.

Bradstreet, Anne. *The Works of Anne Bradstreet in Prose and Verse.* Edited by John Harvard Ellis. New York, 1932.

Bridges, John. *A Defence of the Government Established in the Church of Englande for Ecclesiasticall Matters.* London, 1587.

Brightman, Thomas. *Brightmans Predictions; or, Prophesies.* London, 1641.

——— . *A Commentary on the Canticles.* London, 1644.

——— . *A Most Comfortable Exposition of the Last and Most Difficult Part of the Prophecie of Daniel.* N.p., 1635.

——— . *The Revelation of St. John Illustrated with an Analysis and Scholions.* Leiden, 1616.

——— . *A Revelation of the Apocalyps.* Amsterdam, 1611.

——— . *Reverend Mr. Brightmans Judgement; or, Prophesies.* London, 1641.

——— . *The Workes of That Famous, Reverend, and Learned Divine, Mr. Thomas Brightman.* London, 1644.

Brinsley, John. *The Third Part of the True Watch.* London, 1622.

Brocardo, Jiacopo. *The Revelation of S. Jhon Reveled.* Translated by James Sanford. London, 1582.

Broughton, Hugh. *A Revelation of the Holy Apocalyps.* N.p., 1610.

Bucer, Martin. *De Regno Christi* (1550). In Wilhelm Pauck, ed., *Melanchthon and Bucer.*

Bulkeley, Peter. *The Gospel-Covenant; or, The Covenant of Grace Opened.* London, 1646.

Bullinger, Henry. *The Decades of Henry Bullinger.* Edited by Thomas Harding. 4 vols. Cambridge, 1849.

——— . *A Hundred Sermons upon the Apocalipse of Jesu Christ.* London, 1573.

Burton, Henry. *The Grounds of Christian Religion.* London, 1635.

——— . *Israels Fast.* London, 1628.

——— . *The Seven Vials.* London, 1628.

Byfield, Nicholas. *The Rule of Faith.* London, 1626.

Calamy, Edmund. *Englands Looking-Glasse.* London, 1642.

Calvin, John. *Aphorismes of Christian Religion; or, A Verie Compendious Abridgement of M. I[ohn] Calvins Institutions.* Abridged by John Piscator. London, 1596.

——— . *Institutes of the Christian Religion.* Edited by John T. McNeill. 2 vols. Philadelphia, 1960.

——— . *Institution of Christian Religion.* Translated by Thomas Norton. London, 1562.

Cardwell, Edward, ed. *Documentary Annals of the Reformed Church of England.* 2 vols. Oxford, 1844.

——— , ed. *Synodalia.* 2 vols. Oxford, 1842.

Cartwright, Thomas. *A Commentary upon the Epistle of Saint Paule Written to the Colossians.* London, 1612.

[———— ?]. *The Holy Exercise of a True Fast* (1580). In Albert Peel and
    Leland H. Carlson, eds., *Cartwrightiana* (London, 1951), 118–143.
————. *A Replye to an Answere Made of M. Doctor Whitgifte. . . .* N.p.,
    1573.
————. *The Second Replie of Thomas Cartwright: Agaynst Master Doctor
    Whitgiftes Second Answer touching the Churche Discipline*. [Zurich], 1675.
————. *A Treatise of Christian Religion*. London, 1616.
Chaderton, Laurence. *An Exellent and Godly Sermon . . . Preached at Paules
    Crosse. . . .* London, 1580.
[Chauncy, Charles?]. *Anti-Synodalia Scripta Americana*. Appended to Jonathan
    Mitchel, *Propositions concerning the Subject of Baptism and Consociation of
    Churches . . .* (London, 1662).
Chauncy, Charles, *et al.* "Opinions of Three Ministers on Unnatural Vice,
    1642." Appendix 10 in William Bradford, *Of Plymouth Plantation,
    1620–1647*, ed. Samuel Eliot Morison.
A Christian Letter of Certaine English Protestants. . . . Middelburg, Neth.,
    1599.
Clap, Roger. *Memoirs of Capt[ain] Roger Clap . . .* (1731). In Alexander
    Young, ed., *Chronicles of the First Planters of the Colony of Massachusetts
    Bay, from 1623 to 1636*, 343–367.
Cleaver, Robert. *A Godly Form of Householde Governement. . . .* London,
    1612.
Cobbet, Thomas. *The Civil Magistrates' Power in Matters of Religion Modestly
    Debated. . . .* London, 1653.
"Conference of the Elders of Massachusetts with the Rev. Robert Lenthal, of
    Weymouth. . . ." *Congregational Quarterly*, LXXIV (1877), 232–248.
Cooper, Thomas. *The Blessing of Japheth, Proving the Gathering in of the
    Gentiles, and Finall Conversion of the Jewes*. London, 1615.
Cosin, John. *The Correspondence of John Cosin*. Edited by George Ornsby. Vol.
    I. Publications of the Surtees Society, LII (Durham, 1869).
Cotton, John. *An Abstract; or, The Lawes of New England. . . .* London, 1641.
————. "An Apologetical Preface" to John Norton, *The Answer to the Whole
    Set of Questions of . . . William Apollonius . . .* , trans. Douglas Horton.
————. *A Brief Exposition of the Whole Book of Canticles, or, Song of
    Solomon*. London, 1642.
————. *A Brief Exposition with Practical Observations upon the Whole Book of
    Canticles*. London, 1655.
————. *Christ The Fountaine of Life*. London, 1651.
————. *The Churches Resurrection. . . .* London, 1642.
————. *A Copy of a Letter of Mr. Cotton of Boston*. [London], 1641.
————. *A Copy of a Letter from Mr. Cotton to Lord Say and Seal in the Year
    1636*. In Edmund S. Morgan, ed., *Puritan Political Ideas, 1558–1794*.
————. "Cotton's Reasons for His Removal to New England" (1634). In
    Alexander Young, ed., *Chronicles of the First Planters of the Colony of
    Massachusetts Bay, from 1623 to 1636*, 438–444.
[———— ?]. *A Discourse about Civil Government in a New Plantation Whose*

Design Is Religion. Cambridge, Mass., 1663.

——. *An Exposition upon the Thirteenth Chapter of the Revelation.* London, 1655.

——. *Gods Promise to His Plantations* (1630). *Old South Leaflets* (Boston, n.d.), III, no. 53.

——. *The Grounds and Ends of Baptisme of Children of the Faithfull.* London, 1647.

——. *John Cotton on the Churches of New England.* Edited by Larzer Ziff. Cambridge, Mass., 1968.

——. *The Keys of the Kingdom of Heaven* (1644). In Larzer Ziff, ed., *John Cotton on the Churches of New England,* 69–164.

——. *A Letter of Mr. John Cottons . . . to Mr. [Roger] Williams . . .* (1643). In *The Complete Writings of Roger Williams,* I, 295–311.

——. *Master John Cotton's Answer to Master Roger Williams* (1647). In *The Complete Writings of Roger Williams,* II, 1–240.

——. *The Powring out of the Seven Vials.* London, 1642.

——. *A Practical Commentary . . . upon the First Epistle Generall of John.* London, 1656.

——. *A Sermon Delivered at Salem* (1636). In Larzer Ziff, ed., *John Cotton on the Churches of New England,* 39–68.

——. *Singing of Psalmes a Gospel-Ordinance.* London, 1647.

——. *Some Treasure Fetched out of Rubbish.* London, 1660.

——. *A Treatise: I, Of Faith; II, Twelve Fundamental Articles of Christian Religion; III, A Doctrinal Conclusion; IV, Questions and Answers upon Church-Government.* Boston, 1713.

——. *The True Constitution of a Particular Visible Church. . . .* London, 1642.

——. *The Way of the Churches of Christ in New-England. . . .* London, 1645.

——. *The Way of Congregational Churches Cleared* (1648). In Larzer Ziff, ed., *John Cotton on the Churches of New England,* 165–364.

Coverdale, Myles. *Remains of Myles Coverdale. . . .* Edited by George Pearson. Cambridge, 1846.

Cranmer, Thomas. *Miscellaneous Writings and Letters of Thomas Cranmer.* Edited by John Edmund Cox. Vol. II of *The Works of Thomas Cranmer. . . .* Cambridge, 1846.

——. *The Work of Thomas Cranmer.* Edited by G. E. Duffield. Philadelphia, 1965.

Crowley, Robert. *An Answere for the Tyme, to the Examination. . . .* N.p., [ca. 1566].

[——]. *A Brief Discourse against the Outwarde Apparell. . . .* N.p., 1566.

Dalton, Michael. *The Countrey Justice. . . .* 5th ed. London, 1635.

Dane, John. "John Dane's Narrative, 1682." *NEHGR,* VIII (1854), 147–156.

Danforth, Samuel. *A Brief Recognition of New-Englands Errand into the Wilderness* (1671). In A. W. Plumstead, ed., *The Wall and the Garden: Selected Massachusetts Election Sermons, 1670–1775,* 53–77.

Davenport, John. *Another Essay.* . . . Cambridge, Mass., 1663.

———. *An Answer of the Elders of the Severall Churches in New-England unto Nine Positions Sent over to Them.* London, 1643.

———. *An Apologeticall Reply to a Booke Called: An Answer to the Unjust Complaint of W.B.* Rotterdam, 1636.

[———]. *An Apology of the Churches in New-England for Church Government.* London, 1643.

———. *The Knowledge of Christ.* . . . London, 1653.

———. *Letters of John Davenport, Puritan Divine.* Edited by Isabel MacBeath Calder. New Haven, Conn., 1937.

———. *A Royall Edict for Military Exercises.* . . . London, 1629.

Dent, Arthur. *The Ruine of Rome.* . . . London, 1607.

Dering, Edward. *Certaine Godly and Comfortable Letters.* . . . In *M[aster Edward] Derings Workes.*

———. *M[aster Edward] Derings Workes.* London, 1597.

———. *The Praelections . . . upon . . . Hebrews.* In *M[aster Edward] Derings Workes.*

———. *A Sermon Preached before the Queenes Majestie . . . 1569.* In *M[aster Edward] Derings Workes.*

Dod, John. *A Methodicall Short Catechisme.* . . . Appended to John Dod, *A Plaine and Familiar Exposition of the Ten Commandements.*

———. *A Plaine and Familiar Exposition of the Ten Commandements.* London, 1618.

———. *A Plaine and Familiar Exposition on the Lords Prayer.* 2d ed. London, 1635.

Dow, George Francis, ed. *Records and Files of the Quarterly Courts of Essex County, Massachusetts.* 8 vols. Salem, Mass., 1911–1921.

Downame, George. *A Defence of the Sermon Preached at the Consecration of the L. Bishop of Bath and Welles.* London, 1611.

Draxe, Thomas. *The Worldes Resurrection; or, The Generall Calling of the Jewes.* . . . London, 1608.

Dyke, Jer[emiah]. *A Sermon Preached at the Publicke Fast.* . . . London, 1628.

Eliot, John. *The Christian Commonwealth . . .* [1659]. *MHSC*, 3d Ser., IX (Boston, 1846), 127–164.

———. *The Day-Breaking, If Not the Sun-Rising of the Gospell with the Indians in New-England* (1647). *MHSC*, 3d Ser., IV (Boston, 1834), 1–24.

———. *Indian Dialogues.* . . . Cambridge, Mass., 1671.

———. "John Eliot's Description of New England in 1650." Massachusetts Historical Society, *Proceedings*, 2d Ser., II (Boston, 1885), 50.

———. "The Learned Conjectures of Reverend Mr. Eliot." Preface to Thomas Thorowgood, *Jews in America; or, Probabilities, That Those Indians Are Judaical.* . . .

———. "Rev. John Eliot's Records of the First Church in Roxbury, Mass." *NEHGR*, XXXIII (1879), 62–65, 236–239, 295–299, 413–416.

Eliot, John, and Jonathan Mayhew. *Tears of Repentance . . .* (1653). *MHSC*, 3d Ser., IV (Boston, 1834), 197–260.

Emerson, Everett, ed. *Letters from New England: The Massachusetts Bay Colony, 1629–38.* Amherst, Mass., 1976.

Examen Legum Angliae (1656). In Mark DeWolfe Howe, *Readings in American Legal History*, 86–94.

Fairweather, Eugene R., ed. and trans. *A Scholastic Miscellany: Anselm to Ockham.* New York, 1970.

Fenner, Dudley. *A Brief and Plain Declaration Containing the Desires of All These Faithful Ministers, That Have and Do Seek for the Discipline and Reformation of the Church of England.* London, 1584.

———. *Certain Godly and Learned Treatises.* Edinburgh, 1592.

———. *The Song of Songs.* London, 1587.

[Field, John, and Thomas Wilcox]. *An Admonition to the Parliament* (1572). In W. H. Frere and C. E. Douglas, eds., *Puritan Manifestoes . . .* , 2–55.

Field, Richard. *Of the Church, Five Bookes.* London, 1606.

Fills, Robert, trans. *The Lawes and Statutes of Geneva.* London, 1562.

[Finch, Henry]. *An Exposition of the Song of Solomon: Called Canticles. . . .* London, 1615.

[———]. *The Worlds Great Restauration.* London, 1621.

Fiske, John. *The Notebook of the Reverend John Fiske, 1644–1675.* Edited by Robert G. Pope. Colonial Society of Massachusetts, *Publications*, XLVII (Boston, 1974).

———. "Extracts from the Records Kept by the Rev. John Fiske. . . ." *HCEI*, I, no. 2 (1859), 37–44.

Flavel, John. *The Whole Works of the Reverend Mr. John Flavel. . . .* 2 vols. Edinburgh, 1701.

Force, Peter, ed. *Tracts and Other Papers, Relating Principally to the Origin, Settlement, and Progress of the Colonies in North America. . . .* 4 vols. Washington, D.C., 1836–1847.

Ford, John W., ed. *Some Correspondence between the Governors and Treasurers of the New England Company in London and the Commissioners of the United Colonies in America. . . .* New York, 1970.

The Forme of Prayers and Ministration of the Sacraments . . . (1556). In David Laing, ed., *The Works of John Knox*, 6 vols. (Edinburgh, 1845–1864), IV, 143–214.

Foxe, John. *The Acts and Monuments of John Foxe.* 8 vols. Edited by Stephen Reed Cattley. London, 1837–1841.

———. *Actes and Monuments of These Latter and Perillous Dayes.* London, 1563.

———. *Actes and Monuments of These Latter and Perillous Dayes.* London, 1570.

———. *A Sermon of Christ Crucified.* London, 1570.

———. *A Sermon Preached at the Christening of a Certaine Jew, at London.* London, 1578.

Frere, W. H., and C. E. Douglas, eds. *Puritan Manifestoes. . . .* 1907; New York, 1972.

Gardiner, Stephen. *The Oration of True Obedience* (1535). In Pierre Janelle, ed.

and trans., *Obedience in Church and State: Three Political Tracts by Stephen Gardiner* (London, 1930), 67–172.

Gee, Henry, and William John Hardy, eds. *Documents Illustrative of English Church History*. London, 1896.

The Geneva Bible: A Facsimile of the 1560 Edition. Edited by Lloyd E. Berry. Madison, Wis., 1969.

Gifford, George. *Fifteene Sermons upon the Song of Salomon*. London, 1600.

———. *Sermons upon the Whole Booke of the Revelation*. London, 1596.

Gilby, Anthony. *To My Lovynge Brethren That Is Troublyd about the Popishe Aparrel*. N.p., [ca. 1566].

Good News from New-England (1648). *MHSC*, 4th Ser., I (Boston, 1852), 195–218.

Goodwin, Thomas. *An Exposition of the Revelation*. In John C. Miller, ed., *The Works of Thomas Goodwin*, 12 vols. (Edinburgh, 1861), III.

———. *The World to Come*. . . . London, 1655.

Goodwin, Thomas, et al. *An Apologeticall Narration* (1643). Edited by Robert S. Paul. Philadelphia, 1963.

[———]. "Preface" to John Davenport, *Another Essay*. . . .

Gookin, Daniel. *Historical Collections of the Indians in New England* . . . (1674). *MHSC*, 1st Ser., I (Boston, 1792), 141–226.

Gough, Henry, ed. *A General Index to the Publications of the Parker Society*. Oxford, 1855.

Gray, F. C. "Remarks on the Early Laws of Massachusetts Bay. . . ." *MHSC*, 3d Ser., VIII (Boston, 1843), 191–237.

Great Britain. *Calendar of State Papers, Domestic Series, of the Reign of Charles II. 1629–1631; 1635–1636*.

Greenham, Richard. *The Works of the Reverend . . . M[aster] Richard Greenham*. . . . 3d ed. London, 1601.

Hacket, Roger. *A Sermon Principally Entreating of the Crosse in Baptisme*. . . . London, 1606.

Hall, Joseph. *The Works of Joseph Hall*. Edited by Josiah Pratt. 10 vols. London, 1808.

Hazard, Ebenezer. *Historical Collections*. . . . 2 vols. Philadelphia, 1744.

Hieron, Samuel. *The Workes of Mr. Samuel Hieron*. 2 vols. London, 1635.

Higginson, Francis. *A True Relation of the Last Voyage to New-England, 1629*. In Alexander Young, ed., *Chronicles of the First Planters of the Colony of Massachusetts Bay, 1623–1636*, 214–238.

Higginson, John. *The Cause of God and His People in New-England*. . . . Cambridge, Mass., 1663.

Hildersam, Arthur. *The Doctrine of Fasting and Praier*. . . . London, 1633.

Hill, Don Gleason, ed. *The Record of Baptisms, Marriages and Deaths, and Admissions to the Church and Dismissals Therefrom . . . in the Town of Dedham, Massachusetts, 1638–1845*. Dedham, Mass., 1888.

Hoadly, Charles J., ed. *Records of the Colony and Plantation of New Haven, from 1638 to 1649*. Hartford, Conn., 1857.

Hooke, William. *New Englands Teares, for Old Englands Feares*. London, 1641.

Hooker, Richard. *Of the Laws of Ecclesiastical Polity.* 2 vols. London, 1907.
———. *The Works of Richard Hooker.* Edited by John Keble. 7th ed. 3 vols. Oxford, 1888.
Hooker, Thomas. *The Application of Redemption.* . . . London, 1657.
———. "The Danger of Desertion." In *Thomas Hooker: Writings in England and Holland, 1626–1633,* ed. George H. Williams *et al.,* 221–252.
[———]. "The Preface" to William Ames, *A Fresh Suit against Human Ceremonies in God's Worship.* N.p., 1633.
———. *The Soules Implantation.* . . . London, 1637.
———. *The Soules Preparation for Christ.* . . . London, 1632.
———. *A Survey of the Summe of Church-Discipline.* London, 1648.
———. *Thomas Hooker: Writings in England and Holland, 1626–1633.* Edited by George H. Williams *et al.* Harvard Theological Studies, XVIII. Cambridge, Mass., 1975.
Hooper, John. *The Early Writings of John Hooper.* Edited by Samuel Carr. Cambridge, 1843.
"How Far Moses' Judicials Bind Mass[achusetts]." Massachusetts Historical Society, *Proceedings,* 2d Ser., XVI (Boston, 1902), 274–284.
Hubbard, William. *General History of New England from the Discovery to 1680. MHSC,* 2d Ser., V, VI (Boston, 1815).
Huit, Ephraim. *The Whole Prophecie of Daniel Explained.* . . . London, 1644.
"An Humble Proposal, for the Inlargement of University Learning . . ." (1660). In Samuel Eliot Morison, *Harvard College in the Seventeenth Century,* II, facing 368.
Hutchinson, Thomas. *A Collection of Original Papers . . .* (1769). *The Hutchinson Papers,* 2 vols., Prince Society Publications, II, III (Albany, N.Y., 1865; rpt., New York, 1967 [as Prince Society Publications, I, II]).
———. *The History of the Colony and Province of Massachusetts-Bay.* Edited by Lawrence Shaw Mayo. 3 vols. Cambridge, Mass., 1936.
Jackson, Thomas. *The Works of Thomas Jackson.* 12 vols. Oxford, 1844.
Jacob, Henry. *A Confession and Protestation of the Faith of Certaine Christians.* . . . Middelburg, Neth., 1616.
———. *The Divine Beginning . . . of Christs . . . True Church.* Leiden, 1610.
———. *Reasons Taken out of Gods Word.* . . . Middelburg, Neth., 1604.
Jewel, John. *An Apology of the Church of England.* Edited by John E. Booty. Ithaca, N.Y., 1963.
———. *The Works of John Jewel.* Edited by John Ayre. 4 vols. Cambridge, 1845–1850.
Johnson, Edward. *Johnson's Wonder-Working Providence, 1628–1651.* Edited by J. Franklin Jameson. New York, 1910.
Jones, Phyllis M., and Nicholas R. Jones, eds. *Salvation in New England: Selections from the Sermons of the First Preachers.* Austin, Tex., 1977.
Joye, George. *A Present Consolacion for the Sufferers of Persecucion.* . . . London, 1544.
———. *The Subversion of Moris False Foundacion.* . . . N.p., 1543.
———. *The Unite and Schisme of the Olde Chirche.* N.p., 1543.

Keayne, Robert. *The Apologia of Robert Keayne.* . . . Edited by Bernard Bailyn. New York, 1965.

Keeling, William, ed. *Liturgiae Britannicae.* . . . 2d ed. London, 1851.

Latimer, Hugh. *Sermons and Remains of Hugh Latimer.* Edited by George Elwes Corrie. Cambridge, 1845.

Laud, William. *The Works of William Laud.* . . . Edited by William Scott and James Bliss. 7 vols. Oxford, 1847–1860.

The Laws and Liberties of Massachusetts (1648). Edited by Max Farrand. Cambridge, Mass., 1929.

Lechford, Thomas. *Plain Dealing.* . . . Edited by J. Hammond Trumbull. Boston, 1867.

"A Letter to Oliver Cromwell in 1651. . . . " In Thomas Hutchinson, *The History of the Colony and Province of Massachusetts-Bay*, I, 431–433.

Lever, Thomas. *Sermons.* Edited by Edward Arber. London, 1871.

Luther, Martin. *Martin Luther.* Edited by John Dillenberger. Chicago, 1961.

Mather, Cotton. *Magnalia Christi Americana.* Edited by Thomas Robbins. 2 vols. New York, 1853.

Mather, Eleazar. *A Serious Exhortation to the Present and Succeeding Generation in New England.* . . . Cambridge, Mass., 1671.

Mather, Increase. *A Call from Heaven to the Present and Succeeding Generations.* . . . Boston, 1679.

——— . *The Day of Trouble Is Near.* Cambridge, Mass., 1674.

——— . *A Discourse concerning the Danger of Apostasy.* . . . Boston, 1679.

——— . *An Earnest Exhortation to the Inhabitants of New-England.* . . . Boston, 1676.

——— . *The First Principles of New-England.* . . . Cambridge, Mass., 1675.

——— . *The Life and Death of . . . Richard Mather.* . . . Cambridge, Mass., 1670.

——— . *The Mystery of Israel's Salvation.* . . . London, 1669.

——— . *Renewal of Covenant the Great Duty Incumbent on Decaying or Distressed Churches.* Boston, 1677.

——— . *Some Important Truths concerning Conversion.* . . . Boston, 1684.

——— . "To the Reader." In Samuel Torrey, *An Exhortation unto Reformation* . . . , sigs. A1–A5.

[Mather, Richard?]. *An Apologie of the Churches in New-England for Church-Covenant.* London, 1643.

——— . "Arguments Tending to Prove the Removing from Old England to New . . . to Be Not Onley Lawful, but Also Necessary . . ." (1635). In Increase Mather, *The Life and Death . . . of Richard Mather* . . . , 12–19.

[———]. *Church-Government and Church-Covenant Discussed.* . . . London, 1643.

——— . *A Farewell Exhortation to the Church and People of Dorchester in New-England.* Cambridge, 1657.

——— . "A Letter of Richard Mather to a Cleric in Old England." Edited by B. Richard Burg. *WMQ*, 3d Ser., XXIX (1972), 81–98.

————. "To the Christian Reader." In John Eliot and Jonathan Mayhew, *Tears of Repentance . . .*, 217–225.

[Mather, Richard, and Jonathan Mitchel]. *A Defence of the Answer and Arguments of the Synod Met at Boston in the Year 1662*. Cambridge, Mass., 1664.

Mather, Richard, and William Tompson. *A Modest and Brotherly Answer to Mr. Charles Herle. . . .* London, 1644.

Mede, Joseph. *The Key of the Revelation. . . .* London, 1643.

————. *The Key of the Revelation. . . .* 2d ed. London, 1650.

————. *The Works of . . . Joseph Mede*. 3d ed. London, 1672.

Metcalfe, Michael. "To All the True Professors. . . ." *NEHGR*, XVI (1862), 279–284.

Miller, Samuel. *Presbyterianism the Truly Primitive and Apostolical Constitution of the Church of Christ*. Philadelphia, 1835.

Milton, John. *Of Reformation touching Church Discipline in England*. Edited by Harry Morgan Ayres. In *The Works of John Milton*, 18 vols. (New York, 1931–1938), III, pt. 1, 1–80.

Mitchel, Jonathan. *A Discourse of the Glory to Which God Hath Called Believers. . . .* 2d ed. Boston, 1721.

————. *Nehemiah on the Wall in Troublesom Times. . . .* Cambridge, Mass., 1671.

Mitchel, Jonathan, *et al. Elijah's Mantle*. Boston, 1722.

"A Modell of Church and Civill Power. . . . " Segmentally entered in Roger Williams, *The Bloudy Tenent of Persecution*, in *The Complete Writings of Roger Williams*, III.

Moody, Robert E., ed. *The Saltonstall Papers . . .* , vol. I, *1607–1789*. *MHSC*, LXXX (Boston, 1972).

Morison, Samuel Eliot, *et al.*, eds. *The Winthrop Papers*. 5 vols. to date. Boston, 1929–.

Morton, Nathaniel. *New England's Memorial. . . .* Cambridge, Mass., 1669.

Murray, Iain, ed. *Sermons of the Great Ejection*. London, 1962.

Musculus, Wolfgangus. *Common Places of Christian Religion*. London, 1563.

Napier, John. *A Plaine Discovery of the Whole Revelation of St. John. . . .* Edinburgh, 1593.

New Englands First Fruits. . . . London, 1643. Reprinted as appendix D in Samuel Eliot Morison, *The Founding of Harvard College*, 420–446.

Noble, John, and John F. Cronin, eds. *Records of the Court of Assistants of the Colony of the Massachusetts Bay, 1630–1692*. 3 vols. Boston, 1901–1928.

Norton, John. *The Answer to the Whole Set of Questions of . . . William Apollonius . . .* (1648). Translated by Douglas Horton. Cambridge, Mass., 1958.

————. *The Heart of N—— England Rent at the Blasphemies of the Present Generation. . . .* London, 1660.

————. *The Orthodox Evangelist*. London, 1654.

Oakes, Urian. *New-England Pleaded With. . . .* Cambridge, Mass., 1673.

————. *The Soveraign Efficacy of Divine Providence*. . . . Boston, 1682.

————. "To the Christian Reader." In Increase Mather, *The Day of Trouble Is Near*, 1–2.

Osborne, Francis. *The Works of Francis Osborn*. . . . 8th ed. London, 1682.

Overal, John. Dedication to King James I. In John Ayre, ed., *The Works of John Jewel*, IV, appendix 4, 1306–1312.

Owen, John. *The Works of John Owen*. 12 vols. Edinburgh, 1862.

Owen, John, *et al*. *Strength out of Weaknesse*. . . . *MHSC*, 3d Ser., IV (Boston, 1834), 149–196.

Paget, John. *A Defence of Church-Government*. . . . London, 1641.

————. "Mr. [John] Paget's Twenty Propositions to Mr. [Thomas] Hooker with His Answer Thereto." In Raymond Phineas Stearns, ed., *Congregationalism in the Dutch Netherlands: The Rise and Fall of the English Congregational Classis, 1621–1635*, 105–113.

Pagit, Eusebius. *A Godly Sermon: Preached at Detford in Kent . . . 1572*. London, 1586.

Pareus, David. *In Divinam Apocalypsin S. Apostoli et Evangelistae Johannis Commentarius*. Heidelberg, 1618.

————. *A Commentary upon the Divine Revelation*. . . . Translated by Elias Arnold. London, 1644.

[Parker, Matthew]. *A Briefe Examination for the Tyme, of a Certaine Declaration*. . . . N.p., [ca. 1566].

Parker, Robert. *An Exposition of the Powring out of the Fourth Vial*. . . . London, 1650.

————. *The Mystery of the Vialls Opened*. . . . London, 1650.

————. *A Scholasticall Discourse against Symbolizing with Antichrist in Ceremonies*. . . . N.p., 1607.

Parker, Thomas. *The Visions and Prophecies of Daniel Expounded*. . . . London, 1646.

A Parte of a Register. . . . N.p., [1593].

Peel, Albert, ed. *The Seconde Parte of a Register*. . . . 2 vols. Cambridge, 1915.

Perkins, William. *A Commentarie or Exposition upon the Five First Chapters of the Epistle to the Galatians*. . . . Cambridge, 1604.

————. *A Godly and Learned Exposition upon the Three First Chapters of the Revelation*. 3d ed. London, 1607.

————. *William Perkins, 1558–1602, English Puritanist; His Pioneer Works on Caşuistry: "A Discourse of Conscience" and "The Whole Treatise of Cases of Conscience."* Edited by Thomas F. Merrill. Nieuwkoop, 1966.

————. *The Workes of That Famous and Worthy Minister of Christ, Mr. William Perkins*. 3 vols. London, 1635.

————. *The Work of William Perkins*. Edited by Ian Breward. Appleford, England, 1970.

Peter, Hugh. *A Dying Fathers Last Legacy to an Only Child*. . . . Boston, 1717.

————. "The Fifteen Articles and *Covenant* of Mr. Hugh Peter, Minister of Rhotterdam." In Champlin Burrage, *The Early English Dissenters in the Light*

of Recent Research (1550–1641), 2 vols. (Cambridge, 1912), I, 302–303.
————. *Good Work for a Good Magistrate. . . .* London, 1651.
"A Petition to the Parliament in 1651." In Thomas Hutchinson, *The History of the Colony and Province of Massachusetts-Bay*, I, 428–430.
A Platform of Church Discipline Gathered out of the Word of God (1648). In Williston Walker, *The Creeds and Platforms of Congregationalism*, 194–237.
Plumstead, A. W., ed. *The Wall and the Garden: Selected Massachusetts Election Sermons, 1670–1775.* Minneapolis, Minn., 1968.
The Prayer-Book of Queen Elizabeth, 1559. . . . London, 1890.
Preston, John. *The Breast-Plate of Faith and Love.* 5th ed. London, 1634.
Pulsifer, David, ed. *Records of the Colony of New Plymouth.* 12 vols. Boston, 1861.
[Rainolds, John]. *An Answere to a Sermon Preached the 17 of April Anno D. 1608, by George Downame. . . .* N.p., 1609.
Records of the United Colonies of New-England. In Ebenezer Hazard, ed., *Historical Collections . . .* , II.
The Reformation of Religion by Josiah. . . . N.p., [1590].
Rickey, Mary Ellen, and Thomas B. Stroup, eds. *Certaine Sermons or Homilies* (1623). Facsimile. Gainesville, Fla., 1968.
Ridley, Nicholas. *The Works of Nicholas Ridley. . . .* Edited by Henry Christmas. Cambridge, 1841.
Robinson, Hastings, ed. and trans. *The Zurich Letters. . . .* 3 vols. Cambridge, 1842–1847.
Rogers, Ezekiel. "Ezekiel Rogers's Will." *Documents from the Harvard University Archives, 1638–1750*, IV, *Documents, 1638–1722* (Colonial Society of Massachusetts, *Publications, Collections*, XLIX [Boston, 1975]), 98–101.
Rogers, John. *The Doctrine of Faith. . . .* 3d ed. London, 1629.
Rogers, Richard. *Seven Treatises. . . .* London, 1603.
Rogers, Thomas. *The Catholic Doctrine of the Church of England. . . .* Edited by J.J.S. Perowne. Cambridge, 1854.
Roxbury Land and Church Records: A Report. 2d ed. Boston, 1884.
[Sampson, Thomas]. "Certain Humble Petitions. . . ." In John Strype, *Annals of the Reformation . . .* , III, pt. 2, 278–302.
————. *A Warning to Take Heede of Fowlers Psalter.* London, 1578.
Saravia, Adrian. *Of the Diverse Degrees of the Ministers of the Gospell.* London, 1591.
Shepard, Thomas. *The Autobiography.* In Michael McGiffert, ed., *God's Plot: The Paradoxes of Puritan Piety, Being the Autobiography and Journal of Thomas Shepard*, 33–77.
————. *The Church-Membership of Children, and Thier Right to Baptisme.* Cambridge, Mass., 1663.
————. *The Clear Sun-shine of the Gospel Breaking Forth upon the Indians in New-England. MHSC*, 3d Ser., IV (Boston, 1834), 25–67.
————. *God's Plot: The Paradoxes of Puritan Piety, Being the Autobiography and Journal of Thomas Shepard.* Edited by Michael McGiffert. N.p., 1972.

————. *Journal.* In Michael McGiffert, ed., *God's Plot: The Paradoxes of Puritan Piety, Being the Autobiography and Journal of Thomas Shepard,* 81–238.

————. "Thomas Shepard's Election Sermon, in 1638." *NEHGR,* XXIV (1870), 360–365.

————. "To the Reader." In Peter Bulkeley, *Gospel-Covenant; or, The Covenant of Grace Opened.*

————. *Wine for Gospel Wantons.* . . . Cambridge, Mass., 1668.

————. *The Works of Thomas Shepard.* 3 vols. Boston, 1853.

Shepard, Thomas, Jr. *Eye-Salve.* . . . Cambridge, Mass., 1673.

Shurtleff, Nathaniel B. *Records of the Governor and Company of the Massachusetts Bay in New England.* 5 vols. Boston, 1853–1854.

Sibbes, Richard. *The Brides Longing for Her Bride-groomes Second Comming.* London, 1638.

————. *The Complete Works of Richard Sibbes, D. D.* Edited by Alexander Balloch Grosart. 7 vols. Edinburgh, 1862–1864.

Smith, Henry. *The Sermons of Master Henry Smith.* . . . London, 1628.

Starkey, Thomas. *An Exhortation to the People.* . . . London, [1540?].

[Sternhold, Thomas, et al.]. *The Whole Book of Psalms Collected into English Meter.* London, 1575.

Stoughton, William. *New-Englands True Interest.* . . . Cambridge, Mass., 1670.

Strickland, John. *Mercy Rejoycing against Judgement; or, God Waiting to Be Gracious to a Sinful Nation.* London, 1645.

Stubbes, Philip. *Anatomy of the Abuses.* . . . London, 1583. Reprint, New Shakspere Society, *Publications,* 6th Ser., IV, VI (1877, 1879).

Taylor, Jeremy. *The Whole Works of the Right Reverend Jeremy Taylor.* Edited by Reginald Heber. 15 vols. London, 1822.

Taylor, Thomas. *Christs Victorie over the Dragon.* . . . London, 1633.

————. *A Commentarie upon the Epistle of St. Paul Written to Titus.* Cambridge, 1612.

T.H. "To the Reader." In Edward Johnson, *The Wonder-working Providence.* . . . (London, 1654).

Thorowgood, Thomas. *Jewes in America; or, Probabilities That the Americans Are of That Race.* London, 1650.

————. *Jews in America; or, Probabilities That Those Indians Are Judaical.* . . . London, 1660.

Tillam, Thomas. *The Two Witnesses.* . . . London, 1651.

————. "Uppon the First Sight of New-England, June 29, 1638." In Harrison T. Meserole, ed., *Seventeenth-Century American Poetry* (Garden City, N.J., 1968), 397–398.

Torrey, Samuel. *An Exhortation unto Reformation.* . . . Cambridge, Mass., 1674.

————. *Mans Extremity, Gods Opportunity.* Boston, 1695.

————. *A Plea for the Life of Dying Religion.* . . . Boston, 1683.

[Travers, Walter]. *A Defence of the Ecclesiastical Discipline Ordayned of God to Be Used in His Church, against a Replie of Maister Bridges.* . . . N.p., 1588.
———. *A Full and Plaine Declaration of Ecclesiastical Discipline.* . . . Leiden, 1617.
Tuckney, Anthony. "To the Reader." In John Cotton, *A Brief Exposition with Practical Observations upon the Whole Book of Canticles.*
Tyndale, William. *The Beginning of the New Testament Translated by William Tyndale* (1525). Edited by A. W. Pollard. Oxford, 1926.
———. *Doctrinal Treatises.* . . . Edited by Henry Walter. Cambridge, 1848.
———. *Expositions and Notes on Sundry Portions of the Holy Scriptures, together with "The Practice of Prelates."* Edited by Henry Walter. Cambridge, 1849.
———. *The Work of William Tyndale.* Edited by G. E. Duffield. Philadelphia, 1965.
Tyndale, William, John Frith, and Robert Barnes. *The Whole Works of W[illiam] Tyndall, John Frith, and Doct[or Robert] Barnes.* London, 1573.
Udall, John. *Amendment of Life.* London, 1588.
———. *A Demonstration of the Truth of That Discipline, Which Christ Has Prescribed in His Word, for the Government of His Church, in All Times and Places, until the End of the World* (1588). Edited by Edward Arber. London, 1880.
———. *The True Remedie against Famine and Warres.* . . . London, n.d.
Underhill, John. *News from America.* . . . London, 1638. *MHSC,* 3d Ser., VI (Boston, 1837), 1–43.
Ursinus, Zacharias. *Commentary on the Heidelberg Catechism* (1616). Translated by G. W. Williard. Grand Rapids, Mich., 1950.
Vane, Henry, Jr. "A Brief Answer to a Certain Declaration." In Thomas Hutchinson, *A Collection of Original Papers* . . . , I, 84–96.
Vermigli, Peter Martyr. *The Common Places of the Most Famous and Renowned Divine Doctor Peter Martyr.* . . . London, 1583.
Ward, Nathaniel. *The Massachusetts Body of Liberties.* In Edmund S. Morgan, ed., *Puritan Political Ideas, 1558–1794,* 177–203.
———. *The Simple Cobler of Aggawam in America* (1647). Edited by P. M. Zall. Lincoln, Nebr., 1969.
Ward, Samuel. *Jethro's Justice of Peace.* London, 1627.
Welde, Thomas. *An Answer to W.R. His Narration.* . . . London, 1644.
Whately, William. *Prototypes; or, The Primary Precedent Presidents out of the Booke of Genesis.* . . . London, 1640.
White, Francis. *A Treatise of the Sabbath Day.* London, 1635.
White, John. *The Planters Plea; or, The Grounds of Plantations Examined* . . . (1630). In Peter Force, ed., *Tracts and Other Papers, Relating Principally to the Origin, Settlement, and Progress of the Colonies in North America* . . . , II.
Whitfield, Henry. *Strength out of Weaknesse; or, A Glorious Manifestation of the Further Progress of the Gospel among the Indians in New-England* (1652).

MHSC, 3d Ser., IV (Boston, 1834), 149–196.

Whitfield, Henry, *et al. The Light Appearing More and More towards the Perfect Day* (1651). *MHSC*, 3d Ser., IV (Boston, 1834), 101–147.

Whitgift, John. *The Works of John Whitgift*. Edited by John Ayre. 3 vols. Cambridge, 1851–1853.

Whiting, Samuel. *John Cotton's Life and Letters*. In Alexander Young, ed., *Chronicles of the First Planters of the Colony of Massachusetts Bay*.

The Whole Booke of Psalmes, Collected into English Meter. London, 1575.

The Whole Booke of Psalmes Faithfully Translated into English Metre. Cambridge, Mass., 1640.

Wigglesworth, Michael. *The Day of Doom. . . .* Edited by Kenneth B. Murdock. New York, 1966.

————. *The Diary of Michael Wigglesworth, 1653–1657: The Conscience of a Puritan*. Edited by Edmund S. Morgan. New York, 1965.

Wilcox, Thomas. *A Discourse touching the Doctrine of Doubting*. Cambridge, 1598.

————. *The Summe of a Sermon, Preached at Sowthell. . . .* London, 1597.

————. *The Works of That Late Reverend and Learned Divine, Mr. Thomas Wilcocks. . . .* London, 1624.

Wilkinson, Henry. *Babylons Ruine, Jerusalems Rising*. London, 1643.

Wilkinson, John. *An Exposition of the Thirteenth Chapter of the Revelation of Jesus Christ*. N.p., 1619.

Willard, Samuel. *The Child's Portion. . . .* Boston, 1684.

————. *Covenant-Keeping the Way to Blessedness. . . .* Boston, 1682.

————. *Reformation the Great Duty of an Afflicted People*. Boston, 1694.

————. *Rules for the Discerning of the Present Times. . . .* Boston, 1693.

————. *The Sinfulness of Worshipping God with Men's Institutions. . . .* Boston, 1691.

————. *Useful Instructions for a Professing People in Times of Great Security and Degeneracy. . . .* Cambridge, Mass., 1673.

Williams, Roger. *The Complete Writings of Roger Williams*. 7 vols. New York, 1963.

Wilson, John. *A Seasonable Watch-word unto Christians against the Dreams and Dreamers of This Generation. . . .* Cambridge, Mass., 1677.

Wilson, John, *et al. A Copy of the Letter . . . to Mr. John Dury. . . .* Cambridge, Mass., 1664.

Winslow, Edward, ed. *The Glorious Progress of the Gospel, amongst the Indians in New England . . .* (1649). *MHSC*, 3d Ser., IV (Boston, 1834), 69–98.

Winstanley, Gerrard. *The Law of Freedom in a Platform; or, True Magistracy Restored. . . .* London, 1652.

Winthrop, John. *The History of New England from 1630 to 1649*. Edited by James Savage. 2 vols. 1853; New York, 1972.

————. "John Winthrop's Defense of the Negative Vote." *WP*, IV, 380–391.

————. "A Model of Christian Charity." In Edmund S. Morgan, ed., *Puritan Political Ideas, 1558–1794*, 76–93.

————. "On Arbitrary Government." *WP*, IV, 468–483.

———. "A Reply in Further Defense of an Order. . . ." *WP*, III, 463–476.

Wood, William. *New Englands Prospect*. London, 1634.

Young, Alexander, ed. *Chronicles of the First Planters of the Colony of Massachusetts Bay . . . from 1623 to 1636*. Boston, 1846.

SECONDARY SOURCES

BOOKS

Ahlstrom, Sydney E. *A Religious History of the American People*. New Haven, Conn., 1972.

Albanese, Catherine L. *Sons of the Fathers: The Civil Religion of the American Revolution*. Philadelphia, 1976.

Alexander, H. G. *Religion in England, 1558–1662*. London, 1968.

Allen, David Grayson. *In English Ways: The Movement of Societies and the Transferal of English Local Law and Custom to Massachusetts Bay in the Seventeenth Century*. Chapel Hill, N.C., 1981.

Andrews, Charles M. *The Colonial Period of American History*. 4 vols. New Haven, Conn., 1934–1938.

Auerbach, Erich. *Mimesis: The Representation of Reality in Western Literature*. Translated by Willard Trask. Garden City, N.Y., 1957.

Axtell, James. *The Invasion Within: The Contest of Cultures in Colonial North America*. New York, 1985.

Babbage, S. B. *Puritanism and Richard Bancroft*. London, 1962.

Bailyn, Bernard. *The New England Merchants in the Seventeenth Century*. New York, 1964.

Ball, Bryan W. *A Great Expectation: Eschatological Thought in English Protestantism to 1660*. Leiden, 1975.

Barbour, Hugh. *The Quakers in Puritan England*. New Haven, Conn., 1964.

Barbour, Hugh, and Arthur O. Roberts, eds. *Early Quaker Writings, 1650–1700*. Grand Rapids, Mich., 1973.

Baritz, Loren. *City on a Hill: A History of Ideas and Myths in America*. New York, 1964.

Battis, Emery. *Saints and Sectaries: Anne Hutchinson and the Antinomian Controversy in the Massachusetts Bay Colony*. Chapel Hill, N.C., 1962.

Bauckham, Richard. *Tudor Apocalypse*. Oxford, 1978.

Becker, Carl L. *The Heavenly City of the Eighteenth-Century Philosophers*. New Haven, Conn., 1932.

Beek, M. Van. *An Enquiry into Puritan Vocabulary*. Groningen, 1969.

Bercovitch, Sacvan. *The American Jeremiad*. Madison, Wis., 1978.

———. *The Millennium in America*. Brochure, AMS Press series. New York, 1980.

———. *The Puritan Origins of the American Self*. New Haven, Conn., 1975.

Berens, John F. *Providence and Patriotism in Early America, 1640–1815*. Charlottesville, Va., 1978.

Billias, George Athan, ed. *Law and Authority in Colonial America: Selected Essays*. Barre, Mass., 1965.

Blench, J. W. *Preaching in England in the Late Fifteenth and Sixteenth Centuries*. Oxford, 1964.

Bloch, Ruth H. *The Visionary Republic: Millennial Themes in American Thought, 1756–1800*. Cambridge, 1985.

Boas, George. *Essays on Primitivism and Related Ideas in the Middle Ages*. Baltimore, 1948.

Boorstin, Daniel J. *The Americans: The Colonial Experience*. New York, 1964.

Bowden, Henry Warner. *American Indians and Christian Missions: Studies in Cultural Conflict*. Chicago, 1981.

Brawley, Benjamin. *A History of the English Hymn*. New York, 1932.

Breen, T. H. *The Character of the Good Ruler: A Study of Puritan Political Ideas in New England, 1630–1700*. New Haven, Conn., 1970.

————. *Puritans and Adventurers: Change and Persistence in Early America*. New York, 1980.

Bremer, Francis J. *The Puritan Experiment: New England Society from Bradford to Edwards*. New York, 1976.

Breslow, Marvin A. *A Mirror of England: English Puritan Views of Foreign Nations, 1618–1640*. Cambridge, Mass., 1970.

Brown, Alexander. *The Genesis of the United States*. 2 vols. Boston, 1890.

Brown, Richard D. *Modernization: The Transformation of American Life, 1600–1865*. New York, 1976.

Burg, B. R. *Richard Mather of Dorchester*. Lexington, Ky., 1976.

Burke, Peter. *Popular Culture in Early Modern Europe*. New York, 1978.

Burnet, Gilbert. *The History of the Reformation of the Church of England*. 7 vols. Oxford, 1865.

Bush, Sargent, Jr. *The Writings of Thomas Hooker: Spiritual Adventure in Two Worlds*. Madison, Wis., 1980.

Calder, Isabel MacBeath. *The New Haven Colony*. Hamden, Conn., 1970.

Capp, B. S. *The Fifth-Monarchy Men: A Study in Seventeenth-Century English Millenarianism*. London, 1972.

Chadwick, Owen. *The Reformation*. Baltimore, 1964.

Chapin, Bradley. *Criminal Justice in Colonial America, 1606–1660*. Athens, Ga., 1983.

Chaplin, Jeremiah. *The Life of Henry Dunster: First President of Harvard College*. Boston, 1872.

Cherry, Conrad. *God's New Israel: Religious Interpretations of American Destiny*. Englewood Cliffs, N.J., 1971.

Christianson, Paul. *Reformers and Babylon: English Apocalyptic Visions from the Reformation to the Eve of the Civil War*. Toronto, 1978.

Clark, Peter. *English Provincial Society from the Reformation to the Revolution: Religion, Politics, and Society in Kent, 1500–1640*. London, 1977.

Clebsch, William A. *England's Earliest Protestants, 1520–1535*. New Haven, Conn., 1964.

Cochrane, Arthur C., ed. *Reformed Confessions of the Sixteenth Century.* Philadelphia, 1966.

Cockburn, J. S., ed. *Crime in England, 1550–1800.* Princeton, N.J., 1977.

Cohen, Charles Lloyd. *God's Caress: The Psychology of Puritan Religious Experience.* New York, 1986.

Collinson, Patrick. *Archbishop Grindal, 1519–1583: The Struggle for a Reformed Church.* Berkeley, Calif., 1979.

———. *The Elizabethan Puritan Movement.* Berkeley, Calif., 1967.

Coolidge, John S. *The Pauline Renaissance in England: Puritanism and the Bible.* Oxford, 1970.

Cragg, Gerald R. *Freedom and Authority: A Study of English Thought in the Early Seventeenth Century.* Philadelphia, 1975.

Craig, Hardin. *The Enchanted Glass: The Elizabethan Mind in Literature.* Oxford, 1936.

Craven, Wesley Frank. *The Colonies in Transition, 1660–1713.* New York, 1968.

Cremin, Lawrence A. *American Education: The Colonial Experience, 1607–1783.* New York, 1970.

Davidson, James West. *The Logic of Millennial Thought: Eighteenth-Century New England.* New Haven, Conn., 1978.

Davies, Horton. *Worship and Theology in England.* 5 vols. Princeton, N.J., 1970.

———. *The Worship of the English Puritans.* Westminster, 1948.

Davis, J. C. *Utopia and the Ideal Society: A Study of English Utopian Writing, 1516–1700.* Cambridge, 1981.

Deane, Samuel. *History of Scituate, Massachusetts, from Its First Settlement to 1831.* Boston, 1831.

Dickens, A. G. *Reformation and Society in Sixteenth-Century Europe.* London, 1966.

Drake, Francis S. *The Town of Roxbury.* . . . Roxbury, Mass., 1878.

Dunn, Richard S. *Puritans and Yankees: The Winthrop Dynasty of New England, 1630–1717.* 1962; New York, 1971.

Eliade, Mircea. *Cosmos and History: The Myth of the Eternal Return.* Translated by Willard R. Trask. 1954; New York, 1959.

———. *Mephistopheles and the Androgyne: Studies in Religious Myth and Symbol.* Translated by J. M. Cohen. New York, 1965.

———. *Myth and Reality.* Translated by Willard R. Trask. New York, 1963.

———. *Myths, Dreams, and Mysteries: The Encounter between Contemporary Faiths and Archaic Realities.* Translated by Philip Mairet. New York, 1960.

———. *The Sacred and the Profane: The Nature of Religion.* Translated by Willard R. Trask. New York, 1959.

Elliot, Emory. *Power and the Pulpit in Puritan New England.* Princeton, N.J., 1975.

———, ed. *Puritan Influences in American Literature.* Urbana, Ill., 1979.

Elton, G. R. *England under the Tudors.* London, 1955.

Emerson, Everett H. *John Cotton*. New York, 1965.

Erikson, Kai T. *Wayward Puritans: A Study in the Sociology of Deviance*. New York, 1966.

Eusden, John Dykstra. *Puritans, Lawyers, and Politics in Early Seventeenth-Century England*. 1958; Hamden, Conn., 1968.

Firth, Katharine R. *The Apocalyptic Tradition in Reformation Britain, 1530–1645*. Oxford, 1979.

Flaherty, David H., ed. *Essays in the History of Early American Law*. Chapel Hill, N.C., 1969.

Foote, Henry W. *Three Centuries of American Hymnody*. Cambridge, Mass., 1967.

Foster, Stephen. *Notes from the Caroline Underground: Alexander Leighton, the Puritan Triumvirate, and the Laudian Reaction to Nonconformity*. Hamden, Conn., 1978.

———. *Their Solitary Way: The Puritan Social Ethic in the First Century of Settlement in New England*. New Haven, Conn., 1971.

Froom, Le Roy Edwin. *The Prophetic Faith of Our Fathers: The Historical Development of Prophetic Interpretation*. 4 vols. Washington, D.C., 1946–1954.

Gay, Peter. *A Loss of Mastery: Puritan Historians in Colonial America*. Berkeley, Calif., 1961.

Gellner, Ernest. *Thought and Change*. London, 1964.

Gerrish, Brian, ed. *The Faith of Christendom: A Source Book of Creeds and Confessions*. Cleveland, Ohio, 1963.

———. *Grace and Reason: A Study in the Theology of Luther*. Oxford, 1962.

Gildrie, Richard P. *Salem, Massachusetts, 1626–1683: A Covenant Community*. Charlottesville, Va., 1975.

Gilpin, W. Clark. *The Millenarian Piety of Roger Williams*. Chicago, 1979.

Greenslade, S. L. *The English Reformers and the Fathers of the Church*. Oxford, 1960.

Greven, Philip J., Jr. *Four Generations: Population, Land, and Family in Colonial Andover, Massachusetts*. Ithaca, N.Y., 1970.

Gura, Philip F. *A Glimpse of Sion's Glory: Puritan Radicalism in New England, 1620–1660*. Middletown, Conn., 1984.

Hall, David D. *The Faithful Shepherd: A History of the New England Ministry in the Seventeenth Century*. Chapel Hill, N.C., 1972.

———, ed. *The Antinomian Controversy, 1636–1638*. Middletown, Conn., 1968.

Haller, William. *The Elect Nation: The Meaning and Relevance of Foxe's Book of Martyrs*. New York, 1963.

———. *Liberty and Reformation in the Puritan Revolution*. New York, 1955.

———. *The Rise of Puritanism*. . . . 1938; Philadelphia, 1972.

Haller, William, Jr. *The Puritan Frontier: Town-Planting in New England Colonial Development, 1630–1660*. 1951; New York, 1972.

Hambrick-Stowe, Charles E. *The Practice of Piety: Puritan Devotional*

Disciplines in Seventeenth-Century New England. Chapel Hill, N.C., 1982.

Haraszti, Zoltán. *The Enigma of the Bay Psalm Book.* Chicago, 1956.

Harbison, E. Harris. *The Christian Scholar in the Age of Reformation.* New York, 1956.

Haskins, George Lee. *Law and Authority in Early Massachusetts: A Study in Tradition and Design.* New York, 1960.

Hatch, Nathan O. *The Sacred Cause of Liberty: Republican Thought and the Millennium in Revolutionary New England.* New Haven, Conn., 1977.

Headley, John M. *Luther's View of Church History.* New Haven, Conn., 1963.

Heppe, Heinrich, and Ernst Bizer. *Die Dogmatik der evangelisch-reformierten Kirche.* Neukirchen, 1958.

Heyrman, Christine Leigh. *Commerce and Culture: The Maritime Communities of Colonial Massachusetts, 1690–1750.* New York, 1984.

Hilkey, Charles J. *Legal Development in Colonial Massachusetts, 1630–1680.* 1910; New York, 1967.

Hill, Christopher. *Antichrist in Seventeenth-Century England.* London, 1971.

———. *The Century of Revolution, 1603–1714.* New York, 1961.

———. *Society and Puritanism in Pre-Revolutionary England.* 2d ed. New York, 1967.

———. *The World Turned Upside Down: Radical Ideas during the English Revolution.* New York, 1972.

Hill, W. Speed, ed. *Studies in Richard Hooker: Essays Preliminary to an Edition of His Works.* Cleveland, Ohio, 1972.

Hillerbrand, Hans J., ed. *Erasmus and His Age: Selected Letters of Desiderius Erasmus.* New York, 1970.

Hirsch, Emanuel. *Hilfsbuch zum Studium der Dogmatik. . . .* Berlin, 1951.

Hofstadter, Richard. *Anti-Intellectualism in American Life.* New York, 1963.

Holifield, E. Brooks. *The Covenant Sealed: The Development of Puritan Sacramental Theology in Old and New England, 1570–1720.* New Haven, Conn., 1974.

Howe, Mark DeWolfe, ed. *Readings in American Legal History.* Cambridge, Mass., 1949.

Howell, Wilbur Samuel. *Logic and Rhetoric in England, 1500–1700.* Princeton, N.J., 1956.

Huizinga, Johan. *Men and Ideas: History, the Middle Ages, the Renaissance.* Translated by James S. Holmes and Hans van Marle. London, 1960.

Hunt, William. *The Puritan Moment: The Coming of Revolution in an English County.* Cambridge, Mass., 1983.

Innes, Stephen. *Labor in a New Land: Economy and Society in Seventeenth-Century Springfield.* Princeton, N.J., 1983.

Jong, J. A. de. *As the Waters Cover the Sea: Millennial Expectations in the Rise of Anglo-American Missions, 1640–1810.* Kampen, 1970.

Kellaway, William. *The New England Company, 1649–1776: Missionary Society to the American Indians.* New York, 1961.

King, John N. *English Reformation Literature: The Tudor Origins of the*

Protestant Tradition. Princeton, N.J., 1982.

Knappen, M. M. *Tudor Puritanism: A Chapter in the History of Idealism*. 1939; Gloucester, Mass., 1966.

Knott, John R., Jr. *The Sword of the Spirit: Puritan Responses to the Bible*. Chicago, 1980.

Kunz, Erhard. *Protestantische Eschatologie: Von der Reformation bis zur Aufklärung*. Freiburg, 1980.

Labaree, Benjamin W. *Colonial Massachusetts: A History*. Millwood, N.Y., 1979.

Lake, Peter. *Moderate Puritans and the Elizabethan Church*. Cambridge, 1982.

Lamb, J. A. *The Psalms in Christian Worship*. London, 1962.

Lamont, William M. *Godly Rule: Politics and Religion, 1603–60*. London, 1969.

Langdon, George D., Jr. *Pilgrim Colony: A History of New Plymouth, 1620–1691*. New Haven, Conn., 1966.

Laslett, Peter. *The World We Have Lost*. 2d ed. New York, 1972.

Leff, Gordon. *The Dissolution of the Medieval Outlook: An Essay on Intellectual and Spiritual Change in the Fourteenth Century*. New York, 1976.

———. *Medieval Thought: St. Augustine to Ockham*. Baltimore, 1958.

———. *William of Ockham: The Metamorphosis of Scholastic Discourse*. Manchester, 1975.

Le Huray, Peter. *Music and the Reformation in England, 1549–1660*. New York, 1967.

Leverenz, David. *The Language of Puritan Feeling: An Exploration in Literature, Psychology, and Social History*. New Brunswick, N.J., 1980.

Lewalski, Barbara Kiefer. *Protestant Poetics and the Seventeenth-Century Religious Lyric*. Princeton, N.J., 1979.

Little, David. *Religion, Order, and Law: A Study in Pre-Revolutionary England*. New York, 1969.

Liu, Tai. *Discord in Zion: The Puritan Divines and the Puritan Revolution, 1640–1660*. The Hague, 1973.

Lockridge, Kenneth A. *A New England Town, the First Hundred Years: Dedham, Massachusetts, 1636–1736*. New York, 1970.

Lovejoy, Arthur O., and George Boas. *Primitivism and Related Ideas in Antiquity*. Baltimore, 1935.

Lowance, Mason I., Jr. *The Language of Canaan: Metaphor and Symbol in New England from the Puritans to the Transcendentalists*. Cambridge, Mass., 1980.

Lowens, Irving. *Music and Musicians in Early America*. New York, 1964.

Lucas, Paul R. *Valley of Discord: Church and State along the Connecticut River, 1636–1725*. Hanover, N.H., 1976.

McConica, James Kelsey. *English Humanists and Reformation Politics under Henry VIII and Edward VI*. Oxford, 1965.

McCusker, John J., and Russell R. Menard. *The Economy of British America, 1607–1789*. Chapel Hill, N.C., 1985.

McGee, J. Sears. *The Godly Man in Stuart England: Anglicans, Puritans, and the Two Tables, 1620–1670*. New Haven, Conn., 1976.

McLoughlin, William G. *Revivals, Awakenings, and Reform: An Essay on Religion and Social Change in America, 1607–1977.* Chicago, 1978.

McNeill, John T. *The History and Character of Calvinism.* London, 1967.

——. *Modern Christian Movements.* Philadelphia, 1954.

Manschreck, Clyde Leonard. *Melanchthon: The Quiet Reformer.* New York, 1958.

Marchant, Ronald A. *The Puritans and the Church Courts in the Diocese of York, 1560–1642.* London, 1960.

Martz, Louis L. *The Poetry of Meditation: A Study in English Religious Literature of the Seventeenth Century.* New Haven, Conn., 1954.

Maruyama, Tadataka. *The Ecclesiology of Theodore Beza.* Geneva, 1978.

Mead, Sidney E. *The Lively Experiment: The Shaping of Christianity in America.* New York, 1963.

Merton, Robert K. *Social Theory and Social Structure: Toward the Codification of Theory and Research.* 2d ed. New York, 1968.

Middlekauff, Robert. *The Mathers: Three Generations of Puritan Intellectuals, 1596–1728.* London, 1971.

Miller, Perry. *Errand into the Wilderness.* New York, 1956.

——. *The New England Mind: From Colony to Province.* Cambridge, Mass., 1953.

——. *The New England Mind: The Seventeenth Century.* 1939; Cambridge, Mass., 1954.

——. *Orthodoxy in Massachusetts, 1630–1650.* Boston, 1959.

Miller, Perry, and Thomas H. Johnson, eds. *The Puritans.* Rev. ed. 2 vols. New York, 1963.

Minter, David L. *The Interpreted Design as a Structural Principle in American Prose.* New Haven, Conn., 1969.

Morgan, Edmund S. *The Puritan Dilemma: The Story of John Winthrop.* Edited by Oscar Handlin. Boston, 1958.

——. *The Puritan Family: Religion and Domestic Relations in Seventeenth-Century New England.* Rev. ed. New York, 1966.

——. *Visible Saints: The History of a Puritan Idea.* New York, 1963.

——, ed. *Puritan Political Ideas, 1558–1794.* Indianapolis, Ind., 1965.

Morgan, John. *Godly Learning: Puritan Attitudes towards Reason, Learning, and Education, 1560–1640.* Cambridge, 1986.

Morison, Samuel Eliot. *Builders of the Bay Colony.* Rev. ed. Boston, 1958.

——. *The Founding of Harvard College.* Cambridge, Mass., 1935.

——. *Harvard College in the Seventeenth Century.* 2 vols. Cambridge, Mass., 1936.

——. *The Intellectual Life of Colonial New England.* 2d ed. New York, 1956.

Morris, Christopher. *Political Thought in England: Tyndale to Hooker.* London, 1953.

Morris, Richard B. *Studies in the History of American Law, with Special Reference to the Seventeenth and Eighteenth Centuries.* 2d ed. Philadelphia, 1958.

Mullinger, James Bass. *The University of Cambridge.* 3 vols. Cambridge,

1873–1911.

Murdock, Kenneth Ballard. *Increase Mather: The Foremost American Puritan.* Cambridge, Mass., 1925.

Neill, Stephen. *Anglicanism.* Baltimore, 1960.

Noble, David W. *The Eternal Adam and the New World Garden: The Central Myth in the American Novel since 1830.* New York, 1968.

———. *Historians against History: The Frontier Thesis and the National Covenant in American Historical Writing since 1870.* Minneapolis, Minn., 1965.

Nuttall, Geoffrey F. *The Holy Spirit in Puritan Faith and Experience.* 2d ed. Oxford, 1947.

———. *Visible Saints: The Congregational Way, 1640–1660.* Oxford, 1957.

Oberman, Heiko. *The Harvest of Medieval Theology: Gabriel Biel and Late Medieval Nominalism.* Grand Rapids, Mich., 1967.

Olin, John C., ed. *John Calvin and Jacobo Sadoleto: A Reformation Debate: Sadoleto's Letter to the Genevans and Calvin's Reply.* New York, 1966.

Olsen, V. Norskov. *John Foxe and the Elizabethan Church.* Berkeley, Calif., 1973.

Parker, T. H. L., ed. *English Reformers.* Philadelphia, 1966.

Pauck, Wilhelm, ed. *Melanchthon and Bucer.* Philadelphia, 1969.

Pearson, A. F. Scott. *Thomas Cartwright and Elizabethan Puritanism, 1535–1603.* Cambridge, 1925.

Pomfret, John E., and Floyd M. Shumway. *Founding the American Colonies, 1583–1660.* New York, 1971.

Pope, Robert G. *The Half-Way Covenant: Church Membership in Puritan New England.* Princeton, N.J., 1969.

Post, R. R. *The Modern Devotion: Confrontation with Reformation and Humanism.* Leiden, 1968.

Powell, Sumner Chilton. *Puritan Village: The Formation of a New England Town.* Middletown, Conn., 1963.

Powers, Edwin. *Crime and Punishment in Early Massachusetts, 1620–1692: A Documentary History.* Boston, 1966.

Powicke, Maurice. *The Reformation in England.* 1941; London, 1961.

Prall, Stuart E., ed. *The Puritan Revolution: A Documentary History.* Garden City, N.Y., 1968.

Pratt, Waldo S. *The Music of the Pilgrims: A Description of the Psalm-Book Brought to Plymouth in 1620.* Boston, 1921.

Putnam, Eben, ed. and comp. *Lieutenant Joshua Hewes: A New England Pioneer, and Some of His Descendants. . . .* N.p., 1913.

Reeves, Marjorie. *The Influence of Prophecy in the Later Middle Ages: A Study in Joachimism.* Oxford, 1969.

Rose-Troup, Frances. *John White, the Patriarch of Dorchester. . . .* New York, 1930.

Rossiter, Clinton. *Conservatism in America.* New York, 1955.

Roszak, Theodore. *Where the Wasteland Ends: Politics and Transcendence in Postindustrial Society.* Garden City, N.Y., 1972.

Rupp, E. G. *Studies in the Making of the English Protestant Tradition (Mainly in the Reign of Henry VIII)*. Cambridge, 1966.

Rutman, Darrett B. *American Puritanism: Faith and Practice*. Philadelphia, 1970.

———. *Winthrop's Boston: Portrait of a Puritan Town, 1630–1649*. Chapel Hill, N.C., 1965.

Sanford, Charles L. *The Quest for Paradise: Europe and the American Moral Imagination*. Urbana, Ill., 1961.

Scholes, Percy A. *The Oxford Companion to Music*. 10th ed. Edited by John Owen Ward. London, 1970.

———. *The Puritans and Music in England and New England: A Contribution to the Cultural History of Two Nations*. London, 1934.

Segal, Charles M., and David C. Stineback, eds. *Puritans, Indians, and Manifest Destiny*. New York, 1977.

Shuffelton, Frank. *Thomas Hooker, 1586–1647*. Princeton, N.J., 1977.

Simpson, Alan. *Puritanism in Old and New England*. Chicago, 1955.

Smith, H. Shelton, Robert T. Handy, and Lefferts A. Loetscher. *American Christianity: An Historical Interpretation with Representative Documents*. 2 vols. New York, 1960–1963.

Smith, James Morton, ed. *Seventeenth-Century America: Essays in Colonial History*. Chapel Hill, N.C., 1959.

Solberg, Winton U. *Redeem the Time: The Puritan Sabbath in Early America*. Cambridge, Mass., 1977.

Sprunger, Keith L. *The Learned Doctor William Ames: Dutch Backgrounds of English and American Puritanism*. Urbana, Ill., 1972.

Spufford, Margaret. *Contrasting Communities: English Villagers in the Sixteenth and Seventeenth Centuries*. Cambridge, 1974.

Staedtke, Joachim. *Die Theologie des jungen Bullinger*. Zurich, 1962.

Stannard, David E. *The Puritan Way of Death: A Study in Religion, Culture, and Social Change*. New York, 1977.

Stearns, Raymond Phineas, ed. *Congregationalism in the Dutch Netherlands: The Rise and Fall of the English Congregational Classis, 1621–1635*. Chicago, 1940.

Stoever, William K. B. *"A Faire and Easie Way to Heaven": Covenant Theology and Antinomianism in Early Massachusetts*. Middletown, Conn., 1978.

Strype, John. *Annals of the Reformation*. 4 vols. in 7. 1824; New York, 1968.

———. *Ecclesiastical Memorials. . . .* 6 vols. Oxford, 1822.

———. *The Life and Acts of John Whitgift. . . .* 3 vols. Oxford, 1822.

———. *The Life and Acts of Matthew Parker. . . .* 3 vols. Oxford, 1821.

———. *The Life of the Learned Sir John Cheke. . . .* Oxford, 1821.

Temperley, Nicholas. *The Music of the English Parish Church*. 2 vols. Cambridge, 1979.

Thrupp, Sylvia L., ed. *Millennial Dreams in Action: Studies in Revolutionary Religious Movements*. New York, 1970.

Tichi, Cecelia. *New World, New Earth: Environmental Reform in American Literature from the Puritans through Whitman*. New Haven, Conn., 1979.

Tolles, Frederick B. *Meeting House and Counting House: The Quaker Merchants of Philadelphia, 1682–1763*. Chapel Hill, N.C., 1948.

Toon, Peter, ed. *Puritans, the Millennium, and the Future of Israel: Puritan Eschatology, 1600 to 1660*. Cambridge, 1970.

Torrance, T. F. *Kingdom and Church: A Study in the Theology of the Reformation*. Edinburgh, 1956.

Trevor-Roper, H. R. *Religion, the Reformation, and Social Change, and Other Essays*. London, 1967.

Trinterud, Leonard J., ed. *Elizabethan Puritanism*. New York, 1971.

Tuveson, Ernest Lee. *Millennium and Utopia: A Study in the Background of the Idea of Progress*. New York, 1964.

———. *Redeemer Nation: The Idea of America's Millennial Role*. Chicago, 1968.

Vaughan, Alden T. *New England Frontier: Puritans and Indians, 1620–1675*. Boston, 1965.

Vaughan, Alden T., and Francis J. Bremer, eds. *Puritan New England: Essays on Religion, Society, and Culture*. New York, 1977.

Verkamp, Bernard J. *The Indifferent Mean: Adiaphorism in the English Reformation to 1554*. Athens, Ohio, 1977.

Wakefield, Gordon Stevens. *Puritan Devotion: Its Place in the Development of Christian Piety*. London, 1957.

Walker, Williston. *The Creeds and Platforms of Congregationalism*. 1893; Boston, 1960.

Wall, Robert Emmet, Jr. *Massachusetts Bay: The Crucial Decade, 1640–1650*. New Haven, Conn., 1972.

Walzer, Michael. *The Revolution of the Saints: A Study in the Origins of Radical Politics*. New York, 1969.

Ward, John William. *Andrew Jackson: Symbol for an Age*. New York, 1962.

Watters, David H. *"With Bodilie Eyes": Eschatological Themes in Puritan Literature and Gravestone Art*. Ann Arbor, Mich., 1981.

Weber, Max. *The Protestant Ethic and the Spirit of Capitalism*. Translated by Talcott Parsons. New York, 1958.

Weber, Timothy P. *Living in the Shadow of the Second Coming: American Premillennialism, 1875–1982*. 2d ed. Grand Rapids, Mich., 1983.

Wendel, François. *Calvin: The Origins and Development of His Religious Thought*. Translated by Philip Mairet. New York, 1963.

Whitaker, E. C. *Martin Bucer and the Book of Common Prayer*. Great Wakering, England, 1974.

Whitney, Lois. *Primitivism and the Idea of Progress in English Popular Literature of the Eighteenth Century*. Baltimore, 1934.

Williams, Peter W. *Popular Religion in America: Symbolic Change and the Modernization Process in Historical Perspective*. Englewood Cliffs, N.J., 1980.

Williams, Robin Murphy. *American Society: A Sociological Interpretation*. 2d ed. New York, 1960.

Wilson, John F. *Public Religion in American Culture*. Philadelphia, 1979.

————. *Pulpit in Parliament: Puritanism during the English Civil Wars, 1640–1648*. Princeton, N.J., 1969.

Wilson, Robert J., III. *The Benevolent Deity: Ebenezer Gay and the Rise of Rational Religion in New England, 1696–1787*. Philadelphia, 1984.

Winslow, Ola Elizabeth. *John Eliot: "Apostle to the Indians."* Boston, 1968.

Wood, Gordon S. *The Creation of the American Republic, 1776–1787*. Chapel Hill, N.C., 1969.

Woodhouse, A. S. P., ed. *Puritanism and Liberty: Being the Army Debates (1647–49)*. 2d ed. Chicago, 1951.

Woodhouse, Hugh Frederic. *The Doctrine of the Church in Anglican Theology, 1547–1603*. London, 1954.

Wrightson, Keith, and David Levine. *Poverty and Piety in an English Village: Terling, 1525–1700*. New York, 1979.

Young, Christine Alice. *From "Good Order" to Glorious Revolution: Salem, Massachusetts, 1628–1689*. Ann Arbor, Mich., 1980.

Ziff, Larzer. *The Career of John Cotton: Puritanism and the American Experience*. Princeton, N.J., 1962.

————. *Puritanism in America: New Culture in a New World*. New York, 1973.

ARTICLES AND ESSAYS

Anderson, Virginia DeJohn. "Migrants and Motives: Religion and the Settlement of New England, 1630–1640." *NEQ*, LVIII (1985), 339–383.

Appleby, Joyce. "Value and Society." In Jack P. Greene and J. R. Pole, eds., *Colonial British America: Essays in the New History of the Early Modern Era* (Baltimore, 1984), 290–316.

Avis, P. D. L. "Moses and the Magistrate: A Study in the Rise of Protestant Legalism." *Journal of Ecclesiastical History*, XXVI (1975), 149–172.

Baker, J. H. "Criminal Courts and Procedure at Common Law, 1550–1800." In J. S. Cockburn, ed., *Crime in England, 1550–1800* (Princeton, N.J., 1977), 15–48.

Beales, Ross W., Jr. "The Half-Way Covenant and Religious Scrupulosity: The First Church of Dorchester, Massachusetts, as a Test Case." *WMQ*, 3d Ser., XXXI (1974), 465–480.

Bercovitch, Sacvan. "The Historiography of Johnson's Wonder-Working Providence." In Alden T. Vaughan and Francis J. Bremer, eds., *Puritan New England: Essays on Religion, Society, and Culture*, 268–286.

————. "Horologicals to Chronometricals: The Rhetoric of the Jeremiad." In *Literary Monographs*, III, ed. Eric Rothstein (Madison, Wis., 1970), 1–124.

————. "New England's Errand Reappraised." In John Higham and Paul Conkin, eds., *New Directions in American Intellectual History* (Baltimore, 1979), 85–104.

————. "Typology in Puritan New England: The Williams-Cotton Controversy Reassessed." *American Quarterly*, XIX (1967), 166–191.

Bozeman, Theodore Dwight. "The Puritans' 'Errand into the Wilderness' Reconsidered." *NEQ*, LIX (1986), 231–251.

Brauer, Jerald C. "Reflections on the Nature of English Puritanism." *CH*, XXIII (1954), 99–108.

Breen, T. H., and Stephen Foster. "Moving to the New World: The Character of Early Massachusetts Immigration." *WMQ*, 3d Ser., XXX (1973), 189–222.

———. "The Puritans' Greatest Achievement: A Study of Social Cohesion in Seventeenth-Century Massachusetts." In Alden T. Vaughan and Francis J. Bremer, eds., *Puritan New England: Essays on Religion, Society, and Culture*, 110–127.

Bremer, Francis J. "In Defense of Regicide: John Cotton on the Execution of Charles I." *WMQ*, 3d Ser., XXXVII (1980), 103–124.

Brown, Ira V. "Watchers for the Second Coming: The Millenarian Tradition in America." *Mississippi Valley Historical Review*, XXXIX (1952–1953), 441–458.

Brown, Peter. "St. Augustine." In Beryl Smalley, ed., *Trends in Medieval Political Thought* (New York, 1965), 1–21.

Buchanan, John G. "Puritan Philosophy of History from Restoration to Revolution." *HCEI*, CIV (1968), 329–348.

Capp, Bernard. "*Godly Rule* and English Millenarianism." *Past and Present*, no. 52 (Aug. 1971), 106–117.

Christianson, Paul. "Reformers and the Church of England under Elizabeth I and the Early Stuarts." *Journal of Ecclesiastical History*, XXXI (1980), 463–482.

Clouse, R. G. "The Rebirth of Millenarianism." In Peter Toon, ed., *Puritans, the Millennium, and the Future of Israel: Puritan Eschatology, 1600 to 1660*, 42–65.

Cohn, Norman. "Medieval Millenarism: Its Bearing on the Comparative Study of Millenarian Movements." In Sylvia A. Thrupp, ed., *Millennial Dreams in Action: Studies in Revolutionary Religious Movements*, 31–43.

Collinson, Patrick. "Towards a Broader Understanding of the Early Dissenting Tradition." In C. Robert Cole and Michael E. Moody, eds., *The Dissenting Tradition: Essays for Leland H. Carlson* (Athens, Ohio, 1975), 3–38.

Crouse, Nellis M. "Causes of the Great Migration, 1630–1640." *NEQ*, V (1932), 3–36.

Delbanco, Andrew. "The Puritan Errand Re-Viewed." *Journal of American Studies*, XVIII (1984), 343–360.

"Dudley, Thomas." In *Dictionary of American Biography*.

Eliade, Mircea. " 'Cargo Cults' and Cosmic Regeneration." In Sylvia A. Thrupp, ed., *Millennial Dreams in Action: Studies in Revolutionary Religious Movements*, 139–143.

———. "Paradise and Utopia." In Frank E. Manuel, ed., *Utopias and Utopian Thought* (Boston, 1965), 260–280.

Elliott, J. H. "Revolution and Continuity in Early Modern Europe." *Past and Present*, no. 42 (Feb. 1969), 35–56.

Elton, G. R. Review of *The Puritan Lectureships*, by Paul S. Seaver. *Historical Journal*, XIII (1970), 803–805.

Eusden, John D. "Natural Law and Covenant Theology in New England, 1620–1670." *Natural Law Forum*, V (1960), 1–30.

Foster, Stephen. "The Godly in Transit: English Popular Protestantism and the Creation of a Puritan Establishment in America." In David D. Hall and David Grayson Allen, eds., *Seventeenth-Century New England* (Colonial Society of Massachusetts, *Publications*, LXIII [Boston, 1984]), 185–238.

Friesen, Abraham. "The Impulse toward Restitutionist Thought in Christian Humanism." *Journal of the American Academy of Religion*, XLIV (1976), 29–45.

Gaustad, Edwin S. "Restitution, Revolution, and the American Dream." *Journal of the American Academy of Religion*, XLIV (1976), 77–86.

George, C. H. "Puritanism as History and Historiography." *Past and Present*, no. 41 (Dec. 1968), 77–104.

Goebel, Julius, Jr. "King's Law and Local Custom in Seventeenth Century New England." In David H. Flaherty, ed., *Essays in the History of Early American Law*, 83–120.

Greene, Jack P., and J. R. Pole. "Reconstructing British-American Colonial History: An Introduction." In Greene and Pole, eds., *Colonial British America: Essays in the New History of the Early Modern Era* (Baltimore, 1984), 1–17.

Grislis, Egil. "The Hermeneutical Problem in Richard Hooker." In W. Speed Hill, ed., *Studies in Richard Hooker: Essays Preliminary to an Edition of His Works*, 159–206.

Hall, Basil. "Puritanism: The Problem of Definition." In *Studies in Church History*, II, ed. G. J. Cuming (London, 1965), 283–296.

Hall, David D. "Understanding the Puritans." In Herbert J. Bass, ed., *The State of American History* (Chicago, 1970), 330–349.

Harrison, Frank Ll. "Church Music in England." In *The New Oxford History of Music*, IV, *The Age of Humanism, 1540–1630* (London, 1968), 465–519.

Haskins, George L. "The Beginnings of Partible Inheritance in the American Colonies." *Yale Law Journal*, LI (1941–1942), 1280–1315.

Heimert, Alan. "Puritanism, the Wilderness, and the Frontier." *NEQ*, XXVI (1953), 361–382.

Hoopes, James. "Art as History: Perry Miller's *New England Mind*." *American Quarterly*, XXXIV (1982), 3–25.

Howe, Daniel W. "Descendents of Perry Miller." *American Quarterly*, XXXIV (1982), 88–94.

Howe, Mark DeWolfe. "The Sources and Nature of Law in Colonial Massachusetts." In George Athan Billias, ed., *Law and Authority in Colonial America*, 1–16.

Hudson, Winthrop S. "Fast Days and Civil Religion." In *Theology in Sixteenth- and Seventeenth-Century England* . . . (Los Angeles, 1971).

Hughes, Richard T. "A Civic Theology for the South: The Case of Benjamin M. Palmer." *Journal of Church and State*, XXV (1983), 447–467.

————. "From Civil Dissent to Civil Religion—and Beyond." *Religion in Life*, XLIX (1980), 268–288.

Kaminsky, Howard. "Wyclifism as Ideology of Revolution." *CH*, XXXII (1963), 57–74.

Kearney, H. F. "Puritanism and Science: Problems of Definition." In Charles Webster, ed., *The Intellectual Revolution of the Seventeenth Century* (London, 1974), 254–261.

Kobrin, David. "The Expansion of the Visible Church in New England, 1629–1650." *CH*, XXXVI (1967), 189–209.

Lamont, William. "Puritanism as History and Historiography: Some Further Thoughts." *Past and Present*, no. 44 (Aug. 1969), 133–146.

————. "Richard Baxter, the Apocalypse, and the Mad Major." *Past and Present*, no. 47 (May 1972), 68–90.

McGiffert, Michael. "American Puritan Studies in the 1960's." *WMQ*, 3d Ser., XXVII (1970), 36–67.

————. "Covenant, Crown, and Commons in Elizabethan Puritanism." *Journal of British Studies*, XX, no. 1 (Fall 1980), 32–52.

Maclear, James Fulton. " 'The Heart of New England Rent': The Mystical Element in Early Puritan History." *Mississippi Valley Historical Review*, XLII (1955–1956), 621–652.

————. "The Influence of the Puritan Clergy on the House of Commons, 1625–1629." *CH*, XIV (1945), 272–289.

————. "New England and the Fifth Monarchy: The Quest for the Millennium in Early American Puritanism." *WMQ*, 3d Ser., XXXII (1975), 223–260.

Mead, Sidney E. "The Rise of the Evangelical Conception of the Ministry in America (1607–1850)." In H. Richard Niebuhr and Daniel D. Williams, eds., *The Ministry in Historical Perspectives* (New York, 1956), 207–249.

Miller, Perry. "Declension in a Bible Commonwealth." In Miller, *Nature's Nation* (Cambridge, Mass., 1967), 14–49.

————. "Errand into the Wilderness." In Miller, *Errand into the Wilderness*, 1–15.

Moran, Gerald F. "Religious Renewal, Puritan Tribalism, and the Family in Seventeenth-Century Milford, Connecticut." *WMQ*, 3d Ser., XXXVI (1979), 236–254.

Morgan, Edmund S. "The Historians of Early New England." In Ray Allen Billington, ed., *The Reinterpretation of Early American History* (New York, 1968), 41–64.

————. Letter. *WMQ*, 3d Ser., XIX (1962), 642–644.

————. "New England Puritanism: Another Approach." *WMQ*, 3d Ser., XVIII (1961), 236–242.

Murrin, John M. "Review Essay." *History and Theory*, XI (1972), 226–275.

Oberholzer, Emil. "Puritanism Revisited." In Alden T. Vaughan and George Athan Billias, *Perspectives on Early American History: Essays in Honor of Richard B. Morris* (New York, 1973), 193–221.

Oberman, Heiko. "The Shape of Medieval Thought: The Birthpangs of the

Modern Era." *Archiv für Reformationsgeschichte*, II (1973), 13–33.

Perzel, Edward S. "Landholding in Ipswich." *HCEI*, CIV (1968), 303–328.

Pope, Robert G. "New England versus the New England Mind: The Myth of Declension." In Alden T. Vaughan and Francis J. Bremer, eds., *Puritan New England: Essays on Religion, Society, and Culture*, 314–325.

Prest, Wilfrid R. "The Art of Law and the Law of God: Sir Henry Finch (1558–1625)." In Donald Pennington and Keith Thomas, eds., *Puritans and Revolutionaries: Essays in Seventeenth-Century History Presented to Christopher Hill* (Oxford, 1978), 94–117.

Reeves, Marjorie. "History and Eschatology: Medieval and Early Protestant Thought in Some English and Scottish Writings." *Medievalia et Humanistica*, N.S., IV (1973), 99–124.

Reinsch, Paul Samuel. "The English Common Law in the Early American Colonies." In Association of American Law Schools, *Select Essays in Anglo-American Legal History*, I (Boston, 1907), 367–415.

Rosenmeier, Jesper. "New England's Perfection: The Image of Adam and the Image of Christ in the Antinomian Crisis, 1634 to 1638." *WMQ*, 3d Ser., XXVII (1970), 435–459.

———. "Veritas: The Sealing of the Promise." *Harvard Library Bulletin*, XVI (1968), 26–37.

Roth, Robert J. "The Philosophical Background of New England Puritanism." *International Philosophical Quarterly*, X (1970), 570–597.

Rutman, Darrett B. "God's Bridge Falling Down: 'Another Approach' to Puritanism Assayed." *WMQ*, 3d Ser., XIX (1962), 408–421.

Schlatter, Richard. "The Puritan Strain." In John Higham, ed., *The Reconstruction of American History* (New York, 1962), 25–45.

Scobey, David M. "Revising the Errand: New England's Ways and the Puritan Sense of the Past." *WMQ*, 3d Ser., XLI (1984), 3–31.

Segal, Robert A. "Eliade's Theory of Millenarianism." *Religious Studies*, XIV (1978), 159–173.

Shipton, Clifford K. "The Locus of Authority in Colonial Massachusetts." In George Athan Billias, ed., *Law and Authority in Colonial America: Selected Essays*, 136–148.

Solt, Leo F. "Puritanism, Capitalism, Democracy, and the New Science." *American Historical Review*, LXXIII (1967–1968), 18–29.

Spalding, James C. "Restitution as a Normative Factor for Puritan Dissent." *Journal of the American Academy of Religion*, XLIV (1976), 47–63.

Sprunger, Keith L. "William Ames and the Settlement of Massachusetts Bay." *NEQ*, XXXIX (1966), 66–79.

Stearns, Raymond Phineas, ed. "Letters and Documents by or Relating to Hugh Peter." *HCEI*, LXXI (1935), 303–318.

Stein, Stephen J. "Transatlantic Extensions: Apocalyptic in Early New England." In C. A. Patrides and Joseph Wittreich, eds., *The Apocalypse in English Renaissance Thought and Literature: Patterns, Antecedents, and Repercussions* (Manchester, 1984), 266–298.

Stout, Harry. "Almost Zion." *Fides et Historia*, XII (1979), 83–88.

————. "Puritanism Considered as a Profane Movement." *Christian Scholar's Review*, X (1980), 3–19.

————. "University Men in New England, 1620–1660: A Demographic Analysis." *Journal of Interdisciplinary History*, IV (1973–1974), 375–400.

Sweet, Leonard I. "Millennialism in America: Recent Studies." *Theological Studies*, XL (1979), 510–531.

Talmon, Yonina. "Millenarism." In *International Encyclopedia of the Social Sciences* (1968).

Tipple, John. "The Robber Baron in the Gilded Age: Entrepreneur or Iconoclast?" In H. Wayne Morgan, ed., *The Gilded Age: A Reappraisal* (Syracuse, N.Y., 1963), 14–37.

Toon, Peter. "The Latter-Day Glory." In Toon, ed., *Puritans, the Millennium, and the Future of Israel: Puritan Eschatology, 1600 to 1660*, 23–41.

Trinterud, Leonard J. "The Origins of Puritanism." *CH*, XX (1951), 37–57.

Tyack, Norman C. P. "The Humbler Puritans of East Anglia and the New England Movement: Evidence from the Court Records of the 1630s." *NEHGR*, CXXXVIII (1984), 79–106.

Warden, G. B. "Law Reform in England and New England, 1620 to 1660," *WMQ*, 3d Ser., XXXV (1978), 668–690.

Waterhouse, Richard. "Reluctant Emigrants: The English Background of the First Generation of the New England Puritan Clergy." *Historical Magazine of the Protestant Episcopal Church*, XLIV (1975), 473–488.

Waters, John J. "Hingham, Massachusetts, 1631–1661: An East Anglian Oligarchy in the New World." *Journal of Social History*, I (1968), 351–370.

Williams, George H. "The Idea of the Wilderness of the New World in Cotton Mather's *Magnalia Christi Americana*." In Cotton Mather, *Magnalia Christi Americana, Books I and II*, ed. Kenneth B. Murdock (Cambridge, Mass., 1977), 49–58.

Wilson, John F. "A Glimpse of Sion's Glory." *CH*, XXXI (1962), 66–73.

Wolford, Thorp L. "The Laws and Liberties of 1648." In David H. Flaherty, ed., *Essays in the History of Early American Law*, 147–185.

Woodward, Kenneth L., and David Gates. "How the Bible Made America." *Newsweek*, Dec. 27, 1982, 44–51.

Yule, George. "Continental Patterns and the Reformation in England and Scotland." *Scottish Journal of Theology*, XXII (1969), 305–323.

Zakai, Avihu. " 'Epiphany at Matadi': Perry Miller's *Orthodoxy in Massachusetts* and the Meaning of American History." *Reviews in American History*, XIII (1985), 627–641.

Zanger, Jules. "Crime and Punishment in Early Massachusetts." *WMQ*, 3d Ser., XXII (1965), 471–477.

DISSERTATIONS

Allen, Crawford Leonard. " 'The Restauration of Zion': Roger Williams and the Quest for the Primitive Church." Ph.D. diss., University of Iowa, 1984.

Alpert, Helle M. "Robert Keayne: Notes of Sermons by John Cotton and Proceedings of the First Church of Boston from 23 November 1639 to 1 June 1640." Ph.D. diss., Tufts University, 1974.

Clifford, Norman K. "Casuistical Divinity in English Puritanism during the Seventeenth Century: Its Origins, Development, and Significance." Ph.D. diss., University of London, 1957.

Clouse, Robert Gordon. "The Influence of John Henry Alsted on English Millenarian Thought in the Seventeenth Century." Ph.D. diss., University of Iowa, 1963.

Coffman, Ralph J., Jr. "Gardens in the Wilderness: Stuart Puritan Reforms and the Diversity of New England Puritanism, 1604–1650." Ph.D. diss., Harvard University, 1976.

Cogley, Richard William. "The Millenarianism of John Eliot, 'Apostle' to the Indians." Ph.D. diss., Princeton University, 1983.

Dufour, Ronald P. "Modernization in Colonial Massachusetts, 1630–1763." Ph.D. diss., College of William and Mary, 1982.

Gilsdorf, Aletha Joy Bourne. "The Puritan Apocalypse: New England Eschatology in the Seventeenth Century." Ph.D. diss., Yale University, 1965.

Hill, Marvin S. "The Role of Christian Primitivism in the Origin and Development of the Mormon Kingdom, 1830–44." Ph.D. diss., University of Chicago, 1968.

Luoma, John Kenneth Reynold. "The Primitive Church as a Normative Principle in the Theology of the Sixteenth Century. . . ." Ph.D. diss., Hartford Seminary Foundation, 1974.

Mooney, Michael Eugene. "Millennialism and Antichrist in New England, 1630–1760." Ph.D. diss., Syracuse University, 1982.

Scholz, Robert Francis. "'The Reverend Elders,' Faith, Fellowship, and Politics in the Ministerial Community of Massachusetts Bay, 1630–1710." Ph.D. diss., University of Minnesota, 1966.

Zakai, Avihu. "Exile and Kingdom: Reformation, Separation, and the Millennial Quest in the Formation of Massachusetts and Its Relationship with England, 1628–1660." Ph.D. diss., Johns Hopkins University, 1983.

INDEX

Abelard, Peter, 52

Additions. *See* Primitivism, religious: additions

Adiaphora, 41, 57–65, 105, 109, 163, 170, 172, 238

Admonition to the Parliament, An [Field and Wilcox], 28, 41–42, 152, 292, 365

Adultery, 165, 174, 179, 180, 181

Ainsworth, Henry, 252n. 27; *The Book of Psalmes*, 142

Albanese, Catherine L., 325, 352

Allin, John, 108–109, 118–119, 131–135

Alsted, John Henry, 215–217, 233; *Diatribe de Milleannis Apocalypticis*, 215

American national mission, 81, 119, 218, 227, 230, 316

Ames, William, 29, 34, 67n. 30, 68–69, 170, 174, 179, 223–225, 303–304 n. 29; *The Marrow of Theology*, 69

Anabaptists, 8, 14n. 4, 22, 32

Ancient constitution, 78

Andrewes, Lancelot, 29

Anglicanism, 12, 25–26, 30, 33, 37–38, 57–65, 71, 72, 74, 143, 162, 164, 316, 320; defined, 7–8; and primitivism, 24–26, 74

Antichrist. *See* Millennialism: and Antichrist

Antinomians, 112, 138, 154, 157, 187, 250, 284, 365, 367; and spiritism, 367–368

Apostolicity, 28, 32, 39, 44, 129, 225–228, 257, 259. *See also* Bible: New Testament; Primitivism, religious: first as normative

Archer, John, 216, 232n. 92, 240

Archetypes, 4, 17, 19, 26, 38–49, 54, 57, 62, 73, 114–117, 121, 127–130, 140, 145, 147, 150, 153–160, 173, 176, 227, 234, 242, 258, 268–280, 288, 292, 294, 302, 306, 317, 320–321, 324, 333, 336, 341, 345

Aristotelian concepts, 18–19, 52, 66

Arminianism. *See* Church of England

Aulnay, Charles de Menon, sieur d', 154–155

Bacon, Francis, 28, 115, 308n. 37

Bale, John, 38, 160, 199, 206–207, 246, 251

Bancroft, Richard, 60, 100

Baptism, 103–105, 107n. 37, 112, 137, 139, 149, 318

Baptists, 137, 157, 329, 331, 366

Barrow, Henry, 143n. 43, 166, 190, 366

Baxter, Richard, 47

Baynes, Paul, 223–225, 317

Bay Psalm Book, 139–150. *See also* Psalms

Beauty. *See* Primitivism, religious: beauty

Becon, Thomas, 160

Bercovitch, Sacvan, 3, 83, 97n. 22, 198 n. 8, 234n. 98, 314–316, 337n. 47, 338n. 50, 341n. 56

Berens, John F., 309n. 41

Bernard, Richard, 37n. 42, 38, 218, 240–241, 243, 247, 249n. 23

Bernard of Clairvaux, 52

Beza, Theodore, 38

Bible, 13–79, 128–129, 140, 144; as supreme book, 13–14, 21, 26, 130, 156, 341, 367; New Testament, 14–15, 24–25, 27, 28, 31–32, 33, 39, 41, 62, 119, 130, 134; as sacred drama, 15–16, 33–39, 46–49, 121, 128, 130, 138–139, 150; Old Testament, 32, 37, 40, 42, 134, 169, 245, 253–255;